# 1 MONTH OF
# FREE
# READING

## at

## www.ForgottenBooks.com

By purchasing this book you are eligible for one month membership to ForgottenBooks.com, giving you unlimited access to our entire collection of over 1,000,000 titles via our web site and mobile apps.

To claim your free month visit:

www.forgottenbooks.com/free965298

ISBN 978-0-260-70451-1
PIBN 10965298

# REPORTS OF CASES

# COURT OF CHANCERY

OF

# ONTARIO.

BY

## ALEXANDER GRANT, BARRISTER,

REPORTER TO THE COURT.

## VOLUME XVIII.

TORONTO:
ROWSELL & HUTCHISON,
KING STREET.

1872.

ROWSELL AND HUTCHISON, LAW PRINTERS, TORONTO.

# A TABLE

OF

# CASES REPORTED IN THIS VOLUME.

---

*Versus* is always put after the plaintiff's name.

## A.

## B.

## C.

## D.                                                                    PAGE

## F.

## G.

## G.

## H.

## H.

## J.

## K.

## L.

## R.

## S.

# A TABLE

OF

# CASES CITED IN THIS VOLUME.

# REPORTS OF CASES

### ADJUDGED IN THE

# COURT OF CHANCERY

#### OF

# ONTARIO,

#### DURING PORTIONS OF THE YEARS 1870 AND 1871.

---

## GILLATLEY V. WHITE.

*Specific Performance—Contract—Statute of Frauds—Amendment—Costs.*

In pursuance of a verbal agreement for the sale of lands, the purchase money being payable by instalments, to be secured by mortgage on the premises bargained for and other lands owned by the purchaser; a deed and mortgage were drawn up, which were signed and sealed by the vendor and mortgagor respectively— neither instrument referring to the other, and the deed expressing that the purchase money had been paid. The vendor and mortgagor took away the respective instruments signed by them for the purpose, as alleged, of procuring the execution thereof by their respective wives. The vendor subsequently refused to perfect the transaction, and on a bill filled by the purchaser for specific performance:

*Held*, that the conveyance so executed by the vendor was a sufficient contract of sale within the Statute of Frauds; that the presumption on the face of such instrument was that the purchase money had been paid; which being admitted by the plaintiff to be incorrect, the purchaser was entitled to a decree for specific performance, paying the price in hand.

In such a case, the evidence having clearly established the bargain as alleged by the plaintiff though his bill omitted to state the terms and mode of payment as agreed upon; the Court offered him the alternative of taking a decree for specific performance, with payment of purchase money in hand; or to amend his bill, setting up the exact terms of the bargaain.

Examination of witnesses and hearing at Sarnia, at Statement. the Autumn Sittings, 1870.

. 1—VOL. XVIII. GR.

This was a suit for specific performance, by a purchaser against his vendor and a subsequent purchaser,
who, it was alleged, had notice of the plaintiff's agreement to purchase the land in question; being the east
half of the northerly three-quarters of lot No. 18, in
the 6th concession of Plympton, containing seventy-five
acres, for the price or sum of $900. It appeared that
according to the agreement, no portion of the consideration was to be paid to the vendor, but, to secure payment, a mortgage upon the property, the subject of the
sale, and also upon some other land owned by the purchaser, was to be executed by him.

The bill alleged that, in pursuance of this agreement,
a deed and mortgage were prepared and *executed* by the
vendor and purchaser respectively; that the deed was
then taken away by the vendor for the purpose of procuring the signature of his wife, upon obtaining which
Statement. he was to transmit it to *Hugh Smith*—the person who
had prepared the instrument—for registration; and that
the mortgage was, in like manner, taken away by the
purchaser for a similar purpose.

Then followed allegations as to the sale to the defendant *Armstrong*, by defendent *White*, and also of notice
to *Armstrong* of the interest of the plaintiff.

The prayer was for specific performance by *White*,
"by delivering to him, plaintiff, a deed of conveyance
of said premises"; and as to the agreement with *Armstrong*, it prayed that it might be cancelled and removed
from the registry.

The cause, having been put at issue, came on for the
examination of witnesses and hearing, at the Autumn
Sittings of 1870, at Sarnia.

The evidence fully sustained the statements of the

bill, and established clearly that the defendant *Armstrong* had actual notice of the transaction between the plaintiff and *White*.

Mr. *S. Blake* and Mr. *Pardee*, for the plaintiff.

Mr. *Moss*, for the defendants.

SPRAGGE, C.—[After stating the facts, to the effect above set forth]. One question raised is, was there or not a perfect execution of the deed, so far as *White* was concerned. It is clearly established that he signed and sealed the conveyance.

The position of the plaintiff is, that there was such perfect execution. Defendant's counsel takes the position that the deed was not perfectly executed by the vendor, but signed and sealed only; and then taken away by the vendor, in order to its execution by his wife, upon which being done it was to be sent to *Smith* (who drew it as a conveyancer) in order to its registration, and that this sending was to be the delivery, and that nothing having been done in the way of the execution of the deed after it was so taken away by the vendor, the execution was not perfected.

I do not think it makes any difference in the case which party is right upon this point. If there was a sufficient contract of sale, the vendor is bound to carry it out. A contract of sale, silent as to the dower of the wife of the vendor, imports that her dower is to be barred. If this conveyance is a sufficient contract in other respects, it is certainly sufficient in that; for the wife is named as a party, and it contains the usual clause as to dower. If the plaintiff is right in his position, that there has been a perfect execution by the deed, it is still only a partial execution of the contract; and the purchaser has a right to come to this Court for a complete execution of it, *i. e.*, on the part of the wife as well as the husband. .Of course the wife may refuse; and it would be against the policy of the law to compel her to part with her dower, either directly, or through the coercion, or fear of coercion, on the part of the husband: but if the husband seeks to excuse himself from the fulfilment of that part of his contract, on the ground that his wife is unwilling to part with her dower, he must set that up. *Non constat*, that in this case the husband has not asked his wife to part with her dower; and, *non constat*, that if asked, she would not be willing to do so.

If, on the other hand, there has been no perfect execution, by the husband, of the conveyance, there has not been even a partial fulfilment of the contract of sale, upon which the purchaser came into Court. Either way, the only question is, whether there has been a sufficient contract within the Statute of Frauds. I will take the case upon the hypothesis of the defendants, that there has been no perfect execution of a conveyance at all.

I think that a contract of sale may be in the form of a conveyance: that what the parties intended to be a conveyance, but which is ineffectual to operate as a conveyance, may still be effectual to operate as a contract of sale; but, of course, it must contain all the terms which are necessary to a contract of sale, in .any other shape. The particulars in which Mr. *Moss* contends that this instrument is defective, is that it does not express the consideration as set out in the plaintiff's bill, in that the purchaser should pay $900, by certain instalments, and should give a mortgage to secure the purchase money. The conveyance contains no recital; it expresses the same consideration money, $900, and admits that it is already paid. Suppose the contract had been that the purchase money should be paid in hand, I see nothing to prevent the vendor coming into Court upon such an instrument, effectual as a contract but not as a conveyance, praying specific performance, admitting that the admission which it contains of the payment of the purchase money was incorrect, and submitting to pay it; just as, upon such an instrument, if the purchase money had been actually paid, he could allege it and pray for specific performance. The case before me differs in this: that the purchaser, while admitting that the purchase money has not been paid, alleges that it was a term of the contract that it was to be paid by instalments and secured by mortgage. The deed, *i. e.*, the contract of sale signed by the vendor, does not shew this; it is shewn by the mortgage, if we can look at. Mr. *Moss* contends that it cannot be looked at, not being signed by the vendor, and the instruments not in terms referring to one another. I have no doubt that the plaintiff may now take a decree for specific performance, paying the purchase money in hand, having leave to present his case, in the alternative that if the Court should be of opinion that the mortgage could not be looked at as part of the contract, and as shewing that the purchase money is payable, as by the mortgage it is made payable, he may have specific performance of what appears upon the conveyance itself, and by his admission that the purchase money is not paid.

But the purchaser naturally desires to have the time for the payment of his purchase money which, looking at both instruments, it is certain that he was to have; and I think his title to this may be placed upon intelligible grounds. Looking at the conveyance by itself, it shews a contract of sale, with the purchase money paid, and the vendor consequently a bare trustee to convey to the purchaser. To entitle the defendant to the consideration money we must look outside this contract of sale, viz., to the admission of the purchaser that it was still unpaid : but then looking at this admission we must look at it and take it as a whole. This purchase money he says was not paid because as yet it was not to be paid, but was payable at the times which he specifies.

Another ground, though one that would involve an amendment of the bill, would be, that in one particular the immediate payment of the purchase money to be inferred from no future time being mentioned. The contract does not express the true agreement of the parties, and should in that respect be reformed—the evidence in support of this would be clear and conclusive and an amendment making this ground of equity would be so clearly in furtherance of justice that I should think it right to allow it. It would be a considerable amendment no doubt, but still one that could not take the defendant by surprise, and one which ought to be allowed rather than that the plaintiff's case should fail through

an objection, which may be technically well founded, but is wholly without merit. The plaintiff may take leave to amend in this respect if he desires it.

This other ground was taken by Mr. *Blake*, that the vendor is bound by the terms of the mortgage, that *Smith* was his agent to receive it, and to register it. *Smith* certainly was the vendor's agent for these purposes, but his agency involved the signing of no paper to bring the case within the Statute of Frauds. I prefer to rest the case upon the other grounds to which I have referred.

Notice to the second purchaser, *Armstrong*, of the plaintiff's purchase is clearly proved. The decree will be for the plaintiff with costs, without, however, the costs of amendment, if the plaintiff should be advised so to amend. If he so amends it must be at his own expense.

## THE ATTORNEY GENERAL V. PRICE.

*Information suit—Costs.*

In this case, reported *ante* volume xv., page 304, the defendant was ordered on argument to pay the costs of the relators.

Hearing on further directions.

Mr. *Moss*, for the relators.

Mr. *Becher*, Q.C., for the defendants.

SPRAGGE, C.—I have read the judgment in the case at law and in this Court. I cannot go behind the decree which establishes the right against the defendant *Price*. He sets up certain contracts under which he had acquired the right of one of the relators ; and certain dealings with the other relators, which, as he contends, displaced the equity upon which the information was founded, or shewed in himself a title to the timber in question. That was really the question between the parties, though there were some minor points. Upon the main substantial question the relators, or rather the Crown in their behalf, succeeded. It is putting the case most favourably for *Price* to treat it as a question of private right between him and the relators; because it is upon contracts and dealings with them that he must rely for any title to the timber at all. He makes no case whatever against the Crown. It is true the decree gives only the value of the timber as it stood, or as lying upon the ground, but that was only a question of degree, and the defendant did not submit to pay to that extent, or even submit that if liable at all it was only to that extent, but insisted upon his own equity, and denied that of the relators, and it was upon that issue that the parties went to a hearing.

The issue then is determined substantially for the relators and against the defendant *Price.* My difficulty

Dec. 24.

Judgment.

has been why the costs up to the hearing were not determined at the time. The probability is, that my brother *Mowat*, before whom the case was heard, contemplated an early disposition of the whole case. He suggested that the parties might agree upon the value of the timber, and save the expense of a reference and proceedings, and said he would then dispose of the whole case and of the costs at once. This was two years ago, and the parties come before me now having, as was suggested by my learned brother, agreed upon the value of the timber. I have conferred with him upon the subject, and he suggests no reason, from recollection or otherwise, why the ordinary rule should be departed from of making the unsuccessful party pay the costs.

Judgment.    The decree disposed of all questions between the parties, except the question of costs and the value of the timber. The defendant *Price* is to pay the costs of the cause, including the costs of the motion for injunction.

----

## SHENNAN v. PARSILL.

*Lien for unpaid purchase money.*

The principle that a vendor, by taking from a purchaser an indorsed note as security for unpaid purchase money does not thereby lose his vendor's lien, is equally applicable where the security given is a bond, in which a third person joins as surety.

A parol agreement in reference to land partly performed by execution of deeds, was enforced.

Examination of witnesses and hearing at Goderich, Autumn Sittings, 1870.

Mr. *Bain*, for the plaintiff.

Mr. *Blake*, Q.C., and Mr. *Ross*, for the defendants.

SPRAGGE, C.—The general question as to the plain- **1871.**
tiff's lien for unpaid purchase money is not, in my
opinion, open after the decision of this Court in *Col-* Shennan.
*borne* v. *Thomas* (a). In that case the purchaser gave v.
a promissory note for purchase money, in which a third January 11.
person joined as surety. In this case a bond was given,
a third person joining in it as surety. There is no
difference in principle between the two, and I must decide
this case upon the authority of the other. There appears indeed to have been some conversation between the
parties as to the surety, the vendor making inquiry as
to whom it was to be ; and expressing himself perfectly
satisfied when he found who it was : but if there was to
be a surety at all, such an inquiry was perfectly natural;
and would not indicate an intention on the part of the
vendor to forego his lien ; if the fact of requiring a
surety at all would not indicate such intention. Besides
it was timbered land, and the purchaser a mill owner
on part of the same lot ; and it would naturally be Judgment.
expected that he would make use of the timber for the
supply of his mill; and so probably diminish the value
of the land. If this may reasonably be suggested as a
reason for requiring security beyond that of the purchaser ; and for seeing that such security was good, the
requiring such security is the less an indication of an
intention to waive the vendor's lien upon the land. The
vendor might reason thus : " Though I have my lien
upon the land, the land itself may be made of less value
by the act of the purchaser ; and therefore I require
security for the payment of the purchase money ; " just
as he might reasonably require security in such a case
although the purchase money were secured by mortgage.
Upon the question of lien for unpaid purchase money, .
my opinion is therefore in favour of the plaintiff.

The defendant then sets up an agreement made, as he
alleges, in December, 1869. There is a good deal of

(a) 4 Grant 102.

evidence in regard to this agreement, but it is not in writing. There is a written proposition by the defendant, and the assent of the plaintiff is indorsed upon it, but with this qualification, "if my attorney, Mr. A. Shaw, thinks it correct to do so," and unfortunately Mr. Shaw did not approve of it, or at least there is no evidence that he did ; and after the first interview at the office of his solicitors he announced that the agreement could not be carried out. Upon being remonstrated with, however, he agreed verbally that he would carry out the agreement, and returned to his solicitor's office and gave instructions that writings should be prepared in order to carry it out. Upon this it was looked upon by the parties as a settled thing, and spoken of as settled ; still it was only an agreement by parol. Further, if the agreement had been put into writing and signed, there was nothing in it to affect the vendor's lien for unpaid purchase money ; though the amount of pur-

chase money would be reduced. It was an agreement respecting an interest in hand and required to be evidenced in writing under the Statute of Frauds. It is in substance this case. A agrees to sell to B certain land, the purchase money to be $1200 : B could not prove by parol that A agreed subsequently to reduce the purchase money to $800. This case was not so simple, because certain things were to be done by the purchaser, but that could make no difference, for in the case I have put, it would make no difference that it was for certain considerations that the purchase money was to be reduced. It might prevent its being *nudum pactum*, but the objection on the statute would still remain.

But it is said there has been part performance ; and though there is some conflict of testimony, I think that acts of part performance are sufficiently proved. One of the terms of this agreement was, that *Parsill* should procure one *Redden* to be his surety, by bond to be given to certain parties to whom the plaintiff had sold small portions of the same lot, that upon the issue of the patent to him *Parsill,* he would make conveyances to such purchasers according to their contracts of sale. To one of these purchasers, *Markle,* a bond was executed in pursuance of this agreement; and a suit instituted by *Markle* appears to have been thereby stayed. In connection with it the plaintiff gave to *Parsill* a telegram to be sent, and which he did send, to Messrs. *Freeman & Craigie,* solicitors, of *Hamilton,* in these words: "Matter *Markle* v. *Shennan and Parsills* arranged.—*John Shennan.*" For some reason difficulties were started by the plaintiff's solicitors in the way of carrying out the agreement, and it was modified to this extent, that *Parsill* should make conveyances to the purchasers above referred to, instead of giving security for future conveyances; and in pursuance of this *Parsill* did make a conveyance of what is spoken of in the evidence as the acre lot, and, as he says, deeds to the other purchasers also. There is some evidence that the other purchasers were not satisfied with these deeds, and the plaintiff became desirous of breaking off the agreement, and subsequently repudiated it.

The plaintiff makes by his bill another case besides that to which I have referred. He asks for an injunction to restrain *Parsill* from cutting timber on the part of the lot purchased by him. That part of the plaintiff's case I disposed of at the hearing. My opinion was, and is, for reasons which I gave at the time, and need not repeat, that the plaintiff's case upon this ground failed.

There was also another point, a minor one, upon which evidence was given. It was as to the proper shape and mode of measuring what is called in the evidence the Seiler lot. I think upon that point the defendant *Parsill* is right.

The result then as to the first branch of the plaintiff's case is, that there was a parol agreement, which by reason of its part performance is binding upon the plaintiff. This is especially material so far as the defendants, the Canada Landed Credit Company, are concerned, for part of the agreement, which I must hold to be proved, though denied by the plaintiff, was that *Parsill* should be at liberty to give a first mortgage on the premises, that is to say, on the land purchased by him directly from the plaintiff, and also on the five acres purchased by *Parsill* from *Markle ;* and should give a second mortgage on the same premises to the plaintiff. It may seem strange that he should consent to a first mortgage being given to some other person than himself, but he had not at first stipulated for any mortgage at all, and it could not be said to be clear that he was entitled to any lien upon the land ; and the mortgage that he was to get, though a second mortgage, was to cover, in addition the *Markle* lot, as well property upon which he had no claim, the purchase money for it having been already

paid to him.

My doubt now is, whether I should dismiss the plaintiff's bill, or decree that the plaintiff is entitled to a lien subsequent to that of the Canada Landed Credit Company for the purchase money remaining unpaid. If the plaintiff had amended, or even at the hearing had asked for an amendment, adopting the agreement set up by *Parsill's* answer, I should have been inclined to grant him a decree either for a lien for the unpaid purchase money, or for a mortgage upon both properties to secure it. As it is, I think I may properly decree a lien in favor of the plaintiff for the purchase money remaining unpaid, postponed however to the mortgage of the Canada Landed Credit Company, and it can of course be only upon the land purchased by *Parsill*, not upon the mill property, and the plaintiff must pay the costs. The plaintiff fails upon all the matters really in contest between him and the defendants, and I must add that the evidence shews him to have acted sometimes in a

vacillating, at other times a vexatious spirit. If *Parsill*
had failed in establishing the agreement which he has
set up, I think I should in any event have refused the
plaintiff his costs. The injunction against cutting timber
is refused, and the bill is dismissed as against the Canada
Landed Credit Company with costs.

## PATERSON v. LAILEY.

*Trustee—Unauthorized investment—Damages.*

Where a trustee is authorized to invest in either of two specified
modes, and by mistake he invests in neither, the measure of his
liability is the loss arising from his not having invested in the less
beneficial of the authorized modes.

Two years before the passing of the Act relaxing the usury laws (22
Vic. ch. 85), a trustee, who was authorized to invest on mortgage or
in government securities, made an investment in Upper Canada Bank
stock, under the impression that such an investment was within his
authority; the stock ultimately turned out worthless; and the
trustee submitted to account for the principal with compound interest
at six per cent. :

*Held*, that this was the extent of his liability, though eight per cent.
might have been obtained on mortgages.

This was an appeal from the report of the Master
charging the plaintiff, a trustee, with compound interest
at (as the appellant contended) too high a rate, on
£1000 of trust money which came to his hands about
4th October, 1856. The Master had charged him
with eight per cent. for one year from that date,
with seven per cent. for the next six months, and
with eight per cent. thenceforward. It appeared that
in October, 1856, the plaintiff invested the money in
Upper Canada Bank stock at par; the bank was then in
good standing, and he supposed an investment in its
stock to be within his authority as trustee, and to be a
prudent investment. He learned his error in both
respects some time afterwards, and he then assumed the

1871.    investment as his own, but he made no new investment

Paterson    for the trust.   A dividend of eight per cent. was paid by
v.    the bank for a year ; but less afterwards ; and finally
Lailey.
the bank ceased to pay dividends and the stock became
wholly valueless.   The plaintiff submitted to pay compound interest at six per cent., but insisted that that was
the extent of his liability

Mr. *Crooks*, Q.C., and Mr. *Hoskin*, for the appeal.

Mr. *S. Blake*, contra.

January 11.    MOWAT, V.C.—By the trust deed the plaintiff was
authorized to invest the money "in mortgages of real
estate or in government securities;" and in *Robinson* v.
*Robinson* (a) it was decided by the Lords Justices, that
where a trustee is authorized to invest in either of two
specified modes, and he fails to invest in either mode,
Judgment.    the measure of his liability is the loss arising from not
having selected the investment which is the less beneficial to the *cestuis que trust*.   The modes authorized in
that case were parliamentary stocks or funds, and real
securities ; and it happened that, in consequence of a
subsequent rise in the stocks, an investment therein
would have proved the more beneficial to the *cestuis que
trust ;* but the Court held that they were entitled to the
principal and four per cent. only.   Before this case there
had been a conflict of authority on the point thus decided ;
but there has been none since, so far as I am aware (b).
To make out, therefore, that the plaintiff is chargeable with
more than he submits to pay, it should be made to appear
that both mortgages and " government securities" would
have yielded more.   The evidence is, that government six
per cent. debentures, the only government securities mentioned in the evidence, were at the time in question
seldom obtainable at less than par, or 'a shade less.'   They

---

(a) 1 DeG. McN. & G. 247.        (b) Knott v. Cattee, 16 Beav. at 80.

are at a premium now, I believe; though of that I see no evidence on the depositions.

Again, the usury laws were not relaxed as respects private persons (a) for nearly two years after the receipt of this money ; and the late Chancellor held in *Smith* v. *Roe* (b) and *Cameron* v. *Bethune* (c), that investments by executors and trustees at six per cent. before such relaxation were not open to objection, and that no liability was incurred by not calling in trust money after the passing of the Act, even though eight per cent. was the ruling rate thereafter paid for the use of money. If, therefore, the plaintiff had invested on mortgage at six per cent. when this money was received, and had continued the investment in the same mortgage at that rate, there is direct authority that he would be chargeable with no more than the interest thus reserved.

It was contended for the defendants, that an invest-  Judgment· ment in bank stock was in effect an investment in trade ; that the plaintiff's investment was specially objectionable, both on that account, and because the stock stood in the plaintiff's own name ; and that it should therefore subject the plaintiff to the increased penalty which the Master has imposed on him. The argument from the erroneous investment having been in bank stock is answered by the case of *Hynes* v. *Redington* (d), in which Lord *St. Leonards* expressly held, that all which an executor who had made an unauthorized investment in bank stock, instead of in government three-and-a-half per cents, should be charged with was the loss sustained by not having invested in the way he was bound to do. The circumstance of the bank stock having been purchased in the plaintiff's individual name is not greater misconduct, at worst, than if he had not invested at all ; and the circum-

---

(a) 22 Vic. ch. 85.  (b) 11 Gr. 316.
(c) 15 Gr. 486.  (d) 1 J. & LaT. at 600, 601.

stance no doubt arose from the Bank Act (*a*) declaring that the bank was not bound to regard trusts of stock.

On the whole case, I am of opinion that the only loss to which the plaintiff's unfortunate mistake subjects him is the loss of the principal and six per cent. interest, as submitted to by him; and that the appeal should be allowed. The plaintiff's costs will be costs in the cause; the respondent's costs will be reserved.

## HENRY v. SHARP.

*Administration suit—Execution creditor—Deficiency of assets.*

The plaintiff and another bought from a testator's executors and trustees certain real and personal estate; the real estate was subject to a mortgage which the vendors agreed to pay; the purchasers paid their purchase money, but the vendors applied the same to pay other debts of the testator, and left the mortgage in part unpaid; the plaintiff having bought out his co-purchaser filed a bill against the executors; a decree by consent was made, giving the plaintiff a lien on the testator's assets, ordering the defendants to pay personally what the plaintiff should fail to realize from the assets, and directing the accounts and inquiries usual in an administration suit; the estate was insufficient to pay all creditors: before the making of the decree a creditor of the estate had obtained judgment against the executors, and the sheriff seized and sold goods of the testator in their hands:

*Held*, that the plaintiff had no right to prevent the creditor from receiving the money.

Statement. This suit related to the estate of *William A. Sharp*, deceased. The bill alleged, amongst other things, that on or before the 1st March, 1869, the plaintiff and one *Andrew Sharp*, whose interest afterwards became vested in the plaintiff, purchased from the defendants, who were executors and devisees in trust of *William A. Sharp*, certain lands and goods of

(*a*) 19 & 20 Vic. ch. 121, sec. 25.

the deceased, for the price of $6000; that part of the land was at that time encumbered by a mortgage for $6000, which the defendants were to pay out of the moneys to be received from the plaintiff and his co-purchaser; that one half of the purchase money was paid by the plaintiff at the time of the purchase; that the other half was duly paid afterwards; but that the defendants in violation of their agreement had paid therewith other debts and liabilities of the testator; and that the holders of the mortgage claimed $2,700 to be due thereon. The defendants by their answer admitted these allegations. On the 1st March, 1870, a Receiver was ordered of the assets of the estate. On the 6th of April, 1870, a decree was made, declaring that the plaintiff had a lien on the assets to have the same applied in discharge of the mortgage, and directing among other things the usual accounts to be taken for the adminstration of the testator's estate. Before the obtaining of the decree, two executions had been placed in the sheriff's hands, the first at the suit of one *Reford* for $492.36, and the other at the suit of one *A. C. Sutherland* for $662.43. Under these executions, the sheriff seized the testator's goods, and made $650.75, which sum remained in his hands. There appeared to be other assets of the estate which were not in the sheriff's hands; but it was alleged that the whole assets of the estate were not sufficient to pay his debts.

The plaintiff thereupon moved to restrain *Sutherland* from proceeding with his suit, or enforcing his execution against the goods seized or against the money in the sheriff's hands.

Mr. *Hodgins*, for the motion.

Mr. *Moss*, contra.

MOWAT, V. C.—Before the passing of the Act to amend the Law of Property and Trusts in Upper

3—VOL. XVIII. GR.

1871.

Henry
v.
Sharp.

Statement.

February 8.

1871. Canada (*a*), a decree in an administration suit did not
Henry
v.
Sharp. subject an execution creditor to an injunction restraining
him from enforcing his execution; but creditors only
who had not obtained judgment were restrained. Then
does the statute afford any support to the application?

The statute places all debts of the testator on the
same footing, in case of a deficiency of assets; and in
the *Bank of British North America* v. *Mallory* (*b*), it
was held by the Chancellor, that in such a case an execution creditor was not entitled to priority over the
testator's other creditors. But the plaintiff's debt is not
a debt of the testator; and it does not appear that there
is any debt of the testator now outstanding other than
the debt due to *Sutherland*. In the administration of
the estate, the executor could claim a due allowance in
respect of the debts which he has paid; and the plaintiff
is entitled to stand in the executor's place to that extent
Judgment. and to that extent only (*c*). It was not suggested that
the executors have any equity to restrain *Sutherland*;
and, the executors having no such equity, it follows
that the plaintiff has none.

The motion must therefore be refused with costs, to be
paid by the plaintiff to *Sutherland*.

———

Mr. *Hodgins* asked that the payment should be
expressed in the order to be without prejudice to any
question as to the plaintiff's right to be repaid out of the
estate. The order was allowed to be drawn up in that
way.

———

(*a*) 29 Vic. ch. 28, sec. 28.        (*b*) 17 Gr. 102.
(*c*) See *Tanner* v. *Carter*, 2 Jur. N. S. 413; *Ewart* v. *Steven*, in the
Court of Error and Appeal, and cases there cited.—*Post* 35.

THE TRUST AND LOAN COMPANY OF CANADA V. FRASER.

*Will, construction of—Estate tail—Power.*

A testator devised certain property to his son *A.*, and to the heirs of
his body lawfully to be begotten, with power to appoint any one or
more of such heirs to take the same :

*Held*, that *A.* took an estate tail; that there was no trust in favor of
his children; and that mortgages theretofore executed by him took
precedence of the claims of the children under an appointment which
he afterwards executed in their favor.

The question in this case was as to the construction
of the following clause in the will of the Hon. *Alexander
Fraser*, deceased : "I give and devise to my son *Archibald Fraser*, and to the heirs of his body lawfully to be
begotten, with power to appoint any one or more of
such heirs to take the same," the property in question.
The will was dated the 24th August, 1853. After the
testator's death *Archibald Fraser*, named in the will,
mortgaged the devised property to the plaintiffs; and in
1867 they foreclosed their mortgages. The children of
*Archibald Fraser* were not parties to the suit; and,
shortly before the making of the final orders therein,
he executed an appointment purporting to give the property to certain of his children under the power in the will.

Statement.

On behalf of the children it was contended, that the
will gave to *Archibald Fraser* a life-estate only, and
created a trust in favor of the children as to the remainder in fee; and that the appointment was valid. The
contention of the plaintiffs was, that *Archibald Fraser*
took an estate tail; that there was no trust; that the
mortgages conveyed to the plaintiffs the fee simple; that
the deed of appointment affected the equity of redemption only; and that this equity had been duly foreclosed.

Mr. *Moss*, for the plaintiffs.

Mr. *Bethune*, for the defendants.

1871.

Trust and
Loan Co.
v.
Fraser.

The following cases were referred to by counsel: *Smith* v. *Death* (*a*), *Brooke* v. *Brooke* (*b*), *Fillingham* v. *Bromley* (*c*), *Howorth* v. *Dewell* (*d*), *Bickley* v. *Guest* (*e*), *Evans* v. *Evans* (*f*), *Jarman* on Wills, page 376.

January 11. MOWAT, V. C.—I have looked into the authorities cited, and to those also which are collected in Mr. *Jarman's* book, 3rd ed., pages 338 to 364. They shew clearly that the proper construction of the will, according to the English authorities, is that set up by the plaintiffs; and it is the English authorities which govern; the Canadian Act abolishing the old law of primogeniture is expressly declared not to " affect any limitation of any estate by deed or will (*g*)."

Judgment.

It follows that the children were not necessary parties to the foreclosure suit; and that, the appointment having been executed *pendente lite*, the children are bound by the suit, and by the final orders which were made therein shortly after the date of the deed of appointmnt.

---

(*a*) 5 Madd. 371.  
(*c*) 1 T. & R. 530.  
(*e*) 1 R. & M. 440.  
(*g*) Consol. U. C. ch. 82, sec. 41.

(*b*) 3 Sm. & Giff. 280.  
(*d*) 29 Beav. 18.  
(*f*) 33 L. J. Ch. 662.

## STEWART v. FLETCHER.

*Will, construction of—Liability of executors in respect of real estate— Administration order—Accounts of timber—Costs of executors.*

A testator devised his farm to minor children, and directed that his executors should rent the same; that no timber should be cut except for the use of the premises; and that the executors should have full power to carry the will into effect: *Held*, that it was the duty of the executors to prevent the executrix from cutting the timber for other purposes.

Under the ordinary administration decree in respect of a testator's real and personal estate, the Master may take an account of timber cut with which the defendants are chargeable.

In an administration suit, the executors were charged with so much of the expenses of the reference as was incurred in the Master's office in establishing charges which they disputed.

Hearing on further directions.

The decree was for the administration of the estate of *William Stewart*, deceased, and contained the usual directions. The Master at Hamilton had made several reports, there having been several successive appeals. According to his final findings, it appeared that the clear surplus of the testator's personal estate, after paying all debts and expenses of administration, was $638.76; that the rents and profits of the testator's farm amounted to $1916; that timber has been cut off the farm to the value of $2932.50; that the testator's widow had supported and maintained their children until her marriage with the defendant *John Aikens*, in June, 1858; that from that date the children had been supported by her and her husband; and that a proper sum to be allowed for their support to October, 1869, would have been $2104.

The testator by his will directed the surplus of his personal estate "to be placed on interest for the benefit of (his) wife and children." His farm was ultimately to go to his children in manner designated in the will;

1871.

Stewart
v.
Fletcher.

and meanwhile he directed as follows : " The farm herein named to be rented, and the proceeds thereof, for the benefit of my wife *Elizabeth* and my children. Should my said wife get married before my said children are of age, the said several amounts to be placed on interest for the benefit of my said children. I also direct that the timber from the said farm to be made use of only for the use of said premises during the time my wife remains my widow. And I do hereby make and ordain my friends *Simeon Jones* and *Daniel Fletcher* my executors, and my wife *Elizabeth* my executrix, to this my last will and testament, giving them full power and authority to carry this my will into full effect."

Mr. *Chadwick*, for the plaintiff.

Mr. *S. Blake*, for defendant *Fletcher*.

The other defendants did not appear.

January 11.

Judgment.

MOWAT, V. C.—Three questions were discussed on further directions. Of these I may notice first, the claim to an allowance for maintenance beyond the rents and the interest on the personal estate. If the personal estate had been invested according to the strict terms of the will, the interest would have amounted to more than the rents fall short of what the Master considered would be a sufficient allowance ; and I therefore think that no additional allowance can be made.

The next question to be noticed is as to the timber. I think that it was not improper to take an account of it under the general orders. Then, does sufficient appear to charge the defendants ? The Master by his first report (10th January, 1870,) found that the rents and profits received by the defendants *Daniel Fletcher* and *Elizabeth Aikens*, and for which they were "both, jointly as well as severally, liable," amounted to $5916. This

sum included their respective receipts for the timber ;
and by an order dated 23rd March, 1870, on an appeal
from the report by the defendant *Fletcher*, the Chancellor, amongst other things, declared, that the Master
ought to have certified what part of that sum was derived
from rents and profits ; and that the Master ought not
to have charged the executors with the value of the
timber cut and taken from the estate, as rents and profits,
but should have reported specially respecting the
same, and should have distinguished the amount thereof
received by and chargeable against each of the executors
separately.

In pursuance of that order, the Master made his report,
dated 3rd June, 1870 ; and thereby found, among other
things, that no portion of the rents and profits had been
" actually received" by *Fletcher*, but that the whole was
received by the executrix and her husband ; and that, of
the produce of the timber cut, *Fletcher* received $7.25,
and the executrix and her husband the rest. From this
report, also, *Fletcher* appealed ; and by the order
made on the appeal, dated 22nd June, 1870, amongst
other things, reciting that " the amounts charged by
the said Master *against the defendants* for timber cut
and taken off the lands and premises in question in this
cause appearing to this Court to be excessive," the
Court allowed the appeal with respect to the value, and
referred the report back to the Master to be reviewed.
By the final report (20th September, 1870), the Master
reduced his finding of the value to $2932.50.

This last appeal of *Fletcher's* shews, that he understood that the Master's report of 10th January, 1870,
meant to find that he was chargeable with the value of
all the timber, jointly with Mrs. *Aikens*, though the
Master found that he had not himself received the proceeds ; and the terms of the order indicate, that the
Chancellor also so read the report, or that all parties

Judgment.

1871.

Stewart
v.
Fletcher.
knew and assumed that to be the case. *Fletcher* does
not now dispute that the Master meant to find him
jointly liable for all the rents. Looking at the first two
reports together, I have no doubt that it was the Master's
intention to find *Fletcher* chargeable with the timber,
though the proceeds had not been actually received by him.

It was argued on the part of *Fletcher*, that, under the
will, he had nothing to do with the timber, and could
not be liable for more than he himself had received on
account of it. The Chancellor on one of the appeals
stated his impression to be, that the will made the executors trustees of the real estate; but he expressed no
opinion as to whether they were liable for the care of
the timber. The will directed, "no timber from the
farm to be made use of, only for the use of said
premises during the time my wife remains my widow."
I think that this imposed a duty on the executors (*a*) as

Judgment. trustees, to see that no timber was taken except for the
use of the premises. The object of the last clause,
"during the time my wife remains my widow," is not
very intelligible. It would seem to mean, either that
after her marrying again the timber might be taken for
any other purpose besides the use of the premises, or
that it was not to be taken even for that purpose
after her marriage; neither meaning is likely to have
been the testator's; grammatically, the clause has the
latter of the two meanings; and there is no reason of
probability any more than of grammar for giving to it the
other meaning. It is quite clear that the widow had no
right to the timber after she should marry, nor indeed
while she continued to be the testator's widow. It was
after her marriage that the timber was cut; and I think
that *Fletcher* should have taken steps, in this Court or
otherwise, to prevent the widow from cutting the timber,

---

(*a*) See *Brown* v. *Higgs*, 8 Ves. 574; *Ward* v. *Butler*, 2 Moll. 533;
Sug. Powers, 8th ed., p. 115, et seq.

if it was in fact cut by her, without his concurrence. But the Master does not find how that was. As the matter stands on the reports and orders, I think that I should hold *Fletcher* chargeable jointly with the widow and executrix. The Chancellor meant the Master to report all the facts relating to the question of his liability for this timber, but the Master has not done so; and, as a general rule, the evidence in the Master's office is not looked at on further directions. But if *Fletcher* is advised that the facts, as they appear from the evidence before the Master, do not sustain the conclusion at which, in reliance on the Master's opinion, I have arrived, as to *Fletcher's* joint liability, I think that, considering all things, I should give him an opportunity of bringing that evidence before me on a further argument, without the formality of an appeal.

1871.

Stewart
v.
Fletcher.

Assuming that he may not care to take advantage of that opportunity, I have considered how in that event the question of costs should be disposed of—which was the only other question argued. I think that the defendants should pay the costs of the reference so far as relates to this timber, and as relates to so much of the surcharge as was allowed against them; that the plaintiff's costs in relation to those matters should be paid by the defendants personally; that the defendants should have the other costs of the reference less what they have thus to pay; that they should have or pay no costs except those thus provided for; and that the plaintiffs should have out of the estate the costs which they are not to receive from the defendants; except the costs up to decree—the late Chancellor having decided, that a bill was unnecessary, and that a common order was sufficient, and having given the defendants their costs up to the hearing.

Judgment.

## GARDINER V. PARKER.

*Landlord and tenant—Fixtures—Greenhouse and machinery.*

A greenhouse, conservatory, and hothouse, affixed to the freehold, were held not to be removable by a tenant. Also, the glass roofs.

But machinery for heating these houses, which rested by its own weight on bricks, and was not fastened to the freehold, was held to be removable. Also, the pipes passing from the boilers through a brick wall into adjoining buildings.

This was a motion to restrain the defendant from pulling down and removing a conservatory, greenhouse, and hothouse, erected by him on certain land afterwards mortgaged by the proprietor to the plaintiff; and from committing any other waste, spoil, or destruction thereon. The plaintiff in a suit against the owner, to which the present defendant was not a party, had foreclosed the mortgage; and he was suing the present defendant in ejectment for the possession of the property.

In answer to the motion, the defendant set up, that he had entered into possession of the land, and made upon it the improvements in question, under a parol agreement with the proprietor; and that, if the parol agreement could not be carried out he was, even as tenant at will, entitled to remove the buildings and the machinery in them, as being mere tenant's fixtures. The principal affidavit filed in support of the motion, stated, that the buildings were "affixed to the freehold, and form part of the inheritance;" and the defendant's affidavit did not shew that not to be the case.

The defendant stated, "that the greater part of the roofs are formed by glass panes, resting on the rafters of the said roofs, and so constructed that they can at any time be easily taken out without in any way injuring or tearing away any part of the frame work;" and that the defendant, after the erection of the buildings, put in boilers, steampipes, and zinc troughs, for the purpose of

heating the buildings. The machinery was thus described
by the builder who put it up : " There are five boilers.
Two of these are in a wooden building, the bottom or
floor of which has been excavated below the surrounding
surface to a depth of about three feet ; the ends of these
boilers rest upon bricks placed upon the said floor or
bottom; there is some brick work surrounding one end of
one of these boilers, and the other end is uncovered
and unfastened ; the other boiler rests of its own weight
upon the bricks under its end, and is surrounded by
brick work, forming a furnace around it, but not touching it ; the whole of the brick structure under and
surrounding said boilers is totally disconnected with
any part of the other buildings, and could be wholly
removed without disturbing or damaging them. From
these boilers a pipe conducts the hot water into the
pipes in the conservatory and hothouse. The rows of
pipes in the said conservatory and hothouse are connected with the pipes for the said boilers by short pipes
which pass through a low brick wall between the said
conservatory and hothouse, and the building in which
the boilers are situate ; these short pipes can be disconnected from the pipes in the conservatory and hothouse
without disturbing the wall or injuring any part of the
buildings or pipes. The pipes in the conservatory and
hothouse are not fastened to the wall or floor, but rest of
their own weight on bricks placed on the floor at intervals of six or seven feet apart." The other boilers and
pipes also were described ; but the description did not
present any peculiarity necessary to be noted.

As to the parol agreement, the defendant's affidavit
and deposition shewed that the circumstances connected
therewith were these : The late proprietor is the defendant's brother-in-law, and was until very lately his legal
adviser ; the defendant, who was desirous of moving
into the City, wished to rent a house, with land near, on
which he could erect such buildings as those in question ;

the proprietor offered, to give the defendant the use of this land on the terms that, in consideration thereof, and of the use of the house adjoining in which two unmarried sisters of the proprietor were interested, the defendant should maintain those two ladies as members of his family ; and that the arrangement was to continue as long as the defendant chose ; but that he was to be at liberty to put an end to it at his discretion. Nothing was said about the defendant's removing the buildings, but he understood that he had that right, and the proprietor did not explain to him that he would not have it. In reliance on the agreement, the defendant took possession of the house and land, and had occupied them ever since ; he removed to the land, buildings and machinery which he had elsewhere, and had them put up at considerable expense ; and he had maintained the two ladies ever since as agreed. He had no notice of the mortgage until within the last few months.

Mr. *McLennan*, and Mr. *Snelling*, for the motion.

Mr. *Moss*, contra.

Mowat, V.C.—If the parol agreement set up had not been acted upon as alleged, the Statute of Frauds would not have been the only difficulty in the way of any attempt on the part of the defendant to enforce the agreement ; but, considering the extent to which the defendant is said to have been induced to act upon it, the large expenditure which he has made, and the professional relation to him of the mortgagor at the time, I am not prepared to say that the bargain, if established at the hearing, may not be found to be enforcible to some extent in this Court. Any indefiniteness in it would have to be considered in the light of the cases which I had occasion to cite on that point elsewhere (*a*) ;

---

(*a*) See the cases cited *Bettridge* v. *G. W. R. Co.*, 3 U. C. E. & A. 91 to 96. Also, *Wood* v. *Hewitt*, 8 Q. B. 913 ; *Lancaster* v. *Eve*, 5 C. B. N. S. 717.

the effect of the professional and confidential relationship of the mortgagor towards the defendant would require attention ; and the position of the plaintiff as mortgagee might have to be regarded with reference to *Holmes* v. *Powell* (a) and other cases. This, however, is matter for consideration at the hearing, and does not form a ground for allowing the defendant to remove the buildings and machinery in the meantime.

Then, looking at the defendant as a tenant at will only, the question would be, whether the buildings and machinery are such fixtures as such a tenant can remove ? A mortgage by the owner does not determine the tenancy before the tenant has notice of the mortgage (b), if then ; and, as well by reason of the uncertainty of a tenure of that kind, as by reason of the defendant being still in possession, I apprehend that he has not lost his right to remove any fixtures which he might have removed while the tenancy subsisted.

If, instead of the question being between a tenant and his landlord's grantee, it had arisen between a mortgagor and mortgagee, or a vendor and purchaser, or an executor and heir, there would be little difficulty in holding the machinery as well as the buildings to be irremovable (c) ; but a tenant has, as against his landlord or his landlord's grantee, the right of removing some things which in the cases suggested the mortgagor, vendor, or executor could not claim.

On the other hand, if the machinery had been put up for purposes of trade, the defendant's claim might have been maintained on authorities which are inapplicable to the case of ordinary tenants. The defendant has been

1871.

Gardiner
v.
Parker.

Judgment.

---

(a) 8 DeG. McN. & G. 572.

(b) *Doe Davies* v. *Thomas*, 6 Exch. 854.

(c) *Walmsley* v. *Milne*, 7 C. B. N. S. 115 ; *Mather* v. *Fraser*, 2 K. & J. 536 ; *Ex parte Ashbury*, L. R. 4 Ch. App. 630.

in the habit of manufacturing wine, and of selling part of what he manufactures; but I did not understand the defendant's counsel to contend that, under the circumstances appearing in the affidavits, the fixtures which the defendant has put up can be regarded as trade fixtures.

Treating the defendant as an ordinary tenant, *Jenkins* v. *Gething* (a) seems an express authority that the buildings are not removable by him.

If the buildings are not removable, the glass roofs appear to be subject to the same rule ; even though these may, as the defendant states, be easily taken off without injury to the frame work of the buildings. For it is well settled that doors and windows put in by a tenant are not removable by him; and the rule in regard to glass roofs cannot be different. In *Buckland* v. *Butterfield* (a), a case of the Marquis of *Townsend* v.

Judgment. —————— was cited by counsel as a case in which it had been expressly " determined that glasses and frames resting on brickwork in a nursery ground were not removable."

Then as to the machinery. In *Jenkins* v. *Gething* a boiler, described as " built into the floor of the greenhouse," was held to be irremovable ; but the pipes, which were connected with the boiler by screws, were held to be removable. That part of Lord *Hatherley's* judgment which refers to the machinery is as follows : " With respect to the boiler, that seems, according to the authorities, to be a fixture. It is not like a pump, easily removable. The question as to the hot water pipes is more difficult. Although they are used as the means of circulating the water from the boiler, still they are connected merely by screws, and might very naturally and easily be altered from time to time, like gas fittings,

---

(a) 2 J. & H. 520.        (b) 4 J. B. Moore, 440, at 443.

and can hardly be treated as mere adjuncts of the boiler. It is a matter of comparatively small importance; but I think upon the whole that I must hold the pipes to be removable by the occupier."

The boilers in the present case do not appear to be "built into the floor of the greenhouse," as the boiler in the case cited was; and four of them seem from the affidavits to be as easily removable as the pipes were in that case, or as the pump was in the case of *Grymes* v. *Boweren* (*a*). The last mentioned was the case cited on that point to the learned Vice Chancellor, now Lord *Hatherley ;* and there the pump, which the tenant was allowed to remove, was attached to a strong perpendicular plank resting on the ground at one end; at the other, fastened to the wall by an iron pin,—which had a head at one end, and a screw at the other, and went completely through the wall. In other cases it has been held, that an ordinary tenant may remove grates, ranges, and stoves, fixed in brickwork; also, furnaces, iron ovens, and the like (*b*).

I have spoken of four boilers. The fifth (called "A" in the sketch) is said to have some brickwork surrounding one end of it; and, as I infer, surrounding it closely; but the description given is not sufficient to enable me to form a satisfactory opinion as to whether it should be considered removable or not.

The learned counsel for the plaintiff contended, that the whole machinery was an essential part of buildings of this kind, and was for that reason irremovable. That view was not taken in *Jenkins* v. *Gething*. In *Lawton* v. *Lawton* (*c*) Lord *Hardwicke* was of opinion that, though a shed of brick or wood erected by a tenant over an engine was irremovable by him, it did not follow that

---

(*a*) 6 Bing. 437.　　　(*b*) See *Amos* on Fixtures, 342, 2nd ed.

(*c*) 3 Atk. 14; see also *Marcus* v. *Burnside*, 17 U. C. C. P. 430.

the engine also was on that account irremovable. The
same view was acted upon in *Shinner* v. *Harman* (a),
and *Whitehead* v. *Bennett* (b).

There is therefore express authority for holding the
pipes and troughs to be removable ; assuming that the
facts in regard to these are as stated on the part of the
defendant.   On the same assumption, four of the boilers
appear to be removable also ; and as to the fifth boiler I
can express no opinion.

I have thus, as requested on the argument, expressed
my opinion as far as I could on all the points in question ;
it having been suggested, that in that case the parties
would probably come to an arrangement without further
litigation.   But should they not agree, I think that the
defendant ought not to remove any part of the machinery
until the hearing of the cause ; as at present I have only
Judgment. the defendant's *ex parte* statement of its condition, and
the plaintiff should have an opportunity, if he desires
it, of having the facts investigated at a formal hearing,
and of having the case as it may then appear, discussed
and considered, before any of the property is removed.
The interlocutory injunction to issue should therefore be
as prayed ; the plaintiff undertaking not to enforce his
*hab. fac. pos.* meantime, and undertaking also to abide
by such order as the Court may make as to damages and
otherwise.

---

(a) 3 Ir. Com. L. N. S. 243.        (b) 27 L. J. Chan. 474.

## O'RIELLY v. ROSE.

*Insolvency—Advertisements of sale—Jurisdiction.*

Advertisements by assignees in insolvency for the sale of property of the insolvent should describe the property and state the title with the distinctness required in equity in the case of advertisements by trustees and other officials.

In case of a sale by an assignee in insolvency being open to objection on the part of the creditors, the remedy of objecting creditors is by application to the County Court Judge, not by suit in Chancery in the first instance.

This was an application by a creditor, suing on behalf of himself and all other creditors of *John Smith*, an insolvent, to restrain the assignee from carrying into effect certain sales made to the other defendants of leasehold and freehold property belonging to the insolvent. So far as regards the leasehold, the defendants alleged (in answer) that there was no intention to carry out the sale, as they had been advised that it was not a valid sale under the act 32 & 33 Vic. ch. 16. As to the freehold land, it appeared that the impeached contract had been entered into after an abortive attempt to sell by auction; and that the contract was sanctioned by a resolution of the creditors. The plaintiff alleged against the sale, that the advertisement was too loose and general; that proper steps had not been taken to effect an advantageous sale by auction; that the meeting of creditors at which the subequent sale was agreed to had not been legally called for that purpose; that the price was inadequate; and that the terms of sale were such as the creditors present had no power to sanction.

Mr. *James McLennan*, for the creditors.

Mr. *Grahame*, contra.

1871.

O'Rielly
v.
Rose.

February 8.

Judgment.

MOWAT, V. C.—I do not find, among the papers left with me, a copy of the advertisement, but I understand it to be open to some of the objections observed upon in various reported cases (*a*). Those objections apply to advertisements by assignees in insolvency as well as to those of other officials or trustees.. But it was argued that it is too late for the plaintiff to raise the question. On the whole case, and after hearing read on the argument the affidavits on both sides with reference to this question, and to the other matters in issue, I was inclined to think that a case for the interference of the Court had not been sufficiently established, even if this Court had original jurisdiction in the matter. Having since arrived at the clear conclusion, that the proper authority to which the plaintiff should resort in the first instance is the County Court Judge, I have not found it necessary to give further consideration to the other questions raised. I think that the 50th section of the late act (*b*) gives the County Court jurisdiction in such a case as the plaintiff desires to set up; and that a resort to this Court in the first instance is unnecessary, and should not be sanctioned. This view is in accordance with the course in England under the bankruptcy laws there (*c*); and is warranted as well by the language of the 50th section of the Act in question, as by the whole scope and spirit of the act.

Injunction refused.

---

(*a*) McDonald v. Cameron, 13 Gr. 84; McDonald v. Gordon, 1 Chamb. 125; McAlpine v. Young, 2 Ib. 177.

(*b*) 32 & 33 Vic. ch. 16.

(*c*) Ex parte Cheetham, 2 D. M. & G. 223; Pike v. Martin, 7 Jur. N. S. 251; Heath v. Chadwick, 2 Ph. 469; and other cases collected, 1 Deac. Bankruptcy, 3rd Ed. 917, 918.

. Ewart v. Steven. [In Appeal.]*

*Agent and trustee, advances to and by—Claim against estate.*

M. was administrator of the estate of S. and was managing the real
estate for the heirs ; he was also one of the executors and trustees
of E. ; there was a sum of $808.55 due for taxes on some property
of the S. estate, and M. paid the same with money of the E. estate,
directing the agent of that estate to charge the amount to the S.
estate ; M. did not enter the amount in his accounts with the S.
estate as a loan, and, on the contrary, in the accounts which he
rendered he took credit for the amount as a payment by himself ;
the heirs knew nothing of the loan until some time afterwards ;
they had not authorized M. to borrow money ; and he was at the
time indebted to them as agent in a sum exceeding the amount
of the taxes ; M. afterwards died insolvent, and indebted to both
estates :

*Held*, in appeal, that the E. estate could not hold the heirs of the S.
estate liable for the $808.55, and was not entitled to a lien therefor
on the property in respect of which the taxes were payable.

This was an appeal from a decree of the Court of Statement.
Chancery as reported *ante* volume xvi., page 93.

At the time of the transaction which gave rise to this
suit, *James McIntyre* was administrator of the estate of
*Andrew Steven*. The widow of *Steven* was administratrix.
She had removed to the United States before the transaction in question, and *McIntyre* appeared to have been
left in sole charge of the estate real and personal. *McIntyre* was also one of the devisees in trust and an executor
of *James Bell Ewart*. *Josiah M. Babington* was
their agent. (Through an oversight, *Babington* is stated
in. the report of the case in the Court below to have
been one of the executors). On the 25th of November,
1865, a sum of money which was due to the *Ewart*
estate on mortgage was paid to *Babington* in *McIntyre's*
office by appointment. When it was paid, *McIntyre* said
that he was in advance to the estates of both *Ewart* and

---

* Present.—Draper, C. J., Richards, C. J., Spragge, C.,
Morrison, J., Mowat, V. C., Gwynne, and Galt, JJ.

*Steven ;* and that he would retain $1000 of the sum paid, for the purpose of paying some taxes on property of the *Steven* estate : and he directed *Babington* to charge the amount to the *Steven* estate.  He handed to *Babington* at the same time a receipt in the following terms :—" Received, Hamilton, 25th November, 1865, from *John Babington*, Esquire, the sum of $1000 in full, to pay taxes on the *V. H. Tisdale* property, and others, to-day ;  the same to be refunded in December with interest.  For the estate of *A. Steven—James McIntyre*, administrator."  This was what took place as stated by *Babington*, the only witness to it.  The property mentioned in the receipt belonged to the *Steven* estate ;  taxes were due upon it to the amount of $808.55 ;  and the property had been advertized for sale for nonpayment of them.  It was not true, however, that *McIntyre* was in advance to either estate ; and, on the contrary, at the date of the loan he was indebted to the *Steven* estate, as the agent thereof, in a sum exceeding the amount of the taxes.  On the same 25th of November, 1865, he deposited to his credit at the bank $810, which it was evident was part of the $1000 ;  and he had no other money then in the bank.  On the same day he gave to the collector of taxes a cheque for the $808.55 ;  which was paid.  In *McIntyre's* accounts with the *Steven* estate, he did not then or subsequently enter the loan from the *Ewart* estate ; but he took credit for the $808.55 as paid by himself; and he rendered accounts which contained that charge.  *McIntyre* afterwards died insolvent, and indebted to both estates.  The present suit was by the representatives of the *Ewart* estate, to make the *Steven* estate responsible for the $1000, and to have it declared that they had a lien therefor on the *Tisdale* property.

The heirs of the *Steven* estate had not authorized *McIntyre* to borrow money to pay the taxes ;  some of the heirs were minors, and not competent to give

such authority: and the questions were, whether such
an authority should be implied, and whether any and
what liability on the part of the heirs arose from what
had occurred.

Mr. *Blake*, Q.C., for the appeal.

Mr. *Crooks*, Q.C., contra.

The judgment of the Court was delivered by

MOWAT, V.C.*—If the plaintiffs are entitled to a decree
against the heirs of the *Steven* estate for the money in
question, the claim of a specific lien on the *Tisdale*
property is not of any practical importance, as the *Steven*
estate is more than solvent. The case of *Clack* v.
*Holland* (a)—which the Chancellor met with after the
appeal—has satisfied him that, looking at the case as of
a loan made by *McIntyre* from a stranger (which was
the view on which the judgment of the Chancellor proceeded), the claim of the plaintiffs is not sustainable.
One question in *Clack* v. *Holland* had reference to sums
advanced by a third person to pay premiums on a policy,
and was stated by the Master of the Rolls to amount to
this (b): "A trustee has received money for the purpose of paying premiums on a policy which it is his duty
to apply, can he, by misapplying that money to his own
use, and borrowing money for the purpose of keeping
the policy on foot, give a valid security to the person who
advances money for that purpose?" and the learned
Judge was clear that he could not. In *Tanner* v. *Carter*
(c) Vice Chancellor *Kindersley* held, that a proctor
employed by an executrix to obtain probate of the will
has no lien on the estate for the costs of obtaining it;
but that after the death of the executrix, if she was not
indebted to the estate, and in that case only, the proctor

February 4.

Judgment.

* SPRAGGE, C., was absent from illness.
(a) 19 B. 275.     (b) P. 276.     (c) 2 Jur. N. S. 413.

1871.  might claim the amount against the estate.  There are

other cases in which the same principle has been acted
upon.  I may refer to *Worrall* v. *Harford* (*a*), *Hall*
v. *Lever* (*b*), *Feoffees of Heriot's Hospital* v. *Ross* (*c*),
*Francis* v. *Francis* (*d*), *Re Wilson & Hughes* in
*Mathews* v. *Morley* in Chancery here (*e*), and *Campbell*
v. *Bell* (*f*).  The Chancellor informs us that none of
these cases was cited to him.

Then does the circumstance that the money was trust
money, and was taken by *McIntyre* from an estate of
which he was himself a trustee, make a difference in
favor of the plaintiffs?  On that point there was no
judgment in the Court below.  *Thorndike* v. *Hunt* (*g*)
is an authority upon it against the plaintiffs.  There a
trustee of two different settlements had applied to his own
use funds which were subject to one of the settlements.
Being afterwards called upon to pay the amount into

Court, he did so with funds which he held under the other
settlement.  The parties for whose benefit the payment
was made had no notice of the source from which the
funds had come; and it was held that the transfer into
Court was in effect a transfer for valuable consideration,
and that those whose funds had been so transferred could
not follow them.  The present case seems *a fortiori;*
for, in the cited case the specific fund still existed;
here the money is gone; the debt of *McIntyre* to the
*Steven* estate had *pro tanto* been paid with it more than
two years before this suit was brought.

*Cooper* v. *Wormold* (*h*) is another case to the same
effect.  There trust funds of the estate of a testator

---

(*a*) 8 Ves. 4, 8.                    (*b*) 1 Hare 571.
(*c*) 12 C. & F 507.                  (*d*) 5 DeG. McN. & G. 108.
(*e*) Unreported on this point;  see 14 Gr. 558.
(*f*) 16 Gr. 115.                     (*g*) 3 DeG. & J. 563.
(*h*) 27 B. 266.  See also Case v. James, 29 B. 512; 3 DeG. F. &
J. 256.

were, on the second marriage of his widow, transferred 1871.
into the names of two persons who were trustees and Ewart
executors of the testator's will, and who were to be v.
Steven.
trustees of the settlement on the intended marriage.
They as such trustees of the settlement executed a
deed declaring the intended trusts, and calling themselves and treating themselves as trustees of the settlement. The bill was by a legatee under the testator's
will claiming the funds as belonging to that estate; but,
marriage being a valuable consideration, and the husband having had no notice before the marriage that the
money was not the lady's own money, the bill was dismissed. The Master of the Rolls in giving judgment
said; " It would confuse all the trusts if, where money
has been transferred to trustees expressly on the trusts of
a particular settlement, these trusts could afterwards be
set aside by other *cestuis que trust* of the same trustees,
saying, 'this money came from another source, you
were trustees of it, and you ought to have known that Judgment.
it came from that source, and you ought not to have
declared any other trusts of it.' The trustee may be
guilty of, and liable for a breach of trust; but in respect
of the money itself, there are other persons who have
become entitled for valuable consideration, and whose
rights are not to be set aside by the fact that the money
came from another source."

On the whole we are of opinion that the decree must
be reversed, and the bill dismissed with costs.

GWYNNE, J.—The learned counsel for the respondents
argued the case as being one of loan by the *Ewart*
estate to the *Steven* estate, but in my judgment it
cannot be so regarded, notwithstanding the receipt
signed by *James McIntyre*, as administrator of the
*Steven* estate, for not only had Mr. *Babington* no
authority to lend the moneys of the *Ewart* estate, nor,
so far as appears, Mr. *McIntyre* any authority to bor-

1871.

Ewart
v.
Steven.

row to bind the heirs of the *Steven* estate; but Mr. *Babington's* own evidence satisfies me that *McIntyre* was acting as principal and *Babington* as agent only in the receipt of the moneys which are sought now to be recovered from the *Steven* estate.

*Babington* says: "A sum of money due the *Ewart* estate, on mortgage, was paid to me in *McIntyre's* office by appointment, and when it was paid *McIntyre* said he was in advance to both the estates of *Ewart* and *Steven, and that he would retain* $1,000 *of the sum paid,* for the purpose, as he said, of paying taxes on the *Steven* property. * * He *also retained* $420, which he told me to charge to him personally; the $1,000 *he told me* to charge to the *Steven* estate."

Judgment.

Now, when *McIntyre* received this money, I have no doubt he had it in his hands as one of the trustees of the *Ewart* estate, and that *Babington*, as agent of the trustees, obeying *McIntyre's* orders, cannot alter the character in which the money came to *McIntyre's* hands.

The case then is resolved into the case of a trustee of one estate, who is also agent of another, applying the moneys come to his hand as trustee, to reinstate moneys of which he had defrauded the estate of which he was agent. These moneys being so applied for the benefit of the *Steven* estate, made the *cestuis que trustent* of that estate, purchasers for value without notice, and the case, as it appears to me, is governed by *Thorndike* v. *Hunt* (*a*), and *Case* v. *James* (*b*).

*Per Curiam.*—Appeal allowed, and bill in Court below dismissed with costs.

---

(*a*) 3 DeG. & J. 563.    (*b*) 29 Bev. 512.

DENISON v. DENISON.

*Will, construction of—Double maintenance.*

A testator (amongst other things) devised certain lands to each of his
two younger children, and directed that the rents should be and
remain to his widow or executors for the education and up-bringing
of the devisees respectively until they were twenty-one, &c. ; and
he also left all the dividends and profits of his bank stock, &c.,
to his widow and executors for the same purpose. The residue
of his estate was to be divided equally amongst all his children.
The rents of the lands devised to one of the younger children were
alone more than sufficient for his education and maintenance :

*Held,* notwithstanding, that he was entitled to a share of the dividends
bequeathed; that the whole income derived from the stocks being
given, the gift could not, in favour of the residuary legatees, be
construed as conditional on being needed for the purpose specified.

This case is reported *ante* volume xvii., page 219.
It was afterwards reheard. The same counsel appeared
for the parties; when, after taking time to look into the
cases, the Court affirmed the decree with costs.

———

BUCHANAN v. SMITH.

*Insolvent Act—Priority of subsequent creditors—Costs.*

An insolvent compounded with his creditors, and had his goods restored to him ; he thereupon resumed his business with the knowledge
of his assignees and creditors, and contracted new debts. It was
subsequently discovered that he had been guilty of a fraud which
avoided his discharge, whereupon he absconded, and an attachment
was sued out against him by his subsequent creditors :

*Held,* that they were entitled to be paid out of his assets in priority to
the former creditors.

In such a case the assignee, as representing the former creditors, was
ordered to pay the costs of a suit brought by the subsequent creditors to enforce their rights.

This case is reported *ante* volume xvii., page 208. It
was reheard at the instance of the defendant.

6—VOL. XVIII. GR.

Mr. *Blake*, Q.C., and Mr. *Proudfoot* for the plaintiffs.

Mr. *Miller*, for defendant.

In addition to the cases cited on the original hearing the following were referred to : *Foster* v. *McKinnon* (*a*), *White* v. *Garden* (*b*).

The Court affirmed the decree except as to costs. No costs had by the decree been given to either party against the other, and the decree was varied in that respect, the defendant being ordered to pay the plaintiffs' costs of the suit and of the rehearing.

---

## COLEMAN v. GLANVILLE.

*Dower—Receiver—Injunction.*

A widow entitled to dower commenced an action therefor against a tenant, to whom, without express authority, the property had been leased by a Receiver in a suit in this Court.
*Held*, that she was not at liberty to proceed in such action without the leave of the Court.

A testator devised his farm to his widow for life, determinable upon her marrying again, and gave to her a certain portion of the dwelling house situate thereon ; and subject to this estate of the widow in the portion of the house, the will shewed an intention that the rest of the house and the farm should be kept in entirety, and be personally occupied and enjoyed by his sons until the youngest should attain the age of twenty-one.
*Held*, that the widow must elect between the provision made for her by the will and dower.
*Held*, also, that a second marriage, after having elected to take under the will, would not resuscitate the right to dower.

In such a case the widow remained on the farm, and received some small sums of money for her own use, but had never had set apart for her exclusive enjoyment the portion of the house devised to her:
*Held*, that these acts did not amount to that deliberate and well considered choice made with a knowledge of rights and in full view of consequences, which is necessary to constitute an election.

---

(*a*) L. R. 4 C. P. 701.          (*b*) 10 C. B. 919.

This was a petition by *Whitwell Hall*, the Receiver appointed in the cause, for the object (amongst others) of having an action of dower instituted by the widow of the testator restrained.

Mr. *Bethune*, in support of the petition.

Mr. *Fitzgerald*, for the widow ; and

Mr. *Arnoldi*, for a younger child of the testator, contra.

STRONG, V. C.—This is a suit having for its object the construction and the execution of the trusts of the will of *Richard Coleman*, deceased. A decree referring it to the Master at Whitby to take the usual administration accounts and directing the appointment of a receiver, was pronounced on the 4th of April, 1864. Under this decree the Master appointed *Whitwell Hall*, the present petitioner, to be receiver. The receiver, on the 17th March, 1869, put *Francis Thomas Coleman*, one of the plaintiffs, in possession of the lands of the estate as his tenant, and this tenancy still continues to exist. The widow of the testator, also one of the plaintiffs, and who, in the early part of the present year, inter-married with *John Camplin*, has lately brought an action of dower against *Francis Thomas Coleman*, the tenant under the receiver, to have dower assigned to her in the lands in his occupation. The receiver now presents a petition seeking to have this action restrained as having been improperly brought without the leave of the Court. It is a rule of the Court, well established, and one which is essential for the due protection of its officers, that no action shall be allowed to be prosecuted against a receiver, or those in possession under him, without the leave of the Court. It is, however, contended on behalf of Mrs. *Camplin*, that this rule does not apply to the present case for two reasons—first, because the action is brought on a paramount title ; and secondly, because it is brought not against the receiver, but

Coleman
v.
Glanville.

against his tenant. I am of opinion that neither of
these objections constitute a sufficient answer to the
petition. It is clear that the first contention has no
foundation in authority, but that on the contrary it is
laid down in numerous cases, that a party seeking
relief on a title, superior to that of the receiver, or of
the party in whose interest the receiver has been
appointed, must apply to the Court which will take care
that either at the hands of the Court itself, or in some
other mode which the Court will sanction, justice is
administered to him. I need not refer particularly to
the authorities as they are collected in Mr. *Kerr's*
Treatise on Receivers (a).

The other ground is equally untenable. The possession of the receiver is that of the Court; and a tenant
under the receiver is therefore virtually the tenant of the
Court, and must be protected as such. It was further

Judgment. objected that the receiver had no power to let for the
term of eight years as he has assumed to do, without the
sanction of the Court, and that having thus exceeded his
authority, the agreement under which the tenant holds is
void. But even although this be so, it can make no
difference; for the tenant if the lease is ineffectual to
assure to him the term must be in possession as the
tenant-at-will, or the mere bailiff of the receiver. It
was not contended that the demandant in the action of
dower had not notice that *Francis Thomas Coleman* was
in possession under the receiver, and it could not have
been so contended, for she was a party to the informal
document by which the present tenancy was created;
and moreover, it appears from the evidence that her
actual attorney in the action at law, though not the
attorney whose name is indorsed on the writ—was the
Master of the Court who appointed the receiver, and to
whom the cause still stands referred. It is clear, therefore, that the action must be stayed.

_____

(a) At pp. 125, 126, and 127.

The costs of the petition, ought of course to follow the event, unless good grounds are shewn for departing from the general rule, and I think no such reasons appear.

As to the pendency of negotiations for stating a special case for the opinion of this Court, that alone would certainly be no ground for refusing the receiver his costs. Then these negotiations were, I think, not unreasonably assumed to be broken off when, on the 14th October, the receiver's solicitors caused the petition to be served, they then having received no answer to their letter of the 8th of October, to Mr. *Dartnell*, the attorney for the demandant, in which they distinctly gave notice that they would proceed unless a stay should be agreed to pending the stating of the case, and which letter Mr. *Dartnell* did not answer until the 14th, the day on which the petition was served. Further, in Mr. *Dartnell's* letter of the 14th, he does not agree to the peremptory requirements of Messrs. *Blake, Kerr & Boyd's* letter of the 8th, that all proceedings in the action shall be stayed pending the settlement of the special case, for he proposes to continue the proceedings and merely to stay trial, which is a counter proposition and not an accession to the terms they had offered. On the whole, I am clearly of opinion that the receiver was right in presenting the petition under all the circumstances, and that he must have his costs against *John Camplin*, who is joined in the action as a co-plaintiff with his wife, and who, I take it for granted, has been served with the petition. Apart altogether from the questions raised by the petition and which I have just decided, I was asked to adjudicate upon the substantial question of the widow's right to dower—and all adult parties consenting, and it appearing to be a mode of proceeding beneficial to the infant parties as calculated to save expense, I agreed to determine it.

The right to dower depends upon the considerations : firstly, whether, under the will of the testator *Richard Coleman*, his widow is called upon to elect between her legal provision by way of dower, and the gifts to her contained in the will ? and secondly, if she is so bound to elect—whether she has already made her election, or has it still open to her to repudiate the benefits conferred by the will and abide by her legal rights. By his will the testator, after giving several legacies to his daughters, gives to his wife an annuity of £25 for life, charged on the realty and payable in quarterly payments, and then he proceeds as follows : " From the time of my death my will is that my said wife shall live and reside in and have to her sole use certain rooms in my house, namely : the square room, clothes room, bed room adjoining, and all the furniture that generally furnishes these rooms to her sole use." The will then, after some provisions of minor importance, proceeds as follows : " But my will

is that if she marry or co-habit with any man, the aforesaid annuity and other privileges shall totally cease, nevertheless, if the guardians or trustees hereafter named, deem it right that my widow and her husband should stay in the house with her family for their welfare and benefit, so be it. Yet, they are under the control, discretion, order, and permission of my guardians, and executors hereinafter named absolutely. My will is touching my wife, as marriage will bar her from claims before named in this my will."

The testator then, subject to the payment of his debts and legacies, gives all the residue of his property to his three sons, *Francis Thomas*, *William John*, and *Albert*, whom he appoints to be his executors ; and he also appoints *Thomas Glanville* and *William Hunt* to be the trustees of his will and the guardians of his children. There is then contained in the will the following direction : " Further, my will is that the property shall be kept together, and no division made before *Albert Cole-*

*man* attains the age of twenty-one years; should either
of the three brothers die before the period *Albert Cole-*
*man* would attain the age of twenty-one years, no
division shall be made before that time that *Albert*
*Coleman,* if living, shall, may, or would, have attained
that age of twenty-one years, the whole property and
all its accruing profits not otherwise given herein as
legacy and annuity shall be kept together before that
time, and then equally divided, share and share alike,
equally between the surviving executors:—legitimate
child or children of either of them shall have a father's
share. The property to be partitioned and divided at
the discretion of the guardians herein named. These
guardians or executors are strictly forbidden to encumber
the freehold estate by mortgage or otherwise. Use the
farm economically." And then was added to the will
after the testatum this clause: " I will neither of my
sons shall bring a wife into the house with my wife and
children before the day and date *Albert* would attain
the age of twenty-one years."

Putting out of question for the present the effect of
the second marriage which has taken place, I have no
doubt but that, according to the proper construction of
this will, the claim of dower is inconsistent with the
enjoyment of this provision which is made for the widow.
The gift of the annuity though charged on all the real
estate would not *of itself* raise a question of election;
this is well established by authority: *Jarman* on Wills.
(*a*), *Holdich* v. *Holdich* (*b*). But by the will an estate
for life determinable upon the widow marrying again, is
given to her in a certain portion of the house situated
upon the farm of which the real estate consists; and
subject to this estate of the widow in a portion of the
house the testator has most anxiously indicated an inten-

1871.

Coleman
v.
Glanville.

Judgment.

(*a*) 2nd Ed. pp. 390, 391, and cases there cited.
(*b*) 2 Y. & C. C. C. 11.

1871.

Coleman
v.
Glanville.

tion that the farm, including the part of the dwelling house not given to the widow should be kept in entirety and be personally occupied and enjoyed by his sons until his youngest son should attain the age of twenty-one, when it was to be divided equally amongst the three sons. This destination of the property wonld be utterly defeated if one-third of it was to be set off by metes and bounds, and assigned to the widow for her dower. The case is therefore to be ruled by a line of authority from which *Small* v. *Brain* (a), *Butcher* v. *Kemp* (b), *Goodfellow* v. *Goodfellow* (c), *Roadley* v. *Dixon* (d), and *Maclennan* v. *Grant* (e), may be selected as cases exactly in point, though none of them is so strong in its circumstances as the present case.

Judgment.

The question then arises, had the second marriage, upon which the dower and bequests were to cease, the effect of remitting the widow to her dower, assuming that she had already elected to take under the will. Upon the reasoning of the cases already cited, and particularly upon what is said by *V. C. Knight Bruce* in *Holdich* v. *Holdich*, I am of opinion that she must, in that case, continue bound by her election, after her second marriage. The principle upon which the rule of construction proceeds, in a case like the present, is that the Court finds the will to contain by implication that which, if expressed, would be in form a declaration that the interest given, though limited to widowhood, should be in lieu of dower, in which case it is plain that there would be no resuscitation of the right to dower if, after electing to take under the will there should, on a second marriage, be a cesser of the estate given *durante viduitate*.

Before proceeding to inquire as to whether there has or has not been an election, it will be convenient to

---

(a) 4 Madd. 125.  (b) 5 Madd. 61.  (c) 18 Beav. 356.
(d) 3 Russ. 192.  (e) 15 Grant, 65.

determine what are the present rights of the widow if
she had not, prior to her late marriage, adopted the
will.

I regard the direction in the will authorizing the
trustees to permit the widow, in the discretion of the
trustees, to occupy part of the dwelling house for the
"welfare and benefit", of the children, as being, as
indeed the testator has himself expressed it to be, a
provision in favor of the children rather than of the
widow, and to amount, to no more than this, that the
trustees may, if they think fit, permit the widow to
perform her maternal duties to the children by living
with them in the house which the testator has fixed
upon as their place of residence, but whether this
permission is to be given or not is to depend on
the uncontrolled discretion of the trustees who, in
exercising their judgment, are to regard the interests
of the children, and not that of the widow. Such
a precarious occupation so dependent on what the
trustees may regard as beneficial to the children, cannot
be regarded as a gift to the widow in recompence for
dower. I think, however, that notwithstanding the
comparatively trifling value of the bequest to the widow
in the case of her second marriage,—I mean the gift of
horse, cow, bed, and furniture,—the principle of the
cases I have already referred to as shewing the effect of
the direction that the land shall be kept entire in the
personal enjoyment of the children applies, and that,
notwithstanding the great reduction of her interest as a
beneficiary under the will consequent on the second
marriage, she must still elect.

Judgment.

The final question then is, had the widow, at the time
she married her present husband in January, 1870,
made her election? for there is no pretence for saying
that she has, since her marriage, done anything which
could bind her.

7—VOL. XVIII. GR.

The evidence shews that she had, from the time of the testator's death in 1859, lived in the house with her family, and superintended the affairs of the household and of the farm; that she had never had set apart for her use, or had any exclusive enjoyment of the particular rooms which had been devised to her; that she had, from time to time, received some small sums of money from the trustees for her own clothing, amounting to about $15 a year; and that a short time before her marriage, and when it was in contemplation, Mr. *Francis Thomas Coleman* paid her $100. Having regard to the decided cases, it is out of the question to say that these acts amount to the exercise of that deliberate and well considered choice, made with a knowledge of rights, and in full view of consequences which is requisite to constitute an election. The cases of *Wake* v. *Wake* (*a*), and *Reynard* v. *Spence* (*b*), are precisely in point. I must therefore declare that it is still open to the widow

to exercise her election between dower and the bequests given her by the will in the event which has occurred of a second marriage. The widow must account for what she has received from the trustees and her son, which she may do by setting the amount off against the arrears of dower which she is entitled to claim.

---

(*a*) 1 Ves. Jr. 335            (*b*) 4 Beav. 103.

## CRAWFORD V. FINDLAY.

*Fixtures—Mortgage.*

On the sale of a woollen factory and machinery, it was stipulated that until the purchase money should be fully paid, the vendees were not to remove the machinery. The vendors afterwards executed a conveyance to the purchasers, and the latter, to secure the unpaid purchase money, executed a mortgage which purported to be of the factory only, and did not mention the machinery :

*Held,* that the covenant against removing the machinery remained in force :

*Held, also,* that the mortgage covered not only the machinery which were fastened with nails or screws ; but also machines which were kept in their place by cleats ; as well as the plates and paper used with the press.

The purchasers resold, their vendee having notice of the covenant, and the vendee subsequently became insolvent.

*Held,* that his assignee in insolvency was not at liberty to remove the machinery by reason of non-registration under the Chattel Mortgage Act or otherwise.

Examination of witnesses and hearing at the Autumn Sittings of 1870, in Hamilton.

Mr. *Burton,* Q. C., for the plaintiff, cited *McDonald* v. *Weeks* (a), *Walmsley* v. *Milne* (b), *Haley* v. *Hammersley* (c), *Re Astbury* (d), *Longbottom* v. *Berry* (e).

Mr. *C. G. Crickmore,* for defendant *Findlay,* referred to. *Schrieber* v. *Malcolm* ( f ), *Gooderham* v. *Denholm* (g), *Patterson* v. *Johnson* (h), *Hope* v. *Cumming* (i), *Trappes* v. *Harter* ( j ), and *Waterfall* v. *Pruniston* (k).

STRONG, V. C.—*William Crawford,* the plaintiff's testator, some years before his death, built a woollen

<sub>Dec. 14.
(1870.)</sub>

---

(a) 8 Gr. 297.

(b) 6 Jur. N. S. 125.

(c) 4 L. T. N. S. 269.

(d) L. R. 4 Ch. App. 630.

(e) L. R. Q. B. 123.

(f) 8 Gr. 433.

(g) 18 U. C. Q. B. 203.

(h) 10 Gr. 583.

(i) 10 U. C. C. P.

(j) 2 C. & M. 170.

(k) 6 El. & Bl. 875.

factory and furnished it with appropriate machinery.
By his will he gave the plaintiffs, his executors, a power
of sale over this property.  The plaintiffs entered into a
contract of sale with three persons, *David Cumming,
Cornell,* and *Fady,* by which they agreed to sell not
merely the land and buildings, but the factory complete,
with all its machinery, as it had been left by the
testator, for the price of $4,000, of which $1,500
was to be paid in cash, and thereupon a conveyance
was to be executed and a mortgage given to the
plaintiffs to secure the unpaid residue of $2,500.  This
agreement contained a covenant on the part of the purchasers, that until the purchase money was fully paid
they would not remove the machinery from the building.
Subsequently, *John Cumming* purchased the interest of
the original purchasers, and proposed to the plaintiff to
complete the purchase in his own name; but this the plaintiffs declined, and insisted on the contract being carried

out by the original purchasers, which was done.  $1,500,
part of the purchase money, was paid, and a conveyance
made to the original vendees, by whom a mortgage for
securing $2,500 to the plaintiffs was executed.  One
instalment of the sum secured by this mortgage was past
due when the bill was filed.  The property is described
in the mortgage, as " all and singular that certain parcel
or tract of land and premises known as Branchton
Woollen Factory."

The evidence shews, beyond question, that without the
machinery the land and building would be a grossly
inadequate security for the purchase money unpaid.

It is clearly established by proof that *John Cumming*
had notice of the covenant not to remove the machinery,
contained in the agreement with the original purchasers.
Subsequently to the execution of the purchase deed and
mortgage, two of the purchasers, *David Cumming* and
*Fady,* conveyed to *John Cumming,* in pursuance of the

contract to sell to him, which had been entered into anterior to the conveyance by the plaintiffs. But *Cornell*
has not yet conveyed, though he was bound by agreement to do so. On receiving a conveyance, *John Cum-*
*ming* entered into the occupation of the factory, and
carried on the business of manufacturing in it until in
the spring of the present year he became insolvent,
whereupon the defendant *Findlay* was appointed his
assignee. Soon afterwards Mr. *Findlay* removed the
machinery from the factory, and this bill was filed
seeking an injunction to restrain *Findlay* from selling
or disposing of the machinery, and also praying that he
should be ordered to return it to the factory.

The machinery, and the mode in which it was affixed,
are described in the evidence as follows :

(1.) An old 'Jack,' fastened by screws through the
feet; (2.) A new 'Jack,' fastened in the same way, and
the plaintiffs witnesses also state that it was fastened by
nails to an upright post; (3.) Three 'Power Looms,'
fastened in the same way, but the defendant's witnesses
assert that they could be raised without removing the
screws; (4.) A 'Spooling Machine,' fastened to the
floor by screws; (5.) A 'Warper,' running on rails
which are fastened to the floor ; (6.) A 'Press,' which
was bolted firmly to the building, this was not removed,
but the plates and papers used with it were; (7.) The
'Picker,' 'Breaker,' 'Condenser,' 'Shears,' 'Gig,'
'Napper,' and 'Duster,' were not affixed, but rested by
their own weight, and were kept in their places by cleats.
Steam power was supplied to the factory in which these
machines stood in the usual way, and all were connected
by belting with the motive power, and it was proved
that each machine was essential to the working of the
factory as a whole.

The learned counsel for the plaintiffs, on this state of

1871.

Crawford
v.
Findlay.

facts, claimed a decree on these two distinct grounds:
First, because the machines in question were fixtures,
and as such were bound by the mortgage of the realty;
Secondly, because the defendant *Findlay* was bound
by the covenant not to remove the machinery contained
in the original contract of sale. Both these cases are
distinctly made by the bill. I am of opinion that the
plaintiffs are entitled to a decree. I think it clear that
all the machines which were fastened by nails or screws
to the freehold are fixtures, and covered by the mort
gage as part of the realty. I include in these the
power looms, for I come to the conclusion on the
evidence, that these looms at the time the mortgage was
executed, were affixed as the witness *Green* described
them. I adopt the statement of *Green*, in this respect,
in preference to that of *Wright*, whose evidence I think
entitled to less weight than that of the former witness.
The plates and papers used with the press, although, of
Judgment. course, not attached in any way to the building, are
to be regarded as constructive fixtures, as articles of
a similar character were held to be by Lord Justice
*Giffard*, in *ex parte Astbury* (a).

As to the machines which were fastened, or rather
kept in their places by cleats only, I have had very
great doubts, and I am perhaps going further than has
been gone in any case yet, in holding them to be fixtures.
But having regard to the facts, that all this property
was sold together, for one indivisible price, not distribu-
tively, as land and chattels, but as a factory, or one
whole concern ; that the mortgage was to secure the
purchase money, not of the land and building only, but
of the land and machinery together ; that this mortgage
described the subject of it as a "factory"; that none of
the machines had been introduced since the mortgage,
but were all comprised in the original sale ; that they

(a) L. R. 4 Ch. App. p. 530.

are all indispensable to the working of the factory, and that without them the mere building would have been a grossly inadequate security; and considering also the facility with which Courts of Equity recognize the constructive transmutation of property, in its nature personal, into realty, and *vice versa*, by the doctrine of equitable conversion, I have come to the conclusion that in the present case I may venture to treat the machines I last referred to as fixtures. I consider, too, that I am countenanced in this decision by the very able judgment in the case of *McDonald* v. *Weeks* (a), where his Lordship, the Chancellor, points out that the question is to be regarded as one of intention. Further, I find directly applicable what is said in the case of *Carscallen* v. *Moodie* (b), where Sir *John Robinson* thus expresses his opinion : "If the building had been put up for the accommodation of any one of the various branches of business that were afterwards carried on in it, and the engines and boilers, and the machinery adapted to that business had all formed parts of one whole, constituting a manufactory of some one kind, it would have been, and is, strongly my conviction, that the Sheriff coming with an execution against the goods of the owner of the building, could not have taken away the shingle machine or carding machine, circular saw, or whatever it was, with a view to which the engine and boiler had been put up in the building, and the whole thing made such as it was; because then I should think all, even the minutest part of the machinery, would have partaken of the freehold character of that with which it was connected, and of which it formed a part; and I could give no reason why, in such a case, it should be lawful to sever a spindle or shaft as a chattel merely because it could be detatched without injury to the building, any more than it would be lawful to take away a mill-stone, or a saw, from a building in which it was in use as part of a grist mill or saw mill."

1871.

Crawford
v.
Findlay.

Judgment.

---

(a) 8 Grant, 297.          (b) 15 U. C. Q. B. at p. 316.

I have also considered the following cases: *Forbes* v.
*Dixon* (a), *Mather* v. *Fraser* (b), *Cullinch* v. *Lumsdell*
(c), *Deyncourt* v. *Young* (d), *Cluna* v. *Wood* (e), *Longbottom* v. *Berry* (f), *Metropolitan Co.* v. *Brown* (g),
*Walmsley* v. *Milne* (h).

As to the case of *Trappes* v. *Harter* (i), cited by Mr.
*Crickmore*, that would seem now to be regarded as very
much weakened, if not completely overthrown by later
cases. See, per *Williams*, J., in *Walmsley* v. *Milne*.

But should I have erred in thus holding these machines, or any of them, to be fixtures, the plaintiffs
have, I think, an undeniable equity entitling them to a
decree on the other part of their case.

The original purchasers would, up to the time of the
execution of the mortgage, have been beyond all doubt
restrained from committing a breach of the covenant
contained in this agreement, by removing the machinery.
I can see no ground for saying that the execution of
the purchase deed (which I assume granted the property
by the same description as that contained in the mortgage) only dealing with the realty, as the defendant
contends, could have operated in any way to discharge
the original purchasers from their covenant in the
executory articles. The defendant insists that both the
purchase and the mortgage deeds passed only land; and
granting this, the covenant which concerned only things
collateral to the land, the machinery, was left untouched.

Then it follows that the insolvent, *John Cumming*,
having before his purchase had notice of the covenant,

---

(a) 12 C. & F. 312.                (b) 2 K. & J. 536.

(c) L. R. 3 Eq. 249.               (d) L. R. 3 Eq. 382.

(e) L. R. 3 Ex. 257, on appl. in Exch. Cham. L. R. 4 Ex. 328.

(f) L. R. 5 Q. B. 123.             (g) 26 Beav. 454.

(h) 7 C. B. N. S. 115.             (i) 2 C. & M. 153.

and having, in fact, agreed to abide by it, would be bound, as his vendors were. And the defendant *Findlay*, can have no greater right than *John Cumming*, being bound by the same equities which affected him.

It was argued against this, however, that the Chattel Mortgage Act applies, and that the covenant is not enforcible for want of registration under that Act.

The answer to this is threefold: First, the Act is not pleaded, and in a case of such hardship on the plaintiffs as this, I certainly would not give leave at this stage to set it up by supplemental answer; Secondly, the covenant is not, in my judgment, a mortgage or charge coming within the Act at all, but a mere stipulation as to how the possession of the machines should be dealt with; Thirdly, even granting that it was within the operation of the Statute, and that the defendant *Findlay*, as representing creditors, is to be considered as entitled to raise all objections which they could insist upon, the Act only avoids a mortgage for non-registration as against creditors of the mortgagor, and *John Cumming* is not the mortgagor. In his character of purchaser *John Cumming*, clearly, could not in equity avoid the covenant under the Act, having had notice before his purchase, and being bound to his own vendors to observe the covenant. As to the defendant *Findlay*, his measure of right as a purchaser can be no greater than that of the insolvent.

There must be a decree for the plaintiffs, with costs, for it makes no difference that Mr. *Findlay* is an Assignee in Insolvency, and took the steps he did for the benefit of the creditors, he must look to the insolvent's estate for indemnity, if he is entitled to any.

*Cornell*, who did not execute the conveyance to *John Cumming*, appeared at the hearing by counsel and con-

8—VOL. XVIII. GR.

sented to be bound by the decree. I am not clear that he is a necessary party, but he may be added as a defendant, and the decree can state his appearance and submission.

---

## McIntosh v. McIntosh.

*Division Court—Interpleader—Equitable claim.*

On an interpleader in the Division Court the jurisdiction of the Judge is not confined to the question of legal property : he may determine the claimant's right to an equitable interest.

This was a motion for an injunction to stay the sale of certain timber by the bailiff of the Division Court of the County of Wellington, under the following circumstances.

Statement. The plaintiff claimed to have an interest in certain timber which was got out by *Duncan McIntosh,* and had been seized under attachment issued from the Division Court of the County of Wellington, against *Duncan,* at the suit of the workmen employed by him in getting out and manufacturing the timber.

The plaintiff alleged that, in October, 1869, he and *Duncan* entered into a verbal agreement, that *Duncan* should get out, manufacture, and deliver to the plaintiff at Galt, 30,000 square feet of pine timber (cubic measure), averaging 50 cubic feet per stick ; 8000 feet of pine, of an average girth of 20 inches, string measure; and 2000 feet of cherry—to be delivered at Galt on the 15th June, then next ; that the plaintiff should pay the defendant therefor at the rate of $110 per 1000 feet in manner following : $30 per 1000 feet, as the timber should be manufactured ; $30 more, on the same being hauled to the bank of the Grand River ; and the residue, on its delivery at Galt ; and that, if *Duncan* should not make due progress with the manufacturing or delivering of the timber, the plaintiff might take the same off Duncan's hands, and complete the contract himself, charging the expense to *Duncan*, and deducting the same out of the contract price. The fact of there having been any such agreement was disputed by the creditors. It was conceded that the plaintiff had made advances to *Duncan*, and that the timber in question in the cause had been got out by *Duncan*. After most of it had been got out, it was marked by *Duncan* with the plaintiff's mark. Subsequently, *Duncan* being behind with his men's wages, some of them took out warrants of attachment, under which the timber was seized before the 6th of June, 1870. The plaintiff then advanced money to *Duncan* to pay these men; and they were paid. *Duncan* thereupon executed to the plaintiff a bill of sale of the timber, reciting therein the agreement, or alleged agreement, already stated.

1871.

McIntosh
v.
McIntosh.

Statement.

The bill alleged, that the plaintiff thereupon took actual possession of the timber, and that after he had so taken possession, certain of the defendants obtained from the Division Court warrants of attachment under which the bailiff seized the timber, and continued to hold it. The plaintiff claiming the property, the necessary proceedings were taken for the adjudication of the matter by the Division Court Judge. The plaintiff put in his claim to the timber, and stated the grounds of his claim to be, " that the said timber was got out, manufactured, and delivered" by *Duncan McIntosh* to the plaintiff " under a contract made between them; and was by the said (plaintiff) accepted and received under said contract, and became and was the property of the said (plaintiff) who was in the possession thereof."

The case came before the Judge for trial on the 27th July, when the claimant failed to appear; and judgment

went against him.  He afterwards obtained a new trial
on payment of costs ;  and the matter came on again for
trial before the same Judge, on the 28th September,
when the witnesses on both sides were examined in open
Court.  On the 14th October, the Judge delivered his
judgment, finding that the property in question " is not
the property of the claimant," and " is the property of
the defendant *Duncan McIntosh*," and ordering " that
the costs of this interpleader be taxed, and paid by the
claimant ; and in the meantime that the amount of the
said costs be taken by the bailiff out of the proceeds
of the goods when sold under the execution in this
cause."  The learned Judge gave his reasons in writing.  His judgment was put in on the motion, from
which it appeared, that he was of opinion, and held,
that, prior to the bill of sale, there had been no agreement to sell the timber, or to deliver it at Galt as
alleged ; that if there had been such an agreement, it

was a fraud on the men and on other creditors, the same
having been fraudulently concealed from them, in order
to enable *Duncan* to get the credit which the apparent
ownership of the timber would give him ; and that the
bill of sale was void under the Insolvency law and otherwise.  The learned Judge was also of opinion that there
had been no delivery of the timber to the plaintiff before
the bill of sale.  At the time of the filing of the bill
executions were in the bailiff's hands at the suit of some
of the defendants.

The bill set up the same state of facts as the plaintiff
had alleged before the Judge ; and it was contended for
the plaintiff, that all which the Judge decided, or had
jurisdiction to decide, was that, as between the claimant
and the creditors, the dry legal property was in *Duncan*
the debtor ; that the plaintiff was still at liberty to insist
that he had the equitable title ; or at all events that he
had a lien for his advances.    .

Mr. *Dalton McCarthy*, for the plaintiff.

Mr. *Hodgins* and Mr. *Chadwick*, for the defendants.

MOWAT, V.C.—I am of opinion that the jurisdiction of the learned Judge was not confined to the adjudication of the dry question as to the legal property in the timber. His jurisdiction in such cases, is to "adjudicate upon the claim, and make such order between the parties in respect thereof, and of the costs of the proceedings, as to him seems meet." (*a*) I see no reason whatever for limiting this provision within the narrow bounds contended for by the plaintiff. The language is abundantly large enough to embrace all equitable questions of property, as well as all legal questions; and it is impossible to suppose that the legislature meant to compel equitable claimants to go into the Court of Chancery for the adjudication of their rights in respect of the small matters to which the jurisdiction of the Division Court Judge is ordinarily applied. The Chancellor in *Westbrooke* v. *Browett* (*b*) held that this Court should not entertain jurisdiction in such cases; and parties would therefore be absolutely without a remedy if the Division Court Judge has no jurisdiction. To compel parties interested in chattels of small value to go into Chancery, or to file a bill on the equity side of the County Court, while the County Courts had an equity side, would, in effect though not in form, be giving them no remedy. Here the amount happens to be considerable, but the question is not affected by that accident. The Division Courts, in the exercise of their ordinary jurisdiction, are not mere Courts of common law, but are entitled, I apprehend, to take cognizance of all money demands within the amount limited by the statute, whether such demands are in their nature legal or equitable; and the Court or Judge is to

---

(*a*) Consol. U. C. ch. 19, sec. 175, p. 166.　　(*b*) 17 Gr. 339.

1871.

McIntosh
v.
McIntosh.

"make such orders, judgments or *decrees* thereupon as appear to him just and agreeable to equity and good conscience;" and it is declared that "every such order, judgment, and decree shall be final and conclusive between the parties" (*a*). Under the interpleading jurisdiction it is not with a money demand that the Judge has ordinarily to deal, but with questions of property in chattels; and in such cases the legislature has not required that the Judge should give judgment for one party or the other *simpliciter;* but has authorized him, as seems to me to be the plain reading of the Act, to mould his order, judgment, or decree, so as to meet the justice of the case. The letter of the enactment warrants, if it does not demand, this construction; it is the construction which justice to suitors and general convenience require; and which is in accordance with the spirit of the enactment giving jurisdiction to the Courts in ordinary suits, and defining the

Judgment. principles which are to govern the Judge in the exercise of that jurisdiction.

Reference was made by the learned counsel for the plaintiff to the jurisdiction given by the statute to the Superior Courts of common law and to the County Courts (*b*). But the language there is much more limited than that employed in the Division Court Act. Where there is no consent or default, what the Superior Law Courts are to do is, "to order the claimant to make himself defendant in the same or some other action, or to proceed to trial on one or more feigned issue or issues, and also direct which of the parties shall be plaintiff or defendant on such trial;" and the judgment in every such action or issue is to be final. The legislature considers that, with certain limited exceptions, all equitable matters, of an amount

(*a*) Consol. U. C. ch. 19, sec. 55, p. 145.
(*b*) Consol. Stat. U. C. ch· 30, sec. 23.

or value which, if the question were legal, would be within the jurisdiction of these Courts, should be disposed of in Chancery; but there is no occasion for inferring from this that the Legislature meant to reserve for Chancery equitable demands or questions which, if legal, would belong to the Division Courts; and there would be no propriety in construing the language of the Division Court Act with reference to this subject, as the common law Courts find it necessary to construe the very different language which regulates their jurisdiction.

I think, then, that the Judge had jurisdiction to dispose of the question as to the equitable as well as to the legal title of the plaintiff; and that he has disposed of it.

Assuming that to be so, it was further argued, that he had no jurisdiction to determine whether the plaintiff had an equitable lien on the timber; that he has not in fact decided that question; and that the plaintiff did not raise the question before bringing the present suit. I see no solid ground for this objection to the jurisdiction, any more than for the other objection to it. I see no reason why the Judge might not have found and adjudged, that, as between the claimant and the creditors, the property seized belonged to the debtor, subject to the plaintiff's lien, if he had a lien; or why a Judge, in the exercise of this jurisdiction, may not find according to the very truth of the case, whatever that may be. It is impossible that parliament can have meant that he should adjudge simply, that the property is the debtor's, and is not the claimant's, when the claimant has a lien upon it to perhaps the full value. If the Judge had the jurisdiction, I apprehend that the claimant was bound to insist on his alleged lien before the Judge; and was not at liberty to confine the contest before the Judge to the question of property merely, and to reserve for another Court the question of lien, founded as that claim is on precisely the same allegations of fact as he made before the Division Court. On that point I refer to *Henderson* v. *Henderson* (a) and The Marquis of *Breadalbane* v. The Marquis of *Chandos* (b). But the Judge does seem to have in effect decided the question ; for in his judgment he not only negatived most of the allegations on which the claim depends, but he expressed an opinion that, while " in equity *Peter* may have had a claim of lien for his advances, his advances do not appear to be any more entitled to a preference than the claims of *Duncan's* other creditors for wages and materials which went as much to produce the timber as the money advanced by the claimant." And he directed the costs to be paid by the claimant, and to be taken by the bailiff in the meantime out of the " proceeds of the goods when sold under the execution in the cause."

Judgment.

Looking at all the materials before me, I see no reason for apprehending, that, without the interference of this Court, injustice will be none ; and I am of opinion that the interlocutory injunction asked for should be refused.

———

The motion was afterwards reheard before the Vice Chancellors, when

Mr. *Moss* and Mr. *McCarthy* appeared for the plaintiff:

Mr. *Hodgins* and Mr. *A. Chadwick*, for the defendants.

The judgment of the Court was delivered by

_____

(a) 3 Hare at 114, 115.          (b) 2 M. & C. at 732, 733.

STRONG, V. C.—I think the order of the Vice Chancellor was perfectly right. Assuming, in favour of the plaintiff, that he had a good equitable lien, it was within the jurisdiction of the County Court Judge to entertain the claim of the plaintiff, founded on such a title, and he has conclusively determined that claim against the plaintiff. The words of the statute are large enough to embrace equitable claims, and convenience is strongly in favour of the jurisdiction.

All that makes against such a construction is, that a different interpretation has been put upon the Interpretation Act applicable to Courts of Law; but at the time this last statute was enacted, it would have been considered an anomaly to have subjected any controversy involving equitable considerations to the adjudication of a Court of Law, which was then supposed to possess neither the machinery nor experience essential for the decision of such questions. No such reasons applied to the Division Courts, which are not bound to follow any formal mode of procedure in matters of interpleader, and whose fitness to decide equitable questions is recognized by the fifty-fifth section of the Act. It therefore appears to me, that the words of section 175, being sufficiently large to include equitable claims, we are not called upon, either by any argument derived from inconvenience, or by reason of any repugnancy arising from other provisions of the Act, to give to these words a less comprehensive meaning than they *prima facie* import.

The County Court Judge having jurisdiction to decide the question of lien, his order must, of course, be taken to be conclusive; and this Court cannot enter upon an inquiry as to what points of law were actually brought under his judgment by the parties.

The order refusing the injunction must be affirmed, with costs.

9—VOL. XVIII. GR.

1871.

McIntosh
v.
McIntosh.

February 28.

Judgment.

### Scott v. Scott.

*Will, construction of—Master's reports.*

The testator, after devising a parcel of land to each of his three sons,
  directed his executors to collect the debts due to him, and out of
  the money so collected to pay his debts, funeral and testamentary
  expenses and legacies; and he charged the deficiency on two of the
  parcels which he had devised; by a subsequent part of his will, he
  gave his household furniture, and other personal chattels, to his
  wife, for her own use, except the piano, which he gave to one of his
  daughters; there was no other residuary clause in the will:

*Held,* that the whole of the testator's residuary estate, except the
  debts due to him and the piano, went to the wife, exonerated from
  the debts which the testator owed.

To avoid expense, questions which arise in the Master's office on
  the construction of a will should, where practicable, be left for
  decision by the Court on further directions, instead of being brought
  before the Court by way of appeal from the Master's report.

This was an appeal, by the testator's widow, from
Statement. the report of a local Master.

The suit was for the administration of the estate of
*Thomas O. Scott,* senior, who died on the 13th September, 1868. An administration order was made on
the 18th March, 1870. On the 14th December, 1870,
the Master at Hamilton made his report; and, against
some of the findings in this report, three of the persons interested under the will appealed, viz., *Abigail
Scott,* the testator's widow, and *Thomas O. Scott,* and
*Alva Green Scott,* two of his sons. The principal
question discussed on the appeal was the proper construction of the will. The will was as follows:—

" The last will of *Thomas O. Scott,* of the Township
of Brantford, in the County of Brant, Esquire:

" I will and devise to my son *Thomas O. Scott,* his
heirs and assigns, the 100 acres of land which he now
occupies off the south-east side of my farm; on the

terms and conditions mentioned in a certain agreement entered into between me and him, bearing date the 28th day of July, 1862, which said 100 acres is particularly described therein.

" I will and devise to my son *Alva Green Scott*, his heirs and assigns, the house and premises in which I now live, with 70 acres of the farm adjoining to and parallel with the 100 acres above devised to my son *Thomas O. Scott*, the said 75 acres to be of uniform width, and extending the whole depth of my said farm, and including the house and premises now occupied by me.

" I will and devise to my son *James, Winnett Scott*, his heirs and assigns, the residue of my said farm being the north-west part, and containing about 58 acres; and I charge upon the same the payment of a certain mortgage for $1,000, on the front part or gore of my said farm, and made for my said son *James Winnett's* accommodation.

" I appoint my sons, *Thomas O. Scott*, and *James Winnett Scott*, and friend *Thomas Batson*, executors of this my will, requiring them to get, collect, and get in with all convenient despatch, all debts owing to me; and, out of the moneys so collected by them, and the $1 000 payable by my son *Thomas*, under the said agreement herein before referred to, to pay and discharge all debts owing by me, and my funeral and testamentary expenses; and after the payment of all my just debts, funeral and testamentary expenses, to pay to my daughter, *Clarissa Ann Batty*, wife of *John Batty*, *Abigail Adeline Burkholder*, and *Mary Eliza Scott*, $500 each; and to my grandchild, *Hester Jane Scott*, $400; payable as hereinafter mentioned; and in case sufficient moneys shall not come into the hands of my said executors to pay the said legacies and debts

properly payable by them, including the payment of a
certain mortgage on my whole farm for about $1,000,
held by one *Kerr*, of Hamilton, I order that such deficiency shall be equally made up and paid by my sons,
*Alva Green* and *James Winnett*, and shall be a charge
on the lands respectively devised to them.

" The $500 payable to my daughter, *Clarissa Ann
Batty*, shall be charged with the payment thereout of
about $480 and interest due by the said *John Batty*,
being the portion of the moneys received by the said
*John Batty*, out of the $1,000 mortgage held by said
*Kerr*, of Hamilton, on my whole farm.

" In case of the death of my said grandchild, *Hester
Jane* before she arrives at the age of 21 years or before
marriage, the money devised to her, shall be equally
divided among my children above named.   But in case
of my said grandchild *Hester Jane* marrying, or arriving at the age of 21 years, then the money devised to
her shall be forthwith paid to her by my said executors.

" I will and devise that my dear wife, *Abigail*,
during her natural life, and my daughter, *Mary Eliza*,
until she marries or arrives at the age of 21 years,
shall reside with my son, *Alva Green*, in the house I
now occupy ; and that my sons, *Alva Green* and *James
Winnett*, support and maintain comfortably my said
dear wife and daughter *Mary Eliza*, and bear equally
the expense of such support and maintenance.

" I bequeath unto my said wife, *Abigail.* all my
household furniture and other personal chattels for her
own use ; except the piano, which I bequeath to my
said daughter *Mary Eliza*.   The above provision for
my dear wife is not to be in lieu of any dower she
may be entitled to in the lands devised to my sons, or
other lands.

" I will and direct that the charge upon the lands
devised to my sons, *Alva Green* and *James Winnett*, to
make up any deficiency of moneys required for the
purpose of paying my just debts, funeral and testamentary expenses, and legacies shall be made up by
them as follows : one half of such deficiency in four
years, and the other half of such deficiency in five
years, from the time of my decease.

" In witness whereof, I have hereunto set my hand
and seal, this 28th July, A. D. 1862.

Mr. *E. Martin*, for the appellants.

Mr. *G. Martin*, contra.

Mowat, V. C.—The Master has treated the bequest
to the widow as confined to household furniture and
articles *ejusdem generis*, and as not including farming
stock and implements, &c. I think that this construction is not correct. I think that the argument for it is
outweighed by the other provisions of the will, viewing
these in the light of the decided cases cited and
others (a). The testator directed his executors to collect the debts due to him, and "out of the money so
collected," and the $1,000 which he specifies, to pay
his debts and funeral and testamentary expenses ; and,
after the payment of these, to pay certain legacies
which he gives : the deficiency he charges on his real
estate. The testator thus indicates an intention to
charge his liabilities and legacies on part only of his
personal estate, and to make good the deficiency from
his real estate. The purpose of this he shews by the
subsequent clause, in which he bequeaths to his wife
all his "household furniture and other personal chattels for her own use, except the piano"—which he gives

_____

(a) See the cases collected, Hawkins on Wills, 288, 289 ; 2 Jarman, 3rd ed. 715, *et seq.*

**1871.**

Scott
v.
Scott.

to one of his daughters. Unless this clause covers the whole residuary estate, the will contains no residuary clause; the expression "personal chattels" is, confessedly, sufficient, but for the reference to the piano, to carry the whole residue. The piano, I apprehend, is "household furniture"; and the place of the word in the clause, does not necessarily imply that the testator regarded the piano as a personal chattel which was not furniture. He clearly meant also, that his wife should have such of his personal chattels as were not household furniture. The debts due to him he had already disposed of; and I think that the expression "other personal chattels," must be construed as covering all the testator's residuary personal estate, except the debts due to him. That was probably the testator's actual intention; any other construction rests on too slight and conjectural a basis for judicial adoption.

Judgment.

It was conceded that whatever particulars were covered by this clause were exonerated from the testator's debts; that is, as between the persons claiming under the will.

A further question argued was whether, as between the devisees, *Alva* and *William* on the one hand, and the legatees on the other, each of the two devisees named is liable for half only, so that in case the land devised to either should prove insufficient to pay half the deficiency, and the land devised to the other should be more than sufficient, the legatees have a right to come on the latter half for what may be wanting; in effect, whether the legacies are a charge on both parcels, or half only on each parcel. The Master has decided this point in favour of the legatees, and I agree in that construction.

I think it was said that the testator, after making his will, mortgaged one of these two parcels. If so, the mortgage debt is not, as between the devisees, to be charged on that parcel only, but is to be charged equally on the two parcels, like the unsecured debts. The will bears date in 1862.

Another point argued was, as to the sufficiency of the evidence of the executors' assent to the legacy to the widow. I think that the evidence is sufficient.

I believe that these observations dispose of all the grounds of appeal, except those which are merely formal. I presume that no reference back will be necessary; and that the order to be drawn up on the appeal can contain the proper corrections of the findings of the Master.

The report in this case is unnecessarily diffuse. I may also observe, that it is ordinarily more convenient and less expensive, to argue questions on the construction of the will when the cause comes on upon further directions, than by way of appeal from the report.

There will be no costs of the appeal.

## GRAY v. HATCH.

*Trustees, removal of—Reversionary interest—Assignee in insolvency—*
*Taxes—Dismissal on further directions—Costs.*

The insolvency of a trustee, or his leaving the country in debt to
reside in a foreign country, is a sufficient ground to remove him
from the trust.

An insolvent's reversionary interest in an estate passes to his assignee,
and entitles the assignee to maintain a suit in a proper case for the
appointment of new trustees, and for an account of the estate: But
the court refused to make an order for the sale of such reversionary
interest.

The devisee of a life estate in all a testator's property, is bound to
keep down the annual taxes on the land, and they form a first
charge on the testator's interest.

The costs payable out of an estate to persons not trustees thereof,
were directed to be taxed between party and party only.

On further directions, a bill was dismissed, with costs, as respected
some of the original plaintiffs; they having no right to sustain such
a bill.

Statement.   This was a suit by the assignee in insolvency of
*Joseph Hatch,* and some execution creditors of *Joseph*
and *James Hatch,* both of whom had a beneficial interest in the residue of the estate of their father *John
Hatch,* subject to the life estate of the testator's widow.
The testator, by his will, devised and bequeathed the
residue of his estate, real and personal, to his sons, the
said *Joseph* and *James Hatch,* and one *Henry Peers,*
their heirs, executors, administrators, or assigns, or the
heirs, &c., of the survivor, to sell and dispose of the
same, but so far as related to the real estate, with the
consent and approbation of the testator's widow; and
to apply the proceeds, first, to pay his debts and funeral
expenses, and then, to invest the balance in the purchase of government securities or in bank stock, or in
real securities; to pay to his wife, during her life, the
annual rents, interest or dividends, or authorize her to
take, receive, and retain the same for her own use;

and after her death, to convey and assign the said residue amongst his children equally. If any of them should die before the period of division, leaving issue, such issue was to have the parent's share. The will contained provisions for the appointment of new trustees, in the place of any dying or being desirous of being discharged from the trust, or neglecting or refusing to act therein before all the trusts should be fulfilled.

After the making of the will, *Henry Peers*, one of the trustees, died, and no one was appointed in his place; *Joseph Hatch* became an insolvent under the Act; and *James Hatch*, having fallen into debt, left the country and went to California. An advertisement was subsequently issued by the trustees *Joseph* and *James Hatch*, for the sale of a considerable part of the testator's property under circumstances of suspicion; and, their creditors being apprehensive that the intention was to realize the testator's estate and to transfer the proceeds to another country, the assignee of *Joseph* and some execution creditors of *Joseph* and *James* respectively, filed the bill in this cause, and applied for, and obtained an injunction to restrain the sale.

On the 3rd May, 1867, the cause was brought on for hearing at Woodstock.

It was there objected that there was a misjoinder of plaintiffs, but the Court held that advantage could not then be taken of this objection.

On the merits, the Court continued the injunction against the trustees, *Joseph and James Hatch*; directed all accounts to be taken of the testator's estate, real and personal, in the usual terms; an inquiry as to what sums were due by *Joseph* and *James*

10—VOL. XVIII. GR.

1871.

Gray
v.
Hatch.

Statement.

*Hatch,* or either of them, to the plaintiffs respectively, or any or either of them, for which the latter had a lien, on the interests of *Joseph* or *James,* in the lands of the testator; also, as to other incumbrances on such interest; it was referred to the Master (at Woodstock), to appoint a Receiver of the principal sums derived from past sales of real estate, and to appoint new trustees; and further directions and costs were reserved.

The decree as drawn up and settled between the parties, contained an error as to the costs of the injunction, which was corrected by a subsequent order. It also directed, besides the above mentioned matters, an account of the rents received by the widow, as well as by the trustees; a declaration that the interest of *Joseph Hatch, James Hatch,* and *John Hatch,* respectively, in the lands devised by the testator, was subject to the lien of the plaintiffs for the amount of the respective executions placed by them, or any or either of them, in the Sheriff's office, against the lands of the said *Joseph, James,* and *John Hatch,* or any or either of them, and a direction that the Receiver should get in, not merely the principal sums derived from past sales of real estate, but all sums whatsoever payable in respect of sales of any part of the estate.

In pursuance of this decree, the Master made his report, and the case having come on for further directions, the following judgment was given by

Judgment.  STRONG, V. C.—This case was argued on the assumption that all the plaintiffs were execution creditors of certain of the *cestuis que trust ;* this however is not so, as *Gray,* one of the plaintiffs, sues in the character of assignee of *Joseph Hatch.* As to the plaintiffs other than *Gray,* who are all execution creditors and seeking

satisfaction of their judgments, I am of opinion that
they are entitled to no relief. As against the unsold
lands they can have no decree, because the widow has
a right to the enjoyment of this part of the estate in
specie, until a sale by the trustees with her consent;
and the lands cannot, I think, be sold subject to the
widow's life estate, because that would be injurious to
her rights, by interfering with the trust for conversion,
or at least prejudicing it to a considerable extent. As
to lands converted before bill filed, it is clear the
execution creditors can have no relief (a). The judgment is in no way a charge upon the fund so formed;
and as regards both this portion of the estate and the
personalty, the judgment creditors cannot claim relief
analagous to that afforded to attaching creditors at
law : *Gilbert* v. *Jarvis* (b), *Horsley* v. *Cox* (c). The
execution creditors ought not, therefore, to have been
made parties, and if they had been the only plaintiffs,
the bill would be dismissed with costs; but as they are
joined with *Gray*, who, as the assignee of *Joseph
Hatch*, can maintain the bill, the proper order as to the
execution creditors will be to direct that they pay to
the defendants so much of the costs of the suit as have
been occasioned by their having been made parties.
This point not having been taken or argued at the
original hearing at Woodstock before my brother
*Mowat*, he did not then dismiss the bill against these
parties.

Then as to the proper decree to be made, regarding
*Gray* as sole plaintiff, in his character of assignee of
*Joseph Hatch*; I think, in the first place, that the
widow was bound to pay the taxes on the unconverted
lands, and that these taxes formed a first charge on the
income derivable from realty (d).

---

(a) Foster v. Blackstone, 1 M. & K. 297 ; Lewin on Trusts; Ed. 3, 653.
(b) 16 Gr. 294.        (c) L. R. 4 Ch. Ap. 92.
(d) Biscoe v. Van Bearle, 6 Gr. 438.

*Margin notes:* 1871. Gray v. Hatch. Judgment.

*James, Joseph,* and Mrs. *Hatch* must pay into Court the balances found due from them respectively. Mrs. *Hatch's* interest, as tenant for life, is liable to make good the amount for which she is found indebted, and the Receiver may be continued if requisite to effectuate this. But Mrs. *Hatch* is also entitled to have all the income which has accrued pending the suit set off against her liability, as found by the report, and if necessary it must be referred to the Master to adjust this account; the amount found due from Mrs. *Hatch* being satisfied, the Receiver should be discharged. All moneys should be invested as directed by the will, and the decree must declare Mrs. *Hatch,* subject to her liability to make good her debt to the estate, entitled to the income derived from the investments as well as from the unsold real estate.

I give no costs against *James* or *Joseph,* nor do I give them any except those occasioned by the joinder of the execution creditors, which I have already disposed of. All the other defendants should have their costs out of the estate. The Receiver must be ordered to pass his accounts and pay any balance into Court, and for this purpose, and to fix the Receiver's allowance, there must be a reference to the Master.

---

The cause was subsequently reheard, on further directions, at the instance of the defendant *Sally Hatch,* the widow of the testator. The Judges before whom the cause was reheard, were the Vice Chancellors, the Chancellor being absent from illness.

Mr. *S. Blake,* for the widow and other parties.

Mr. *Barrett,* for the plaintiff.

The judgment of the Court was delivered by

1871.

Gray
v.
Hatch.

Feb. 23.

MOWAT, V. C.—On the rehearing of this cause on further directions, the learned counsel for *Sally Hatch* contended that the bill should have been dismissed against the plaintiff *Gray*, the assignee of *Joseph Hatch*; as well as against the execution creditors. If that were so, the defendant should have appealed from the original decree. But both myself and my brother *Strong* are clear that the assignee in insolvency was entitled to maintain the suit; that the insolvent's reversionary interest in the testator's estate passed to his assignee, under the Insolvent Act; that he was entitled to have the amount ascertained and the estate secured; and that for this purpose it was necessary that the accounts of the testator's estate should be taken.

The removal of the two sons as trustees is objected to, but their removal was based on well settled principles. One of them had, after the testator's death, become insolvent under the Act; the other had left the country and gone to California, and there were unsatisfied executions against him in the Sheriff's hands; and no one had been appointed in the room of the trustee who had died. Any one having an interest in the management and safety of the estate, was entitled under such circumstances to come into equity; and the substitution of new trustees, and the appointment of a Receiver meantime, if required, were matters of course.

Judgment.

It appears that new trustees were approved of by the Master, but the estate has not been transferred to them; nor had any one taken steps for the purpose until the cause came on for further directions. The Master appointed a Receiver also, but it seems that he has never acted. Instead of being appointed Receiver of the principal sums only, according to my note at the hearing, the decree directed the Receiver to get in all sums; and we are now told that nobody has been collecting since before the making of the decree. Who is to blame for all this does not appear on the papers now before us; but it is certainly greatly to be regretted, that a valuable estate like this should have been for so long a time tied up unnecessarily.

There should have been no account directed of rents received by the widow. .It is a usual direction in an administration order, for an account to be taken of rents received by the trustees or executors; but it is most unusual to take an account of rents received by the beneficial devisee, and in the present .case no possible object was to be gained by such an account. The widow was entitled, for her own use, to the rents which she had received, and she was accountable for them to no one. The oversight having occurred in drawing up the decree, the account should have been waived by all parties; and if any of them had been so unreasonable as to object to that, an application should have been made to the Court to correct the decree, which correction must have been made at once. We cannot say that one party is much more to blame than another for the useless expense incurred in taking this account, but the estate should not be charged with it.

With this exception, to which the attention of my learned brother was not drawn on further directions, the plaintiff *Gray* is clearly entitled, by the practice of the Court, to have his costs as between party and party out of the *corpus* of the estate. The defendants, to whom the order gave costs, are also entitled to them, but between party and party only. The Receiver may be discharged at once. The new trustees can now receive and apply all moneys.

With these variations, the decree on further directions will stand. The co-plaintiffs, against whom the the bill has been dismissed, do not complain of the decree in that respect. There will be no costs of the rehearing.

## HENDERSON V. BROWN.

*Vendor and purchaser—Covenant against incumbrancers—Set off—Right of retainer.*

On the sale of land, which was subject to a prior mortgage which the vendor had given, and which was not then due, the vendor executed a covenant to the purchaser *B.* covenanting that he had not incumbered the property, and the purchaser *B.* executed a mortgage for his unpaid purchase money. The intention was, that the vendor should pay the prior mortgage, but he failed to do so; after it became due, he sold and assigned *B's.* mortgage to the plaintiff, who had notice of all the facts; the plaintiff afterwards obtained an assignment of the prior mortgage, and *B.* paid off the same:

*Held,* that *B.* was entitled to apply on his mortgage the money so paid by him to the plaintiff. [STRONG, V.C., dissenting.]

The plaintiff's bill was for the foreclosure of a mortgage executed by the defendant to one *Sando,* and assigned to the plaintiff. The defendant set up that he had purchased the property from *Sando;* that the mortgage was for part of the purchase money; that *Sando* had previously given a mortgage to one *Hughes* which he (*Sando*) agreed with the defendant to pay off; that the defendant had been compelled to pay this mortgage; and he claimed to set off or retain the amount as against his mortgage now sued on. The cause came on for hearing before Vice Chancellor *Strong,* who pronounced a decree in favor of the defendant, because the late decisions in this Court were in his favour; his Honor intimated, however, that his own opinion was against those decisions.

The plaintiff thereupon reheard the cause, and it was argued before the Chancellor and the Vice Chancellors.

Mr. *Fitzgerald,* for the plaintiff.

Mr. *Moss,* for the defendant.

1871.        SPRAGGE, C.—I take these short material facts to be
~~~~~       established in evidence; that upon the sale by *Sando*
Henderson
v.          to *Brown*, the mortgage money due to *Hughes*, and
Brown.
            which had not then accrued due, was to be paid by
Feb. 23.    *Sando;* that *Brown* received the conveyance, paid
            purchase money on account, and gave the mortgage for
            the balance upon that understanding and agreement;
            and that *Henderson* took from *Brown* an assignment
            of the mortgage, with notice of the agreement between
            *Sando* and *Brown*, and with notice that the mortgage
            was for unpaid purchase money.

            There are some principles applicable to this case that
            I apprehend will not be controverted.  The right of
            the purchaser before conveyance to apply unpaid
            purchase money in paying off incumbrances is one.
            Another is, that an assignee of a chose in action takes
            subject to the equities to which his assignor was
Judgment.   subject.

            I have met with a case which resembles this in
            several of its features; *Lacey* v. *Ingle* (a) decided by
            Lord *Cottenham*.  The question was between a pur-
            chaser and the assignee for value of purchase money.
            The assignee had got in an incumbrance, and claimed
            to tack his claim for unpaid purchase money, to that
            incumbrance.  The judgment of Lord *Cottenham* covers
            so much of the ground that is in contest in this suit,
            that I cannot do better than quote from it.  " The real
            question is, whether as against the defendant, the
            assignee of the purchase money, she (the purchaser)
            can justify the application of part of it, in payment of
            *Wilkinson's* charge, and in relieving the estate pur-
            chased by her from such charge.  As against *Rogers*
            (the vendor) her right so to do could not be disputed,
            whatever may have been the relative position of the

            _____
                        (a) 2 Ph. 413.

defendant and *Wilkinson ;* and I cannot understand
how the defendant, purchasing from *Rogers* his title to
the purchase money, can have a larger right than the
assignor had." His Lordship then refers to the
assignee's claim to tack, and to the question of notice
in relation to it, and says: " How can the defendant
say that he had not notice of the plaintiff's right to
apply her purchase money in paying off any incumbrances affecting the estate, when his agreement recites
the plaintiff's agreement of purchase under which that
right arises. That he did not know of *Wilkinson's*
charge is nothing, as he had notice of the plaintiff's
right to pay off any charge, and it is against that equity
he is now contending." I have quoted the latter part
of Lord *Cottenham's* judgment for the sake of the clear
recognition that it contains of the right of a purchaser
to apply unpaid purchase money in the discharge of
incumbrances. I do not think myself that it was
necessary to prove notice to *Henderson.*

The case of *Lacey* v. *Ingle* differs from this, just in
two points; one, that in this case it was a mortgage
given for purchase money, not the mere right to receive
purchase money that was assigned ; the other, that the
purchaser had received a conveyance. The latter is
probably the distinction that will be relied on by the
assignee.

I confess I feel great difficulty in seeing the force of
this distinction. It seems to rest upon a notion that
the purchaser in accepting a conveyance with the covenant of the vendor against incumbrances, elected his
security. He would properly take such a covenant
even if there had been an express agreement in writing
that in the event of the vendor's failing to pay off
incumbrances the purchaser should be at liberty to apply
unpaid purchase money to that purpose. It is the
clear equity of the purchaser before conveyance, why

should it not survive the conveyance? Admitting that the covenant of the vendor was intended to apply to to it, it is going very far to say that the covenant was intended to supersede the equity; that it is to be construed into an abandonment of such a plain, natural, equitable right as the one in question.

The case of *Woods* v. *Martin* (a) is an authority in favour of the continuance of the equity after conveyance; the purchaser in that case being allowed to apply unpaid purchase money in the payment of head rents, although the existence of the incumbrance, though not the amount, was known at the time of the conveyance; and there was a covenant against incumbrances. Lord *St. Leonards* says of this case, (b) "the relief appears to have been properly administered." I would refer also to the remarks of the same learned author upon *Tourville* v. *Naish (c)*, and the conse-

quences he deduces from it.

I do not myself feel any doubt that purchase money retains its character of purchase money, notwithstanding that a mortgage upon the purchased premises is given to secure it, and that it retains with it all the equities incidental to its having that character. In *Galt* v. *The Erie and Niagara R. W. Co.* (d) I had to consider whether the vendor's lien was affected by his taking such a mortgage; and came to the conclusion that it was not. I refer to the case instead of repeating the authorities and reasons which I thought led to that result. I apprehend that the converse of the proposition will hold good; that if it is purchase money for the equities of the vendor, arising out of its having that character, it must be so in favor of the purchaser as well.

---

(a) 11 Ir. Ch. 148.              (b) V. & P. 552.
(c) V. & P. 752.                 (d) 15 Grant 637.

Assuming notice to be necessary; *Henderson* had notice that the mortgage of which he took an assignment, was for unpaid purchase money; and even if he had not notice of the mortgage to *Hughes*, it would, as put by Lord *Cottenham*, be nothing, as he had notice of the purchaser's right to pay off any charge.

In *Tully* v. *Bradbury* (a), a case decided by the late Vice Chancellor, there was a bond given by the vendor to the purchaser to indemnify him against a prior mortgage; the purchaser giving a mortgage for the balance of purchase money with a covenant for payment. These instruments, the late Vice Chancellor said, indicated a clear intention to his mind that the balance of the purchase money should be paid irrespective of the prior incumbrance, and that no lien should exist upon it for the discharge of the incumbrance.

In a subsequent case, *The Church Society* v. *McQueen* (b), in which, however, *Tully* v. *Bradbury* does not appear to have been cited, the late Chancellor held a purchaser who had given a mortgage for unpaid purchase money entitled, as against an assignee of the mortgage, to apply unpaid purchase money in discharge of a prior incumbrance of which the assignee had notice. Mr. *Fitzgerald* distinguishes the later of these two cases, by assuming that the mortgage contained no covenant for payment. I do not think this is to be assumed, the presumption is, that it did, as such a covenant is usual; an exception from ordinary practice is not to be presumed. If it did contain such a covenant the cases are in conflict; taking the reason for his decision given by the late Vice Chancellor, there is, however, this distinction, that in the earlier case it does not appear that the assignee of the mortgage had notice that it was given for unpaid purchase money. While in the latter case it seems that this did appear.

(a) 8 Grant 561.    (b) 15 Grant 281.

1871.

Henderson
v.
Brown.

The authorities from the English and Irish Courts to which I have referred, the latter approved by Lord *St. Leonards*, support the case decided by the late Chancellor, and is, I think, in accordance with reason and justice.

I have not thought it necessary to touch upon the question of set-off.

I think the decree should be affirmed with costs.

MOWAT, V.C.—On the 22nd July, 1858, one *Stephen Sando*, being owner of the property in question, subject to a mortgage which he had executed in favor of one *John Hughes*, for £150, sold and conveyed the property to the defendant *William Brown*. The conveyance contained a covenant that the vendor had not incumbered the property. *Brown* was aware of the mortgage; but *Sando* promised to pay it when due, and *Brown* relied on his doing so. *Brown* paid £100 down on account of the purchase money, and gave a mortgage on the property for the balance, viz., £150, payable in three instalments of £50 each, on the 1st August, in the years 1860, 1862, and 1864, respectively. It does not appear whether the sum paid down was applied on the mortgage to *Hughes* or not; but when the transaction was completed, it appears that less than £50 was unpaid on that mortgage, and that the amount would not become due until January, 1859. It was not then paid; and afterwards, viz., on the 20th July, 1859, *Sando* assigned *Brown's* mortgage to one *Robert Henderson;* and gave the assignee security against the prior mortgage on other property which seems to have turned out worthless. *Sando* gave *Henderson* a bond also, contemporaneously with the assignment, conditioned that *Sando* should pay the mortgage to *Hughes*, or cause it to be paid, and should keep *Henderson* harmless and

Judgment.

indemnified in respect of the same. Shortly after
this transaction *Henderson* paid off *Hughes*, and took
an assignment of his mortgage. *Brown* subsequently
paid to *Henderson* the amount of this mortgage; and
*Henderson's* representative has filed the present bill
to enforce *Brown's* mortgage. *Brown* sets up that he
is entitled to credit for the amount which he paid on
*Hughes's* mortgage; and his right so to claim was the
question argued on the rehearing of the cause.

1871.

Henderson
v.
Brown.

I believe that we are all agreed, that if *Sando* had not
assigned the mortgage which he received from *Brown*,
*Brown* would be entitled as against *Sando* to the credit
*Brown* now claims. On this point the law appears to
be clear (a). An observation in Lord *St. Leonard's*
book (b), that "it seems that, if the conveyance be
actually executed the purchaser can obtain no relief,
although the money be only secured," has reference to
relief against an incumbrance not covered by the covenants contained in the conveyance, as appears by the
antecedent context of the observation, as well as by
what follows.

Judgment.

Is *Sando's* assignee equally bound? It is to be borne
in mind, that *Hughes's* mortgage was over due at the
time of the assignment, and that *Henderson* bought
with notice of *Sando's* deed to *Brown*, and therefore
with notice of the covenant therein against incumbrances. In regard to these facts there is no contest.

Against the assignee, is the long-established general
rule, that the purchaser of a chose in action takes
subject to all the equities which existed between the
debtor and the assignor. That amongst these equities

---

(a) See Dart on Vend. 3rd ed. 525; Rawle on Cov. 3rd ed. 636 et
seq.; Beasley v. Darcy, 2 S. & L. 403 n.; Tourville v. Naish, 3 P. W.
307; and cases cited post.

(b) 14th ed. 551.

**1871.**

Henderson
v.
Brown.

is the right of set-off, has been held in many cases (a). One of the latest cases on the point is *Watson* v. *The Mid-Wales R. W. Co.* (b) in the English Court of Common Pleas. The plaintiff there was seeking to enforce a bond which had been assigned; the defendant wished to set-off rent which had accrued *after* the assignment on a lease made previously. The Court negatived this claim; but upon what ground? Chief Justice *Bovill* observed, that no case had been cited where equity had "allowed against the assignee of an equitable chose in action a set-off of a debt arising between the original parties *subsequently* to the notice of assignment, out of matters not connected with the debt claimed, nor in any way referring to it." *Montague Smith, J.*, said: "If the debt sought to be set-off in an action brought on behalf of the assignee of a debt, had existed at the time of the transfer, equity would not interfere to restrain the legal set-off which the parties

Judgment. had. But here, at the time of transfer and notice, no debt existed to be set-off. It is said that, if debts are accruing mutually under independent contracts, neither of which is due at the time of the transfer, the right of set-off exists; if at the time of action brought upon one of them, the liability of the other has ripened into a debt actually due. But the time to be looked at is, not the time of action brought, but the time when the transfer was made and notice given, and the rights of parties must be determined by the state of things then existing." It may be assumed for the purposes of the

---

(a) See Priddy v. Rose, 3 Mer. 86 ; Hopkins v. Gowan, 1 Mol. 561 ; Morris v. Livie, 1 Y & C. C. C. 380 ; Moore v. Jervis, 2 Coll. 60 ; Cole v. Muddle, 10 H. 186 ; Smith v. Parke, 16 Beav. 115; Cockell v. Taylor, 15 B. 103 ; Cavendish v. Geaves, 24 B. 163 ; The Unity Joint Stock Mutual Banking Association, v. King, 25 B. 73 ; Irby v. Irby, *Ib.* 632; Willes v. Greenhill, 29 B. 376 ; Barnett v. Sheffield, 1 DeG. McN. & G. 371 ; Wilkins v. Sibley, 4 Giff. 442 ; Clarke v. Faux, 2 Russ. 320; Re Natural Alliance Insurance Co., Ashworth's case, 7 L. T. N. S. 64 ; Alliance Bank v. Holford, 16 C. B. N. S. 460.

(b) L. R. 2 C. P. 593.

present case, that the restriction on the rights of the
assignee is as the learned judges stated.

That the doctrine applies where the chose in action
assigned is a mortgage, is clearly settled. The circumstance that a mortgagee takes a legal estate in the land
on which the debt is secured was expressly held in
*Matthews* v. *Wallwyn* (a) to make no difference in
favor of the assignee. The Lord Chancellor there
observed : "It is true there is a legal estate or term;
but it must be apparent on the face of the title, that it
is not an absolute conveyance of the term or legal
estate, but a security for a debt; and the real transaction is an assignment of a debt from *A* to *B;* that
debt collaterally secured by a charge upon real estate.
The debt therefore is the principal thing; and it is
obvious, that if an action was brought upon the bond
in the name of the mortgagee, as it must be, the
mortgagor shall pay no more than what is really due
upon the bond; if an action of covenant was brought
by the covenantee, the account must be settled in that
action. In this Court the condition of the assignee
cannot be better than it would be at law in any mode
he could take to recover what was due upon the
assignment." I refer also to *Williams* v. *Sorrell* (b),
*Smith* v. *Parkes* (c), *Parker* v. *Clarke* (d), *Davis* v.
*Hawke* (e), and *McPherson* v. *Dougan* (f). Indeed
the general doctrine has long been beyond dispute. (g)

In *The Church Society* v. *McQueen*, Chancellor
*VanKoughnet* applied the rule to a case which is not
distinguishable in its circumstances from the present;

---

(a) 4 Ves. at 128.                    (b) 4 Ves. 389.
(c) 16 B. 115.                        (d) 30 Beav. 54.
(e) 4 Gr. 394.                        (f) 9 Gr. 258.
(g) Norrish v. Marshall, 5 Madd. at 481. See per Lord Ch.
Barnard v. Hunter, 2 Jur. N. S. at 1213 ; Church Society v. McQueen,
15 Gr. 281.

1871.

Henderson
v.
Brown.

and the decision of the late Vice Chancellor *Esten* in *Tully* v. *Bradbury* (*a*), though it was against the right of set-off there claimed, proceeded on the ground that set-off is allowable,° only when "the necessity for making the arrangement, occurs, and not before; and if one of the funds has been *previously* alienated it does not arise at all." The learned Vice Chancellor thus made the distinction stated in the case in the Common Pleas.

In *Hanford* v. *Moseley* (*b*), and *Alliance Bank* v. *Halford* (*c*), effect was given to this right, in favor of the purchaser, as against the mortgagee's assignees in bankruptcy, as being an equity to which a purchaser and mortgagor is entitled under the general law of the Court, though the rights of third parties, viz., the assignees in bankruptcy and the creditors, had intervened. In *Woods* v. *Martin* (*d*) the same equity was

Judgment. enforced against a purchaser of the mortgage. Mr. *Dart*, in his book on Vendors, expresses an opinion that the equity would not prevail against a purchaser "*without* notice, and who previously to taking the assignment had ascertained from the purchaser the existence of the debt" (*e*); but the learned writer does not suggest, nor am I aware that any one else has ever suggested, any doubt, that the equity prevails against an assignee *with* notice.

It has been held in several cases (*f*) that, after a conveyance has been executed, if the purchase money has been actually paid, it cannot be recalled or followed by the purchaser, or its appropriation or application

---

(*a*) 8 Gr. 561.

(*c*) 16 C B. N. S.

(*e*) P. 525.

(*b*) 3 Hare at 572.

(*d*) 11 Ir. Ch. 148.

(*f*) Thomas v. Powell, 2 Cox. 394; Tylee v. Webb, 14 Beav. at 17; Miller v. Pridden, 26 Law J. Chan. 183; Cator v. Earl of Pembroke, 2 B. C. C. 282.

interfered with, in consequence of the discovery or
existence of an outstanding incumbrance or other defect
in the title. But it is to be remembered, that, even in
those cases in which a set-off is clearly claimable
against a chose in action, if the party pays the debt
against which the set-off would have been claimable,
he retains no lien on the money so paid; his opportunity of claiming the set-off is gone both at law and in
equity. It is one thing to hold, that money paid
cannot be recalled or specifically followed; and quite
another thing to say, that the purchaser is not permitted to withhold from an assignee unpaid purchase
money with a view to its application to pay an outstanding incumbrance, which the vendor or assignor
should have paid before the assignment, and of which
the assignee was aware when he took his assignment.
This distinction was expressly recognized in very early
cases (a), and is in accordance with all subsequent
authority. I am of opinion that the decree was right,
and should be affirmed.

*1871.*

*Henderson
v.
Brown.*

*Judgment.*

STRONG, V. C.—The facts of this case as they appear
in evidence are as follows: *Stephen Sando,* being the
owner of the property comprised in the plaintiff's
mortgage, subject to a mortgage to *Hughes,* on 22nd
July, 1858, sold and conveyed the mortgaged land to
the defendant, who, on the same day, executed the
mortgage which is the subject of this suit, securing
the purchase money to *Sando.* The purchase deed
executed by *Sando* contained the usual limited vendor's
covenant against incumbrances, and *Brown* had notice
of the outstanding mortgage to *Hughes,* which was
within this covenant. Subsequently, and on the 20th
July, 1859, *Sando,* for valuable consideration, transferred *Brown's* mortgage to *Henderson,* who afterwards

---

(a) Maynard v. Mosley, 3 Sw. at 625; Anon. Freem. C. 118, p.
107; &c.

12—VOL. XVIII. GR.

procured, likewise for value, an assignment of *Hughes's*
mortgage.  *Sando,* in his evidence, states that he told
*Henderson* that *Brown's* mortgage was given for the
purchase money, and *Henderson* must therefore be
taken to have notice of this fact.

*Henderson* took from *Sando,* as indemnity against
the mortgage to *Hughes, Sando's* bond, and also an
assignment of a contract of purchase of certain land.
*Henderson* compelled *Brown* to pay off part of the
mortgage to *Hughes.*  Upon this state of facts, *Brown,*
in his answer to the bill of *Henderson's* administratrix
to foreclose *Brown's* own mortgage, claims the right to
set off the amount which he has been compelled to pay
in respect of the mortgage to *Hughes.*

At the hearing I expressed an opinion adverse to
the defendant's contention, but the case of *The Church
Society* v. *McQueen* being cited, and ascertaining also
on inquiry from both his Lordship the Chancellor
and my brother *Mowat* that they had made decrees in
accordance with that case, I thought it my duty to
follow it as an authority rather than the earlier and
conflicting case of *Tully* v. *Bradbury* (a), and I accordingly made the decree now under review.

The case being now to be regarded as free from the
authorities I have mentioned, none of which were
decisions of the full Court, I have been unable to come
to any conclusion other than that I originally stated.

In the first place, to clear the case of any compli-
cations, it may be said that the circumstances of an
indemnity having been taken by *Henderson* against
*Hughes's* mortgage, and of this latter incumbrance
having been got in by *Henderson* himself, and the

(a) 8 Grant, 561.

partial. payment sought to be set off having been
made to him, have not and could not have been
used as foundations for any arguments in favour of
the defendant.

'. The abstract question which is presented for decision
may therefore be thus stated : A purchaser who has
taken a conveyance. and given a mortgage for the
purchase money, has been compelled to pay off a
charge forming an incumbrance within the covenant
contained in his. purchase deed, of which he had
notice at the time of his purchase. Can he, in such
a case, set off or retain what he has so paid out of
the purchase money remaining secured, against an
assignee for valuable consideration of the mortgage—
the assignee having had actual notice that the mortgage had been given to secure purchase money, and
his assignment being prior in point of time to the
payment by the mortgagee of the outstanding incum- Judgment.
brance ?

It is clear that there is not here any room for the
application of the doctrine of equitable set-off. This
is settled by the late case of *Watson* v. *Mid-Wales
R. W. Co.* (a), which, whilst it establishes that. the
assignee of a chose in action is liable to a right of set-
off which is perfect as against the assignor at the date
of the assignment, also disaffirms the proposition that
he is subject by way of set-off to a claim which did
not ripen into a debt as against the assignor until
after the transfer. The first branch seems to be an
extension of the doctrine of equitable set-off, for it is,
in effect, treating the cross demands as extinguishing
each other *ipso jure*, which Sir *George Turner*, V. C.,
in *Freeman* v. *Lomas* (b), says is not the true principle. It is, however, a fair and reasonable rule, and

---

(a) L. R. 2 C. P. 593.          (b) 9 Hare, 109.

I can see no objection to it. But applying this rule and its limitation to the present case, it is clear that the defendant is not entitled to set off the amount which he paid on account of *Hughes's* mortgage, inasmuch as that payment was not made until after the transfer of *Brown's* mortgage by *Sando* to *Henderson*.

It is, however, argued that, although there may be no right of equitable set-off in the strict sense, yet the defendant has a right to retain (rather than set-off) out of his unpaid purchase money secured by the mortgage of which foreclosure is sought, a sum equal to that which he has been compelled to pay towards satisfaction of the incumbrance against which he has his vendor's covenant for indemnity ; or, in other words, that he has a lien on the unpaid purchase money to that extent. And it is on this view that the judgment of the Court proceeds.

Judgment.

It may be conceded that, if the mortgage had remained unpaid in the hands of *Sando*, and the defendant had not had notice of the mortgage to *Hughes* at the time of his purchase, the defendant would have been entitled to this right of retainer or stoppage—something differing from set-off, as is explained by Lord *Cottenham* in the case of *Cherry* v. *Boultbee* (a).

Then it must be admitted that *Henderson* had notice of this equity of the defendants, for he clearly had actual notice that the mortgage from *Brown* to *Sando* was for purchase money, and that *Hughes's* mortgage was an outstanding incumbrance, and notice of the vendor's covenant must be imputed to him because that was contained in a deed which formed part of his title. The case is therefore reduced to the naked

---

(a) 4 M. & C. 442.

question of law, is the defendant, as against *Henderson*,
an assignee under the circumstances stated, entitled to
the same measure of equitable right which he could
have insisted upon against *Sando* ?

The only reported cases in this Court are those of
*Tully* v. *Bradbury* and *The Church Society* v. *McQueen*,
which, as I have said, are in direct contravention of
each other. *Tully* v. *Bradbury* proceeds on the sound
distinction that this lien on the purchase money for an
incumbrance within the covenant does not exist when
the purchaser has notice of it at the time of his purchase ; the course adopted by the purchaser in such a
case of taking a covenant and not insisting on the
incumbrance being discharged out of the purchase
money, before completion, indicating a clear intention
not to rely on the lien, but on the personal liability of
the vendor merely ; and this, I should have thought,
applied in full force in the present case, and ought
alone to be decisive against the defendant, had it not
been for the case of *Woods* v. *Martin* (a). There are,
however, I think, other grounds for coming to a conclusion in the plaintiff's favour.

In the English reports, so far as I can find, there is
but one decided case touching the question, that of
*Cator* v. Lord *Pembroke* (b), and this, which is not
referred to in either *Tully* v. *Bradbury*, or *The Church
Society* v. *McQueen*, seems to be an authority for the
plaintiff.

There Lord *Bolingbroke*, being tenant for life of a
settled estate, with a power of sale, granted an annuity
charged on his life estate, and then exercised the
power of sale. The purchaser having no notice of the
charge, which was fraudulently concealed by the ven-

---

(a) 11 Ir. Ch. 148.       (b) 1 B. C. C. 301; S. C. 2 B. C. C. 282.

dor, paid his purchase money, with which stock was purchased and transferred into the names of the trustees of the settlement; the vendor then assigned his interest, as tenant for life, of this stock, to purchasers for value. Subsequently, the purchaser having discovered the outstanding incumbrance, filed a bill to establish a lien on the vendor's life interest in the stock, which still stood in the names of the trustees. The case was first heard before the Lords Commissioners, who, according to the report in 1st *Brown's* Chancery Cases, determined against the purchaser, upon the ground that the assignees of the vendor's life interest in the stock, were purchasers for valuable consideration without notice. The case subsequently came on to be reheard before Lord *Thurlow*, who, according to the Report in 2 B. C. C. 282, affirmed the decree, saying that the plaintiff must have failed, even though there had been no assignment of the vendor's

life-interest in the suit and the suit had been against the trustees.

Both Lord *St. Leonards* and Mr. *Dart* treat this case as being a governing authority on the present question. Mr. *Dart* (a) considers it as determining that the purchaser whose purchase money is secured by a mortgage which has been assigned, is not entitled to a lien for an incumbrance within his vendor's covenant, which he has been obliged to pay off, when the assignee of the mortgage has had no notice and has paid a valuable consideration; and he observes that what Lord *Thurlow* says in his judgment on the rehearing, is to be regarded as dictum only.

Lord *St Leonards*, on the other hand (b), recognizes Lord *Thurlow's* judgment as correctly propounding the law, which is stated by Lord *St. Leonards* in

---

(a) 4th Ed. p.　　　　　(b) *Vide Sugden's* V. & P. Ed. 14, 553.

these words: ."The purchaser has no lien on the purchase money after. it is appropriated by the vendor,"
which is clearly against the purchaser in the present case.

I do not think Mr. *Dart* is warranted in saying that
Lord *Thurlow's* opinion was mere dictum, for Lord
*St. Leonards* deduces from it the important principle
I have stated, and which it is manifest, from the report,
the decision was intended to be rested upon. I find
therefore, that the authority of Lord *Thurlow* and
Lord *St. Leonards* is in favour of the plaintiff, and
this, I think, ought to outweigh the opinion of Mr.
*Dart*, who appears to assign an unsound reason for
restricting the lien, as he admits must be done when
the assignee is a purchaser for value without notice.

I do not regard the case of *Woods* v. *Martin* as
an authority against the plaintiff, but the contrary;
as there the assignment of the security for purchase
money was impeached as fraudulent against the purchaser, and determined so to be upon the evidence,
and much stress is laid upon this, which would have
been entirely immaterial if the assignee had taken
subject to the same equities which bound the vendor.
In my opinion, the solution of any difficulty in ex-
plaining the authorities, is to be found in this mode of
regarding the equitable rights of the parties. So long
as the mortgage for purchase money remains in the
hands of the vendor, the purchaser has a potential, as
distinguished from an actual equity, inasmuch as he
has the power to apply the money in paying off incumbrances which the vendor ought to discharge; but he
must exercise this right whilst the mortgage belongs to
the vendor, for it is intercepted so soon as, by a transfer
of the mortgage, the fund which the purchaser has had,
up to that time, the right to appropriate, ceases to
belong to the vendor and becomes the money of the

*Judgment.*

assignee. After assignment, the purchaser has no more right, as against his assignee, to stop the money than in the ordinary case of the assignment of a chose in action unsecured the debtor has to set-off against the assignee a debt existing, but not payable at the time of the transfer; and that this cannot be done is decided by the case of *Watson* v. *The Mid-Wales Railway Company,* before cited.

Apart from authority, and having regard to the freedom with which mortgage securities are dealt with by way of assignment in this country, it would appear to be a much more convenient course to tell the purchaser, in a case like the present, " that he has chosen his remedy," and to leave him to an action on the covenant, than to entangle the assignee of a mortgage for purchase money in the equities of the mortgagee, not arising from his character of mortgagee, but out of a totally different relationship with his mortgagor— that of vendor and purchaser; and I think this argument is not answered by the consideration that the assignee ought to apply to the mortgagor before taking his transfer, for this would manifestly be no complete protection to him since there might be outstanding an incumbrance created by the vendor unknown to either the purchaser or the assignee, and which, if the purchaser should be compelled to pay, he would, upon the principle established by the judgment of the majority of the Court in the present case, be entitled to recoup himself for out of the unpaid purchase money secured by the mortgage.

Upon the whole, I am compelled, with great respect for the opinion of the majority of the Court, to hold that the plaintiff ought not to be charged with the sum paid by the defendant on account of the mortgage to *Hughes.*

## CAMPBELL v. YOUNG.

*Riparian proprietors—Bracket boards—Statute of Limitations.*

The use of bracket boards on a mill dam is such an easement as the
Statute of Limitations will protect.

The parties to the suit were riparian proprietors on March 8.
the river Otonabee. The plaintiff complained, amongst
other things, of the use of bracket or flash boards on
the defendants' dam. The defendants proved to the
satisfaction of the Court, that they had used such
bracket boards for twenty years, and they claimed the
benefit of the Statute of Limitations.

Mr. *Moss*, appeared for the plaintiff.

Mr. *S. Blake*, for the defendants.

It was contended for the plaintiff, that an easement Statement.
of this kind was one to which the Statute of Limitations did not apply, and the following amongst other
authorities were cited:

*Moore* v. *Webb* (a), *Davies* v. *Williams* (b), *Wardle*
v. *Brocklehurst* (c), *Murgatroyd* v. *Robinson* (d), *Tickle*
v. *Brown* (e), *Beasley* v. *Clarke* (f), *Warburton* v.
*Parke* (g), *Beamish* v. *Barrett* (h), *Flight* v. *Thomas* (i),
*Buell* v. *Ford* (j), *McKechnie* v. *McKeyes* (k), Brown
on Stat. Lims. 400.

For the defendant, it was argued, that these authorities did not apply; that the Statute of Limitations

---

(a) 1 C. B. N. S. 673.　　　　(b) 16 Q. B. 546.
(c) 1 Ell. & Ell. 1058.　　　　(d) 7 El. & B. 391.
(e) 4 A. & E. 369.　　　　　　(f) 2 Bing. N. C. 705.
(g) 2 H. & N. 64.　　　　　　(h) 16 Gr. 318.
(i) 8 Clk. & F. 231.　　　　　(j) 10 U. C. C. P. 206.
　　　　　(k) 9 U. C. Q. B. 563.

1871.    had been expressly held in the American Courts to affect
~~~~~    easements of this kind; and that that view was in
Campbell.  accordance with the spirit of the English law; referring
   v.
 Young.   to *Cowell* v. *Thayer* (a), *Pierce* v. *Travers* (b), *Bolivar
         Manufacturing Co.* v. *Neponset Manufacturing Co.* (c),
         *Sumner* v. *Tillerton* (d), *Moyse* v. *Stilman* (e), *Marcly* v.
         *Shultz* (f), *Hynds* v. *Shultz* (g), *Angell* on Watercourses,
         sec. 380; Consol. Stat. U. C. ch. 88, secs. 37, 39, 40.

At the close of the argument, MOWAT, V. C., held,
that such an easement was protected by the Statute,
and that there was sufficient evidence of twenty years
user to entitle the defendants to a decree.

---

## McDONALD v. McKAY.    [IN APPEAL.*]

*Timber limits—Statute of Frauds.*

The plaintiff, being entitled, according to the usage of the Crown, to
a license for certain timber limits, on the 3rd December, 1863, took
out a license in the name *J. N. & Co.*, and delivered the same to
them upon a verbal agreement for obtaining advances on the security thereof; *J. N. & Co.* procured these advances from a bank, and
deposited the license by way of security. In December, 1864, the
plaintiff took out a new license in the name of *J. N. & Co.*, and
they assigned the same to the bank as a further security. The
plaintiff having made default, the bank sold the limits with the
knowledge of, and without any objection by, the plaintiff.
*Held*, in appeal, that though there was no writing shewing the agreement between the plaintiff and any of the other parties, the sale was
binding on him; and a bill impeaching it was dismissed with costs.
[DRAPER, C. J., and SPRAGGE, C., dissenting.]

---

(a) Metc. 253.        (b) 97 Mass. 306.      (c) 16 Pick. 241.
(d) 7 Pick. 198.      (e) 24 Conn. 27.       (f) 29 N. Y. 352.
(g) 39 Bar. 600.

\* *Present.*—DRAPER, C. J.; RICHARDS, C. J.; VANKOUGHNET, C.*;
SPRAGGE, V. C.†; MORRISON, WILSON, GWYNNE, and GALT, JJ.

*Died before judgment was given.
†Was appointed Chancellor before judgment.

The plaintiff in his bill alleged that, being possessed of a Crown timber license, he, on the 17th October, 1862, entered into an agreement with the defendants, *Jeffery* and *Noad*, to the effect that they should advance money to the plaintiff to enable him to get out timber from the timber limits in the season of 1862–3; and that, in the month of December then next, the plaintiff would assign the license to them, which they should hold as a security for the advances to be made in that season; that he accordingly did assign the license absolutely in terms to *Jeffery* and *Noad*, but that it was in fact a mortgage security only for such advances; that on the 31st of October, 1863, all the advances which had been made by *Jeffery* and *Noad*, in pursuance of the above agreement, were repaid; and that they were in fact indebted to plaintiff, in respect of the transactions of the the season, in about $2000 : and the plaintiff averred that then, and from thenceforward he had been unable to obtain a re-assignment of the timber license; that *Jeffery* *Noad* were bare trustees of it for the plaintiff; and the bill alleged that the defendants pretended that there was a subsequent agreement between plaintiff and *Jeffery* and *Noad* for further advances to be made to the plaintiff on the security of the said limits; that at a period subsequent to the said 31st of October, the plaintiff was indebted to *Jeffery* and *Noad* in a large sum and that plaintiff gave them authority to sell the said limits, and assented to the sale thereof by *Jeffery* and *Noad ;* and that the intention and effect of the said written agreement was to confer a power of sale; "*but your complainant charges the contrary of such pretences.*"

The bill then alleged that the plaintiff himself procured renewals of the said timber license for the years 1863–4, 1864–5, and that the same was, in April, 1866, renewed to the defendant *Noel,* for the season of the years 1865–6.

1871.

McDonald v. McKay.

Statement.

The bill further alleged that in the latter end of the year 1864, *Jeffery* and *Noad* became insolvent; and being indebted to the Quebec Bank in a large sum of money, an agreement was entered into between them, that *Jeffery* and *Noad* should assign the license to the Bank; and for that purpose should execute a transfer to defendant *Noel*, an agent of the Bank, in trust for the Bank; that accordingly, by an instrument, dated the 18th February, 1865, *Jeffery* and *Noad* assigned the license to *Noel;* and that the Bank pretended to have entered into a verbal agreement with defendant *McKay* for the sale of the limits to him, for $1200; but the plaintiff asserted that no beneficial interest passed to *Noel* or *McKay*, and that *Noel*, the Bank, or *McKay*, had no interest in the license, except as trustee for the plaintiff; that no valuable consideration was given by *Noel* or the the Bank, for the assignment to *Noel;* that no transfer was ever executed by *Noel* to *McKay;* that at the time

of the assignment to *Noel*, and of the pretended sale by the Bank to *McKay*, the Bank and *McKay* respectively had notice of plaintiff's title to the limits; that *McKay* paid no valuable consideration for the limits; that in the winter of 1865-6, the defendants *Burnett* and *Bannerman*, in conjunction with *McKay*, had cut timber on the limits; and the bill submitted that *McKay*, *Burnett*, and *Bannerman*, should be enjoined against trespassing and waste; and that it should be declared that the plaintiff was entitled to the license, and to the renewal thereof; that the defendant *Noel* should be declared to be a trustee thereof for the plaintiff; and that if it should appear that any sum was due by the plaintiff to *Jeffery* and *Noad* at any time since the 31st October, 1853, and if it should be determined that the said limits should be held by the defendants *Jeffery* and *Noad*, or any of the other defendants, or their assigns, as a security for any such sums, the plaintiff submitted that he was entitled to redeem the same upon payment of any excess of such rents and profits of the said limits since the defendants *Noel, McKay, Burnet,* and *Banner-man,* had gone into possession.

The Court below having made a decree in favour of the plaintiff, as reported ante volume xv, page 391; the defendants, other than *Jeffery* and *Noad,* appealed therefrom, on the following, amongst other, grounds :—

That the plaintiff had no more than a redeemable interest in the said timber limits, and could obtain relief only upon payment of what was due upon account taken, of all the several years' dealings between the parties; that all the interest of the plaintiff in the said timber limits was sold after due notice, and his title thereto was thereby destroyed; that in equity the plaintiff should be estopped from saying that the said limits were not validly pledged for subsequent advances, and validly sold, as he acquiesced therein, and caused the defendants to alter their position and to advance money upon the faith of their having the said limits as a saleable security in their hands; that by the pleadings the issue between the parties is whether or not there was in fact an agreement for subsequent advances, and such an agreement was proved and subsequent advances were made in pursuance thereof; that *The Quebec Bank* and *McKay* were purchasers for value of the said limits without notice of the plaintiff's alleged claims; that by the deposit of the timber license with *Jeffery* and *Noad,* and the transfer thereof to them absolutely and by allowing the same to remain with them, subject to their disposal, there was created by the plaintiff an equitable mortgage on the said limits by deposit of documents of title thereof; and that inasmuch as the plaintiff had absolutely assigned the limits in question, it was not necessary to have any agreement in writing to constitute such limits a continuing security for subsequent advances, and the Statute of Frauds did not apply to such a case.

In support of the decree, it was contended that as the advances made in pursuance of the written assignment were paid off or discharged long prior to the filing of the plaintiff's bill of complaint, such assignment had become null and void; that the subsequent verbal agreement for future advances, between the plaintiff and *Jeffery* and *Noad*, was for an interest in or concerning land, and therefore void, to all intents and purposes, by reason of the fourth section of the Act for prevention of frauds and perjuries (a); that the said agreement related to timber then uncut and formed part of the realty, which timber was not severed therefrom in contemplation of law, so far as the validity of the said verbal agreement was concerned; and it could be dealt with only as an interest in or concerning land; that the pretended sale of the plaintiff's interest in the premises passed nothing, by reason of the vendors having no interest therein at the time of sale; that the alleged acquiesence of the plaintiff in such agreement did not give it any force or validity, either at law or in equity, and the defendants were bound to know that the said agreement was null and void; that the Quebec Bank and the defendant *McKay* had notice of the nature of the dealings between the plaintiff and *Jeffery* and *Noad*, and therefore they were not purchasers for value without notice; and that the assignment and delivery of the documents to *Jeffery* and *Noad*, being made for a specific and expressed purpose, the assignees could not convert them into a different security, nor hold them for any other purpose than that for which they received them, save by some valid agreement between the parties, and there never was any such agreement.

Mr. *J. A. Boyd*, for the appellants.

Mr. *McGregor*, contra.

(a) 29 Charles II., chapter 3.

DRAPER, C. J.—The question presented for decision is, whether the verbal agreement for the season of 1863–4, operated to transfer the plaintiff's rights and interests, in and under the license which he had transferred to *Jeffery* and *Noad*, as a security for their transactions during the previous season ; and upon which transactions they had no claim against him : in other words, whether such an agreement is not within the fourth section of the Statute of Frauds requiring it to be evidenced by a writing.

The authorities appear to me to establish that this agreement is within the statute. A purchaser of growing trees which he is to cut down, hew into timber, and haul away, must, of necessity, have a right to enter upon the land on which such trees are growing; and must acquire a possession sufficient to enable him to cut, and to hew the trees when cut, and to remove the timber so manufactured. Trees, although the growing produce of the land, do not constitute its annual profits, as growing crops of potatoes or turnips do.

The cases on this point are considered in *Evans* v. *Roberts* (a).

But, independently of such authorities and of the reasons upon which they are grounded, the Consolidated Statutes of Canada, chapter 23, appears to me conclusive of the question. Section 2 declares that a license issued in conformity with the statute, shall confer, for the time being on the licensee "the right to take and keep exclusive possession" of the lands therein described ; and shall vest in the holder of such license all rights of property whatever in all trees, timber, and lumber cut within the limits during the term thereof.

*1871.*

McDonald
v.
McKay.

January 12.

Judgment.

(a) 5 B. & C. 829.

McDonald
v.
McKay.

Judgment.

It appears to me impossible to hold that the right to take and keep exclusive possession of land, does not amount to an interest in the land. And an agreement to transfer such license is an agreement to transfer the right which the license confers. The plaintiff had such interest, and he verbally agreed to transfer it; and the agreement was within both the letter and spirit of the Act. The case of *Kelly* v. *Webster* (a) does not seem to me so strong, and certainly is not stronger than this; and *Smith* v. *Surman* (b), is so plainly distinguishable as to be an authority in the plaintiff's favour rather than against him; for *Littledale*, J., treats the fourth section as relating to contracts (for the sale of the fee simple or of some less interest than the fee), which give the vendee a right to use the land for a specific period. Here, our statute gives the licensee the right to " take and keep *exclusive* possession" of the lands with the right to cut the trees; and gives him the absolute property in all the trees cut by others without his consent, within his limits, and while his license is in force.

For these reasons I agree with the learned Judge in the Court below that the agreement required to be in writing, because it related to an interest in lands.

Mr. *Boyd*, however, also endeavoured to sustain the defence, upon the footing of an equitable mortgage by deposit of papers or documents with *Jeffery* and *Noad*, by the plaintiff, as a security for advances to be made by them to him, in order to carry on operations for a second season (1863–4).

I do not find any sufficient foundation in fact on which to build up any such conclusion. The only apparent support for it seems to be in the evidence of Mr. *Jeffery*.

---

(a) 12 C. B. 283.                    (b) 9 B. & C. 561.

He says : " I deposited with the Bank, early in November, 1864, the *license papers* which I held from McDonald ;" but there is no statement that the plaintiff was in any way a party to this arrangement, or was made aware of it until afterwards, or that he ever assented to it. Nor is it explained what is meant by the " license papers." The agreement of 1862 was not one of them, for Mr. *Jeffery* says he did not deposit it with, or inform the Bank that it existed. The transfer of the license for the season of 1862–3 (which, by the way, was the only license for the limits in question in this suit granted in plaintiff's name) was, it is to be presumed, in the Crown Timber Office, as it is referred to as Transfer No. 825, in Exhibits E. and F., which purport to be extracts from the License Book. The licenses mentioned in those exhibits were, the first, to plaintiff; the second, to *Jeffery* and *Noad*. The first expired in April, 1863; the latter, in April, 1864; and neither of them were (apart from the agreement of 1862), the titles or documents relative to plaintiff's title to these limits in November, 1864; and the first of them must have come into the hands of *Jeffery* and *Noad* under the agreement of 1862. I think, therefore, the defence fails as to this pretence.

On the whole I am opinion the appeal should be dismissed with costs.

RICHARDS, C. J.—The original transaction between the plaintiff and *Jeffery, Noad & Co.*, was this : In October, 1862, they entered into an agreement in writing with the plaintiff, in which reference is made to the timber limits now in dispute, of which plaintiff was the owner ; and *Jeffery, Noad & Co.* agreed to make him certain advances on the timber which was to be gotten out on those limits to the extent of $6000. The timber was to be marked *J. McD.*, which was to signify that it was the property of *Jeffery, Noad & Co. McDonald*

14—VOL. XVIII. GR.

1871.

McDonald
v.
McKay.

Judgment.

1871.
McDonald
v.
McKay.

was to bring it to market to Quebec, and *Jeffery, Noad & Co.*, were to sell it, and were to get five per cent. commission on all they sold, as well as interest on the advances. It was further agreed that plaintiff would, on or about the 1st December, 1862, transfer to *Jeffery, Noad & Co.* all his interest in the timber limits on the Bonnechere River, so as to vest in them all the rights which plaintiff then enjoyed—which rights he bound himself to maintain by the regular payment of the Crown dues. Then follows this important paragraph : " It is further agreed that the said transfer is made as a security to the said *Jeffery, Noad & Co.*, for the payment, of any, balance arising on this transaction."

On the 22nd December, 1862, plaintiff made an absolute assignment of these limits to *Jeffery, Noad & Co.*, in pursuance of the agreement ; this assignment was recognised by the Crown Lands Department, and Judgment. *Jeffery, Noad & Co.* then appeared on the books of the office as the absolute owners of the limits.

The plaintiff being successful in his timber operations of that year, repaid *Jeffery, Noad & Co.* all their advances.

In the fall of 1863 plaintiff made another arrangement with *Jeffery, Noad & Co.* Mr. *Noad's* evidence is, " he proposed, and I agreed that my firm should continue to make advances upon the same terms as we had done under our written agreement for the then ensuing season. * * He agreed that the same interest should be charged, and that we should continue to hold the limits as security, The plaintiff asked myself that our firm should allow him to buy the deep river limits, and that when purchased they also should be held as security and transferred in like manner to our firm."

The renewal of the license for the season of 1863–4, was obtained by the plaintiff in the name of *Jeffrey & Noad.*

The plaintiff's operations in 1863–4 were not so
successful as they were in the previous season ; and he
was desirous of raising in the summer of that year $3000
more, which he supposed the timber got out the prior
season would be sufficient to pay, as well as the advances
made by *Jeffery, Noad & Co.*, to enable him to get it
out. And he also (24th September, 1864,) then assigned to them the Deep River limits as further security.
These limits are not now in question in this suit.

*Jeffery, Noad & Co.* agreed to make the further
advance of $3000, which they did by giving their note
for $2000 to plaintiff, which he got discounted at the
Quebec Bank, and by accepting his (plaintiff's) draft for
$1000, which plaintiff had discounted through the agent
of the Quebec Bank, at Ottawa.

*Jeffery, Noad & Co.*, early in November, 1864,
deposited with the Quebec Bank the license papers
which they had received from plaintiff : they deposited
them by way of security for the note for $2000 and the
draft of $1000, and informed plaintiff they had deposited
the licenses with the Bank, and transferred them to the
Bank as collateral security, as *Jeffery, Noad & Co.*
could not meet the note and draft at maturity. This
was in November. In the same fall, in the month of
November, plaintiff said he wished to work the limits
during the winter, and asked *Noad* to assist in procuring
the sanction of the Bank. *Noad* told him in the summer
of 1865, that unless he redeemed the limits, the Bank
would sell them. He made no particular remark until
the limits were sold.

*Jeffery, Noad & Co.* stopped payment on the 4th or
5th of November, 1864. *Noad* did not tell the Bank of
the agreement of 1863, when he deposited the license
with them.

After the failure of *Jeffery, Noad & Co.*, plaintiff obtained advances from a person in Ottawa; and before that person would make the advances he required the consent of *Jeffery, Noad & Co.* and of the Bank to his using the limits. Plaintiff received the advances, and told this person that the license was transferred to *Jeffery*, and the limits, as security for a balance of $3000. On the limits being offered for sale, in 1865, plaintiff came to the same person, and wished him to buy them from the Bank, and give $1200, that being the price asked for them. This person, who was called as a witness, thought them insufficient security for $1200.

The Bonnechere-limits were transferred to Mr. *Noel*, the agent of the Bank, on the 18th of January, 1865; and he had them advertised for sale, but did not succeed in obtaining a purchaser.

In May. 1865, the Vice President of the Bank, Mr. *Ross*, spoke to *McKay* about purchasing the limits, and the Cashier of the Bank agreed to sell to *McKay* for $1200. Mr. *Jeffery* was sent for to get his consent; and he thought it was best to sell them for that price. Mr. *Ross* informed the Bank that his firm would pay the amount. The answer states the President of the Bank informed him in a letter of the acceptance of his offer.

The limits were advertised in the Ottawa papers for sale in August and September, 1865. After they were advertised, plaintiff saw the agent of the Bank, referred to the advertisement, and did not complain of it, or object to it.

After the acceptance of the offer, *McKay* apparently entered into arrangements with parties to work the limits, and paid the agent of the Bank $40 to pay the Government dues on the renewal of the license. The amount of the $1200 was afterwards placed to the credit of the notes.

Plaintiff gave *McKay* notice on the 3rd November, 1865, that the agreement, transferring the limits to *Jeffery, Noad & Co.*, was null and void, and that he claimed the limits as his property.

The parties with whom *McKay* had arranged to go on and work the limits, had before this, I infer, engaged men, and incurred expense for the purpose of carrying out that arrangement.

The plaintiff, in his amended bill, states that he procured the renewals of the license for the season of 1863–64, and also the season of 1864–65. The license for the season of 1863–64, when produced, appears to be dated 3rd December, 1863, and was issued in the name of *Jeffery & Noad*. The former license for 1862–63, was dated 19th December, 1862, issued in the name of plaintiff, and under his name in that license, was noted "Transfer to *Jeffery & Noad*, No. 825."

At the date of the new license, taken out by plaintiff in 1863 (December, 1863,) for the season of 1863–64, he was not indebted to *Noad & Co.*, for advances made under the first agreement; and the license was his, to do with as he pleased. If he had required *Noad & Co.* to assign it to him, he could have compelled them to do so; and they could have then said if they would go on making him advances on the security of these limits, as they then were, or not. But instead of doing this, he, either in good faith, intending that *Jeffery, Noad & Co.* should have the security of these limits as he had agreed they should have, renewed the license in their name, and probably sent it to them, for the answer shews they handed the licenses to the Bank, or he to lull them into security, and make them believe they had this security, renewed these licenses in their name and now seeks to take advantage of the act which was well calculated to deceive them. He, by his conduct, induced them to continue their advances to him by placing that in their hands which was in fact a substantial security; and he now wishes to deprive them of that very security. I do not think this can be done either in law or equity.

The renewal again of the same license on the 31st of December, 1864, in the name of *Jeffery, Noad & Co.*, after they had informed him of its being transferred to the Bank; the conduct of plaintiff in getting *Jeffery* to apply to the Bank to allow him to use the limits in that season; the application and consent to allow him to do so; the knowledge that the Bank was offering them for sale, and no objection being urged against it; the interests of third parties being affected by these acts and this conduct of the plaintiff; and the undoubted fact

Judgment. that the plaintiff did agree that these limits should stand as a security to *Jeffery, Noad & Co.* for the further advances for the business of 1863-64; and the very money, which the Bank holds the licenses to secure, having passed directly from the Bank into the plaintiff's own pocket, all shew how grossly unjust the plaintiff's pretensions in this matter now are.

I think we may well hold that there is quite enough shewn, in the acts and conduct of the plaintiff to justify us, in this case, in refusing to declare that these limits, which were granted by the Crown to *Jeffery, Noad & Co.* were held by them as trustees for this plaintiff without any right on their part, or that of their assignees to consider them in their hands as charged with the liabilities which all parties believed and intended should attach to them. To do so, I think would be grossly unjust; and I have not been convinced by the arguments urged on behalf of the plaintiff, that we are bound to do so by any rule, either in law or in equity.

SPRAGGE, C.—I believe it is the opinion of a majority of the Court, that the plaintiff's bill ought to be dismissed; and the ground of that opinion I understand to be, that, assuming that the assignment of October, 1862, was only by way of security for the transactions of that season, as it certainly was, and is in terms expressed to be, there was something more than parol agreement in the two subsequent years, that the timber limits assigned should stand as security for transactions between the same parties of the like character in the two subsequent seasons. That the true equity of the defendants consists in this, that in each of those two subsequent years the license assigned by the plaintiff to *Jeffery & Noad*, was renewed by the plaintiff himself; and by him deposited with *Jeffery & Noad*, as security for their advances to him in those subsequent years respectively. That they were renewed by the plaintiff himself, is alleged in his bill; and it also appears by the bill, that during those two years, the limits were worked by the plaintiff himself for his own use; and this he could not do without a renewal of the license, year by year. The renewals of the license could be only in the name of *Jeffery & Noad*, they standing as assignees. There is no direct evidence of a deposit of the licenses by the plaintiff. The only evidence upon the point is that of *Jeffery*: that early in November, 1864, he deposited with the Quebec Bank certain licenses: these licenses, it appears by his evidence, were for the timber limits in question, and for other timber limits in which also the plaintiff was interested, and they were, as I gather from the evidence, licenses for the season of 1864–65. By that evidence this fact only is proved, that in November, 1864, *Jeffery & Noad* had in their possession a license for that season. How that license came into their possession is no where shewn. It is only an inference, and, as I think, not a necessary inference, that it came there by deposit from the plaintiff for security for advances. It may have been so, or it

1871.

McDonald
v.
McKay.

Judgment.

may not. The renewals by the plaintiff were for his own purposes. When made, *Jeffery & Noad* were the only persons who could be recognised by the Crown Timber Department as entitled to the documents. They would naturally look for the custody of the documents, by reason of the parol agreement that they should hold the limits as security for subsequent advances, and would ask them from the department as of right. If we might speculate upon probabilities we might say that it was quite as likely that these renewal licenses—supposing that for both years they came to the hands of *Jeffery & Noad*—came there by delivery from the public department, as they were there by deposit from the plaintiff.

If a deposit of these documents, and their deposit for a specified purpose, is the foundation of the defendants' equity, it is a fact, or rather they are facts, which it was necessary for the defendants to establish by evidence. Instead of evidence we have only conjecture; and it seems strange that Mr. *Jeffery* was not asked anything about it. But, independently of the weakness of the evidence upon this point, there is that which, in my humble judgment, should make it impossible to establish it as the equity upon which a Court can properly found a decree in favour of the defendants. Neither in the answers, nor in the argument in the Court below, nor in the reasons of appeal, nor in argument in this Court, has this ground been taken. I concede that it is competent to give effect to a point which has not been taken in argument; but to give or to refuse relief upon a ground of equity not taken by the pleadings, is against the rules of a Court of Equity, as it is of a Court of Law. The exception in equity is, where evidence has been given upon the assumption that the point to which evidence has been directed, is raised by the pleadings. That is not the case here. Not a tittle of evidence was given with a view of shewing that there was a deposit of licenses to create an equitable mortgage. The omission to ask Mr. *Jeffery* how the renewal licenses came to the hands of his firm, is convincing evidence of this. I may at the same time observe that, if the question had been asked, it might have been properly objected that the point was not made by the pleadings.

1871.

McDonald
v.
McKay.

The point is not made by the pleadings. *McKay* is the only defendant who has answered at length: the other defendants (with the exception of *Jeffery & Noad*, against whom the bill is taken *pro confesso*,) adopting for the most part the answer of *McKay*. *McKay's* answer takes this ground, that there was a written agreement that the timber limits should stand as a security for the transactions of the season of 1862–63; and that there are subsequent parol agreements in respect of the two subsequent seasons; and that the subject matter of these agreements was personal property; and the evidence was given, and the case was argued upon the assumption that these were the points in question.

Judgment.

Then, to come to the appeal. If counsel for the appellants had taken the ground that there was a deposit of title deeds in the two subsequent years, whereby an equitable mortgage was created, he would have been asked to point to the reason of appeal which warranted the taking of this ground. No such ground is taken by the reasons of appeal. No such fact is alleged as that a deposit of the licenses was made in those years. Indeed the language of the reasons rather excludes such a hypothesis. To take the seventh: "Because by the deposit of the timber license with *Jeffery & Noad*, and the transfer to them absolutely, and by allowing the same to remain with them, subject to their disposal, there was created by the plaintiff an equitable mortgage on the said limits by deposit of documents of title thereof." Here, if anywhere (or following this), the fact of subsequent deposits and the equitable rights flow-

McDonald
v.
McKay.

ing therefrom, might be expected to be fonnd if at all. But it is plain, from the language of this "reason," that it refers to the transaction of October, 1862, and not to any subsequent transaction. None of the reasons of appeal point directly or impliedly to the ground now proposed to be taken.

If the judgment be reversed upon the ground now taken, it will be upon ground not raised in pleading, upon ground to which no evidence has been directed, and upon ground not taken in the reasons of appeal. It would, in my judgment, be most unsafe, as well as in contravention of well established rules of pleading and practice, to adjudicate upon such grounds.

WILSON, J.—Why did the plaintiff, in December, 1863, pay the fees, and renew in the name of *Jeffery & Noad*, if he did not owe them money? Or, if he had not agreed for advances for the ensuing year? He commenced his operations for that year in September.

Judgment.

*Jeffery, Noad & Co.* had, therefore, all along the legal title; and, I think, by the plaintiff's consent and act; and they are entitled to retain it, or those who claim from them, are entitled to retain it until their claim is paid.

That the plaintiff must have known the legal title was in *Jeffery, Noad & Co.*, by reason of his own payments and renewals in their name, is very plain. He notified the Crown Lands Office on the 3rd of November, 1865, that the agreement was at an end which he had made in 1862. Why did he not do so before that time?

It is only consistent with the fact that the legal estate was permitted to remain in *Jeffery, Noad & Co.*, so far as the plaintiff could affect it; and it was done, too, solely by his own act of renewal in their name; and it was to be of some use to them, which could only be by its remaining as security for the advances made after the first year.

I think, according to *Ex parte Witbread* (a), the charge against the plaintiff for the future advances has been made out; and that the appeal should be allowed.

GWYNNE, J.—Upon these pleadings, and this evidence, I take it to be established that by the agreement of October, 1862, *Jeffery & Noad* were only to have a lien on the license then assigned to them for the advances of that season ; and that at the close of the season there was nothing due to them upon the footing of the security. The plaintiff then had, as he contends, a right to call for a re-assignment of the license ; but whether because of the parol agreement that it should remain in the hands of *Jeffery & Noad*, as security for advances to be made by them during the then coming season, or for some other reason, the plaintiff did not call for such re-assignment. *Jeffery & Noad*, although being the persons appearing on the books of the Crown Lands Office to be entitled to a renewal, took no steps themselves to procure a renewal. It is part of the plaintiff's case, that on the 3rd of December, 1863, he paid the Government charges himself, and procured a license for the season terminating in 1864, to be granted to *Jeffery & Noad ;* and he must have delivered it, or caused it to be delivered to them. By that act, whatever might be the secret trust upon which *that license* was so delivered to *Jeffery & Noad*, to be held by them, the plaintiff placed them in the position of appearing to the world as the persons entitled to deal with the license. *Jeffery & Noad* were then, as it appears to me, possessed of *that grant*, not merely in virtue of the assignment of the license or grant of 1862, but by the superadded act of the plaintiff in procuring

Judgment.

_____

(a) 16 Ves. 209.

the grant for 1863–64, to issue to *Jeffery & Noad*, and delivering it or causing or procuring it to be delivered to them for some purpose or other of the plaintiff's; his so dealing with the grant must have been to promote and advance some object of his own. I find it then as a fact established by the evidence of *Jeffery* that in August, 1864, while *Jeffery & Noad* were so in possession of the license granted on December 3rd, 1863, the plaintiff applied to them for pecuniary accommodation, which they obtained for him at the Quebec Bank upon the faith and assurance of the agreement, verbal it is true, made in August, 1863, that *Jeffery & Noad* should hold and deal with the license as collateral security for these advances, amounting to $3000. The advances were not made by the bank upon the security of the license, but *Jeffery & Noad*, through their names procured the advances at the bank for the plaintiff upon the faith that they should retain and deal with the license as collateral security for these advances.

Now at that time, according to the plaintiff's contention *Jeffery & Noad* held the license solely in the character of agents and trustees for the plaintiff. The legal estate was by the plaintiff's act (confirmed by procuring the license to be granted on December 3rd, 1863) vested in *Jeffery & Noad*, and the agreement that *Jeffery & Noad* should hold and deal with the license as security for the advances might well, I think, be taken by *Jeffery & Noad* as authority competent to be given by a principal to his agents without writing.

I find it also as a fact established in the case that in November, 1864, *Jeffery & Noad* in pursuance of what they deemed to be the authority given to them by the plaintiff in August, deposited the license so granted in December, 1863, with the bank as collateral security for the advances made by the bank, and which the plaintiff received; and hence the bank, at the time, had

no reason whatever to doubt the right to deal absolutely
with the license. I do not see why that deposit was
not a good, equitable deposit of the license with the
bank, by *Jeffery & Noad* as agents of the plaintiff.

I find it as a fact established by the evidence that
the fact of this deposit of the license with the bank was
immediately after it was made, communicated by *Jeffery*
to the plaintiff, and that he not only did not object to
it, but *by his acts and conduct ratified and confirmed it.*
Upon the fact of its being a good and valid deposit the
plaintiff in November, 1864, asked *Jeffery* to assist him
in procuring the *sanction of the bank* to his working
the limits in the winter of 1864. In the same month he
applied to *McGillivray* to make him advances ; he declined doing so unless plaintiff should procure the consent of the bank, who, as *McGillivray* had heard, had
an interest in the license. The plaintiff accordingly
obtained the consent of the bank and upon the faith of it,
procured the required advances from *McGillivray*,
thereby affirming the right of the bank by virtue of the
deposit of the license. Subsequently and on the 30th
December, 1864, while the bank were so, with the knowledge of the plaintiff, in possession of the license granted
on December 3rd, 1863, the plaintiff himself procures a
further license for the year 1864 and 1865, to be
granted to *Jeffery & Noad*, and procures this also to be
delivered to them. They immediately and in the month
of January, 1865, assign it formally to *Noel*, as a
trustee of the bank, who then became entered in the
books of the Crown Lands Office as assignee of the
license, and the plaintiff does not afterwards pay any
further fees to Government or procure any further renewals of the license to be made.

I find it is a fact established in evidence that *Jeffery*
informed the plaintiff in the summer of 1865 that unless
he redeemed the limits the bank would sell them. I

find that he was aware of, and saw the advertisement published by *Noel*. I find that he never objected to the right of the bank to sell, but dealt with *Noel* in recognition of that right, and tried to procure him to become purchaser of the limits from the bank; he applied to *McGillivray* for the like purpose and asked him to buy them from the bank and told him the price asked by the bank, namely, $1200. He got money from *McGillivray* to go to Quebec to get *Ross & Co.*, as the plaintiff said, to *buy the limits from the bank*, and to work them himself under *Ross & Co.*, and when he heard that the bank had sold to *McRay* he made no complaint further than that he expressed to *Stevenson*, the cashier of the Bank of Quebec, his regret that the limits had been sold, *as he wished Mr. Supple to have bought them for him ; and he went to Jeffery* and asked him to intercede with the bank to cancel the sale to *McRay* as he hoped to get Mr. *Supple* or some one else to buy the

limits for him—this he said to *Jeffery* on several occasions.

Under these circumstances it appears to me that the deposit of the license of the 3rd December, 1863, by *Jeffery & Noad* with the bank was a good equitable deposit, binding on the plaintiff; that the subsequent assignment by him to the bank of the license which he (plaintiff) procured to be issued on the 3rd of December, 1864, was a good legal assignment, for valuable consideration, (by *Jeffery & Noad* in pursuance of authority given by the plaintiff in August, 1864, when the arrangement for the $3000 to be obtained through the bank was made) to *Noel* as trustee of the bank, and moreover that the plaintiff has so recognized the dealing of the bank with the limits and the advertisement for sale, and the sale by *Noel* to *McRay*, that the plaintiff cannot now be permitted to dispute the right of the bank to sell. There is no pretence or suggestion of the sale having been improvidently conducted ; no case of that kind is

made by the bill Upon the pleadings and evidence, I
think that the plaintiff should not, under the circumstances, be permitted to dispute the sale, and that the
bill as against all the defendants should be dismissed
with costs.

---

## HENDRY v. ENGLISH. [IN APPEAL]*

*Mill-dam.—Parol agreement.*

C contemplated the erection of a saw mill on land which he owned,
but he required the privilege of backing water on the lands of four
other persons having lands further up the stream ; from three of
these persons he obtained, through the agency of the fourth of them
(E), the right, by deed, of backing the water to whatever extent
would be occasioned by a dam nine feet high. The fourth (E) verbally gave the same right but executed no writing. C thereupon
erected a dam seven feet six inches high, but finding this insufficient
he some years afterwards desired to raise it further.

*Held*, by the Court on appeal, [SPRAGGE, C., and MOWAT, V. C., dissenting,] That E.'s agreement was not binding to any greater extent
than C. had taken advantage of in erecting his original dam.

The plaintiff *Charles Hendry*, claimed under one
*John Clark,* who was the locatee of the Crown of a lot
of land in the township of Maryborough, in the County
of Wellington, who, in 1854, built a saw mill thereon;
the township having been recently settled.

Statement.

The point involved in the case may be thus briefly
stated :—*Clark* contemplated the erection of a saw mill,
having on his land a partial mill site only, not having
sufficient head of water, and was therefore desirous of
obtaining the privilege of backing water on the lands of
persons further up the stream. The evidence in the

---

[*Present.*—DRAPER, C. J., RICHARDS, C. J., HAGARTY, C. J.,
SPRAGGE, V. C.,* MORRISON, J., WILSON, J., MOWAT, V.C., GWYNNE,
and GALT, JJ.]

* Was appointed Chancellor before judgment was given.

cause shewed that the settlers desired to have the saw mill erected, both as a matter of convenience and advantage, and as a means of enhancing the value of their lands. From the three persons immediately above him he bought, in some instances through the intervention of *English*, the right, and obtained conveyances, that is grants of easements; from the defendant he did not obtain any grant or writing of any kind.

The defendant commenced proceedings at law against the plaintiff for damage done to his land by reason of the backing of the water, and the present suit was instituted to restrain such action on the ground of acquiescence, &c. The defendant answered the bill denying the acquiescence alleged, and setting up the Statute of Frauds in bar of the plaintiff's right to the relief prayed.

The cause came on for the examination of witnesses and hearing at the sittings of the Court in Guelph, when a decree was pronounced by [the then] Vice Chancellor *Spragge* giving the plaintiff a right of damming back the water for the purposes of the mill; whereupon a decree was drawn up declaring that the plaintiff had the right of so damming back the water, by any dam erected or to be erected on the site of the old dam, not exceeding nine feet in vertical height, measuring from the surface of the stream when at an average height.

From this decree the defendant appealed, alleging as grounds therefor the following, amongst other, reasons: That there was no agreement by the defendant to allow the plaintiff to construct a dam or to flood the defendant's land; that if there was any agreement it was too indefinite and too uncertain to allow the plaintiff to act upon it, or to enable him to obtain any benefit from it; that if there was an agreement, it did not permit the raising of a dam to a height nearly so great as the present dam, or the flooding the defendant's land to the extent to which the same has been, and is being flooded and the defendant is injured to an extent which in any event was never contemplated or agreed upon ; that there has been no part performance to take the case out of the Statute ; that there could be no part performance of an agreement so uncertain and indefinite, if any there was ; that there was no acquiescence on the part of the defendant, but on the contrary, he continually objected, and brought actions at law, and in other ways denied the right contended for by the plaintiff, and that in any event the decree goes too far, and allows a dam higher than the present one.

1871.

Hendry
v.
English.

In support of the decree the plaintiff assigned the following, amongst other, reasons against the appeal, that there was an agreement by the defendant to allow *John Clark*, through whom the plaintiff claims to construct a dam and flood the defendant's land as stated in the said bill; that the defendant stood by, and saw and encouraged the said *John Clark* to incur great expense in erecting his dam, and knew that the same would flood the said land, and did not forbid the said *John Clark* to continue; that the Statute of Frauds does not apply to the case ; and that the action brought by the defendant was brought in fraud and bad faith, and was properly restrained by the decree of the Court below.

Mr. *Strong*, Q.C.,* for the defendant.

Mr. *Blake*, Q. C., contra.

DRAPER, C. J.—I do not in any respect question the law, as stated by the learned Judge in the Court below, that if a landholder under a verbal agreement, or, what amounts to the same thing; under an expectation

Judgment.

Feb. 5th
(1870.)

---

* Was appointed Vice Chancellor before judgment was given.
16—VOL. XVIII. GR.

created or encouraged by another landowner, that if
he will do a certain thing involving the expenditure
of money, he will grant him a certain privilege upon
his own land; and if upon the faith of such promise
or expectation the first-named landowner lays out
money in doing what it was contemplated he should
do, with the knowledge of the other landowner, and,
without objection by him, a Court of Equity will
compel the other landowner to give effect to such promise or expectation. But I am not satisfied that this
case as presented by the plaintiff, warrants the application of the doctrine, I apprehend it is only applicable in this Court on the ground of fraud; and that
the Court will prevent a party using the Statute of
Frauds to sustain or further a fraud. But the burden
of proof lies wholly on the plaintiff, who charges such
a fraud upon the defendant. In my judgment the
plaintiff here has not sustained the charge.

Judgment.

My brother *Gwynne* has suggested to me another
ground upon which he thinks the decree wrong. All
which *Clark* derived from *English* was from a parol
license given by him to raise the water; from his acts
confirmatory of his willingness that it should be raised,
and from *Clark's* expending money, on the faith of
that license, in raising a dam to a certain height—from
seven feet to seven feet and a half. This license was
merely personal, as I understand him to think; and
could not be considered as appendant or appurtenant to
the land conveyed by *Clark*. That *Clark's* conveyance
to *Stinson*, from whom the plaintiff derives title, did not
in law or equity pass more than *Clark* actually had
in possession when he executed it; and that conceding
it passed the right to overflow the appellant's land to
the extent to which *Clark* had overflowed it, it passed
no more; whereas the respondent was insisting on a
right to raise the dam to nine feet, and had raised it
to eight feet two inches.

I have not been able to see my way with sufficient clearness, to adopt this conclusion, and if I thought the case was made out in fact, I should require more time to consider the matter. The case of *Child* v. *Douglas* (a) appears to me at present to go a long way in support of the plaintiff's contention, though in that case the question did not arise upon a matter resting on parol or verbal license, but on covenants.

Yielding, on the question of fact, to the opinion of my learned brothers, and thus assuming that an easement was vested in *Clark* as against the appellant, the question arises to what extent the easement goes. It is a *parol* license, made good and binding on the grantor, by the erection of a dam and the expenditure of money. I think this fixed the respondent to the construction he thus placed on the parol license, and that when he sold and conveyed the land, he sold with it the easement as then shewn by actual enjoyment and exercise.

I concur, therefore, in varying the decree by declaring that the plaintiff is entitled to raise, keep, and maintain the dam at present erected on the mill property of the plaintiff, in the pleadings mentioned as against the defendant, and by means of such dam, or any other dam hereafter to be erected on the site of the present dam, to throw back the water of the stream in the pleadings mentioned upon, and to flood all such part or parts, portion, or portions of the lands of the said defendant, also in the said pleadings mentioned, being lot number sixteen in the ninth concession of the township of Maryborough, in the County of Wellington, as now are, or shall, or may from time to time, or at any time hereafter, be flooded or damaged by reason, or means, or in consequence, of any such dam, provided

*1871.*

*Hendry*
*v.*
*English.*

Judgment.

---

(a) Kay, 560.

always that the dam erected, or to be erected as aforesaid, shall not raise said water at such dam beyond a
head of seven feet six inches ; and this Court doth .
further order and decree that the injunction issued in
this cause. bearing date the first day of June, 1868,
be, and the same is hereby made perpetual, and that
if the plaintiff shall so desire, a further perpetual injunction do issue out of this Court restraining the
defendant, his servants, agents, and workmen, from
bringing any other action. or doing, or causing to be
be done, any other act, or taking any other proceeding
whereby the plaintiff may be hindered, or deferred, or
interfered with, in raising, keeping, or erecting his
dam.

No costs in the Court below, nor of this Court.

SPRAGGE, C.—The argument in appeal has not at all
changed my view of the law applicable to this case.    I
believe, indeed, that the learned Judges who dissent
from my judgment, differ from me only in this, that
*Clark*, the builder of the mill, between whom and the
defendant, the original agreement was made, having
put up a dam of a less height than the dam, standing at
the date of the bringing of the action by the defendant,
exhausted the equitable right, which he had acquired
under the agreement, and by acting upon it, by the
erection of the mill.

The substance of the agreement was, that *Clark*
should be at liberty to erect a dam of such height as
might be necessary for the proposed saw mill ; the same,
however, not to exceed nine feet ; and he did put up a
mill upon the faith of that agreement, and of the grants
of easement which he had obtained from other proprietors of land.    If, through bad judgment, he at first put
up a dam of insufficient height, I can see no reason why
he should not raise it, or put up another dam of such

height as might be necessary, provided he did not exceed the limit of nine feet. It was still within his agreement, which by necessary implication extended to the maintaining as well as the putting up of a dam.

We cannot see, and no one is warranted in saying, that *Clark* would have incurred the expense that he has incurred, or that he would have put up a mill at all, if the privilege he acquired from *English* as well as from other proprietors, had been less extensive than it was ; for instance, if it had been limited to seven feet or eight feet : the legal conclusion is that what he did, he did upon the faith of the agreement that he had ; and what he did in the first instance, in the way of acting upon it, has nothing to do with the case. It did not, and could not limit the right which he had acquired. His manner of exercising his right was praiseworthy ; he so exercised it as to do as little damage as possible to his neighbours ; and was so moderate in its exercise that he built his dam to a less height than was necessary ; his mill worked but imperfectly ; it ran slowly. It was found necessary to raise it, and at its present height (greatly within the limit of the nine feet) there is no evidence that it is higher than is necessary for the efficient working of the mill, nor has it been contended that it is so.

In my judgment acquiescence has nothing to do with the case, and I am not prepared to say that there has been any acquiescence that would bar the defendant's legal right. What the plaintiff's case is rested upon is not acquiescence, but upon encouragement and agreement on the part of the defendant, upon the faith of which expenditure was incurred by *Clark*. The parties themselves put certain limits to the easement which *Clark* was to enjoy : a dam no higher than should be necessary, and at any rate not to exceed nine feet. Why should this Court put limits to the easement not put by the parties themselves. There is no evidence to shew that the first dam erected was to be the measure of the easement, and I can see no reason why this Court should make it so. Taking the true ground of the plaintiff's equity, and following it out to its legitimate consequence this Court cannot, in my humble judgment, make it so.

Since the argument of this case upon appeal it has occurred to some of the learned Judges of this Court, of the Common Law Bench, that, assuming that *Clark* had an equity arising out of what passed between him and *English*, to maintain a mill-dam on his own premises, as adjudged in his favor by the Court below; that that equity did not pass to the assignee of the land. The point is a new one. The case was argued for the defendant by my brother, *Strong*, (then at the bar), in the Court below, and on appeal. I have often heard my learned brother contend that certain equities are

personal equities only, and were confined to the parties between whom they arose; but on neither of the occasions on which he argued this case, has he contended that the equity in this case was a personal one; nor is that ground taken by the answer.

It is not, in my opinion, in the nature of a personal equity. It was in *Clark* as owner of land. If it did not pass to his assignee of the land, he himself had not that full dominion over the land as he held it, which is an ordinary incident of ownership. But besides the reason arising out of the nature of the equity, there is authority that an equity of this character does pass to an assignee of land. For this I refer to *Child* v. *Douglas* (a) before the present Lord Chancellor, then Vice Chancellor. An owner of land laid it out for building in plots, and with streets. The defendant in the suit was the purchaser of one of the plots, and covenanted

---

(a) Kay 560.

with the vendor not to build within a certain distance
of any of the streets. The plaintiff in the suit was the
purchaser several years afterwards, of a neighboring
plot, from (virtually) the same owners. Several questions arose, among them that which is thus discussed
by the Chancellor. "Then (a) it is argued that if the
landlord assign to other persons the reserved property,
the assigns cannot have the benefit of this covenant.
But that was the very case of *Whatman* v. *Gibson* (b).
Each party there was an assign under those who were
parties to the original covenant, and though there were
reciprocal covenants in that case, yet there can be no
doubt, supposing that the plaintiff there had been the
purchaser of the last house, and the vendor had entered
into no covenants with him, he would still have been
entitled to the benefit of the defendant's covenant."

I have felt some difficulty throughout in seeing how
reciprocity could have anything to do with the question.
Where part of the remaining property of the original
vendor has been sold to another person, who must be
considered to have bought the benefit of the former
purchaser's covenant, and more especially when the
subsequent purchaser, has entered into a similar covenant on his own part, he must be considered to have
done this in consideration of those benefits, and even
whether he actually knew, or was ignorant that this
covenant was, in fact, inserted in the other purchase
deeds, because he must be taken to have bought all the
rights connected with his portion of the land."

Neither the bill, nor the argument of counsel, nor the
judgment of the Court, proceeded upon the ground of
specific performance of the covenant, nor is the case
among those referred to in Mr. *Fry's* Treatise on that
branch of Equity Law; but upon the equity arising out

1871.

Hendry
v.
English.

Judgment.

---

(a) At p. 571.          (b) 9 Sim. 196.

of the stipulation of the defendant, that he would not use his property in a particular way, to come to a Court of Equity to restrain him from so using it; and upon that equity passing to a purchaser, from the person in whom it originally existed. The question arose in that case upon an application for an injunction, and upon an appeal to the Lords Justices, the order was reversed, but on grounds other than that for which I have cited it. There is also the case of *Whatman* v. *Gibson* (a) referred to by the Chancellor, which is in affirmance of the same principle, and *Eastwood* v. *Lever* (b) before the Lords Justices.

I confess it never occurred to me that if *Clark* was entitled to this equity, his assignee of the land would not have the same equity. In my judgment the assignee is so entitled.

Judgment.  The conduct of this defendant has been most unconscientious. What he attempted was nothing less than a gross fraud upon *Clark*, and those claiming under *Clark*. Whether he contemplated this fraud when he gave encouragement, and made the agreement with *Clark*, is known to himself alone, but the spirit in which he acted afterwards is well shewn in the evidence of *Hudson*, who, in the course of his examination, swore : " I worked the mill for Mr. *Clark*. I was the foreman about the saw mill. I remember Mr. *English* coming to the mill the spring after *Clark* had sold the property. He wanted the water taken down. He wanted to put up his line fence. He demanded the water should be taken down. Mr. *English* stated, as far as I understood that he wanted the water down, and to be kept down. Mr. *Clark* appeared surprised at this, and said to *English* that he had given him the right to flood. Mr. *English* said he had not given him the right, and *Clark*

---

(a) 9 Sim. 196.          (b) 33 L. J. Chy. 355.

said he could prove it. *English* said if he had given
him a right, it was only verbal, there was no writings.
The property had now changed hands, and he did not
consider it was binding. I don't mind *Clark* saying
anything further, but that he could not take it down
then ; that he had induced him to put up the mill, and
that without a dam the mill would be rendered useless.
*English* made no answer to this that I mind of. I don't
mind *Clark* saying anything further than that *English*
had induced him to build the mill, and that if it had not
been for *English* and others of his neighbors, he would
not have went on with the mill. Mr. *English* still held
out that he had never given anything that he considered
binding. He admitted after *Clark* had said he could
prove it and had named some of the witnesses, that he
had given him the right to flood ; but that there was
no writings or anything binding in law. This was after
*Clark* had said that *English* had induced him to build
the mill."

The evidence of *Wilson* and others is to the same
effect, and he has followed this up by attempting to
enforce his strict legal right; and by denying by his
answer the conduct on his part, and the agreement with
*Clark*, which are proved most convincingly against him
by numerous witnesses.

At the hearing of the cause I thought both the law
and the facts of the case so clear, that I did not think
it necessary to reserve judgment; and were it not that
some learned Judges, whose opinion is entitled to
respect, think differently, I should feel equally clear
upon the case now. My judgment, at any rate, leads me
to the same conclusion. The paper printed as my judgment consists merely of my notes made at the hearing.

The decree as drawn up is erroneous and not in
accordance with my judgment. The plaintiff is not

entitled absolutely to a dam of the height of nine feet, but to a dam of such height not exceeding nine feet as may be necessary to the proper working of a saw mill on the plaintiff's land : and this I think sufficiently appeared from my notes. I ought, at least, to have been referred to by the counsel or solicitor for the plaintiff, and by the officer of the Court, before the decree was drawn in its present shape.

MOWAT, V. C., concurs in judgment of the Chancellor.

GWYNNE, J.—The basis upon which the plaintiff rests his title to the relief prayed is contained in the 7th, 8th, 9th, and 23rd paragraphs of his bill, and · is as follows :—

7. " The said late *John Clark* before the erection of the mill and mill-dam hereinafter mentioned, offered to purchase from the said *Samuel English* the right to throw back the water of the said river Canestoga, as aforesaid, upon such portion of the west half of said lot number sixteen as might be necessary for the purposes of the said proposed mill and mill-dam, but the said *Samuel English* refused to accept any compensation of any kind whatever for the said right, alleging as a reason that the mill would, when built and in operation, be of great benefit to him, and increase the value of his farm, and that throwing back the water on his said lot, aforesaid, could not do him much harm, or that it would be trifling or words to that effect, and on all the said occasions, he told the said late *John Clark* to build and erect the said saw mill and dam, and gave the said late *John Clark* full and free permission to throw back the water of the said west branch of the said river Canestoga, on the said west half of the said lot sixteen, only stipulating that the water should be let down when the said *Samuel English* should desire to put up his line fence.

8. "Trusting in and relying upon the representations and promises made by the said defendant *Samuel English*, the said late *John Clark*, in the year of our Lord, 1854, caused to be erected at great expense a saw-mill and mill-dam as aforesaid.

9. "While the said mill and mill-dam were being erected, and ever since the erection thereof, the said *Samuel English* continued to reside on the said west half of the said lot sixteen, and was aware of the erection thereof, and that the said late *John Clark* was spending his money and erecting his dam and mill on the faith that the said defendant would not object thereto, and would not seek to disturb him in the use thereof.

23. "That the said dam erected by the late *John Clark* was originally eight feet above the ordinary level of the river, and that the present dam is not over eight feet two inches above the average height of the water in the said river."

Now it appears to me that the allegations in the 7th, 8th, and 9th paragraphs assert a claim to the relief prayed either upon two separate and distinct principles, or upon one only. The principle asserted in the 7th paragraph is that while the erection of the mill and dam was a matter only in contemplation, and before they were erected and built, or any thing was done towards their erection, the defendant gave to *Clark* full and free permission by the erection of a dam across the river upon *Clark's* own property to throw back the water of the said river on the west half of lot number sixteen. Now if such full and free permission was given in an effectual manner, and granting that the permission related to a dam of the height mentioned in the third paragraph, namely : not exceeding the height of nine feet in vertical height, measuring from the surface of the water of the stream ; the permission would undoubtedly operate as a grant of an easement affecting the defendant's land to such extent as such a dam would affect the land, but to be effectual it must needs be by deed. Then the eighth paragraph alleges in effect that *Clark* relying upon this permission erected the dam in the year 1854.

If it be true then that he erected the dam upon the faith of that permission, he must, as it seems to me, stand or fall accordingly as that permission has been given effectually or not: but here it has not been given effectually, and the benefit of the Statute of Frauds is claimed by the answer, so that the plaintiff's case must rest alone upon the sufficiency of the other principle which is contained in the ninth paragraph, which in substance is, that the defendant having, as alleged, encouraged *Clark* to erect the dam which was erected, "and having stood by and seen *Clark* proceed with the erection of the dam, and having seen him spending his money and erecting the said dam and mill on the faith that the defendant would not object thereto, and would not seek to disturb him in the use thereof," should be estopped from interfering with the dam so erected.

Now, it appears to me to be obvious that upon this principle of Equity, the rights of *Clark* and of the plaintiff as claiming through him, must, of necessity, be limited to the height of the erection, which the defendant so stood by and observed in progress of erection, and assisted in erecting and by his acquiescence countenanced; and which is the work which the bill alleges that *Clark* erected in virtue of the encouragement and acquiescence of defendant. When *Clark*, or his assigns, at a future period after the complete erection of the work said to be so acquiesced in, assert the right, adversely to the defendant, of raising from time to time the height of that erection, until the maximum height of nine feet is attained, they must found their right so to do upon some other title than the previous acquiescence, which as it appears to me is exhausted by the first erection; and here they have no such other title to rest upon than the ineffectual parol permission, alleged to have been given, prior to the commencement of the original work.

It may be admitted to be established in evidence that it was the interest of the defendant, in 1854, before the dam was erected, and that he so considered it to be, that there should be) a dam and saw mill erected on the site in question; but whether such dam should be of any given height for such purpose of utility and whether there should be any necessity for its penning back the waters of the river upon defendant's land, to any, and if any, what extent, are totally different questions, and upon which, to say the least, considerable doubts were entertained, not only by the defendant, but by *Clark* himself, as appears by the evidence.

It appears that *Clark*, prior to his commencing to erect the dam and prior to his obtaining from *Justason*, whose lands adjoined his, the deed of the 24th March, 1854, had a survey made of the river to the limits of his own lands, and ascertained thereby that he could not erect a dam of a greater height than five and a half or six feet, without penning back water upon *Justason's* lands; it was therefore necessary that he should secure *Justason's* permission, which he did by deed, before he should commence to work, unless he should be content with erecting a dam of such a height only as should keep the waters penned back within the limits of his own land.

*Zadok* and *John Justason*, and *Wooley*, three witnesses called by the plaintiff, speak of conversations between themselves, respectively, and the defendant and *Clark*, before the latter commenced the work;

but they all say that in these conversations nothing
whatever was said as to what was to be the height of
the dam. The chief testimony upon which the plaintiff relies is that of *Richard* and *Jessie Roe*. *Richard
Roe* says, that he heard some conversation between
*Clark* and *English* before the mill was built, one in
particular at *Clark's* house. Mr. *English* said to Mr.
*Clark*, " what about our mill ?" *Clark* said he wanted
to get the privilege right before he commenced the mill.
*English* said he did not think there would be the least.
difficulty about the privilege ; he knows as a fact that
*English* was negotiating between *Blackwell* and *Clark*
on behalf of *Clark* ; *Blackwell* was *English's* brother-
in-law ; *Clark* asked defendant how it would be in
regard to his part ; defendant said to *Clark*, how much
head will you have by raising the water on my land to
highwater mark, Mr. *Clark* said he would have nine
feet ; *English* said, you are welcome to it Mr. *Clark* ;
*Clark* replied, he would like to have it done all at one
time, and have a clear title. *Clark* said to *English* "I
never expect to go over high water mark ;" *English*
said to *Clark*, all I require of you is that you will take
the water down when I want to build my line fence ;
*Clark* said he did not think he would flood defendant's
land further than high water mark. Now, all this
evidence applies to the parol license before the work
was commenced. Then *Jessie Roe* says, that she has
heard conversations between *Clark* and *English* before
the erection of the mill about its erection ; on one
occasion she speaks of *English* saying to *Clark*, "' If
you will go on with the mill I will do all I can to help
you.' I cannot say how he meant to help him ; *Clark*
said he was obliged to him." This also relates to the
parol license.

Witness then says, that she was present at the raising
of the mill and that *English* was there also. This witness heard *Clark* say he might flood back a piece on

*English* ; *English* said he was quite welcome ; *Clark* said he thought he would flood back on *English* that he would level it and see ; that *English* left *Clark* when he said he would get it levelled, and that at the time of this conversation he does not think that either *Clark* or *English* had any idea of flooding ten acres of defendant's land ; this is the quantity which by other witnesses appears to be flooded by the present dam.

Whether *Clark* did or not, after the conversation spoken of by *Jessie Roe*, make the levels spoken of does not appear ; a jury perhaps might infer that he did ; if they might we may infer so also ; and if he did, then we might infer as a consequence that the dam which he did erect was as high as he conceived anything which had passed with the defendant warranted him in erecting ; but whether he did or whether he did not, we find, that having obtained from *Zadok Justason* the deed of the 24th of March, 1854, he proceeded to erect what, in so far as this defendant is concerned, we must, I think, take to be the contemplated dam. The defendant, it may be admitted, was aware of the progress of this erection, assisted in it, and had a material interest in its construction.

It may be admitted, for the sake of argument, also, that upon the strength of the doctrine of acquiescence, he has precluded himself in equity from asserting at law a right inconsistent with the existence and maintenance of the construction as completed, but that construction being completed, the doctrine of acquiescence can go no further. If a stranger begins to build on my land, supposing it to be his own, and I, perceiving his mistake, abstain from setting him right, and leave him to persevere in his error, a Court of Equity will not allow me afterwards to assert my title to the land on which he had expended money on the supposition that the land was his own. It considers that when

I saw the mistake into which he had fallen it was my duty to be active and to state my adverse title. The application of the doctrine of acquiescence in such a case is simple; but it appears to me to be very different when a person makes an erection upon his own lands which may or not turn out to be injurious to me; with reference to a construction such as the dam in this case, *Clark* had a perfect right, without the concurrence of any one, to erect such a dam as would not pen back the water further than the limits of his own land. With the aid of the deed of *Zadok Justason*, he had a perfect right to erect it of such a height, within the limit in that deed prescribed, as should not pen back the water beyond the limit of *Justason's* land. In like manner as to *Wooley* and *Blackwell*, from whom, however, he did not obtain deeds until after the dam was erected; but as to the defendant the doctrine of acquiescence does not apply until something was done with his acquiescence affecting his lands, and the application of the doctrine is limited to what was done by *Clark*, in the doing of which the defendant acquiesced.

Now, what was done by *Clark* was, that he erected a dam from seven to seven feet six inches high, according to the evidence of *Hudson*, who measured it several times. That dam, as appears by the evidence, penned back water upon the defendant to a greater extent, as is said, than either he or *Clark* contemplated. When that dam was erected, all was completed to which the doctrine of acquiescence can attach; it is a misapplication of that doctrine to construe its sanctioning something further yet to be done still more prejudicial to the defendant, whenever *Clark*, or his assigns, might find it to their interest to raise the dam; for a thing to be done at any indefinite time increasing the extent of the easement then acquiesced in by *Clark*, affecting the defendants lands, some other title must be shewn than that of acquiescence, which, in my judgment, must be

limited to the dam originally constructed, and no further acquiescence in anything done subsequently to the
completion of the original dam is alleged or pretended.
But the evidence fails to satisfy my mind that *Clark*
entertained the idea, that as against the defendant he
had ever acquired any right to maintain the dam he
had erected, much less to raise that dam from time to
time until he attained the height of nine feet, granted
him by the others. When three years after the erection of the dam, and after *Clark* had sold to *Sutton*, the
defendant sued *Clark* for the wrongful damming back
of water upon defendant, by the dam which *Clark*
erected, *Clark* then filed no bill in assertion of the
title now asserted. Immediately upon the writ being
served in July, 1857, or before it was served he and
*Stinson* went to the defendant for the purpose of purchasing from him the right, which it is now contended
*Clark* already had, and failing to agree with him he
eventually paid the damages sought to be recovered in
that action for the injury then already sustained.

Assuming, however, that *Clark* may have been mistaken in his view of his rights, and that it does now
appear that he could have insisted upon his right to
maintain the dam as first erected, I am of opinion that
nothing has occurred which upon any recognized principle of equity justifies us in affirming a decree which
restrains the defendant from recovering at law for any
damages sustained by him, by reason of the increased
height of the present dam above that which was originally erected by *Clark*. I am unable to understand
how *George Stinson*, the grantee from *Clark* of the
land on which the dam was erected acquired an easement in the defendant's land greater than that which
had been enjoyed for the three years previously as consequential upon the dam then already erected and in
existence. If he did, it must have been by some title
different from a grant or prescription, or even acquies-

18—VOL. XVIII. GR.

cence by the defendant in anything already done. I can see no mode by which a right of extending the easement could pass to *Clark's* assignees, unless it be that the parol license given by the defendant, such as it was, as appearing in the evidence can be construed in a Court of Equity to be equivalent to a covenant, both the benefit and burden of which, runs with the land : in that doctrine I cannot concur.

----

### RASTALL v. THE ATTORNEY GENERAL.   [IN APPEAL.*]

*Jurisdiction of Chancery—Recognizance in criminal cases.*

The Court of Chancery has no jurisdiction to give relief to sureties on a recognizance in a criminal proceeding.

A recognizance which was expressed to be the joint and several recognizance of the prisoner and his sureties was acknowledged by the sureties only ; and the prisoner was discharged without his acknowledgment first having been obtained :

*Held*, that the sureties were liable. [SPRAGGE, C., MOWAT and STRONG, V. CC., dissenting.]

This was an appeal by the *Attorney General* from a decree of the Court of Chancery as reported *ante* vol. xvii, p. 1, on the following, amongst other grounds ; that the plaintiffs were by the recognizance severally bound as principals for the due appearance of the defendant *Henry Rastall*, to stand his trial, whether the latter was bound thereto by recognizance or not ; that the object of the recognizance was solely to secure the appearance of *Henry Rastall* to stand his trial on a criminal charge, and not to secure a debt or money payment ; and consequently the law relative to money-bonds is not applicable to this case ; that the plaintiffs, in their bill, do not

----

* *Present.*—DRAPER, C. J., RICHARDS, C. J., SPRAGGE, C., MORRISON, J., MOWAT, V. C., GWYNNE, J., GALT, J., and STRONG, V. C.

allege any special fact which would entitle them to relief in a Court of Equity. They do not allege that any fraud was practised on them ; nor that they lost any-thing by the non-execution of the recognizance by *Henry Rastall* ; and if their position was not as good as if *Henry Rastall* had executed the recognizance, their own negligence was the cause ; that in this, as in all similar cases, the Crown rely chiefly, if not wholly, on the bail, and not on the personal recognizance of the accused, which is generally formal, and that it would be dangerous to the public peace and safety to discharge bail in such cases, where there was room for collusion between the accused and his bail. For anything that appears to the contrary, *Henry Rastall* may have been prevented from executing the recognizance by the plaintiffs or their agents.

In support of the decree it was contended that it should be sustained for the following reasons : that the plaintiffs never agreed to become bound for the appearance of *Henry Rastall* for trial, in the manner or under the circumstances in which it is sought to make the plaintiffs liable ; that the only risk the plaintiffs agreed to assume, was for the appearance of *Henry Rastall* for trial, on condition that he should be bound in a penalty of $2000 to appear, and the plaintiffs never agreed to the increased risk which would have rested upon them if they were responsible for the appearance of *Henry Rastall* while he was under no obligation to appear ; that the said *Henry Rastall* was illegally dis-charged out of custody, and the order for his discharge was upon a condition precedent, which was not complied with ; that while the Crown acts through its officers or agents, and has a right to claim, and claims the advan-tages of their acts, their omissions in respect of such acts should have the like effect when third parties are affected, as if the transactions were between subject and subject ; and that the reasons given for the judgment in the Court below, are sufficient in law and equity to sustain said judgment.

Mr. *McGregor*, for the appeal.

Mr. *Spencer*, contra.

DRAPER, C. J.—The plaintiffs' bill states that *Henry Rastall* was committed by two Justices of the Peace to the common gaol in the County of Huron for trial, at the then next sittings of a Court of Competent Jurisdiction, on a charge of larceny ; that, after such commitment, an order was made by the County Judge to admit him to bail—himself in $2,000 and two sureties each in $1,000, and that he applied to the plaintiffs to become such sureties, and they consented ; that a recognizance was prepared, dated the 11th July, 1868, by which the said *Henry Rastall* was to become bound in the sum of $2,000, and the plaintiffs each in the sum of $1,000, and at the foot of it is written, "Taken and acknowledged the day and year first above mentioned, at Goderich, before us," which was signed by two Justices of the Peace for the County of Huron, and was also signed by the two plaintiffs ; the condition of the recognizance being, that *Henry Rastall* should appear at the next Court of competent jurisdiction to be holden for the said county, and there surrender himself into the custody of the gaoler, and plead to any indictment to be found against him for the offence charged, &c.

The bill further states that the plaintiffs entered into the said recognizance and became bound thereby as sureties for *Henry Rastall* in $1,000 each, and that immediately after, the Justices who took the plaintiffs' recognizance, without requiring *Henry Rastall* to enter into it, delivered their warrant to the gaoler to discharge *Henry Rastall* from custody, and he was discharged,

and has never entered into any recognizance pursuant to
the Judge's order, but left the country. That the first
Court of competent jurisdiction held within the county
of Huron, after the recognizance was entered into by the
plaintiffs, was the Court of Quarter Sessions of the Peace,
at Goderich, on the 8th September, 1868, at which the
Grand Jury found true bills against *Henry Rastall* for
larceny, and he did not surrender himself, and although
he was duly called in Court, did not appear, &c. By reason
of which default the Court of Quarter Sessions declared
the recognizance to be estreated, and the sums for which
the plaintiffs appeared by the recognizance to be liable,
were declared to have been forfeited to the crown, and
the recognizance was duly entered on the roll of estreated
recognizances and the roll with a writ of *fi. fa.* and *capias*
thereon was delivered to the sheriff of Huron, and is now
in his hands in full force.

That the plaintiffs entered into the recognizance upon
the representation that *Henry Rastall* should, before
being discharged from close custody of the gaol, also
enter into the recognizance to appear, and they would
not have incurred the liability except upon that representation, and they charge that the Justices should not
have delivered their warrant to the gaoler to discharge
*Henry Rastall* from close custody until he should have
entered into the said recognizance, and by reason of him
not being a party to it their liability under it was materially altered and increased without their consent. And
they pray to have the recognizance delivered up to be
cancelled, or for a perpetual injunction to restrain the
sheriff from proceeding on the writ.

The Attorney General put in an answer, stating that
it was as much owing to the negligence of the plaintiffs
as to any other cause that *Henry Rastall* did not "execute" the recognizance, and they might have got him
to execute it. And he denies any representations to the

1871.

Rastall
.v.
Attorney
General.

plaintiffs that *Henry Rastall* should " execute " the recognizance before being discharged.

The plaintiffs went into evidence, and proved and put in a copy of the Judge's order for bailing *Henry Rastall*, also a copy of the warrant of deliverance, signed by the two justices, which recites that *Henry Rastall* " *entered into his own recognizance* and found sufficient sureties for his appearance."

The cause was heard by way of motion for decree by consent as against the Attorney General on an admission that " *Henry Rastall* did not enter into the recognizance ; also that there was nothing to prevent the plaintiffs from going to gaol and seeing to the execution of the recognizance by all parties."

Judgment.

The argument took place before *Strong*, V. C., who considered the case to rest on the same principles as a case between subject and subject, observing that " a recognizance is a contract of record," and that in his opinion, there was no reason why the same rule should not apply to sureties under such contracts as to them whose obligations are created by bond. The case may therefore, be regarded as if it were that of a Crown debt created by bond. Then, it is clear that on the Revenue side of the Court of Exchequer in England, relief can be obtained by Crown debtors on equitable grounds and this by express enactment of the statute. The Statute of 33 Henry VIII., c. 39, no doubt makes provision for the subject's right in every case of bonds and specialties to the Crown, as well as gives new modes of enforcing the debts of the Crown, but, whether to enforce the latter or to afford the former, the Court must be strictly speaking in possession of the case. An extent will not be issued until the debt to the Crown has by commission or by other means been, *prima facie* at least, established and made a matter of record in the Court—in the case of a bond, for example, by being delivered into Court.

It appears to me indispensible in the first place to consider how far the statutes of the Provincial Legislatures affect the subject.

The 34 George III., chapter 2, (Upper Canada), erected the Court of King's Bench, and gave to that Court all such powers and authorities as by the law of England were incident to a Superior Court of Civil and Criminal Jurisdiction, with all rights, incidents, and privileges as at the time the first Act took effect, were used exercised and enjoyed by any of the Superior Courts of Common Law at Westminster in England, with power to hold plea, in all manner of actions, &c., as well criminal as civil, real, personal, and mixed, by such process and course as are provided by law, &c. ; to hear and determine all issues of law, and (except where otherwise provided), with a jury to determine all issues of fact and give judgment and award execution, in as *full* and *ample* a manner as *then* (1794), could be done in the Courts of Queen's Bench, Common Pleas, or " *in matters which regard* the King's revenue (including the condemnation of contraband or smuggled goods), by the Court of Exchequer in England."

The Court of Chancery, in its present form, derives its existence from the joint operation of 7 William IV., chapter 2, (Upper Canada) and 12 Victoria, chapter 64. These statutes, together with 13 and 14 Victoria, chapter 50, 16 Victoria, chapter 159, and 20 Victoria, chapter 56, define the jurisdiction of the Court with one exception. The last mentioned Act, after conferring jurisdiction on the Court in some matters not before given, adds : " the like power and authority as the Court of Chancery in England" possessed on the 10th June, 1857, " as a Court of Equity, to administer justice in all cases in which there may be no adequate remedy at law."

Then it is further enacted by 28 Victoria, chapter 17, s. 2, (passed 18 March, 1865), that " the Court of Chancery in Upper Canada shall have the same equitable jurisdiction in matters of Revenue as the Court of Exchequer in England possesses."

In *Miller* v. *Attorney General* (a), *VanKoughnet*, C., had (in 1862) decided that the Court of Chancery had no jurisdiction, as the matter was one which specially regarded the Revenue ; and the jurisdiction affecting it had been vested in the Courts of Common Law.

This decision possibly gave rise to the statute 28 Victoria, chapter 17, s. 2.

British statute, 5 Victoria, chapter 5 (passed 5th October, 1841), transferred and gave to the High Court of Chancery (on the 15th of that month) " all the power, authority and jurisdiction of the Court of Exchequer as a Court of Equity, and all the power, authority, and jurisdiction which had been conferred upon, or committed to, the said Court of Exchequer by, or under the special authority of, any Act or Acts of Parliament (*other than* such power, authority, and jurisdiction, as shall *then* be possessed by, or be incident to, the said Court of Exchequer as a Court of Law, or *as shall then be possessed by the said Court of Exchequer, as a Court of Revenue,* and not heretofore exercised or exercisable by the same Court sitting as a Court of Equity) * * * to all intents and purposes, in as full and ample a manner as the same might have been exercised by the Court of Exchequer, if this Act had not been passed."

This statute was considered (in 1845) in the case of *The Attorney General* v. *The Corporation of London*(b) when Lord *Langdale*, M. R., held that the jurisdiction which had been possessed by the Court of Exchequer, sitting as a Court of Equity in suits instituted by the

*Judgment.*

(a) 9 Grant 558. (b) 9 Jur. 570.

Crown respecting matters of revenue, was transferred
thereby to the Court of Chancery, and he overruled a
demurrer, objecting that the Court of Chancery had no
original jurisdiction to entertain Revenue cases at the
suit of Crown, and that this statute did not confer such
jurisdiction.

In 1846, the same question was raised in the Court of
Exchequer in the *Attorney General* v. *Halling* (a), upon
an information in the nature of a bill filed on the Equity
side of the Court ; and that Court differed from Lord
*Langdale's* judgment, and held, that notwithstanding
the Act of 5 Victoria, the Court of Exchequer retained
all its actual and incidental jurisdiction, equitable as
well as legal, which it had as a Court of Common Law,
together with its proper jurisdiction, as a Court of
Revenue for the collection of the Revenues of the Crown
whether the jurisdiction be exercised after the forms of
common law or equity—but that it has lost all jurisdiction as a Court of Equity between its officers and Crown
debtors and the other subjects of the realm which was
before incident to it as a Court of Revenue and was
exercised by it as a mere Court of Equity.

In *Miller* v. *The Attorney General*, the late Chancellor adopts this decision of the Court of Exchequer as
the true exposition of the statute, and our statute 28
Victoria, follows that interpretation by giving to the
Court of Chancery the same equitable jurisdiction in
matters of revenue as the Court of Exchequer in England possessed when this Act was passed.

In giving judgment the learned Chancellor said,
" the statute 34 George III., chapter 2, which constituted the Court of King's Bench, appears to me to have
given to that Court all the powers which the Court of

---

(a) 15 M. & W. 687, and See Attorney General v. Sewel, 4 M. & W. 77.

Exchequer in England then possessed, in the matters which regard the King's Revenue," and in a preceding sentence, he suggests that if (which was not then the case) the Court of Chancery in this Province possessed the powers which were transferred in England to it by the 5 Victoria, it would not follow that our Court of Chancery was the sole tribunal in which parties to claims by the Crown in respect of the revenue, might have relief, or would at all interfere if the Court of Common Law had power to do Equity. That the Courts of Common Law have the same equitable powers to give relief in suits affecting the revenue that they possess in ordinary cases will not be questioned. Those ordinary powers are not, and as I apprehend were not, intended to be taken away by the statute 28 Victoria. They were long before exercised by the Court of King's Bench, of Upper Canada, in *Rowand* v. *Tyler* (a), in which case the defendant having covenanted with the plaintiff to give him a lease of certain premises, the latter assigned the covenant before any breach thereof, and the assignee brought an action against the defendant in the plaintiff's name. The defendant procured a release from the plaintiff (they two combining to defraud the assignee) and pleaded this release, to which a replication, alleging this fraud, was put in, and the parties went to trial, when the Court refused to admit the evidence, as the record then stood, but afterwards set aside the plea and ordered that the release should not be made use of at the subsequent trial. The powers of the Courts of Common Law, in entertaining equitable defences and giving relief have also been extended by the Common Law Procedure Act. We are not however, called upon in this case to decide, whether the Act 34 George III., gave to the Court of King's Bench, the equitable jurisdiction in matters of revenue which the Court of Exchequer possessed. That jurisdiction, adopting the course of procedure and plead-

---

(a) Decided in Michaelmas Term, 5 Wm. 4.

ing of Courts of Equity, certainly has never been exercised in Upper Canada by the Courts of Common Law,
and if it were held that they possessed it, the Act of 28
Victoria has given to the Court of Chancery a concurrent jurisdiction.

It is necessary, however, to refer to other Provincial
Statutes which regulate the estreating of recognizances
and the subsequent proceedings for enforcing them.

By the Consolidated Statute of Upper Canada,
chapter 117, ss, 34, 5; provision is made relative to
estreats. In regard to forfeited recognizances, before
any Court of Oyer and Terminer or General Gaol Delivery, or before any Court of Assize and *Nisi Prius*, the
Clerk of Assize is required within twenty-one days from
the adjournment of such Court, to enter and extract
upon a roll in duplicate such forfeited recognizance,
and to sign the rolls. One of these rolls is to be transmitted to the office of the Clerk of the Crown and Pleas
of the Queen's Bench on or before the first day of the
term next succeeding the Court before which the recognizance was forfeited, and the other shall be sent by the
Clerk of Assize with a writ of *fieri facias* and *capias* to
the sheriff of the county in and for which the Court was
holden, which writ shall be an authority to the sheriff
for levying or for the taking into custody the bodies of
the persons named therein, in case goods and lands cannot be found, whereof the sums required can be made
" and every person so taken shall be lodged in the common gaol of the county, until satisfaction shall be made
or until the Court of Queen's Bench or Common Pleas,
upon cause shewn as hereinafter mentioned makes an
order in the cause, and until such order has been fully
complied with."

In like manner the Clerk of the Peace is to extract
and enter upon a roll in duplicate, all recognizances

forfeited by or before any Court of General Quarter Sessions of the Peace, one copy to remain in his own office, the other to be sent by him, with a writ of *fi. fa.* and *capias*, according to form given, which makes it returnable into the Court of Quarter Sessions, annexed, to the sheriff of the county where the Court was held ; such writ to be an authority to the sheriff, to levy or arrest as above stated. And every person so taken shall be lodged in the common gaol of the county until satisfaction be made, or until the Court of Quarter Sessions of such county, upon cause shewn by the party as hereinafter mentioned, makes an order in the case, and until such order has been fully complied with. The 11th section provides that the Court of Queen's Bench or Common Pleas, or Court of General Quarter Sessions into which any writ of *fi. fa.* and *capias* issued under the Act, is returnable, *may* inquire into the circumstances of the case and *may* in its discretion, order the discharge of the whole of the forfeited recognizance or

sum of money paid or to be paid in lieu or satisfaction thereof, and may make such order as may to such Court appear just. The case of *Rex* v. *Hankins* (a), is upon a similar statute in England, and is adverse to the plaintiffs.

That case differs only from the one now in judgment, in the words of the respective enactments. The British statute, 3 George IV., ch. 46, sec: 5, provides that the Court of General or Quarter Sessions before whom any person so committed to gaol or bound to appear, shall be brought, is hereby authorized and *required* to inquire into the circumstances of the case, and *shall, at its discretion,* be empowered to order the discharge of the whole of the forfeited recognizance or any part thereof, or if the party be in custody the said Court is empowered either to remand such party to custody, or, upon the

---

(a) 1 McL. & Y. 27.

release of such party from the whole of the forfeited recognizance, to order his discharge. Our statute is less imperatively worded. It does not *require*, but enables or empowers the Superior Courts and the Court of General Quarter Sessions to *inquire*, and says they may in their discretion afford relief. I fail to see any substantial or reliable distinction between the two enactments. Ours gives to the Quarter Sessions a power they had not before, to afford relief to the subject in certain cases after inquiry, and in their discretion. I apprehend this form of words gives the subject a right to the inquiry and to the relief, which latter is no more than a matter of discretion on the circumstances appearing under either statute. *Hankins's* case is approved of and followed in *Rex* v. *Thompson* (a).

According to the law of England, a recognizance is said to be estreated when it is extracted or taken out from among the other records and sent up to the Court of Exchequer, where the party and his sureties, having become by the forfeiture of the recognizance, the King's absolute debtors, are liable to be sued for the several sums in which they are respectively bound (b).

Such recognizances are to be transmitted in the first instance to the proper officer of the Court where the trial is to be; and when they are for the appearance of a party at the Assizes, the Judges of Oyer and Terminer are to determine whether they should be estreated. A like power is vested in Justices of the Peace, where the recognizances relate to offences cognizable at the Sessions. All such estreats were by the Statute of Westminster, first to come into the Court of Exchequer, "for that Court is the true centre into which all the King's revenue and profit ought to fall." And *Manning* states generally that all estreats of fines, issues, recognizances,

1871.

Rastall
v.
Attorney
General.

Judgment.

---

(a) 3 Tyr. 53.　　(b) 4 Black. Com. 253.　　(c) 2 Inst. 197.

1871.

Rastall
v.
Attorney
General.

&c., are transmitted into this Court from both Houses of Parliament; from the Courts of Queen's Bench and Common Pleas, and from the office of Pleas in the Exchequer; from the Justices of Assize, Justices of the Peace, and other jurisdictions. And the statute 33 Henry VIII. ch. 39, gave to this Court, among other things, power and authority when any person from whom a debt or duty to the King was demanded, shewed in the Court sufficient cause and matter in law, reason and good conscience in bar or discharge of such debt or duty, and sufficiently proved the same, to judge and allow the proof and acquit and discharge such person. But the practice appears to be, that a party moving for a discharge must bring in a *constat* of the recognizance (a), &c., (*i. e.*, a certificate from the Clerk and Auditors of Exchequer, certifying what appears on the record,) because the motion is in the nature of an account, and then a man must charge himself before he can be discharged; and if the Court of Exchequer were asked to exercise the power to discharge, it was necessary to shew to them that by the records of that Court he was charged with the debt or duty (b).

Judgment.

It needs scarcely be said that the powers, legal or equitable, of the Court of Exchequer to enforce payment or otherwise to deal with a forfeited recognizance cannot attach until such recognizance has been duly estreated into that Court (c). It seems equally clear that the powers and authorities vested by the 34 George III. (Upper Canada), as to matters which regard the revenue, in the Court of King's Bench, cannot be exercised in regard to a forfeited recognizance until it has been estreated into or transmitted to that Court; and as the 28 Victoria gives to the Court of Chancery no addition to its former juris-

(a) Exch. Prac. 316; 4 & 5 W. & M. ch. 24; 3 & 4 Wm. IV. ch. 99; Sec. 4 Inst. 117.

(b) Gilb. Ex. 191; Harper v. Holden, 3 Tyr. 580.

(c) Rex v. Pellow, McL. 111; Rex v. Thompson, 3 Tyr. 53.

diction except the same equitable jurisdiction in matters
of revenue as the Court of Exchequer in England possesses, it would seem to follow that a recognizance not
estreated into a Court to which our Legislature has given
similar powers and authorities in matters of revenue to
those possessed by the Court of Exchequer in England,
will not be the subject of equitable any more than of
legal jurisdiction in this province. In other words the
estreat of a recognizance into a Court having the jurisdiction of the Exchequer as a Court of Revenue is a
necessary preliminary to the exercise of either the legal
or equitable jurisdiction. When the 34 George III. was
passed it was contemplated that all forfeited recognizances should be estreated into the Queen's Bench.
The change which has been made by Provincial legislation, in dealing with forfeited recognizances and
enforcing payment thereof, has been already pointed
out. The recognizance in the present case is one forfeited before the Court of Quarter Sessions, which Court
has authority to inquire into the circumstances, and
may in its discretion order the discharge thereof, or of
the money to be paid in lieu or satisfaction thereof, and
may make such order thereon as may to such Court
appear just. There appears to me to be great difficulty,
if not impossibility, in holding that the Court of Chancery has any jurisdiction over the forfeited recognizance,
unless the case of *Rex* v. *Hankins* is disregarded.

The case of *Colebrooke* v. *The Attorney General* (a)
was mentioned to me by the learned Chancellor as
tending to shew that I have taken too narrow a
view of the jurisdiction of the Court of Chancery
in this case, and as shewing that notwithstanding
our statute, the plaintiffs had a right to file their bill for
relief. With great submission, that case does not appear
to me to have any application, and decides nothing

1871.

Rastall
v.
Attorney
General.

Judgment.

---

(a) 7 Price, 146.

more than that the Court of Exchequer retained the jurisdiction which they formerly had over the auditors of the Prest, over a different set of officers appointed under a (then) recent Act of Parliament, for the discharge of analogous duties relative to the public accounts.

The greater part of the cases cited by the counsel for the respondents relate to the relief given by Courts of Equity to sureties in cases where they have entered into security upon the faith of representations or upon the expectation and belief, that something further was to be done in relation thereto which was not done, and so the surety's position or liability was different from that which he intended to enter into, or where some subsequent act or omission of other parties had altered the original position of the surety and affected his intended liability.

Were this case certainly one to which such decisions are applicable, I agree both in the statement of them and of their effect contained in the judgment of the learned Vice Chancellor, which is appealed from. But we have to consider whether they are so applicable, I have seen no case, certainly none was referred to, where the Court of Exchequer in England has granted the relief asked for in this bill, to parties who were bail for a prisoner charged with felony.

One important distinction presents itself *in limine* between sureties in civil matters and bail in a criminal proceeding. Payment by a surety for the amount for which he has become bound is a full equivalent to the creditor for the default of the principal in not paying that amount, but payment of the penalty named in a recognizance of bail is no satisfaction to the community for the escape of a criminal, it is rather in the nature of a fine or penalty for wilfully or negligently permitting the criminal to escape.

It is not in all cases indispensable that the party accused should be present or enter into the recognizance in order to its validity. In 2 *Hale* (a) it is laid down that the true and regular bail is not only a recognizance in a sum certain, but also a *taking to bail*, and the form is given stating that the sureties received (the accused) to bail, taken and detained for the suspicion of a certain felony, each in a several sum to be made of their respective goods, lands and tenements if he (the accused) did not appear; and it is added " this is the form of a bail where the principal is either an infant or in prison, and so absent, and thereupon a warrant issues under the hand and seal of him that takes the bail for his enlargement, called a *liberate*." Very like the present case.

And *Hawkins* (b) says it seems to be the practice of the King's Bench in admitting a person to bail who is actually present in Court upon an indictment or appeal of felony, &c., to take a several recognizance to the King in a certain sum from each of the bail that the prisoner shall appear at a certain day and also that the bail shall be liable for the default of such appearance, body for body. This latter clause has become obsolete, and even when it was in use persons so bound were not liable on a forfeiture to be punished as the prisoner, if convicted, might have been, but only to be fined (c). Nevertheless it confirms the distinction taken between the undertaking of bail for a prisoner charged with crime and the engagement of a surety in a civil case, as for the payment of a debt. The liability of the accused was not satisfied or discharged, and the liability of the bail to be *fined* may, for all that appears, have been no *discharge* of their recognizance. The liability of the accused to be tried certainly continued.

It is further to be observed that his bail are in law the keepers of one who has been committed for felony or

---

(a) Pl. C. 126. (b) Bk 2 ch. 15 s. 83. (c) See 2 Str. 911.

20—VOL. XVIII. GR.

treason (a). A man's bail are looked upon as his gaolers of his own choosing, and he is for many purposes esteemed to be as much in the prison of the Court by which he is bailed, as if he were in the actual custody of the proper gaoler. It seems certain that if the party bailed be suspected by his bail as likely to deceive them, he may be detained by them, and enforced to appear according to the condition of the recognizance, or may be brought before justices of the peace by whom he shall be committed, unless he find new sureties (b); and *Petersdorff* (c) adds, that bail in a criminal case may seize their principal on a Sunday.

Moreover, in this case, the recognizance following the form given by statute is several, not joint, and this also creates a distinction. In *Underhill* v. *Howard* (d) Lord *Eldon* considers it. His first observation is in favor of the plaintiffs' contention as to the right to equitable relief by giving up the bond, that is, if the same rules

govern this case, as govern in regard to sureties in civil matters, namely, that where a man executes a bond meaning it to be the joint bond of himself and another who does not execute, *it is the several bond of the former*, but he may have it delivered up as contrary to the intention. His Lordship further adds, " if he is only a several obligor he has no remedies over against any one." The application for equitable relief involves the admission of legal liability.

The decision in *Jones* v. *Orchard* (e) turned wholly on a question of liability to pay the prosecutor's costs. There is however one observation of *Jervis*, C. J., which is to be noticed. " There cannot be a good express promise to indemnify against the consequences of non appearance, the law cannot therefore imply one." He

---

(a) Hale P. C. 325.    (b) Hawk Bk 2 ch. 15 s 3.    (c) On Bail 515.
(d) 10 Ves. 212, 225.    (e) 16 C. B. 614 1 Jur. N. S. 936.

observed however that it was not necessary to decide whether it would be illegal to indemnify against the consequences of not surrendering in a criminal case, but if it were necessary to determine that point, the Court was inclined to think that such a promise would be illegal as it would be against public policy to allow a contract between an offender and his surety to indemnify the latter in case of his non appearance. That case was where the indictment was for misdemeanor, it would *a fortiori* be illegal in a case of felony.

In *Cripps* v. *Hartnoll*, (a) the plaintiff had become surety for the appearance of a third person at the request of the defendant, and it was held in the Exchequer Chamber, that it was not within the 4th section of the Statute of Frauds. In giving judgment, *Williams*, J., drew the distinction between bail in a civil and in a criminal proceeding, and said, " I think that where bail is given in a criminal suit, there is certainly no debt or duty which can be considered due to the surety from the party on whose behalf the recognizance was given."

It does not appear by whom the recognizance was prepared. If it be treated as done by the justices as a record of what was taken and acknowledged before them, and was, as such returned by them to the Court of Quarter Sessions, it would, *prima facie* at least, prove that *Henry Rastall* had acknowledged it, and the very foundation of the bill would be uprooted ; but the answer admits that he was no party to it, and then the justices should not have certified the recognizance as entered into by him before them, nor have issued the warrant of deliverance to the gaoler, reciting what was untrue. In the absence of any explanation, and the plaintiffs are not called upon to give any, the conduct of the magistrates seems to have been negligent, to say the least of it.

1871.

Rastall
v.
Attorney
General.

Judgment.

(a) 4 B. & S. 414.

Upon a careful consideration of the whole case I have·
arrived at the following conclusions:—

1. That this forfeited recognizance never having been
estreated into the Queen's Bench, was not a record of
that Court, sitting as a Court of Revenue, and that the
powers conferred on that Court and on the Court of
Chancery, similar to those possessed by the Court of
Exchequer in England in matters of revenue, did not
attach upon, and could not be exercised in regard thereto.

2. That there is so broad a distinction between the
position of sureties in civil matters and that of bail in
criminal cases, especially in cases of felony, that the
principle upon which Courts of Equity act in granting
relief to the former class, are inapplicable to the latter.

3. That even if the last preceding proposition may
require further investigation, yet the absence of any
Judgment. direct authority shewing the exercise of such an equitable jurisdiction by the Court of Exchequer in England
in a similar case of a recognizance of bail for a prisoner
charged with felony affords a strong reason for with-
holding its exercise here. The possible consequences of
such a precedent upon the due administration of justice
in criminal prosecutions, strengthen this reason for non
interference.

RICHARDS, C. J.—As to the jurisdiction of the Court
to grant the relief prayed for in the bill, the case of
*The King* v. *Thompson*, (a), seems conclusive. The
English Statute on which that decision is based, does
not in effect differ from our own, under which this recognizance was declared forfeited. The conclusion of the
article under the head of "Estreat," in *Tomlins'* Law
Dictionary, is, "The Court of Exchequer has no jurisdic-

––––––––––––––––––––––––––––––––––––––

(a) 3 Tyr. 53.

tion over estreats not returned to it, *e. g.*, estreats of
recognizance to try a traverse at the Quarter Sessions ;
the Sessions only have jurisdiction to relieve,"and the case
in 3 *Tyrwhitt* is referred to. *The King* v; *Hankins*, (a)
was referred to in *The King* v. *Thompson*, as an authority on which that decision was based. There is a note by the
Reporter to that case stating that in no known case has
the principle of that decision been departed from ; though
the question has been repeatedly brought before the Court,
and special reference is made in the note to the equitable
jurisdiction conferred on the Court of Exchequer by 33
Henry VIII., ch. 39 ; and the reporter comes to the conclusion, though that statute was not referred to in the
argument or judgment, that nevertheless it makes no difference in his view as to the right of the Court to grant
relief, for inasmuch as the party in default " not being
now to be impleaded, sued, vexed, or troubled for the debt
in the Exchequer, that Court cannot have authority under
33 Henry VIII., cap 39, sec. 79, to discharge him."

Judgment.

In *Ex parte Pellow*(b) the Court of Exchequer assumed
jurisdiction because the recognizance in fact had been
estreated into the Court.

I think the conclusion arrived at by the Chief Justice
of this Court, that the Court of Chancery had no jurisdiction in the matter, is correct ; and that the appeal must
be allowed, on this ground, and the 'bill in the Court
below dismissed with costs.

In the main ground, however, on which the judgment
of the learned Vice Chancellor proceeded, I cannot concur ; not that the views expressed are not correct in
themselves as applied to an ordinary case of principal
and surety, but that those rules apply to a recognizance
of bail given in a criminal case, I have not been able to
convince myself.

---

(a) M'Cl. & Y. 30.        (b) M'Cl. 111.

The facts and circumstances usually accompanying the case of security for the payment of money and the rights of sureties to contribution between themselves or to indemity from the principal form so important an element, in considering the question of how far these rights may be affected by the omission or negligence of the parties to whom the security is given, that the rules applicable to that class of cases can hardly apply to a recognizance to the crown entered into by the party who receives as bail a criminal charged with felony.

*Tomlins'* Law Dictionary, under the head of "Bail," gives the origin of the term from the French and Greek, and says it signifies to deliver into hands. Under the same head it is stated bail and mainprise are often used promiscuously in our law books, as signifying one and the same thing, and agree in the notion that they save a man from imprisonment in the common gaol, his friends undertaking for him, before certain persons for

Judgment.

that purpose authorized, that he shall appear at a certain day and answer whatever shall be objected to him in a legal way (*a*). The chief difference is, that a man's mainpernors are barely his sureties, and cannot imprison him themselves, to secure his appearance, as his bail may, who are looked upon as his gaolers, to whose custody he is committed, and, therefore, may take him upon a Sunday, and confine him to the next day, and then surrender him (*b*).

In the anonymous case in 6 *Modern* 231, the Court use this rather quaint language, "The bail have their principal always upon a string, and may pull the string whenever they please, and render him in their own discharge; they may take him up even upon a Sunday, and confine him until next day, and then render him for the

---

(*a*) 2 Hawk, P. C., c. 15, sec. 29, 4 Inst. 180.
(*b*) 6 Moo. 231; Lord Raymond, 706.

entry in this Court is '*traditui in bellum,*' &c., and the 
doing it on a Sunday is no service of process, but rather 
like the case where the sheriff arrests by virtue of a process of Court on Saturday, and if the party escapes he may 
take him upon a Sunday, for that is only a continuance 
of the former imprisonment." Under the same head of 
*Tomlins*' Law Dictionary : " In admitting a person to 
bail in the Court of Queen's Bench for felony, &c., 
a several recognizance is entered into to the King 
in a certain sum from each of the bail that the 
prisoner shall appear at a certain day, &c., and also 
that the bail shall be liable for the default of such 
appearance, body for body. And it is at the discretion of the justices of the peace in admitting any 
person to bail for felony to take the recognizance in a 
certain sum, or body for body ; but when a person is 
bailed by any Court, &c., for a crime of an inferior nature, the recognizance ought to be only in a certain 
sum of money, and not body for body (*a*). * * * 
If bail suspect the prisoner will fly, they may carry him 
before a justice to find new sureties, or to be committed 
in their discharge."

In *Hale's* Pleas of the Crown (*b*), a form of the 
recognizance is given from *Lambert's* justice (*c*), on 
which it is observed, " this is the form of bail where the 
principal is either an infant or in prison, and so absent ; 
and thereupon a warrant issues under the hand and 
seal of him that takes the bail for his enlargement, 
called a *liberate.*"

" But if he be bailed by a justice of the peace before 
commitment, or if committed and brought into the Court 
of Queen's Bench or Sessions to be bailed, then the 
party himself is also bound and sometimes the recog-

1871.

Rastall 
v. 
Attorney 
General.

Judgment.

---

(*a*) 2 Hawk. P. C., c. 15, sec. 83.          (*b*) Vol. ii., p. 126.
(*c*) Lib. 1 cap. 23, p. 264.

nizance is simple with a condition added for his appearance, and sometimes the condition is contained in the
body of the recognizance *ut supra ;* only that it is to be
remembered that when any person is bailed for any misdemeanor either upon the return of an *habeas corpus,* or
otherwise the return or record ought to be first filed, and
a *committetur marescallo* entered, and then bail taken; for
all persons that are bailed in the King's Bench are *de
facto* or in supposition of law first supposed to be *in cus-
todia marescalli.* The advantage of this kind of bail is
this, that it is not only a recognizance in a sum certain,
but also a real bail, and they are his keepers, and may
be punished by fine beyond the sum mentioned in the
recognizance if there be cause, and may re-seize the prisoner if they doubt his escape and bring him before the
justice or Court, and he shall be committed and so the
bail be discharged of his recognizance."

Judgment. In *Petersdorff* on Bail, p 309, the general form of a
recognizance of bail is given similar to that taken in
this case. At p. 510 it is stated " the principal and bail
usually acknowledge themselves respectively to owe to
the King a named sum which it is said should not in
general be less than £40 payable on the contingency
of the defendant's omitting to appear at the appointed
place of trial."

But if the party be a *feme covert* or infant, and
therefore incapable of entering into a recognizance, or
if already in gaol, or from any cause precluded from attending, the sureties alone must be named in the recognizance, and the whole sum, intended to be inserted as
the security for the appearance of the offender, must be
equally apportioned between them ; and it seems that the
Court may in all cases dispense with the principals joining in the acknowledgment. (*d*)

---

(*d*) 2 Hawk. P. C. 126.   1 Bacon Ab. vol. 1, p. 497. (K.)

The case of *Cripps* v. *Hartnoll*, reported in the Exchequer Chamber (a) contains the latest exposition of the law on the subject of bail in criminal cases on some of the points discussed in this case. *Erle*, C. J., said in the argument, "Is there any instance of an action by bail in a criminal case against the principal who has absconded?" In argument reference is made to a statement contained in *Highmoore* on Bail, and repeated with approval in *Petersdorff* on Bail, to the effect that when bail in a criminal proceeding have been compelled to pay the penalty in consequence of the recognizance becoming forfeited they are entitled to recover all the expenses they have incurred incidental to that situation. *Williams*, J., said, "Does he give any authority for that?" and, in giving the judgment of the Court, *Pollock*, C. B., said, "Here bail was given in a criminal proceeding, and when bail is given in such a proceeding there is no contract on the part of the person bailed to indemnify the person who became bail for him. This is no debt, and with respect to the person who bails this is *hardly a duty*."

The proceeding by warrant of attorney in a civil suit, has some analogy to this. There, if two or more persons join in a joint warrant purporting to be given by three parties but executed by two only, the third having refused it has been holden to be an incomplete instrument and not enforcible. But it might be otherwise if the warrant authorized a judgment against any one or more of the parties, and not simply a judgment against all (b).

In the case referred to in *Adolphus* and *Ellis*, the counsel, in moving the rule to enter judgment against one of two defendants, said, "With respect to severing the defendants, the Court in ——— v. *Hobson* (c) refused to allow a judgment to be entered up against two only

*1871.*

*Rastall*
v.
*Attorney General.*

*Judgment.*

---

(a) 4 Best and Smith, 416.
(b) Chitty's Arch., 8 ed. p. 854 ; Jordan v. Farr, 2 A. & E. 437.
(c) 1 Chitty's Reports, 314.

1871.

Rastall
v.
Attorney
General.

of three parties who had given a joint warrant of attorney; but they added, had the warrant been joint and several judgment would have been granted; that is the present case." The Court granted the rule. In that case the defendants had given a warrant of attorney to the plaintiff authorizing him to appear for them or either of them to receive a declaration and to suffer judgment, &c. (a).

I think we should require very strong reasons to draw us to the conclusion that the rigid rules of construction as to the liability of sureties for ordinary debts should be held to apply to parties who enter into the recognizance of bail in criminal cases that are felonies. The nature of the obligation is so entirely different from that of the ordinary security for the payment of money. It may be entered into without the prisoner being present, or in any way a party to it. It need not be with a money penalty and the bail cannot recover from the prisoner any sum that he may have paid to discharge his liability, and there can be no contribution between the bail on such a recognizance as this, for, as is usually the case in these cases, the bail are each severally bound; and it may so happen that the bail are bound in different amounts, one from the other.

Judgment.

Besides, the circumstances under which bail is given are so very different from the payment of, or security for the payment of, a debt. There the creditor has an interest in obtaining security for the payment of his money, something more than the mere promise of the debtor; he obtains that when a surety is offered, who becomes a promissor to him that the debt will be paid under certain circumstances, and when it is paid principal and surety are both discharged. But in a criminal case the Crown has no interest in allowing the accused to go at large: it seeks no security for his forthcoming

(a) Harris v. Wade et al. 1 Chitty Rep. 322.

on the day of trial : his body is in custody and will be produced when wanted. The bail on the other hand are pressing to have their friend. delivered into their charge, to be taken care of, and they undertake to be liable for his being brought forward when he is wanted. Sometimes under a pecuniary penalty, and sometimes by the pledge of body for body, and it is said they are liable to be punished beyond the sum mentioned in the recognizance, if there be cause. They enter into a recognizance, and the prisoner is handed over to them. For many purposes, he is considered still to be in the custody of the law, and the bail, and each one of them, I apprehend, may take him and surrender him in discharge of his liability. If the party bailed fails to appear, the recognizance may be estreated, a fresh warrant issued for his apprehension, and if arrested, he may be tried and punished precisely in the same manner as if he had not been bailed, or had appeared to save his bail ; and the bail cannot recover from him the money they have been compelled to pay for his default.

1871.

Rastall
v.
Attorney
General.

Judgment.

Again, a recognizance is something more than a mere bond, but even in a bond, where the parties are severally bound it is said to be the same as if they were all separate bonds. But when a recognizance is for money lent, though it is not a perfect record until entered on the roll, yet when entered, it is a recognizance from the first acknowledgement, and binds persons and lands from that time (a).

If a party in a judicial proceeding makes an acknowledgement which may be enforced against him alone, but in which others may be also joined, but are not necessarily so, such as an action against the joint and several makers of a promissory note, if one allows judgment to go against him by *nil dicit*, the plaintiff may take that

---

(a) Hob. 196.

judgment, though he commenced his action against both and declared against both. If the defendant wished to avoid a judgment against himself individually, he should have taken care that the other defendant was also permitting the same kind of a judgment.

Here these plaintiffs deliberately entered into an engagement, which was in the nature of a judgment confessed, that each would be bound to pay a certain sum if a third party whom it is said they supposed would be also bound to pay twice as much did not appear before a certain Court on a certain day. They are the parties who are to be discharged from the acknowledged debt, and ·they are the parties to have everything done which they think will enable them to discharge their obligation. This seems to me to be the technical view of the subject and one also which in the interest of the public is most desirable to be upheld.

Judgment.     It is the friends of the accused who are the actual parties in procuring the bail ; it is they who are offered as bail ; it is they who have him in custody, after he is bailed ; and it is their interest to create or avail themselves of technical difficulties to avoid the liability they have consented to undertake to serve their friend ; whilst no one has the same direct personal interest in seeing that everything is done in due form to compel the bail to discharge their duty—of producing the party whom they have in custody to take his trial for the offence charged against him.

These plaintiffs have created by their own voluntary act a liability to the crown to serve their friend. They say that he ought to have been bound with them to have afforded them greater security, and they supposed he would have been so bound. The ready and proper answer is, "You could have refused to be bound until he was; your solemn engagement on your own behalf did not

necessarily require his undertaking a similar engagement on his own behalf, but if you desired that for your
security, you could have had it or you could have
declined becoming bail." The technical nature of a
recognizance differs from that of a bond. The difference being chiefly in this, that the bond is the creation
of a fresh debt or obligation, *de novo*. The recognizance
is an acknowledgment of a former debt upon record with
condition to be void on performance of the thing stipulated. This being either certified to, or taken by, the
officer of some Court is witnessed only by the record of
that Court, and not by the party's seal; so that it is not
in strictness properly a deed, though the effects of it are
greater than a common obligation, being allowed a priority in point of payment and binding the lands of the
cognizor from the time of enrolment on record.

We have not been referred to a single case either in
the Courts of Law or Equity, or in the Exchequer, in
England, where an application on the grounds taken
here has been successful or has ever been made. This
omission seems to me a strong ground for our not making a precedent, in this country, in a matter which may
have such a serious effect in the administration of justice,
as inducing parties who enter into recognizances for the
forthcoming of prisoners on a certain day, to suppose
they may discharge themselves from that liability by any
other means than the production of the party accused.

I need not repeat what has been so often said: "It is
the interest of the public that every person charged
with crime should be tried; so that if he be innocent,
that innocence may be properly ascertained and made
known; or, if he be guilty, that he may be convicted and
punished."

If the friends of parties who are accused, are allowed
to go through the form of acknowledging a recognizance,

and by so doing get their friends released from custody, and when called on to produce them, say the form was technically wrong on some hidden equitable grounds, and the magistrate gave the order for the discharge when he ought not to have done so, and they are therefore to incur no liability, and their friends are to be free from all risk of punishment, having fled from justice through their aid and conduct, it seems to me that public justice will suffer though the criminals, and their friends may not.

If we looked at the obligation contracted by the plaintiffs as a mere pecuniary one, and to be subject to the ordinary rules applicable to such obligations, the judgment of the learned Vice-Chancellor is undoubtedly correct. I do not think that the principles applicable to that kind of obligation attach to a recognizance several in its character to compel the forthcoming of a person to answer a criminal charge, who has been, Judgment. according to the legal result of their becoming bail, delivered to the custody of the cognizors in consequence of the undertaking entered into by them. I am therefore of opinion, both on the ground of the want of jurisdiction in the Court, and on the merits, that the plaintiffs fail ; that this appeal should be allowed ; and the bill in the Court below dismissed with costs.

SPRAGGE, C.*—The decree made in this case is, in my judgment, right. The cases cited shew that the case falls within the definition of revenue cases, of which the Court of Exchequer has cognizance; and the 2nd section of our Provincial Statute, 28 Victoria, chapter 17, gives to our Court of Chancery the same equitable jurisdiction in matters of revenue as the Court of Exchequer in England possesses.

If the question had arisen upon a bond or other agreement between subject and subject, it would, in

* Was absent from illness, and his judgment was read by V. C. Strong.

my opinion, be a case in which a Court of Equity would grant relief. I mean in a case where the undertaking is in the same terms, each undertaking for himself, and there being, consequently, no·contribution as between sureties, there would still be the equity of the sureties against the principal, which, however, would probably stand independently of his being a party to the instrument. Still, assuming this to be so, it would become a very intelligible element of consideration with a party about to become a surety, whether his principal, or whether one named as a co-surety, were also becoming bound or not; and this would apply with peculiar force in a case of this nature. In ordinary cases the principal is already under a personal pecuniary obligation, while here it arises from the instrument, if at all. A person might be quite willing to become a surety if his co-surety were a brother of the principal, and if the principal were also bound, and be unwilling, because feeling less safe, if either of these were not bound with him. His right to relief rests upon this, that the contract to which his name is appended is not the contract that he agreed to enter into, nor is it the same with only nominal or immaterial differences; but it is essentially different—so different that a man might well be content to enter into the one, and not content to enter into the other. The course of the Attorney General in the suit does, indeed, assume the existence of the equity in the abstract. He does not demur, but sets up by answer what he submits to be an answer to the equity of the plaintiffs' bill. He sets up that it was as much through the negligence of the plaintiffs as from any other cause that the prisoner did not execute the recognizance, a fact not sustained in evidence: there appears, indeed, to have been negligence, but it was the negligence of the local officials—not of the gaoler, however, for the warrant of discharge recites that the prisoner had "entered into his own

Judgment.

1871.

Rastall
v.
Attorney
General.

recognizance, and found sufficient sureties for his appearance." The answer of the Attorney General further sets up that one of the plaintffs is the prisoner's brother, a fact wholly immaterial to the question in issue; and further, that no representation was made to the plaintiffs that the prisoner should, before being discharged, execute the recognizance. As to the latter, if the instrument had been a bond or other agreement between subject and subject, the names of the parties appearing as they do upon this recognizance, there could be no doubt, I apprehend, that the presenting of the instrument in such form to any party who executed it, would be a representation to such party that it would be executed by all whose names appeared upon the instrument as parties to execute it.

I see no reason for a distinction between such an instrument and the instrument in question in this cause. Nor do I see that any distinction arises from

Judgment. the nature of the instrument, or the mode in which it is entered into. It is an instrument of suretyship; not only are the parties to it (other than the prisoner himself) styled sureties in the order for admission to bail and the warrant of discharge, but their position is essentially a position of suretyship; that position arising when one engages to be answerable for the debt, default, or miscarriage of another. As a rule, the form of the instrument is immaterial, so as it does not come within the mischief of the Statute of Frauds. Its being matter of record, cannot, I apprehend, alter its legal effect. It seems scarcely logical to say that instruments, alike in terms as to the engagement entered into, shall be construed differently as to their legal effect, because the one is a matter of record and the other a matter not of record. It is clear that, whether solemn instruments under seal, as a deed or bond, or whether not under seal, formal or informal, a formal writing, or a memorandum note or letter, all

are construed according to their terms, not according
to their nature. An engagement of record must, I
think, be interpreted in the same way. My conclusion,
then, shortly, is, that the plaintiffs are entitled to be
relieved because the instrument against which they
seek relief is not the instrument that they agreed to
enter into, but one essentially different. It is impossible
to say that they would have agreed to become bound
by such an instrument as is sought to be enforced
against them.

MOWAT, V. C.—If this were a case between subject and subject, it seems to me clear that the sureties
would be entitled to the relief which the decree
gave to the plaintiffs. A recognizance of bail in a
private suit cannot be different from a bail bond to
the sheriff, as to the necessity of all becoming bound before the transaction is, in the view of equity, complete,
or binding on any one of them; and a bail bond to the
sheriff cannot be different in that respect from any other
bond of suretyship which parties may execute.

I also agree with the Court below, that there is no rule of
law on which a case between the Crown and a subject
can, by a tribunal having jurisdiction over it, be distinguished from a similar case between subject and subject.
It seems to me impossible to hold, that a recognizance of
bail in a private suit, and a recognizance of bail in a criminal proceeding, differ essentially as to what is necessary to make them complete and binding in equity;
or that in the latter case the prisoner's acknowledgment
of the recognizance is a mere formality, which those acting for the Crown can disregard. The practice is, to require a prisoner to enter into such a recognizance, as
well as for his bail to do so; and the order of the County
Court Judge in this case expressly required this, and
named $2000 as the sum in which the prisoner was
to be bound, and $1000 as the sum in which each of the

sureties was to be bound. The prisoner's acknowledgment of the recognizance was considered to afford some
additional security that he would be forthcoming to take
his trial; and the sureties were entitled to have that
security taken, whatever it amounted to. On well settled
principles of equity, they have a right to say, that all
which they were asked to do, all which they contemplated
doing, all which they really did, was to bind themselves
on condition of that security being taken. The prisoner
was not in fact delivered to them; they were not
present when he was discharged from custody; and it
is not shewn that they did anything to waive their right
to have the recognizance regarded as incomplete and
ineffectual until it had been acknowledged by all parties
according to its tenor and purport.

But it is objected that the Court of Chancery had no
jurisdiction in the matter.

It appears by the learned Vice Chancellor's notes of
the argument in the Court below, that counsel for the
Attorney General expressly waived any objection on
the ground of jurisdiction. The Attorney General on
behalf of the Crown was then content (as he reasonably
might be) that the question of equity raised should be
decided in Chancery, instead of the plaintiffs being sent
to the Court of Quarter Sessions to have the point determined; and the objection is not now distinctly raised, if
it is raised at all, even in the reasons of appeal. It is
said to be a rule of the common law that the Sovereign
by his prerogative may sue in what Court he pleases.
If this doctrine applies to our Ontario Courts, ought it
not to follow that, in case, when sued in Chancery in respect of a matter not within the ordinary jurisdiction of
that Court, the Crown submits to the jurisdiction, and
judgment is against the Crown on the merits, the question of jurisdiction should no longer be open to either
party? and that the Attorney General should not be at

liberty for the first time on an appeal to this Court, to object to the jurisdiction whose action he had invited?

If the objection had been taken, would it have been good? Had the plaintiffs a remedy by bill in equity?

That depends on the question whether there is at the present day a remedy by bill in a like case in the Court of Exchequer in England? The jurisdiction of that Court over such cases existed before 33 Henry VIII., ch. 39, sec. 79; and this ancient jurisdiction was exercisable, though no suit by the Crown were pending there against the debtor; and, in some cases, at all events, though the recognizance, if any, had not been estreated into the Court. The cases of *Attorney General* v. *Halling*, (a), *Hix* v. *Attorney General* (b), *Pawlett* v. *Attorney General* (c), *Cawthorne* v. *Campbell* (d), *Ex Parte Durrand* (e), and *Colebrooke* v. *Attorney General* (f), appear to me to be sufficient to shew that. The equitable jurisdiction of the Court of Exchequer in such cases was expressly given to the Court of Chancery in this country by the Statute 28 Victoria, chapter 17, sec. 2 (g).

So far I think that the judgment below was correct. But *Pellow's* case (h), *Hankin's* case (i), and *Thompson's* case (j), seem to me to shew that the ancient jurisdiction which there was in the Court of Exchequer in such a case, was taken away by the Acts 3 George IV., ch. 46, and 4 George IV., ch. 37; and the terms of those statutes correspond so closely with the terms of our Consolidated Act respecting estreats (k), that I am

1871.

Rastall
v.
Attorney
General.

Judgment.

---

(a) 15 M. & W. 687.    (b) Hardres, 176.    (c) Ib. 465.
(d) 1 Anstr. 205.    (e) 3 Anstr. 743.
(f) 7 Pri. 146; see also 7 Co. 19; Manning's Exch. Pr. 102; and authorities referred to in the cases cited in the judgment.
(g) See Baker v. Ranney, 12 Gr. 228; Westbrook v. Attorney General, 11 Gr. 330; Comp. Attorney General v. Halling, supra.
(h) McCl. 111.    (i) McCl. & Y. 27,    (j) 3 Tyr. 53.
(k) Con. Stat. U. C. ch. 117,

unable to say there is any ground for distinguishing them.

It has been suggested, that these decisions only shew that there is now no jurisdiction by summary motion under the Statute, 33 Henry VIII., ch. 39, and that they do not affect the question as to the general jurisdiction by bill. But that does not seem to be so. The Statute of Henry VIII. is not once mentioned in any one of the three cases. In *Pellow's* case (a) the motion was to discharge a recognizance which had been estreated into the Court of Exchequer from the Borough Sessions in Oke-hampton, in Devonshire. The Court granted the motion ultimately, on the ground, that "the recognizance had been in fact estreated into it, and consequently the party had no other remedy but this application, in order to prevent the issuing of process;" but before these circumstances were pointed out, the Court "had suggested a doubt whether, since the passing of the Acts mentioned,

their jurisdiction in matters of this nature was not completely taken away; being inclined to think that the party could only be relieved by applying to the Justices in Sessions." In *Hankin's* case, the application was similar; and the decision was in accordance with the doubt so expressed in *Pellow's* case: that the Statute 3 George IV., ch. 46, secs. 5 & 6, having required applications for relief in these cases to be made to and determined by the General or Quarter Sessions, that had become the "sole jurisdiction" for the purpose; and that the Court of Exchequer could not "interfere at all;" that "there would be an incongruity in the recent statute contemplating the continuance of its former jurisdiction in this Court, in view of the provisions which the Statute contains." In *Thompson's* case a like view was taken, the Court holding, that they had now no jurisdiction over recognizances forfeited at Quarter Sessions but not estreated into the

---

(a) 15 George IV.

Court of Exchequer. There the Sessions had recommended the application to be made to the Exchequer; but, nevertheless, the Court felt it necessary to refuse to interfere. It thus appears that both the language of the Court and the reasoning on which it proceeded in these cases, point to an entire want of jurisdiction, and not merely to a want of jurisdiction by a summary mode of procedure. I think that the Court was of opinion, that the Legislature in passing the Statutes of George IV. meant to give jurisdiction to the Quarter Sessions to the entire exclusion of the Court of Exchequer, in the cases to which those two statutes were applicable.

I do not find that the jurisdiction of the Court of Exchequer over revenue matters by bill, has any other foundation than its summary jurisdiction in such matters. As I have already said, the jurisdiction existed before the Statute of 33 Henry VIII., ch. 39; and it is not confined to cases within that Statute. That Act did not point out the mode in which the jurisdiction which it gave to the Courts therein mentioned (and of which Courts the Exchequer is but one) was to be exercised; and I apprehend that it was exercised by plea, motion or bill, according as the case required, and that the Acts of 3 George IV. and 4 George IV. did not take away that jurisdiction as exercised in one mode any more than in another. The Lord Chief Baron in *re Durrand* said of the authority which the Court of Exchequer possessed in matters of revenue, that (*a*) it "may be exerted in two shapes; either by motion or petition to the Court, or by the more formal method of an information by the Attorney General, or a bill against him; each of these is the proper mode of application in different cases. Thus, in the ordinary applications to take off an *insuper* improperly imposed; to remove the hands of the sheriff

1871.

Rastall
v.
Attorney
General.

Judgment.

---

(*a*) 3 Anstr. at 746.

on an improper levy, and the like, a motion is the proper mode of obtaining the assistance of the Court. But, where the nature of the question, or the intricacy of the circumstances, renders it impossible to come at the justice of the case on motion, the more formal mode, by bill or information, must be resorted to.''

The judgments in *Ex parte Colebrooke* (a) shew that the summary jurisdiction is-not confined to recognizances estreated into the Court, or to cases where a suit by the Crown is pending in the Court.

To pass by intermediate authorities, I would further refer to the able and elaborate judgment of Lord Chief Baron *Pollock*, in *Attorney General* v. *Halling*, (b), in which his Lordship gave this exposition of the law on the subject : "It is not strictly correct to say of (the Court of Exchequer) that in matters of revenue, it sits as 'a Court of Equity.' It sits as a Court of Revenue having ancient forms of equitable procedure. * * The books on the subject of our practice lay it down that, in our Court, the justice done to the public is attempered with a salvo of private rights and equities, and that the foundation of the equitable discretion and moderative power of the Barons is traceable to sources more remote than any writs from the Royal grace, or any Acts at present extant emanating from the Legislature. Thus, cases repeatedly occur in our ancient records of purely equitable beneficial proceedings, founded on the ancient law and custom of the Exchequer, upon mere equitable prayer, and permitted expressly in consideration of the equity raised, and often disclosed on summary proceeding. Then, again, all kinds of equitable matter, raised either on suggestion, petition or plea, were dealt with, and parties furnished with summary means of asserting their rights against

*Judgment.*

---

(a) 7 Pri. 87.          (b) 15 M. & W. at 697 *et seq.*

the Crown, and having the same determined at once by
the Court, in a way wholly dissimilar to the practice of
any other Court, and presenting a peculiar union of
legal and equitable procedure. This summary exercise
of the Court's authority, in ease and equitable relief of
the subject, wherein their interference would appear by
the precedents to be almost without limit, is intimately
connected and bound up with the inherent equity of the
jurisdiction of the Court of Revenue. Therefore, both
by the peculiar comprehensiveness of the power of
pleading in revenue, and the equitable interference of
the Court by summary motion on all sorts of equities
shewn, a very important security to the subject, in
matters otherwise of very stringent and almost arbitrary
proceeding, as well as great facility and saving of
time to the Crown, mainly depend on this inherent
equity in revenue." It is this "inherent equity in
revenue," which, according to the decision in that case,
was left in the Court of Exchequer after its general
equity jurisdiction was abolished; and it appears clearly
from the Lord Chief Baron's exposition of the law and
practice, to be as much exercisable by one mode of procedure as by the other; by motion, as by bill; one
form or the other being selected according as one or the
other is more adapted to the proper litigation of the case.

The result is, that I find myself unable to resist the
conclusion, that the Court of Exchequer in England has
not now jurisdiction to entertain a bill of this kind, and
that, consequently, in the present case, the Court of
Chancery in this Province had not such jurisdiction
either; if the express waiver of the objection to the
Court below was not sufficient to remove the difficulty.

STRONG, V. C.—Some of the grounds upon which
the judgment of the Court below proceeded, have not
been disputed either in argument or in the opinions of
the members of this Court.

1871.

Rastall
v.
Attorney
General.

Judgment.

'It is not denied that the plaintiff would, if he had entered into an ordinary contract by speciality with a subject, under the circumstances, admitted in the present case, have been entitled to relief in equity. Nor is it disputed that the effect of the Statute 28 Victoria, chapter 17, was to transfer to the Court of Chancery all the equitable jurisdiction which the Court of Exchequer in England, sitting as a Court of Revenue, possessed at the time of the passing of the Act 31 George III. Moreover, no authority has been produced to shew that there exists any reason founded on grounds of policy or otherwise for distinguishing the liability of a surety in a recognizance of bail in a case of felony, from that of any other Crown debtor, as respects the right to insist as against the Crown on a discharge on grounds of equity, which is assured to all such debtors by the express words of the Statute 33 Henry VIII., chapter 39. On the contrary, the only authority bearing on this part of the case is that of Lord Chief Baron *Gilbert*, who in his work on the Exchequer in the passage hereafter quoted, distinctly controverts this objection. But it is determined by a large majority of the members of this Court, that the decree of the Court of Chancery ought to be reversed for want of jurisdiction, a ground not raised by the answer of the Attorney General, expressly waived by counsel at the bar in the Court below, and not alluded to in argument in this Court.

It is said that the recognizance having been estreated into the Court of Quarter Sessions the right to be relieved from that estreat and from liability on the recognizance, even on equitable grounds, is to be sought at the Sessions, which it is said has under the Consolidated Statute of Upper Canada, 22 Victoria, chapter 117, exclusive jurisdiction.

From this opinion I respectfully differ. In the cases of *Ex parte Colebrooke* and *Colebrooke* v. *The Attorney*

*General* (*a*), the jurisdiction of the Court of Exchequer to give equitable relief to Crown debtors was fully discussed both in the arguments of counsel and the judgments of the Court. The case was one of great importance as regarded the amount involved, and indeed the reporter in a note which he appends, states it to have been a cause of great public interest. There it was expressly decided after two arguments and much deliberation, that under the Statute 33 Henry, VIII., the Court had jurisdiction to relieve, and would relieve debtors to the Crown, upon equitable grounds, on a bill filed against the Attorney-General, and that although there was no liability of the debtor under any record of the Exchequer, and notwithstanding that no proceeding had been taken to enforce the debtor's liability.

This case, which was not cited in the Court below, is in my judgment conclusive in favour of the plaintiffs.

The great authority of Chief Baron *Gilbert* can also be adduced, for in his book on the Exchequer, at page 191, after referring to the Statute 33 Henry VIII., he says: "The Court of Exchequer have power to discharge all debts and duties due to the King upon any equity disclosed, and it is by virtue of this Act they discharge recognizances."

This passage at least shews that a recognizance stands on no higher ground than any other Crown debt.

The authorities relied on as determining the want of jurisdiction are, I understand, the cases of *The King* v. *Hankin* (*b*), and *The King* v. *Thompson* (*c*). These were cases in which applications were made in the

---

(*a*) 7 Price, pp. 84 and 160.
(*b*) McClelland & Young, 27.   (*c*) 3 Tyr. 53.

Exchequer in summary form by motion, for relief against recognizances which had been estreated at the Sessions; and it was held that such applications could not be entertained as the recognizances were not records of the Court of Exchequer, and that the relief ought to be sought in the Quarter Sessions, which, under an Act similar to the Consolidated Statute of Upper Canada, already referred to, had power to give discharges. These decisions, I venture to think, do not conflict with the case of *Colebrooke* v. *The Attorney General*, or with the view taken in this case in the Court below, but are susceptible of a plain distinction.

It is, of course, well known that every Court of Common Law has an equitable jurisdiction, by means of which it exercises control over its own records, and to a certain extent restrains its suitors from making an inequitable use of its process. This jurisdiction is enforced by summary modes of proceeding, that is to say, by rule or order, and is of course, confined to cases and proceedings actually pending, and where the record belongs to the Court to which the application is made.

It was this jurisdiction which was invoked in the cases of *Rex* v. *Hankin* and *Rex* v. *Thompson*, and which was declined, on the ground, as I understand these cases, that the Court could not deal summarily with the records of another Court.

This was wholly beside the question of the right to relief by virtue of a general equitable jurisdiction, to be administered according to the established course of Courts of Equity upon bill filed, and which it had been determined in the case of *Colebrooke* v. *The Attorney General*, the Court of Exchequer possessed.

This latter jurisdiction was entirely independent of the possession of the record, and was not, in my judgment, taken away by the Statute which provided for recognizances being estreated into the Court of Quarter Sessions.

It being established, as I think, by the authorities already quoted, that before the passing of the Statute 3 George IV., chapter 46, relief would have been given against a recognizance on grounds of equity, on bill filed and proceedings being taken according to the established course of Courts of Equity, the effect of the construction given to the Consolidated Statute of Upper Canada, 22 Victoria, chapter 117, in this case must be to treat that jurisdiction as entirely abolished for it is out of the question to suppose that it was intended to transfer it and provide that proceedings should be taken by bill in the Court of Quarter Sessions.

The consequence is, that a Crown debtor by recognizance claiming equitable relief, can now only seek it by a summary application to the Quarter Sessions founded on affidavit evidence, the effect of the Consolidated Statute being now held to be by implication to abolish the former mode of proceeding by bill.

Judgment.

In other words, there, having been originally a clear equitable jurisdiction to relieve against recognizances on bill filed, it is held to be totally abrogated by an Act of Parliament, providing merely that recognizances shall be estreated into the Court of Quarter Sessions, instead of the Court of Queen's Bench, as formerly.

Speaking with great deference such a construction of the Statute seems to me at variance with all principle. Supposing the Consolidated Statute of Upper Canada, 22 Victoria, chapter 117, had never been passed, and the original provision that recognizances should be estreated into the Court of Queen's Bench, had remained in force when equitable jurisdiction in matters of revenue was

1871.
Rastall
v.
Attorney
General.

conferred by the 28 Victoria, chapter 17, on the Court of Chancery, might it not in that case have been said, by a parity of reasoning with that which has prevailed here, that a bill for relief against a recognizance would not have lain.  And if it could have been so said, then the mere circumstance of two distinct jurisdictions, which, up to a certain time had been administered in the same Court, being distributed and given to two distinct Courts would have had the effect of annihilating one of the most important of these jurisdictions.

This, it seems to me is precisely what is now being done by the judgment in this appeal.

I admit that all depends upon the question of the original jurisdiction of the Court of Exchequer under the Statute of 33 Henry VIII., to give relief against recognizances on bill filed according to the course of Courts of Equity; but this I take to be determined by the cases of *Colebrooke* v. *The Attorney General,* and the authority of *Gilbert* on the Exchequer; and this being established I am unable to see how the jurisdiction has been either abolished or transferred.

*Judgment.*

I think the appeal should be dismissed.

## HOWARD V. HARDING.

*Mortgagor and mortgagee—Solicitor—Sale.*

Where a sale takes place under a power contained in a mortgage, and
the sale is not properly conducted through the fault of the solicitor,
the mortgagor, or any other party interested as well as the mortgagee, has a right to institute proceedings complaining thereof.

In case of such a sale the solicitor of the mortgagee cannot become
the purchaser, though the proceedings for the sale were not taken
in his name, and it was not shewn that any loss had occurred by
reason of his being the purchaser.

In 1859 the plaintiff joined as surety for one *George
Garner*, and with him, in making several promissory
notes, payable at different dates, and the plaintiff,
through the default of *Garner*, was compelled to pay
them.

Shortly before the first note fell due, *Garner* made
a voluntary conveyance of the land in question—east
half of lot 26 in the 6th concession of West Nissouri—
to his son, *William A. Garner*, who thereupon incumbered the property by executing a mortgage with a
power of sale to one *Irvin Pool*.

Upon payment of the several notes endorsed by the
plaintiff, he obtained a judgment against *George Garner*
for the amount paid as his surety, and issued execution
thereon; but before that time, and during the pendency
of such action, the younger *Garner* re-conveyed to his
father, and by collusion obtained two judgments at
law against him, and sued out execution against the
lands of his father. The plaintiff thereupon filed his
bill in this Court, and obtained a decree declaring such
judgments and executions of the son fraudulent and
void as against the plaintiff and others, the creditors
of *George Garner*, and declaring plaintiff's execution
to form a lien and charge upon the said land, and
ordering the sale of it to satisfy the plaintiff's claim.

Meanwhile, default having been made in payment of *Irvin Pool's* mortgage, steps were taken by him to sell the land under the power of sale in the mortgage, and the land was sold a few days before the plaintiff obtained his decree, and was purchased by the defendant *Harding*, a practising barrister and solicitor, who acted for *William A. Garner* in procuring the judgments and executions against his father, and also had defended the *Garners* in the suit in this Court, in which the plaintiff had obtained the decree.

*Harding*, shortly after his purchase, sold the land to the defendant *McVane*, and took a mortgage to secure payment of part of the purchase money. This mortgage he assigned to the defendant Mrs. *Adams*.

The proceedings to sell the land under the power of sale, were so taken by a Mr. *O'Loan*, a solicitor, but the plaintiff alleged that the defendant *Harding* was the actual solicitor of *Pool*, and that the several papers and notices were drawn in his own office; and that he merely used *O'Loan's* name for the purpose of concealing his own position in the matter.

This, however, the Court held was disproved by the evidence.

The bill was filed for the purpose of setting aside the sale and mortgage; and the re-sale as fraudulent; for leave to allow the plaintiff to redeem *Pool's* mortgage, and for an injunction against any sale of the property before decree.

The cause came on for the examination of witnesses at the sittings of the Court in Guelph, in the Spring of 1870.

Mr. *George Murray*, for plaintiff.

Mr. *S. Blake*, for defendant *Harding.*

Mr. *Moss*, for defendants *McVane* and *Adams.*

The Court being of opinion that the plaintiff had failed to establish the case set up, dismissed the bill with costs. In delivering judgment the following observations were made with reference to some points of law which had been raised in the argument :—

SPRAGGE, C.—The position taken by Mr. *Blake*, that, when a sale under a mortgage is conducted by the solicitor of the mortgagee, and that sale is not properly conducted, through the fault of the solicitor, the mortgagee is the only party entitled to complain, I dissent from. I think the mortgagor whose property may have brought a less price, or any other who is prejudiced by the wrong or error of the solicitor, has a right to complain.

The mortgagee with power of sale, is a trustee in the matter of any sale under the power. If he conducted the sale wrongly, he would be answerable to his *cestui que trust;* and if the wrong is that of his agent, he is equally answerable.

The position taken by Mr. *Moss*—that where a sale is conducted *in fact* by a solicitor for the mortgagee, such solicitor becoming the purchaser at the sale, he can hold his purchase if it be not known that he was solicitor, because the sale is not thereby damped ; unless it be shewn that there was something wrong in the conduct of the sale, or that a less price was obtained— I dissent from also. What is done in the case supposed, is a wrong : the solicitor has placed himself in a false position ; in a position in which there is a conflict between his duty and his interest. His duty was, so to fix the time, and place, and terms of sale, and to give publicity to it, to appoint the auctioneer, and so

to conduct it in all respects, as to obtain the highest
price for the land : his interest is, so to do all this
that *he* may obtain it at the lowest price. I am supposing that he is the directing mind and hand, though
undisclosed—that he is the real solicitor conducting
the proceedings of the sale, in the name of another.
It may be said that he did not contemplate a purchase
when he settled all these proceedings ; but that is a
matter always easy of assertion ; and the affirmative,
that he did actually contemplate a purchase by himself,
is a matter difficult of proof. If the law will allow
him, in such a case, to purchase, he may always settle
these proceedings, having in his mind the possibility
of his becoming a purchaser. The rule, I take to be,
and it is the only safe rule, that where there is, or
may be, a conflict of duty with interest, it is against
good policy that a party should be allowed to act, and
that if he does act, and obtains a benefit from it, the
law will not allow him to hold that benefit.

I think the rule is as broad and comprehensive as I
have stated it. I refer particularly to the case of the
*City of Toronto* v. *Bowes*, and cases referred to in the
judgments delivered in that case, as reported in Mr.
*Grant's* Reports, Volumes IV. and VI., and on appeal to
the Privy Council, in 11 *Moore.*

1871.

THE CITY BANK V. SCATCHERD.

*Practice—Administration suit—Costs.*

In case a creditor brings an administration suit after being informed that there are no assets applicable to the payment of his claim, if the information appear by the result to have been substantially correct, he may have to pay the costs of the suit.

This was a suit by creditors of *John W. Kermott* and another on behalf of the plaintiffs and all other creditors interested, under a deed of assignment, dated 3rd May, 1856, and executed by the debtors to the defendants as trustees. The defendants themselves were creditors; the deed gave a preference to them and others, and provided that the residue should be applied in discharge *pari passu* of the unpreferred debts of the assignors, provided that the creditors to whom the same were owing should come into the assignment within 60 days from its date. The plaintiffs' bill was filed in 1863; and, to excuse the delay, the plaintiffs alleged that until shortly before the filing of the bill they had not been aware of the nature of the assignment. They claimed to be preferred creditors. This claim was at the hearing (30th April, 1864,) found against them, and the bill was dismissed. The cause was afterwards reheard; and a decree was made (21st December, 1864), allowing the plaintiffs to come in as unpreferred creditors, directing the usual accounts, giving the defendants their costs to the hearing, and reserving further directions and subsequent costs.

It appeared from the pleadings, that before the filing of the bill the defendants had informed the plaintiffs that the assets were not sufficient to pay the preferred creditors; that the defendants before suit had given to the plaintiffs an abstract of the affairs of the estate, and had given to them liberty to inspect the books;

24—VOL. XVIII. GR.

and that the plaintiffs had availed themselves of this liberty; but the bill complained that the statement rendered to them was not sufficiently minute. No evidence as to these matters was gone into at the hearing.

On the 2nd December, 1870, the Master at London made his report, shewing, that most of the assets capable of being realized had been realized before the suit; that no further sum had been realized since the suit was instituted; that the assets still outstanding consisted of two small mortgages, and some mortgaged property of which the trustees had obtained the equity of redemption; and that all the assets when realized would not be sufficient to pay the preferred creditors. The only question argued on further directions was, as to the costs of the suit.

Mr. *Morphy*, for the plaintiffs.

Mr. *Meredith* and Mr. *Rae*, for the defendants.

MOWAT, V.C.—The plaintiffs claimed the costs of the suit since decree. They had been informed by the trustees before any of these costs were incurred, that the assets were not sufficient to pay even the preferred creditors; but counsel for the plaintiffs argue, on the authority of a case in *Price, Sharples* v. *Sharples (a)*, that notwithstanding such notice they were entitled to have the accounts taken at the cost of the estate; and further, that if all the debts due to the debtors had turned out to be good, there would have been something for the general creditors. The plaintiff in *Sharples* v. *Sharples* was a residuary legatee, as well as a creditor, and costs were given against him as a creditor. But the case has never been

_____

(a) 13 vol. p. 745.

followed in Chancery, so far as it purports to decide that the right of a residuary legatee who brings an administration suit, to receive out of the estate the costs incurred in it, was not affected by previous notice of the insufficiency of the assets. The case is cited in *Miller* v. *McNaughton (a)*, but not with reference to that peculiarity. In *Miller* v. *McNaughton* neither the statement nor judgment mentions that there was a deficiency of assets; I have had the Chancellor's note-book examined, and am informed that it contains no reference to any allegation of that kind; and I have myself read the report which was before the Court for the purpose of further directions, and I find that it did not indicate that there would be a deficiency. Whether there did turn out subsequently to be a deficiency, I do not know; but it is quite certain that the judgment did not proceed on such an assumption. The case in *Price* is cited, in *Daniell's* Practice, as an authority for the right of a party to costs where there is no deficiency *(b)*. As to the bad debts in the present case, it was seven years after the assignment that the bill was filed, and the plaintiffs might very fairly have been satisfied that unsecured debts which the trustees had failed for that time to collect were uncollectable; and there is no reason for supposing that the plaintiffs in fact regarded any of them as good, or that they filed the bill in reliance on these debts proving collectable. But if they did think them collectable, it now appears that they were wrong in thinking them so; and the settled rule is, that, where a party is informed that there are no assets to pay his demand, and he, notwithstanding, files a bill for administration, but the result shews that there are no assets applicable to his claim, he is not entitled to his costs. In such a case the only question is, whether he ought not to pay the costs of the defendants.

1871.

City Bank
v.
Scatcherd.

Judgment.

---

(a) 11 Gr. 308.  (b) 4th ed. pp. 1308, 1309.

1871.        It is hard that assets which belong to others should
⌣            have to be applied to the payment of costs created by
City Bank    a party who has no interest in such assets, and who
Sc at cherd. brings his suit after information of the fact. - But there
v.
             is a conflict of authority as to whether in such a case a
             plaintiff loses his own costs merely, or should also pay
             the costs of the defendants.                    •

             *King* v. *Bryant (a)* is an express authority for the
             defendants.   The following is the judgment of the
             Master of the Rolls in that case : " Where a creditor's
             suit is properly commenced and prosecuted by a simple
             contract creditor, and the assets are realized in the suit,
             he will be entitled to payment of his costs, although the
             estate is deficient for the payment of the specialty
             creditors.   Every creditor has a right to have an
             account of the assets, but it does not follow that he is
             to be indemnified out of the assets of others, against
Judgment     every expense which he may rashly or injudiciously
             incur.   Here the suit was neither properly commenced
             nor prosecuted.   The plaintiff has thought fit to carry
             it on in the face of information as to the state of the
             assets, which turned out to be perfectly correct, for the
             state of the assets, the existence of the specialty debt,
             and the Master's report, are not now questioned.   The
             plaintiff, therefore, has proceeded at his own peril, and,
             the representations made before suit and on the answer
             turning out to be perfectly accurate, he must pay the
             costs of the suit.   The defendant must have her extra
             costs out of the fund, and the remainder will belong to
             the judgment creditor."

             *Bluett* v. *Jessop (b)*, *Thompson* v. *Clive (c)*, *Fuller* v.
             *Green (d)*, are to the same effect; and the rule as stated
             in *Morgan & Davey* on Costs is in accordance with

             ───────────────────────

(a) 4 Beav. 460.        (b) Jac. 240.        (c) 11 B. 475.
(d) 24 B. 217, and see Loomes v. Stotherd, 1 S. & S. 461 a.

these cases *(a)*.  In other cases the plaintiffs have not  1871.
been charged with the defendant's costs *(b)*; but the  City Bank
circumstances of some of these cases were peculiar;  v.
and in a conflict of authority on such a point I have  Scatcherd.
to consider what is the better rule.

The assignment was a mortgage, so far as the
defendants and the preferred creditors were concerned; and, under all the circumstances of the case,
I think that the plaintiffs should pay the defendants'
costs (as between party and party) up to the decree on
further directions.  Any further proceedings which
the parties interested may desire to take with a view
to the estate being wound up under the direction of
the Court, being now taken voluntarily on their part,
I think that the plaintiffs should not be charged with
the costs of such proceedings.  With the consent of the
preferred creditors, the decree now to be made might
leave the realization of the remaining assets and the  Judgment.
distribution of the proceeds, as well as of the fund in
Court, to the trustees, if the parties choose.  The extra
costs of the trustees as between solicitor and client,
not payable by the plaintiffs, will be payable out of
the estate.

---

*(a)* P. 137.

*(b)* Robinson v. Elliott, 1 Russ. 598; Ottley v. Gilby, 8 B. 602;
Attorney General v. Gibbs, 1 DeG. & S. at 161; Sullivan v. Bevan,
20 Beav. 399.

1871.

## BUTLER v. CHURCH.  [IN APPEAL.*]

*Practice—Appeal by married woman—Specific performance—Statute of Frauds—Pleading—Parties.*

Where a married woman defended a suit in Chancery without a next friend, it was held that the husband and wife could appeal to this Court without any next friend.

Coutinued possession by a tenant coupled with acts inconsistent with his previous tenancy, is sufficient part performance to let in parol evidence of a contract of sale.

A vendor devised his estate to trustees, and on a division of the estate among the *cestuis que* trust the trustees conveyed to one of them the sold property : these facts appeared on a bill by the purchaser against the grantee for specific performance : the defendants set up by answer that the executors and trustees were necessary parties : the Chancellor at the hearing over-ruled the objection and the Court of Appeal sustained the decree. [DRAPER, C. J., and GWYNNE and GALT, J J., dissenting.]

*Quære,* whether in order to exclude parol evidence of a contract it is necessary for a defendant who denies the contract to claim the benefit of the Statute of Frauds.

This was an appeal by the defendants *Susan Church* and *Coller M. Church* her husband, against the judgment of the Chancellor as reported ante vol. xvi., page 205, decreeing specific performance of a parol agreement on the grounds that the executors and trustees under the last will and testament of *William Hodgins*, the testator in the pleadings mentioned, should have been, but were not parties to this suit; that no agreement in writing was shewn sufficient to satisfy the Statute of Frauds, and no sufficient evidence was adduced by the plaintiff to take the case out of the operation of that statute ; and that the evidence adduced did not establish the plaintiff's case, nor entitle him to a decree, and that the weight of evidence was in favor of the defendants.

Statement.

_____

* *Present.*—DRAPER, C. J. ; RICHARDS, C. J. ; HAGARTY, C. J., WILSON, J. ; MOWAT. V. C. ; GWYNNE, J. ; GALT, J.

In support of the decree the plaintiff contended that
the decree being an exercise of discretion was not
appealable; that the executors and trustees other than the
defendant *Coller M. Church,* were not necessary parties
to the suit; that such an objection could not in any
event be taken by the appellants, because, if tenable, it·
could only be so-on behalf of the respondent, who was
the purchaser; but no such objection existed inasmuch
as the legal estate was conveyed to the appellant *Susan
Church* by the other trustees, and no personal representative was a necessary party; but, if so, the appellant
*Coller M. Church* is a sufficient party in that character;
that the appellants, not having pleaded the Statute of
Frauds, could not in any event rely thereon or insist that
the respondent should be required to prove that there
was an agreement in writing; that the respondent did
not profess to rely upon a written agreement; and the
appellants, seeing such to be the case upon the respondent's bill in Chancery, had by their answer waived any
right to call upon the respondent to prove anything
further than a parol agreement; that there were sufficient acts of part performance to take the case out of
the operation of the Statute of Frauds ; that the weight
of evidence was in favor of the respondent, and sufficient
to entitle him to a decree for specific performance, and
that the appellants have waited and taken the account
in the Master's office for the purpose of ascertaining the
result thereof, and the same being against the appellants,
no discretionary power could then or would in any
event in a suit for specific performance be exercised in
favor of the said appellants. The respondent also objected
that it was not competent for a married woman to appeal
without naming a next friend.

Mr. *C. S. Patterson* and Mr. *J. C. Hamilton,* for the
appellants.

Mr. *Fitzgerald,* contra.

1871.

Butler
v.
Church.

Statement.

1871.    HAGARTY, C.J.—I think that a parol agreement to
sell the land at £650, payable with interest, as *Butler*
could pay, is fairly proved.

I also think there is evidence that from 1856, when
the verbal contract was made,-there was a change in
the dealings. That before that time the rent was paid
in shares. Since that time numerous payments were
made in money. There is no pretence that there was
any bargain for an increased rent from 1856, and except
on the theory that a contract of purchase had been
made it is almost impossible to understand on what
principle the payments were made, as they vary so much
from year to year, repelling the idea that any fixed
yearly payment existed.

Thus we find in the books £60 paid in 1857, besides
the £20 in the preceding October when the bargain was
said to be made; £47 15s. in 1858; £23 4s. 3d. in
1859; £39 16s. 6d. in 1860; £51 15s. in 1861;
£51 15s. in 1862; £46 15s. 9d. in 1863; about the
same in 1864; £44 in 1865; £47 10s. in 1866. Six
per cent. on £650, the purchase money, would be £39
per annum. In the absence of any other contract than
that to pay in shares it is very hard to understand this
system of payment, except on the idea of a contract of
sale.

Judgment.

Lord *Cranworth*, in *Nunn* v. *Fabean* (a) (a case of a
parol contract by a tenant in possession), says, "But here
I am not driven to rely on this evidence, because I think
that there was clear part performance by payment of
the Michaelmas rent at the increased rate fixed by the
agreement."

*Wells* v. *Stradling* (b) is to the same effect.

_____

(a) L. R. 1 Ch. App. 40.          (b) 3 Ves. 378.

I think the rule is clearly laid down by Sir *W. Grant*
in *Frame* v. *Dawson* (a) : " It is necessary to shew a part
performance; that is, an act unquestionably referring to,
and resulting from, the agreement, and such that the
party would suffer an injury amounting to fraud by the
refusal to execute that agreement. \* \* The principle
of the cases is, that the act must be of such a nature
that if stated would of itself infer the existence of some
agreement, and then parol evidence is admitted to shew
what the agreement is."

In *Ex parte Hooper* (b) Lord *Eldon* says, " As to
the cases of part performance, the authorities say that
the act, to be considered part performance, must be in
its nature almost necessarily done in pursuance of such
alleged contract."

There is a summary of the authorities in Vendors and
Purchasers, 152 (14th ed.): " Possession by a tenant
cannot be deemed a part performance, unless the landlord accept an additional rent upon the foot of the
agreement."

Most of the authorities are reviewed and commented
on with great clearness by the late Chancellor *Blake*, in
*Jennings* v. *Robertson* (c), from *Lester* v. *Foxcroft* (d)
to 1852.

He considers the doctrine of part performance to fall
within the general principle of a party by words or by
conduct making a representation to another, leading him
to believe in the existence of a particular state of facts,
and if that other person has acted on the faith thereof,
the party making the representation shall not afterwards
be allowed to say the facts were not as he represented
them to be.

---

(a) 14 Ves. 387.      (b) 19 Ves. 479.
(c) 3 Grant, 513.      (d) 1 White and Tudor.

It might well be urged here that *Hodgins*, if he were alive, allowed *Butler* to act for many years, and to pay much money, on the faith of a verbal bargain to sell the farm to him at a named price, and should not now be heard denying that any such bargain existed.

That it did in fact exist I have very little doubt on the evidence, inconsistent as it may be in some particulars and open to much hostile criticism, as all such dealings usually are. The evidence of defendant *Church* as to what *Hodgins* told him the summer he died, would remove any doubt of there having, at all events up to that time, been an existing contract.

I do not feel pressed by any difficulty as to the absence of any express term of payment : the payment, of the whole purchase money is alleged, and this, if true, puts an end to any question on that head. It was quite competent I presume for *Hodgins* to have agreed to let him pay a fixed sum for the land as he was able, and payment being accordingly made removes all difficulty.

I am most reluctant to see any of the wise provisions of the Statute of Frauds in any way weakened or disregarded, but I think, on the evidence before us in this case, we are justified in holding, on the authorities, that the parol agreement, which I think was very clearly proved, was acted on and partly performed by both parties for a series of years to the extent of raising such an equity against the vendor as would make it a fraud in him to refuse to complete the contract.

RICHARDS, C.J., WILSON, J., and MOWAT, V.C., concurred therein.

DRAPER, C. J.—The first question appears to be whether the defendants can avail themselves of the protection of the Statute of Frauds, having neither pleaded it nor set it up in the answer.

In addition to the two cases decided by V. C. *Knight Bruce* which were referred to in the judgment appealed from, the same learned Vice Chancellor, in effect decided in the same way in *Baskett* v. *Cafe* (a).

But in the case of *Ridgway* v. *Wharton*, which was cited for the appellant, Lord *Cranworth* said, where a defendant admits the agreement, if he means to rely on the fact of its not being in writing and signed and therefore invalid, he must say so, otherwise he is taken to mean, that the admitted agreement was a written agreement, good under the statute, or else that on some other ground it was binding on him; but when he denies or does not admit the agreement, the burden of proof is altogether on the plaintiff, who must then prove a valid agreement capable of being enforced. The decree was for the defendant, and it was carried to the House of Lords. Lord *Cranworth* himself stated he had fallen into an error, and agreed with Lords *Brougham* and *Chelmsford* on this point, which had not engaged his attention, that there was a signed paper, not containing sufficient particulars of the alleged agreement, but which referred to another signed paper, in which those particulars were fully stated, and that the two, being connected by parol evidence, constituted a binding contract. But no dissent was even hinted at, upon the rule of pleading as above stated; and Lord *Chelmsford* went very fully into the case in his judgment.

It is true that Mr. *Lewis*, in his Treatise on Equity Drafting (230) in a note, states that *Ridgway* v. *Wharton* is overruled by *Holding* v. *Barton;* but on referring to the case it will be found not to relate to the Statute of Frauds, but to the necessity for pleading the Statute of Limitations.

On the other hand in *Heys* v. *Astley* (b) *Turner*, L.J., said, "It is not necessary in the view I take, to give any

---

(a) 4 De. G. & Sm. 388.　　　　(b) 12 W. R. 64.

1871.

Butler
v.
Church.

opinion on *Ridgway* v. *Wharton* though I agree in the conclusions arrived at in that case, having regard to the uniform course of pleading which has always prevailed." I cannot infer from this language that *Sir George Turner* disapproved of the passage of Lord *Cranworth's* judgment which I have partially extracted, and in 1 *White & Tudor's* Leading Cases, at p. 639 (2nd ed.), the first part of the passage is referred to as authority.

It appears to me that the plaintiff must prove, in the words of Lord *Cranworth*, a valid agreement, capable of being enforced, as he has stated it in his bill. The defendants have as far as in their position was possible denied any contract, and put him to the proof of it. Proof of a parol agreement without more cannot, as appears to me, be proof of a *binding* agreement capable of being enforced. Here the plaintiff alleges part performance. The cases resemble *Monday* v. *Jolliffe* (a), in the allegation of a parol contract, part performance, and denial of any binding contract. There specific performance was decreed on proof of the parol agreement and part performance.

Judgment.

There is no proof of any agreement in writing ; the statement in the bill negatives the idea of any : then what was the parol agreement, and by what acts alleged and proved is it sustained ?

The language of the statute is plain enough as to the present case. "No action (which has been held to include suits in Equity) shall be brought whereby to charge any person upon any contract or sale of lands * * unless the agreement upon which such action shall be brought or some memorandum or note thereof shall be in writing signed by the party to be charged therewith." It is objected on behalf of the respondent, as I have already observed that the appellants have waived the benefit of the statute, though they have denied any contract what-

---

(a) 5 My. & C. 167.

ever. Still, as numerous cases shew, part performance

will take the case out of the statute, on the ground that
were the exception not allowed, the statute would be
made a cover for, instead of a prevention of fraud ; and
under that exception the right to relief rests not merely
on the contract but on what has been done under it.
The question whether enough is proved to take the case
out of the statute, must be considered.

I think the plaintiff proved a parol agreement with
*Hodgins* for the sale, by the latter, of the premises in question, to this extent that the subject of sale was ascertained,
and the price was fixed payable with interest, but no
time within which payment was to be made was limited.
By claiming specific performance, on paying whatever
may be found due, the appellant has so far fixed the
time or left it to the Court to fix the time within which
the payment must be completed. The bill alleges that
all is paid, whether that be so or not, is a matter of Judgment.
account not before this Court.

As to part performance the bill sets up possession
under the agreement, and clearing the land and making
valuable improvements; such as building a barn and
stable, and planting an orchard. It is also alleged that
at the time of making the agreement he paid *Hodgins*
£20 on account of the £650, the price of the land.

To begin with possession. The plaintiff, about the year
1842, became tenant to *Hodgins*. The bill states upon a
lease of the contents of which nothing is shewn. Plaintiff's
son William swears his father went into possession of
it in February of that year, giving, by way of rent, half
the produce, and that he has been improving the place
ever since, clearing the land and having three or four of
his boys working with him. The witness left the place
in 1852. The evidence shews the alleged contract was
made in October, 1856. There has been no apparent dif-

1871. ference shewn between the possession before or after that
day. In *Savage* v. *Carroll* (a) Lord Chancellor *Manners*
said, "whether the possession be an unequivocal act
amounting to part performance must depend upon the
transaction itself, whether it be so circumstanced that it
can be referred only to a contract of sale, if it be so the
party may go into evidence of the terms of that contract.
Here, without the aid of the parol contract the possession must be referred to the previously existing tenancy."
And in *Brennan* v. *Bolton* (b) Lord Chancellor *Sugden*
remarks, "if a man is in possession of land as tenant,
a mere parol agreement cannot have any operation in
law, there is nothing but the subsisting tenancy to which
this Court can refer any act which may have been done
when it is consistent with his character as tenant. His
remaining in possession is a mere continuance of the
character which he all along filled; and any act which
may be thus referred to a title distinct from the agreement cannot be considered as operating to take the case
out of the statute."

-As to improvements. At the date of this parol agreement the plaintiff had been in possession well on to fifteen years paying rent by the delivery of half the produce. The lot contained 125 acres. Plaintiff's son,
*Richard*, says, "the whole of it was chopped some
seventeen years ago, [that would be about 1851]; last
summer we stumped and ploughed about 9 acres; we
were clearing up every year before that; about seven
acres were stumped and cropped in the year before last
[1866]; * * there was an old barn upon the place;
I recollect a fair at Richmond, when it was said my
father agreed to buy the place; we *put up a stable before that and one barn*—the first of the two now on the
place; the roof of the old barn fell in, and we pulled it
down six or seven years ago; we put up the new barn
in the same place; * * thirteen apple trees were

*Butler*
v.
*Church.*

Judgment.

_____

(a) 1 Ball & B. 282.          (b) 2 Dr. & W. 349.

planted last spring" [1867]. On cross-examination he said, "I do not call land cleared until after it is stumped, not while it is in pasture ' * * ; *it had been all logged-off* seventeen years ago except about two acres." *William Butler* said, " when my father went into possession there were between thirty and forty acres cleared." He also said one of the two barns now on the place was put up before he left. The only change which took place about thirteen years ago, evidently alluding to the time of the fair at Richmond, is thus stated by *Richard Butler*, " We did not continue to carry half the produce to Mr. *Hodgins* up to the time of his death. There was a change about thirteen years ago : my father after that paid him money in my presence."

It is clear that the plaintiff, while he was tenant, cleared in the ordinary sense, not stumped, the 125 acres, less the forty or fifty which were cleared when he entered into possession. "It was all logged-off seventeen years ago." During his admitted tenancy he built a stable and one barn. It is not asserted that the plaintiff had any claim upon *Hodgins* for erecting these buildings, nor for clearing, nor fencing, which is also mentioned by *Richard Butler*, and it must be inferred that the terms on which he held, precluded him from claiming on those accounts. Then the building a second barn on the land since 1856 would be as consistent with a tenancy as with a purchase.

The change to a money payment is, however, shewn by the evidence of two books of account which belonged to *Hodgins* and are marked respectively A and B. Book A commences in 1850, which is eight years after the plaintiff went into possession. It ends with an entry under the date of 26th March, 1863. It is headed " Account of the grain received from *Benjamin Butler* on shares for the past year." In 1850 he is credited with certain deliveries of grain to which a price is affixed, and with two deliveries to which there is no price, but at the prices given for the first, the payment in that year was £26 8s. 9d. The entries continue of the same character, year after year, more frequently without figures than with, and always of grain till 1865, when, in January, there are three entries with the amounts carried out, being together £40 13s. 9d., and in December of the same year are two entries, which, at the prices allowed in January, would amount to £8 4s., making the value of the grain delivered in that year £48 17s. 9d. In 1856, up to the 3rd March, are entries of grain, but no prices; but at the prices of the preceding year the sum is £30 5s., and then follows this entry, "1856, Oct. 14, Received from *Benjamin Butler* the sum of £20," which would make the sum paid in that year £50 5s. From that date to the end of this book the entries are nearly all of cash payments.

Judgment.

Book B is a transcript of Book A from the entry under date October 14, 1856, and it continues down to 26th January, 1864. It is kept in the same manner as Book A. The credits are mostly for cash; but there are a few for farm produce and meat, and one for labor in a former year. There is not a word to indicate why the payments were made. The largest sum paid in any one year was £60, the lowest (in 1859) £23 4s. The average of the ten years, beginning with 1857, is £45 14s. 8d., nearly, which, in view of the evidence of the land being more extensively brought under tillage, is probably not more than would have been paid if the land were rented on shares. Without the aid of the parol evidence of the agreement, it cannot be asserted that the payment of £20 in October, 1856, was purchase money. In *Ridgway* v. *Wharton*, to which I have already referred, two papers were connected together by parol evidence to shew a contract in writing within the statute. But that will not help in this case, for instead of two signed papers, which, connected together, made up the entire contract, there is no writing whatever which shews anything connected with the alleged contract, for the entry in *Hodgin's* books is no evidence in the plaintiff's favor without assuming the existence of the parol contract. And again Lord *Redesdale* says, " it has always been considered that payment of money is not to be deemed part performance to take a case out of the statute, (*a*) and it is stated in *Sugden's* Vendors and Purchasers (*b*) " it seems to be settled that part payment of money is not part performance." The great reason is that the statute expressly says with regard to goods part payment shall operate as part performance and therefore silence with regard to lands indicates the absence of such intention.

And with regard to part performance generally, the reason for holding that it takes a case out of the statute is, that it is a fraud for one party to refuse to perform after performance by the other on the faith of the agreement. However, the evidence must be clear and convincing that the acts relied upon as part performance were done exclusively under the agreement, and not *diverso intuitu*. I do not find that convincing proof here for the act of building a barn, clearing and fencing land, had all been done while the plaintiff was unquestionably a tenant as well as after his asserted purchase.

If, therefore, the answer had set up the statute in words, I feel no doubt his bill ought to have been dismissed (*c*), nor would this be so unjust as it might appear at first sight, for money paid upon a consideration that has failed, may be recovered back. But it is insisted on his behalf that the defendants, by not expressly claiming, have waived the benefit of the statute.

---

(*a*) 1 Sch. & L. 40.          (*b*) 124, 13th ed.
(*c*) Cooth v. Jackson, 6 Ves. at 37.

26—VOL. XVIII. GR.

1871.
~~~~~
Butler
v.
Church.

Judgment.

</div>

The Bill evidently is framed so as to claim performance of a parol contract, as is evinced by the allegations of part performance, which are introduced to take the case out of the statute. Without these I apprehend a demurrer would lie for want of shewing an agreement in writing or any note or memorandum thereof signed (*a*). This is consistent with *Spurrier* v. *Fitgerald* (*b*), where Sir *W. Grant* says, if the plaintiff alleges a written agreement the defendant will be reduced to the necessity of pleading the statute and supporting the plea by an answer, whereas as is said in *Whitchurch* v. *Bevis* (*c*), if the bill had stated the agreement generally, a demurrer might have been allowed. Here the defendants were under the necessity of answering, and they deny any agreement, whether one in compliance with the statute or one which, as the bill is framed is taken out of it. In the first case some writing must be proved; in the second, a parol agreement taken out of the statute by part performance. I think this is what Lord *Cranworth* meant when he spoke of a valid agreement capable of being enforced. It may be different where as in *Skinner* v. *McDouall* (*d*), the denial in the answer is, what at law would be called a negative pregnant, alleging that no formal note of the agreement was made and no binding agreement ever existed which was rejected in that case.

There are cases as noticed in the judgment in the Court below, in which a result contrary to that which I deduce from Lord *Cranworth's* language has been reached. I may be in error in my interpretation. I have supposed that he had in his mind the mandatory force of the words " No action shall be brought," &c., and meant that a defendant who denied any agreement existed on which the plaintiff could charge him—cast

---

(*a*) 5 D·G. McN. & G. 41.         (*b*) 6 Ves. at 555.

(*c*) 2 B. C. C. 559.             (*d*) 2 DeG. & S. 265; 12 Jur. 741.

upon the plaintiff the onus of proving an agreement in accordance with the statute, or one so evidenced as to come within the exception established by Courts of Equity in order to prevent the statute being made a cover for fraud. The rule as to claiming the benefit of the statute appears to me to be one of procedure—the exception is one of substantial merit founded upon principles of equity. If I am wrong in this interpretation it will only exemplify what the learned Chancellor in giving judgment in the case plainly intimates, that however Equity Judges doubt the propriety of some previous decisions which break in upon the Statute of Frauds, they uphold them all equally even where merely regulating a matter of practice.

If I am right as I venture to hold on this occasion, and Lord *Cranwoth* meant what I have assumed, I prefer to follow him than to adopt the opinions of others who readily adhere to decisions of which from time to time they express their misgivings.

I agree with the judgment in the Court below—that there was no necessity to bring other parties before the Court—but in my opinion the plaintiff's bill ought to have been dismissed.

GWYNNE, J.—*Picard* v. *Hine* (a) is an authority that the defendant *Susan Church* having appealed by her next friend, the record, as it is with the other defendant *Coller M. Church*, also an appellant, is not open to the preliminary objection taken.

That it is necessary for the plaintiff to entitle him to a decree upon this record, to prove not only an agreement for the purchase and sale of the land in question, *but also* a part performance of that agreement appears

1871.

Butler
v.
Church.

Judgment.

---

(a) L. Rep. 5 Chy. Ap, 274.

to me to be clear, both upon principle and upon authority, although the benefit of the Statute of Frauds has not been claimed by the answer.

The judgment by Lord Chancellor *Cranworth* in *Ridgway* v. *Wharton* (a) must be taken to express the undoubted law and practice of the Court. Upon this point his judgment was based upon that of Lord *Eldon* in *Cooth* v. *Jackson* (b). Lord *Eldon* there says, "If a plaintiff's title to relief stands both upon the fact of a parol agreement *and* part performance of that agreement, there must, in some stage of the cause be *proof* that there was a parol agreement *and* a part performance of *that* agreement, by which I mean some parol agreement certain and definite in its terms, and to which those acts of part performance can be clearly and certainly referred.". *Heys* v. *Astley* (c) cannot affect the doctrine laid down in *Ridgway* v. *Wharton* ; 1stly. Because the observations of Lord Justice *Knight Bruce* upon the point are wholly beside the question which was before him for decision, for he says, "Assuming the doctrine of part performance not to have any application to the case, I am still not satisfied that upon any view whatever, the Statute of Frauds has any application. 2ndly. Because the case before him was one of an admitted written agreement signed by parties, the question raised being the extent and operation of the agreement ; and 3rdly. Because Lord Justice *Turner* there declares that the rule as laid down in *Ridgway* v. *Wharton*, is conformable with the uniform course of pleading which has always prevailed. A short reference to the cases cited in opposition to the rule will clearly establish the correctness of Lord Justice *Turner's* remarks. The cases cited by Mr. *Tripp* in his book at page 54, note *p*, in support of the position, that "unless a defendant

---

(a) 3 DeG. M. & G. at p. 689.      (b) 6 Ves. 88.

(c) 12 W. R. 64.

insist by his answer upon the Statute of Frauds he cannot avail himself of it at the hearing, although he denies the agreement set up by the bill," are *Clifford* v. *Turrell* (a) and *Baskett* v. *Cafe* (b). In *Clifford* v. *Turrell* the Statute of Frauds was not sought to be relied upon. There was an agreement signed by both parties with a consideration therein stated, and what the plaintiff set up was a case of equitable fraud, namely, that he refused to execute the agreement as it was, nor unless provision should be made therein for securing to the plaintiff a small annuity, and that the defendant procured him to sign the agreement as it was by a collateral agreement to give him the annuity; and the question was, whether the additional consideration of the annuity, it not being part of the consideration named in the instrument, could be permitted to be proved, and upon the authority of *Rex* v. *Scammonden* (c) it was decided that it could, and plaintiff was permitted to prove the parol agreement for the annuity, as it was only adding to the consideration and not inconsistent with it; and because the defendant had procured plaintiff to sign the agreement as it stood upon an express collateral agreement that he would give the annuity. The case proceeded upon a principle wholly unaffected by the Statute of Frauds. In *Baskett* v. *Cafe* the case alleged in the bill was not of a parol agreement partly performed. The bill did not state whether or not the trust, of which the plaintiff claimed the benefit, was or not in writing, but it set forth the whole transaction in virtue of which the defendant, by the written consent and authority of one *Watt*, had acquired from an insurance company the assignment of an annuity granted by *Watt*, as whose assignee in bankruptcy the plaintiff claimed by virtue of an order in bankruptcy, to try the right of the defendant to retain to his own benefit the

1871.

Butler
v.
Church.

Judgment.

---

(a) 1 Y. & Col. C. C. 138.　　(b) 1 DeG. & S. 388.

(c) 3 T. R. 474.

Butler
v.
Church.

Judgment.

assignment of the annuity beyond the amount advanced by him to the company therefor. The report does not state what the defendant's answer contained, but by the judgment of the Vice Chancellor *Knight Bruce*, at page 398, it sufficiently appears that it contained admissions which, with the evidence, enabled the Vice Chancellor to decide as he did, without any reference to the Statute of Frauds, that the defendant purchased the assignment of the annuity as a trustee for *Watt*, and that he could only hold it as security for his advances and his costs in the transaction, with interest. In *Sutherland* v. *Briggs* (a), referred to by the learned Chancellor in his judgment, the point does not arise, nor does the judgment of the Vice Chancellor contain any expression of opinion upon it. That case was, in his judgment, supportable upon two grounds : first, that before the plaintiff expended his money upon the land of which he claimed the right to have a lease executed to him, one *Frampton*, under whom the defendant claimed, with notice of the agreement, had agreed to grant the plaintiff a lease of a field commensurate with his interest in a house of which the plaintiff also had a lease from *Frampton* as an inducement to, and consideration for, his doing the repairs, alterations, and improvements which, being proposed by *Frampton*, the plaintiff executed; and, secondly, that there was sufficient consideration (which was disputed) to support an agreement which was come to between the parties, and was drawn up in *Frampton's* handwriting, and signed by the plaintiff, whereby it was agreed that the rent of £69, which had been paid by plaintiff for the house alone, should be increased to £80, for house and field together.

The Vice Chancellor was also of opinion that, as in *Mundy* v. *Joliffe* (b), before Lord *Cottenham*, the plaintiff's case shewed a parol agreement and a clear

---

(a) 1 Hare, 26.                (b) 5 M. & C. 167.

part performance of it. In *Parker* v. *Smith* (a), the 1871. case made by the bill was of an agreement made out by various letters and documents, and acts done in pursuance of the letters ; but the defendants, who were assignees of a bankrupt, by their answer admitted all the various letters and documents mentioned in the bill, and they submitted that the offer of the bankrupt, contained in some of the letters, to accept a reduced rent and to grant a new lease to two only of the original lessees, was purely voluntary, without any valid consideration ; and that not being completed at the time of the bankruptcy could not be carried into effect unless under the direction of the Court, and they submitted whether the signing by the bankrupt, *Hugh Parker* the elder, of the words " approved by me, *H. Parker*," at the foot of the memoranda mentioned in the bill was duly signing such memoranda. That answer was an admission of the agreement contained in the letters and documents mentioned in the bill, whatever effect as a memorandum in writing within the statute might be, and upon the acknowledged rule, would have precluded the defendants from claiming the benefit of the Statute of Frauds at the hearing if not insisted upon in the answer. Afterwards the case came up again when it was agreed that the bill should be treated as amended to introduce into it certain facts contained in these affidavits, setting forth a parol agreement preliminary to, and explanatory of, the documents mentioned in the bill, which documents were themselves acts done in pursuance of the parol agreement, and that to such amended case it should be considered that the defendant's answer did claim the benefit of the statute ; but that was reasonable upon this amendment being made by consent in this manner, for the answer still remaining on record as an admission of the agreement contained in the documents alleged in the bill, it would still be necessary to insist upon the statute in the answer in order to open that objection at the hearing.

Butler<br>v.<br>Church.

Judgment.

--------------------------------

(a) 1 Col. 608.

In *Skinner* v. *McDouall* (a) the plaintiff claimed to make out the agreement of which she claimed the benefit upon certain letters which had passed between her and her agent, and her agent and the defendant. The defendant's answer in substance admitted the letters, but disputed their effect, and it was upon the ground of such admission that plaintiff's counsel successfully insisted that the defendant could not, at the hearing, claim the benefit of the statute, not having insisted upon it in his answer.

In reality, then, no case has been cited wherein it has been held that, if the case made by the bill be of a parol contract partly performed, and that both the contract *and* part performance are denied by the answer, the plaintiff can succeed upon proof only of the parol contract, without any proof of any act of part performance. If such a rule should prevail, then, although a bill alleging a parol contract only, without some act of part performance, would be demurrable (b), yet if to avoid a demurrer a plaintiff should falsely allege acts of part performance, and the defendant should rest his defence upon a denial of the parol contract and of any act of part performance, the plaintiff would be able to succeed by proving only that part of his bill which, if it stood alone, would be demurrable; although the allegation that there had been any act of part performance was utterly without foundation. If I should find authority for such a position, which appears to me to be so repugnant to the doctrines of pleading, and to sound sense, I should not, sitting in this Court at least, feel bound to accede to it, unless it was the decision of some Court of appellate jurisdiction.

The question which arises upon the merits of the case is one which may present itself in different lights to different persons. For myself, I must say that, after

---

(a) 2 DeG. & Sm. 265.        (b) Wood v. Midgely, 5 DeG. M. & G. 41.

the most careful consideration that I am able to give
the case, I cannot satisfy my mind from the evidence
that any act whatever has been done by the plaintiff
under the terms of, or by force of any agreement of
• purchase and sale; or which can be unequivocally
referred to such an agreement, assuming such an agreement to have been finally concluded between the plaintiff
and the deceased, of which fact also the evidence fails
to satisfy me.

1871.

Butler
v.
Church.

[The learned Judge then entered into a minute examination of the evidence, and concluded that in his opinion
the bill should be dismissed with costs.]

GALT, J., concurred in the views expressed by the
Chief Justice.

Judgment.

*Per Curiam—Appeal dismissed with costs*
[DRAPER, C. J., GWYNNE and GALT, JJ.,
dissenting.]

---

## HANCOCK v. McILROY.

*Practice—Married woman moving without next friend—Evidence of debtor
after death of creditor.*

On an appeal against the report of the Master by a married woman
and her husband, defendants in the suit, it is not necessary that
the married woman should have a next friend; such case differing
from an application by a married woman alone.

In a suit by the assignee of a mortgage, brought against the mortgagors (who had covenanted with the assignee that the whole mortgage money was due), one of the mortgagors is not a competent
witness to prove a payment to the mortgagee in his life time.

This was an appeal from a report made under a
decree of reference in a foreclosure suit, and was heard
by Vice Chancellor *Mowat.*

27—VOL. XVIII. GR.

The appeal turned chiefly on the evidence, and at the close of the argument was dismissed with costs.

The points stated in the head note were ruled by the Court after argument.

Mr. *S. Blake,* for the appeal.

Mr. *McMichael*, Mr. *English*, and Mr. *Hoskin*, contra.

---

WALKER v. NILES.

*Chattel mortgage—Interest—Mistake—True copy—Statement.*

An immaterial variation between a chattel mortgage and the copy subsequently filed does not invalidate the re-filing.

A mistake in the number of the lot where the chattels were, was held to be immaterial under the circumstances.

The statement annexed to the affidavit filed with the copy of the mortgage, did not give distinctly all the information required by the Act, but the affidavit and statement together contained all that was necessary : *Held*, sufficient.

The statement contained an item of $2.25 as paid for re-filing, which the mortgagee had no right to charge : *Held*, not to vitiate the instrument.

A chattel mortgage was given for $1070 ; it afterwards appeared that the amount was made up in part of a promissory note made and given by the mortgagee to the mortgagor at the time of the execution of the mortgage, and not paid for some months afterwards : *Held*, that in the absence of fraud the mortgage was valid.

Statement. The plaintiff in this case having obtained a writ of execution against the defendant, the sheriff seized under it certain chattels (amounting to $921), which were claimed by one *Samuel Doolittle*, under a mortgage thereof given to him by the defendant before the

issuing of the writ.  This claim was sent for trial be- 1871.
fore a jury at the assizes, and resulted in a verdict
for the claimant, subject to certain questions as to the
validity of the mortgage in point of law.  These questions were afterwards discussed before Vice Chancellor
*Mowat* by

Walker
v.
Niles.

Mr. *S. Blake*, and Mr. *Kerr*, (of Cobourg), for the
claimant.

Mr. *Moss*, contra.

MOWAT, V. C.—The mortgage in question in this
cause was given to secure $1070 with interest.  Of
this sum, it appears from the evidence that part,
viz., $500 or $550, was for a promissory note made
and delivered by the mortgagee to the mortgagor
at the time of the execution of the mortgage, and
not paid until some months afterwards.  It was
argued, that such a mortgage was invalid; that if
not necessarily invalid the fact of that portion of the
mortgage money being for this note should have
been stated in the mortgage; and that the mortgagee's
affidavit was to the extent of that sum incorrect in
saying that the mortgagor was justly and truly indebted to the mortgagee in the amount of the mortgage money.  Apart from the Act for the registration
of chattel mortgages, it is clear that this objection is
not sustainable.  It would, perhaps, be sound policy for
the Legislature to require that chattel mortgages should
set forth the exact nature of the debt; and one sees
the danger of fraud which arises from a transaction
like the present.  But it is conceded that the plaintiff
*Walker* has failed to make out that there was any
fraud in the present case; and there is no rule of law
forbidding such a transaction as this was—provided
that it be honest and *bona fide*, or requiring that it
should be set forth in the mortgage.  The mortgagor

March 8

Judgment.

1871.

Walker
v.
Niles.

accepted the note as cash, and the amount thereby became a debt from him; but if the mortgagee could not truly make the affidavit in such a case, it would follow, according to *Baldwin* v. *Benjamin* (a), recognized in *Mathers* v. *Lynch* (b), that the case is not within the operation of the Act, and that compliance with any of the provisions of the Act was unnecessary in order to the validity of the transaction. The circumstance of a note having been given by the mortgagee for $500 (or $550) distinguishes the case from *Robinson* v. *Patterson* (c).

The next objection was, that the mortgage had not been duly renewed after the expiration of the year. The Act requires, that within thirty days next preceding the expiration of the year, "a true copy" of the mortgage should be filed, "together with a statement exhibiting the interest of the mortgagee in the property

Judgment.

claimed by virtue thereof, and a full statement of the amount still due for principal and interest thereon, and of all payments made on account thereof;" and an affidavit of the mortgagee, "stating that such statements are true," &c. It was said, that the paper filed as a copy of the mortgage was not a true copy; and that the "statement" filed did not contain the particulars which the statute requires.

The incorrectness of the copy is this: The copy describes the chattels as one span of horses, &c., one piano, &c., "being now in the possession of the mortgagor, and in the house and barn and on the premises occupied by him, situated on lot number *ten* on the broken front concession of the township of Haldimand." The mortgagor did not occupy number ten, but did occupy number two. If this mistake had occurred

---

(a) 16 U. C. Q. B. 52.          (b) 28 U. C. Q. B. 354.
(c) 18 Ib. 55.

in the mortgage as well as the copy, the mistake would not have vitiated the mortgage (a) ; the number of the lot might be rejected as surplusage, the description otherwise being sufficient within the authorities to identify the chattels for the purposes of the Act (b). But the original mortgage has, in place of the distinctly written word *ten,* a scribble which may be read *two* or *ten*; which the writer intended for *two*; and which the person who made the copy read and copied as *ten.* Is this variation fatal ? In *Armstrong* v. *Ausman* (c) the copy had given as the mortgagor's name *Montgomery,* while the mortgage had named him *Mongomery,* omitting the *t ;* the copy had also *he* for *him,* and *they* for *them* ; had the word *his* where it was not in the original ; had not the word *the* where it was in the original ; and gave the name of a subscribing witness while there was no subscribing witness to the mortgage. It was not therefore a true copy, according to the strictest sense of that expression; but nevertheless it was held to be a true copy within the meaning of the Act. All the Judges appear to have agreed that none of the variances except the last was material on the point ; and as to the last, there was a difference of opinion, but a majority of the Judges held that that was immaterial also ; and one of them in giving judgment made the following remarks, which appear to be just : " It is always understood * * that in transcribing, some different words may be used and others left out, provided the sense or meaning is not altered, and then the instrument itself is not vitiated ; and if the instrument itself be good, I do not see but the same rule will prevail with the copy, and that in common parlance such variations do not prevent our saying it is a true copy. * * The re-filing of a security must be done in consequence of a security having previously

---

(a) White v. Haight 11 Gr. 420.

(b) See Mills v. King, 14 U. C. C. P. 223.

(c) 11 U. C. Q. B. 498.

1871.

Walker
v.
Niles.

existed, and been registered and filed; and the one is necessarily by its very terms a continuation of the other; and therefore on searching or looking at the last it shews that the security had existed before. It does not appear to me that the addition of the name of a witness renders it less a copy of the other, and I do not think the addition vitiates." A copy for some purposes would not be sufficient if it varied as this does; but what is the purpose of this copy? The original is filed with the same officer as the copy, and is as open to inspection by every body; and the erroneous word does not ascribe to the mortgage a different legal effect or operation. It having been decided that it is not necessary that every word in the one should be the same as in the other, I cannot satisfy myself that any slip in copying, which has not the effect of ascribing a different effect to the original from what the original bears, can be regarded as vitiating the re-filing.

Judgment. Nor, considering that the original is there for inspection, and forming the best opinion which I can of the purpose of requiring the subsequent filing of a copy, do I wish to be understood as intimating an opinion that any mistake which might affect the construction of the instrument in some respect or other, should, on that account, be held necessarily to vitiate the proceeding. If the variation was not inadvertent, the case might be very different.

The " statement " filed was as follows :—

" STATEMENT.

"1868.

           Amount of mortgage consideration,   $1,070 00
" Jan. 4.     " Interest thereon..................     64 20
           " Paid the renewal ..............     2 25

                              $1,136 45

           SAMUEL DOOLITTLE.

" Dated at Cobourg, 23rd Dec., 1869."

These particulars, if they stood alone and were verified by an affidavit swearing only that "such statements are true," would seem insufficient according to *O'Halloran* v. *Sills* (a); but it was admitted that the averments of the affidavit, if they can be read to supplement the so-called "statement," are sufficient to remove the objection. The mortgagee swears, amongst other things, "that there is still justly due and owing to him, on account of said mortgage, the sum of $1,136.45, as shewn by the subjoined statement." The affidavit and statement are written on the same side of the same leaf; and, as together they gave all the particulars required by the Act, the question is, whether this is insufficient, because the "subjoined statement" does not of itself contain a statement of the particulars which in *O'Halloran* v. *Sills* neither the statement nor the affidavit contained? The error there was, in omitting to state "either that the amount stated to be due is due on the mortgage, or on the debt secured by it; or that it is due to the mortgagee, or that he is still interested in the property as mortgagee; he may have assigned it [it was said], and the assignee may have been paid, and yet the statement as it stands may be true." The affidavit had "only set out that the mortgagor is indebted to the mortgagee in the sum mentioned as set forth in the statement, without specifying upon what account."

By the Act 12 Victoria., ch. 74, the statement was required, but no affidavit of verification was necessary; the affidavit is an addition made by the statute 20 Victoria. The term "statement" is not a technical one; and any paper containing in any form the necessary information would be a statement. A sworn statement is as much a statement as if it were not sworn. I see no objection, under either statute, to the statement being

---

(a) 12 U. C. Q. B. 465.

1871. in the form of an affidavit, for neither statute prescribes
the form. What is material obviously is, that certain

Walker
v.
Niles.

information should be given, and that that information
should be sworn to; and, considering that the Courts
have found themselves constrained to sanction a
departure from the strict letter of the statute in the
decision already referred to, as to the filing of a true
copy of the mortgage, and in the description which
shall be deemed a sufficient description of the chattels
under the Act (a), as well as in other cases not deemed
to interfere with the substantial and true intention
and policy of the Act (b), I perceive no principle on
which to hold that every particular that the statute
requires must be in a paper distinct from the affidavit,
and must be expressed in terms embodying all the information, without any reference to, or assistance from,
the affidavit. Against this view there are some observations of Chief Justice *Draper*, in *O'Halloran* v. *Sills*

Judgment. (c), and no observations of a Canadian Judge can have
more authority than his; but, as the opinion which he
there expressed on this point was not necessary for
the decision of the case before him, and does not
appear to have been concurred in by the other Judges,
I have come to the conclusion, after considerable hesitation, that I am not at liberty to act on the view
which his Lordship intimated on this point, in opposition to what seems to myself the spirit of the later
authorities, and the just and equitable construction of
the statute.

It was further contended, that the mortgagee had
no right to charge the $2.25 "paid for renewal," and
that his including it in the statement vitiated the
statement. In *Fraser* v. *The Bank of Toronto* (d) an

---

(a) Powell v. Bank of Upper Canada, 11 U. C. C. P. 303; Mills v.
King, 14 *ib.*, see 240, 241; Mathers v. Lynch, 28 U. C. Q. B., at 365.
(b) Mathers v. Lynch, 28 U. C. Q. B. 354.
(c) Supra.                         (d) 19 U. C. Q. B. 381, at 388.

objection was taken that the mortgagee had included
three days' extra interest, which on the sum due would
be about one pound. The Court held that he had not
included too much; but said also: "We should never
hold the object of refiling to be defeated, and the
security lost, by a mistake of that kind, if there was a
mistake. Clearly no fraud was intended, and the act
was complied with, even if the amount due was by
any inadvertence stated at a few shillings too much."
I think the charge in the present case falls within the
principle of these observations, and does not avoid the
re-filing.

The plaintiff *Walker's* motion must therefore be
refused with costs.

---

## RAE V. GEDDES.

*Vendor and purchaser—Acceptance of title.*

An abstract of title and the title deeds having been sent to a purchaser
in November, 1869, at his own request, for the purposes of examination and advice, he retained the same for a considerable time, intimated no objection to the title, and in correspondence with the
vendor's solicitors implied that he was content with the title; but in
June, 1870, he claimed the right of investigating it afresh :

*Held,* that by the lapse of time and the letters which he had written he
had impliedly accepted the title.

On a sale by a person whose title is derived under a Chancery purchase, a question as to whether the legal estate was effectually conveyed to him under such purchase is, on a subsequent sale of the
property, a question of conveyance, not of title.

On the 28th September, 1869, the defendant entered
into an agreement for the purchase, from the plaintiff,
of six lots of land on King Street, in the City of Hamilton, at the price of $2,000, one fourth cash, and the
residue in five equal annual instalments with interest.

28—VOL. XVIII. GR.

1871. The defendant's object in purchasing was to use the
ground as a site for a chapel and school house.
Afterwards the Building Committee disapproved of so
much land being taken, and the defendant, in consequence, wrote to the plaintiff's solicitors requesting to be
relieved from the contract; and proposing, if that
request should not be acceded to, that, in carrying out
the transaction, other persons whom he named should
be substituted for himself, as grantees of some of the
lots. The proposal to rescind was declined; and as to
the alternative proposal, the answer was in these terms:
" With regard to the details of the conveyance and
mortgage, I will consult the convenience of the members
of the Committee in every possible way; and I would
consider the plan named by you as perfectly satisfac-
factory." That letter was dated the 6th of October,
1869.

On the 14th of October, the plaintiff's solicitors wrote
to the defendant, stating that, if he had named any
one to examine into the title of the King Street lots,
on his advising them, they would be prepared to proceed therein at once. On the 6th of November the
defendant replied as follows: " Have you an abstract
of the title to the property we have agreed to purchase
from Dr. Rae? If so, would you kindly furnish us
with it, and we shall then be prepared to close the
negotiation. An early answer will oblige."

On the 11th of November the abstract was sent.
This document did not contain the full particulars
usual in English abstracts, but was in the short form
ordinarily adopted in this country. It began with the
title of *James Mills*, which was stated, in the letter
that accompanied the abstract, to be well known and
established, and which the solicitors presumed the
defendant would not wish to go behind, but they offered
to give the antecedent title if the defendant desired it.

Rae
v.
Geddes.

Statement.

The plaintiff's title appeared by this abstract to be a
registered title, and to be derived under a deed from
*Mills* to *John W. Hunter*, in 1838, and a sale by this
Court of the estate of *Hunter* in these and other lots
to the plaintiff, in 1853.

1871.

Rae
v.
Geddes

The abstract, on being received by the defendant,
was delivered by him to Mr. *Martin*, solicitor, who
was a member of the Building Committee. Being
desirous of inspecting the deeds, &c., Mr. *Martin* asked
the defendant to write for them. The defendant wrote
accordingly on the 17th of November, and stated in his
letter that on seeing these, they would be better able
to judge " whether they desired anything further." The
deeds, &c., were sent on the 19th of November, and, on
being received by the defendant, were immediately
delivered by him to the solicitor.

From the time of thus receiving the abstract and
deeds, in November, until June following, neither the
defendant nor any one for him made any objection or
requisition in regard to the title, or gave any intimation
that the title was not satisfactory, or that the defendant or those associated with him " desired anything
further."

Statement.

Several weeks after the deeds had been sent, viz., on
the 17th December, the plaintiff's solicitors wrote to
the defendant pressing " to have the sale concluded as
speedily as possible."

The defendant delayed answering that letter until
the 28th. In his letter of that date he asked nothing
further in regard to the title ; and said that he saw no
reason " why the sale might not be concluded during
the first week in January ;" he proposed the names of
persons whom he wished to substitute in the conveyance of some of the lots, for those he had named in

October ; asked whether the plaintiff's solicitors had
any objection that the deeds should "be prepared
accordingly, and forwarded for execution, together
with the first payment;" and promised that on hearing
from them he would "see the matter immediately attended to."

.The plaintiff's solicitors appear, from a subsequent
letter, to have thereupon written to the plaintiff, who
resided in Europe, informing him of the letter of the 28th,
and stating that he might confidently expect the first
payment to be remitted in ten days. They also wrote to
the defendant, (29th December,) acceding to his proposal to get the deeds prepared, and expressing their
desire to have the transaction completed by the first
week in January.   However, it was not completed then.
On the 8th of January the defendant wrote to the
plaintiff's solicitors, informing them that in endeavoring to conclude the arrangements for the purchase,
he had met with fresh and unexpected difficulties ;
that the persons who were to take some of the lots had
declined doing so ; and that as soon as he had anything
decided to communicate, he would do so.   In consequence of these difficulties, the defendant had further
correspondence with the plaintiff's solicitors, and with
the plaintiff himself, with a view to induce them to
relieve him from his purchase.   This correspondence
came to an end in May, 1870.   Messrs. *Martin & Bruce*
then commenced a correspondence as the defendant's
solicitors.  The plaintiff's solicitors insisted that the title
had been accepted, but intimated that they were willing
to give any further satisfaction in regard to it which
might be desired.   The defendant's solicitors declined
to consider the title, as long as the plaintiff denied their
right to object.   The present bill was therefore filed on
the 18th of July, 1870.

The cause came on for hearing at the Spring Sittings
of the Court in Toronto, in 1871.

The only point argued by the counsel was, whether the defendant had or had not a right to insist upon a reference to the Master to inquire whether there was a good title, or whether he had not waived his right to having a good title shewn; counsel for the plaintiff contending that what had taken place in the course of the correspondence between the parties amounted to an acceptance of the title.

Mr. *James MacLennan,* for the plaintiff.

Mr. *Bethune,* for the defendant.

MOWAT, V.C.—The only issue raised by the pleadings is, whether the defendant had accepted the title or waived his right to any further investigation of it. To establish the acceptance or waiver, counsel for the plaintiff relied on the lapse of time before any objection had been made, and on the defendant's correspondence, particularly his letter of the 29th December; counsel for the defendant disputed the sufficiency of this evidence. The defendant deposed that he had not intended to accept the title; and his counsel argued that waiver was matter of intention; that there can be no waiver without an intention to waive.

Lord *St. Leonards* says, that "the question in each case is one of fact; did the purchaser mean to waive, and has he actually waived, his right of examining the title? although his intention will be inferred from his acts, and no direct expression of it is required. His silence, as we shall see, may be tantamount to the clearest expression of being content with the title" (*a*). "A purchaser may by simple acquiescence be held to have waived objections to the title, although he has not taken possession" (*b*). The Court does "not allow

*1871.*

*Rae
v.
Geddes.*

*April 5.*

*Judgment.*

_____

(*a*) V. & P. 14th ed. p. 342.     (*b*) *Ib.* 446.

a purchaser to dispute his acts which constitute an acceptance of the title shewn, by afterwards saying that he did not so intend them" (a).

In the present case, there is the "silence" of the defendant and the solicitor as to any objection, from the 11th November when the abstract was sent, and the 19th November when the deeds, &c., were forwarded, until the month of June following. A much shorter silence, in the case of so simple a title as this abstract shewed, would afford just ground for inferring the purchaser's contentment with the title, and his acceptance of it, than in case of the long and complicated titles which are the rule on English sales. But in *Pegg* v. *Wisden,* before the Master of the Rolls (b), "a purchaser having retained the abstract for five months, made no objection to the title, but simply required the vendor to verify the abstract with the title deeds; held, that he must be deemed to have accepted the title."

There is, however, not merely the lapse of time without any objection being intimated; but there is the correspondence, which deals with other matters in connection with the completion of the purchase, and asks for nothing further than had been furnished in regard to the title. I think that the plaintiff's solicitors' reading of the letter of the 29th December, as intimating the defendant's contentment with the title, was a natural and reasonable reading of it. I think that that letter, and the subsequent letters of the defendant, implied that nothing further was required as to the title; and that all which remained was, the arrangements for paying the money, and the conveyances. The loss of time for making the title acceptable, between December, 1869, and June following, evidently arose from the

---

(a) Bown v. Stenson, 24 Beav. 631; Margravine of Anspach v. Noel,
1 Madd. 310.                    (b) 16 Beav. 239.

reliance of the plaintiff's solicitors on that position of
the defendant; and I think that the defendant is
bound by it. I refer to *Fleetwood* v. *Green* (a), *Bur-*
*roughs* v. *Oakley* (b), *Clive* v. *Beaumont* (c), *Simpson*
v. *Sadd (d)*, and *Sweet* v. *Meredith* (e).

On behalf of the defendant, there was offered in
evidence a correspondence which had passed between the
plaintiff's and defendant's solicitors since the suit was
begun. For the plaintiff it was objected, that this correspondence was no evidence of anything in the pleadings;
that it is inadmissible without a supplemental answer,
and that, if received, the plaintiff should have an
opportunity of shewing that it was expressly agreed
that this correspondence should be without prejudice.
Counsel for defendant did not apply for leave to file a
supplemental answer. I reserved the question, and on
consideration, am of opinion that this correspondence
must be excluded. It may save expense, however, if I *Judgment.*
say that the only material question which appears
from this correspondence, is, whether the legal estate
in the property was effectually conveyed by the deeds
which have been executed in completion of the
plaintiff's purchase at the Chancery sale; and that
was held in *Jumpson* v. *Pitchers (f)* to be an objection, not of title, but of conveyance.

I think that the plaintiff is entitled to a decree with
costs.

---

(a) 15 Ves. 594.                    (b) 3 Sw. at 170, 171.
(c) 1 DeG. & Sm. 397.
(d) 2 Sm. & Giff. at 475; S. C. 4 D. M. & G. 673.
(e) 8 Jur. N. S. 637; see also cases *supra*.
(f) 1 Colly. 13.

1871.

BRIGHAM V. SMITH.

*Practice—Appeal from the Master—Statute of Limitations.*

An objection of the Statute of Limitations cannot be made by an
appellant against the Master's report without having been taken
before the Master.

March 8.     This was an appeal from the Master's report allowing the claim of a creditor, one *McPherson*.   The chief
objection urged on appeal was that the claim had been
barred by the Statute of Limitations.

Mr. *Fitzgerald*, for the appeal.

Mr. S. *Blake*, contra.

The Court held that, the objection not having been
taken in the Master's office, it was not open to the
plaintiff on appeal.

———

PHILLIPS V. ZIMMERMAN.

*Dower, arrears of—Gift to heir.*

Where the annual value of a widow's dower was not large, and she
made no demand for it, but resided on the property with her son,
the heir, during his life, she having no intention of claiming
dower, a claim for arrears against his estate after his death was
refused.

On an appeal in this case from the report of the
Master at Brantford, dated 4th February, 1871, the
question argued was, the right of the widow of *Jacob
Zimmerman* to arrears of dower.   Her husband had
died intestate 19 years before, leaving *Elias Zimmerman*, their son, his heir-at-law.   Up to that time they
were all living on the farm in respect of which the
present question arose.   The widow was about 60

years old when her husband died. She continued to
live on the place with the son until the death of the
latter on the 14th May, 1869. The son died unmarried.
For the last ten years of his life (whether longer did
not appear), he had employed a housekeeper, who did
most of the work of the house, his mother giving some
assistance. In the widow's evidence she said, that a
housekeeper could do all the work ; that formerly she
had many a time done it all herself; but that at the
time of giving her evidence she was too old to do much.
It further appeared from her evidence, that she had
had some money of her own ($600), which she had
received after her husband's death; that she had lent
part of this money ; and that she had used part in
buying furniture for the house, and part towards her
own support; how much for these purposes respectively,
she did not state. She further said, that during her
son's life she had never claimed dower ; that as long
as he lived she would have said nothing about it ; and
that she had not expected to survive him.

1871.

Phillips
v.
Zimmerman.

The Master at Brantford by his report found, that
the widow was entitled to six years' arrears of dower,
the Master being of opinion, (1) that the absence of a
demand for dower was no bar in equity as between a
widow and the heir-at-law, and (2) that her services and
the use of the furniture were more than equivalent to
the support which she had received from her son. His
opinion on both points was controverted on the appeal.

Mr. *W. N. Miller*, for the appeal.

Mr. *Wilson*, contra.

Mowat, V. C.—A demand is necessary to entitle a
widow to recover arrears at law ; and the 'right to
dower is a legal right in regard to which equity in
most respects follows the law. The first question for

March 8.

Judgment.

29—VOL. XVIII. GR.

the Master in the present case was, whether as between the widow and heir, the rule in equity is not different ?

In *Dormer* v. *Fortescue (a)* Lord *Hardwicke* declared the rule to be, that if the widow was obliged to come into equity because of the existence of an outstanding term, or because she could not, without the aid of an equity Court, ascertain the lands out of which she was dowable, the Court would give her arrears from the time her title had accrued, and not merely from the time of her demand. Originally the Court seems to have assumed jurisdiction in dower on the ground of special circumstances such as Lord *Hardwicke* thus referred to ; but now no special circumstances are necessary to sustain such a suit. *Curtis* v. *Curtis (b)* seems an express authority that in all cases in which the Court entertains jurisdiction, mesne profits are given against the heir from the death of the husband ; and

Judgment.

that view was acted on by Sir *William Grant* in *Oliver* v. *Richardson (c)*.

Referring to the text books, I find that Mr. *Roper* states the law in accordance with these cases (*d*). In *Tudor's* Real Property Cases (*e*) it is laid down, that " in equity she may have an account of the rents and profits from the death of her husband ;" and in *Seton's* Forms the direction given is for an account from the husband's death (*f*). On the other hand, it appears from Lord *Redesdale's* book on Pleading (*g*) that his opinion was, that the rule of law should be followed, " unless particular circumstances had occurred to warrant a departure from the course of common law;" and in a note reference is made to *Curtis* v. *Curtis* as if it were an exceptional case, as far as it was a case in

---

(*a*) 3 Atk. 124.          (*b*) 2 B. C. C. 620.
(*c*) 9 Ves. 222.          (*d*) P. 453, &c.
(*e*) P. 71.               (*f*) See also 1 St. Eq. Jur.
(*g*) See p. 145, 5th ed.      sec. 625.

which "this rule had not been observed." *Oliver* v. 1871.
*Richardson* is not referred to. Mr. *Jacobs* in his notes
to Mr. *Roper's* book took the same view (*a*).

But if there is some conflict of authority as to
whether, in the absence of any demand, a widow is
*primâ facie* entitled to arrears, the absence of any
demand may be at all events a material element for
consideration where the amount is small, and the widow
has, since the husband's death, continued to live on the
property with her son, and received her support,
wholly or mainly, from him. In such a case there are
some analogies which more or less support the view of
the appellants. A joint tenant, or tenant in common,
cannot claim arrears from a co-tenant who has occupied
their joint property, unless the claimant was excluded
from the possession. Where a husband has paid for a
wife's apparel and provided for her private expenses,
she cannot, after his death, claim arrears of pin money;
or if a wife has tacitly permitted her husband to receive
the income of her separate property, and he has applied
it from year to year for their common benefit, she cannot afterwards claim the money from his estate (*b*). So,
the intention of a parent in favor of a child, as made
out by circumstances, has been enforced in equity after
the parent's death (*c*). Dower is defined to be that
estate which a widow acquires in a certain portion of
her husband's real property after his death for her
support and maintenance (*d*); and though the fact of
her receiving such support and maintenance from the
heir may be no absolute bar at law, in case by a
demand for dower she has entitled herself to mesne
profits there (*e*), yet where the amount to which she
was entitled would be so moderate a sum as $90 a

*Judgment.*

---

(*a*) P. 454, 2nd ed.; see Bright on Husband and Wife, p. 419, *et seq.*
(*b*) 1 Wh. & Tud. 457.
(*c*) See Long v. Long, 16 Gr. 242, and cases there cited.
(*d*) 1 Cruise 151.      (*e*) Robinett v. Lewis, Draper, 269.

1871. year, and the widow, instead of demanding dower,
Phillips lives on the property with her son, the heir, as she had
v. done with her husband, and is shewn by her own
Zimmerman. confession to have had no intention of claiming dower
against her son, I think that, in general, she ought not
to be permitted after her son's death to set up a claim
for arrears against his estate. I think that in the
present case, if the widow's dower was of greater
value than her support, after making all just allowances,—which I am not prepared to say on the
evidence that it was,—a gift of the difference may,
and should, be inferred; and that such a gift is so far
enforcible in equity, that she may not be permitted
afterwards to enforce against her son's estate a claim
for arrears (a).

On the whole I think that the appeal should be
allowed, without costs as respects the widow; the
Judgment appellants will receive their costs out of the estate.

---

### GILPIN V. WEST.

*Trustee and cestui que trust—Purchase by trustee from one cestui que trust.*

By virtue of a will *A.* had a life interest in certain lands, with remainder to the plaintiff in fee. The land was afterwards sold at sheriff's
sale under circumstances which made the sale void in equity, and
the purchaser a trustee for the devisees. *A.* (the life-tenant) for
valuable consideration conveyed his life-interest to the purchaser:
*Held*, that the plaintiff could not claim the benefit of that transaction.

Examination of witnesses and hearing at the Spring
Sittings of 1871, at Cobourg.

*Samuel Gilpin,* by his last will, devised the south-
half of lot No. 5 in the 7th concession of Seymour to

---

(a) See Long v. Long, 16 Gr. 239; S. C. on rehearing, 17 *ib.* 251.

*Mary Carr*, his daughter, for life; remainder to the
Rev. *George Carr*, her husband, for life; remainder to
the plaintiff in fee. The three devisees survived the
testator, but *Mary Carr* was dead before the filing of
the bill. The plaintiff was a minor at the testator's
death, and had recently come of age. One of the
executors proved the will for the purpose of giving
to the defendant *William West* a confession of judgment, to which he thought that in justice *West* was
entitled. The executor did not act otherwise in the
affairs of the estate. Judgment was entered on this
confession; execution was issued against the testator's lands; and the devised property was sold thereunder to one *James West*, who bought for *William
West*, and conveyed to him immediately after receiving the sheriff's deed.

At the hearing, the Vice Chancellor held, that the
debt claimed by *William West* was not due; and that,
under circumstances proved, the sheriff's deed and
the deed to *William West* were void in equity against
the plaintiff.

The bill prayed, that these deeds might be declared
void against both the plaintiff and *Carr;* and that if
any legal interest passed thereunder, *William West*
should be declared a trustee of it for the plaintiff and
*Carr*, and should convey the same to them. *Carr*,
however, by his answer, stated that he had conveyed
his interest to *William West*, and he disclaimed all
further interest in the property. It appeared by the
evidence that this conveyance was after suit, but in
pursuance of an agreement made previously.

Mr. *James MacLennan* and Mr. *S. M. Jarvis*, for the
plaintiff.

Mr. *Blake*, Q.C., and Mr. *Armour*, Q.C., for defendants.

*1871.*

Gilpin
v.
West.

Statement.

MOWAT, V. C.—Counsel for the plaintiff claimed that *William West* having, by means of the impeached transactions, become a trustee for the plaintiff, the plaintiff was entitled to the benefit of the purchase by *West* from *Carr*. I reserved judgment as to this point, and on reflection I am clear that the plaintiff is not so entitled. *West* by means of the impeached deeds was a trustee for *Carr* as to his life interest, and for the plaintiff as to the remainder in fee; and had a perfect right, as between himself and the plaintiff, to purchase for *West's* own benefit the interest of *Carr*, the other *cestui que trust*. That accords with what I held in *King* v. *Keating (a)*; one point in the subsequent case of *Baldwin* v. *Thomas (b)* was to the same effect; and I know of no authority to the contrary.

The decree, therefore, will declare the two impeached deeds to be void in equity against the plaintiff; will declare *William West* to be a trustee for the plaintiff of any legal interest which *West* may have in the remainder in fee after *Carr's* death, and will vest the same in the plaintiff accordingly. *West* will pay the plaintiff's costs. The defendants, being friendly to one another, do not desire, I presume, any adjudication with respect to their costs as between themselees.

---

(a) 12 Gr. 29.                    (b) 15 Gr. at p. 122.

## GORDON V. HARNDEN.

*Vendor and purchaser—Construction of agreement—Title to be shewn—*
*Waiver.*

*A.* agreed to sell to *B.* "all his right, title, and interest," in certain
specified property "owned by" *A.*, and to "give a good and sufficient deed of the said land free of all incumbrances:"
*Held*, that the vendor was bound to shew a good title.

Before an abstract was asked for, the purchaser had sold small portions of the land, and he and his vendees had cut down some of
the wood thereon; but the vendor, notwithstanding, promised
afterwards to give an abstract as demanded, and delivered an
abstract accordingly:
*Held*, that the plaintiff was entitled to have this abstract verified.

Hearing at Whitby Spring Sittings, 1871.

This was a suit upon a contract entered into
on the 2nd April, 1870, for the sale of a lot of
land in the township of Reach. The agreement
was in writing, signed by both parties, and was as Statement.
follows: "This agreement witnesseth, that *Benjamin
Harnden* of the first part, yeoman, and *Adam Gordon*
of the second part, merchant, bargain as follows: That
the said party of the first part does hereby sell all his
right, title, and interest, to the said party of the second
part, in the north-half of the south-half of lot No. 7,
in the 3rd concession of the township of Reach, in the
County of Ontario, or the whole of the said portion
of land owned by said party of the first part, the same
being fifty acres more or less,—on condition that the
said party of the second part pays to the said party of
the first part the sum of $1,615 of lawful money of
Canada; the payment of $15 of the said sum is hereby
acknowledged; and the remaining portion of the said
sum on or before the 1st day of December next ensuing;
on payment of which sum being duly made or tendered,
the said party of the first part will give a good and
sufficient deed of said land, free of all incumbrances,
to said party of second part."

Mr. *S. Blake* and Mr. *Gordon*, for plaintiff.

Mr. *Fitzgerald* and Mr. *P. Hurd*, for defendants.

June 24.　MOWAT, V.C.—The first question argued was, whether the defendant *Harnden* was bound to shew a good title. Looking at the whole instrument, I think that it does not contain enough to relieve him from that ordinary obligation of a vendor. That which is sold is described to be " all his right, title, and interest," in the lot. But it is to be remembered, that an ordinary agreement to sell land is stated in the books to be " an agreement to sell the whole of the vendor's interest therein;" and that "such interest, if not described, will be inferred to be an estate in fee simple " (*a*).

Whatever might be thought of the words referred to, if they had stood alone in the contract in question, the meaning of the parties seems to me, upon consideration, to be made sufficiently certain by the land being described as " owned " by the vendor, and by his undertaking " to give a good and sufficient deed of said land, free of all incumbrances."

It was argued, that the plaintiff had waived his right to a good title, if he ever had such a right. The waiver relied on was, his selling at auction part of the lot, in small parcels, on the 12th November, 1870, and the cutting down of a considerable quantity of the wood after that date by the plaintiff and his vendees. The defendant was present at this auction ; he encouraged those present to buy ; and he knew that it was for the sake of the wood, and of nothing else, that the parcels were being bought. I have no doubt, however, that he expected then that the plaintiff's purchase would be carried out by the 1st December. The abstract had

---

(*a*) See Dart's Vendors and Purchasers, 4th ed., p. 104.

not yet been called for. If these sales, and the sub-sequent cutting of the wood, amounted to a waiver of the plaintiff's right to call for the title, their effect in that respect was removed by the defendant's subsequent proceedings. Shortly before the 1st December, the plaintiff demanded an abstract. Mr. *Hurd*, the defendant's solicitor, at an interview with the plaintiff's solicitor, on the 13th or 14th December, promised to furnish an abstract, and to produce the title deeds, the plaintiff's solicitor consenting to accept what is called a Registrar's abstract, instead of the more full document to which a purchaser has a right. On the 29th December, the abstract was delivered to the plaintiff; the plaintiff's solicitor, being satisfied with the title as shewn by this abstract, applied, on the 2nd January, 1871, to Mr. *Hurd*, by letter, for the title deeds and evidences of title ; on the following day, the defendant personally promised the plaintiff that these should be furnished; and, on the strength of that promise, he obtained from the plaintiff $75 on account of the purchase money. The delivery of the abstract is sufficient alone to answer the argument that the question of title had been waived; and if the plaintiff was entitled to an abstract, he was entitled to have it verified, even if the defendant had not promised the deeds.

The defendant, however, it seems, was not ready to produce the deeds, and, unfortunately, was advised that he was not bound to produce them. He therefore commenced an action at law for the purchase money, and the plaintiff filed the present bill to restrain the action, and to have the deeds and other evidences of title produced for inspection, and for further relief. The plaintiff is content with the title as shewn by the abstract, subject to its being verified ; and I think that the prayer of the bill is sufficient to enable me to make the decree to which, in that view, the plaintiff

1871.

Gordon
v.
Harnden.

Judgment.

is entitled. I am satisfied that the plaintiff has been guilty of no wilful delay, though it is to be regretted that he was so late in applying for the abstract; this delay evidently arose from his not having at an earlier period referred to a solicitor, not having perceived occasion to refer to him before ; and cannot, in view of what occurred afterwards, militate against his now obtaining the decree, as to costs and otherwise, to which, in the absence of that circumstance, he would have been entitled. The decree, therefore, will declare, as in *Southby* v. *Hutt* (a), that the purchaser has accepted the title as set forth in the abstract, subject to the same being verified ; and will refer it to the Master to inquire and state whether the defendant can make out and verify the title so set forth. If he can, the contract is to be specifically performed ; an account taken of the purchase money, with interest from the 1st December, 1869, less the costs of the present suit; and the other usual directions given. If the title cannot be verified, further directions and costs had better be reserved.

---

## THE TRUST AND LOAN CO. OF CANADA V. BOULTON.

*Mortgage—Release of portions—Pleading—Usury—Amendment.*

First mortgagees with a power of sale released portions of the mortgaged property to the mortgagor : *Held*, that this did not give priority to a subsequent incumbrancer, with respect to the remainder of the property ; but might render the first mortgagees responsible to the second for the fair value of the parcels released.

An assignment to the Trust and Loan Company of a valid existing mortgage bearing more than eight per cent. interest, is not necessarily void.

The Court will not at the hearing of a cause allow an amendment or supplemental answer to let in evidence necessary for a defence of usury.

Hearing at the Kingston sittings, in the spring of 1871.

---

(a) 2 M. & C. at 219.

This was a suit of foreclosure by the plaintiffs, as assignees of a mortgage, against *Harriet Boulton*, the owner of the equity of redemption. The mortgage was dated the 30th December, 1843, and was given by the defendant's father, the Hon. *George S. Boulton*, to one *Jacob Corrigal*, to secure $2,400, with interest at six per cent., payable in 1845. On the 13th of June, 1849, the mortgage being unpaid was transferred by the executors of *Jacob Corrigal* to one *William Corrigal*. On the 2nd of July, 1849, *William Corrigal* assigned it to one *Nourse*. *Nourse* died, and *William Corrigal* being his executor, assigned the mortgage on the 15th of January, 1868, to *Asa Allworth Burnham*. On the 9th of February, 1869, a deed was executed by *Burnham* and the mortgagor, whereby the latter admitted $2,080 to be due on the mortgage, and agreed to pay interest thereon at ten per cent., and charged the property therewith; and in consideration thereof *Burnham* extended the time for paying the principal to the year 1871. On the 10th of April, 1869, *Burnham* transferred the mortgage to the plaintiffs.

The defendant's interest in the property is as a mortgagee, and as devisee of the equity of redemption. On the 20th of July, 1848, the Hon. *George S. Boulton*, the mortgagor, executed a second mortgage on the same premises to certain trustees for the defendant and her sister, Mrs. *Beck;* and on the 30th of January, 1854, the trustees transferred this mortgage to their *cestuis que* trust. On the 14th of February, 1869, the mortgagor died, having devised the mortgaged premises to the defendant.

Mr. *James MacLennan*, for the plaintiffs.

Mr. *Crooks*, Q. C., for the defendant.

MOWAT, V. C.—Two defences are set up. The first is, that, without the defendant's consent, and with full

*margin:* 1871.

Trust and Loan Co.
v.
Boulton.

June 24

Judgment.

1871.

Trust and
Loan Co.
v.
Boulton.

knowledge of the second mortgage, certain portions of the mortgaged property were released and discharged from the first mortgage, viz., by *Burnham*, on the 16th of May, 1868, to one *Striker*, and one *Meredith*, respectively; and the same parcels by *Jacob Corrigal*, previously. The defendant insists that the effect of these releases was, to wholly discharge the first mortgage, even as to the remaining portions of the mortgaged property. It was proved that *Corrigal* and *Burnham* were aware of the second mortgage when their respective releases were executed. But it appears, that, before any of the releases were executed, *Boulton* had made sales of the released parcels, and had executed conveyances to *Striker* and *Meredith*, the purchasers; that *Jacob Corrigal's* release was executed in 1865; that it was made to the mortgagor himself for the benefit of the purchasers; and that (as the deed shews) it was executed on the application of the mortgagor, and because the remainiug property was

Judgment. considered " abundantly sufficient to secure the amount due thereon." It is clear that this instrument had not the effect of releasing the remainder of the property, as between the parties to it (*a*). As between the first and second mortgagees, the effect would have been to postpone the first to the second (*b*), but for the circumstance stated in the bill, that the first mortgage contained a power of sale. Under that power, *Corrigal* was entitled to sell and convey any parts or portions of the mortgaged property; and he was entitled to foreclose in respect to the remainder of the property. If he conveyed for a nominal consideration only, he may have been responsible to the second mortgagees for the fair value of the parcels conveyed; and the present holders of the first mortgage may be in the same position; but these are matters for the Master's office.

---

(*a*) Crawford Armour, v. 13 Gr. 576.
(*b*) Bank of Montreal v. Hopkins, 9 Gr. 495, S. C. 3 E. & App. 459; Schoole v. Sall, 1 Sch. & L. 176; Gurney v. Seppings, 2 Ph. 40; Lockhart v. Hardy, 9 B. 349.

When *Burnham's* releases were executed to *Striker* and *Meredith* (16th May, 1869), the parcels named in these releases had ceased to be subject to the mortgage; and these releases clearly had no effect on *Burnham's* position.

The other defence is, "that the plaintiffs by the operation of the laws respecting interest, and by the terms of their charter and act of incorporation, are precluded from holding or enforcing the said indenture of mortgage in the bill mentioned, the interest thereupon reserved being at a higher rate than eight per cent. per annum; and that the said indenture of mortgage and assignment to the plaintiffs were and are in their hands void and of no effect, being in contravention of the said laws respecting interest, and in violation of the limitations and prohibitions imposed in and by the said charter and acts relating to the said plaintiffs, and that it should be so declared accordingly."

Now, the *bona fide* purchase of a valid mortgage at any rate by a private individual, was never within the operation of the usury laws; and an assignment to the plaintiffs of such a mortgage cannot be void under the usury laws, whatever it may be under the plaintiffs' charter and the acts of the legislature having express reference to the plaintiffs (a). If their purchase of a mortgage bearing ten per cent. is void under these acts, it must be because the sum they paid for it would yield to them more than eight per cent., and not merely because the mortgage reserved more than eight per cent. But the answer contains no allegation with reference to the amount which the plaintiffs paid for the mortgage, and rests this defence on the other ground, namely, that the mortgage reserved ten per

---

(a) 7 Vic. ch. 63, sec. 2; 8 Vic. ch. 96, sec. 2; 13 & 14 Vic. ch. 138, sec. 5.

cent. It would be contrary to the course of the Court, as I understand it, to allow an amendment or supplemental answer in case of a defence of this kind, or to look at any evidence bearing on it which is not in support of the allegations of the answer (*a*).

I think that the plaintiffs are entitled to a decree with the usual reference as to incumbrances. I make no special order as to costs ; the plaintiffs' costs will be dealt with as in ordinary cases of foreclosure.

---

### GRAHAM v. YEOMANS.

*Trustee for sale, duty and responsibility of.*

It is the duty of a trustee for sale to use all diligence to obtain the best price ; and where a trustee sold property at private sale, without previous advertisement, at a price lower than other persons were willing to give, and did not first communicate with these persons though informed of offers of the higher price made by them to one of the *cestuis que* trust ; the trustee was held responsible for the loss.

In such a case, the absence of any fraudulent motive in the trustee is no defence ; nor is evidence of witnesses that the property was worth no more than the trustee obtained for it.

The trustee deposed that he had disbelieved the statement of the *cestui que* trust :
*Held*, no excuse for not testing the truth of the statement by reference to the parties.

Statement.  Hearing at the sittings of the Court, at Kingston, in the spring of 1871.

The plaintiffs were the seven children of *Henry Graham*, who died on the 14th December, 1863 ; having first made his will, directing, that part of his estate

---

(*a*) See Emmons v. Crooks, 1 Gr. 159.

should be sold to pay his debts; that the residue should go to his children; and that his widow should be supported on his estate with them as long as she remained his widow. At the time of his death he was owner in fee of a lot of land in Camden, subject to a mortgage for $288.28 in favor of the defendant *John Yeomans*, which had become due in the previous March; this lot was the family homestead. The testator had also a leasehold interest in another lot (which was variously valued at from $400 to $600); and some farm stock and other chattels. The executors were *John Pomeroy*, since deceased, and *Richard Dowling*, a defendant in the cause. The executors did not prove the will until the 5th May, 1864; and they left the property, real and personal, in possession of the widow until after that date. All the children were then infants; the eldest of them came of age in February, 1870; the others being still minors when the cause was heard.

After the executors had proved, they were sued in the Division Court for the amount of an account due by the testator to one *Ham;* and, judgment having been recovered and execution issued, the chattels of the testator in the hands of the widow were seized by the bailiff. There appeared to have been an execution about the same time in the hands of the bailiff against the widow personally. *Yeomans* had before this offered to the executors $1000 for the homestead; others had applied to the widow, and offered a higher price, but had always replied to these that she did not wish to sell. She wished to save the homestead, and she hoped to do so by the leasehold and some of the other chattel property being sold; but the executors thought that these would not bring enough, and they decided, against the wishes and expostulations of the widow, that the homestead must be sold. On the 9th May, 1865, *Yeomans* placed the mortgage in the hands of a solicitor. On the 11th May, the bailiff's sale took place; and *Yeomans*, at the request of the executors, bought in a span of horses (the only chattels offered for sale) and settled the execution. He did this under an agreement with the executors that they might have the horses on paying the sum bid by him. Their means of doing this was to be by a sale of the land. *Yeomans* appeared to have about this time renewed his offer to buy at $1000; the executors now accepted the offer; told the widow that if she would release her dower they would pay to her one-third of the purchase money; to this she consented, on the persuasion of the executor *Pomeroy;* and she executed a release accordingly; the executors left with her the horses and other chattels, paid some debts for her, and in one way or other paid to her, or accounted to her for, the amount agreed upon. During the transactions of May, before the sale to *Yeomans* was made, the widow had informed the executors of the higher offers which had been made for the property, and by whom they had been made. *Dowling* deposed, that the executors had asked her to see these parties; but if so, she did not see them again; and the sale to *Yeomans* was closed without any of them being communicated with. The property had not been advertised for sale, either in any newspaper, or by handbill; and it was not suggested at the hearing that the executors had applied to more than one person, a man named *James McGuire*, to buy. Who this *McGuire* was, and why he, and he alone, was applied to, did not appear.

The bill impeached the sale on the ground of fraud and collusion; it also charged that the executors took no steps to sell the property to the best advantage, or to obtain the best price therefor; and that the sale was at a gross sacrifice and undervalue, and was a breach of trust on the part of the executors.

Mr. *James MacLennan* and Mr. *P. Cameron,* for the plaintiffs.

Mr. *Crooks,* Q. C., and Mr. *Price,* for the defendant *Yeomans.*

Mr. *Machar,* for the defendant *Dowling.*

MOWAT, V. C.—At the close of the argument, I expressed my opinion that the evidence did not establish
fraud or collusion on the part of the purchaser. As to
the value, the evidence was conflicting, as evidence of
value almost always is ; but the defendants produced
several respectable witnesses competent to speak on the
point, and whose opinion was, that the property was not
worth more than $1000 ; the highest evidence of value
fixed it at $1500. Upon the whole evidence,—whatever
opinion I might have formed as to preponderance one
way or the other, or as to what the executors might
probably have got for the property by taking measures
which they did not take,—I was unable to say that the
plaintiffs had shewn that the purchase was at an
undervalue so obvious as to afford notice to the purchaser of a breach of trust by the executors in selling
at such a price.

The plaintiffs have established that the property had
not been previously advertised ; and no doubt it should
have been ; for the executors, so far as appears, took
no other means of securing the best price. They
appear to have thought that the widow was the
person to look after the interests of the children, and
that her acquiescence or inaction was a sufficient justification for what they did. Now it is a well settled
and well known rule, that a trustee is bound to sell
under every possible advantage to all his *cestuis que*
trust, and for that purpose to use all reasonable diligence to obtain the best price. The concurrence of the

widow in the sale, however reluctantly given, may have deprived her of the right of complaining of the sale; but her conduct did not bind the infant *cestuis que* trust, who are now suing; for it was to the executors, and not to the widow, that the testator entrusted the sale of the property, and the protection of the interest of his children therein.

But it is another settled rule, that a person who purchases from trustees in good faith, and without fraud or collusion on his part, is not " bound to inquire what steps have been antecedently taken for the purpose of promoting the sale (a)." A sale so made is allowed to stand, and relief for the misconduct of the trustees is given in the form of a decree against them to make good the loss which their misconduct occasioned.

Now, for the purpose of obtaining a personal decree against trustees in the case of a private sale, the mere absence of any previous advertisement is not sufficient; a sale without advertisement at a fair price may, under circumstances, be free from objection; but the additional fact, which is admitted here, that the executors had notice from the widow of higher offers having been made for the property, and did not communicate with the parties named before accepting *Yeoman's* offer, shews negligence on their part which places their liability beyond reasonable controversy (b). The defendant *Dowling* says, that, though the widow told him of these offers, he did not believe her. The parties lived near; it would have been easy to ascertain the truth of her statements; and it is not now denied that they were true. The defendant's neglect to inquire was at his own peril; that is the settled doctrine in the matter of notice; and, since he did not choose to

---

a) Davey v. Durrant, 1 DeG. & J. at 538; Borell v. Dann, 2 H. 440.

(b) See Hughes v. Williams, 12 V. 493.

take the trouble of communicating with the parties named, or of advertising the property, he must be content to bear the consequences of his unfortunate and (so far as appears) unreasonable incredulity.

The observations of the Court in *Marriott* v. *The Anchor Reversionary Company* (a) may be cited as illustrative of the law applicable to these circumstances. Thât was the case of a sale of a vessel by a mortgagee at an alleged undervalue. After referring to the want of an advertisement, the learned Judge said : " I have looked carefully and with great regret through the case of the defendants, to see what, through their agents, they did in order to inquire for a purchaser. Did they go about, if they did not advertise in the newspapers, or advertise by handbill, for a purchaser ? Did they go to any person or persons whom they can name, and ask that person or those persons to purchase ? The plaintiff's case is very clear, for the plaintiff says he told them when they were going to take possession, that he wished they would not, for he was negotiating the sale of her with the Waterman's Co. The defendants say that that was a mere pretence—that there was no negotiation for a sale to that company. The plaintiff positively swears there was. Did the defendants, who took possession with a view to a sale, go to the Waterman's Co. and ask whether they were disposed to buy her—whether it was true they were in negotiation for the purchase ? There is no evidence of the kind. It does not appear, although they were told that this particular intending purchaser was inquiring, or that there was some negotiation for the sale of the vessel to him, that they took the least trouble at all upon the subject. *   * I can come to no other conclusion than that justice can only be done between these parties by directing that, upon an

(a) 7 Jur. N. S: 155,

1871.

Graham
v.
Yeomans.

inquiry to be pursued in Chambers, it shall be ascertained what is a fair sum to charge these defendants with as the value of the ship at the date when they took possession."

General evidence has been given by some of the defendants' witnesses, that it was known that the property was for sale.   But a notion of that kind, amongst it is impossible to say how many persons or how few, did not relieve the executors from the duty of diligence.   The property was mortgaged; executors have not as such the power of selling real estate; the heirs were minors; the widow was (with her family) in possession of the property; she had been allowed by the executors to manage the estate, and she had been announcing to all applicants that she did not wish to sell the homestead.   Some of them may, notwithstanding, have looked to a sale as probable; though when, or how, or by whom, would be, and (as appears from the evidence) actually was, matter of uncertain conjecture. The case was thus one which in a peculiar manner rendered desirable authoritative information to the public and to any who had a disposition to buy; whether such information should be given by means of newspaper advertisements or of hand bills or otherwise.   It is not suggested that any fear was entertained that *Yeomans* would withdraw his offer, if not promptly accepted; the contrary is clear.

Judgment.

As to the amount of loss, I think that $400 would be a fair sum to name, with interest from the 29th of May, 1865.   *Dowling* claims to be due to the executors a balance of $39.67.   It would probably be for the interest of the estate to assume that balance to be correct, rather than to incur the expense and risk of a reference.   If the plaintiffs are so advised, the decree against *Dowling* would be for the balance, and the costs of the suit so far as relates to *Dowling*.

This relief is not specifically prayed by the bill. It is unnecessary to consider whether the plaintiffs are entitled to it under the general prayer; as if not, I think that I should not refuse liberty to amend; and in either case, I think that the defendant *Dowling* should have an opportunity of shewing by affidavit that he has been prejudiced by the absence of an alternative prayer for this relief. On being satisfied of that, I shall make such order as justice may require. The decree will not be drawn up until 1st September.

*1871.*

*Graham
v.
Yeomans.*

If no application is made meantime, a decree will go, dismissing the plaintiff's bill as to *Yeomans* with costs, and giving as against *Dowling* the relief which I have mentioned.

---

### STORM v. CUMBERLAND.

*Partnership—Statute of Limitations—Division of losses.*

In partnership suits the defence of the Statute of Limitations is not available unless six years have elapsed before the filing of the bill since the dealings of the partners wholly ceased.

A partnership was formed between two civil engineers and architects, the profits of which were to be divided in shares of three-fifths and two-fifths. During the continuance of the partnership they invested moneys of the partnership in the purchase of real estate which resulted in a loss:

*Held*, that the loss was to be borne by the partners in the same proportions as they were to share the profits and loss of their other business.

Appeal from the report of Mr. *Turner*, Accountant.

The first and ninth grounds of appeal were argued together, and were as follows:

*Statement.*

1. "That the said Accountant has erroneously, and improperly, included as a payment made by the above

1871.

Storm
v.
Cumberland.

named defendant, on account of the partnership in the proceedings in this cause mentioned in the first schedule to his said report, the item following, that is to say: Law expenses paid Mr. *Harman*, $439.65; and the net profits of the said partnership, as stated in the said schedule, should therefore be increased by the said last mentioned sum, and, for that also the said net profits, in the said first schedule stated, at the sum of $58,970.-43, is erroneous and incorrect, and largely in excess of the correct amount thereof; for the sums which appear in the second schedule to the said report, together with those which the said plaintiff contends have been omitted from the said second schedule, ought to be deducted from the said sum of $58,070.43, and the balance thereof should be found to be the net profits of the said partnership.

Statement.

9. The said plaintiff also complains and excepts to the said report, for that the said Accountant has erroneously stated the account between the said plaintiff and the said defendant; that admitting that the gross receipts of the said firm to have been as in the said report stated, namely, the sum of $78,432.21, and admitting the expenditure of the said firm to have been as in the said report stated, namely, the sum of $19,461.78, (less the sum of $439.65 referred to in the objection No. 1, of this notice, that is the sum of $19,-022.13,) the said Accountant should have added to the said sum of $78,435.21 the respective sums advanced by the said respective partners; and the said accountant should have added to the said sum of $19,022.13 (the amount of the said expenditure) the amount or sum paid or expended by the said partnership on the investment account, (the said Accountant having treated the said investment account as a partnership transaction,) and then the said Accountant should have deducted the said sums of the said two last mentioned accounts, that is the said $19,022.13 and the total of

the said investment account from the said gross receipts, **1871.**
and have found the balance as the net profits of the
said partnership, divisible among the said partners in
the proportion of two-fifths to the said plaintiff, and
three-fifths to the said defendant, in other words the
said Accountant should have stated an account as
follows :

| | |
|---|---|
| By gross receipts.................... | $78,432.21 |
| By advances by plaintiff.........$ | |
| By      do      by defendant.......$ | ———— |
| Total (gross) | |

| | |
|---|---|
| To cash expended as per report $19,461.78 | |
| Less objected to..................... 439.65 | |
| | |
| $18,022.13 | |

To cash expended on investment
account as in the said report
mentioned, together with the
additions claimed on this
appeal.......................... $———— ————
Balance net profits......... $

and have found that of this balance the said plaintiff
was entitled to two-fifths and the said defendant to
three-fifths. The said Accountant should then have
stated an account with the said plaintiff, crediting him
with his said share of net profits, and his said advances,
and debiting him with his said drawings, and found
the balance. The said Accountant should also have
stated an account with the said defendant, crediting
him with his said share of net profits, and his said
advance, and debiting him with his said drawings, and
found a balance."

The 2nd, 4th, 6th, 7th, and 8th objections to the
report were allowed; the 3rd was abandoned at the
hearing; and are not of sufficient general importance
to require to be further noted.

The 5th objection to the report was as follows :
"That the said Accountant has erroneously and improperly omitted to give the said plaintiff credit, as and
for moneys advanced by him on account of the said
partnership, in the second part of the said 3rd schedule
to his said report, for the following sums, that is to say :

For books purchased in England, &c., for
    the library of the said partnership......$ 463.04
1862, sundries as per books of account... 1,774.49
1863, sundries as per books of account...   621.03

Mr. *Snelling,* for the appeal.

Mr. *G. D. Boulton,* contra.

The following cases were referred to, *Robinson* v.
*Alexander,* (a) *Tatam* v. *Williams,* (b) *Wood* v. *Scoles*
(c) and *Collyer* on Partnership, 376.

Judgment.    SPRAGGE, C.—As to $439.65, law expenses, the ob-
jection must be allowed.

I stated my impression to be that the Accountant was
right in not charging the losses upon the land transactions against the receipts of the partnership dealings
referred to him. Even if the land transaction was a
partnership dealing between them, as probably it was,
it is not the partnership dealing or any part of it that
is referred to the Accountant. If the reference was
large enough to cover both, the Accountant would properly keep them separate, and state the profits and
losses, as the case might be, upon each; leaving the
Court to adjust and settle the rights of the parties on
further directions.

---

(a) 8 Bli. N. S. 352.        (b) 3 Hare, 347, 357.
(c) L. R. 1 Ch. App. 369.

I do not see that the Accountant has gone wrong. If
he has erred, it has been in taking any account in
respect of the profits and loss upon the land transactions. The bill was for an account of the dealings of
the parties as partners, in the business or profession of
architects and civil engineers, and it was that, that
was referred to the Accountant. That business being
profitable, the partners invested a portion of the profits
in the purchase of lands, with a view to selling them
again ; as they no doubt anticipated, at a profit. Upon
that business there was a loss, and the Accountant has
found a certain sum of loss as the result of those transactions, and he has stopped there.

The plaintiff finds fault with this, and says that he
should have charged the losses against the architect
business. I think, as I have said, that he was right in
not doing so.

The plaintiff also takes this position that in
the land transactions which he says, correctly probably, was a partnership dealing it is to be assumed
that the profits were to be in the same proportion as it
was agreed that they should be in the architect business, and he has cited a number of authorities in
support of the position, that in the event of loss upon
partnership dealings, the rule of law is, that they are
borne in the same proportion by the partners as they
had stipulated that profits should be borne.

That may be the rule, but none of the cases cited
establish it to be so. In the first place, I am not prepared to say that it is to be assumed that in the land
transactions either profit or loss were to be otherwise
than equal. The profits out of which the purchases
were made belonged to the parties in unequal proportions, but all that that amounts to is, that a larger
proportion of capital was contributed by one party than

*1871.*

*Storm
v.
Cumberland.*

*Judgment.*

Storm
v.
Cumberland.
by the other, and proves nothing as. to the proportion of profit and loss; and that the defendant was to have the same proportion of profit as in the architect business lies at the very foundation of the plaintiff's position.

But, however, the fact or the 'law may be, I have nothing to do with it upon this appeal. It was not within the province of the Accountant to decide these questions, and he has properly abstained from deciding them. If the plaintiff can raise them upon further directions that is another thing, with which upon this appeal I have nothing to do. The first objection therefore is disallowed. The 9th objection involves the same question, and is also disallowed.

Judgment.
The 5th objection raises the question of the Statute of Limitations. The plaintiff's claim is, that with his private means he made certain purchases; among other things, books for the use of the partnership, in other words, that he made advances to the partnership. The defendant objects the Statute of Limitations. The advances were made more than six years before the filing of the bill, but the partnership was dissolved within six years. This at least applies to some of the items mentioned in this objection. It seems to me that the Statute of Limitations does not apply.

Accounts between partners are, or rather before the Mercantile Law Amendment Act of 1856, were held in England to be within the analogy of the exception of merchant's accounts in the Statute of James (a), and in *Tatam* v. *Williams*, Sir *James Wigram* after observing that the cases at law which appear to have been commonly argued upon as affording an analogy in questions between partner and partner, after a dissolution of partnership, and those

--------

(a) Robinson v. Alexander, *supra*.

which fall within the exception as to merchants accounts in the Statute of Limitations, proceeds to say
that he understands the law to be settled "that if all
dealings have ceased for more than six years the statute
(even between merchant and merchant their factors and
agents) is a bar to the whole demand, except when the
proceeding is an action of account or perhaps an action
upon the case for not accounting." Here six years have
not elapsed since the dealings between the partners
have ceased or had not at the filing of the bill.

Mr. *Boulton* mentioned that he had an authority the
other way. He has not produced it. It is probably
since the passing of the Act of 1856. The account
must be taken as to these items without reference to
the Statute of Limitations.

Is must be referred back to the Accountant to alter
his report in the particulars in which objections are
allowed. It is not a case for costs to either party.

———

The cause was again brought on by the plaintiff by
way of appeal from the certificate of the Accountant.
The certificate was as follows :

- "In pursuance of the order made in this cause, bearing date the 6th day of April last, I have been attended
by the solicitors of the above named plaintiff and
defendant respectively, and upon proceeding thereunder
to review the former report therein referred to, the following claim and submission with respect thereto was
made before me on behalf of the said plaintiff.

"Mr. *Snelling* for plaintiff submits and claims that
on review of the report the Accountant following the
judgment of his lordship the Chancellor, should only
take an account of the partnership business as architects,

and should reject from the accounts taken under the old report all items referring to the land transactions. But if he takes an account of both the architect business and the land transactions, then he should give effect to the Chancellor's judgment on appeal, in which he says. 'Even if the land transaction was a partnership dealing between the parties, as probably it was, it is not the partnership dealing or any part of it, that is referred to the Accountant. If the reference was large enough to cover both, the Accountant would probably keep them separate, and state the profits and losses as the case might be, upon each; leaving the Court to adjust and settle the rights of the parties on further directions.'

" Mr. *Snelling* asks the Accountant, if he takes the account to keep them separate and to state the profits or losses, as the case may be upon each, or if he does not take the account, then to limit his report to the architect business simply.

" Upon which I rule that by the former report herein, no account having been in effect taken or intended to be taken, of the profit or loss upon the land transactions, but only on the architect business, and the land transactions being referred to, and any finding with respect to the same being only intended to apply so far as was necessary to complete the accounts of the other business, and to shew the application of the profits thereof, it is not now competent for the Accountant in the face of the judgment and the order on appeal, and without a special direction in that behalf, to disturb the manner in which the account of the architect business has been already taken."

The same counsel appeared for the respective parties.

This appeal was heard before the Chancellor, and was allowed with costs.

The case subsequently came up for further directions and as to the question of costs before Vice Chancellor MOWAT, when it was determined that the loss upon the land transactions should be borne by the parties respectively in the same proportions as they were to share the profits of the general partnership; and that the costs of both parties should be paid in the manner usual in partnership cases, other than the costs incurred in contesting the liability of the defendant to bear three-fifths of the losses on the land transactions; as to those costs the defendant was to pay them.

1871.

Storm
v.
Cumberland.

---

## CRIPPEN v. OGILVIE. [IN APPEAL.*]

*Mortgage—Release of equity of redemption—Parol trust—Lapse of time.*

A., who was greatly addicted to drinking, gave to B. a mortgage to secure a small debt; the property was worth at least seven times the debt; and the rent of half the property, for three years, would have paid off the claim: but five years before the debt was payable, A., without any additional consideration, released his equity of redemption to B.; and B. was allowed to remain in possession for seven or eight years after the mortgage debt was paid off by rents. A majority of the Judges of the Court of Appeal were of opinion and held (affirming the decree of the Court below) that the facts and evidence shewed that the release was given on a parol trust, for the benefit of the mortgagor and his family, and that to set up the release as an absolute purchase, was a fraud on B., against which the Court should relieve, notwithstanding the lapse of time and the death of some of the witnesses.

This was an appeal, by the defendant, from the decree of the Court below, as reported, *ante* Volume XV., page 490.

Statement.

---

* *Present.*—DRAPER, C. J., RICHARDS, C. J.,* VANKOUGHNET, C.,†
HAGARTY, C. J., SPRAGGE, V. C.,‡ MORRISON, WILSON, GWYNNE, and
GALT, JJ.

* Was absent when judgment was delivered.
† Died before judgment was given.
‡ Was appointed Chancellor before judgment was given.

1871.

Crippen
v.
Ogilvie.

Mr. *Strong.* Q.C.,* and Mr. *Blake*, Q.C., for the appellant.

Mr. *S. M. Jarvis*, contra.

February 5.  DRAPER, C. J.—I think the respondent has succeeded in proving that from 1850, up to, probably, 1860, he was a confirmed drunkard, disposing of whatever available means he had in order to gratify this degrading passion. Indeed, one of his witnesses carries it to an excess for the purposes of this case, in suggesting, as his conviction, that the respondent would be the same now as in 1855, but that he has exhausted his means and shattered his constitution, so that he can no longer purchase liquor or long resist the destructive consequence of an insane perseverance in the abuse of it. We are only concerned in inquiring into his habits and mental condition, so far as they bear upon his transactions, in 1854 and 1855, with the appellant.

Judgment.

The respondent examined the defendant as a witness, and he swore that the respondent spoke to him in the spring of 1855, several times, about making the deed of his property, saying that *he* could not hold to the property, and he wished the defendant to take it. That defendant was to advance a sum of money to pay Dr. *Denmark*, and to take up the bond given by the vendor of the land, binding himself (the vendor) to convey to the respondent, which bond the respondent had deposited with Dr. *Denmark* as security for a debt. The amount due to the vendor ($100) was paid when the mortgage was given to the defendant, who had agreed with respondent's son, to indorse as payment on this mortgage the value of any work the son might do for defendant. Dr. *Denmark* was dead before this deed was given, and one *Rowed* (since dead) was his executor. The bargain

---

* Was appointed Vice Chancellor before judgment was delivered.

between the respondent and the defendant was made in
*Rowed's* office, who was Clerk of the Division Court;
the consideration for the deed was sworn by the defendant to have been the $160, the cost of two journeys to
Cobourg, where the vendor lived, and the sum to be paid
to *Rowed*, as executor—and the deed was executed
before this last sum was paid. The defendant swore he
did pay *Rowed*; the sum, he thought, was $57; that
the sum actually advanced by him was the $160, $12
the cost of the mortgage, and $20 due to himself.
He stated that the respondent's wife and son urged him
to take this deed. On 3rd May, 1855, defendant leased
the house, and half an acre of the land, to the respondent for five years, at $24 per annum; and the re-
spondent's son, in 1856, paid $36 on account of the
rent.

The proof of the execution of the deed impeached is
very clear, both as to the fact, and the respondent's
capacity to understand it. Two of the subscribing witnesses prove this, as well as that *Rowed* prepared and
read it over to the respondent, whose wife and son were
present.

Against this is the evidence of *Archibald McColl*,
said to be the brother of the respondent's wife. All he
knows of this part of the transaction, he professes to
have learned from the defendant in two conversations,
in March, 1855; the first disclosing a scheme to deceive
the respondent into the execution of a deed, when he
would not know what he was doing; the second, boast-
ing of the successful accomplishment of the plan.

I cannot help noticing the improbability of these
statements, and the improbability that the defendant
made them, as is represented. The man who could have
made them, was as shameless as he must have been dishonest, and even more imprudent than either. Accord-

ing to *McColl*, the defendant deliberately, and on con-
sultation with lawyers, planned a gross fraud, one feature
of which was, "to keep the plan a secret," and he
begins by disclosing it, without any sufficient motive,
for *McColl's* aid was neither asked nor wanted. It is
true, he asserts that he would have nothing to do with
it, but he does not inform us that any proposal was
made to him. And the defendant has no sooner executed his design, than he boasts to *McColl* that having got
the plaintiff so that he did not know his right hand from
his left, he had procured the wished-for deed. Either
the subscribing witnesses to the transaction have sworn
falsely, or the defendant uttered a deliberate, and for
his own evil purposes, assuming them, a most useless
falsehood; or *McColl's* invention, or imagination, has
taken the place of his memory. It is plain, from his
own testimony, he misunderstood the actual position of
things; either he confuses the mortgage with the deed,
Judgment. or he was not aware that the latter was an absolute
conveyance.

The learned Chancellor had an advantage not easily
to be overrated, that of seeing the witnesses under examination, and his conclusion alone makes me hesitate
in adopting an opposing view of the effect of the
evidence. But I have gone over it again and again,
and taking first the case which the respondent asserts as
his ground for relief, and then the proof he has adduced
to support it, I cannot agree in the decree that has
been pronounced. I do not think there is any difference
between the learned Chancellor and myself, as to the
principles applicable to the case asserted, but I differ
from the conclusion, that a case is proved to which those
principles are applicable, and the only plausible theory,
the only reasonable explanation which can aid the decree
seems to be this: that the respondent's wife and son,
apprehensive that the respondent would dissipate all his
property, and confiding in the defendant, who, already

a mortgagee of the premises, it is assumed, engaged to
take an absolute conveyance thereof, to hold for their
benefit, and to become a trustee for them—united with
them, to get a deed from the respondent without his
obtaining any consideration for the property, and without
any intention or expectation on the defendant's part that
he was to become the beneficial owner. The defendant's
evidence is opposed to this. Its only support is in
*Archibald McColl's* testimony, and that consists in the
statement which he says the defendant made to him in
March, 1855, and on which I have remarked.

Independently of the absence of any such case from
the bill, and admitting the possibility of this theory, I
cannot find in the evidence a sufficient foundation for it.
And I think it ought not, after so many years delay,
and after the death of two witnesses—one of whom (the
respondent's son) must, and the other (*Rowed*) most
probably would, have given testimony most material—
to be adopted, unless upon very clear evidence. It may
be said, the defendant has not alleged in what respect
the evidence of these witnesses would have helped his
case; but he could scarcely be expected to anticipate
that a ground would be taken against him, which the
plaintiff never suggested, and in regard to which they
could, as I have suggested, have related what actually
took place.

Judgment.

I have not overlooked the advantageous bargain (*a*),
which the defendant had made, if it were sustained;
nor am I insensible to the duty, I might say privilege,
which belongs to a Court of Equity to defeat a fraud
practised on a man who has weakened himself, both in
mind and body, by long continued and gross intemperance. On the other hand, the respondent must prove
his case, not only that by persistence in evil habits he

---

(*a*) See Moth v. Atwood, 5 Ves. 845.

33—VOL. XVIII. GR.

has weakened or destroyéd his powers of self-guidance
or self-protection, but he must also shew the fraudulent
manner in which advantage has been taken of him.

I need not go so far as to say that the defendants'
case is free from suspicion, on the contrary, I do not
like the complexion of it; but I cannot, on the pleadings
and evidence, hold that the respondent has entitled himself to relief.

SPRAGGE, C.—Since the argument of this case upon
appeal, I have reconsidered it very carefully; and have
been unable to come to any other conclusion than that
at which I arrived upon the hearing of the case before
myself. As to the facts of the case; especially in relation to the habits and mental condition of *Crippen;* as to
the weight to be attached to the evidence of *McColl* and
*Black;* and as to the value of the land, I claim only

what is accorded to every judge of fact before whom
witnesses have been examined; to be more competent
to judge of them than it is possible for those to be who
have heard the case only upon appeal.

As to the law of the case, I applied it to the best of
my judgment; and I do not upon reflection see that I
was wrong. If I was wrong, I think it was in laying
less stress upon the gross, the absurd inadequacy of
price, than I ought to have laid upon it. Taken in connection with the habits and mental condition of the man,
and the circumstances attending the transaction, the
conclusion to my mind is irresistible that he was grossly
imposed upon; how, for what purpose, and by what
means, I have suggested in my former judgment. It is
not necessary, however, that we should be able to see
*how* the imposition was brought about: the Court may
infer that it has been brought about, that fraud has been
practised, from the result.

This case seems to me to come under the well-recognized head of fraud, which is thus expressed in the oft-quoted language of Lord *Hardwicke* in the *Earl of Chesterfield* v. *Janssen* (a): " Secondly, it (fraud) may be apparent from the intrinsic nature and subject of the bargain itself, such as no man in his senses, and not under delusion would make, on the one hand, and as no honest and fair man would accept on the other." Every word of this is strictly applicable to the transaction set aside by the decree appealed from. It would be difficult, indeed, to imagine a case which contained stronger internal evidence of its being brought about by imposition and fraud.

The impression produced upon my mind upon hearing the evidence was, that a gross fraud had been committed; and that the death of *Dougald Crippen* had in all human probability aided the defendant in the non-disclosure of the truth. I cannot believe that he and his mother were aiding and assenting, and the latter a party to an absolute sale to the defendant (without a secret trust) without believing them to have been actually imbecile; the utter folly of such a bargain would be so great.

In addition to the cases to which I referred in my former judgment, I would refer to *Longmate* v. *Ledger* (b), before Sir *John Stuart*, and *Clarke* v. *Malpas* (c), before the present Master of the Rolls. In both of these cases there was inequality between the contracting parties, but not greater inequality than existed between the parties to the transaction in question. These cases, are neither of them so strong, for setting aside the transaction as the one now in appeal.

I have not much to add to what I said in my former judgment on the subject of the delay in bringing this

1871.

Crippen
v.
Ogilvie.

Judgment.

(a) 2 Ves. 125; 1 W. & T. 287.  (b) 2 Giff. 163.
(c) 31 Beav. 80.

suit, I felt it to be a difficulty in the plaintiff's way, but upon consideration it did not appear to me to be an insuperable difficulty; and for this I have already given some reasons.

I desire now to add upon that head, that it would not be in accordance with principle to visit the plaintiff *in pœnam* for his delay. There is no reason to suppose that the plaintiff purposely and advisedly abstained from bringing this suit. If there were, I grant that everything should be presumed against him; but his wretched condition until after the death of his son sufficiently accounts for the delay until that time; and his poverty accounts for further delay afterwards. There was no wilful lying by until evidence should be lost to the defendant, by the death of witnesses, or otherwise; and the question resolves itself into this, whether by the delay that has occurred there is reason to believe that the defendant has lost evidence which would have displaced the plaintiff's case. I concede that the delay having occurred through the fault of the plaintiff, though without any fraudulent intent on his part, the Court should see that the defendant is not prejudiced thereby. At the date of *Rowed's* death, there had been no such delay as to disentitle the plaintiff to relief. The defendant does not shew when *Bailey* died. If he complains that he has lost *Bailey's* evidence through the delay of the plaintiff, it is for him to shew that *Bailey's* death occurred at a time when it would have been great delay on the part of the plaintiff not to have brought his suit. Strictly, upon the case as it stands, the defendant does not shew that he has lost the evidence supposing it would have been in his favor, of either *Rowed* or *Bailey* by the plaintiff's delay in bringing this suit. But at any rate the defendant is not prejudiced, if it be assumed in his favor that these persons if living would have testified to their belief in the sobriety and intelligence of the plaintiff at the execution of the deed; and it is not suggested by the defendant that they could speak to any other point. Assuming that they would have testified to their belief in his sobriety and intelligence ever so strongly, the fact of the nature of this bargain being what it is still remains, the fact, that is, that it is such a bargain "as no one in his senses, and not under delusion would make on the one hand, and as no honest and fair man would accept on the other," and so "fraud is apparent from the intrinsic nature and subject of the bargain itself." The case may fairly be looked at in that view. Take first the bargain itself, and if it is of such a nature as to come within Lord *Hardwicke's* definition, it cannot stand, merely because some three or four persons who were present at the execution of the instrument by which it was carried out, testified ever so strongly that the grantor appeared to them to be perfectly sober, and to understand what he was doing. In this view the habitual drunkenness, and at least habitual incapacity for business of the plaintiff, may be discarded as unnecessary to his case. But when his habits and their consequences are also taken into account, his case is greatly strengthened; as there is in such case something to aid the presumption, or rather there comes in a second presumption; and his case is then brought within Lord *Hardwicke's* definition of a third kind of fraud which he says (in the same case) may be presumed from the circumstances and condition of the parties contracting; and this (he adds) goes further than the rule of law, which is, that "it must be proved, not presumed." In this case there is the double presumption arising from the nature of the bargain; and, the condition of one party to it, of the party on whose part it is improvident.

But there is still the evidence of the son that has been lost by his death in 1863; but, is the loss of his evidence a loss to the defendant? My own conviction is, that it is not. That he could, if living, give important evidence, I have no doubt; but it is utterly incredible

*1871.*

*Crippen
v.
Ogilvie.*

Judgment.

that he and his mother could have joined in inducing the unfortunate man whose habits had made him almost an imbecile, to sell absolutely to the defendant upon the terms that the defendant claims that he did. The plaintiff's case is sufficient without the son's evidence. It is the defendant who must be in a position to say that it is lost to him. To me it seems impossible that the son's evidence could be of benefit to the defendant, because if alive and giving evidence, to make that to support the transaction he would prove that he was imbecile, which it is certain that he was not; or that he joined with his mother in committing a fraud upon his father, and that for the benefit of a stranger. The transaction is explicable without resorting to such a violent presumption, and it is shortly this : the wife and son wished to save a helpless drunkard from his own improvidence : the defendant aided them in doing it, and then played them false, and claimed the land for himself. That is,

Judgment. in my opinion, the proper inference from the whole of the evidence, and it appears to me unintelligible upon any other hypothesis. I shall regret very much if the defendant were enabled to sustain the defence, in my judgment a dishonest one, which he has set up.

HAGARTY, C. J.—The plaintiff seems in the statements in the bill, most doubtful as to how he should present his case : whether, as having, while intoxicated, executed a deed of which he did not understand the effect; or that he was induced, by defendant's representations and influences, to execute the deed to defraud his creditors, and on some parol trust.

It has been suggested that the most probable account of the transaction is, that the plaintiff's wife and son induced him to execute the absolute conveyance to defendant, with a view to protect the property from plaintiff's own possible folly, and the chances of his being defrauded out of it by others; and that defendant joined them in the design, they having confidence in his honesty.

In this way the deed was procured by his family's persuasions, less than by any active practice of defendant.

. This view I did not understand the plaintiff's counsel to urge before us. We may, of course, uphold a decree on any available ground. I do not read the bill as presenting such a case; but I am told we should if necessary amend the pleading so as to admit it. In this aspect the defendant may have accepted the conveyance in good faith, but afterwards, tempted by the rise in value, have determined on keeping it for himself; or he may have from the begining, resolved to deceive those who trusted him.

I am strongly of opinion that the case fails as to avoidance of the deed, on the ground of intoxication.

The evidence for the plaintiff is wholly silent as to his state at the time of execution; that for the defence reasonably clear, especially at such a distance of time.

The whole burden of proof of intoxication must be on the plaintiff. I think he wholly fails in that branch of his case. The general evidence is just what might have been expected in any case where men after the lapse of years are questioned as to the capacity of one whom they remember as a great drunkard.

The presence of his wife and son, the character of *Rowed*, by whom the papers were drawn; and the direct testimony of *Catharine Brown* and *William Smith*, who were present; all tend to repel the belief that plaintiff did not know what he was doing.

It has been also suggested that this is a case where a mortgagee, by unfair pressure and taking advantage of his position, has extorted a release of the equity of redemption from the mortgagor.

I am unable to see evidence sufficient to lead to this conclusion. The only evidence pointing to any direct action of defendant, is that of *Archibald McColl*. From it I gather that defendant spoke as if he were acting in concert with the son *Dugald Crippen*. "He (defendant) said, they would pretend the deed was some other document connected with the mortgage, and see and get plaintiff to sign it." Again: "that he had a scheme, which was, that they would get him, when he did not know what he was doing, and get him to sign a deed of the property to *Ogilvie* so as to hold the property from *Gibb, Miller*, and others." This points to the obtaining the deed from plaintiff by fraud when drunk. I have already stated my disbelief in the assertion that he signed the deed without knowing its effect. I cannot believe that the son was colluding with defendant to obtain an unfair bargain from the father, on the ground of defendant being mortgagee making an unfair use of his position and power.

The only plausible view is, I think, that suggested since the argument,—that plaintiff, and his wife, and son, all knowingly joined in conveying the land absolutely to defendant for plaintiff's protection, either as against his own folly or the apprehended fraud of others. There is much to support that view. *Dugald Crippen* is spoken of as a steady industrious man, very kind to his parents: He lived eight years after the deed sought to be impeached, and seems to have done nothing. Had any fraud been practised on his father by which a valuable property was taken from him, he would hardly have remained passive so many years.

The only explanation of his conduct seems to be, that the impeached deed was made with his full concurrence.

In fact, he was a party to it with his father, in consequence of an assignment of Major *Campbell's* bond for a deed having been made to him by his father in May, 1854, some days before the date of the mortgage. I am satisfied of the genuineness of the deed of 1855, as made by plaintiff, knowing its effect, and with the full assent of his family. In 1859, during *Dugald's* life, it is stated that Mr. *Dumble*, on behalf of plaintiff in *McColl's* presence, offered the defendant the full amount due on the mortgage. It is not shewn whether this was done with or without *Dugald's* sanction or knowledge. I incline, on the whole, to believe that the property was in 1855, absolutely conveyed to defendant on a secret or parol trust, to hold it for the benefit of plaintiff or his family. If, therefore, the difficulty as to the proof of such a trust under the Statute of Frauds can be surmounted, I must be prepared to support the decree. I see no other satisfactory view of the position of the parties. I feel a growing reluctance to relieve parties, who, if they have rights, sleep on them for a long period of years, till the persons best qualified to testify the truth are dead, and the facts are fast fading from the memory of the living.

*1871.*

*Crippen*
*v.*
*Ogilvie.*

*Judgment.*

If there be obscurity in such a case, it is the plaintiff's misfortune, if not his fault. It is his duty to make the case reasonably clear, before he should ask a Court to take the seal off his deed. If the trust can be legally proved, I incline to enforce it under the circumstances.

I am utterly unable, under the view I take of the facts, to see my way to take the case out of the Statute of Frauds. To those who take a different view of the facts, this difficulty may not present itself. To me, it is simply insuperable ; and I am not inclined, for the purpose of redressing a wrong, to run counter to what appears to me to be the plain provisions of the law.

GWYNNE, J.—After a careful perusal of the pleadings and evidence in this case, I must say that my mind has

34—VOL. XVIII. GR.

been impressed with a strong conviction that the conduct of the defendant, in asserting the absolute beneficial interest in this property to be vested in himself, is
most unconscientious, and that he, of all persons, has
least reason to complain that he is prejudiced, by being
unable to produce the evidence of *Rowed* and *Dugald
Crippen,* who are both dead.

If they were living, I entertain the belief that whatever defence the defendant might have set up to this
bill, it would have been of a wholly different character
from that which he has set up. But, however strong
may be my conviction of the falsehood and uncon-
scientiousness of the defendant's defence, and however
much I may deplore his success, I cannot interfere to
prevent that success, if the principles of law which he
invokes interpose themselves for his protection.

Judgment.  The defendant, in order to shew that he had given to
the plaintiff valuable consideration for the conveyance
to him of the equity of redemption in the mortgaged
premises, which is the impeached deed, over and above
the amount secured to the defendant by the mortgage ;
in the 4th paragraph of his answer says: "The said
plaintiff, in or about the month of March, 1855, being
embarrassed, *applied to me for further sums* of money,
*in order to pay off* a further lien upon the said property,
in favor of *Henry Boyd,* executor to one *Robert
Denmark,* and certain other claims against him; that I
advanced the sum of $60, *and,* at the urgent request of
the said plaintiff, paid off the said lien of the said *Henry
Boyd, and* certain *other sums the exact amount of which*
I am now unable to state." And in the 5th paragraph,
he says: "The said plaintiff, representing himself to be
unable to pay off the said mortgage to me, agreed to
convey the said property absolutely to me, in full satisfaction of said mortgage, and in consideration of the
further sums *so advanced by me, and* in pursuance of

said agreement, did by indenture, dated the 14th day of March, 1855, convey the said property to me absolutely." And in the 6th paragraph, he says: "The consideration of the said deed is expressed to be the sum of £40, whereas it was, in fact, the sum of $272, *and the latter amount was intended to be inserted in the said deed, but by some mistake or inadvertence the said sum of £40 was inserted; the said sum of $272 was the actual* consideration for the said deed." And in the 8th paragraph, he says: "It was at the plaintiff's own suggestion, *that if I would make said further advances* he would, *in consideration thereof*, and in satisfaction of said mortgage, convey *his interest* in the said property to me."

Now at the time that the defendant represents the plaintiff to have been so embarrassed by the pressure of the mortgage debt, as to be urging the defendant to accept a conveyance of the whole property absolutely, in consideration of a further advance, not exceeding, according to defendant's own shewing, about $80, there was not a farthing due upon the mortgage, for interest or principal, and there was upon the premises, independently of the house in which plaintiff lived, a store which, according to the testimony of defendant himself, and one *Miller*, was worth £25 per annum rent, and which rent the defendant acknowledges having received, at any rate, for three years, subject to some deductions for improvements, the amount of which he does not state.

The mortgage is dated the 22nd May, 1854, it was to secure £48 principal, payable, with interest for the same, in manner following (extracted from the mortgage), "the principal money to be paid within six years from the date of these presents, and interest thereon at the rate of *nine* per centum per annum, to be paid yearly, on the 22*nd of May*, in each year, till the principal debt is paid, as aforesaid, *provided always*, and it is agreed, that said party of the first part may pay any moneys on account of *said principal at any time, and the interest on* such payments shall cease thereafter."

Now before the impeached deed of the 14th of March, 1855, was executed, *McColl*, in his evidence, says that the defendant, speaking of the contemplated execution of that deed, said that whenever *Dugald* (the plaintiff's son, who is shewn to have been a steady, industrious young man, a carpenter by trade) would be able to pay the mortgage money, he would take it from him; that *Dugald* had already paid him some money on the mortgage, he did not know what, but not exceeding £8, and defendant said "he would *put* the amount he got from *Dugald* (that is, indorse it,) on the mortgage shortly."

Judgment. The truth of this evidence of *McColl's* does, I confess, appear to me to be placed beyond all reasonable doubt, when we find a gentleman of the strict habits of integrity and preciseness, which Mr. *Rowed* is represented to have been, inserting, shortly after, in the deed of the 14th of March, 1855, the precise sum of £40 as the consideration of that deed, being the principal sum secured by the mortgage, less this identical sum of £8. I think also, that every probability establishes the truth of this further portion of *McColl's* evidence, when he says that on meeting the defendant again, in the end of that month of March, he informed *McColl* of the deed, which is now impeached, having been executed, and added, "the amount due me is exactly £40, and that is the amount put in the mortgage."

Assuming, then, that in March, 1855, the true amount of *principal* due to the defendant, upon the security of the mortgage of May, 1854, was this £40, and that the defendant, in truth, made no further advances in consideration of the deed of March, 1855, and assuming, as I think we fairly may, that the three years rent of £25 per annum, acknowledged to have been received by the defendant, were received in the three years next ensuing the execution of the latter deed, and adding these sums to the $36.20, also acknowledged by the defendant to have been received from *Dugald* in the year 1856, as the defendant says, it is true, upon the lease, we shall find that after every reasonable allowance is made for deductions, from the £25 per annum rent, for improvements, the defendant was over-paid the whole principal and interest, secured by the mortgage of May, 1854, before, *in the terms of that mortgage, the principal was payable.*

I propose now to test the defendant's veracity by his own oral examination, taken at the hearing. He says: "I am grantee in deed B (the impeached deed); plaintiff spoke to me several times about making that deed, it might first be a month before the date of it. He came to my house; it was in the spring of 1855; he first told me he could not hold the property, and wished me to take it: *I was to advance* a sum to pay Dr. *Denmark*, and to take up a bond he had given in security—the bond I refer to, is exhibit C." This bond is not the plaintiff's at all, but the original bond, given by *Campbell* to plaintiff, and which had been paid off by the money loaned by the defendant on the mortgage of May, 1854: we shall see, by and bye, how the defendant professes to explain this: he proceeds on his examination to say:—"The bargain was made in Mr. *Rowed's* office. *Rowed* was *Denmark's* executor. The bond was void when the deed was given. The price for the deed to me was *to be* what I had paid already: the cost of going twice to Cobourg, and the amount due to Rowed. *I did not hear of the debt to Rowed until the evening we got there.*"

Now, in his answer, he has stated that "the plaintiff, being embarrassed, *applied* to him, in March, 1855, for further sums of money *to pay off* a further lien on the property, in favor of *Henry Boyd*, Dr. *Denmark's* executor, and certain other claims." And above, in the early part of his examination, he says, as I understand him, that when the plaintiff first came to defendant's house, about a month before the execution of the deed, his object was to obtain an advance *to pay* Dr. *Denmark, and to take up* a bond he had given in security.

Defendant, in his examination, proceeds to say : "We went to the office to have the deed drawn, and get the matter arranged, and give the plaintiff a lease." Before they went to *Rowed's* he says : "The bargain was, that I was to take a deed for the amount due." I suppose he means " secured " on the mortgage (for nothing was Judgment. due), "and give him the lease;" and again, "I told him several times I would not take the deed ;" and again, " I went with him to *Rowed's* to take a deed of the property for the amount due on the mortgage, and give him a lease, as *he owed a good many debts, and could not hold it. I don't know who was to receive the rent from Hunter. I know nothing about the bargain.* I had nothing to do with the lease to *Hunter.* I know he had a lease. I was not to receive the rent."

Now, upon this evidence, how is it possible to conceive that the plaintiff had ever applied to the defendant to obtain any advance to pay off *any* lien held by Dr. *Denmark's* executor upon the property ; or how is it possible to conceive that a person intending to become an absolute purchaser of property, part of which was under lease, was, although the absolute purchaser, to have nothing to say to the lease or the rent issuing thereunder ? And with whom was the bargain made ? It could not have been with the plaintiff, whose object,

as stated in the answer, was to obtain an advance to pay 1871.
Dr. *Denmark's* executor a debt due to that estate, which
it now appears the defendant never heard of until, in Crippen
pursuance of a bargain which must, as I submit, have v. Ogilvie.
been made between the defendant and some person other
than the plaintiff, the defendant went to accept a deed,
and give back a lease merely for the amount already
secured to him by his mortgage.

The defendant says : "I know nothing about the
bargain;" that is, the bargain by which, although
becoming absolute purchaser of all the property, he was
to have nothing to do with the lease of part of the
premises to *Hunter*, or to the rent issuing thereon.
Between whom, then, could this bargain have been made
so materially affecting the purchaser's rights? The
defendant further says : " There was no bargain between
me and the plaintiff about this lease;" and yet he was
to have nothing to do with it. 'He must surely, then, Judgment.
for some reason or other, have made the bargain for the
purchase of the plaintiff's property with some person
other than the plaintiff.

But, to proceed with the examination, the defendant
further says, " *Rowed* told me he had a claim of about
$60, which plaintiff borrowed, and left bond C. as secu-
rity. I agreed to pay this debt. *Rowed* told me I
would have to pay it. Plaintiff was agreeable to it."
This was the debt which, in his answer, he says the
plaintiff *applied to him for an advance to pay*, and which
in another place he swears he never heard of until now,
*Rowed*, for the first time, mentioned it; and immediately upon its being mentioned, defendant agreed to
pay, and " plaintiff was agreeable to it." He proceeds :
" I merely said to Mr. *Rowed* that I would pay him the
claim he made ;" and again, " I agreed to pay no more
than *Rowed's* claim beyond the mortgage." In his
answer, he had stated, " the plaintiff, being embarrassed

in or about the month of March, 1855, *applied to me* for further sums of money, *in order to pay off* a further lien on the said property in favor *Henry Boyd*, executor, to one *Robert Denmark*, and certain other claims against him. I *advanced* the sum of $60, and *at the urgent request of the said plaintiff*, paid off the said lien to the said *Henry Boyd, and certain other sums*, the exact amount of which I am now unable to state." In his examination he proceeds as to this debt: "I *advanced* no money when I took the deed; but I assumed the debt to Mr. *Rowed*, but no others;" and again: "I paid *Rowed* $57 on the debt to *Denmark, I think*."

Now, can there be one word of truth in all this about the debt to *Denmark ?* Not one particle of it is proved. That there ever was such a debt does not appear. No entry of any such appears in *Rowed's* books. The defendant only ventures to swear that *he thinks* he paid Judgment. *Rowed* $57 on it. No evidence of any such payment is offered. It is out of the question to treat *Ogilvie's* own note to *Rowed* for $50, dated April 2, 1858, and paid in instalments of $24, the 22nd December, 1860, and $35, on the 24th December, 1863, as payments on any debt that had been due by plaintiff to *Rowed*. But is not the whole story incredible ? Is it credible that *Rowed* held the forfeited bond of *Campbell* to *Crippen*, forfeited before the mortgage of May, 1854, was executed and paid, when that mortgage was executed, *as security for a debt ?*

If this precise man of business had such a debt due to the estate of which he was executor, what difficulty would he have had in getting security upon the property by mortgage executed by *Crippen ?* Then, looking at the bond we find indorsed on it the following, executed by the plaintiff, in the presence of Mr. *Rowed* himself, on the *9th day of May*, 1854: " Know all men by these presents, that I, *Samuel Crippen*, do hereby transfer all

my right and title to the within bond and therein mentioned property, to my son *Dugald Crippen*.". Now, is it
credible, that if Mr. *Rowed* held this bond as a security
for a debt due by. *Crippen* there would be no memorandum on the bond to that effect? or, that he would
have been a party to the assignment by the plaintiff to
his son? or that he could have treated this deed as
having any effect after the execution of, the deed by
*Campbell* to the plaintiff, and the mortgage by plaintiff
to defendant, of the 22nd of May, 1854?

Then, *William Smith,* a witness to the impeached
deed, and who was present the whole time it was being
prepared by Mr. *Rowed, did not hear any claim of Mr.
Rowed's or Dr. Denmark's spoken of, nor could he be
certain that Mr. Rowed went and got a bond.*

Neither did *Catharine Brown,* another witness, and
also present when the deed was prepared, *hear anything
about any debt due to Mr. Rowed or Dr. Denmark
spoken of;* and these are the defendant's own witnesses.

But, to close the defendant's examination. He says:
" The lease was not given at the time the deed was
drawn. *Rowed* was not asked to draw the lease"—(which
they went to him for the express purpose of getting
drawn). " He only drew the deed. I did not give the
plaintiff a written agreement for a lease. * * After the
mortgage," that is, the deed of May, 1854, " I told
*Dugald Crippen* that if he would work for me, I would
indorse for the amount upon the mortgage. *I took the
deed because his wife and son urged me to do it,* as they
preferred being under me. I had agreed before to
indorse the son's work on the mortgage." And again:
" I expect I gave the lease on the date of it—on 3rd of
May, 1855. Archer wrote it for me. Plaintiff's son
suggested that he should draw it. The son and I
arranged to get it drawn. The plaintiff never gave me

35—VOL. XVIII. GR.

any money; but the son gave me money. The son earned it, I expect. There was only one copy of the lease, which I kept."

Taking, then, the defendant's own statement of the transaction, it presents, I think, the most singular narrative of the circumstances attending a *bona fide* absolute purchase by the defendant of property, three years' rent of no more than the half of which, according to the defendant's own shewing, was sufficient to pay the whole debt secured to the defendant by a mortgage upon the property, the principal of which would not become due for upwards of five years ; and the interest upon which, in the meantime, was payable annually to the amount of $13.50.

There are but three ways to my mind of accounting for the transaction :

1. That this wretched, drunken imbecile, which the evidence establishes the plaintiff to have been, was totally incapable of understanding what he was doing, although perhaps kept temporarily sufficiently sober to go through the form of executing the deed which stripped him of all his valuable property ; or,

2. That the plaintiff, with a full knowledge of what he was doing, and trusting to the defendant's honor, conspired with the defendant to divest himself of all his property to defraud his creditors, of whom, however, we hear of the existence of none, except from what is stated by witnesses to have been mentioned by the defendant himself, and these to an inconsiderable amount ; or,

3. That the wife and son of this unhappy sot, who "sold his carpenter's tools and every thing he could lay his hands on," to gratify his insatiable thirst for ardent spirits, which, from the description given of him,

1871.

Crippen
v.
Ogilvie.

had completely robbed him of his intellect, fearing that he would, for the like purpose, dispose of all his property, and reduce them, as well as himself to destitution, formed a contrivance with the defendant to procure the plaintiff to execute a deed to him for the purpose of saving it for the benefit of the wife and son, upon an arrangement made between them and the defendant, which, by reason of the son's death, cannot now be proved, to the effect that the defendant, upon his mortgage debt being paid, should hold the property for their benefit : they being perhaps advised that a deed of gift to the son direct, would still leave the property at the mercy of some unscrupulous person who might induce the imbecile husband and father to sell it to them.

I confess I have no doubt in my own mind, from reading the evidence, that this latter was the real transaction; and, so thinking, it explains sufficiently to my mind, Mr. *Rowed's* part in suffering the deed to be executed, and perhaps in assisting to get it executed.

Judgment.

Under the circumstances detailed in evidence of the plaintiff's miserable conduct and character, many a good man might think that he was doing a kind, humane, and praiseworthy act, in procuring him to put it out of his power utterly to ruin himself and family without stopping to inquire whether the plaintiff was perfectly competent to understand the extent and nature of the obligation which his friends were putting him under to them, or caring to inquire whether the plaintiff approved of their motives and friendly interference.

This view of the case also seems to me to give the complexion of truth to Mr. *McColl's* testimony of what at the time was said of the transaction by the defendant, who, at that time, I doubt not, was acting the part of a friend in concert with the wife and son, and entertained no design of setting up this claim of an absolute purchase, which, now that Mr. *Rowed* is dead, and the son is dead, he ventures to assert, and who, regarding *McColl* also as a friend of the family, would have had no motive to suppress the circumstances attending a transaction which, at that time, he deemed to be, and possibly was, praiseworthy.

Entertaining, as I do, this view of the case, all that remains is to inquire whether the decree can be affirmed or not, upon the grounds, or any of the grounds laid by the plaintiff in his bill as constituting his equitable title to relief.

During the argument I felt much pressed with the force of the arguments urged by the able counsel for the defendant. No one can be more impressed than I am with the importance of requiring plaintiffs to state accurately in the bill the basis upon which they claim the interposition of the Court, and of the necessity that the evidence should accord with, and support the statements of the bill, so that the judgment may be always *secundum allegata et probata*. But when I see a defendant setting up as his defence an absolute purchase for good consideration, which he himself disproves; and when I find him leaning upon principles of law to support him in the consummation of what, from his own lips, I am satisfied, is a gross fraud, I think that we should be astute to support, if possible, the plaintiff's case, and not be too particular in criticising his pleading.

Now, in this case, the chief ground upon which the plaintiff rests his claim for relief, namely, that condition of mental degradation to which his own sottish habits had reduced him, explains (or if it be established, as I think it is, that such was his general condition,) the difficulty which the plaintiff must have had in presenting his case to the Court.

Now, that we have seen the evidence, I think that no
very considerable amendment in the plaintiff's statement
in his bill will bring the pleadings and the evidence into
accord.  As, for example, if the fifth paragraph of the
bill should be made to state that the plaintiff's wife and
son, being apprehensive that the plaintiff should for the
gratification of his intemperate habits, sell the said property, and waste the proceeds in the indulgence of those
habits, contrived a scheme, in concert with the defendant,
whereby they should procure the plaintiff to execute a
deed of the property to the defendant, upon some arrangement made between the wife and son and the defendant,
that upon payment of the mortgage by the son, the
defendant should hold the property for their benefit;
and that accordingly the wife and son and the defendant,
well knowing the plaintiff's mental condition to be such
that he was utterly incapable of understanding the
nature or effect of what they required him to do, exercised their influence upon him, and procured him to
execute the deed which is impeached, although he was
utterly incapacitated by the condition to which his mind
was reduced by his intemperate habits, from appreciating
or understanding the nature or effect of the transaction.

*Black's* evidence also supports the view that this is a
true representation of the transaction.  He says : " In
1857, I had a conversation with *Ogilvie* : he said he had
taken a deed of plaintiff's property to save it for him
and his family.  He said he expected to get into trouble
with *Crippen* on that account.  He said, *Miller* wanted
to undermine him, and take it from him.  He said, he
took the property with the intention of giving it back
again on payment of the principal and interest.  He
said, he had received some rent for interest."

The rent, here referred to, no doubt was the $36.20,
paid by *Dugald*, in 1856, and which defendant indorsed
on the lease, the only copy of which that was ever exe-

1871.

Crippen
v.
Ogilvie.

Judgment.

cuted, he retained in his own possession from the day it was executed.

Upon this lease the plaintiff never paid a shilling of rent, nor does any appear to have been demanded of him. I do not attach much weight to the fact of the defendant having in the summer of 1859, refused to receive the mortgage money when tendered by Mr. *Dumble*, as establishing laches; for *Dugald*, the son, was then living, and the general condition of the plaintiff was much the same as it was in 1855; and, assuming as I do, that *Dugald* and the defendant understood each other, it would have been easy for the son to exercise an influence upon the father sufficient to prevent him from proceeding against the defendant.

In *Anderson* v. *Elsworth* (a), a bill was filed by the heir-at-law against the grantee of a deceased lady by a
Judgment voluntary deed executed in her life-time, the grounds for relief stated in the bill were: " That the execution of the deed by the deceased was obtained by the defendant and her husband while the deceased was residing with them, and while she was unable to read and write, and was in a state of bodily infirmity and mental incapacity, which rendered her wholly unable to understand the meaning or effect of any deed or other document, or any matter of business; and she could not have been, and was not in fact aware of what she was doing, or of the object, meaning, purport, or effect of the deed, when she executed the same."

It was proved that she had consulted with her solicitor upon the matter before the deed was prepared; that her object, as she stated to her solicitor, was, that the property should not go to her heir, nor to any one, but this grantee, whom she was resolved to give the property to.

(a) 7 Jur. N. S. 1047.

She was desirous of effecting her purpose in the cheapest way possible. Her solicitor suggested a deed as a cheaper mode than by will; and, accordingly, she selected that mode, and gave him instructions to prepare the deed.

The grounds of relief laid in the bill were wholly disproved; and although the plaintiffs were claiming as volunteers, the deed was set aside because it contained no clause of power of revocation, and because the Vice Chancellor thought that although the deceased grantor was perfectly capable of understanding the matter, the solicitor had not sufficiently explained to her the effect of such a clause being omitted from the deed. The only consequence of the decree being made upon a point not made by the bill, was, that it was to set aside the deed without costs.

When I find a mortgagee setting up as an absolute purchase a deed in effect conveying to him the equity of redemption in property worth at least seven times the amount secured upon the mortgage; and when we find that done for no additional consideration whatever, five years before the mortgage money became due; and when we find that three years' rent of the half of the property was abundant to pay the whole mortgage security; and that the mortgagee declares the *deed was forced upon him ;* and that in fact it was for the benefit of the mortgagor that it was executed; and when we find the mortgagor to be the drunken imbecile which he is represented to have been here, a Court of Equity would be indeed impotent if it was unable to redress so great a wrong, or if it should be deterred from stripping the mortgagee of the benefits of a deed so obtained, because he has been permitted to receive the rents issuing from half of the estate for about seven or eight years longer than he should have been, and after the rent received must have paid off his mortgage security in full.

1871.

## Box v. The Provincial Insurance Company.
## [In Appeal.*]

*Sale of wheat, part of a larger quantity—Warehouseman's receipt.*

A warehouseman sold 3,500 bushels of wheat, part of a larger quantity which he had in store, and gave the purchaser a warehouseman's
receipt, under the statute, acknowledging that he had received from
him that quantity of wheat, to be delivered pursuant to his order
to be indorsed on the receipt. The 3,500 bushels were never
separated from the other wheat of the seller :

*Held*, by the Court of Appeal [Spragge, C., and Morrison, and
Gwynne, JJ., dissenting] that the purchaser had an insurable
interest.

This was an appeal by the plaintiffs from the decree
of the Court below, pronounced on the re-hearing of
the cause as reported, *ante* volume xv., page 337, affirming the decree made on the original hearing, dismissing
the bill with costs.

Statement.

The facts appearing in the case were shortly these :
*Robert Todd* was a warehouseman, carrying on business at Seaforth, he had from time to time, during the
latter part of 1866 and the beginning of 1867, purchased considerable quantities of wheat, which were
placed together, according to their qualities, as spring
or fall wheat in his warehouse, and from time to time,
during the same period, he had sent away to market or
delivered to purchasers various quantities of the wheat
in the warehouse.   Other wheat dealers had also deposited during the same period, parcels of wheat in his
warehouse, and had disposed of and removed part of
the quantities which they were thus entitled to.

*Todd* sold to plaintiffs, acting through *Carter*, one of
their firm, 3,500 bushels of wheat, which he represented
to be owned by him and to be then in his warehouse,

---

* *Present.*—Draper, C.J., Richards, C.J., Hagarty, C.J., Spragge,
V.C., Morrison J., Wilson, J., Mowat, V.C., Gwynne, J.

and received payment for it, and the evidence shewed

that more than that quantity belonging to him, though mixed with the wheat of other parties, was at the time of this sale in the warehouse. Besides the oral evidence of the sale, given by a party present when it was made, there was put in a receipt given to *Carter* by *Todd*, in the following terms: "Received in store from *George Carter*, owner, 3,400 [bill stated 3,500] bushels No. 1 spring wheat, to be delivered pursuant to his order to be endorsed hereon. This is to be regarded as a receipt under the provisions of Statute, 22 Victoria, chapter 20, being 22 Victoria, chapter 54 of the Consolidated Statutes of Canada, and the amended Statute 24 Victoria, chapter 23. Seaforth, C. W., 30 January, 1867—*Robert Todd*." Endorsed "Jany. 31, 1867. *George Carter*, Deliver to order of Messrs. *Box*, and *Summerville*, and *George Carter*."

On the 15th of March, 1867, the plaintiffs, *Box, Summerville*, and *Carter*, insured $5,000 on wheat in store in the warehouse, which *Todd* occupied, and obtained an insurance receipt from the defendants' agent. On the 18th of March the storehouse was destroyed by fire, and the grain in it consumed or greatly damaged, a part only being saved from entire destruction.

The defendants, it was shewn, had refused to pay the plaintiffs anything or to issue a policy to the plaintiffs.

Mr. *Blake*, Q. C., for the appellants. The only question presented on this appeal is, did there or not exist an insurable interest in the wheat on the part of the plaintiffs at the time the insurance was effected? The Chancellor determined that he had no such interest, because at the time plaintiffs had not 3,500 bushels in store their own property; although there was a larger quantity in bulk, out of which plaintiffs were to obtain 3,500 bushels. Under these circumstances he contended the property in the wheat passed. *Todd* could not be heard to deny, after giving the receipt, that there were 3,500 bushels of spring wheat in his warehouse belonging to *Box & Company*.

Mr. *Duggan*, Q. C., and Mr. *Moss*, contra—The effect of the transaction between *Todd* and the plaintiffs was a contract, on *Todd's* part, to sell to the plaintiffs a certain quantity of spring wheat out of a larger quantity then in his warehouse. If there were 3,500 bushels of spring wheat, it is clear it did not all belong to *Todd*, neither could he have owned so large a quantity of wheat as was there. They also contended that the provisions of the statutes, 22 and 24 Victoria, did not apply to this case. The first of these enactments only enabled the owner of grain who had stored it, to transfer the receipt he obtains from the warehouseman, by indorsement, to a bank or private individual as a collateral security to such bank for any note discounted

in the regular course of business, or of any debt due to a private person : the second act simply extended the prior statute by enabling the owner of grain, being a warehouseman, to give a receipt and indorse it.

Here, neither Act applies. The first only gives the power to an owner who has goods stored, to transfer them to a bank or other creditor by simple indorsement over of the warehouse receipt ; but the question which arises here is, did the plaintiffs by the transaction between themselves and *Todd* become owners of any portion of the grain in *Todd's* warehouse. The second only enables the *owner*, being a warehouseman, to transfer by this short mode his property to a bank, &c.; unless, however, a party be from the first *owner* he cannot take advantage of the Act. The warehouse receipt *per se* derives no authority from these enactments, as transferring property from the owner who has it there, to a purchaser.

This case is distinguishable from *Clark* v. *The Western Assurance Company* (a), as the point in dispute here, did not arise in that case. The defendants in that action contended that the plaintiff was bound to prove the identity of the grain destroyed with that insured : the insurable interest there was admitted in the first instance. Here the warehouse receipt is the only evidence of transfer of property and it is only a contract of sale ; under it the plaintiffs acquired a right of action against *Todd* their vendor, if he did not deliver to them the 3,500 bushels, severing it from the larger quantity ; they acquired however no property in any specific 3,500 bushels of such larger quantity, and it follows that they had not any insurable interest in the quantity so contracted for.

Mr. *Blake*, Q. C., in reply. It may be admitted for the sake of argument that the statute in respect of these warehouse receipts is not directly applicable to this case. But *Todd* having received a valuable consideration, acknowledges that he has 3,500 bushels of wheat belonging to the plaintiffs, by giving this receipt : thus establishing the relation of warehouse-keeper and depositor between himself and them.

*Seagrave* v. *The Union Marine Insurance Company* (b), *Robertson* v. *French* (c), *Stockdale* v. *Dunlop* (d), *Aldridge* v. *Johnson* (e), *Busk* v. *Davis* (f), *Hale* v. *Rawson* (g), were (amongst other cases) referred to.

DRAPER, C. J.—The material question raised between the parties and the only one pressed before us on the argument, is whether on the 30th of January, 1867, *Carter*, and subsequently through him the plaintiff

1871.

Box
v.
Provincial
Ins. Co.

Judgment.

---

(a) 25 U. C. Q. B. 209.　　　(b) L. R. 1 C. P. 306.
(c) 4 East 130.　　　　　　　(d) 6 M. & W. 224.
(e) 7 El. & B. 857.　　　　　 (f) 2 M. & S. 397.
(g) 4 C. B., N. S. 85.

became the owners of the wheat mentioned in the receipt, whether they had an insurable interest in wheat in the warehouse at the time of the insurance and of the fire.

Considering the judgment of the learned Chancellor in the cause, together with the evidence which was given, which shews that wheat belonging to *Todd*, and wheat belonging to other persons, was delivered and received · into the warehouse both before and after the sale to *Carter* by *Todd;* that it does not appear that in any instance was wheat so delivered, kept separate and apart from other wheat of similar description and quality ; that the practice recognized in our courts in more than one decided case, is that each kind of wheat—say fall wheat, No. 1, or No. 2 ; or spring wheat, No. 1, or No. 2—should be mingled with other wheat of similar kind and quality already received in store; that during all the period from the earliest delivery into the warehouse until the fire, large quantities of wheat were delivered out for and on account of the parties who deposited and who held warehouse receipts without reference or inquiry as to the fact whether the grain so delivered out was the identical grain delivered in by the respective parties to whom such receipts were given ; the question raised by the defendants is a very important one to dealers in grain who deposit their purchases in the manner indicated—not requiring their grain to be kept separate from the grain of other parties stored in the same warehouse.

The course of dealing with grain so received into such warehouses, has become familiar and well understood and is, I believe, correctly stated in the judgment in *Clark* v. *The Western Assurance Company* (a), to the following effect, that the warehouseman receives grain, giving a receipt to the depositor for the quantity, and

(a) 25 U. C. Q. B. 209.

designating the kind, class, or quality, which receipt
amounts to an undertaking by the warehouse-keeper to
deliver the same quantity of a like description of grain to
such depositor, or any other person lawfully authorized
by him to receive it, but not (in the absence of any
special agreement,) to an undertaking to re-deliver to
each depositor the identical grain stored by him.
·Neither the Consolidated Statutes of Canada, chapter
54, section 8, nor the Amending Act, 24 Victoria, chapter 23, section 1, affect this well-understood and long-
established course of dealing.

The primary object of the Legislature in these acts
seems to have been to enable the incorporated banks in
the Province of Canada to afford larger facilities to
commercial transactions. To some extent they also
give an advantage to private persons. They enable the
owner or the person entitled to receive any cereal grains,
goods, wares or merchandise for which such owner or
person entitled held—(1) a bill of lading (2) a specification, in case of timber, or (3) a receipt given by a
warehouseman, miller, wharfinger, master of a vessel
or carrier, for such cereal grains, &c., stored or deposited
in any warehouse, mill, cove, or other place in the
Province, or delivered to a carrier for carriage, by
indorsement on such receipt, &c., to transfer the same
to such bank, or to any person for such bank, or to any
private person or persons *as collateral security for the
due payment of any bill of exchange or note discounted
by such bank in the regular course of business, or of any
debt due to such private person*, and the receipt so
indorsed shall vest in such bank or person from the date
of such indorsement the right and title of the indorser
to such cereal grains, &c., subject to retransfer in the
event of the bill, note, or debt being paid when due. A
power of sale to be exercised after ten days' notice, if
the endorser does not pay, is given to the indorsee,
subject however to these limitations that no such cereal

1871.

Box
v.
Provincial
Ins. Co.

Judgment.

grains, &c., can be held in pledge for more than six months, and that no such transfer can be made by way of collateral security for any bill, note or debt which was not negotiated or contracted at the same time with the indorsement of the bill of lading, specification or receipt. It was further provided that if the warehouse-man, miller, wharfinger, master of a vessel, or carrier who might, as such, give a receipt for cereal grains, &c., and who also was as owner, or in any capacity other than warehouseman, &c., authorized to receive such grain, &c., indorsed such receipt or any acknowledgement or certificate intended to answer the purposes of such receipt; the receipt, &c., so indorsed should be as valid and effectual for the purposes of the Act as if the giver and indorser thereof were not one and the same person.

But the introduction into the receipt given by *Todd* to *Carter* of the words "this is to be regarded as a receipt under the provisions of the Statute 22nd Victoria," &c., will not alter the real character of the transaction between those parties, which was simply a sale to *Carter* of certain wheat, represented as lying in *Todd's* warehouse and belonging to *Todd*, though the receipt itself represents *Todd* as receiving into his warehouse from *Carter* 3,400 bushels of wheat, of which the latter was owner. *Todd* was not pledging his wheat as collateral security to *Carter* for a debt, neither did *Todd* as debtor indorse a receipt, certificate, or acknowledgment, signed by himself, as warehouseman, to *Carter*. The actual transaction was not one, which by force of the statute, would make the receipt when indorsed operate as a transfer of the wheat mentioned in it.

The statutes referred to in the receipt do not affect the question. There is a sale and payment, the property sold being a named quantity of *Todd's* wheat, part of, and not severed from, a larger quantity of wheat belonging to *Todd*, and possibly, and even probably, in part to other owners; and notwithstanding the receipt I think, to borrow Lord *Campbell's* language in *Aldridge* v. *Johnson* (a), that the property in this wheat did not become absolutely vested in the plaintiffs "until the appropriation and separation of a particular quantity, or signification of assent to the particular quantity, the property is not transferred." There is nothing in the facts before us to afford ground for applying the principle that where the owner of grain, or wine, or oil, mixes either with similar articles belonging to another he loses his own property through his own wrongful act, for here the intermixture preceded the sale to *Carter*. Nor do I think the principle asserted in *Gillett* v. *Hill* (b), applicable to this case. If the decision depended upon the legal transfer of the property as being indispensable to the creation of an insurable interest I should concur in the judgment of the learned late Chancellor.

But I am of opinion that under the circumstances in evidence the plaintiffs had an insurable interest. And Mr. Vice Chancellor *Mowat* treating the evidence as sufficient to establish the intention both of *Todd* and of *Carter*, that the property should pass, arrived at the same result when the case was in the court below. I think there is great force in his remarks upon the effect which should be given to *Todd's* receipt. From the moment it was given, *Todd* was virtually estopped (not using the word "estopped" in the strict legal sense) from denying that he had the specified quantity of wheat as *Carter's* property. To the authorities cited as to the effect of intention, I would add *Young* v. *Matthews* (c).

If it were necessary for the decision of this case, I incline to think it might be properly held, considering the course of dealing in regard to the storage of grain already adverted to, that after the receipt was

*1871.*

Box
v.
Provincial
Ins. Co.

Judgment.

(a) 7 E. & B. at 899.    (b) 2 C. & M. 530.    (c) L. R. 2 P. C. 127.

1871.

Box
v.
Provincial
Ins. Co.

given nothing remained to be done for the purpose of passing the property, by *Todd* in his character as vendor; he had assumed the duty as warehouseman to weigh out and deliver to the lawful holder of his receipt the quantity specified therein. Suppose *Carter* had actually delivered wheat purchased elsewhere to be stored by *Todd* in this warehouse, and had taken this receipt, and the wheat had been mixed with wheat of a similar quality already stored, it could not, I apprehend, be denied that *Carter* would have an insurable interest. I am not able to find a substantial reason why the same result should not follow upon the receipt given under the fact of sale and payment which are in evidence.

But independently of this view, I think it clear that the plaintiffs had an insurable interest. In *Lucena* v. *Craufurd*, (*a*) (in Dom. Proc.) *Lawrence*, J., in answer to one of the questions put by the House of Lords

Judgment.

to the Judges, after stating the general nature of the contract of insurance, says: "It is applicable to protect men against uncertain events which may in anywise be of disadvantage to them, not only those persons to whom positive loss may arise by such events occasioning the deprivation of that which they may possess, but those also who in consequence of such events may have intercepted from them the advantage or profit which, but for such events, they would acquire according to the ordinary and probable course of things." He further cites as good law a decision of Lord C. J. *Willes*, adding that according thereto " the impossibility of valuing" the loss " *and not the want of property*," may afford the sole reason why a particular interest is not insurable. The language of Lord *Eldon* in the same case seems to me clearly in favor of the plaintiff. He says, in reference to what is an insurable interest :

---

(*a*) 2 N. R., at p. 301.

" Nor am I able to point out what is an interest unless it be a right in the property or a right derivable out of some contract about the property which in either case may be lost upon some contingency affecting the possession or enjoyment of the party."

In the present case the plaintiffs had purchased and paid for a fixed quantity of wheat, and were entitled to a delivery upon demand. The property was not absolutely vested in them because the wheat bought was mixed with a larger quantity, but they clearly had a " right derivable out of some contract," about the wheat, and that right might be lost if the wheat was destroyed by fire before they required a delivery. I think this was an insurable interest.

I am therefore of opinion that the conclusion of *Mowat*, V. C., was right, viz: that the decree should declare the defendants liable to indemnify the plaintiff against the loss in a sum not to exceed $5,000.

Judgment.

The question as to the quantity of wheat which *Todd* had in fact, and which would be applicable to the plaintiffs under his receipt, was but little discussed in the Court below; we think therefore the case should be referred back to that Court, with the declaration that the plaintiff had an insurable interest in whatever wheat, (if any) would be applicable under the receipt, to the fulfilment or satisfaction of the plaintiffs' purchase from *Todd*. If no wheat, the bill to be dismissed with costs. If any, the defendants to pay the amount arising from the loss and costs of suit.

SPRAGGE, C.—The judgment of His Lordship the Chief Justice of this Court concedes the general question, that by a sale of an unsevered portion of a larger quantity, the property does not pass. I do not propose to go over the same ground, but will only refer to some cases in affirmance of that doctrine, not cited in the judgment, in the Court below, of the late learned Chancellor, nor, I believe, in the judgment just delivered : *Godts* v. *Rose* (a), *Logan* v. *LeMesurier* (b), *Campbell* v. *Mersey Docks and Harbour Board* (c). There is also the case of *Clay* v. *Harrison*, which I will refer to upon another branch of the case, and there are several other cases.

His Lordship also says, and I agree with him, that the introduction into the receipt by *Todd* to *Carter* of the words "this is to be regarded as a receipt under the provisions of the Statute 22nd Victoria," &c., does not alter the real character of the transaction between those parties, which was simply a sale to *Carter* of certain wheat represented as lying in *Todd's* warehouse, and belonging to *Todd ;* though the receipt represents *Todd* as receiving into his warehouse, from *Carter*, 3,400 bushels of wheat of which the latter was the owner.

I agree also as to the course of trade in dealings of this nature, and that the Courts, in dealing with questions arising out of these transactions, properly take notice of what is the course of trade.

The judgment of my brother *Mowat* upon the rehearing proceeded upon the ground that it was the intention of the parties that the property should pass to the plaintiffs ; and that the law, carrying out the intention of the parties, transfers the property where it appears to be the intention of the parties that it should be transferred. The learned Chief Justice adopts this reasoning.

I do not feel it necessary to go into the law upon this point, *i.e.*, as to the effect of intention, because I cannot

---

(a) 17 C. B. 229.          (b) 6 Moore P. C. 116.
(c) 14 C. B. N. S. 412.

see in the dealings of these parties any manifestation of intention that the property should pass. Without the warehouse receipt there was nothing more than a contract of sale. Then what is the effect of the receipt? Its office and object are two-fold: to evidence the contract of sale, and to enable the purchaser to use it under the Act as collateral security for advances. It must be read by the light of the recognized ordinary course of trade, and with reference to the Statute. The Statute itself does not confer the property or make it pass in a case where, without the Statute, the property would not pass. The receipt, then, styles *Carter* the owner: with what intent? In order to change the property? In order to give to their dealing a character, or to make their relative positions different from what they would be otherwise? 1 think, certainly not. There is nothing in their dealing to shew this to be the object. The real object is manifested by the reference to the Statute at the foot, viz., in order to its use as a collateral security for advances. The word "owner," or "owners," appears really to be nothing more than a stereotyped form meaning only depositors, or party entitled to receive. The point here is, whether, *between these parties themselves*, it was intended that any particular legal effect should be given to the use of this word, and whether it was used in order to vest property; because the question is, whether, *in fact*, the property was thereby changed, that depending upon the fact whether or not it was the intention thereby to change it; unless we can see that it was used with that *intuitus*, it is simply worthless as an indication of intention, and the general law applying to unsevered property applies; and the receipt was only a contract of sale put into a particular shape in order to its use under the Statute.

In the English case, referred to by my brother *Mowat*, *Woods* v. *Russell* (a), the intention to transfer the property was unequivocally manifested. The person for

1871.

Box
v.
Provincial
Ins. Co.

Judgment.

---

(a) 5 B. & Al. 942.

1871.

Box
v.
Provincial
Ins. Co.

whom the ship was being built desired to have it registered in his own name, and the builder gave a certificate
in order to its registry; and beyond all this, the registry
could not be effected without an oath of ownership.
There is nothing at all like this in the case before us.
He refers also to *Clark* v. *The Western Ins. Co.* (a),
but in that case the point taken in this case was not
taken, and it is not authority in this Court. My learned
brother refers to other cases by name only. In one of
them, *Whitehouse* v. *Frost* (b), it was stipulated that the
oil sold should be at the risk of the purchaser. In
another, *Woodley* v. *Coventry* (c), the purchaser resold
to a third person, and the original vendors recognized
the title of the third party, and the case proceeded
mainly upon the ground of estoppel. *Pooley* v. *Budd*
(d) proceeded upon the ground of trust. The vendors
gave the purchasers a lien upon the goods sold; and
Lord *Romilly* was of opinion that, taking all the allegations in the bill to be correct (the question arose upon

Judgment.

demurrer), the vendors must, by their own admission,
have ceased to have any interest in the thing sold at the
time when the lien was created. So far as *Pooley* v.
*Budd* may be looked upon as an authority for the
position that property in unsevered goods passes by
contract of sale, supposing it an authority for that position at all, the weight of authority is against it.

My position upon the question of property in this
case is, that unless the Court sees that as between the
parties to this sale of grain, there is an intention manifested that the property in the grain should pass to the
purchaser, so as to take it out of the general rule that
property does not pass upon a sale of unsevered goods,
then the actual property in the goods did not pass; the
vendor did not cease to be owner, the purchaser did not
become owner.

(a) 25 U. C. Q. B. 209.          (b) 12 East 614.
(c) 2 H. & C. 164.               (d) 14 Beav. 34.

In regard to the question of estoppel. As between the vendor and purchaser, the former, it is said, is estopped from controverting that which is alleged in the document. Two things are alleged: one, that the purchasers were owners; the other, that the vendor had in store a certain quantity of wheat belonging to them. Assuming that the vendor is estopped as to both, it does not follow that the Insurance Company is estopped. They certainly are not estopped from shewing that the quantity of wheat stated in the receipt was not in store; and I apprehend that they are not any more estopped from shewing that the plaintiffs were not owners. There is nothing in the nature of the document to prevent third parties, at any rate, if not the parties themselves, from shewing the truth.

It is not contended that, even if there was *no change of property* in the grain sold by *Coleman* to the plaintiffs, the latter had at any rate an *insurable interest.* That position involves this: that, upon a contract of sale, the property in the thing agreed to be sold remaining in the vendor, the purchaser has an insurable interest in the thing which is the subject of the contract. I think that this is not law. I refer upon this point to *Clay* v. *Harrison* (a), *Fragano* v. *Long* (b), *Stockdale* v. *Dunlop* (c), *Sparkes* v. *Marshall* (d). In some of these cases it was held that the assured had an insurable interest, but they are nevertheless authorities for the position that upon a contract of sale, the thing sold remaining in the custody of the vendor, the purchaser has not an insurable interest; because in all those cases the Court laid hold upon the goods sold being dispatched by the vendor, or some other circumstance, indicating change of property, all which would have been unnecessary if the contract of sale were in itself sufficient. The earliest

Judgment.

(a) 10 B. & C. 99.  (b) 4 B. & C. 219.
(c) 6 M. & W. 224.  (d) 2 Bing. N. C. 761.

of these cases, *Clay* v. *Harrison*, resembles this case in all essential circumstances, as well as in principle. The question arose. upon a special case, from which, as noted by the reporters, and from the statement of the case, it appears that certain timber dealers in St. Petersburg agreed to sell a quantity of deals to a merchant in Hull, and shipped them on board a ship bound for Hull. The ship was wrecked off Elsinore, and the agent of the vendors stopped the goods *in transitu* at Elsinore. I cannot do better than transcribe the note of the learned reporter at the end of the case : "It appears from the special case, that by the contract between the bankrupt and the vendors, the latter were to supply a cargo of timber. There was no bargain for any specific ascertained chattel, but the vendors were at liberty to supply any timber answering the description of that ordered ; and, consequently, no property passed till the cargo of timber was appropriated by the vendors to the vendee, by the delivery on board the ship. The subsequent

stoppage *in transitu*, supposing it had only the effect of revesting the possession in the vendors, and placing them in the same situation as if they had not parted with the goods, destroyed the effect of that delivery which was the only circumstance which vested the property in the vendee ; and consequently the property revested in the vendors. They then were exactly in the same condition as if the goods had always remained in their warehouses ; and in that case the bankrupt would have had no interest in the goods : his rights, if any, would have rested in contract merely." The judgment of the Court was, that after the stoppage *in transitu* the purchaser had no property in the goods insured, and therefore that the action on the policies of insurance could not be supported. Mr. *Arnould*, in his treatise on Insurance, under the head "Insurable Interest of Vendor and Vendee," states the law to be that the party insuring must "have an interest, legal or equitable, in the subject of insurance during the pendency

of the risk, and until and at the time of loss. If, therefore, the insurable interest depends upon a sale, the
vendee must have acquired a complete title to the thing
insured at some time during the risk, and before the
loss, otherwise he can recover nothing on his policy; "
(a) and he reiterates this in almost the same terms :
" Unless the sale vests in the purchaser an absolute title
to the thing insured during the risk, and before the loss,
he has no insurable interest." The authorities to which
the learned writer refers seem to me to bear out his
proposition.

To recur once more to the position of the parties.
*Coleman*, in this case, like the timber dealers in *Clay* v.
*Harrison*, having (or assuming to have) a commodity in
bulk in his warehouse, agrees to sell a certain quantity
thereof. He gives a paper, which admittedly does not
describe the true nature of the transaction between them,
in which he calls the purchaser "owner." In the timber
case, also, a paper was given beginning " Sold Mr. So-
and-so, two 'cargoes of deals, deliverable." It then
sets out quantity, price, mode of payment, and how to
be shipped. If it had been an insurance against fire,
and the timber had been burned, the assurer could not
have recovered. There is literally nothing in the case
before us to distinguish it from that case, except the
use of the word "owner," and that word, used *alio
intuitu*, viz., to give currency to the document. No
setting apart, no appropriation of any kind. I find
difficulty in understanding of what tangible thing he
was owner. He might, by a figure of speech, be called
owner of a right to have a certain quantity of wheat
delivered to him; but how he was owner of any wheat
I confess I cannot see; and unless he was owner, the
wheat was the subject of contract only, and no insurable interest passed to the vendee. We were referred to

1871.

Box
v.
Provincial
Ins. Co.

Judgment.

---

(a) Sec. 121.

Box
v.
Provincial
Ins. Co.

*Davies* v. *The Home Ins. Co.* (a) in this Court; but in
that case there was property in the party insured.
We are also referred to the language of Lord *Eldon*, in
*Lucena* v. *Craufurd* (b), when his Lordship was in the
Common Pleas. Some of the language used by his
Lordship in his definition of what is an insurable interest
may be wide enough to comprehend the case of any
purchaser of goods ; but definitions are sometimes found
to be at fault when they come to be applied to particular
cases, as his Lordship's definition certainly is if intended
to comprehend the case of an ordinary purchaser. The
decided cases upon the point are, of course, entitled to
more weight.

Judgment.

Supposing the Court to be of opinion that the plaintiffs were not, in fact, owners, but still that they had
an insurable interest, they are not, as I think, entitled
to recover, because they untruly described their interest.
The rule, as laid down by Lord *Tenterden*, in *Crowley*
v. *Cohen* (c), is, that " although the subject matter of
the insurance must be properly described, the *nature of
the interest* may in general be left at large ;" and if it
had been left at large in this case, there would have
been no difficulty on that score. But in one of the
queries put to the plaintiffs as applicants for insurance
the question of the nature of their interest was pointedly
put to them thus : " State fully the applicants' interest
in the property insured ; whether owner or otherwise."
And to this the answer was " owners." If they had
some insurable interest, but still were not owners, the
answer was untrue ; and, as stated by Mr. *Arnould*,
" a policy must in *all* cases state correctly, and in *some*
specifically, *what* is insured (d) ;" and he states the true
proposition to be that laid down by Lord *Tenterden*.
I will upon this point only refer to some cases in which

---

(a) 3 U. C. E. & A.                (b) 2 N. R. 321.
(c) 3 B. & Ad. at 485.             (d) Sec. 14.

this point has arisen : *Glover* v. *Black* (a), *Palmer* v. 1871.
*Pratt* (b), *Carruthers* v. *Sheddon* (c). . These were cases
where the insurance was general, not describing the
nature of the insurer's interest, and the Courts laid stress
upon that circumstance in sustaining the actions on the
policies. I confess, however, I should be unwilling to
defeat the plaintiffs upon this ground, as I suppose they
believed themselves to be owners. The point, I believe,
was not taken in argument ; at least I have not noted it.

Upon the whole, I have ;not come- to the conclusion,
to which I belive a majority of the Court has come, that
the judgment of the Court below is wrong.

HAGARTY, C. J.—I agree in the judgment just pronounced by the learned Chief Justice of this Court.

As soon as it is conceded that there was at the time
of effecting the insurance a sufficient quantity of wheat,
although not severed from a larger quantity, to answer
the appellants' warehouse receipt, the latter had an
insurable interest. If there be any meaning in the
various propositions laid down in *Lucena* v. *Craufurd*
and the text books which adopt that case as declaratory of the true principles of insurance,I think I am
bound to hold the appellants had an insurable interest.

As between them and *Todd*, the latter had declared
in writing that he had received into his store and
held for them the specified quantity of wheat. It
seems to me that had he refused to deliver, they could
have maintained trover against him on his express
written declaration of having that specific property
in his hands belonging to them, and if the wheat in
the warehouse had been destroyed by fire uninsured,
and under such circumstances that *Todd* as bailee would

Box
v.
Provincial
Ins. Co.

Judgment.

---

(a) 1 W. Black. 423.　　(b) 2 Bing. 185.　　(c) 6 Taunt. 14.

38—VOL. XVIII. GR.

not be liable for loss by accidental fire, the loss would fall on the appellants. I hardly think if they brought trover or an action against *Todd* for non-delivery, and he set up the destruction by fire that they could insist that the property had not passed to them, or that it was not their property that was destroyed.

I do not think that this case can be decided on the law as laid down as to unascertained or unseparated property passing between vendor and vendee. In an insurance case, *Joyce* v. *Swann* (a), the question was whether there was an insurable interest in plaintiff, and there was a contest as to whether the property in certain goods shipped had passed to him or not. *Willes*, J., says, after holding that it did pass, "I am inclined to go further, for it appears to me that if what was done by *Swan and Co.*, was to put the goods on board the vessel with the intention of fulfilling Mr. *Carter's* (the real plaintiff) order even if by reason of some special

circumstances the property did not pass on shipment, yet by reason of the risk, the buyer might insure the cargo in respect of the interest he had in it. It is like the case I put of a tenant bound by a covenant to insure, though he had no longer any interest in the house, yet by reason of his covenant he had an interest in the insurance." See the same facts in *Seagrave* v. *Union Insurance Company* (b). In the case before us I think the appellants' interest in the wheat was one which a Court of Equity would protect. If they had bought or contracted to buy half of a pile of wheat in *Todd's* warehouse, and *Todd* or others were about destroying or taking the whole out of the country, equity would, I think, interfere. The law is very clearly laid down by Lord *Westbury* in *Holroyd* v. *Marshall* (c) "a contract for the sale of goods, as for example 500 chests of

---

(a) 17 C. B. N. S. 84. (b) L. R. 1 C. P. 505.
(c) 33 L. J. Cb. at 196.

tea was not a contract which could be specifically performed, because it did not relate to any chests of tea in particular, but a contract to sell the 500 chests of a particular kind of tea which are now at my warehouse in Gloucester, was a contract relating to specific property, and which would be specifically performed."

In that case the question was as to whether certain machines brought into mortgaged premises in addition to, or substitution for, other machinery already mortgaged should, be held under the mortgage. It was conceded that the new machinery would not pass at law on such a contract, but the Court of Equity interfered, and protected it from the execution creditor of the mortgagor. It appears to me there can be no doubt of the mortgagees in that case having an insurable interest in all new or substituted machinery. I also refer to *Wilson* v. *Martin* (a), and to *Davies* v. *The Home Insurance Co.*, in appeal.

*Judgment.*

I think the appellants entitled to the relief prayed.

GWYNNE, J.—The late learned Chancellor, as I understand his judgment, dismissed the plaintiffs' bill upon this principle, that inasmuch as the plaintiffs took the interim insurance receipt, as upon a policy, to be effected upon 3,500 bushels of wheat which the plaintiffs represented themselves to be the owners of, and that as, in the judgment of the learned Chancellor, they had not the 3,500 bushels, or any part of it, as their own property, but had only a right to claim some as yet unascertained 3,500 bushels from *Todd*, or damages in lieu of it, the insurance which they effected fails, and cannot be enforced. The learned Chancellor says in his judgment, " the questions are, had they an insurable interest in an unascertained quantity of 3,500 bushels of

(a) 11 Ex. 684.

wheat, if they had, *was it that interest* which they insured,
or did they insure *as the owners of a specific quantity of
3,500 bushels*, and if so insuring" (that is, as owners of
a specific quantity when they were not) " can they insist
that under it" (that is, a policy so effected,) " they have
a right to protect themselves to the extent of the
damages which they could recover from *Todd* for the
non-delivery of the wheat when called for ?".

*William Currie*, a witness called by plaintiffs, says,
" I know *Robert Todd*; I recollect seeing him on the
30th of January, 1867, in company with Mr. *Carter*.
On that day a sale of 3,500 bushels of No. 1 spring
wheat was made by *Todd* to *Carter*; I drew the receipt"
(exhibit 'A', that is the warehouse receipt signed by
*Todd*) "and *Todd* signed it in my presence. A few
days after I was in the warehouse, and there was then
fully 3,500 bushels of No. 1 wheat: so far as I know
the sale was completed on the 30th January in *Lloyd's*

Judgment.

Hotel, Seaforth; *part of the price was paid in cash at
the time, and the balance was to be sent by express*."
This balance if paid must have been paid at some time
*after* the warehouse receipt was given, and being so paid
the terms of that receipt are not entitled to that weight
which the learned Vice Chancellor *Mowat*, attaches to
them in his judgment. I agree with the learned Vice
Chancellor that it is the intention of the parties to the
contract that is to govern. *Reeve* v. *Whitmore* (a)
sufficiently shews that; but that the intention shall
govern is a principle not unknown in Courts of Law, the
difference being, that whereas by the rules of law, operation can be given to it only in respect of things having
existence at the time the contract is entered into,
Equity is restricted by no such limitations, but will give
effect to the intention so as to enable it to operate upon
things coming into existence; and in the case of goods

(a) 9 Jur. N. S. 243.

in existence so situated as to be incapable of delivery at law, the contract will attach in equity, if it was the intention of the parties that it should, upon *some particular goods ;* which *specific* goods the Court can without difficulty or uncertainty compel the delivery of.

If then only a portion of the purchase money had been paid by the plaintiffs, and the balance was agreed to be paid at a future time, it appears to me, but natural to assume, that the vendor did not intend the contract to be concluded, or that any property either at law or in equity should pass to the vendee, *unless nor until the balance should be paid,* and when that balance should be paid, we must inquire what the contract was in order to determine what was the intention of the parties, and whether it was that the contract should attach upon any, and if any, what particular wheat ; *but on this point the evidence is wholly silent.* It does not appear to me to be sound reasoning to argue that because *Todd* might by reason of the warehouse receipt be estopped in an action of trover at the suit of the plaintiffs, the truth should also be shut out in this *suit,* although the very issue raised between the plaintiffs and defendants, affects the truth of that receipt, and raises the express question whether the plaintiffs had that property in the thing insured, which they averred that they had in order to induce the defendants to insure, and which they now allege in their bill. Now assuming the truth to be, that in fact no wheat of the plaintiffs was ever received by *Todd,* and that the warehouse receipt which admits that there was, is untrue, and that in truth only a small portion of the purchase money was paid by the plaintiffs to *Todd* at the time the contract was entered into, and that the agreement and intent of the parties was, that until payment of the balance the contract itself should be incomplete, and that the plaintiffs should have no claim against *Todd* to recover back the amount paid in cash, and that the intent and object of the warehouse receipt was, that *Todd* should give it, and the plaintiffs receive it, solely for the purpose of enabling the plaintiffs to raise money upon it, to enable them to pay to *Todd* the balance of the purchase money, *and that it had not been used for that purpose*, would *Todd* in an action of trover brought by the plaintiffs, before they had ever made any use of the warehouse receipt, and before therefore the interest of any third person had been prejudiced by the giving of the receipt, and before the condition of the plaintiffs had been altered by reason of it, be estopped at law from setting up these facts in defence of the action. I think that he would not. Between the original parties to a receipt for money, the party giving it is not estopped from shewing that the receipt is untrue, and that he in fact never received any of the money, why then should he be estopped from shewing that a receipt for goods is untrue, and from shewing what the truth of the transaction was? and that it was in reality one between vendor and vendee for the sale of 3,500 bushels generally, not of any specific wheat. The general doctrine is, that a party is at liberty to prove that his admissions not under seal are untrue, and is not estopped or concluded by them *unless another person has been induced by them to alter his condition* (a). So the giving a delivery order for goods in dock does not estop the party giving it from setting up that no possession had been given, the situation of the parties not having been changed in consequence (b). Then if (as we must assume from the evidence of the only witness called by the plaintiffs themselves to prove the purchase of the wheat) only part of the purchase money was paid at the time the warehouse receipt was given, and the balance was to be paid at a future time, it is obvious that in a Court of Equity upon an issue involving a question as to what were the terms of the contract, whatever might be

(a) Heane v. Rogers, 9 B. & C. 577.
(b) Lackington v. Atherton, 7 M, & G. 360.

the proper ruling at law as to the effect of the receipt, in an action of trover, the receipt so given can afford *in itself* no evidence of what the contract in reality was, and if the contract was not to have complete effect until the payment of the balance, upon what specific wheat was the contract by intention then to operate? In fact we have no evidence of what the contract and intention of the parties was.

I have said this much upon this point because it appears to me, in view of the fact that *Currie*, the plaintiffs' own witness, disproves the truth of the receipt, and of the fact that it was not until six weeks after the contract was entered into, nor until the vendor had absconded, that the plaintiffs claimed to be the owners of wheat, as stored by them in the warehouse, and as such effected this insurance, too much stress has been laid upon the effect of this receipt as establishing the fact of the plaintiffs' having had an insurable interest in any particular wheat. Upon the best consideration I have been able to give the case I am of opinion that the decree of the learned Chancellor should be affirmed.

The plaintiffs in the bill rest their whole claim to relief upon the allegations that they were originally owners of the wheat before it was stored in *Todd's* warehouse, and that being such owners they stored the wheat in the warehouse, and that as such owners they effected the insurance with the defendants and took the interim insurance receipt which is the subject of this suit. These allegations are denied by the answer and put in issue in the cause. The actual truth of these statements then became not only examinable, but the onus of proving them was cast upon the plaintiffs. They accordingly produce the warehouse receipt of the 30th of January, 1867, and they call a witness to prove it. That witness proves it to have been signed by *Todd*, but at the same time he proves the admission contained in it to be *untrue;* he further proves that instead of its being true, as represented in the receipt, that the plaintiffs then stored wheat of their own with *Todd*, the transaction was one of a contract then entered into for the sale by *Todd* to the plaintiffs of 3,500 bushels of No. 1 spring wheat, upon which part of the price only was paid in cash by the plaintiffs at the time this warehouse receipt was given, and the balance of the purchase money was agreed to be paid by the plaintiffs at a future time.

Now inasmuch as no estoppel arising from the admissions contained in the receipt can preclude the defendants in this suit from disputing its truth, and inasmuch as the plaintiffs themselves, upon whom lay the onus of proving the truth of the title alleged in their bill, have disproved the truth of the receipt upon which they relied, it is obvious, they cannot fall back on the receipt itself as, operating by way of estoppel, establishing their title to the wheat to be as alleged in the bill; I submit that in law in an action of trover at the suit of the plaintiffs against *Todd*, the receipt could not operate as an estoppel to bar him from shewing the truth to be that the transaction was a contract for the sale of wheat generally, not of any specific wheat, for breach of which an action for damages only would lie; but whether it could or could not, it cannot have such an operation in this suit to bind the defendants who are only liable under their contract in case the plaintiffs were either at law, or in equity owners of some specific wheat, then in store, which their own evidence in my judgment wholly fails to establish.

This same witness, *Currie*, called by the plaintiffs, does not profess to say whether *Todd* had or had not any No. 1 spring wheat of his own in the warehouse at the time of his entering into this contract. The only other witness called by the plaintiffs upon this point, namely *William Broadfoot*, says: " I think *Todd* had

more than 3,500 bushels of No. 1 spring wheat in the
warehouse at the date, the 30th January, 1867, when
the plaintiffs purchased the 3,500 bushels from *Todd.*"
But it appears from the evidence that *Todd* was a warehouseman, and that large quantities of the wheat of
other owners were then in the warehouse, and I do not
understand *Broadfoot's* evidence to go to the length of
saying even that " he thinks" *Todd* had of his own
property in the warehouse 3,500 bushels or any quantity
of No. 1 spring wheat, or that if he had any it was
in any manner separated from like wheat belonging to
any other person. I take his evidence to be that he
thinks there were more than 3,500 bushels of No. 1
spring wheat in the warehouse on the 30th January,
1867, but to whom belonging he does not say. Now we
see by the evidence the frauds of which this man *Todd*
and his warehousekeeper were guilty, that they together
and *Todd*, perhaps also separately, concocted false warehouse receipts to such an extent that at length they both
absconded from the Province. In the course of his
business, whether fraudulently or mistakenly does not
in my judgment signify, *Todd* procured his own servant
*Coleman* to execute, as and in the character of warehouseman, three several documents purporting to be
warehouse receipts under the statute dated the 27th
December, 1866, the 4th and 10th January, 1867, whereby respectively *Coleman* acknowledged to have received
from *Todd*, as owner, 1000 bushels of No. 1 spring
wheat ; 600 bushels of spring wheat and 1000 bushels
of spring wheat, but of what quality the two last were
does not appear. Then it appears by the evidence that
upon the 18th of January, 1867, *Todd* actually received
into this same warehouse 1,800 bushels of spring wheat
and on the 29th of January, 1,800 more bushels of
spring wheat but of what description is not stated, the
property of *Gilpin* and *Currie.*

Then *Currie* says, that five days after the 30th of

January he was in the warehouse, and then saw 3,500 bushels of spring wheat No. 1 beyond the quantity of wheat stored in the warehouse when *Gilpin* and *Currie's* had been stored on the 29th of January, and he says that he could not distinguish between *Gilpin* and *Currie's* wheat and *Todd's*, nor could he say where *Gilpin* and *Currie's* wheat lay. Now *Broadfoot* says that he cannot say whether or not he was in the warehouse on the 30th of January, 1867, he says, however, "that they were buying every day;" and it would seem that they were also selling nearly "every day." Now I think it no unfair conclusion to be arrived at upon this evidence that the 3,500 bushels No. 1 spring wheat which *Currie* says were in the warehouse five days after the 30th of January, in excess of what there had been on the 29th of January, were not there at the time of the contract between *Todd* and the plaintiffs on the 30th of January. Then admitting, for the sake of argument, the warehouse receipts of the 27th of December, 1866,

and the 4th and 10th of January, 1867, to be invalid, as not coming within the provisions of the statute relating to warehouse receipts, I cannot see how the plaintiffs can avail themselves of any such invalidity, for as it is the intention of the parties to the contract of the 30th of January, which is undoubtedly to govern, we cannot presume that it was the intention of the parties that *Todd* was selling and the plaintiffs purchasing any part of the wheat intended to be represented by these receipts, whether they were valid or whether they were invalid, upon the faith of which, as valid, *Todd* had raised money at the banks sa appears in evidence, or that it was any part of the plaintiffs' contract with *Todd* that they should be treated as invalid; and assuming them to be valid or intended by *Todd* to be regarded as valid, then I do not see upon the evidence that *Todd* had at the time of his entering into the contract with the plaintiffs any wheat of his own to represent that contract.

. If we are to assume that *Todd* had 3,500 bushels of
No. 1 spring wheat of his own in store when the contract
was entered into, and that this was the particular wheat
intended to be sold, I do not see how that fact will enable
the plaintiffs to recover in this suit, for it being in evidence that *Todd* was buying and selling daily, it is quite
probable that the wheat in store when this contract was
made, was removed by *Todd* long before he absconded
and before the 15th of March, when the plaintiffs insured;
it will not do to say that the plaintiffs are no parties to
any fraud, and that the wheat ought to be there and
was there unless fraudulently removed by *Todd*; that is
no answer to the defendants, who may reply that they
did not insure *Todd's* integrity. He had absconded in
fact when the plaintiffs insured, and the defendants took
the risk upon the plaintiffs' guarantee that there was
then wheat of theirs in the store. The burden of
establishing the fact lay on the plaintiffs, and in a case
where so many frauds appear to have been committed by
*Todd*, it is but reasonable that the defendants should hold
the plaintiffs to strict proof of their case; it is surely
contrary to all principle to hold the defendants to be
responsible because *Todd's* frauds may render it difficult
or impossible for the plaintiffs to establish their case by
sufficient evidence.

I see nothing in the evidence which warrants us in
holding that the contract operated or was intended to
operate upon any particular wheat then existing, the
property of *Todd*, or thereafter to be acquired by
him. It cannot, in my judgment, upon the evidence
adduced, be regarded in any other light than simply a
contract to be complete only when the balance of the
purchase money agreed upon should be paid, for the sale
of 3,500 bushels of wheat, which may or may not have
then been owned by *Todd*, but not affecting any specific
wheat so as to pass the property at law or to enable a
Court of Equity to declare that the contract has attached

1871.

Box
v.
Provincial
Ins. Co.

Judgment.

1871.  upon any specific parcel.  In *Holroyd* v. *Marshall,* (a)
Lord Chancellor *Westbury,* clearly elucidates the doctrine

Box
v.
Provincial
Ins. Co.

which affects the case : " A contract for valuable consideration, by which it is agreed to make a present
transfer of property, passes at once the beneficial interest,
provided the contract be such as a Court of Equity will
decree a specific performance of : the vendor becomes a
trustee for the vendee, subject of course to the contract
being one to be specifically performed.  A contract for
the sale of goods, as for example, 500 chests of tea, is
not a contract which would be specifically performed,
it does not relate to any chests of tea in particular ;
but a contract to sell the 500 chests of a particular
kind of tea, which are now in my warehouse at Gloucester, is a contract relating to specific property",
(namely, those particular 500 chests) " and which would
be specifically performed.   The buyer may maintain a
suit for the delivery of a specific chattel when it is the
subject of a contract, and for an injunction, if necessary,

to restrain the seller from delivering it to any other
person."

So here, I can find no evidence of any contract which
either at law or in equity can attach upon any specific
3,500 bushels of wheat.  No bill for specific performance
of a contract, the terms of which the plaintiffs fail to
prove could be sustained, nor could any injunction have
been obtained, at the plaintiffs' suit from anything which
appears in evidence, to restrain *Todd* from dealing with,
as his own, any specific 3,500 bushels of wheat.  It
follows then, in my opinion, that as the plaintiffs have
failed to shew that there were on the 15th March, 1867,
any specific 3,500 bushels, or any other quantity of
specific wheat situate in the warehouse which was
destroyed by fire in which the plaintiffs had any interest
perfect in law, or capable of being enforced in equity in

---

(a) 9 Jur. N. S. 215.

virtue of any contract relating thereto, or any specific
3,500 bushels, or any other specific wheat situate in the
warehouse, by the loss of which, by the risk insured against
the plaintiffs can be said to have been damnified, the bill
cannot be sustained, the whole burden of proving the
case alleged in their bill lay upon the plaintiffs, and they
having failed to establish their title as alleged, and in
virtue of which the insurance was to have been effected,
is in itself sufficient in my judgment to demand the
affirmance of this decree.

It would, I think, be very calamitous if upon such
evidence as has been adduced here, insurance companies
could be held responsible, or if upon a bill alleging title
as owners the plaintiffs, disproving that title, should still
be entitled to succeed upon the surmise of some insurable
interest unsuggested and undefined, and the nature and
extent of which it seems to me at least to be difficult to
express or determine.

This case is quite distinguishable from *Davies* v. *The
Home Insurance Co.*, for that case proceeded upon the
principle that in the opinion of the Court the plaintiffs
had an interest capable of being enforced in equity
in and upon the identical specific goods which were
insured. *Seagrave* v. *The Union Marine Insurance
Co.* (a), seems to me to conclude this case in favor of
the defendants. There A who had been in the habit
of buying guano largely from B and Company, at prices
which were settled at the beginning of each year, wrote
to them on the 14th of February ordering a shipment
of 100 tons provided freight did not exceed six shillings
and six pence. On the 16th B and Company wrote in
answer, "We have succeeded in fixing the schooner *Anne
and Isabella* to carry about 115 tons at your limit of
six shillings and six pence per ton. We presume we may

---

(a) L Rep. 1 C. P. 305.

1871.

Box
v.
Provincial
Ins. Co.

Judgment.

value upon you at six months from the date of shipment at £10 per ton ;" adding in a postscript, "please say if you purpose effecting insurance at your end." On the 3rd March A wrote, "I am favored with yours of the 26th. You say, 'we presume we may charge you £10 per ton net cash.' I really cannot understand this, when I know that Mr. L. supplies your guano in Scotland at £9 15s. net there to dealers. Besides I look, as heretofore, for the special allowance made to me at the origin of our transactions ; and now that we are making some changes, it may be as well that I should know how we are to get on for the future ;" and he concluded with a request that some flowering shrubs should be sent him in charge of the captain. On the same day A. effected an insurance upon the guano, per *Anne* and *Isabella*, for £1200. The guano was shipped on the 4th of March by B and Company under a bill of lading, making it deliverable to B and Company or their assigns, and was lost on the voyage. It was held that A had no

insurable interest, because the contract was incomplete, the letters not amounting to a contract in the opinion of the Court. Now there the goods were specific, but the contract being incomplete, A had no interest in the goods in virtue of any contract. So here, assuming the contract to be complete for some but no specific wheat, the same result follows, that the plaintiffs have no interest in any specific goods in virtue of any contract relating thereto.

It was decided there also, that although the bill of lading was made " deliverable to B and Company or their assigns," they had no insurable interest, because, although they dealt as principals with A, still in fact they were acting as agents of D, whose property the guano was, and it was held that D alone, who was the owner of the property, had the insurable interest.

So here, no property in any specific wheat having by

the contract passed out of *Todd*, the vendor, capable of being enforced in equity or complete at law, he alone continued to be the owner of any wheat, if any there was in the warehouse, not belonging to other owners, who had stored with him; and so he alone had the insurable interest which the plaintiffs claim in this bill to have been in them, and he seems to have insured to the full amount of any wheat he had.

The plaintiffs have in my opinion wholly failed to establish the issue, the burden of proving which lay upon them, and the decree therefore of the learned Chancellor dismissing their bill with costs should be affirmed, and the appeal should be dismissed with costs.

1871.

Box
v.
Provincial
Ins. Co.

---

## The Town of Dundas v. The Hamilton and Milton Road Company. [In Appeal.*]

### *Canal intersecting road—Injunction.*

An Act of Parliament having provided that it should be lawful for a Canal Company to cut a channel across a certain highway, and to erect, keep, and maintain a safe and commodious bridge across the canal; and the bridge, after being erected, having become unsafe through the default of the Canal Company, an incorporated Road Company, which had acquired the road, made several endeavours to get the bridge repaired, but all of them having failed, through the insolvency of the Canal Company, the Road Company at length commenced the erection of a fixed bridge, which would have the effect of impeding the navigation of the canal:

*Held*, reversing the decision of the Court below, that they had not any right to do so, and a permanent injunction was granted restraining them [Spragge, C., and Mowat, V. C., dissenting].

This was an appeal by the plaintiffs, the Corporation of the Town of Dundas, against the decree pronounced by the Court of Chancery, as reported *ante*, Volume

Statement.

---

* *Present.*—Draper, C.J., Richards, C.J., Spragge, C., Morrison, J., Mowat, V.C., Gwynne and Galt, JJ.

XVII., page 31, on the grounds (amongst others) that, upon the pleadings and evidence, the plaintiffs were entitled to a decree for an unconditional injunction to restrain the Hamilton and Milton Road Company from committing the injury complained of in the bill to the Desjardins Canal in the pleadings mentioned; that the terms imposed by the Court of Chancery, and on the observance and performance of which the said Court would only issue an injunction to restrain the said Road Company in the commission of the acts complained of, are such as the said Court should not have imposed, and are, in effect, a denial of all beneficial relief herein to the plaintiffs; that the plaintiffs, as a municipal corporation, have not, and cannot legally possess, funds which would enable them to pay and fulfil the terms and conditions of the said decree; that the judgment and decree of the Court of Chancery assume that the Desjardins Canal Company were guilty of a nuisance in excavating their canal through Burlington Heights, and thus severing the ancient highway, in the pleadings mentioned, when such act was made lawful and authorized by Statute 16 Victoria, chapter 54; that the said judgment and decree further erroneously assume that the Road Company were, in consequence of the alleged non-repair of the bridge over said excavation, justified in creating a nuisance as a remedy therefor; that the Statute in that behalf and the general law give an appropriate remedy to the Road Company and to the public for such alleged non-repair of the said bridge; that the Hamilton and Milton Road Company were not in any way to acquire, nor can they legally occupy or possess the line of road attempted to be newly constructed, and which leads across the lands of the Canal Company and other proprietors, nor have they any legal right or authority as a Road Company to construct or maintain the said bridge complained of in this cause, or any similar structure, and such maintenance is and always has been an illegal act; that the road and bridge

newly attempted to be constructed by the said Road
Company were not, and may never be, accepted by the
public in lieu of, or in substitution for, the ancient
travelled highway aforesaid, and should plaintiffs therefore pay and perform the conditions of the said decree,
the liability of the Canal Company to maintain the said
bridge would still continue; and that the proceedings
of the Road Company in endeavouring to obstruct the
navigation of the said canal was *mala fide* and collusive
in the interest of the Great Western Railway and others,
and not in that of the public, and was not justified by
the alleged non-repairs of the said bridge or otherwise.

In support of the decree the Road Company assigned
the following (amongst other) reasons: that the Desjardins Canal Company had no rights in the premises except upon the terms of keeping the bridge in question
in perfect repair, which liability to repair was a continuing one, and when once neglected these rights of
the Canal Company ceased for ever; that the Canal
Company, having wilfully neglected and refused to
comply with the terms upon which alone they had the
right to keep open their canal, such rights were forfeited, and their canal became a nuisance, which might
be abated in any manner by those injured by such
nuisance; that the Road Company, in doing the acts
complained of by the plaintiffs, were simply abating
the nuisance, which they were entitled to do as against
the plaintiffs, as they cannot stand in any higher position
than do the Canal Company under whom they claim;
that under the circumstances proved, the rights of the
Canal Company in the premises, and of the plaintiffs,
as growing out of the same, were forfeited, and a Court
of Equity has no power to relieve against forfeiture in
such a case as the present; that the Canal Company
and the plaintiffs, by their acts in the premises, their
determination not to build or repair, their defiance of
the process of the Court of Common Law, and their

1871.

Town of
Dundas
v.
Hamilton
and Milton
Road Co.

Statement.

1871.

Town of
Dundas
.v.
Hamilton
and Milton
Road Co.

laches, have disentitled themselves to any relief in a
Court of Equity; that the plaintiffs, if entitled to any
relief in the premises, are only entitled thereto upon
the terms of their complying with the requirements
upon which alone they are entitled to interfere with the
road in question, and the Court below, as the condition.
of granting relief to the plaintiffs, simply directed
them to do that which, in strictness, they should have
shewn that they had done before bill filed; that although,
for years before the filing of the bill, the bridge in question was dangerous and unfit for travel, yet the plaintiffs
and the Canal Company, although frequently called
upon to do so, never took any step to repair the same
until after the Road Company had entered into contracts for the completing of the works complained of
in the bill, and such steps then taken by the plaintiffs
were not taken for the *bona fide* purpose of repairing
the said bridge, but merely for a pretence in order to

enable them to apply to the Court of Chancery to
restrain the proceedings of the Road Company; that
the plaintiffs, not having applied for relief until this late
period, obtained the same on terms most favorable to
them, and chose rather to accept the relief upon those
terms than to dismiss the bill, and they cannot therefore
now complain of the terms upon which such relief was
granted; that the Road Company have not been guilty
of any nuisance, nor have they colluded with the Great
Western Railway Company, or any others, in obstruct-
ing the canal; but they have constructed *bona fide*, as
they lawfully might, their road and bridge in such
manner as cannot, under the circumstances, be complained of by the plaintiffs; that although a remedy is
given to the Road Company by Statute for the non-
repair of the bridge in question, yet such remedy does
not deprive the Road Company of any other remedies
they may possess, but such remedy is merely cumulative;
and that, in place of dismissing the plaintiffs' bill with
costs, the Court below gave to them the largest measure

of relief it was possible to give them, having regard to the pleadings and evidence in the cause.

1871.

Town of
Dundas
v.
Hamilton
and Milton
Road Co.

The defendants, the City of Hamilton, also opposed the varying of the decree on the grounds that the decree is fair and just under all the circumstances of this case, and will work substantial justice to all parties interested, and is the only decree that could properly have been made on the pleadings and evidence adduced; and because the decree makes proper and reasonable provision for the erection and maintenance of a good and sufficient bridge over the canal of the defendants, the Desjardins Canal Company : the remedy by indictment against the Canal Company mentioned in the plaintiffs' reasons of appeal having been tried, and having proved ineffectual by reason of the said Canal Company having no property and effects out of which the fine imposed could be levied.

The Attorney General also opposed the appeal on the grounds that the terms imposed by the decree are reasonable and proper under the circumstances; that the bridge across the canal erected by the Desjardins Canal Company was a public nuisance, so found by a jury, and one which the Company ought to have abated long before the commencement of this suit; that the Company acted in bad faith when they began to repair the old bridge, their object being to prevent the Hamilton and Milton Road Company from having a good and safe road, and the plaintiffs acted in collusion with the Company for that purpose; the Company, in fact, being wholly controlled by the plaintiffs, and sustained by them for the purpose of keeping the said road in an unsafe condition for the special benefit of the town of Dundas, which has benefited largely by the unsafe condition of said road, the same being the principal inlet into the city of Hamilton from the north, north-east, and northwest; that the decree of the Court does not

Town of
Dundas
v.
Hamilton
and Milton
Road Co.

assume that the said Company were guilty of a nuisance
in excavating their canal through Burlington Heights,
and thus severing the ancient highway in the pleadings
mentioned; that the Road Company were not guilty of
creating a nuisance by erecting a proper bridge over
the canal; that neither the Statute in that behalf nor
the general law gives the Road Company an adequate
or sufficient remedy for the said nuisance committed by
the Canal Company; that the Road Company were
authorized to acquire, and did legally acquire, the new
line of road in the pleadings mentioned; and they had,
and have, a legal right to construct and maintain the
bridge complained of by the plaintiffs; that, by the
decree, if the plaintiffs perform the conditions thereof,
they will not be liable to maintain the said bridge over
the excavation, nor subjected to any other unreasonable
or improper burden; and that the proceedings of the
Road Company, in constructing the new road and bridge,
were *bona fide*, and fully justified under the circumstances
appearing in the pleadings and evidence herein.

The defendants the Road Company, filed a cross-
appeal, on grounds agreeing substantially with those
assigned by the Company in opposition to the appeal
of the plaintiffs.

Mr. *Crooks*, Q.C., and Mr. *Hoskin*, for the Town of
Dundas.

Mr. *Miles O'Reilly*, Q.C., Mr. *Blake*, Q.C., and
Mr. *McGregor*, contra.

September 3.
(1870.)

Judgment.

DRAPER, C. J.—The defendants the Desjardins
Canal Company, by a series of arrangements with the
defendants the Great Western Railway Company,
agreed to change the original outlet of their canal; to
allow the Railway Company to fill up part of the channel;
and to carry their railway over the place so filled up,

and to adopt a new out-let by means of a [cut through 1871.
the Burlington Heights, which cut (upwards of 100 feet
deep) severed a public highway.   They also agreed to
pay the Railway Company £13,000 for digging this cut
and for erecting a bridge to re-unite the several portions
of the highway.   The plaintiffs became sureties for the
Canal Company and have paid large sums to the Railway Company ; and they are holders of a mortgage on
the canal and the tolls thereof by way of security.

Town of
Dundas
v.
Hamilton
and Milton
Road Co.

The   defendants the Hamilton and Milton Road
Company, are a corporation erected under the Statute of
Canada, relating to road companies, and have permission from the defendants the City of Hamilton, to carry
their road within the corporate limits of the City.   The
road, as first constructed by this Company, was connected
with the bridge above alluded to.

The Railway Company under their agreement erected
a suspension bridge across the cut; but in or about
1857 this bridge was destroyed by heavy winds.   The
Railway Company replaced it by a wooden bridge.   This
in 1866 required much repair, which being neglected
the Canal Company were indicted and convicted of a
public nuisance, and after ineffectual attempts to be
relieved from the conviction, they were sentenced to
pay a fine of $8,000.   Execution was issued against
their lands and goods, but is at present stayed by
injunction.

Judgment.

Recently the Road Company have begun to construct
a new road from a point north of the canal, which road
is being made on and up to each side of the canal at a
level, about sixty feet below the bridge above mentioned,
and they have declared their intention to extend over
the canal a fixed and permanent bridge at a height
of about fifty feet above the level of the water ; the
effect of which will be to close the navigation of the

canal to schooners and such other masted vessels as now navigate it.

The old wooden bridge has been repaired. Its condition was reported on, on 8th December last, by a Civil Engineer specially engaged, and he considered that with proper attention it will be good for two years, as mentioned in a report of 'his, dated in October preceding.

The plaintiffs instituted this suit to obtain an injunction against the Road Company from proceeding to erect the iron bridge, or any other bridge, and from doing any act which might tend to impede the navigation of the canal.

The Road Company in their answer set forth the 28th section of the Statute of Upper Canada, which incorporated the Canal Company, and which required them to construct and maintain bridges for the passage of carriages, wherever they should cut into or through any highway, and the 5th section of the Statute of Canada, which made it lawful for the Canal Company, or the Railway Company, permanently to close the former channel, and to erect and maintain a bridge across the cut through the Burlington Heights, under the authority of which Act the cut was made.

They asserted that the wooden bridge was built across the cut, without the consent of the Canal Company, and that both these Companies denied any liability to repair the same, and they say that if the bridge is repaired upon the plan adopted, it will not be safe for public travel. That the dilapidated state of the bridge has so lessened the travel over their road, and that they are daily sustaining heavy loss in the diminution of their tolls.

That they ineffectually endeavoured to come to some arrangement with the Canal Company for repairing the high bridge, and then came to an arrangement with the defendants, the City of Hamilton, whereby they agreed to extend their toll road into the City, and to erect and maintain a fixed bridge across the canal at their own cost; and the corporation of the City agreed to lend them, at nominal interest, $5,000 to assist them ; that they entered into this arrangement to protect their property from destruction, having been advised that the keeping a sufficient bridge across the canal was a continuing condition, and that by the failure to perform it, the right to obstruct the highway by means of the canal was forfeited and gone, and any one might lawfully restore the said highway in the cheapest and most convenient way, and they insist that by the neglect to repair the bridge, the canal, where it intersects the highway, has become, and is a nuisance, and the right of the Canal Company to obstruct and intercept the highway by means of the canal is at an end ; and that they and the City of Hamilton were legally entitled to enter into and carry out their said arrangement, and for that purpose to place a fixed bridge across the canal.

1871.

Town of
Dundas
v.
Hamilton
and Milton
Road Co.

Judgment.

The Court of Chancery granted an injunction, restraining the Road Company from in any way interfering with the navigation of the canal, but the injunction was not to issue unless certain conditions were complied with which the plaintiffs accepted, reserving a right to appeal against the decree and against the terms imposed as conditions of relief.

1st. That the plaintiffs shall first, at their own expense, erect in connection with the new road of the Road Company a new bridge which shall not interfere with the navigation of the canal, and shall have proper approaches thereto in connection with the said road.

2nd. That plaintiffs' shall pay the damage, if any, which the Road Company have sustained by the non-

1871.

Town of
Dundas
v.
Hamilton
and Milton
Road Co.

repairs of the old or high-bridge, and any further compensation, if such there be, which should be justly made
for their past expense on the new road and bridge.

3rd. That proper provision be made for opening and
closing the new bridge, in case the plaintiffs should
build a draw or swing-bridge ; and for the repair thereof
at the plaintiff's expense.

And an Engineer was named to superintend the erection of the new bridge, and for the purpose of ascertaining and determining the several payments and other
matters stated in the second and third conditions above
set forth, and unless the plaintiffs complied with them
the bill was dismissed with costs.   If they fulfilled
them, they were to pay the defendants their several
costs of suit.

Judgment.     Against this decree the plaintiffs have appealed, contending that they should have had an injunction without
such terms against the Road Company ; that the terms
are in effect a denial of all beneficial relief; that as a
Municipal Corporation they have no funds to be applied
as the conditions require ; that the decree assumes the
Canal Company were guilty of a nuisance in severing
the highway by the cut through the Burlington Heights,
and that the Road Company were consequently justified
in creating another nuisance, by way of remedy, for the
first, and that the road newly constructed by that Company is not in law a substitute for the old highway,
though the decree assumes it to be so; and the construction of this road was resolved on and executed
*malâ fide* and in collusion in the interests of the Great
Western Railway and others.

The Road Company have also entered a cross appeal,
chiefly for the reasons following : That the plaintiffs
cannot stand on a better footing than the Canal Com-

pany, whose rights were dependent on their keeping the high-bridge in repair, and made the canal a nuisance which might be abated, as the neglect to keep and maintain a sufficient bridge was a forfeiture of the right to have the canal; that the Road Company were simply abating a nuisance which was positively injurious to them. That a Court of Equity cannot relieve against such a forfeiture, and if otherwise, the conduct of the Canal Company disentitles them to relief; that the steps taken by that Company towards repairing the bridge were a mere pretence, to enable them to apply for an injunction; that the terms imposed by the Court of Chancery, being such as that Court cannot properly enforce, that Court should have dismissed the bill as no case was made for an absolute unconditional injunction.

The plaintiffs do not, nor indeed could they with any shew of reason, contest the liability of the Canal Company to keep in repair and maintain the high bridge. Their Act of Incorporation provided for the construction of a bridge or otherwise re-establishing the communication in every case in which they should cut into any highway, in order to conduct their canal through the same, and, (what does not seem to have been noticed in the prosecution of the Canal Company, or in later proceedings,) subjected them to a penalty of £5 per day for every day during which they should neglect this duty, and although this Statute does not in express terms provide for the maintenance of the re-establishment of the communication, I feel no doubt that the duty extended so far, and the later Statute (16 Victoria) passed *in pari materia* may, so far as the Canal Company is concerned, be treated as declaratory of the intention of the first.

I will only further observe as to that Statute—that I see nothing in the judgment of the Court of Queen's Bench on that indictment, which goes further than to.

1871.
Town of
Dundas
v.
Hamilton
and Milton
Road Co.
determine the liability of the Canal Company. The Court treats that Act, though permissive in form, as mandatory in effect. The Canal Company were alone before them, and they were not called upon to express; nor did they express any opinion, whether the Great Western Railway Company, to whom it gave authority for one purpose, are not equally bound with the Canal Company to the erection and maintenance of the bridge in question. The present case does not involve a determination of that point.

The contention of the Road Company—both in their defence and cross-appeal—is two-fold : first, that all the rights, franchises, and privileges, conferred upon the Canal Company are forfeited by their neglect and omission to repair the high-bridge ; and second, that the cut across the Burlington Heights is a nuisance in law ; and that they, being injured by it, have a right to abate it.

As to the first point, I agree with what I take to be the opinion of the learned Vice-Chancellor in the Court below, that there is no such forfeiture established ; that the work of repairs having been actually completed, and the old bridge being, according to Mr. Shanly's evidence, good for a period not yet expired ; so much of the Road Company's contention fails. As to the second point, even conceding that the allowing the high-bridge to get out of repair amounted to a breach of a continuing condition, and that the conviction of the Canal Company establishes, as a matter of fact, that breach, it does not appear to me that the forfeiture of the franchises of that Company is thereby legally complete. The grant of these franchises was a Legislative Act, and, though it is to be assumed to have been passed for the use and advantage of the shareholders, yet the recital to it shews that the public advantage was also in contemplation. Moreover, the owners of vessels navigating

the canal, and persons using it for the transmission of 1871.
their produce and other merchandize, have interests
which are not to be overlooked. It requires a legal Town of
Dundas
proceeding of record to repeal a charter from the v.
Hamilton
and Milton
Crown for a cause of forfeiture expressed in it; and a Road Co.
charter granted by Act of the Legislature cannot, in
my opinion, be repealed or annulled unless by some
proceeding which has not yet taken place. I do not
overlook the very broad language in the case of *Regina*
v. *The Inhabitants of Ely* (a); but I think the Road
Company are seeking to give it a practical application
which it will not bear. The *dictum* relied on is—"The
condition which was necessary to legalize the cutting
the first drain was, and is, a continuing condition; the
instant it was broken the indefeasible rights of the
public revive, and the cut becomes a nuisance." As
applicable to the case in which that *dictum* was uttered
I entirely agree in it. The question pending arose on
an indictment for the non-repair of the bridge, and I Judgment.
have no doubt the indictment would have been equally
sustainable if it had been for cutting across the highway,
which cutting rendered the bridge necessary. As in
the case of *Rex* v. *Kerrison* (b), where the indictment
was also for not repairing, rendered necessary by cutting
through a highway, under the authority of an Act for
improving the river Wavenay, *Bailey*, J., observed:
"The indictment might have charged them with cutting
across the highway, and if they had pleaded the Act of
Parliament the Court would have determined on it that
they had power only to make the cut *sub modo*, that is,
providing a substitute for the public." But I am quite
satisfied that in neither case did the learned Judges
mean that the rights and beneficial use of the respective
cuttings were forfeited and gone; that in the first case,
the old Bedford River might be filled, and thereby the
lands drained be overflowed again, or in the other, that

---

(a) 15 Q. B. 827.                    (b) 3 M. & S. 526.

1871.

Town of
Dundas
v.
Hamilton
and Milton
Road Co.

the improved navigation of the river Wavenay might be stopped by a bridge in continuation of the intercepted highway, which would seriously impede or entirely hinder vessels in the use of it.

The cross appeal should, in my opinion, be dismissed with costs.

We come then to the plaintiffs' appeal, which involves mainly, if not exclusively, this question, whether the terms on which an injunction is ordered are such as the Court ought under the circumstances to have imposed? I am not prepared to concur altogether in an observation contained in the judgment of the learned Vice Chancellor. In alluding to the *dictum* in the *Queen* v. *Ely*, on which I have already remarked, he says: "If applicable, it follows that the Road Company were but exercising a strict legal right, when, after the long

Judgment.  delay of the Canal Company to repair their bridge, the Road Company set about making a bridge of their own, and the making of the necessary approaches to it."

There is a distinction to be observed between nuisances of commission and those of omission or mere neglect. In the case of the *Earl of Lonsdale* v. *Nelson* (a), *Best*, J., says: "Nuisances of commission are committed in defiance of those whom such nuisances injure, and the injured party may abate them without notice to the person who committed them; but there is no decided case which sanctions the abatement, by an individual, of nuisances from omission, except that of cutting the branches of trees which overhang a public road or the private property of the person who cuts them."

The indictment on which the Canal Company were convicted was for non-repair of a bridge, an act which,

_____

(a) 2 B. & C. 302.

though a nuisance, is one of omission. If, therefore, the Road Company had entered upon and taken possession of the old bridge, in order to repair it, they would, I am inclined to think, have been guilty of trespass, at least, unless a reasonable time for repairing had elapsed, and after notice to the Canal Company.

But further it appears that the right of abating, as the Road Company claim to exercise it, goes very far beyond the right given by law to a party to abate a nuisance which is injurious to him. The right which the Road Company had, was to have a particular highway, as I understand, the only highway which the cut through the Burlington Heights intersected, restored by a bridge. That right was infringed by allowing the bridge to become unsafe and out of repair, and this was the only nuisance of which the Canal Company were guilty and consequently the only nuisance which the Road Company were injured by. The argument of the Road Company leads to this :—that to abate this nuisance they may construct a new road—for a public highway—which as it did not exist when the cut was made, could not have been intersected by it, and in respect of which, therefore the Canal Company had committed no nuisance; and that in the line of such new highway they may construct a bridge, of such a character that it will prevent a class of vessels, which have ordinarily navigated this canal from doing so in future. It amounts in effect to this—that to abate a nuisance of omission in one place, where it injures them, they may erect a nuisance in another place where it injures the party guilty of the first nuisance. The language of the learned Vice Chancellor, inadvertently no doubt, if correctly reported, appears to sanction this pretension—which I think to be wholly untenable. Moreover, the new road which the Road Company have constructed and which is intended to be carried across the cut by the fixed bridge complained against, may not

1871.

Town of
Dundas
v.
Hamilton
and Milton
Road Co.

be a work within their legitimate power and authority.
It must be assumed that their original road, had its
points of commencement and termination as well as its
line of direction set out in the instrument which under
the Consolidated Statute Upper Canada, chapter 49, they
must have filed in order to become a Corporation, and
that in constructing it so as to connect with or pass over
the then existing public highway, which passed over the
high-bridge they followed the description which that
instrument contained. Unless they have acquired some
new authority subsequently, they can have no pretence
for erecting a bridge across the cut and over the canal,
as a part of an entire new line of highway, and to substitute such bridge and highway for the former one. For
all that is shewn—the statutory obligation on the Canal
Company to maintain the high-bridge continues and there
is no obligation in law on the Canal Company to assist
the Road Company in any other way than by affording

and maintaining a sufficient bridge on the old site.

I presume it will not be seriously contended that a
fixed bridge which would prevent masted vessels, sloops,
schooners, &c., from navigating this canal, would not be
indictable as a nuisance. The language of *Park*, J., in
delivering the opinion of the Judges before the House of
Lords, in *The Mayor, &c., of Lyme Regis* v. *Heneley* (a),
removes any doubt as to this canal being a matter of
general and public concern.

I therefore have the misfortune to look upon the
position of the parties in a somewhat different light from
the view taken by the learned Vice Chancellor, and as a
consequence should vary the decree that has been made.

I agree that the Canal Company should effectually
restore the communication over the cut, by a bridge (to

---

(a) 1 Bing, N. C. at p 238.

be approved by an Engineer to be named by the Court,) connecting the several portions of the old highway. This is the duty, permanently imposed by their Act of Incorporation and also by the Statute, 15 Victoria without prejudice to their claiming (if they have a claim) contribution from the Railway Company. I cannot but see that if the defendants the Road Company could have sustained their claim to erect and maintain a permanent fixed-bridge, the Railway Company would be relieved from any liability, which they may be subject to, as to the high-bridge under the 15th Victoria, and that they would also be relieved from much inconvenience and interruption to their business, in having to admit such vessels as will be excluded from the canal if the Road Company's new fixed-bridge were sanctioned.

1871.

Town of Dundas v. Hamilton and Milton Road Co.

I think it should be referred to the Master to ascertain any loss the Road Company have sustained, by reason of the non-repair of the old bridge, if they desire it, and that on paying or securing to the Road Company, the amount, if any, of the said loss sustained by the Road Company, a perpetual injunction should issue, to restrain the Road Company, &c.

Judgment.

I incline to give no costs of the plaintiffs' appeal to any one; but I think the Road Company should pay the costs of their cross appeal, and that the plaintiffs should pay the costs in the Court below of all the defendants except the Road Company.

RICHARDS, C. J., concurs.

SPRAGGE, C.—There are some points as to which I believe all the members of the Court are agreed. They agree that there was no forfeiture of the franchise of the Canal Company by reason of their omission to repair the bridge, and on the other hand that the duty created by the statute to keep and maintain, as well as to erect, a safe and commodious bridge over and across the cut referred to in the Act, was a continuing obli-

1871.
Town of
Dundas
v.
Hamilton
and Milton
Road Co.

gation; and further, that that obligation has not been observed by the Canal Company. These two last points were necessarily determined against the Company by their conviction upon the indictment for nuisance in omitting to keep the bridge in repair.

I think further, that it can admit of no doubt that this omission of the Company has been in a very high degree prejudicial to the Road Company; to such an extent that if the injury had been created by an act of commission, instead of by the omission of a duty, it would have been their clear right to remove it, in order to their being reinstated in their rights; and if in order to their being effectually reinstated in their rights they had necessarily expended money, it would be just, and would be in the power of the Court, to make the reimbursement of the money expended a condition to any relief granted to the Canal Company

Judgment.

Two grounds are suggested why the reimbursement of money expended by the Road Company should not be reimbursed to them: one, that the leaving the bridge unrepaired was a nuisance of omission, not of commission, the former being removable or remediable by the party aggrieved only in one or two specified instances. The other ground is, that the expenditure was *ultra vires*.

Upon the first ground the *Earl of Lonsdale* v. *Nelson (a)* is referred to, and his Lordship the Chief Justice has quoted from the judgment of *Best*, J. The language of the learned Judge, in continuation of that quoted, is material: "The permitting these branches to extend so far beyond the soil of the owner of the trees (*i.e.*, branches overhanging a public road or private property) is a most unequivocal act of

_____

(a) 2 B. & C. 222.

negligence; which distinguishes this case from most
of the others that have occurred. The security of
lives and property may sometimes require so speedy a
remedy as not to allow time to call on the person on
whose property the mischief has arisen to remedy it.
In such cases an individual would be justified in
abating a nuisance from omission, without notice."
From this it is quite clear that *Best*, J., by no means
meant to put the case of the overhanging branches of
trees as the only nuisance of omission which the
injured party might abate. It scarcely indeed comes
within the category of cases requiring so speedy a
remedy, for the sake of security of life or property, as
to justify the abatement of the nuisance without notice.

If the leaving the branches of trees to overhang is an
act of such " unequivocal negligence" as to warrant their
removal by a party aggrieved, surely the omission to
repair this bridge was a *multo fortiori* an act of unequivocal negligence, and the *consequences* of the
omission are in the like proportion; in the case of the
trees some inconvenience, and perhaps some pecuniary
damage :—in the case of the bridge the danger to life
and property; the very consequences pointed at by
Mr. Justice *Best* as justifying the abatement of a
nuisance from omission by the party aggrieved. The
case put by the learned Judge is one of imminent
danger to life and property, requiring so speedy a
remedy as not to afford time to call on the person
whose omission of duty it is that has caused the
danger, to remove the cause. In such case he holds
the party aggrieved excused, as in reason he must be,
from giving notice. Now, though the circumstances of
such a case differ from those in the case before us, the
reasoning and the principle apply. They are that, in a
case the necessities of which are of such a character as
to warrant the party aggrieved in himself applying a
remedy to the nuisance, he may lawfully do so. Mr.

1871.

Town of
Dundas
v.
Hamilton
and Milton
Road Co.

Justice *Best* after saying that in such cases as he had put an individual would be justified in abating a nuis-ance from omission without notice, goes on to say : " In all other cases of such nuisances, persons should not take the law into their own hands, but follow the ad-vice of Lord *Hale*, and appeal to a Court of Justice." In this case there was an appeal to a Court of Justice ; and this Canal Company was adjudged to be in the wrong ; and punishment for the wrong was awarded. But that adjudication has been practically a dead letter. Lord *Hale* advised parties aggrieved to appeal to a Court of Justice, assuming that they would thereby obtain a remedy.

But here there has been no remedy. The case after the judgment at law remained as much a case of danger to life and property as ever it was, the necessity for abating it as great as ever. There were two ways of abating it : one by appealing to the law ; the other by doing that which is lawful where the necessity warrants it, the abatement of the nuisance, be it a nuisance from omission or commission, by the hand of the party aggrieved. Here the remedy by appeal to the law practically failed. Upon that the party injured had either to sit down helpless under the injury because it was a nuisance from omission, or to apply a remedy himself as he might clearly do if the nuisance was what is called a nuisance from commission. I do not think that the distinction between these two classes of nuisances can be carried in reason, or is carried by authority, to such an extent as this. In my humble judgment, the necessity which existed for having a safe and commodious bridge for the use of travellers on the defendant's road was such, as to justify them, after the failure of any effectual remedy at law, to apply a remedy themselves. The necessity, under the circum-stances, was their warrant ; and the wrong which made the necessity, being one of omission can, in reason,

make no difference. I think the distinction between
the remedies of parties aggrieved by nuisances of omission, and those aggrieved by nuisances of commission,
will be found to consist in this : that in the latter class
of cases, the party abating the nuisance need not shew
any necessity for abating it ; while in the former class,
a necessity must be shewn : a necessity once shewn, the
right to abate the nuisance is made out. Nothing can
be more clearly made out than the necessity in this
case.

But it is said that the Road Company, in abating
the nuisance of the Canal Company, committed one
themselves. So far as this objection rests upon the
assumption that the Road Company had not authority,
apart from the interference with the navigation of the
canal, to construct a road and bridge where they have
constructed it, the answer to the objection is, that no
such objection and no facts upon which to found such an
objection, are taken by the plaintiffs' bill. If such an
objection were intended to be made, one would naturally
look for it in that part of the bill where the works of
which the plaintiffs complain are stated. Paragraph
13 would lead the Road Company to conclude that
there was no complaint on that head. It runs thus :

"The said defendants the Hamilton and Milton
Road Company, are now engaged in building a new
road from a point on the present roadway owned by
them and used as a public highway, to the north of
the said canal, and the said new road is now being
built up to the banks of the said canal on both sides
at a height of about fifty feet above the waters of the
said canal, being at a level of about sixty feet lower
than the present bridge and road."

If there was any ground of complaint on that score,
it should have been stated. It is impossible for us to
say that it would not have been satisfactorily answered.

1871.

Town of
Dundas
v.
Hamilton
and Milton
Road Co.

Judgment.

1871.

Town of
Dundas
v.
Hamilton
and Milton
Road Co.

Suppose, indeed, that the Road Company had not authority to make such road, and, in doing so. were trespassers upon the property of others, it does not follow that the plaintiffs can set that up. Is it not setting up a *jus tertii?* And, again, it is not shewn that there was any other place along which they could have constructed their road. The Canal Company were wrongdoers, and I assume, in discussing this point, that the Road Company was justified *ex necessitate* in doing whatever was really necessary to preserve the continuity of their road. I grant that their acts were limited by the necessity for them ; and that they were bound to do what was imposed by that necessity, in such a way as would be least injurious to the Canal Company, so as the expense to themselves were kept within reasonable limits. I do not think they would be bound to incur any very-great expenditure, because doing so would be advantageous to the Canal Company.

The question here is whether they should be reimbursed at all, or should receive any compensation for their expenditure in providing a substitute for the bridge, which the Canal Company were bound to keep in repair.

The plaintiffs have only shewn that the Road Company bridge will impede the passage of masted vessels up this Canal; they have not shewn that the Road Company could have placed their bridge at any place where the passage of masted vessels would not be impeded. Then how have they placed the Road Company in the wrong. The Road Company has been forced by the wrong of the Canal Company to provide a new bridge. For aught that appears they could place it at no other place than that in which they did place it. If so, the expense was rightly incurred and the wrong doers are now complaining of that which is in truth a consequence of their own wrong. The nuisance which the plaintiffs retort upon the Road Company is, that, by the bridge they have erected, masted vessels are

1871.

Town of
Dundas
v.
Hamilton
and Milton
Road Co.

prevented from passing up the Canal, whereby the tolls of the Canal Company are diminished. The diminution of tolls is what gives the plaintiffs a *locus standi* in Court. The answer to this is that the Canal Company is the *origo mali*. The Road Company has done, from necessity, what the wrong of the Canal Company forced them to do.

I have discussed these points at some length because His Lordship the Chief Justice has in his judgment given prominence to them as elements of consideration. I confess that in my own view the question lies in a much narrower compass. What the plaintiffs have come into Court for is an injunction; a species of relief, which the Court grants or refuses in its discretion; and consequently upon such terms as in its discretion appear to be just. This is well put by Mr. *Kerr* in his book on Injunctions. "The existence of the jurisdiction is never of itself a reason for its exercise. The Court is in each case guided by its own discretion, and will not interfere unless it is satisfied that the case is one in which the jurisdiction can be properly and beneficially exercised, and ought in fact to be exercised. * * * The superior powers which a Court of Equity possesses of adapting its decrees to the special circumstances of each particular case, of adjusting cross equities, of laying down the conduct to be observed by the several parties to the suit: of imposing terms, and generally of doing justice in the most minute detail," &c. Now, in this view, the question, what a party aggrieved by a nuisance arising from omission of duty, may or may not do, is out of the case; the Court is not trammelled by any such considerations: the simple question is, what is reasonable and just between the parties, looking at all the circumstances of the case.

It was the opinion of my brother *Mowat*, and I agree

1871.

Town of
Dundas
v.
Hamilton
and Milton
Road Co.

with him, that it was the wrong of the Canal Company, whether a wrong of omission or commission is in this view immaterial, that forced upon the Road Company the necessity of building a bridge for their road. When the wrongdoers came for an injunction to prevent the completion of the bridge, it necessarily became a question whether the Road Company ought not to be recouped for the expenditure, which the wrong of the Canal Company had made necessary. If it was reasonable and just that they should he so recompensed, the propriety of making it a term of relief by injunction, is obvious. The reasonableness and justice of the terms imposed appear to me, I confess, very clear : and but for the contrary opinion entertained by a majority of the Court, I should have felt no doubt that they were rightly and properly imposed in this case.

MOWAT, V.C., retained the opinion expressed by him
in the Court below.

GWYNNE, J.—Long prior to the month of June, 1852, the Desjardins Canal Company had constructed a canal, leading along a natural watercourse from Dundas to the waters of Burlington Bay, under the powers contained in their Act of Incorporation, 7 George IV., chapter 18.

In the month of June, 1852, the Great Western Railway Company having occasion to cross the canal, and being desirous of closing it up by the erection of an embankment of considerable height across it, near its entrance into Burlington Bay, came to an agreement with the Canal Company, executed under the seals of the respective companies, dated 7th day of June, 1852. This agreement recited that in the construction of the railroad, it was *necessary* to carry the same across the Desjardins Canal. That the Canal Company for the improvement of the canal, desired to make a new channel or outlet, therefor, through Burlington Heights, in the vicinity of the then channel or outlet. *That the filling up of the then existing channel or outlet would be an advantage to the Railway Company.* That the Canal Company and the Railroad Company had agreed that the new channel should be opened at a place (indicated on plans annexed to the agreement, and) where the channel has in fact been cut and now is; and that the then existing channel should be closed and filled up at a point where the railroad was then being and has since been constructed, and that the railroad might pass over the said filling without a bridge; or by any means the Railway Company might think proper to adopt. That it had been agreed by and between the said companies that the cost and expense *of effecting the said change of channel,* should be borne jointly by the said companies in the proportion and manner following : namely, that the said Canal Company should contribute £12,500, and the Railroad Comapny *the residue, whatever the same might amount to.* That the Canal Company, not being in possession of funds sufficient, it was agreed that the Railway Company should execute the works necessary to effect the said changes and improvements, and the Canal Company should give security to the Railway Company for the proportion agreed to be advanced by it towards the completion of the works ; and in consideration of the premises, the Railway Company covenanted with the Canal Company, that the Railway Company should and would with all due diligence, and with the use of all means within their power, well and sufficiently do, perform, erect, execute, and complete the excavation, bridges, and all and singular other the works, matters and things mentioned, and contained in the specifications and plans thereunto annexed, according to and agreeably with the said specifications ; " using all available means that can or may be adopted for the completion of the same, and furnishing and providing of good quality all the material therefor."

1871.

Town of
Dundas
v.
Hamilton
and Milton
Road Co.

The sum of £12,500 agreed to be paid by the Canal Company as its contribution toward the completion of these works appears to have been raised to £13,000, for, on the same 7th June, 1852, the Canal Company executed a mortgage to the Railway Company, of the Canal, &c., to secure payment of £13,000.

This indenture, which is between the same parties, recites the occasion which the Railway Company in constructing their railway, had to cross the canal, and that the Canal Company propose to make a cut through Burlington Heights, and that it was desirable that the improvement and completion of the canal should be carried on simultaneously, with the construction of the railroad, *and that the making of the alterations,* (in the course of the canal,) *would be beneficial to the Railway Company,* and that the Railway Company had therefore agreed to lend and advance to the Canal Company the sum of £13,000, *being the amount the said Canal Company are to contribute to assist in effecting the same,* " the railway Company agreeing, if the consent of the Government can be obtained, to make and finish the said proposed cut or channel, and to fill up the now existing outlet, and to advance, lay out and expend the above sum in so doing, as well as a further large sum of money out of the proper funds of the Railway Company, which will be necessary therefor."

Judgment.

At the time of the execution of these instruments, there was no Legislative authority which authorized the proposed new cut, or the severance of the highway effected thereby; nevertheless the Railway Company relying, no doubt, upon having Legislative sanction given to their acts, proceeded with the works under the agreement. Accordingly in the then next session of Parliament and on the 10th November, 1852, an Act was passed recognizing the works then in progress, by the Great Western Railway Company, under their agreement with the Canal Company, and the 5th section enacted that it should "be lawful for the Desjardins Canal Company or the said Great Western Railway Company to permanently close, shut, and fill up the channel or course of the present canal at its eastern extremity, and at the place where the line of the Great Western Railroad crosses or intersects the said channel, or course of the said canal, and to erect, keep, and maintain a safe and commodious bridge over and across the opening or cut through the said Burlington Heights, for all Her Majesty's liege subjects, their horses and carriages, free of toll at all times thereupon, and thereby to pass and repass."

Now, from this section it would seem to have been contemplated by the Legislature, that the same persons who should permanently close up the then existing channel, should be the persons who should erect and maintain the bridge across the new channel substituted for the one closed up.

The Act then referring to the works as in progress and legalizing them, recognizes them as constructed under the agreement between the two companies. Now we cannot read this agreement, I think, without coming to the conclusion that it was certainly as much, if not more, in the interest of, and for the benefit of, the Railway Company, that the old cut was closed up, and that *therefore the new cut was made necessary.*

The old cut was, in fact, closed up by the Railway Company, and the embankment closing it is their property ; as between the two Companies it might be an important question, whether the £13,000 agreed to be paid by the Canal Company as *their whole contribution* towards the cost and expense of "effecting the change of channel," did not subject the Railway Company to maintain as well as erect the bridge *as a continuing incident to the change of channel*; or whether the Rail-

43—VOL. XVIII. GR.

*Marginal notes:*

1871.

Town of Dundas
v.
Hamilton and Milton Road Co.

Judgment.

1871.

Town of
Dundas
v.
Hamilton
and Milton
Road Co.

way Company having in fact closed up the old channel by an embankment upon which their railway is constructed, and which is their property, are not persons *equally* liable with the Canal Company, within the provisions of section 5 of 16 Victoria, chapter 54, to erect and maintain the bridge; we are not called upon in this case to decide such a question; but that the Railway Company, at one time, entertained the apprehension that they were under some obligation to maintain the bridge is, it appears to me, an important element of which we cannot lose sight in the proceedings which have occasioned the question which this case does present for our decision.

As between the public and the Canal Company, the case of *The Queen* v. *The Desjardins Canal Company* decides, and I think correctly, that the Canal Company are under an obligation to the public of maintaining and repairing the bridge. That case decided that

Judgment. the bridge was not in a fit state of repair. It still remained, however, in use by the Hamilton and Milton Road Company. That Company, while the bridge was being used by persons who paid them tolls for access upon their roads to and from Hamilton across the bridge for the passage of loaded teams over the bridge, varying in number from 127 to 410 per day, conceived the design, which they have proceeded to carry into effect, of erecting a fixed bridge across the canal at such a lower level as would effectually close the canal for all time to come against masted vessels ; and, towards the expense incident upon this project, the Great Western Railway Company, who appear at one time to have entertained, not perhaps unreasonably, the apprehension that *they* were under some obligation to contribute towards the maintenance of the upper bridge, agreed to pay $15,000 to the Hamilton and Milton Road Company, if the design of that Company should be matured to legal perfection, and confirmed by Act of Parliament. The Road Company now assert their right

to do this act, which the Canal Company regard as an
irreparable trespass and injury to their property and
rights, upon the contention that the Canal Company
having been convicted on an indictment for a nuisance
in suffering the upper bridge to fall into disrepair the
Road Company have a right to abate such nuisance;
and that the erection of the bridge at the lower level
in such a manner as to close the canal against masted
vessels is merely an abatement of the nuisance of which
the Canal Company have been guilty, and is therefore authorized; that the right, in fact, to maintain the
canal at all is gone, and that the defendants might, if they
had pleased, have filled it up by an embankment. But
this argument proceeds upon a very apparent fallacy,
for the maintenance of the upper bridge where the old
highway is intersected, is not, that I can see, the less
an obligation upon the Canal Company and all other
companies or persons, if any there be, originally liable
to maintain that bridge, because another bridge is
erected by the Road Company at a lower level; nor can
the erection of a bridge at the upper level with any
propriety be termed an abatement of the nuisance of not
maintaining a bridge at the upper level in a proper state
of repair. The evidence shews that in fact for the
present the nuisance of which the Canal Company was
convicted *is* abated by the repair of the high level
bridge; for the Engineer appointed by the Court to
inspect it and point out the necessary repairs, reports
them almost completed in November, 1869, and that the
bridge was and would continue to be in sufficient repair
for at least two years. It is insisted that the *Queen* v. *The
Inhabitants of Ely* (a) is an authority for the defendants'
contention; but that case only decides that persons
entitled to maintain the cut for their peculiar benefit,
and not the public, are the persons liable to maintain
the bridge, and indictable as for a nuisance if they
neglect that obligation. To make that case applicable to

1871.

Town of
Dundas
v.
Hamilton
and Milton
Road Co.

Judgment.

---

(a) 15 Q. B. 827.

1871.

Town of
Dundas
v.
Hamilton
and Milton
Road Co.

the defendants' contention, it would require to have been
held that the bridge across the cut which drained the
Bedford level having become impassable, it was competent for any person to have treated the cut itself as a
nuisance, and to stop it up, and to render it useless for
the purpose for which it was constructed, namely, of
draining the Bedford level.

The bridge which has been erected by the Hamilton
and Milton Road Company at the lower level, is not in my
opinion shewn to be an authorized and legal construction
at all, and the plaintiffs therefore as mortgagees of the canal
were entitled to an injunction, simple and unconditional,
in the terms of the prayer of their bill, and with costs.

The appeal of the plaintiffs should, in my opinion, be
allowed, and the injunction ordered in the terms of the
prayer of their bill, with costs.    And the appeal of the
defendants, the Hamilton and Milton Road Company,
should be dismissed with costs.

Judgment.

MORRISON and GALT, JJ., concurred.

> *Per Curiam.*—Cross-appeal of defendants dismissed
> with costs ; decree to be varied by referring it to
> the Master to inquire what, if any, loss the Road
> Company have sustained by reason of the non-
> repair of the old bridge, and consequent loss of
> tolls—if Road Company desire such reference.  On
> payment, (or securing payment, by bond, in the
> penal sum of $2,000, to be approved of by the
> Master,) of the amount of such loss, a permanent
> injunction to issue restraining the defendants, the
> Hamilton and Milton Road Company, their work-
> men, servants, and agents, from in any way inter-
> fering with the navigation of the canal.    Plaintiffs
> to pay the costs of all the defendants—other than
> the Road Company—in the Court below.    No
> costs of plaintiffs' appeal to either party. [SPRAGGE,
> C., and MOWAT, V. C., dissenting].*

---

* This cause has since been carried to the Privy Council on an appeal
by the defendants the Road Company.

## TOTTEN v. DOUGLAS. [IN APPEAL.]*

*Mortgages—Fraud on creditors—Assignee for value without notice.*

An insolvent person executed to his son a mortgage for $1000, of
which $400 was a pretended debt to the son, and $600 a pretended
debt to his mother. The son subsequently, under an arrangement
with the father, transferred the mortgage to *C.*, who was the holder
of notes of the mortgagor to the amount of $600, which he gave
up to the mortgagee, and he paid in cash $400 to the mortgagee.
*C.* had notice of the character of the mortgage, but the transaction
with him was *bonâ fide :*

*Held,* ,that he was entitled to claim for the full amount of the security,
in priority to subsequent execution creditors of the mortgagor.
[MOWAT, V. C., dissenting].

This was an appeal by the defendants *Nesbitt* and
*Cook* from a decree of the Court below, as reported *ante*
Volume XVI., page 243. The grounds of the appeal
appear sufficiently in the judgment.

Mr. *Read,* Q. C., Mr. *Moss,* and Mr. *J. A. Boyd,*
for the appellants.

Mr. *Blake,* Q. C., and Mr. *McLennan,* contra,

The judgment of the Court was delivered by

GWYNNE J.—If the estate which was conveyed by the [Judgment.]
mortgage executed by *Alexander Douglas,* in favour of
his son *James,* still remained vested in *James,* I think
the transaction would be open to impeachment, as a
mortgage fraudulent and void as against the creditors of
*Alexander,* under the 13th *Elizabeth,* chapter 5; but
*James Douglas* having conveyed that estate to *Cook,*
and *Cook* having conveyed it to *Nesbitt,* before any steps
had been taken to impeach and avoid the mortgage, we
have now to decide what is the effect of these two
separate alienations of the estate.

* *Present.*—DRAPER, C. J., RICHARDS, C. J., SPRAGGE, C., MOWAT,
V. C., GWYNNE and GALT, JJ.

The statutes of 27 Elizabeth, chapter 4, and 13 Elizabeth, chapter 5, being *in pari materia,* decisions under the one statute afford apt illustration of the doctrine to be applied in *consimili casu,* in the construction of the other (*a*).

In cases arising under 27 Elizabeth, chapter 4, it was, at a very early period, determined in *Rodgers* v. *Langham* (*b*) that " where a feoffment was made without good consideration, or even by fraud, and that the feoffee enfeoffs another for valuable consideration, and then the original feoffor makes a feoffment for valuable consideration, yet the former will prevail *by effect of the reference*"—the valuable consideration given to the voluntary or covinous feoffee supported the *original feoffment* : the original feoffment was said to be made good by this matter occurring *ex post facto* before the feoffment had been in fact avoided, by a subsequent feoffment for value by the original feoffor.

In *George* v. *Milbank* (*c*), Lord *Eldon* applied this principle in favour of a purchaser for value of an interest in a sum of money from a person claiming under a voluntary appointment as against the general creditors of a deceased person upon the administration of his estate. He proceeded, as is said by Lord Justice *Turner* in *Payne* v. *Mortimer* (*d*), upon the ground that the assignee for value from the voluntary appointee had a superior equity to the general creditors of the settlor, the appointor. Speaking of the case of *Rodgers* v. *Langham*, Lord *Eldon* says: " In the case in Siderfin, the " settlement is expressed to be *by covin*—the reason " as stated is this, that though a voluntary feoffment is " bad as between *a creditor* and the feoffee, yet it is " good between the feoffor and feoffee—the consequence

---

(*a*) Notes to Twyne's case, 1 Smith's L. C.

(*b*) Sid. 133.  (*c*) 9 Ves. 190.  (*d*) 5 Jur. N. S. at 750.

" is that the feoffment of the voluntary feoffee is good " *against* creditors."

In *Daubeny* v. *Cockburn* (a), Sir *William Grant* states the principle thus : " In the case of a convey- " ance of a man's own property or an appointment of " property over which he has a power unlimited as to " objects, he who pays a consideration to the voluntary " grantee or appointee may, constructively, be held to be " in the same situation *as if he had in the first instance* " *paid it to him by whom the estate had been granted or* " *the power executed.*"

In Doe *Newman* v. *Rusham* (b), Lord *Campbell* re- ferring to *Rodgers* v. *Langham* says : " It has been " constantly held that if the person to whom a voluntary " conveyance is made, sells and conveys for value, that " *which was in its creation* a *voluntary* conveyance and " voidable by a purchaser, *becomes good* and unavoidable " by matter *ex post facto, and will be considered* as " *made upon valuable consideration.* This, however, is " not by the operation of the Statute of Elizabeth, but " rather by excluding that operation."

By this last observation I understand him to mean, that, inasmuch as a voluntary deed is good between the grantor and grantee, an alienation for value by the vol- unteer grantee passes the estate to his vendee ; and, con- sequently, there is nothing left which the original grantor could pass to a purchaser for value from him ; that which was *sub modo* voidable had passed completely to a purchaser for value from the volunteer grantee, and so the case is taken out of the Statute—the operation of the Statute upon a sale for value by the original grantee is excluded.

Lord *Campbell* in the same case at p. 361, explains

---

(a) 1 Mer. at 638.    (b) 16 Jur. at 362.

the principle upon which voluntary conveyances are held
fraudulent and void as against a subsequent purchaser,
to be, that by selling the property for a valuable consideration, the seller so entirely repudiates the former voluntary conveyance, and shews his intention to sell, as
that it shall be taken *conclusively against* him and the
person to whom he had conveyed voluntarily that such
intention existed when the conveyance was made and
that it was made in order to defeat the purchaser.

It is plain, then, that a voluntary or covinous conveyance within the Statute of 27 Elizabeth, is voidable
only, and that this is good and valid until avoided ; the
act which avoids it being the sale by the grantor to a
purchaser for value *before* the volunteer grantee shall
have conveyed for value. Upon the instant of such a
sale being perfected by the original grantor, the voluntary conveyance becomes absolutely void as against
the purchaser for value, insomuch that a conveyance
thereafter made by the voluntary grantee for value to a
purchaser ignorant of the character of the voluntary conveyance, and without notice of the subsequent sale for
value, passes nothing.

Such a person, as said by Lord Justice *Turner*, in
*Lloyd* v. *Attwood* (a), merely stands in the position of
being assignee of an estate which the statute *has made*
void ; but if the voluntary grantee conveys for value before the voluntary grantor avoids his voluntary conveyance by a sale for value, the estate passes absolutely to
the purchaser for value from the volunteer grantee, and
thenceforth the operation of the statute in favour of a
purchaser for value from the original grantor is excluded;
*he* then is in the position of the person *who takes nothing.*

Now a deed within 13 Elizabeth, ch. 5, is equally
voidable only as one within 27 Elizabeth, ch. 4—that is

---

(a) 5 Jur. N. S. at 1331.

to say, it is as good against the grantor and all persons
except his creditors, as a voluntary deed is within the
Statute of 27 Elizabeth, good against the grantor and all
persons except subsequent purchasers for value from the
same grantor—it is subject also to the same incident of
being able to pass the estate absolutely to a *bona fide*
purchaser for value from the fraudulent grantee, as in
the case of a deed within the Statute of 27 Elizabeth.

1871.

Totten
v.
Douglas.

It has been often said that the Statute 13 Elizabeth, ch.
5, is but declaratory of the common law, and that no deed
can be avoided under the statute which could not equally
have been avoided under the common law—without the
statute. When, then, a creditor seeks to avoid a deed
as fraudulent against him, it is to the principles of the
common law that he appeals; and although a Court of
Equity has concurrent jurisdiction with the Courts of
Common Law, to set aside such a deed, still the principles of decision in both Courts must be the same. The
Common Law being the rule of decision, the deed cannot be avoided in a Court of Equity, or dealt with there,
upon any other principle than that upon which it would
be avoided in the Court of Common Law, namely, the
principles governing fraud in the eye of the common
law and of the statute; all rules and doctrines which are
peculiar creatures of the Court of Equity in the administration of purely equitable principles, must of necessity
be excluded, and can have no place whatever in an inquiry whether or not a deed is void, as fraudulent, upon
the principles of the common law, or in the eye of a
Statute declaratory of the common law. I must therefore enter my earnest protest against the idea that a
doctrine which is essentially and 'peculiarly a *creature
of a* Court of Equity in the administration of equities,
namely, that, *a plea of purchase for value without notice
presents no defence, unless the whole purchase money has
been paid before plea pleaded*,—has any application
whatever in the decision of the case before us.

Judgment.

44—VOL. XVIII. GR.

Granting, then, the mortgage executed by *Alexander Douglas* to his son *James*, to have been void in the hands of *James* as against *Alexander's* creditors, *James* nevertheless, until a creditor interfered, retained under the mortgage the estate and the interest created thereby, but before any creditor interfered this estate and interest had passed out of *James*, and the first question, is, whether it had so passed out of him to *Cook*, to whom the mortgage was assigned, as to be capable of being followed in the hands of *Cook* by a creditor of *Alexander's* who could have avoided it in the hands of *James Douglas*, and, second, when the mortgage was assigned by *Cook* to *Nesbitt*, whether or not it so passed to *Nesbitt* as to be capable of being avoided as it could have been if still in the hands of *James Douglas*, the original mortgagee.

*Morewood* v. *The South Yorkshire Railway Company* (a) is a comparatively recent case at law and the most recent which I have been able to find, which appears to have a direct bearing upon the point in issue. It was a case of interpleader between plaintiffs who claimed certain goods by bill of sale from one *Watson*, and the defendants who claimed as execution creditors of *Watson*.

The facts were that on the 4th February, 1848, *Watson* had conveyed the goods by bill of sale, by way of mortgage to *Morewood*, one of the plaintiffs, to secure £300. There was evidence from which a jury might infer that this bill of sale was fraudulent and void, within 13 Elizabeth, ch. 5, as against the defendants, but on the 13th May, in the presence of *Watson*, *Morewood*, assigned the goods to *Bayne* by way of mortgage, to secure £250 then paid by *Bayne* to *Morewood*. *Bramwell*, B., told the jury that it was not material whether the transfer to *Morewood was fraudulent* or not. If *Bayne* advanced

--------

(a) 3 H. & N. 798.

his money in good faith and *Watson* stood by while
*Morewood* mortgaged to him, neither *Watson* nor the
defendants could dispute the validity of the transaction.

The jury found that the assignment to *Bayne* was
*bona fide* so far as he was concerned. *Bovill* moved for
a new trial for misdirection—his contention was, that
assuming the bill of sale to *Morewood* to have been
fraudulent as against the defendants, the conveyance was
utterly void by 13 Elizabeth, ch. 5, and that *Morewood*
therefore had nothing which he could convey to *Bayne*—to
this *Watson*, B., observes, "section 6 provides that nothing
therein contained shall extend to any estate or interest
in land, &c., conveyed *bona fide* and upon good consideration, to any person not having notice or knowledge
of the fraud,"—and *Pollock*, C. B., says, " *Void* does
not mean utterly and absolutely void, but void *sub modo*
and here before the question of the validity of the bill
of sale arose, the property was divested out of the first
assignee." In giving judgment, *Pollock*, C. B., says:
" There will be no rule : assuming the assignment to
*Morewood* to have been fraudulent within the Statute of
13 Elizabeth, ch. 5,—*Bayne* having taken *bona fide* by a
conveyance made by *Morewood in the presence, and
with the assent of Watson*, has a good title."

*Judgment.*

*Watson*, B., says,—" The conveyance to *Morewood*
was only void as against creditors, *Morewood* retained an interest until some creditor interfered, the 5th
sec. of 13 Elizabeth, ch. 5, only does what justice would
require, and makes *Morewood's* transfer for value good.
In the case of a deed void as against creditors there
must be an election to avoid the deed, but before any
election the property was gone out of *Morewood*."

*Bramwell*, B., says,—" *Watson*, a person possessed of
goods, puts them into the hands of another,—that other
with his assent sells the goods to *Bayne*, a *bona fide* pur-

chaser. *Watson's* creditor then says, that inasmuch as the title must be traced through a *mala fide* purchaser he is entitled to treat the sale to *Bayne* as null. To that there are two answers. If the transfer operated as between the *mala fide* purchaser and *Bayne,* the title of the *mala fide* purchaser was defeasible ; but before any step was taken to defeat such title, the property passed. If the first transfer had no operation, then the *bona fide* purchaser took directly from the original owner."

These observations of *Bramwell*, B., in relation to 13 Elizabeth, seem to coincide with the opinion of Sir *William Grant* as to cases within 27 Elizabeth, expressed in *Danberry* v. *Cockburn*, viz. : that he who pays the consideration to the voluntary grantee, may, constructively, be held to be in the same situation as if he had in the first instance paid it to him by whom the estate had been granted— and with the opinion of Lord *Campbell*, expressed in *Doe Newman* v. *Rusham*, to the effect that the consideration paid to the voluntary grantee will enure to support the voluntary conveyance, so that *it* will be considered to have been made upon valuable consideration—and with the principle of *Rodgers* v. *Langham*, that the valuable consideration given to the voluntary feoffee will operate by reference back so as to support the original feoffment, which by this payment *ex post facto*, *is made good*, and with the conclusion from that case drawn by Lord *Eldon*, that the consequence is that the feoffment of a voluntary feoffee is good against creditors.

It appears then that a *bona fide* sale by a covinous grantee, is as good against the creditors of the grantor under 13 Elizabeth, as it is against a purchaser from the grantor for value under 27 Elizabeth ; and the transaction, attending a transfer from the covinous grantee, may amount to, and may be held to be, a transaction directly between the original grantor and the assignee of the covinous grantee.

It becomes then important to determine what was the substance of the transaction in virtue of which *Cook* became assignee of the mortgage. He appears to have been a creditor upon promissory notes of *Alexander Douglas* to a considerable amount, in fact, to an amount about four times greater than the claim of the plaintiff *Baker*. When he first heard of the mortgage to the son he had reason to be anxious about his own position and would have been justified in taking measures to protect himself. If then he had gone to the father and son and had complained that the mortgage was a fraud upon him as a creditor of *Alexander Douglas*, and had threatened to take proceedings to avoid it, and if under the influence of such threats the father in consideration of $400 paid to him in cash by *Cook*, and of notes of his own in favour of *Cook*, to the amount of $600, given up by *Cook* had executed a mortgage to him for $1000, that mortgage, however assailable it might be in whole or in part as a preference to a creditor, under the provisions of the Insolvent Act, it never could have been assailed under 13 Elizabeth by any creditor of *Alexander Douglas*. Now, if the substance of the transaction which did take place is equivalent to such a security given to *Cook*, I do not think that we can avoid a transation in substance unimpeachable by reason of the form which it assumed.

The learned Vice Chancellor was of opinion that " *Cook's* negotiation for the purchase of the mortgage was with the mortgagor, and that the son merely acquiesced in, and carried out what his father had agreed to."

I confess I am strongly of the same opinion, and it is because I entertain that opinion that I think the plaintiff is not entitled to have a decree made in his favour. In the view which I take it is a matter of no importance what was the motive or consideration for the father making the mortgage to the son, for it is upon the assumption that there was no consideration which could have supported it standing alone and consistently with *Cook's* belief that it had been executed in June with an intent fraudulent as against creditors, that I hold, in accordance as I think with the principles laid down in *Morewood* v. *The South Yorkshire Railway Company*, and with the other cases quoted above ; and with *Wood* v. *Dixie*, and all the cases of that class down to *Alton* v. *Harrison* (a), the subsequent transaction between *Alexander* and *James Douglas* on the one part and *Cook* on the other, to be unassailable under the 13 Elizabeth, although as I have said it may be assailable under the provisions of the Insolvent Act.

Concurring with the Vice Chancellor, I think that *Cook* negotiated with the father that in consideration of *Cook* giving up over-due notes of the father to the amount of $600, and of a present cash advance of $400, he *Cook* should be secured to the extent of $1000 by a mortgage on

the father's property, and that upon the notes being given up and the cash advance made through the hands of the son, *Cook's* security should be perfected by an assignment by the son to *Cook* of the mortgage of the 18th June. In pursuance of this arrangement, and upon the faith of its being perfected, *Cook* gives up the notes to the amount of $600, and made the cash advance, and thereupon the son, by the direction of the father, assigned the mortgage to *Cook*. I have not the slightest doubt in my own mind as a juror, that in fact, and in truth, it never entered the heads of any of the parties to this arrangement with *Cook*, that he should hold subject to any secret trust in favour of *Alexander Douglas* or *James ;* and that the consideration given by *Cook* was *bona fide* given by him for the express and sole purpose of repayment to himself of the notes for $600 given up, and the actual advance of the $400.

---

(a) L. Rep. 4, Ch. Ap. 622.

Now, the consideration so given by *Cook*, upon the
authority of *Rodgers* v. *Langham*, operated by reference
back to support the original mortgage—it operated, upon
the authority of *Doe Newman* v. *Rusham*, so to support the original mortgage that it shall be deemed to
have been executed for the consideration given by *Cook*.
To apply the judgment of *Pollock*, C. B., in *Morewood*
v. *South Yorkshire Railway*: *Cook* had a good title,
having taken *bona fide* by a conveyance made by *James
Douglas*, with the assent and by the direction of his
father *Alexander*; in the words of *Bramwell*, B., it operated to make *Cook*, the *bona fide* purchaser, take directly
from *Alexander Douglas*, the original owner; and, in the
words of Sir *William Grant*, it operated constructively
to place *Cook* in the same situation as if the consideration given by him, had been paid *to him by whom* the
mortgage had been granted. But on the assumption,
which I think is warranted by the evidence, that the bargain was made by *Cook* with *Alexander*, and that the
assignment was made by the son by the direction of the
father, it needs no constructive interpretation, for it is
the natural interpretation of what took place, to enable
us to hold that the consideration given by *Cook* passed
directly to *Alexander*, although it came by his direction
through the hands of the son. The son was in fact no
more than the agent of the father in the transaction.
This being the substance and operation of the negotiations between *Cook* and *Alexander*, which became matured
and completed by the assignment made to *Cook*, I
cannot see wherein this case differs from *Wood* v. *Dixie*
and that class of cases which holds, that a security given
for an actual advance made, or partly for an advance
made and partly to prefer a creditor for an old debt,
where there is no secret trust in favour of the grantor, is
unassailable under the statute of 13 Elizabeth, although
it may be under the Insolvent Act in this country, or the
Bankruptcy Acts in England. I can see no reason why
*Cook* who was one of *Alexander Douglas's* largest credi-

tors should be deprived of a benefit which, as it seems to me, he has obtained for good consideration, upon the allegation that the security he has obtained is a fraud upon *Alexander Douglas's* general creditors, for the purpose of enabling the plaintiff *Baker*, another creditor, to sweep away the same property from the general creditors as well as the purchaser creditor *Cook;* nor do I see how we can deprive *Cook* of the benefit which he has obtained without overruling the authority of *Wood* v. *Dixie* so recently confirmed in this Court, in *Smith* v. *Moffatt* (a), and in the Court of Appeal in Chancery in England, in *Alton* v. *Harrison*—wherein it was held as settled beyond doubt, as this Court had also held, that the *bona fides* referred to in the statute means an execution of the instrument for the actual purpose of passing the estate honestly to the vendee or mortgagee, claiming under it; and not as a mere cloke for retaining a benefit to the grantor.

But assuming the mortgage to have been impeachable in the hands of *Cook*, notwithstanding the consideration given by him, it was assigned by *Cook* to *Nesbitt*, before the bill in this case was filed and before any proceeding had been taken by a creditor to avoid it, and the question remains whether or not it is impeachable in the hands of *Nesbitt*, at the suit of the plaintiffs. For my own part, acting as a juror, I cannot say that there is anything in the evidence sufficient to warrant the conclusion, that the assignment to *Nesbett* was otherwise than for good consideration, *bona fide* paid without notice of any fraud; he is in my judgment entitled to be regarded precisely in the same position as, in the case of *Morewood* v. *The South Yorkshire Railway Company*, *Bayne* was after the finding by the jury that the assignment to him was *bona fide*, so far as he was concerned. It does not appear that the learned Vice Chancellor

---

(a) 28 U. C. 486.

formed an opinion upon this point unfavourable to *Nes-*
*bitt.* The decree in so far as he is concerned 'seems to
proceed upon the assumption that, assuming the consideration given by *Nesbett* to have been *bona fide* given and
him to be free from fraud, nevertheless, that as he had
paid to *Cook* for the assignment only $500 in cash and
had given his note for the balance, he must lose the benefit of the assignment, not only as respects the amount
secured by his note, but also as respects the $500 ac-
tually paid by him in cash upon the faith of the security,
and that he must stand or fall upon the sufficiency of
*Cook's* estate, and interest in the mortgage ; upon a
principle which is the peculiar creature of the Court of
Chancery ; namely, that a person pleading a purchase
for valuable consideration, without notice, must have
paid the whole of his purchase money before plea pleaded,
in order to obtain the benefit of the plea.

Whether this rule is not confined, in its application,
to the case of a defence offered by plea which is in bar
of discovery, it is unnecessary now to inquire; because in
my judgment the rule invoked has no application whatever to the case before us.

In a case before Lord *Westbury*, *Phillips* v. *Phil-*
*lips* (a), he traces the doctrine to the elementary principles from which it has sprung. That case shews that
the doctrine is purely a creature of a Court of Equity
and that its application is confined exclusively to the
dealing of that Court with equitable estates, or pure
equities as distinct from estates.

Now, it needs not, as it appears to me, much argument
to shew that a claim to set aside a deed as fraudulent
and void against the plaintiff as a creditor of the grantor,
is—neither the assertion of an equitable estate nor of

---

(a) 8 Jur. N. S. 145, S. C. 5 L. Times, N. S. 655.

any equity as distinguished from an estate, nor of any right peculiar to a Court of Equity to administer—it is the assertion of a common law right, confirmed by the Statute of 13 Elizabeth, which right is cognizable in a Court of Equity equally as in a Court of Law, and must be determined upon the principle of the Common Law as recognized by the Statute which are common to both jurisdictions and not upon, or by the aid of, any peculiar doctrine which is the creature of the Court of Chancery designed for the purpose of dispensing and regulating *equities*, their *rights and priorities*.

True it is, that an issue is presented whether or not the assignment to *Nesbitt* is sustainable as having been executed for good consideration *bona fide* given by him without fraud on his part, but that issue necessarily arises upon the charges which the plaintiff's bill must contain assailing the assignment, the onus of impeaching which successfully, lies upon the plaintiff; the issue in no sense arises as by way of a defence set up of a purchase for valuable consideration without notice, within the application of that doctrine as above explained by Lord *Westbury*. The question to be determined is precisely the same as if the issue arose in a Court of Law, as it might have arisen, and is identical with that which arose in *Morewood* v. *the South Yorkshire Railway Company*, namely: Granting the mortgage to be impeachable in the hands of *Cook*, was it assigned by him to *Nesbitt* for any, and if any, for what consideration, and was such consideration, if any there was given, valuable and *bona fide*; that is honestly and really given by *Nesbitt* without fraud in the eye of the common law, or of the statute, upon his part—to the extent of the consideration, if any, so given by *Nesbitt*. The mortgage cannot be impeached in his hands whatever may have been the amount of the consideration and whether the whole agreed upon had or had not been paid before bill filed, or whether the whole amount was or not paid in cash. The amount only becomes of importance upon the question of redemption arising ; and redemption implies the validity of the mortgage for whatever sums *Nesbitt* advanced upon the security of it.

Now, upon a trial at law, there can be no doubt that if the consideration given by *Nesbitt* consisted of $500 in cash, and his note for $500, payable to *Cook's* order at a future day, $1000 represents the consideration so given, whatever may have been the cash value of the note; and if *Cook* transferred the note for value, it represents the amount actually received by *Cook*, less the amount which he allowed, if any, upon the transfer of the note as discount for converting it into cash.

The fact of the note remaining still in *Cook's* hands undisposed of, could not alter the fact that it constituted part of the consideration given by *Nesbitt*, and that such consideration was given *bona fide*.

It would be a singular thing, as it appears to me, if the fact of *Cook* having or not having negotiated the paper, which he received as part of the consideration *bona fide* given by *Nesbitt* could alter, or in any manner detract from, *Nesbitt's bona fides* in giving the consideration. Now, that same *bona fides* of *Nesbitt*, assuming *Cook's* possession of the mortgage to be impeachable, is sufficient to protect *Nesbitt*, so as to prevent the possibility of a decree in Equity or a judgment at common law being sustained declaring the mortgage to be fraudulent and void in his hands as against the plaintiff—the principle governing the decision must be the same in whatever Court the issue is tried. All application of that peculiar doctrine which Lord *Westbury* calls the creature of the Court of Chancery, whatever may be its incidents where applicable, must then of necessity be excluded, and we must determine the point upon *Nesbitt's bona fides* in giving the consideration which he did give and not di-

vest him of his security because of the existence of a fact
which is perfectly consistent with the utmost *bona fides*,
and with the utter absence of all fraud upon his part. In
the view which I take, the application of the *Commercial Bank* v. *Wilson* is excluded, for I proceed upon the
assumption that the original mortgage was, in the hands
of *James Douglas*, fraudulent and void as against creditors, and confine myself to the inquiries whether the
consideration given by *Cook* under the circumstances in
which it was given is sufficient upon the authorities to
have sustained the mortgage in his hands to any amount ;
and assuming it not to be, then whether upon the same
principle the consideration given by *Nesbitt*, is sufficient
to sustain it in his hands to any amount.

Whether, therefore, we regard alone the consideration
given by *Cook* or that given by *Nesbitt*, I am of opinion
the mortgage in the hands of *Nesbitt* cannot be set aside
as fraudulent and void under the Statute of Elizabeth, at
the suit of the plaintiff, whatever might be the result of a
case made by the assignee in insolvency, under the provisions of the Insolvent Act ; and that the plaintiff's bill
therefore, in so far as it prayed such relief should be
dismissed with costs.  I do not find, upon the evidence
before us, whether the period of redemption mentioned
in the mortgage has or not arrived ; if not then
as a redemption suit, the bill is premature (*a*).
Under the circumstances the order I think should
be, that the plaintiff's bill so far as it prays to set
aside the mortgage in the hand of *Nesbitt* as fraudulent
and void against the plaintiff and others, creditors of
*Alexander Douglas*, should be dismissed with costs ;
and that the suit should be remitted to the Court of
Chancery, to be there entertained as a redemption suit ;
when if it appear that the period of redemption has not
arrived, the bill should be dismissed wholly ; but if it has,
should be proceeded with as a redemption suit.

Judgment.

---

(*a*) Skeeles v. Shearly, 3 My. & Cr., 112, 120.

MOWAT, V.C.—The defendant *Cockshutt* has not been made a respondent, and it seems to me that in his absence it would be equally against principle and against practice to vary the decree to his prejudice and the prejudice of those whom he represents. In *McQueen's* Practice of the House of Lords (*a*), the rule is stated to be, "that all persons who were made parties in the Court below, must be made parties, or cited to appear as parties, in the House of Lords." So strict is this rule that the circumstance, "that the decree or order complained of may be considered to be right and unobjectionable in so far as it affects the interest of certain parties to the suit, is no reason for omitting to make those parties, parties to the appeal. * * A person made a party below in the character of trustee, but who by his answer stated that he had never acted as trustee, and who had made no appearance at the hearing, was nevertheless ordered to be summoned as a party to the appeal. So, also, a party who had not only made no appearance at the hearing, but against whom the cause had been heard upon a sequestration." In the present case counsel for the plaintiffs, who are the only respondents, called attention to the want of parties ; but it is not in their interest, but in the interest of the absent party, that his presence is essential. He happens to have a large interest under the decree as it stands, the property being worth about three times the plaintiff's debt, and the absent party *Cockshutt*, as representing the creditors under the insolvency, having therefore an interest in the property under the decree to twice the amount of the plaintiffs' interest. To reverse the decree as respects *Cockshutt* on such a record, I humbly think, is impossible.

The circumstance that this Court does not hear more than two counsel for the respondents, and that we have

---

(*a*). p. 123.

already heard two on behalf of the plaintiffs, has been suggested as a reason for giving judgment on the record as it stands. But the counsel heard were not *Cockshutt's* counsel; he had no voice in selecting or instructing them, as he would have had if he had been a respondent; and it is obviously no reason for not hearing a party, or for giving judgment against him in his absence, that counsel for another party had argued the case for him.

As to the merits, I have failed to see that the decree was wrong. If the transaction between the *Douglasses* and *Cook* is to be treated as a mortgage by *Alexander Douglas* to *Cook*, the case is, a mortgage for $1000 given by an insolvent person in consideration of the mortgagee's paying to the assignor $400 in money, in satisfaction of one fictitious debt, and $600 in promissory notes of the mortgagor, in satisfaction of another fictitious debt, the purchaser having notice that the debts were fictitious. Can such a transaction be valid? To hold it valid would, I apprehend, be going far beyond *Wood* v. *Dixie*, or any other case which has hitherto been decided against creditors. I am assuming here that *Cook* had sufficient notice of the real character of the mortgage which he was bargaining for. If payment of the consideration to a fraudulent mortgagor or grantor does not necessarily, according to modern decisions, make the mortgagee or grantee a party to the fraudulent use which the mortgagor or grantor may make of the money, surely if, with notice of the fraud, the party paying discharges with his own hand fictitious debts, he must be treated as so far a party to the fraud on the real creditors, that he cannot maintain the transaction as valid against them.

Taking the transaction in the way most favorable to the appellants, the consideration for the mortgage to *Cook* was, his own legal debt for $600, and money paid

for the transfer (with notice) of a fictitious debt of $400. 1871.
Now, *Commercial Bank* v. *Wilson* (a) is an express decision that, where a consideration is in part valuable, and
in part a pretence to defeat creditors, the security is void
as to both. The case was of a judgment; but the decision
proceeded on grounds of a general kind. The Chief
Justice said: "Being tainted with actual fraud, and to
a great extent, it should not be upheld as to any
part, but in the words of the Statute 13 Elizabeth,
ch. 5, sec. 2, being made 'of fraud, collusion, and
guile, with intent to delay, hinder, or defraud creditors
of their just and lawful actions and debts, it must
be deemed and taken (as against the plaintiffs who
are judgment creditors) to be clearly and utterly
void, frustrated, and of no effect.' The Court does
not in such cases attempt, or (as it has been said)
they will not condescend, to go into the consideration
whether any and what part of the fraudulent judgment
may not have been founded in a just and legal demand.
I refer to *Sanders* 66, note *q; Twyne's* case, 3 Coke
83; and *Thomas's* note to that case; 2 *Coke's* Reports,
p. 222, note *w; Hobart's* Reports, 14. * * If this
was not so held, the statute would fail greatly in its
effect, for then parties would be in a situation to attempt
such frauds without risk of loss of anything real in case
of detection. * * The principle, that under the very
words of the statute, the judgment, if fraudulent as to
part, is utterly void as against the creditor whose action
is attempted to be defeated by it, puts an end to all
argument. We have so applied the principle in other
cases in this country, and must equally do it in this."

The same principle was acted upon in this Court in
*Crawford* v. *Meldrum* (b). That was the case of an
absolute conveyance which was (no doubt) meant to be a
real transaction; part of the consideration was a *bond*

Totten
v.
Douglas.

Judgment.

---

(a) 14 Gr. 473.          (b) 3 E. & A. 101.

*fide* debt; the other part was the result of a transaction which was invalid against creditors; and the former standing alone was an inadequate consideration for the property. The deed was set aside in toto.

If the present case is not disposed of by those decisions, I would further observe, that what we have to deal with is, not the case of a merely voluntary convey-ance to *James Douglas*, but of a conveyance made to him with express intent to defeat creditors. I think it clear that between these two classes of cases there is an essential distinction; and that it is only in one exceptional case that they are treated as one and the same.

The Statute 27 Elizabeth, ch. 4, enacted, that every con-veyance of land " for the intent and purpose to defraud and deceive" future purchasers should be void against such purchasers. Now under this statute it is true that, at an early period, it was held that every conveyance by way of gift, however honest, was void against a subse-quent purchaser from the grantor; though that determi-nation has often been regretted by learned Judges (*a*), and was only followed because it had been acted upon, and many titles had in consequence become' dependent on it. It has, therefore, been followed wherever strictly applicable; but the Courts have declined to extend the rule so as to embrace all cases to which it might logically have been held applicable. Thus, a prior voluntary deed is not void against a subsequent purchase from the heirs or devisee of the voluntary grantor (*b*); nor against a purchase from a second voluntary grantee of the donor. To maintain such purchases, the prior voluntary deed must be shewn to have been actually fraudulent, and not merely to have been voluntary. The Courts have

---

(*a*) Pulvertoft v. Pulvertoft, 18 Ves. at 90 ; &c.

(*b*) See 1 Smith's Lead. Ca. 25, 26, &c.

also refused to hold the voluntary deed to be fraudulent 1871.
and void where the donee disposed of the property for
value before the sale by the donor; or where the purchase from the voluntary grantor was for a grossly
inadequate price (a). It is plain, therefore, that a
voluntary conveyance, not otherwise objectionable, is
not treated under the Statute 27 Elizabeth, as for all
purposes on the same footing as a conveyance executed
with express intent to defraud.

Further : Though the Statutes 13 Elizabeth and 27
Elizabeth are in *pari materiâ*, the application to cases
under the one statute of decisions under the other, has
to be made with caution. A deed void against a
purchaser under the one statute, may be valid against
a creditor under the other statute; and *vice versa*. Thus,
a deed of gift made by a party not indebted, and without fraud, may be perfectly valid against creditors; but
the mere circumstance of its being voluntary would,
according to the decisions, make it invalid against a
subsequent purchaser. So, I apprehend, though a
sale for value would necessarily defeat a prior deed
of gift, yet if the sale was an express contrivance of
both parties for the very purpose of defrauding creditors, it might be void against them. The cases of fraudulent settlements on marriages illustrate the latter
proposition (b).

It manifestly therefore does not follow as of course,
that, because a voluntary conveyance, executed in good
faith, may be made effectual by a subsequent sale by
the grantee, a voluntary conveyance executed with express intent to defraud creditors is in the same position.

Totten
v.
Douglas.

Judgment.

---

(a) Metcalf v. Pulvertoft, 1 V. & B. 184 ; Upton v. Basset, Cro. Eliz.
445 ; Doe v. Rutledge, Cowp. 705 ; Parry v. James, 16 East 212.

(b) Columbine v. Penhall, 1 Sm. & Giff. 228 ; see Dart on Vendors,
4th ed., p. 827.

That in such a case a purchaser who had no notice of the fraud should not be affected by it, is just and reasonable; is in accordance with the letter and spirit of both Statutes of Elizabeth; and is agreeable to the general doctrine of equity. But what the appellants had to make out was, that notice makes no difference.

It would be a strange thing so to hold in equity. The rule there is (and no equitable doctrine is better established than this), "that the person who purchases an estate (although for valuable consideration) after notice of a prior equitable right, makes himself a *mala fide* purchaser, and will not be enabled by getting in the legal estate to defeat such prior equitable interest. * * A purchaser, with notice of a right in another, is in equity liable to the same extent, and in the same manner, as the person from whom he made the purchase" (a). Why should the creditors of a fraudulent debtor be alone excluded from the benefit of this just doctrine? In the absence of authority to that effect, no such exception surely can be admitted. This doctrine of notice is the sole occasion in many instances of a plaintiff's resorting to equity instead of bringing his suit at law (b).

I am not aware of more than five reported cases in which a question has arisen between creditors and a purchaser from their debtor's voluntary grantee; and all of them except one, which is a case in *Siderfin's* Reports, either assert or imply that to maintain the purchase against creditors, it must be shewn, either that the gift was *bona fide* and valid against creditors, or that the purchaser had no notice of its true character. In the case in *Siderfin* (c) nothing is said as to notice.

*George* v. *Milbanks* (d) is the next case. There the purchasers expressly claimed " by assignment for valu-

---

(a) See White and Tudor, p. 39, et seq.          (b) Ib.
(c) Rogers v. Laugham 1 Sid. 133.          (d) 9 Ves.

able consideration without notice;" and the plaintiffs, on the other hand, contended that the defendants could "not be considered as purchasers without notice." Lord *Eldon*, in giving judgment, said: "The circumstances of notice are not immaterial;" and he proceeded to comment upon them. The valuable consideration there was marriage; and as to that circumstance, the Lord Chancellor remarked: "There is no difference between a voluntary settlement made good by a subsequent marriage, and one made good by a subsequent advance of money."

In *Meggison* v. *Foster* (a) a person gave a voluntary bond for £5000; the bond was afterwards included in the ante-nuptial marriage settlement of the obligee; subsequently to the marriage the obligor became bankrupt, and his assignees insisted that the bond being voluntary was void against creditors. The Court maintained the settlement, but expressly on the ground, not that the marriage alone made the voluntary bond valid against creditors, but that the obligor was in solvent circumstances when he gave the bond, and that there was no dishonesty or unfairness in it. The parties there appear to have had notice that the bond was voluntary; and the judgment therefore implies that if the bond had been open to objection, the assignment of it for value would not have been valid.

*Judgment.*

*Payne* v. *Mortimer* (b) was a similar case, and was decided on the same ground.

*Morewood* v. *The South Yorkshire Railway Co.* (c) was a case at law. There the purchaser had no notice of the fraudulent character of the conveyance to his vendor; and the head note of the case is, that the

---

(a) 1 Y. & C. C. C. 335         (b) 4 DeG. & J. 447.
(c) 3 H. & N. 798.

conveyance to the purchaser "being *bona fide*, and without notice, his title was good against the creditors." That such notice was immaterial, was therefore not supposed by the learned reporter to have been the view of the Court; and I have no doubt that it was not. *Watson*, B., pointed out during the argument, that the statute excepted from its operation "any estate or interest conveyed *bona fide* and upon good consideration, to any person not having notice or knowledge of the fraud;" and in giving judgment he referred to the same enactment as only doing "what justice would require, and makes the transfer for value good." Notice is not expressly referred to by any of the learned judges in pronouncing judgment; but, notice not having been alleged against the purchaser, and the argument on the other side having been that the conveyance being fraudulent was utterly void against them, the case seems clearly no authority for more than the reporter has noted as the point decided in it.

The authorities at law are thus not sufficient to maintain *Cook's* purchase as against the creditors of *Douglas*. But if they had been, I do not see how the purchase could be maintained in equity without violating one of the best settled and most important doctrines of equity. That doctrine requires us to hold, that, whatever the rights of the plaintiffs would have been against the fraudulent grantee *James Douglas*, they must be the same against a purchaser from *James Douglas* with notice.

It has been suggested that, the deed being impeached on the ground of fraud, for which it might have been impeached at law, the jurisdiction of law and equity in such cases being concurrent, the relief can only be granted in equity against persons who could be reached at law. To this it is sufficient to answer, that it is a mistake to assume that the jurisdiction of equity in cases of frauds on creditors is only concurrent and co-extensive with the jurisdiction at law; for it is well settled that equity can give relief to creditors in cases in which the law recognizes no right in the creditors. Thus, where a conveyance was valid as between an insolvent vendor and his vendee, but part of the consideration was for the benefit of the vendor's family; though at law the creditors could not have reached this part, yet the Court held that it was liable in equity to their claims (a). So, where a man has a general power of appointment over a fund, and exercises his power by a deed or will in favor of volunteers, his appointment may be unimpeachable at law; but in equity the property appointed is subject to the claims of the creditors of the appointor, in preference to his appointees (b). Then, an owner of equitable estates may make a fraudulent conveyance of them—Is notice immaterial in such cases because it would be immaterial if the estates were legal? Or is the materiality of notice to depend altogether on whether the debtor's estate was legal or equitable? It is impossible to avoid all sorts of anomalies without holding that the equitable doctrine of notice applies in all cases.

As to *Nesbitt's* position, I observed in my judgment on the first hearing below, that "the nonpayment of the whole of his purchase money was admitted at the bar to make it essential for him to sustain *Cook's* purchase" (c). I assumed the same thing in my judgment at the second hearing; and on looking at my notes of the argument on that occasion, I do not find that anything had been urged before me in favor of a different view. Besides, the question is immaterial for any substantial purpose. *Cook* is a man of wealth, and *Nesbitt* has his covenant. *Cook's* object in assigning to him, there is little doubt,

---

(a) French v. French, 6 DeG. McN. & G. 95; Neale v. Day, 4 Jur. N. S. 1225.

(b) See the cases, 2 Wms. Exrs. 1557.     (c) 15 Grant, at 131.

was to intercept the plaintiffs' right; and there is the strongest indication that *Nesbitt* purchased to assist *Cook* in his purpose, and not as an ordinary business transaction. *Cook*, notwithstanding his assignment to *Nesbitt*, retained the mortgage deed; and *Nesbitt* bought without investigation of the title, or of the particulars of the property. To any extent that he now fails to retain the mortgage, he has his remedy against *Cook;* and the defence on this point, as on every other, is thus in substance *Cook's* own defence still. But if a party in whose hands land is liable to the claim of another, intercepts that claim by selling the land to a purchaser for value without notice, the purchase money which he receives is in equity subject to the claim, and applicable to its liquidation. In every view, therefore, the case should be disposed of according to the equities between the plaintiff and *Cook*, unaffected by the transfer to *Nesbitt*.

Judgment.

The result is, that I still think that the decree was right, and should not be changed, even if the assignee in insolvency (who has a larger interest than the plaintiff) were a respondent to the appeal.

Order.

*Order*—That the bill in the Court below, so far as the same seeks to set aside the mortgage from *Alexander Douglas* to *James Douglas*, and the assignments thereof, as void as against plaintiff and others, the creditors of the said *Alexander Douglas* be, and the same is, hereby dismissed with costs, to be paid by the plaintiff to the defendants; without prejudice, however, to the right of *Ignatius Cockshutt* to file a bill to enforce his claim in repect of the matters in the said bill mentioned : Order, that the case be remitted back to the said Court of Chancery to entertain the same as a redemption suit in case the time for redemption has arrived, but, if such time has not arrived, then and in such case the said bill of complaint, shall be dismissed out of the said Court with costs.

## McIntyre v. The Canada Company.

*Statute of Limitations—Amendment at hearing.*

A person who had been in possession of lands for upwards of 20 years wrote to the heir of the true owner, acknowledging his title as such heir:

*Held,* that such acknowledgment having been made after the title by possession was complete, did not take away the statutory right which possession gave.

An acknowledgment to a party's trustee is sufficient to take a case out of the Statute of Limitations.

*P,* being in possession of land of which he was not the owner, made a verbal gift of the land to *C,* but afterwards ejected him. *C* then obtained a conveyance from the owner. More than 20 years had elapsed from the time that the Statute of Limitations began to run in favor of *P* against the true owner:

*Held,* that *C's* possession did not interrupt in *C's* favor the running of the Statute; that the owner being barred, *C,* his grantee, was barred also.

The defence of the Statute of Limitations being allowed at the hearing to be put in by supplemental answer :

*Held,* on rehearing, that the plaintiff should have an opportunity of controverting this defence.

Rehearing.

The original decree pronounced by Vice Chancellor *Strong,* dismissed the bill with costs.                    Statement.

*Francis McIntyre,* in his lifetime, contracted with the defendants, the *Canada Company,* for the purchase of the land in question, and went into possession with his brother *Patrick,* and remained in possession until his death, in 1840. The purchase money was partly paid during the lifetime of *Francis,* and the residue by *Patrick* after the death of *Francis. Francis* died intestate and without issue, leaving his brother *James,* who resided in Europe, his heir-at-law. The plaintiff was another brother, and was younger than those named. He came to this country in 1849, and in

1868 obtained a conveyance from the heir of *Francis*. The plaintiff had possession of the property at one time, and was ejected by *Patrick*. No conveyance had been executed by the *Canada Company*, and the bill was for a conveyance. *Patrick*, who was a defendant, claimed the property as his, but did not prove any title except by length of possession. The *Canada Campany* submitted to convey to either, as the Court should direct. The other facts appear sufficiently from the judgment of the Court on rehearing.

Mr. *McGregor*, for the plaintiff.

Mr. *Moss*, for the defendant.

The judgment of the Court was pronounced by

MOWAT, V. C.—On the evidence as it stands, I think that the decree of my brother *Strong* was right. *Francis* died in 1840, and *Patrick* remained from that time in sole possession. This possession would have ripened into a title in 1860 but for the absence of *Francis's* heir from the Province. In 1862 the Legislature did away with the distinction between persons resident and persons not resident in the country, and made the Act retrospective except as to suits commenced before the 1st July, 1863 (*a*). The present suit was not brought until long after that date. The plaintiff has proved that, in 1864, *Patrick* wrote a letter to the heir of *Francis*, acknowledging his title; but an acknowledgment after a title by possession is complete, does not take away the statutory right which possession gave.

The plaintiff swore that *Patrick*, in 1859, made a verbal gift to him of this land and of every thing else which he had in the world; that the plaintiff was in

_____

(*a*) 25 Vic., ch. 20.

possession of the land under this gift for eight years
and ten months, when *Patrick* ejected him; that they
lived together on this place for the first three or four
years after the verbal gift; and that, from the time
*Patrick* left, the plaintiff was in sole possession. So
far as appears, that verbal gift, if made, was not binding on *Patrick;* the plaintiff is not the heir of *Francis,*
but only the grantee of the heir, and he did not acquire
the heir's interest (if any) until 1868. The plaintiff's
possession was therefore as much against the heir of
*Francis* as *Patrick's* possession was, and did not prevent the Statute from running against the heir.

The defendant did not, by his answer, set up the
defence of the Statute of Limitations. My brother
*Strong* gave him leave at the hearing to amend his
defence in that respect, but declined to allow the plaintiff to amend his bill, and have a future opportunity of
giving evidence, to meet that defence, believing that he
had no other evidence. It is quite probable that my
brother was right in that supposition; but if the plaintiff
really has other evidence, he should, of course, have the
opportunity of adducing it. Counsel for the plaintiff
mentioned, amongst other things, that the *Canada
Company* had received letters from *Patrick* within
twenty years after the death of *Francis,* acknowledging
the title. The *Canada Company* being (until barred by
lapse of time) trustee for *Francis* and his heir under
the contract of sale, I think that a written admission to
the *Company* by *Patrick* during that period, would
take the case out of the Statute up to the date of such
admission; and that the plaintiff should have an opportunity of producing these letters. It will not be necessary, I suppose, that the case should be delayed until
next sittings for that purpose; and, unless the plaintiff
shews by affidavit that he has other material evidence,
the matter may be disposed of here.

Judgment.

I observe that expense has been incurred by means of a foreign commission to prove the heirship of the person through whom the plaintiff claims. The plaintiff, and *Patrick*, and *Francis*, were brothers ; and it is not fitting that *Patrick* should have compelled the heirship to be proved. Having reference to the General Order No. 124, I think that the defendant should not have the costs of, and incidental to, the commission, however the other costs may be ultimately disposed of.

---

### ROSAMUND V. FORGIE.

*Riparian proprietors—Mill-dams—Construction of covenant in equity.*

On a sale of a mill site the vendor covenanted to secure to the vendee sufficient water for certain manufacturing purposes ; the deed did not state how the water was to be supplied ; but a dam was then standing which afforded the necessary supply, and it did not appear that the covenantor had any other way of securing it :

*Held*, that he or any one claiming under him was not entitled to a decree for the removal of this dam without supplying sufficient water in some other way.

*Held*, also, that the grantee, his heirs and assigns, were entitled to use the water for other purposes, provided no more was used than the specified manufactures had required and used.

After the conveyance, other persons, unconnected with either party, erected mills above the dam, and used part of the water : *Held*, that this did not relieve the grantor, or those claiming under him by subsequent deeds, from the obligation to supply his first grantee with water so far as the maintenance of the dam was a discharge of this obligation.

Certain riparian owners filed a bill against another riparian owner to restrain him from maintaining a dam ; other persons were interested in maintaining the dam, whom the plaintiffs did not prove any title to interfere with ; and one of the plaintiffs had sold a mill-site to the defendant on verbal representations which implied that he was to have the benefit of the dam : The Court *held*, that if the plaintiffs had any claim against the defendant, the proper course was to leave them to their legal remedy against him ; and the bill was dismissed with costs.

This suit, and a cross-suit by the defendant *Forgie*, related to a dam at the head of *Coleman's* Island, on

a river called the Mississippi, which flows past the
village of Almonte, county of Lanark. In the first suit,
*Bennet Rosamund, William Rosamund,* and *George
Stephen,* were the plaintiffs, and *James Forgie* and
*John Baird* were the defendants. The plaintiffs in
that suit were the defendants in the other suit: *Baird*
was not a party to the latter suit. All these persons
had mills affected by this dam. The mills of *Forgie*
and *Baird,* respectively, were above the dam, and these
parties wanted the benefit of the dam: the mill of
*Rosamund & Co.* was below the dam, and they claimed
to be entitled to the flow of the water without any
obstruction. These differences were the matters in
issue in the two suits. There were several other persons interested in the dam being maintained, who
were not parties to either suit.

*Daniel Shipman,* the patentee of all the land in
question, conveyed 52 acres of it to one *Boyce,* in 1830.
On the 11th February, 1846, *Boyce* re-conveyed to
*Shipman* and his heirs two acres of this parcel, and
the deed contained the following provision: "The said
*J. K. Boyce* agrees to let the said *Daniel Shipman,*
his heirs and successors, have the privilege of joining
a mill-dam to the north shore on the north side, where
a dam is now erected, of such a height as will secure
to the said *Daniel Shipman,* his heirs and assigns,
sufficient water for carrying on wool-carding and cloth
manufacturing; but it is understood the said *J. K.
Boyce* reserves to himself and his heirs the privilege
of altering the shape of the aforesaid dam, provided
he does not lower the head of water thereby."

On the 11th March, 1847, *Shipman* sold and conveyed to one *Allan McDonald* an acre and a quarter
of the two-acre-parcel; and this deed contained the
following provision: "The said *Daniel Shipman*
agrees to secure to the said *Allan McDonald,* his

1871.

Rosamund
v.
Forgie.

heirs and assigns, sufficient water for carrying on wool-carding and cloth-manufacturing; and also the privilege of the water passing off into the river by the present channel below the cloth-dressing shop, by deepening the same." There was a carding-mill on this parcel at the time of the conveyance; and *McDonald*, immediately afterwards, erected a cloth factory; and he thenceforward carried on, upon the premises, a wool-carding and cloth-manufacturing business until the 1st December, 1846, when he sold the property to *Forgie*. During all this time he, with the aid of *Shipman* and others interested, kept up the dam in question; and it was by means of this dam that he obtained a supply of water for his mills. *Forgie* added machinery, &c., for the manufacture of cabinet-ware, window-sashes and blinds, &c.; and he had been in possession ever since his purchase. He claimed, by virtue of the covenant contained in *Shipman's* deed to *McDonald*, and also by virtue of long possession, to be entitled to keep up the dam.

Mr. *S. Blake* and Mr. *Bethune* for *Forgie* and *Baird*, contended, that as the evidence in the cause established an uninterrupted possession of the premises in question for a period of twenty-three years, *Forgie* was entitled to the assistance of the Court in retaining peaceable

Argument. possession of the easement enjoyed by him and those under whom he claimed during all this time : *Brown* on the Statute of Limitations R.P. 340; *Angell* on Water Courses, sec. 383 ; *Cowell* v. *Thayer* (a), *Pratt* v. *Lamson* (b), *Hulme* v. *Shreve* (c), *Jackson* v. *Harrington* (d), *Marcly* v. *Shultz* (e). The title was not interfered with until 1870, and then only a partial interruption. *Forgie* had a right to make the dam staunch which had always existed on the property. The flume now in use is shewn to be the same size as that originally

---

(a) 5 Met. 253.                    (b) 2 Allen 284.

(c) 3 Green Ch. N. S. 116.    (d) 2 Allen 242.    (e) 29 N. Y. R. 354.

constructed, the use of which had been acquiesced in during the whole time of the possession, and such acquiescence is sufficient to shew that the respective rights of the parties as to the easement had been agreed upon ; and the easement goes with the conveyance of the land : *Cruske* v. *Huffinan* (a), *Edinburgh Life Assurance Co.* v. *Barnhart* (b).

It is shewn that the defendants were all aware of the erection of the mills by the plaintiff, and their construction ; and after so long an acquiescence in the enjoyment of them, they will not be permitted to assert a right to prevent the continued enjoyment of the easement : *McKellip* v. *McIlheney* (c), *Liggins* v. *Inge* (d), *Lampman* v. *Milks* (e), *Warren* v. *Munroe* (f), *Nuttall* v. *Bracewell* (g), *Sanders* v. *Newman* (h), were referred to.

Mr. *Moss* for *Rosamund & Co. Forgie* places his right to relief on two distinct grounds ; first, title by prescription ; second, under a contract with *Shipman*, through whom he derives title from the owner. The title by prescription is not established, and as against defendants we contend that he could not acquire it. The dam in question is [not on either the lands of the plaintiff or of the defendants. Now an easement must be attached to the property of the person setting up the claim thereto ; in other words, there must be the dominant and servient tenement ; here *Forgie's* land would be the dominant, and the land affected by the dam, the servient tenement.

The deed to *Coleman* was made in 1851, at which time the prescription commences ; until that date there

1871.

Rosamund
v.
Forgie.

Argument.

---

(a) 27 U. C. Q. B. 116.
(c) 4 Watts. 317.
(e) 21 N. Y. 510.
(g) L. R. 2 Ex. 1.

(b) 17 U. C. C. P. 63.
(d) 7 Bing. 682.
(f) 15 U. C. Q. B. 557.
(h) 1 B. & Al. 258.

was a unity of possession in *Shipman :* it is impossible, therefore, by force of the existence of such title to create or establish any easement in those claiming under him, by the existence of the dam.

The cases cited by the other side to shew that *Forgie* is entitled to retain and repair the dam at the height it originally was, are all American cases ; those are opposed to the English authorities which shew that the question which governs in such a case is, what damage has been sustained, or rather what amount of water has been diverted by the party claiming the easement, not what the height of the dam has been: *Crossley* v. *Lightowler* (a).

An easement, we admit, may be used in a different way from what it originally was ; but, it must be used in such a manner as not to cause any damage other than the previous user did.

The American cases go to shew that a mill-owner may overflow adjoining lands to a reasonable extent, but this is done under the provisions of a Statute passed permitting such overflowing on making compensation for damages sustained by the owner of the land. No such rule exists either in England or in this country.

*The City of Springfield* v. *Harris* (b) fully illustrates the American doctrine as to the rights and liabilities of riparian proprietors.

*Cowell* v. *Thayer* is the governing case for the position asserted by the plaintiff, that he had a right to repair and tighten the old dam ; but unless that case is consistent with English authority, it cannot be of any assistance to this plaintiff in the claim he now sets up : what we

---

(a) L. R. 3 Eq. 296.                    (b) 4 Allen 494.

contend for is, that the old dam having been shewn to
be of a poor construction and leaky, the plaintiff had
no power, even if the right to the easement had been
acquired by prescription, to make it of a different construction and stauncher, thereby damming back a
greater amount of water than had been formerly
penned back by the owners of the mill: *Mentz* v.
*Dorney* (a).

MOWAT, V. C.—The covenant in the deed from *Ship-*   
*man* to *McDonald* does not expressly refer to the dam
in question, but, looking at the surrounding circumstances, it is plain that it was by means of this dam
that both parties contemplated that the supply of
water should be secured. It was by means of this
dam that the supply was always in fact obtained;
and it does not appear that *Shipman* had any other
way of securing it. I think that no one claiming
under *Shipman* is, as against the covenantee, his
heirs or assigns, entitled in equity to the removal
of the dam, without supplying sufficient water in
some other way.

It is proved that *Forgie* does not use more water
for all his mills than was formerly used for the wool-
carding and cloth-manufacturing mills alone, there
having been a great improvement in the machinery
employed, which enables much more to be done with
the same amount of water than formerly. The throat
through which the water passes to the mills is the
same as before the new works were added; the wheel
is also the same; and the weight of the whole evidence
is, that no more water is used than before the new factory was added.

It was suggested that, since 1847, other mills have
been built above the dam; that water kept back by

---

(a) 22 Penn. St. 519.

the dam is used for these mills; and that *Shipman*, his heirs or assigns, are not obliged to supply to *Forgie* what is withdrawn for these mills. The owners of these mills are not parties to the present suits; and whether their withdrawal of water is rightful or wrongful towards *Shipman*, his heirs or assigns, I do not see how the acts of strangers can relieve him, or those claiming under him by subsequent deeds, from the obligation which by his covenant he had assumed in favor of *McDonald* and his assigns; so far, at all events, as permission to maintain the dam would be a discharge of that obligation.

Independently of the covenant, the Statute of Limitations affords another ground for maintaining the dam. I have said that *McDonald* had the use of the water from 1846 to 1866; and *Forgie* has had possession ever since—considerably more than 20 years before either of the present suits was brought.

Judgment.

The defendant *Baird's* land consists (as I understand) of three-quarters of an acre, the residue of the two acres re-conveyed by *Boyce* to *Shipman*, and another parcel, which is part of what *Shipman* retained after conveying the 52 acres to *Boyce*. *Bennet Rosamund* subsequently became the proprietor of the land so now owned by *Baird;* and he sold and conveyed the same to *Baird* in February, 1865—consideration, $3,350. It was after this transaction, viz., on the 23rd May, 1866, that *Rosamund & Co.* became entitled to the land which they now own. It was as a mill-site, or supposed mill-site, that the land so sold to *Baird* had any value; it was this dam which, either principally or wholly, gave the land value as a mill-site; the land was commended by *Bennet Rosamund* to *Baird* in the negotiation as adapted for the purpose; there was a grist-mill on the property at the time; and *Baird* bought, as *Bennet Rosamund* well knew, with the view of repairing the grist-mill and erecting a woollen-factory, and in the faith that he was entitled to the use of the water for the purpose of these mills, by means (amongst other things) of this dam. *Baird*, after his purchase, repaired the grist-mill accordingly, and built the woollen-mill, at an expense of several thousand dollars, before *Rosamund & Co.* acquired their property. Under these circumstances, I do not think that *Bennet Rosamund* can now claim in equity an injunction against *Baird* to restrain him from having the advantage of the dam, on the faith of which he bought the property and expended his money upon it. What interest the other partners have, as between them and *Bennet Rosamund*, does not appear. *Forgie's* interest alone is sufficient for the maintenance of the dam; other persons, not parties to the suit, are also interested in its maintenance; and, if *Rosamund & Co.* have any claim against *Baird*, the proper course seems to me to be, to leave them to their legal remedy against him. These considerations dispose of the suit of *Rosamund & Co.*, which must be dismissed with costs.

In the other suit, *Forgie* is entitled to a decree for the preservation of the dam; but the condition of it twenty years before suit, being a matter in controversy, requires consideration, in order to determine the form and extent of the decree. The dam needed repairs from time to time, and was consequently in a better condition at one time than at another. The year 1857 was one of the periods at which repairs were made; and the evidence is conflicting as to whether or not the repairs then made rendered the dam materially tighter than it had been made when repaired on previous occasions. The condition in which those repairs put the dam was for ten years acquiesced in by all parties concerned. This long delay has created difficulty in ascertaining how the fact was; but, where evidence is conflicting, every presumption is to be

*1871.*

*Rosamund v. Forgie.*

Judgment.

made in favor of that evidence which has been corroborated by years of acquiescence and of dealing
with the various properties which the dam affected,
either beneficially or injuriously. I think that the
proper conclusion from the whole evidence is in favor
of the rightfulness of the repairs of 1857. (a).

The decree on *Forgie's* bill will therefore declare
him entitled to maintain the dam in the condition in
which it was after the repairs of 1857; will restrain
the defendants *Rosamund & Co.*, from interfering
with his putting the dam into that condition (it having
lately been destroyed by them), and with his keeping
it in that condition; and from destroying, removing,
or injuring the same; will direct an inquiry as to
damages; and will give to the plaintiff the costs of
the suit.

---

## FARLEY v. STARLING.

*Dower in respect of timber cut—Injunction suit, costs of.*

In case of land of which a widow is dowable, but in which her
dower has not been set out, if the timber is cut down she is
entitled to the income arising from one-third of the amount
produced.

In such a case the widow had reason to apprehend that the owner
intended to fell the whole of the wood; it was shewn that in fact he
had no such intention; but he had an opportunity of undeceiving
her, and did not avail himself of it:
*Held*, that proof that he had not the intention imputed to him did not
exempt him from liability to the costs.

On the 23rd May, 1868, the plaintiff's husband
died, seised in fee simple in possession of a lot of
land in the township of Sidney, a considerable part
of which was in wood. On the 10th December,

---

(a) Cotching v. Bassett, 32 B. 101.

1870, the defendant became the purchaser of the lot
under a decree of this Court in a partition suit. His
purchase was subject to the plaintiff's right of dower.
After his purchase he commenced cutting down wood
on the lot for the purpose of fulfilling a contract which
he had entered into for supplying wood to the Grand
Trunk Railway Company; and he had a large number of
men at work on the lot. The plaintiff was apprehensive
that he meant to cut down the whole of the wood;
and she therefore, on the 7th February, 1871, addressed
to him a letter referring to her right of dower; and to
his cutting down and removing the timber; giving him
notice that she claimed to be entitled to as much of
the wood as she would require for her firewood during
her life, and also for fencing her third of the land, and
requesting him to desist from further cutting or removing the wood or timber on the lot until her share of
the land should be set apart for her. This letter was
delivered to the defendant on the morning of the 8th
February. The defendant did not answer it or desist
from cutting; and the plaintiff, in consequence, on the
10th February, addressed to the plaintiff another letter,
stating that she wished it to be distinctly understood
that she claimed sufficient wood off the lot to fence
her portion thereof, and for firewood during her life;
requesting him to state whether he intended to set
apart for her on the lot enough wood for these purposes; and adding, that if he did so intend the matter
might be now arranged; and that if not, she would be
compelled to take steps to enforce her rights. The
defendant paid no attention to this letter; and proceeded with his work. On the 15th the plaintiff filed
her bill for an injunction, and for her dower; and
shortly afterwards an interlocutory injunction against
further cutting was granted.

Two of the plaintiff's step-sons, acting in her interest,
had conversations with the defendant about his cutting

the wood; their statements and the statement of the defendant were somewhat at variance as to what took place on these occasions; but it appeared from the defendant's own evidence that he did not then admit the plaintiff's right to any firewood.

The cause came on for the examination of witnesses and hearing at the Sittings of the Court at Belleville, in the Spring of 1871.

Mr. *L. Wallbridge*, Q.C., for the plaintiff.

Mr. *Blake*, Q.C., and Mr. *C. Bell*, for the defendant.

June 24.

Judgment.

MOWAT, V.C.—The defendant seems to have acted with considerable temper; and, though it appears now from the evidence of himself and his witnesses, that he had no intention of cutting down all the wood, and that the quantity which he had always meant to leave standing until some future season far exceeded what the plaintiff would be entitled to, yet he did not choose to say this to the plaintiff or to her sons. The excuses he has made for this in his deposition are insufficient, and indeed frivolous. I think that the circumstances amply justified the plaintiff's apprehension that he meant to denude the lot of all the wood; and justified her proceedings to restrain his doing so.

The defendant by his answer to the plaintiff's bill admitted her right to dower, and stated that since the filing of the bill he had set off a third of the land for her acceptance, and that she had refused to accept it. It turned out, however, that he had offered it in full of her claim for dower and costs; that she was willing to accept it for her dower alone; but that she insisted on receiving her costs. Unless the plaintiff is willing that she should have this parcel for her dower alone,

there will be the usual reference for assigning her
dower.

The plaintiff, by an amendment which was introduced
into her bill after answer, claimed to be entitled to the
interest on one-third of the proceeds of the timber
which the defendant had cut. At the hearing her
counsel offered to accept the parcel set out for her and
the costs of the suit, in full discharge of this claim as
well as of her dower; but the plaintiff declined the
offer.

The case of *Bishop* v. *Bishop* (a), which Mr. *Wallbridge* cited, is an express decision that " if timber be
cut down upon estates of which a widow is dowable,
before her dower is set out by metes and bounds, the
dowress is entitled during her estate to the income
arising from one-third of the fund produced by the
sale of the severed timber." This case was recognized
in the subsequent case of *Dickin* v. *Hamer* (b). The
defendant appears from the evidence to have received
over $750 for what he has cut. If the parties choose
to accept that amount as correct, the plaintiff's interest
in it will be equal to, say, $15 a year, from say 1st
March. But either party is entitled to a reference as
to the amount, at the peril of the costs of such reference.

I think that the plaintiff is entitled to the general
costs of the suit; except of the reference (if necessary)
to assign dower, as to which there will be no costs.

---

(a) 10 Law J. Chan. 302.
(b) 1 Drew. & Sm. 284. See Tooker v. Annesley, 5 Sim. 235.

1871.

Merchants'
Bank
v.
Morrison.

MERCHANTS' BANK v. MORRISON.

*Registry—Constructive notice—Priorities.*

The registration of a deed is not constructive notice of the grantor's
interest in land not comprised in it; and has not the same effect in
that respect as actual notice of the registered deed might have.

Two mortgages were successively taken and registered which, by mistake, omitted a certain parcel of ground which both were meant to
contain. The second mortgage was subsequently assigned for value,
without actual notice of the first mortgage; and the assignee afterwards acquired the legal estate from the original vendor's grantee,
who was entitled to hold it for unpaid purchase money:

*Held*, that the assignee of the second mortgage was entitled as against
the first mortgage to hold the legal estate until the second mortgage
should be paid.

Statement.

On the 25th November, 1856, the late *David Roblin*
executed a mortgage on certain land to *George Moffatt*
to secure £1968 16s. 9d.; and on the 4th July, 1857,
he executed a second mortgage on the same land to
*Joseph A. Woodruff* to secure £5000, the amount of a
loan made to the mortgagor by *Samuel Zimmerman*.
It was intended that these mortgages should embrace a parcel of land adjoining the land described
in them. Of this parcel the mortgagor had not
acquired the legal estate, but he had contracted to
purchase it, and had built his house and made
other improvements upon it. After his death, viz.,
on the 15th February, 1864, one of his sons,
*David Allen Roblin*, paid the vendor of this parcel the
balance due to him in respect of the purchase money
and got a conveyance of the land to himself. It was
not until some time after this that the holders of the
mortgages discovered that the descriptions therein did
not cover this parcel; and they thereupon filed separate bills against *David Allen Roblin* and the other
heirs of the mortgagor, for the rectification of the
mortgages. The first mortgage was then owned by the
plaintiffs, and the second mortgage by the defendant.

The defendant was not a party to the plaintiffs' suit, and the plaintiffs were not parties to the defendant's suit. The defendant was the first to obtain a decree (5th April, 1869,) and thereby the legal estate became and was vested in him. The decree was with costs, and *David Allen Roblin* received credit for the $150 which he had paid to the vendor.

1871.

Merchants'
Bank
v.
Morrison.

The present bill was for a declaration that the plaintiffs having the first mortgage on the land therein described are entitled to the first charge also on the omitted parcel; and the bill prayed consequential relief. The defendant resisted this claim; asserted by his answer that at or before the mortgage was assigned to him, or at or before he paid the valuable consideration in respect of which the assignment was made, he had no notice of the plaintiffs' claim; alleged the registration of his decree; and claimed the benefit of the Registry Acts. The bill did not allege notice to the defendant of the first mortgage at or before the time of the assignment to the defendant (1st August, 1857); the only notice which it charged was notice of the plaintiffs' present claim before the filing of the defendant's bill for the rectification of his mortgage. There was no evidence of notice, either at or before the time of the assignment of 1st August, 1857. It appeared that the mortgagor was an intimate friend of all the parties; and they seemed to have relied on his representations as to the title, without even the precaution of examining the Registry before the execution of the mortgage to *Woodruff*, or of the assignment to the defendant. The Court inferred that they were not aware of the mortgage to *Moffatt* until subsequently; as the property subject to that mortgage was not a good security for half the amount of the second mortgage.

Statement

Mr. *Moss*, for the plaintiffs.

Mr. *S. Blake* and Mr. *Bethune*, for the defendant.

Mowat V.C.—The omission to examine the Registry does not enable the defendant to cut out the plaintiffs' mortgage, so far as it affects the property described in it; for the Act 13 & 14 Victoria, ch. 63, sec. 8, made the registration notice to all persons subsequently acquiring an interest in the *same* lands. Had the defendant had actual notice of that mortgage before he acquired the second mortgage, there would be considerable reason for holding that he considered, or must be taken to have considered, that that description comprised the parcel in question, and that he considered and had notice that the plaintiffs' mortgage embraced, or was meant to embrace, that parcel. But I cannot construe the statute as giving to registration the effect of notice to that extent. The registration is notice of the party's interest in the land comprised in the registered instrument, but is not constructive notice of his interest in other land not comprised in it.

June 24

Judgment.

I must treat the defendant, therefore, as having acquired his original equity without any notice of the equity now claimed by the plaintiffs. The effect of that is, that he had an equal equity with the holders of the first mortgage; and that he was entitled to avail himself of the legal estate, if he could acquire it, as a *tabula in naufragio.* The equities being equal, and the defendant having priority at law, the settled doctrine of equity entitles the defendant to hold the legal estate, as against the plaintiffs' equity, until his debt is paid. The rule on this point has been so long established, and is so well settled, that it would be useless to cite the authorities bearing on it. The principal of them are collected in Messrs. *White & Tudor's* note to *Marsh* v. *Lee* (a). Notice before the defendant acquired the legal estate is in such a case wholly immaterial, as the same authorities shew.

It was contended, that the circumstance of the legal

(a) 1 Lead. Ca. Eq. 3rd ed. 550.

estate having been acquired by the defendant during the pendency of the plaintiffs' suit for rectification, and after they had obtained a decree for an account in a foreclosure suit against the mortgagor's heirs, prevented the defendant from availing himself of the legal estate for the purpose mentioned. But the authorities negative that view *(a)*.

It was further contended, that *David Allen Roblin* was a dry trustee for the parties, according to their priorities; and that, according to the cases, the transfer of the legal estate by such a trustee is not permitted to affect such priorities. To this it is sufficient to answer, that he was not a dry trustee; that he had a right to hold the property as a security for the $150 which he had paid to the vendor; that he was in effect first mortgagee of the parcel in question to the extent of that money; and that the case is under these circumstances not distinguishable from the cases in which the doctrine invoked by the defendant has been allowed to operate.

I think that the bill must be dismissed with costs.

*1871.*

*Merchants' Bank v. Morrison.*

Judgment.

---

(a) See Marsh v. Lee, 2 Ventris 337; Wortley v. Birkhead, 2 Ves. senr. 574; Bates v. Johnson, Johns. 304.

ELMSLEY V. MADDEN.

*Charitable bequests—Superstitious uses.*

A testator bequeathed £100 to the Society of St. Vincent de Paul, and directed the residue of his estate to be converted into cash, and paid to the House of Providence. These were voluntary unincorporated associations.

*Held,* that so far as they could be paid out of personalty these legacies were good ; and should be paid over to the persons having the management of the pecuniary affairs of the institutions named.

A bequest by a member of the Roman Catholic Church of a sum of money for the purpose of paying for masses for his soul, is not void in this Province.

The bill in this cause was originally filed by the late Hon. *J. Elmsley,* as executor of one *James Flynn,* who had left by his will a bequest of £100 to the Society of St. Vincent de Paul ; £15 to be expended in paying for masses to be said for the soul of the testator, and the residue, after certain other bequests, to be converted into cash, and paid to the House of Providence ; and the bill prayed a declaration as to the validity of these bequests.

At the original hearing of the cause, in 1865, a decree was made referring it to the Accountant to inquire (amongst other things) as to the truth of the statements in the bill respecting the House of Providence and the Society of St. Vincent de Paul.

In pursuance of this decree, a report was made, dated 18th November, 1870, whereby it was found that the House of Providence is an institution founded for educational and charitable purposes, and has several branches, one in Toronto and others in various places in Canada, and is under the superintendence of the Sisters of St. Joseph, a Society incorporated under the Statute 18 Victoria, chapter 225 ; that the Society of St. Vincent de Paul is a Society instituted by members of the Roman Catholic Church in Toronto and elsewhere, for the following objects: to encourage its members, by example and counsel, in the practice of a Christian life; to visit the poor, and afford them religious consolation; to give elementary instruction to poor children; and to undertake any other charitable work to which the resources of the Society are adequate.

The cause having been brought on for further directions upon this report,

Mr. *McLennan*, for the heir-at-law of *Flynn*, who claimed against the will, contended that the bequest of £15 for masses was void under the Statute; that the House of Providence and Society of St. Vincent de Paul were not definite legal persons, and the bequests to them were void for this reason: *Shelford* on Mortmain, p. 664; *Jarman* on Wills, 189; *Ommaney* v. *Butcher* (a), *Morrice* v. *Durham* (b), *Nash* v. *Morley* (c), *Attorney General* v. *Powell* (d), *Clark* v. *Taylor* (e), *Cary* v. *Abbott* (f). He also contended that such bequests could be held valid, at any rate, only in regard to the personalty: Doe *Anderson* v. *Todd* (g).

Mr. *J. C. Hamilton*, for the other defendants, contended that it was shewn by the report of the Master that the House of Providence and Society of St. Vincent de Paul, represented by his clients, were charitable institutions within the legal definition of that term, and that the bequests to them were valid. As to the bequest for masses, the English authorities are not in point, the Imperial Act against superstitious bequests not being applicable to the circumstances of this Province, or introduced by our constitutional acts,

(a) 1 T. & R. 260.
(b) 10 Vesey, 522.
(c) 5 Beav. 77.
(d) 1 B. & B. 145.
(e) 1 Drewry, 642.
(f) 7 Ves. 490.
(g) 2 U. C. Q. B. 82.

1871.

Elmsley
v.
Madden.

or the Treaty of Paris: citing (amongst other autho_
rities), *West* v. *Shuttleworth* (a), *Heath* v. *Chapman* (b),
*Wilcox* v. *Wilcox* (c), *Stuart* v. *Bowman* (d), *Whicker*
v. *Hume* (e), *Campbell* v. *Radnor* (f), *Mayor of Lyons*
v. *East India Co.* (g), *Attorney General* v. *Stewart* (h),
*Tudor's* Leading Cases on Real Property, page 480;
Consol. Stats. Canada, ch. 17, sec. 7.

Mr. *Donovan*, for the plaintiff, also contended for
the validity of the bequests, stating a large sum had
been already paid over on account thereof.

June 28.

Judgment.

STRONG, V. C.—The questions for decision in this
case which came before me on further directions, were;
as to the validity of certain bequests contained in the
will of *James Flynn*, the testator mentioned in the
pleadings. One of these bequests was a direction to
the executor to appropriate £15 for masses to be
offered for the happy repose of the testator's soul, to
be apportioned in a particular manner between clergymen named in the will and the officiating clergymen
of the City of Toronto; another disputed legacy was
the gift of £100 to the Society of St. Vincent de Paul;
another was the gift of the residue to the House of
Providence.

It was alleged in the bill that the Society of St.
Vincent de Paul and the House of Providence were
both charitable institutions. By the decree it was,
amongst other things, referred to the Master to inquire
as to the character of these two institutions, and the
Master, by his report, has found that they are institutions established for the purposes set forth in the

---

(a) 2 My. & K. 684.          (b) 2 Drew. 417.
(c) 2 L. C. Jur., 1, and Appendix.    (d) 2 L. C. L. R. 369.
(e) 14 Beav. 509; 1 DeG. M. & G. 506; 7 H. & Ca. 126.
(f) 1 Br. C. C. 271.          (g) 1 Moore, P. C. C. 293.
(h) 2 Mer. 143.

report, and which clearly shew them both to be charities, either within the Statute of 43 Elizabeth, chapter
4, or by analogy to that Statute (a).

The objection to the first legacy (for masses) was
that it was void as a bequest for superstitious uses.

I am very clearly of opinion that this is not so, but
that, on the contrary, the gift in question is free from
any taint of illegality.

The definition of a gift to superstitious uses is given
in *Boyle* on Charities, at page 242, as follows: " One
which has for its object the propagation of a religion
not tolerated by the law." This description is manifestly inapplicable to the legacy in question. By our
law, all bodies of Christians enjoy equal toleration,
unless, indeed, the privileges guaranteed to the Roman
Catholic Church by the capitulation of Quebec and
Montreal, and the Treaty of Paris, 1763, and the
Quebec Act, 14 George III., chapter 83, which directs
that in Canada the free exercise of the Roman Catholic
religion shall be enjoyed, give that Church peculiar
rights and privileges. This question was much discussed
in the argument before me, but I do not feel called upon
to determine it, as, for the first reason I have given, it
is clear that there is nothing in our law which prevented the testator from appropriating this sum of
money to a purpose which his religion had taught him
was one of importance to his spiritual welfare. I may
say, however, that a reference to *Forsyth's* Constitutional Law shews that there is weight in Mr. *Hamilton's*
argument as to the effect of the treaties and Statute
above referred to.

---

(a) See cases collected in Tudor's Leading Cases on Real Property;
Notes to Corbyn v. French, Walsh v. Gladstone, 1 Ph. 290; Attorney
General v. Gladstone, 13 Sim. 7.

Then I am of opinion that the legacies to the two societies of St. Vincent de Paul and the House of Providence are perfectly good. Any objections to them on the score of illegality is answered by the observations I have already made, and by the cases of *Walsh* v. *Gladstone* and *Attorney General* v. *Gladstone*, before cited.

It is contended, however, that these gifts are void because neither of these societies are corporations. But this objection is clearly not sustainable in the face of the numerous authorities, which shew that gifts to voluntary charitable associations are certainly recognized and carried out. *Tudor's* Charitable Trusts, page 19; *Wellbeloved* v. *Jones* (a), and *Attorney General* v. *Gladstone*, and *Walsh* v. *Gladstone*, cited above, are examples selected from a great number of cases. All these legacies, so far as they can be given out of personalty, must therefore be good. In the case of the Society of St Vincent de Paul, the amount of the bequest must be divided equally among the four Presidents mentioned in the will. In respect of this society it is clear that no scheme is requisite, and that the Attorney General need not be a party, as the legacy is to form a part of the general funds of the society (b). In the case of the House of Providence I have more doubt as to dispensing with a scheme, but as it appears to me, from what the Master finds to be the object of this institution, that the application of this legacy to the general purposes of the charity will in effect carry out the testator's intentions, I direct that the amount of the residue, consisting of personalty, be paid over to the head of the Sisters of St. Joseph, who I understand are intrusted with the management of the pecuniary affairs of the House of Providence.

All parties must have their costs out of the estate.

Judgment.

---

(a) 1 S. & S. 40.      (b) Wellbeloved v. Jones.

1871

# THE BANK OF TORONTO V. FANNING [IN APPEAL.*]

### Tax titles.

*Held*, per RICHARDS, C. J., WILSON, J., MOWAT, V. C., GALT, J., and
STRONG, V. C., that the Statute 27 Victoria, chapter 19, section 4,
cures all errors as regards the purchaser at a tax sale, if any taxes
in respect of the land sold had been in arrear for five years; this
rule applies where an occupied lot has been assessed as unoccupied:
[DRAPER, C. J., doubting: HAGARTY, C. J., and GWYNNE, J., expressing no opinion.]

In a suit to impeach a sale of land for taxes, it appeared that about
20 or 30 acres of the lot were cleared and fenced, and a barn was
erected thereon, into which hay made on these twenty acres was
stored in winter, by the person occupying the adjoining lot under
the authority of the proprietor; no one resided on the twenty
acres; the owner was resident out of the country and had not
given notice to the assessor of the township to have his name
inserted on the roll of the township:

*Semble*, that the lot should have been assessed as occupied.
[DRAPER, C. J., HAGARTY, C. J., and GWYNNE, J., dissenting, who
were of opinion that the lot was properly assessed as non-resident.]

An appeal by the plaintiffs from the decree reported *Statement.*
*ante* volume xvii., page 514; for the following, amongst
other reasons, viz.: that the land in question was
assessed as non-resident for the period in respect of the
non-payment of taxes, whereon the same was sold,
whereas, in fact, the land was for such period occupied,
within the meaning of the Statutes in question; that
the warrant in question, and the advertisement issued
by the Sheriff in pursuance thereof, did not contain
any statement shewing whether or not the land was
patented or unpatented or leased; that during the
period the land was assessed for the taxes in question,
there were goods and chattels thereon from which the
taxes could and should have been levied; and that the
defendants had not proved such a compliance with the
requirements of the Statutes as was necessary in order

---

\* *Present.*—DRAPER, C. J.; RICHARDS, C. J.; HAGARTY, C. J.;
WILSON, J.; MOWAT, V. C.; GWYNNE, J.; GALT, J., and STRONG, V.C.

to support the tax sale, and the conveyance in question issued in pursuance thereof.

The defendants, in support of the decree, assigned the following, amongst other grounds, viz.: that the land in question was properly assessed as non-resident for the period in respect of the non-payment of taxes whereon the same was sold, and was not for such period occupied within the meaning of the Statutes in question; that even if the land was occupied for such period within the meaning of the Statutes in question, and was incorrectly assessed as non-resident instead of as resident, the said alleged erroneous assessment was a proper matter of appeal to the Court of Revision of the municipality in which the land is situate; that no appeal was made to said Court of Revision from any of the assessments in question, and the assessment rolls of the municipality for the said period were all passed by the Court of Revision of the said municipality, and therefore the assessment of said land as non-resident was valid and binding on the appellants and all other parties concerned; that the evidence taken in the case fully proved that the Treasurer's warrant, Sheriff's advertisement, and the sale of the land for taxes, and the conveyance thereof to *Richard Clark*, complied with the statutes in question, and were in all respects regular and correct; that the respondent *Joseph Fanning* was a *bona fide* purchaser for value from the said *Richard Clark*, with a registered title without notice of the alleged erroneous assessment, and of the other defects and irregularities complained of by the appellants; and that the appellants were not entitled to relief in equity by reason of their laches and acquiescence.

Mr. *J. Hillyard Cameron*, Q. C., and Mr. *Snelling*, for the appeal. The question upon which this appeal must ultimately turn, is whether or not the occupation shewn was such as to have prevented the assessor inserting on his roll the land as being unoccupied, in the years 1857, 1860, 1861, 1863, and 1864, and it was

1871.

Bank of
Toronto
v.
Fanning.

for the taxes due in those years that the land was sold. In 1858 the lot was omitted from the non-resident list, and for 1858, the assessor in his evidence swears, that the taxes were paid, although he cannot state by whom. This was sufficient to have induced some greater effort on the part of the assessor, to find out who was the owner, than a mere formal visit to the lot at a season of the year when, unless a dwelling house had been on the lot and occupied, it was most improbable that any one would be in visible occupation of the land. "Residence" and "occupancy" are not the same thing. An owner may be, as in this case we contend he was, in occupation of the lot, although actually resident on an adjoining one.

The Statutes under which the municipal officers professed to act in carrying out this sale are Consol. Stat. U. C. ch. 55, secs. 21, 22, 23, and 24, and chapter 19 of the Acts of 1863, secs. 2 and 5.

Here the evidence shews clearly that the assessor did not properly discharge his duties, as it is evident from the facts appearing in the case, that it required but very little trouble or labour on his part to find out who was the owner of the land. The appellants clearly should not be made to suffer for the assessor's neglect of duty.

Argument,

They referred to *Wilson* v. *Watterson* (a), *Milliken* v. *Benedict* (b), *Green* v. *Watson* (c), *Arthurs* v. *Smathurs* (d), *Jones* v. *The Mersea Docks* (e), *Rex* v. *The Chelsea Water Works* (f), *Blackwell* on Tax Titles, pp. 137, 138, 162; *Burns's* Justice, 30th ed., vol. iv., p. 844 to 865.

Mr. *Moss* and Mr. *Duncan Morrison*, contra. Submitted that the conclusion at which his lordship the Chancellor had arrived, would be sustained by this Court. The assessor here had done all that it was incumbent on him to do for the purpose of ascertaining who was the party properly assessable with the taxes

---

(a) 4 Barr. 214.          (b) 8 Barr. 169.
(c) 34 Casey, 332.        (d) 21 Wright, 40.
(e) 11 H. L. 443.         (f) 5 B. & Ad. 156.

for the land; the law requiring the officer merely to go to the land to be assessed and there find out to whom the property should be assessed. It is shewn that no one resided on the land from the expiration of 1856 or beginning of 1857, when *Lane*, a tenant under the then owner, gave up possession; from thence forward until after the sale which is now impeached, the only occupation which is attempted to be shewn was that some person was in the habit each year of cutting the grass which grew upon the land and making it into hay, which hay it is asserted was stowed away in the barn standing on the premises; but even this slight evidence of ownership had disappeared when the assessor made his annual visit for the purposes of assessment. Section 19, of chapter 55 (C. S.), does not apply to cases like the present—it has no reference to non-resident lands; and section 58, of that Act, shews that the assessor's roll not having been appealed against to the Court of Revision, became binding and conclusive on all parties.

Amongst other authorities, *Hamilton* v. *McDonald* (a), *McDonald* v. *McDonald* (b), *Rex* v. *Welbank* (c), *McCarrall* v. *Watkins* (d), *Scragg* v. *The Corporation of London* (e), were referred to.

Mr. *Cameron*, in reply, referred to *Hall* v. *Hill* (f) *Yokham* v. *Hall* (g).

Judgment.    DRAPER, C. J.—The question is reduced to occupation in 1857, and the evidence of *James Allen*, junior, alone gives any support to the appellants' contention that the lot (No. 76) was occupied during that time. He swears that one *Lane* rented it by a lease dated 5th March, 1856, for two years from 1st April, 1856, and remained in possession, but living on No. 77

---

(a) 22 U. C. Q. B. 136.     (b) 24 U. C. Q. B. 74.
(c) 4 M. & C. 222.     (d) 19 U. C. Q B. 248.
(e) 26 U. C. Q. B. 263, S. C. in Appeal, 28 U. C. Q. B. 457.
(f) 2 U. C. E. & A. 569.     (g) 15 Gr. 335.

nearly a year; leaving in 1856 or 1857. That *John* 1871.
*Allen* went upon the property. "He occupied for the
remainder of *James's* time. *John Allen* never moved
upon the premises; he lived upon the lot opposite, and
cropped the lot" (No. 76).

Bank of
Toronto
v.
Fanning.

There was a barn, but no house on this lot. On No.
77 there was a house and no barn. *Lane* lived in this
house, and no person lived in it after *Lane* left.

The idea entertained of occupation is explained by
the evidence of *Robert Spier*, who first says, "the lot
was always occupied from 1855 or 1856 till old Mr.
*Allen* left it * * I mean by occupation that parties
cut hay in summer." As much might be said of many
marshes, on which hay is made.

Looking at the whole evidence, it is tolerably clear
that as "the assessor generally goes round in winter
time," there was no visible occupation whatever. If
cropped, otherwise than by the crop of hay, in 1857,
it is no otherwise proved than in the evidence of *James
Allen*, junior, who swears he rented to his father for
1858 and 1859. *Murray*, the assessor, swears that in
1857 he found the lot "not occupied," and that in 1855
old Mr. *Allen* told him "to put his son's name down as
owner of the lot."

Judgment.

I adopt the conclusion of the learned Chancellor upon
this unsatisfactory evidence, and think the appeal should
be dismissed with costs.

I incline strongly to concur with the majority on the
question on the Assessment Acts.

RICHARDS, C. J.—I have had the opportunity of
perusing the judgment prepared by my brother *Wilson*,
and concur in the reasons therein stated for dismissing
this appeal.

HAGARTY, C. J.—I think the appeal should be dismissed. I see no reason to question the correctness of
the learned Chancellor's finding on the facts " that there
was no such occupancy of the premises during any of

1871.

Bank of
Toronto
v.
Fanning.

the years that the land was returned as non-resident,"
and that there was a legal assessment.

On this ground therefore I concur in dismissing the appeal.

WILSON, J.—The land was sold for taxes alleged to have been due and in arrear for the years 1857, 1860, 1861, 1863, and 1864.

The sale was on the 1st of November, 1865, under a warrant the precise date of which is not given, but which it must be presumed was issued more than three months before the sale according to the Consolidated Statute of Upper Canada, chapter 55, section 130, under which Statute the sale was made; the warrant would therefore bear date sometime before the 1st of August, 1865.

Leaving the year 1857 out of consideration for the present, there would not have been a portion of taxes due for five years (*a*) (s. 123) at the time when the warrant was delivered to the sheriff.

Judgment

The 29 and 30 Victoria, chapter 53, section 156, or the 32 Victoria, chapter 36, section 155, does not apply as the bill was filed on the 22nd of September, 1868, before the period of limitation therein mentioned had expired.

The sale then, in my opinion, cannot be supported unless the taxes for the year 1857 can be considered as taxes due and in arrear at the time of the sale.

The taxes for that year were not paid, and they were rated in fact upon the land, but upon the land as vacant or non-resident, instead of as occupied and resident land as it is contended should have been done.

The 27 Victoria, chapter 19, section 4, provides that if any taxes in respect to any lands sold by the sheriff after the passing of that Act shall have been in arrear for five years preceding the first day of January in the year in which the sheriff shall sell the said land, and

---

(*a*) Ford v. Proudfoot, 9 Grant, 478; Kelly v. Macklem, 14 Grant, 29; Bell v. McLean, 18 U. C. C. P. 416, 27 Vic., ch. 19, ss. 1, 4.

the same shall not be redeemed in one year after the said sale, such sale and the sheriff's deed to the purchaser of any such lands, provided the sales shall be openly and fairly conducted, shall be final and binding upon the former owners of the said lands, and upon all persons claiming by, through, or under them. The object of the statute was to make the sale valid, although the assessment may not have been quite regularly made, or although there were some other informality or irregularity in the way of the sale being such as would otherwise be a perfectly legal sale, so long as any taxes were in arrear for five years and the land had not been redeemed. The re-enactment of this clause by the 29 and 30 Victoria, chapter 53, section 131, and by the 32 Victoria, chapter 36, section 130, with the addition to it, "it being intended by this Act that all owners of land shall be required to pay the arrears of taxes due thereon within the period of five years, (three years by the last Act), or redeem the same within one year after the treasurer's sale thereof," is very conclusive on this point.

In my opinion the irregular or wrongful assessment of this lot in 1857 as an unoccupied or non-resident lot, instead of its having been rated as an occupied or resident lot, cannot now be impeached.

There was in fact a portion of taxes due upon the lot for five years, and as the sale was made after the passing of the 27 Victoria, chapter 19, that Statute has given validity to the title, which in my opinion might otherwise have been invalid. It is not necessary to say what would, or will, or may constitute an occupant or an occupation, as I am assuming for the purposes of my opinion that the land was occupied in 1857, and was improperly assessed as an unoccupied lot.

If I had been obliged to do so, it is probable, my opinion would have been upon this evidence that the land was not vacant or unoccupied property.

MOWAT, V. C.—During the years that the lot in question was returned as unoccupied, twenty or thirty

*1871.*

*Bank of Toronto v. Fanning.*

*Judgment.*

acres of it were cleared land, and this clearing was
fenced; there was on the place a barn which, though
out of repair, was capable of being used as a barn, and
was from year to year used for storing the hay cut on
this lot, and on the adjoining lot, by the person who was
owner or tenant of the latter, and who cut the hay and
used the barn on the lot in question under the authority
of its proprietor. I feel great difficulty in saying that
this use of the lot did not constitute a sufficient occupation of the lot to make it improper and illegal for the
assessor to return the lot as unoccupied; even though,
when the assessor visited the lot in February or March,
there may have been no hay in the barn. There are
thousands of parcels throughout the country which
belong to persons actually residing on adjoining parcels,
and which it would surely be against the intention of the
law for the assessor indolently to return as unoccupied,
though the visible occupation of them in February or
March is not greater than that of this parcel was. The

analogous cases which were cited to us from the American and English reports, as well as the reason of the
thing, seem to me to support the contention of the
appellants on this point. Land which is in use during
the season seems to me to be occupied within the meaning of the Act, though in winter there is no produce in
the barn, and no person to be seen in the fields. The
19th section of the Assessment Act (*a*) required the
assessors to make "diligent inquiry;" and an inquiry
which does not extend to the occupiers of the adjoining
lots is certainly the reverse of diligent.

But I think that the Act 27 Victoria, chapter 19, section 4, cures the error as regards the purchaser at the
tax sale; that Act confirms the sale if any taxes in
respect of the land sold had been "in arrear" for five
years. Now this land was liable to taxes whether
the proceedings of the assessor had been correct or not;

---

(*a*) Consol. U. C. ch. 55.

for by the 116th section of the Consolidated Act, **1871.**
even the omission of the lot from his roll would not
exempt the land from taxation. That section provides **Bank of**
that, in case of such omission the clerk is in the follow- **Toronto**
ing year to enter the lot on the collector's roll, " as well **v.**
for the arrears omitted as for the tax of that year." **Fanning.**
Therefore the taxes may be in "arrear," according to the
legislative use of the term, though the lot had been wholly
omitted by the assessor ; and if so, they are certainly not
less in "arrear" where the lot has been assessed and
entered on the assessment roll, though under an irregular designation. I am of opinion that on this ground
the decree should be affirmed and the appeal dismissed.

GWYNNE, J.—I do not feel sufficiently clear upon the
point urged, that the conclusion in fact of His Lordship
The Chancellor was wrong, to justify me in arriving
at an opposite conclusion ; and assuming him to be right
upon the fact I agree with his application of the law. I
concur therefore that the appeal should be dismissed. **Judgment.**

GALT, J., and STRONG, V. C., concurred in the views
expressed by *Wilson*, J., and *Mowat*, V.C.

*Per Curiam.*—Appeal dismissed with costs.

---

## LEWIS V. ROBSON [IN APPEAL.*]

*Parol agreement—Contemporaneous covenant.*

An alleged parol agreement said to have been entered into contemporaneously with a covenant under seal, was not permitted to control
the covenant, the parol agreement having been proved by one witness only, whose intention to speak the truth was admitted on all
hands, but the accuracy of whose recollection was not confirmed by
other evidence.

This suit was instituted by *Lewis*, *McPhail*, and
*Foster*, as assignees of certain lands for the benefit of
the creditors of *White*, who was also a plaintiff.

---

* *Present.*—DRAPER, C. J, RICHARDS, C. J., VANKOUGHNET, C.,*
HAGARTY, C. J., SPRAGGE, V. C.,† MORRISON, WILSON, GWYNNE, and
GALT, JJ.

* Died before judgment pronounced.   † Appointed Chancellor before judgment.

It appeared that *White* was (among other debts) indebted to the firm of *Ross, Mitchell & Co.*, who, being insolvents, were declared bankrupts in Scotland, and *Robson*, one of the defendants in this suit, was appointed a trustee for winding up their affairs.

*White's* creditors compounded with him for ten shillings in the pound; and his assignees proposed to convey to *Robson* certain lands to liquidate the debt due to *Ross, Mitchell & Co.* Difficulties were suggested, and according to the plaintiff's statement it was agreed that the assignees should convey to *Robson* by way of mortgage, and if default were made in payment, that *Robson* should foreclose or exercise a power of sale, to be inserted in the mortgage, and that the lands should be taken in full satisfaction of the debts mentioned therein.

A mortgage was thereupon prepared, containing no covenant for payment by the assignees, but *Robson's* solicitor objected, and the assignees relying, as they asserted, on *Robson's* good faith, and being assured that the land would be taken for the debt, executed a mortgage in which they covenanted for payment. They further asserted that *Robson* entered and continued in possession of the property and receipt of the rents and profits.

*Robson* sold the mortgage to the defendant *Rankin*, who asserted that he was an innocent purchaser without notice. The plaintiffs on the contrary asserted that he had notice before the transaction was completed; and *Robson* commenced an action at law against the assignees on their covenant.

The assignees asserted that in settling *White's* affairs they had been in the habit of conveying portions of *White's* lands in payment; that *Robson* knew this, and agreed to accept the lands mentioned in the mortgage in payment, but he represented that in consequence of want of power in himself to accept land as absolute payment or want of power in the assignees to make an absolute conveyance that it was necessary it should be done in the form of a mortgage, but with the distinct understanding that the land was, upon default made, to be taken in full payment.

The plaintiffs prayed an injunction to restrain the suit at law, and the disposing of, or assigning the mortgage, and a declaration that *Robson* took the mortgage in full payment of the debts therein mentioned as due to *Ross, Mitchell & Co.*, and by reason of his accepting the same, the debts had been fully discharged, and that the mortgage might be reformed accordingly, and if assigned to *Rankin*, that it might be declared that he took it with notice.

*Robson's* answer as to the arrangement with the assignees was given on the information of *Fisken*. He asserted that he had ample power under the Bankruptcy Act of Scotland, and he denied that he ever proposed the lands in question should be taken in full payment of the debts due by *White*.

He admitted entering into possession, but said it was in consequence of an agreement indorsed on the mortgage by the solicitor of the assignees.

*Rankin's* answer set forth that the sale of the mortgage to him was *bonâ fide* and for valuable consideration, and he explained that he did not become the purchaser of it until after the commencement of this suit.

Only two witnesses were examined, viz., Mr. *Barrett* (the solicitor for the assignees), and Mr. *Fisken*, who had been one of the firm of *Ross, Mitchell & Co.*

Mr. *Barrett* said his instructions were to prepare a mortgage without a covenant for payment by the assignees.  He did so, and took it to Mr. *Freeland,* who was

solicitor for *Ross, Mitchell & Co.  Freeland* insisted on a covenant by the assignees to pay, stating at the same time that "*it need never be acted on.*"  The witness understood that a mortgage and not an absolute deed was to be given in consequence of some difficulty either by *Robson* as to his power or right to take an absolute deed, or as to the power of *White's* assignees to give one.  He said it was clearly understood with *Freeland* that if a covenant for payment by *White's* assignees was inserted it would never be acted on, and that the land would be taken in full discharge of the debt, but by means of the mortgage ; that the clear understanding was that the assignees were not to be called on to pay.  That he wrote a memorandum which was signed by *Ross Mitchell & Co.,* as follows : " Instead of taking an absolute deed of such lots as under the *above arrangement* would come to us and thereon discharging our

judgment, we are willing to take a mortgage on such lots for the amount of our debt as above mentioned, and give five years for the payment of it, without interest. Upon getting such a mortgage, with clear title, free of all incumbrances, we will discharge our judgment and rely solely upon the said mortgage.—Toronto, 9th August, 1860."  Mr. *Barrett* would not say that *Ross, Mitchell & Co.* were, on taking the mortgage, to abandon all claim on *White* personally : that *White* was to be discharged nor whether the mortgage originally prepared by himself contained a covenant to be entered into by *White.*  He (the witness) had stated in an affidavit made in the cause, that the mortgagee was to exercise the power of sale contained in the mortgage, but in this he was mistaken, as the mortgage contained no such power.  He explained that they were to exercise the powers contained in the mortgage for realizing out of the property, and he supposed there was a power of sale.  He said he told the defendant *Foster,* that *Freeland* insisted on a covenant by the assignees, and proposed that they should covenant as assignees, and he told his clients that they would not be called upon to pay—*but if they had to pay as assignees they had property of White's estate out of which to pay themselves.* Mr. *Barrett* indorsed a memorandum on this mortgage, which he says contained, as far as he knew, the agreement of the parties, and was written upon the assumption that the mortgage was to be treated as an absolute conveyance to the assignees. " It is agreed that the mortgagee shall take immediate possession of the within mortgaged premises, and credit the amount of rents to be received for the same, less the amount which shall be paid for repairs, taxes and insurance on the within mortgage.—Toronto, 14th March, 1862." This was unsigned.

Mr. *Fisken* was the only other witness. He stated that he made the original agreement for the settlement with *White*, according to which, White alone was to give the usual mortgage covenant. He wrote in the name of the firm a letter to *Freeland*, dated 5th April, 1861, enclosing the mortgage put in evidence. In this letter he writes, " *White* only to be bound for the money—property to be insured—surplus rents over payment of taxes, premiums of insurance, and necessary repairs of buildings, to be paid on account of the mortgage. We suppose *White's* letter as to this last will be sufficient if the deed is otherwise in accordance with such arrangement. Mr. *Oswald* will call on you to-morrow with a copy of abstract of title, and give you memorial for registration." Mr. *Fisken* stated that he never altered the instructions, and so far as the assignees were concerned " *they had agreed to look only to the land*;" that he agreed to take *White's* covenant to pay if the assignees would convey ; that after great delay *Freeland* said that he could not get the original agreement carried out, and that *Fisken* had better take the present mortgage as it was the only one he could

1871.

Lewis
v.
Robson.

Statement.

get from *Barrett*, and it was something better than was originally agreed on: that *Freeland* said it was the only one *Barrett* would give.

Mr. *Strong*, Q. C., for the plaintiffs.

Mr. *Blake*, Q. C., for defendants.

VanKoughnet, C.—I cannot distinguish this case from *Major* v. *Major* (a). I confess that case puzzles me. It is at variance with all my notions of law, and yet I do not feel at liberty to act in opposition to its authority. I think it decides that a parol or oral contemporaneous agreement may utterly nullify a written obligation under seal. Here the covenant of the plaintiffs was to pay a certain sum of money at a certain time, accompanied by an express oral agreement, or undertaking, that this covenant was never to be enforced.

Judgment. Although Mr. *Barrett's* memory was not perfect as to some of the circumstances that occurred on the negotiation between the parties and as to the terms of the mortgage itself, yet he is positive that there was an undertaking that the covenant in question was not to be used, and to this I must give credit. Such a covenant was not originally required from the assignees. The plaintiffs, who were merely the trustees of the debtor *White,* who alone was to covenant for payment of the debt— merely giving the land in security. For some reason, not very plain in the evidence, this course was found objectionable. The desire seems to have been that the mortgage should be in the usual form, with the usual covenant for payment, but on the understanding that that covenant was not to be enforced in *personam*. *White* gave a covenant to carry out or perform the covenants of the mortgagor, and the mortgagee or his assignee may have some remedy on this. Doubting the

(a) 1 Drewry, 165.

authority of *Major* v. *Major*, I yet act upon it by
granting an injunction with costs, restraining the defendants *Robson* and *Rankin* from proceeding with the
action at law, and from taking any proceeding to enforce
the covenant against the plaintiffs, other than *White*.

1871.

Lewis
v.
Robson.

From the decree drawn up in pursuance of this judgment the defendants appealed, on the grounds that there
was no proof, or at any rate no sufficient proof, of the
alleged facts upon which the said decree was based; that
the covenant in the mortgage in question cannot be
controlled on parol evidence of the said alleged facts,
and there is no jurisdiction to make the decree; and
that if any relief is to be given to the plaintiffs, the
plaintiff *White* should by the decree be made liable in
the premises.

Mr. *Blake*, Q.C., for the appellants.

Judgment.

Mr. *Strong*, Q.C.,* contra.

DRAPER, C. J.—There is nothing to lead to the conclusion that the mortgage first spoken of by Mr. *Barrett*
was ever executed—and I presume that is the mortgage
referred to in the letter to Mr. *Freeland*, of 5th April,
1861. The mortgage put in evidence was executed
after the communications between Mr. *Barrett* and Mr.
*Freeland*—and as Mr. *Fisken* says, after great delay—
very probably about the date of Mr. *Barrett's* indorsement upon it (14th March, 1862), though it bears date
on the 25th January, 1861—which was the date of the
mortgage inclosed with the letter of 5th April, 1861.

Mr. *Barrett's* memory as to these instruments is not
accurate, for he supposed that the deed that was executed
contained a power of sale—which, however, it does not;

* Was appointed Vice Chancellor before judgment was delivered.

and though . he is certain that the mortgage first prepared by him contained no covenant by the assignee for payment, he cannot say whether there was in it a covenant on *White's* part, nor whether his instructions would have warranted the introduction of such a covenant. The only objection, so far as appears, made by *Freeland* to this mortgage was the absence of a covenant to pay on the part of the assignees. This led to the discussion, but it never was a point of difference whether the conveyance was to be by way of mortgage, nor, whatever the undertaking of the assignees should be, that a right to redeem was to be reserved for the benefit of *White*; and it is clear from Mr. *Barrett's* testimony that there was neither fraud nor mistake in introducing the covenant to pay by the assignee. His statement affirms that the covenant was to be entered into, in form, but subject to an understanding and agreement that it would not be acted on ; and he adds that the land would be taken in full discharge of the debt.

No one has questioned the perfect good faith with which Mr. *Barrett's* statements are made. The inaccuracy of his memory upon a different but not unimportant matter in the transaction ; the total absence of any written memorandum of this parol agreement ; and the account given by Mr. *Barrett* himself, of his conversation with Mr. *Fisken* before the mortgage was assigned to *Rankin*, taken together, make it, in my opinion at least, extremely difficult to say that this agreement is satisfactorily proved. Mr. *Barrett* stated that he spoke to Mr. *Fisken* on the subject of the covenant by the assignees, and was told by Mr. *Fisken* that "he would hold them by it, although the *original* understanding was, that they were not to covenant ; but he said they had given something more than they originally undertook." The natural reply to this surely would have been to the effect if not in the words of Mr.

*Barrett's* evidence "it was clearly understood that if a covenant to pay by the assignees was inserted in the mortgage it would never be acted on," coupled with a reference to the doubts expressed as to sufficient authority to give or to accept a simple absolute conveyance. But Mr. *Barrett* does not say that he gave any such explanation to Mr. *Fisken,* though he states that he called upon *Rankin's* solicitor, and gave him notice of the agreement that the assignees were not to be called upon to pay the mortgage money—and that the solicitor told him the transfer of the mortgage was not then completed—but the time when this notice was given is not fixed, it may have been as stated in *Rankin's* answer after the commencement of this suit.

Let it for the moment be conceded that a parol contemporaneous agreement will nullify a sealed contract; it appears to me that such an agreement, when not followed by some subsequent act or declaration of the party to be bound by it, or in some other independent mode corroborated, should be proved by very clear and satisfactory evidence. If it is all rested upon the testimony of one witness, his evidence should be free from objection, not simply on the ground of personal reputation (which in the present case is fully admitted), but on the score of accurate recollection of, at least, all the important features and details of the transaction, and if not supported by any extraneous evidence, it should not be contradicted by any material part of the writing to be qualified or varied by such parol agreement.

Now, in the present case the question naturally suggests itself, why was not the land conveyed at once in satisfaction of *White's* debt? Mr. *Barrett's* statement as to this is: "I understood that a mortgage instead of an absolute deed was to be given to *Robson,* in consequence of some difficulty either by *Robson* as to his power or right to take an absolute deed, or of the assignees of *White* to give one." Neither of these suggested difficulties are proved to have any existence. *Robson's* authority to accept a deed seems unquestionable, and no reason is suggested why *White's* assignees could give a mortgage in fee, especially if it was to contain a power of sale, and yet could not make a direct sale and conveyance, or why a pretended mortgage should be better than a direct conveyance. I am more inclined to think that under an expectation that by covenanting "as assignees" would charge them only in respect of the assets of *White's* estate, the assignees were willing to covenant in that form, and if that be so, we have a very simple explanation of such a covenant being entered into by them. The original agreement as far as we are made acquainted with its contents, as well as the letter to *Freeland*, of April, 1861, contemplates a mortgage with an undertaking by *White* to pay, and the deed executed is a mortgage, with a covenant by *White*, not indeed in the usual form for payment, but, conditional on the assignees ceasing to represent his estate, that he will fulfil all the covenants in the deed. All this is consistent with there being some liability on the part of the covenantors to make payment, but utterly at variance with any agreement that the covenant should never be acted upon. If this was Mr. *Barrett's* agreement on their behalf, I cannot understand, unless for the purpose of misleading, why *White* should have told them, "if they had to pay as assignees they had property of *White's* estate, out of which to pay themselves."

Upon the respondent's contention, *Robson* has no remedy upon the covenant of the assignees; nor does it appear that he is in a situation to derive any benefit from the covenant by *White*; nor can *Robson*, or *Rankin* as his assignee, get a complete title to the land without obtaining either a release of the equity of redemption, or a decree for foreclosure. The bill is not framed upon the hypothesis that the assignees were to covenant to pay out of the proceeds of *White's* estate, but on the assertion that a covenant entered into by them was not to be enforced; that they were only to convey the legal estate vested in them, and that the land conveyed was to be taken in satisfaction of *White's* debt, though *White* might redeem at any time before the 1st October, 1865. Taking all the evidence into consideration, it appears to me insufficient to support the plaintiffs' case.

The decree was grounded on the authority of *Major* v. *Major* (a), not as a decision which the learned Chancellor approved, but one by which he considered himself bound, and without overruling which he could not dismiss the plaintiffs' bill.

In that case there was a debt due to three sisters, and the debtor executed a bond to them of £500, objecting at the time to giving the bond, and only doing so upon a verbal assurance that it should not be enforced unless the obligees came to want. The three obligees held the bond until one of them died; the survivors then held it, and after the death of one survivor, it remained in the hands of the other until her death. It had by mutual arrangement become hers. Upon this bond there appeared the following indorsement: "This bond is never to appear against (the obligor) witness;" and the names of the two surviving sisters were written; but the name of one was said to have been written by the other who was the last survivor; but if so, it was proved that she wrote her sister's name by her sister's authority. This indorsement was dated eleven years after the date of the bond. *Kindersley*, V. C., held, that without deciding that this writing amounted to a release, the circumstances disclosed an equity against enforcing the bond.

Judgment.

(a) 1 Drewry, 165.

*Wekett* v. *Raby* (a) is perhaps stronger, for there was no contemporaneous agreement not to enforce the bond, but there was the obligee's verbal declaration made on his death-bed to his executrix and residuary legatee, " I have *Raby's* bond which I keep. I don't deliver it up, for I may live to want it more than he ; but when I die, he shall have it : he shall not be asked or troubled for it." After the obligee's death, the executrix being pressed by *Raby* to give up the bond, told him he might be easy, it was safe in her hands ; and if she married she would deliver it to him before. She did marry, and afterwards brought an action on the bond. The House of Lords affirmed the Lord Chancellor's decree, that the bond should be delivered up to be cancelled.

In these and other cases, such as *Aston* v. *Pye* (b), *Eden* v. *Smyth* (c), *Gilbert* v. *Wetherell* (d), *Flower* v. *Marten* (e), there has been an existing debt or obligation, and either some subsequent act done, or express declaration made, by the party entitled to the money, shewing an intention to release or cancel the debt, and in some cases, as in *Eden* v. *Smyth* and *Major* v. *Major* there has been some written evidence of such intention ; and, in *Cross* v. *Sprigg* (f), *Wigram*, V. C., remarking upon *Flower* v. *Marten*, says he does not consider that case to decide any such abstract proposition as that where a creditor by his conduct shews an intention to abandon his rights as a creditor, and treat the debt as a gift to the debtor, equity will not permit the debt to be enforced. It is true Lord *Cottenham* reversed the decree in this case (g), but it was upon an entirely different ground. It appears to me *Major* v. *Major* falls within the other case I have referred to, and is decided upon the particular circumstances, and not upon a

---

(a) 2 Br. P. C. 386, Tomlin's edition ; in the Dublin edition 3 16.

(b) 5 Ves. 350 n.                    (c) 5 Ves. 341.

(d) 2 S. & S. 254.                   (e) 2 Myl. & Cr. 459.

(f) 6 Hare 552.                      (g) 2McN. & G. 113.

general proposition that a parol contemporaneous agreement will make void and nugatory a sealed contract.

The case most resembling the present which I have seen is, that of *Smith* v. *East India Company* (a) (reported on another point in 1 Phill. 50). The plaintiff had proposed to purchase cotton from the defendants, to be shipped on board a vessel of theirs which he commanded. His proposal was accepted with a further proposition that he should be subject to the payment of such freight as the defendants should see fit to demand, for which he must enter into an àgreement. He immediately objected to this, saying he would not take the cotton, if he was to pay any freight for it. Some days after, a bond was presented to him for execution, binding him *inter alia* to pay freight as proposed by the defendants. He objected, but was told on the part of the defendants that the clause as to freight was inserted as a matter of form only, and that it would not be enforced against him and a letter to that effect was written to him by the Secretary of a board of the defendants, and thereupon he executed the bond. Sir *L. Shadwell*, V.C., held that the bond should be controlled by that letter, and restrained the defendants from setting it up as a defence at law, to an action the plaintiff had brought, and from claiming as a set-off in that action the charge for the freight of that cotton. He states the foundation of his judgment thus : " I go by the written instrument which cannot err, and which appears to me to give complete protection to Captain *Smith* against the legal advantage which would arise to the Company from the bond." In the judgment, and introductory to the passage above cited, the learned Vice Chancellor remarks upon " the very odd evidence that has been given, years after the transaction had passed." And I apprehend clearly that no decree such as was pronounced would have been rested upon what Lord *Coke* speaks of as "the uncertain testimony of slippery memory."

(a) 12 Jur. 367.

In our case we have no writing to control the covenant, either contemporaneous or subsequent. The plaintiffs depend upon the conversation between Mr. *Barrett* and Mr. *Freeland*, before the mortgage was executed. I have remarked upon the testimony already ; and without any doubt that Mr. *Barrett* has, to the best of his recollection stated what took place, I cannot but observe that his memory has proved defective, and that some of the facts are very difficult to be reconciled with the understanding which he states was arrived at. I do not think I am bound by authority or warranted by the evidence, which unlike the written instrument may err, to control or disregard the assignees express covenant, and to substitute a new and different contract for it. The deed must, in my opinion, be taken to contain the actual engagements of the parties.

I think the decree should be reversed.

HAGARTY, C. J.—If the law be as contended for by the respondents, we are bound to apply it to any case fairly within its control. We have, at all events, the right to require that where it is sought to avoid a distinct covenant to pay money, by a verbal agreement attempted to be proved by one witness after the lapse of many years, the evidence should be clear and convincing beyond reasonable doubt. In this case, giving Mr. *Barrett* credit for the most sincere desire to speak the truth to the best of his recollection, I must say that his account of the transaction leads me to an opinion on the facts that there was no agreement on the part of the mortgagees not to insist on the covenant to pay. Mr. *Freeland's* death deprives us of much valuable evidence which might have removed our doubts.

I see no adequate explanation as to why the land should be only conveyed by way of mortgage, and still less why, if it must be by way of mortgage, the deed should contain a covenant not intended to be acted upon. A suggestion, but no proof is all that is offered to us. Mr. *Barrett* says he told his clients that he thought that the covenant to pay would make no difference ; that they would not be called upon to pay ; but if they had to pay as assignees, they had property of *White's* estate to pay themselves. " I endeavored to secure the assignees by a covenant from *White*, to save them harmless, though I did not anticipate any trouble to the assignees from their covenant though there was a risk from it of course."

I do not know what writing or covenant Mr. *Barrett* took from *White* to indemnify the assignees against their express contract ; but his getting, or his endeavoring to get, any such, would be utterly inconsistent with the position that the assignees were not to be bound by their covenant. Mr. *Fisken* says, that had the mortgage contained *White's* covenant to pay, without a covenant by the assignees, it would be in accordance with the original intention. *White* only, he says, was to give the usual mortgage covenant, and that *Freeland* told him that the mortgage in its present form was all he could get from *Barrett ;* and that he, *Freeland,* considered the covenant in the present mortgage, by the assignees, better than a covenant by *White* alone. The covenant really contained on *White's* part is only to perform the covenant when the assignees ceased to represent the estate on fulfilment of the trusts. Mr. *Barrett's* evidence wholly fails to satisfy me, how it could be true as stated in the bill, that the property was to be taken for the debt, making it in fact a sale, while a clear right to redeem at the end of nearly five years was reserved, leaving a future proceeding necessary to complete the title. I hardly understand two intelligent professional gentlemen gravely performing this legal comedy. I do Mr. *Barrett* the justice of fully believing that he has forgotten the true bearing of this transaction. A recollection of the character and practice of the late Mr. *Freeland* strongly tends to confirm this impression.

52—VOL. XVIII. GR.

1871.

Lewis
v.
Robson.

Judgment.

The conclusion I draw from the evidence is adverse to the assignees' intention. I think they were to be bound just as the deed expresses them to be. Had I arrived at a different view of the evidence, I should have paused long before accepting as correct the view of the law on which the decree rests; nor am I satisfied that assuming the judgment of *Kindersley*, V. C., in *Major* v. *Major*, to be sound, it must necessarily govern this case. The facts are widely different; and the suggestion that the bond was not intended to be enforced except on the happening of a specified event, was supported by the memorandum signed by the obligees some years later.

I have not seen any other case laying down a principle wide enough to embrace facts such as are now before us. A late case of *McKenzie* v. *Coulson* (a) before *James*, V. C., seems to me much in point on a question like the present. My impression is, that the late learned Chancellor took a stronger view of the general legal bearing of *Major* v. *Major* than the case warrants. It is remarked on in the elaborate case of *Jorden* v. *Money* (b): Lord *Brougham* says, " in *Major* v. *Major*, there was an endorsement on the bond. It had been originally said that it was not to be enforced unless the obligees came to want, and afterwards there was an endorsement signed by two of them, ' that this bond is never to appear against the obligor,' that endorsement had a great effect on the mind of the Vice Chancellor." Again the Lord Chancellor, *Cranworth*, says, " there can be no doubt about that case, the bond was not to be enforced if certain circumstances did not arise, and they did not arise."

If the law really be, as the assignees contend, I can hardly conceive any doctrine so dangerously subversive of the ordinary securities of property. I can understand a

---

(a) L. R. 8 Eq. 368.          (b 5 H. Lords, at 205.

deed being executed under such circumstances as to raise the conclusion that it was only delivered conditionally, as a species of escrow. But where the unqualified and complete delivery is admitted; when it is admitted to be operative in its general purport and design, and to have been acted on for years, it is a startling thing to be told that a covenant proper and usual for such a conveyance, almost of the very substance of the whole transaction, viz., to pay the money in a mortgage of real estate, can be taken out of the deed and wholly avoided by the declaration of a witness years afterwards, that at the execution of the deed it was agreed between the attorneys that it should be inoperative.

As I draw a wholly different conclusion from the evidence from that arrived at in the Court below, I need not further discuss the legal question. I think the appeal must be allowed, and the bill dismissed with costs.

Judgment.

GWYNNE, J.—As to reforming this deed, which can only be done where there is a mutual mistake, appears to me to be out of the question, for the evidence shews very plainly that there was no mistake upon Mr. *Freeland's* part, whose testimony, if he were alive, would, most probably, clear up whatever obscurity there may appear to be cast around the transaction.

I think it probable that if Mr. *Freeland* were alive, he would say if he insisted upon the covenant, being by the assignees instead of by *White*, that he did so because *White* was insolvent and all his estate was transferred to his assignees, and he preferred taking the covenant from them as the persons having the management of *White's* estate, leaving it to them to see that they reimbursed themselves out of that estate ; but, however this may be, the evidence points, not to a case for reformation of a deed, but to a case seeking to vary wholly the terms and effect of a deed upon parol testimony.

**1871.**

Lewis
v.
Robson.

I confess I have not felt the difficulty which appears to have been felt by the learned Chancellor, arising from the decision in *Major* v. *Major*. That case is not an authority for the position that a covenant designedly inserted in a deed, shall be deprived of its legal efficacy upon parol evidence;—that it was inserted upon an agreement that it should have no effect, or in other words, that its designed introduction into the deed should be nugatory: it is, as I understand, an authority only for the position that a deed executed and delivered upon an agreement,

Judgment.

that unless, and until, a certain event should happen it was to have no force, should not have any force until that event happens; it is founded on the doctrine of escrow, and touches not, as I understand it, the doctrine that the terms and effect of a sealed instrument cannot be varied by parol.

*Per Curiam.*—Appeal allowed; decree to be reversed, and bill in Court below dismissed with costs.

---

## THE FREEHOLD PERMANENT BUILDING AND SAVING SOCIETY v. CHOATE.

*Building Societies—Usury Laws.*

Building Societies are virtually exempted from the operation of the usury laws.

In mortgages taken by a building society for advances to borrowing members, it is not necessary to express in the instruments how much of the interest reserved is a bonus in respect of the sum advanced, and how much for interest.

Examination of witnesses and hearing.

In this case the defendant *Ashford* had applied to the plaintiffs for a loan of money, when it was arranged that he should subscribe the books of the Society for stock to the amount of the proposed loan ($10,000) which he accordingly did and executed to them the mortgage now sued on. The present suit was for the sale of the mortgaged premises in default of payment. *Ashford* had conveyed the property to one *Choate*, who was made a defendant to the bill.

1871.

TheFreehold
Permanent
Building and
Saving
Society
v.
Choate.

The objections relied on by the defendants to the plaintiffs' recovery in the suit are clearly stated in the judgment.

Mr. *Blake*, Q. C., and Mr. *McMurrich*, for the plaintiffs.

Mr. *Crooks*, Q. C., for defendant *Ashford*.

Mr. *Moss*, for defendant *Choate*.

SPRAGGE, C.—The first point made by the answer is, in substance, that *Choate*, the mortgagor, became a member of the Building Society (if he became a member at all) only for the purpose of borrowing money at a higher rate than legal interest; and that it was agreed between him and the plaintiffs that he should become a member for that purpose; and this is designated in the answer as a corrupt bargain and unlawful. Mr. *Crooks* very properly concedes that this objection cannot be sustained. The case of *Burbidge* v. *Cotton* (a) is an authority against it; and independently of that authority my own opinion would be against it. I think we have nothing to do with the motives of a party in becoming a member of a Building Society. To inquire into them would introduce subtle and uncertain elements into the consideration of these cases: moreover the statute (b) itself seems to contemplate persons becoming members of Building Societies with the purpose of borrowing: the recital speaks of persons becoming members "for investment therein, *or to obtain the advance of their*

Judgment.

(a) 5 DeG. & S. 17.     (b) 22 Vic. c. 45.

1871.
The Freehold
Permanent
Building and
Saving
Society
v.
Choate.

*shares or share by giving security therefor.''* Thus
contemplating two classes; one class becoming members
as a mode of investing their moneys, another for the
purpose of borrowing upon the security of their .pro-
perty.

It is next objected that what is authorized by the Act
is, that Building Societies may besides interest receive
from any member a bonus on any share for the advance
to him of the same, and that a reservation beyond six
per cent. in any other shape is unlawful.  Upon this
point I agree with the *Canada Permanent Building
and Savings Society* v. *Harris* (a).  In that case there
was a reservation of interest at eight per cent.  As to
that the language of the Court was; "As to the eight
per cent. we are of opinion that we cannot hold it to be
contrary to the Company's act; for by that Act the
plaintiffs were permitted to take, besides interest, any
bonus from a member for his receiving his share in
advance, and we cannot say that the alleged excess of
two per cent. is not a bonus under the name of interest :
the statute does not require that the portion of it which
is bonus shall be called bonus, and it would be a very
rigid construction of the deed to avoid it on the ground
of illegality, when the defendant has not excluded the
presumption which must be made in favour of the deed,
when there is no express averment to the contrary (b).''
Before the repeal of the Usury Laws, if an excess were
taken on a loan, and it was called by the name of
bonus, it was still open to inquiry whether it was not
interest taken contrary to the statute.  Why, therefore, should not the same rule be reversely applied,
and this sum, or a part of it which is called interest,
be shewn to be a bonus?''  In this case it is not
by the name of bonus, or of interest, or partly of each,
that payment for the use of the sum advanced is reserved,

---

(a) 16 U. C. C. P. 54.              (b) Page 60.

but a sum is made payable each half-year which is equal
to ten per cent. on the sum advanced. The rate is
immaterial, as the Act places no limit on the bonus that
a Company may require. The truth is, that what are
termed Building Societies are by the Acts relating to
them virtually exempted from the operation of the Usury
Laws: and as on the one hand an individual or body
subject to those laws could not under any name, bonus,
or otherwise, reserve more than six per cent. upon a loan,
so on the other, these Societies, authorized to receive
more than six per cent. by adding an unlimited bonus to
that rate of interest, are in effect set free from the
restrictions imposed by the Usury Laws upon others:
and it would be looking at the form instead of the substance of their dealings to require it to appear upon the
face of their securities, that so much of the sum payable
half-yearly for the use of the moneys advanced is for
interest at six per cent., and so much for bonus at such
and such a rate. Further, it does not appear that the
sums reserved half-yearly were not based upon a calculation of so much per cent. by way of bonus added
to interest at the rate of six per cent.; and as was said
in the case in the Common Pleas, we are not "to
presume illegality."

A further objection is, that it is not shewn that there
is any rule of this Society whereby the sums reserved
upon this mortgage as a half-yearly payment for the
use of the money advanced are authorized in any shape,
either as interest or bonus, or in part of each, or otherwise: but as I understand the objection, it may be, for
aught that appears, that the half-yearly payments were
the result of a bargain made in this particular transaction, and not founded upon a rate of any kind fixed, by
a rule of the Society. It may be that making a bargain
with an individual borrower as to the sum or rate to be
charged upon the advance would be open to abuse, inasmuch as all, being as they are, in name at least, mem-

1871.

The Freehold
Permanent
Building and
Saving
Society
v.
Choate.

bers of the Society should be upon the same footing: and advantage might be taken of the necessities of some having very urgent need, in exacting from them more than would be required of others. But it does not follow that it would be unlawful; that a mortgage given upon such a bargain would be void. I am referred to Mr. *Scratchley's* book for the form of a table of charges (*a*), but that is a table shewing the re-payments of advances by periodical payments covering principal as well as interest; and I find a similar table in the printed rules of this Society put in. It may be that the rates of interest, to call it by its proper name, are fixed from time to time by the directors, or by some officers of the Society to whom the duty is committed. I cannot assume that this is not so. I should rather assume that it is. But if the fact be that the advance in this case was made without there being any rule fixing the rate at which interest should be charged, I do not see upon what grouud I can say that the mortgage is therefore void. If there was no rule fixing the rate, it would necessarily be fixed by

Judgment. agreement between the borrower and the Society, the latter acting through its proper officer; that would at any rate be presumed.

The decree will be as prayed for, a sale, and for an order against the mortgagor for the payment of the deficiency, if any.

---

(*a*) p. 97.

SANDERSON V. BURDETT.—[IN APPEAL.*]

*Joint Purchase—Personal decree.*

Where a purchase was made by a person in his own name but in reality for the benefit of another, a personal decree against both, for the payment of the purchase money, was held to be correct.

Parol evidence of the agency was held admissible, and the purchaser who entered into the contract in his own name, and who was a defendant, was held a good witness on behalf of the plaintiff against his co-purchaser, the other defendant.

Appeal from the decree of the Court below, as reported, *ante* volume XVI., p. 119, by the defendant, *Cameron.*

Mr. *McMichael,* Mr. *Fitzgerald,* and Mr. *A. Hoskin,* for the appellant.

Mr. *Hodgins,* contra.

The judgment of the Court was delivered by

STRONG, V.C.—There is no pretence for the appel- February 4. lant's contention that the defendant *Burdett* was not a competent witness for the plaintiff against the defendant *Cameron;* the Act of Parliament in force at the time the cause was heard only disqualified parties to the record as witnesses on their own behalf.

Then, the evidence of *Burdett* being admissible, he Judgment. proves that the purchase was made by him for the behoof of *Cameron* and himself as jointly interested from the beginning; and this proposition must be considered as conclusively established, unless *Burdett* is to be deemed unworthy of credit. The appellant can scarcely expect

---

*Present.—DRAPER, C.J., RICHARDS, C.J., HAGARTY, C.J., WILSON, J., MOWAT, V.C., GALT, J.

Sanderson
v.
Burdett.

this Court to review the finding of the Judge in the Court below, in whose presence the witness was examined, upon a mere question of credibility; for, whilst there can be no doubt but that it is open to the appellate Court, in equity causes, to review the evidence, and to come to a different conclusion as to its weight and effect from that arrived at in the Court of first instance, yet this right will not be so exercised as to reverse the finding of the Judge, who heard the cause, upon a mere question of the credibility of a witness, when the evidence as recorded does not appear to be either self-contradictory or improbable, although it may be controverted by that of other witnesses; and this is but giving the same effect to the decision of the Judge in equity, upon questions as to the veracity of the witnesses, as is at law accorded to the finding of a jury. *Santacana* v. *Ardevol* (a); *Reid* v. *The Aberdeen, Newcastle and Hull Steamship Co.*, (b); *Gray* v. *Turnbull* (c); *The Julia* (d); 

Judgment. may be referred to on this head. Now in this case *Burdett's* statements, so far from being inconsistent with the documents, and the conduct of the parties, is rather confirmed by that evidence; and the witness was considered truthful by the learned Chancellor before whom he was examined.

That parol evidence of agency was admissible to charge an unnamed principal in circumstances like the present is established by the well-known case of *Higgins* v. *Senior* (e).

The Statute of Frauds is satisfied by the contract being in writing, signed by the agent, though ostensibly as a principal, and it does not require the agency to be also so evidenced: *Heard* v. *Pilley* (f).

---

(a) 1 Knapp 269.

(b) L. R. 2 P. C. 245.

(c) L. R. 2 Sc. App. 53.

(d) 14 Moo. P. C. 210.

(e) 8 M. & W. 8 34.

(f) L. R. 4 Chy. App. 548.

That the decree rightly contains a personal order 1871.
against *Cameron* is shewn by the reasons given by my Sanderson
brother *Mowat*, in his judgment in the Court below, v.
supported by the authority there cited. From this it Burdett.
appears that a personal decree will be made against a
purchaser for the payment of purchase money in a suit
to enforce a binding lien, which is certainly conformable
to the general practice of Courts of Equity ; and no
contradictory authority being produced, and the form of
decree in general use being as in the present case, the
appeal fails in this respect also; and must be dismissed
with costs.

---

## SHAVER V. GRAY.

*Foreign testator—Administration.*

Where a testator dies in a foreign country leaving assets in this
province, the Court, at the instance of a legatee, will restrain the
withdrawal of the assets from the jurisdiction, notwithstanding that
there may be creditors of the testator resident where the testator
was domiciled at the time of his death ; and that there are no
creditors resident in this Province.

This was a motion for a receiver and injunction,
made under the following circumstances : *Abraham
Martell*, the testator, was, at the time of his death,
domiciled in the State of Iowa. By his will he be- Statement.
queathed several legacies; amongst others, one amounting to $200 to the plaintiff. The defendants were the
executors appointed by the will, which they had proved
both in this Province and in Iowa. One of the assets of
the estate consisted of a mortgage debt secured on land
in this Province, and due by a person living here. This
mortgage debt the defendants, the executors, desired to
get in, and have remitted to Iowa to be applied there with
the other assets in payment of debts and legacies. The ·
plaintiff insisted that she was entitled to an injunction

restraining the transmission of this money beyond the jurisdiction, and to have the amount secured in the hands of a receiver. There were no creditors in this Province.

Mr. *English*, for the plaintiff.

Mr. *Fleming*, contra.

STRONG, V. C.—[After stating the facts as above.] These facts are undisputed. It was, however, contended on behalf of the defendants that the executors were entitled to have the money remitted to the domicile of the testator for distribution there ; that the principal administration and distribution was to be enforced in that forum, and that the administration here was merely ancillary, and there being no creditors here the beneficiaries must resort to the forum of the domicile instead of compelling creditors at the domicile to resort to this forum. These contentions were rested on the principles of comity applicable to cases in which a conflict of jurisdiction arises, and on the supposed inconvenience or other injustice of applying this fund to the payment of legatees here, whilst in the country of the testator's domicile there might be unpaid creditors whose right of prior satisfaction would be defeated. Upon the argument on the motion I thought that the position of the defendants, in one aspect of it, was sustainable, and that the motion ought to be refused ; for it then appeared to me highly reasonable that the executors to whom the testator had entrusted the administration of his assets, persons residing at the domicile, should be placed in possession of the fund in order that they might apply it in the first place in payment of creditors there, leaving those beneficially entitled to the surplus to go to the executors at the domicile to receive the bequests, which it is not too much to infer that the testator intended to be paid there ; and I should have thought that our Courts ought to have entrusted the forum of the domicile with the

*Judgment.*

whole administration. I find, however, that the weight
of authority is against this view. It is true that an
eminent writer on the conflict of laws, Mr. *Westlake*, at
article 300 of his treatise, lays down the rule as follows:
" The administration of the assets to which each local
representative is bound, in the manner we have now
considered, refers to the payment of the debts of the
deceased ; for the principle is, that until these are satisfied the property will be retained within the jurisdition,
but that the surplus then remaining is transmissible to
the deceased's domicile to be distributed by that forum
among his heirs and legatees; " for these propositions two
cases are cited, *Preston* v. *Melville* (a), *Mechlan* v. *Campbell* (b), neither of which, however, supports the text. And
in articles 311 and 312 the learned writer neutralizes the
authority of the passage I have quoted by shewing that
in a much stronger case, when the property has even been
removed abroad, the forum of the ancillary administration will take jurisdiction. The authorities cited by Mr.
*English* from *Williams* on Executors, pp. 1536-7, *Story's*
Conflict of Laws, sec. 513, and the cases of *Dawes* v.
*Head* (c), *Harvey* v. *Richards* (d), *Hervey* v. *Fitzpatrick*
(e), are also strongly in the plaintiff's favour.

The argument derived from the assumed injustice to
the creditors in Iowa, I need scarcely say, has no foundation ; for nothing so contrary to reason and justice could
be effected by any proceedings of this Court as to sub-
vert the order of administration, by paying the legatees
here in priority to the creditors abroad. The rights of the
foreign creditors will be protected by the decree, and they
cannot be prejudiced beyond having to resort to this
forum which, however, it is impossible to deny does
inflict an inconvenience on them. In deference to the
authorities I must grant the motion, but I would suggest

---

(a) 8 C. & F. 1.     (b) 24 Beav. 100.     (c) 3 Pick. 128.
(d) 1 Mason 381.     (e) Kay 421.

1871. in order to save expense, that, instead of an injunction
and receiver, the money should to be paid into Court.
A decree may also, if the parties consent to treat this
motion as a motion for decree, be now pronounced for
the administration of the fund.

---

## O'CONNOR v. CLARKE.

*Interest—Sale of notes.*

A loan of money was made for two months at two per cent. a month,
at the expiration of which time it was contemplated a new arrangement would be made. After the expiry of the two months, no other
arrangement having been effected, the Court held the lender entitled
to claim interest at the rate originally agreed upon, and to sell the
notes held by him as security, to repay himself the amount of his
claim; subject only to the question whether he had sold the notes
for the best price that could be obtained for them; and as to which
the Court directed an inquiry before the Master.

Examination of witnesses and hearing at Sandwich
Autumn Sittings, 1870.

Mr. *O'Connor*, in person.

Mr. *S. Blake*, contra.

SPRAGGE, C.—I take the result of the evidence to be
that the loan was to be in the first place for two months,
at two per cent. per month interest, the promissory
notes in the bill mentioned being given at the time by
way of collateral security; that it was contemplated at
the expiration of the two months that a new arrangement
should be made; that security—probably security upon
land—should be given in place of the notes, and upon
that being done, the rate of interest should be reduced.
This contemplated new arrangement never was made.
It was deferred more than once for reasons which are
explained by defendant *Clarke* in his evidence, until in

*Judgment.*

about a year or more after the loan of the money,
negotiations were entered into for giving security upon
certain land of the plaintiff's. These negotiations fell
through, *Clarke* not being satisfied with the land offered
as security, without retaining the notes as collateral
security.

One of the questions made is, whether *Clarke* was
entitled to the same rate of interest after the expiration
of the two months as he was to have during the two
months. It is certain that it was not in any event to be
reduced to six per cent., for the plaintiff's agent says in
his evidence that he expected it to be ten or twelve per
cent., or understood that it was to be at that rate.

When the giving of the contemplated security was
deferred at the instance of the plaintiff the first arrangement necessarily continued—there was nothing to change
it—the loan was not repaid, and if continued it would
be upon the old terms ; then at what time was there
any change in the terms ? The event upon which a
change was contemplated never took place. It may have
been supposed by the plaintiff that so large a rate of interest would not be exacted when the loan was protracted
so much beyond the time first contemplated : but I do
not see what time I can fix upon as a matter of law
when the rate of interest first agreed upon should cease.
After default the debtor is held bound to pay the same
rate of interest as before default. Whether, therefore,
this loan is to be regarded as payable at the expiration
of two months, unless some further arrangement should
then be made ; which is, I incline to think, the real
nature of the agreement, or to be continued beyond the
two months until some further arrangement should be
made ; either way, the same rate of interest would be
payable after the expiration of the two months. A loan
for two years from the date of the advance, or for a year
from the expiration of the two months, it is not certain

which, appears to have been contemplated ; but I think
no definite period was fixed. Everything beyond the
loan for two months was left as a matter for future
arrangement.

I think that *Clarke* was entitled, after default in payment of the money for the repayment of which the notes
mentioned in the pleadings were given by way of collateral security, to sell the notes. I understood the plaintiff
rather to contend that there was no default, than that
upon default it was not competent to the lender to repay
himself by selling them. That such is the right of the
lender, the following cases are authority : *Pothonier* v.
*Dawson* (*a*), *Tucker* v, *Wilson* (*b*), *Lockwood* v. *Ewer*
(*c*), and the cases referred to in the argument and in
the judgment of the Court in *Pigot* v. *Curley* (*d*), and
in *Martin* v. *Reid* (*e*). I think that in this case there
was a time fixed for payment, and that it had passed.
At any rate it is proved that the plaintiff was notified
by *Clarke* that unless he repaid the loan, he would sell
the notes. If the plaintiff desires an inquiry whether
*Clarke* sold the notes for the best price that could be
reasonably got for the same, he may have a reference
upon that point, upon making known his intention to the
Registrar at Toronto within one month.

The costs, up to and inclusive of the hearing, are to
be paid by the plaintiff. The costs of the reference, if
the plaintiff desires to have one, will be reserved.

---

(*a*) Holt Rep. 385.          (*b*) 1 P. Wms. 261.
(*c*) 2 Atk. 303.          (*d*) 15 C. B. N.S. 701.
(*e*) 11 C. B. N. S. 730.

THE EDINBURGH LIFE ASSURANCE COMPANY V. ALLEN.

*Trustee to sell, mortgage by—Release of suit executed without advice.*

*A.* executed to *B.* a deed of his property in trust, (amongst other things) to convert the same into money. *B.*, under the assumed authority of this deed mortgaged the property:

*Held,* that the mortgage was not authorized by the trust for sale, and was only valid to the extent of *B.'s* beneficial interest (if any) in the premises.

Differences having arisen between the parties, *A.* obtained against *B.* a decree for an account, and large sums were in dispute between them : while the reference was pending, *B.* got a release of the suit prepared for *A.'s* signature : a friend brought *A.* to *B.'s* office, and *B.* there induced *A.* to sign the release in consideration of $150 which he promised to pay; on a subsequent day *A.* went for the money, and then at *B.'s* request executed a quit claim deed of all his interest in the land. There was no evidence of the true state of the accounts at the time of these transactions : *A.* was sober when he entered into them, and he understood their nature ; and *B.* had no fraudulent purpose therein : *B.* was a person of large business experience, *A.* had little, if any, business experience, and his habits were intemperate and thriftless ; and he executed the two instruments without the knowledge of his solicitor, and without advice :

*Held,* that the instruments were void in equity.

This was a proceeding, under the Quieting Titles Act, Statement. for the purpose of trying certain issues directed by an order of the 1st of March, 1871; the trial of which was undertaken by Mr. *Crooks*, Q.C., at the request of Vice Chancellor *Mowat*, under the authority of the Statute 29 & 30 Victoria, chapter 39.

The claimants deduced their title to the property in question under a deed of trust, dated the 19th February, 1855, made by *James Allen* (the father of the contestant) to *John W. Gamble*, and a conveyance by *Gamble* to the claimants dated the 10th November, 1860, which though absolute in form was subject to a defeazance, and admitted to be a mortgage in effect.

54—VOL. XVIII. GR.

The deed of the 19th February, 1855, declared the
same to be in trust for *Gamble* or his heirs, " to sell
and dispose of the same at such time, in such manner,
and for such price as he or they may, in his or their
discretion, think best, so that the price obtained therefor
be not less than six hundred pounds of lawful money
of Canada over and above the aforesaid mortgage;
and to apply the proceeds of such sale as received
by him or them in manner following, that is to
say: Firstly, to retain and pay to himself and themselves all such sum and sums of money, costs and
expenses as he or they may have been put to in
and about the execution of these presents and performance of the trusts herein contained. Secondly, to
retain and pay to the said *John William Gamble*, his
executors and administrators, all and every such sum
and sums of money as are now due and owing from the
said *James Allen* to the said *John William Gamble* for
goods sold and money lent by the said *John William*

*Gamble* to the said *James Allen*, or for money now or
heretofore paid or hereafter to be paid by the said *John
William Gamble* for the use of the said *James Allen*,
for debts of the said *James Allen* contracted prior to
the date of these presents. Thirdly, to pay all expenses
and sum and sums of money that may be paid in
and about perfecting the title to the lands herein
described in the purchaser or purchasers thereof, free
from dower and all other incumbrances. And, lastly,
to pay over the balance of the said purchase money to
the said *James Allen*, his executors, administrators, or
assigns."

On the 29th May, 1867, *James Allen* executed a
release to *Gamble* of a Chancery suit then pending, and
in which *Allen* had obtained a decree for an account of
all moneys paid or advanced, or received by *Gamble*,
according to the terms of the deed of trust, and for
an inquiry as to whether *Gamble* had sold the trust

property under the terms of the deed : further directions and costs being reserved.

On the 24th of June, 1867, *Allen* also executed a deed whereby for the expressed consideration of $150, he granted and released the property to *Gamble* in fee.

· In December, 1869, *Allen* died intestate, leaving the contestant, *Victoria Allen*, and several other children surviving., The contestant, in objecting to the title of the claimants, contended that the release of the 24th of May, 1867, and the deed of the 24th of November following had been obtained without consideration, and by the undue influence of *Gamble* over *Allen*, who from intemperate habits had become incapable of transacting business, and under circumstances which would render these instruments void in equity.

She also contended that the mortgage security of the 18th of November, 1860, was void, as not being author- ized by the deed of trust of the 19th February, 1855.

The order of this Court of the 1st of March last, thereupon directed that the following questions should be tried before a Judge of the Court, viz. : " 1st. Whether the said indenture of mortgage of the 18th of November, 1860, is void as against the said contestant, and all others entitled to the benefit of the said trust deed of the 19th day of February, 1855;" and 2ndly. "Whether the said deed of the 24th day of June, 1867, was void as against the said contestant and the other heiresses-at-law of the said *James Allen* as having been obtained from the said *James Allen* by the undue influence and control of the said *Gamble,* and while the said *Allen* was unfit to transact business."

This order also directed that this matter should be set down for hearing at the then next ensuing Sittings of the Court at the City of Toronto, and that notice should be given to the widow and children of the intestate *Allen*, or such of them as were within the jurisdiction of the Court.

Witnesses were accordingly examined and the cause heard on the 31st of May and 2nd of June.

Mr. *Hillyard Cameron*, Q.C., and Mr. *Kennedy*, for the claimants.

Mr. *Hodgins*, contra.

CROOKS, Q.C.—The following facts were, I think, established by the *viva voce* testimony :—that from 1854 till his decease, *Allen* was addicted to habits of drinking, and his intemperance was such, that he was more frequently drunk than sober until the period of his leaving for the United States, in 1865 ; that from his return in December, 1866, till his death, he was less frequently under the influence of liquor ; that, although *Allen's* intellect had become deteriorated from his great intemperance, he continued till his death capable, when sober, of understanding matters of business in the ordinary way of persons of his station, education, and experience ; that, when he executed the release of the 29th of May and the deed of the 24th of June, *Allen* had sufficient mental capacity to understand their nature and effect, and this is also true with respect to the acknowledgment of the account obtained by Mr. *Gamble*, on the 5th of December, 1861 ; that, in obtaining these several instruments, Mr. *Gamble* acted in the *bonâ fide* belief of the correctness of his account and claim against *Allen*, and that he was in no way seeking to impose upon *Allen*, or to take any advantage of him or his circumstances.

The evidence shewed that Mr. *Gamble* was a person of large business experience, while *Allen* had none,

excepting in so far as he had gained any while shift- 1871·
lessly managing his farm ; and that, after *Allen* left
the property, he spent his time loitering about taverns,
and away from his family. In fact, this disparity
between Mr. *Gamble* and *Allen* led to the deed of trust
of the 19th of February, 1855, being executed, it being
considered by both that Mr. *Gamble* could best dispose
of the property; and, after paying the mortgage and
other debts contemplated, realize a surplus for *Allen.*
It was unfortunate for Mr. *Allen* and his family that
advantageous opportunities for accomplishing this were
frustrated by Mrs. *Allen's* opposition.

Beyond this disparity in business experience, and the
general respect and confidence entertained by *Allen*
towards Mr. *Gamble,* there was nothing in their relations
or in the mental condition of the one, as compared with
that of the other, which would avoid in equity any
transactions between them, unless upon the ground of
fraud, or as being otherwise obnoxious to some equitable
principles.

Such being their relative personal positions, the
release of the 26th of May was obtained by Mr. *Gamble*
under these circumstances :—the suit in Chancery of
*Allen* against him with respect to the trusts of the deed
of the 19th February, 1855, was pending, and the decree
for an account pronounced ; under it his account had been
brought into the office of the Accountant, shewing an
amount claimed by him (after crediting the amount
received from the *Edinburgh Insurance Company*) of
$2,612.68 ; and against this the plaintiff had filed a
surcharge amounting to $6,384, and Mr. *Gamble* had
mortgaged the trust property to the now claimants for
$3,893.33. He admits his anxiety to be effectually rid
of this suit, and he obtains a draft form of release from
his solicitor, has this copied, and *Allen* having been
brought to his office by Dr. *Mahaffey* (who had been

*Allen's* occasional medical attendant), was asked by Mr.
*Gamble* to execute the release, Mr. *Gamble* offering
him $150 as a gift, induced, as Mr. *Gamble* says, by
his destitute circumstances. Without independent advice,
or the opportunity of consulting his or any solicitor, as
to his rights or position, *Allen* executed the release; and
on the occasion of his subsequent visit to Mr. *Gamble*
for the $150 which he had left in Mr. *Gamble's* hands,
Mr. *Gamble*, on his mere request, obtains from him the
deed of the 2nd June. *Allen* was sober on these occasions, and evidently knew the nature and effect of the
instruments ; yet, under the circumstances referred to, I
think it would be contrary to the well-established principle of the Court that these instruments should stand.
I do not think that Mr. *Gamble* intended in any way
to act contrary to what he considered he could right-
fully do in dealing with *Allen* and obtaining this release
and deed of quit claim, but his solicitor should have
advised him that in order to make a settlement of the

trust between him and *Allen* binding, such settlement
should have been arrived at, when *Allen* had the
benefit of proper counsel and advice. *Gamble* was
*Allen's* trustee; and questions were then in issue between
him and *Gamble* as to the management of the trust in
respect of which *Allen* was entitled to be independently
advised, and I do not think that having regard to all
the circumstances attending the execution of the release,
and the deed of quit claim which was merely a consequence of it, either of them can be considered as binding
upon *Allen* or those claiming under him.

The principle of my decision may be best expressed
in the language of Lord Justice *Turner*, in *Rhodes* v.
*Bate* (a), " Persons standing in a confidential relation
towards others cannot entitle themselves to those benefits which those others may have conferred upon them,

(a) L. R. 1 Ch. App. 252.

unless they can shew to the satisfaction of the Court
that the persons by whom the benefits have been conferred had competent and independent advice in conferring them. This, in my opinion, is a well settled
general principle of the Court, and I do not think that
either the age or capacity of the person conferring the
benefit or the nature of the benefit conferred, affects
this principle; age and capacity are considerations
which may be of great importance in cases in which
the principle does not apply, but I think they are of
little, if any, importance in cases to which the principle
is applicable. They may afford a sufficient protection
in ordinary cases, but they can afford but little protection in cases of influence founded upon confidence. And
as to the nature of the benefit, the injury to the party
by whom the benefit is conferred cannot depend upon
its nature."

It was of course necessary to first consider the latter
of the two questions, for, in the event of this being
determined against the contestant, it would have also
disposed of the first issue. In respect to this, the trusts
of the deed of the 19th of February, 1855, are express,
and could only have been fulfilled by a sale of the
property. It contemplates, by its language and its
object, an out and out conversion; and the principle is
clear, as expressed by Lord *St. Leonards* (a), "as a general
rule, there can be no difficulty in saying that a mortgage
under a mere trust for conversion out and out is not
a due execution of the trust." The object of the
trust in the present case was not to raise a sum of
money, in order to pay off a particular charge, but it
was to sell and apply the proceeds according to the
trusts of the deed. The mortgage to the claimants
would therefore be unauthorized and not binding, unless
Mr. *Gamble* had further interests under the deed which

*1871.*

Edinburgh
Life Ass. Co.
v.
Allen.

Judgment.

---

(a) Stoughill v. Anstrey, 1 DeG. M. & G. at p. 643. See also Lewin
on Trusts, p. 315.

1871.

Edinburgh
Life Ass. Co.
v.
Allen.

he could otherwise validly transfer to the claimants. It would appear from the deed and the facts in evidence that Mr. *Gamble* had an interest in the nature of an incumbrance on the property, and to the extent to which he could hold the legal title in the property for the security of that interest, to that extent I think he could well transfer the legal title to the claimants; and the indenture of the 10th November, 1860, would, I think, be effectual to that extent. In *Devaynes* v. *Robinson* (a), the Master of the Rolls, while he held the mortgage not to be authorized, and declared it void, nevertheless declared the mortgagee entitled to stand as a creditor of the estate to the extent to which the mortgage money had been properly applied; and here the trustee could himself hold the land in security for the amount of his own claim against it under the terms of the deed and the transactions between the parties.

Judgment.

My finding, therefore, on the first of the issues referred for the determination of the Court is—

1. That the indenture of the 10th November, 1860, is void as against the contestant and all others entitled to the benefit of the deed of trust of the 19th of February, 1855, but to the extent only to which it purports to convey or assure to the claimants a greater right or interest than that which the said *John W. Gamble* was himself individually entitled to.

2ndly. That the deed of the 24th of June, 1869, is void as against the contestant and the other heiresses-at-law of the said *James Allen*.

---

(a) 24 Beav. 86.

1871.

# THE ATTORNEY GENERAL V. FOWLDS.

*Statute, repeal of, by implication—Indian Lands.*

The Act respecting Indian Lands authorized the Governor in Council
to declare applicable thereto the Act respecting timber on public
lands; an order in Council was issued accordingly; eight years
afterwards another Act was passed which contained a clause authorizing the Governor in Council to declare the timber Act applicable
to Indian Lands, and to repeal any such order in Council and
substitute others, and another clause authorizing the Governor in
Council to make regulations and impose penalties for the sale and
protection of timber on Indian Lands:

*Held*, that the Timber Act continued in force until revoked or altered
by a new order in Council.

On the 29th September, 1870, the Superintendent
General of Indian Affairs granted to the defendant
*Fowlds* a license to cut timber on certain Indian lands
on terms specified in the license. It appeared from the
evidence that the license had been issued in the interest
of the Indians, and that the terms were the highest which
could have been obtained. At the hearing the defendant
was not charged with any impropriety either in procuring a license or in acting under it. The Indians,
however, having been dissatisfied, the license was revoked. The question in issue before the Court was,
whether the license had been legally granted. On that
question depended the defendant's right to the timber
which he had cut before the revocation. This right was
the only matter in issue.

On behalf of the Indians it was contended, that the
supposed authority under which the license had been
issued was not in force at the time of the license
being granted.

The license was in terms of the Consolidated Act, chapter 23, "respecting the sale and management of timber
on public lands." The subsequent Act 23 Victoria, chapter

55—VOL. XVIII. GR.

151, transferred to the province the management of the
Indian affairs, which had previously been managed by the
Imperial authorities.   That Act made the Commissioner
of Crown Lands, for the time being, Chief Superintendent
of Indian Affairs, and enacted, that the Governor in
Council might "from time to time declare the provisions of
the Act respecting the sale and management of the public
lands passed in the" same session, and the Consolidated
Statute as to the timber on public lands,  "or any of
such provisions, to apply to Indian lands or to the timber
on Indian lands; and the same shall thereupon apply
and have effect as if they were expressly recited or embodied in this Act."   Under this Act the Governor in
Council passed an order in Council, dated sixth of May,
1862, declaring the Timber Act thus mentioned to apply
to Indian lands.   This order in Council had never been
revoked; and it was not disputed that, from the time it
was made until the passing of the Act, 31 Victoria,
chapter 42, the provisions of the Timber Act applied to
Indian lands, and had the same effect with respect to
them as if these provisions had been embodied in the
Act 23 Victoria, chapter 151, under which the order in
Council had been issued.

Previous Acts (a), as well as this Act, had authorized the
Governor in Council to declare the laws enacted respecting the sale and management of other public lands to
apply to Indian lands.   Whether this power had ever
been exercised did not appear from the evidence in the
cause.

The Act 31 Victoria, chapter 42, was "an Act providing for the organization of the Department of the
Secretary of State of Canada, and for the management
of Indian and Ordnance lands."   It provided amongst
other things that "the Secretary of State shall be the

_____

(a) 16 Vic. ch. 159, sec. 15; 22 Vic. ch. 22; 23 Vic. ch. 22.

Superintendent General of Indian Affairs, and shall as
such have the control and management of the lands and
property of the Indians in Canada." The Act gave the
Secretary of State some new powers in regard to Indian
lands; authorized the Governor in Council to make regulations from time to time for the protection and
management of such lands and the timber thereon, and
for these purposes to impose penalties (a) ; and it re-en-
acted almost all the provisions of the Act 23 Victoria,
chapter 151, in nearly the same language. It contained
a clause (b) corresponding with the seventh clause of the
previous Act (c) as to the power of the Governor in
Council to apply to Indian lands the Acts, Consolidated
Canada, chapter 23 (timber), and 23 Victoria, chapter
2, but in addition gave the Governor in Council power
to from time to time repeal orders in Council passed
for that purpose, and to substitute others. The part
of the clause referring to Indian lands was as follows: "The Governor in Council may direct that the
said two Acts or either of them, or any part or parts of
either or both of them shall apply to the Indian lands
in the provinces of Quebec and Ontario, or to any of
the said lands, and may from time to time repeal any
such order in Council, and make any other or others
instead thereof." No new order in Council was made
after the passing of this Act.

The cause came on for the examination of witnesses
and hearing at the Spring Sittings 1871, at Lindsay.

Mr. *Bain*, for the informant.

Mr. *Crooks*, Q.C., and Mr. *Moss*, contra.

Mowat, V. C.—The Department considered that, by
virtue of the order in Council of August 23, 1862, the

1871.

Attorney
General
v.
Fowlds.

August 22.

---

(a) sec. 37.        (b) sec. 38,        (c) 23 Vic. ch. 151, sec. 7.

Timber Act continued applicable under the last Act (*a*). The principal argument now urged against this is, that the circumstance of the last Act giving to the Governor in Council authority to apply the previous Acts to Indian lands implies, that they were not to be applicable unless the Governor in Council should thereafter by order in Council make them so.

Now it must be assumed that the Legislature when passing the last Act were aware that the Timber Act was then in force with respect to Indian lands as fully as if its provisions had been embodied in the previous Act (*b*); and it would be a very strong thing to hold that the provisions so in force and known to be in force were intended to be repealed by the form of enactment referred to. Acts of Parliament often contain enactments of old and recognized rules as if they were new, but the Courts do not in such cases hold that such enactments unsettle the existing law; the implied opinion of the Legislature that the provisions are new is not construed as an authoritative declaration that they are new, or as an enactment that the Courts are so to regard them.

It is further to be observed, that the presumption of law is against a repeal by implication. Then, in the present case, the policy of the Legislature at the time of passing the last Act, as shewn by its provisions generally, affords no argument in favor of an intention to repeal by Act of the Legislature; but the contrary. The Timber Act had at this time been applicable to Indian lands for eight years; by the new Act, confessedly, the Governor in Council might at any moment, again put the same Timber Act in force with respect to those lands; the provisions of the Timber Act, when examined, appear as beneficial and desirable for Indian lands as for any other; there might be considerable

---

(*a*) 31 Vic. ch. 42.                    (*b*) 23 Vic. ch. 15.

inconvenience from there being a Legislative repeal 1871.
without any special provision for past matters ; and
I think that such a construction of the new Act is not a
necessary or probable implication. I think that I shall
best carry out the intention of the Legislature, and shall
do no violence to the language of the Act, by holding,
in accordance with the view on which the license now
in question was granted, that, under sections 35 and
37 (a), the Governor in Council had power to, from
time to time, withdraw Indian lands from the provisions
of the Timber Act, and to, from time to time, direct that
they should be again applicable, but that, meanwhile,
and until the Governor in Council should act, the provisions in question continued in force.

The information must therefore be dismissed. I believe the Attorney General raises no question as to the
propriety in that case of the defendant getting his costs.

Attorney<br>General<br>v.<br>Fowlds.

Judgment.

---

## ABELL v. McPHERSON. [IN APPEAL*].

*Patent for invention—Novelty.*

The plaintiff had obtained a patent for an improved gearing for driving
the cylinder of threshing machines ; and the gearing was a considerable improvement : but, it appearing that the same gearing had
been previously used for other machines, though no one had before
applied it to threshing machines—it was *held*, [affirming the decree
of the Court below,] that the novelty was not sufficient under the
Statute to sustain the patent.

This was an appeal by the plaintiff from the decree
pronounced by Vice Chancellor *Mowat* dismissing his
bill with costs ; as reported *ante* Volume XVII., p. 23.

Mr. *Blake*, Q.C., and Mr. *McLennan*, for the appeal.

---

(a) 31 Vic. ch. 42.

* [*Present.*—DRAPER, C, J., MORRISON, J., MOWAT, V. C., WILSON,
GWYNNE, and GALT, JJ.]

1871.        Mr. *Crooks*, Q. C., and Mr. *Hodgins*, contra.

Abell
v.
McPherson.        At the close of the argument the Court intimated an
opinion in favor of the respondents.  On a subsequent
day the Chief Justice said he had since read the Vice
Chancellor's judgment, and, concurring in his conclusion,
he saw no reason for discussing any further the question
of fact upon which it mainly, if not exclusively, turned.

Sept. 8th.    *Per Curiam.*—Appeal dismissed with costs.

---

### HEENAN V. DEWAR.   [IN APPEAL.*]

*Nuisance —Acquiescence.*

In 1861, while defendant was engaged in erecting buildings for a
tannery on land adjoining the plaintiff's premises, the plaintiff encouraged the defendant to proceed with his project ; the buildings
were proceeded with, and business in them was commenced the
same year ; in 1863 additions were made to the buildings with the
plaintiff's knowledge and acquiescence ; and the plaintiff made no
complaint about the business until 1868, though all this time it had
been carried on, and the plaintiff had been residing on the premises
adjoining

*Held,* [affirming the decree of the Court below,] that by his conduct
he had debarred himself from obtaining relief in equity on the
ground of a tannery being a nuisance.

Statement.        This was an appeal by the plaintiff from the decree of
the Court below dismissing the bill with costs ; as
reported *ante* Volume XVII, page 638.

For the facts, reference is made to that report.

Mr. *Crooks*, Q.C., and Mr. *Cattanach*, for appellant.

Mr. *S. H. Blake,* contra.

---

*     [*Present.*—DRAPER, C. J., MORRISON, J., MOWAT, V. C., WILSON,
GWYNNE, and GALT, JJ.]

DRAPER, C. J.—In the conclusion at which I have arrived, I mainly rely on the evidence of the plaintiff's own conduct in regard, 1st. to the encouragement given by him to the defendant to go into the tanning business, and therefore to put up the requisite buildings and works; and, 2nd, to his silent acquiescence for several years after the plaintiff had acted in pursuance of such encouragement. In the face of this it would require very strong, almost incontrovertible, evidence of nuisance, before an injunction should issue to prohibit the defendant from continuing the business, thereby rendering his outlay and investment an immediate, and perhaps, in some respects, a total loss. I do not find in the evidence adduced by the plaintiff, and met as it is on the part of the defendant, enough to warrant a decision which must inevitably produce such a result, or to lead me to think that the judgment of the Court below ought to have been other than it was. My opinion at the close of the argument was against the plaintiff, and I have on consideration found no satisfactory reason for altering it. The complaint in respect to the hair was the only thing that made me hesitate, and this not being, as the Vice Chancellor remarks in his judgment, complained of in the bill, is not, so far as I see, of sufficient consequence in its effects as regards the plaintiff to call for the suppression of the defendant's tannery, though, if continued, it may entitle the plaintiff to damages at law.

I think the appeal should be dismissed with costs.

*Per Curiam.*—Appeal dismissed with costs.

1871.

Heenan
v.
Dewar.

Sept. 8.

Judgment.

BARKER v. ECCLES.　[IN APPEAL.*]

*Mortgage—Priorities—Merger.*

There were two mortgages on certain land. *O.,* having notice of the
second mortgage, bought the first mortgage, and, at or about the same
time, the equity of redemption, and gave to the party who was selling
to him the first mortgage a new mortgage for the sum *O.* was to pay
therefor. *O.* conveyed portions of the land to his sons in terms
subject to the mortgage which he had so given; and he afterwards
paid that mortgage off :

*Held,* [affirming the decree of the Court below,] that these facts were
not sufficient evidence of an intention to merge under the statute
22 Victoria, chapter 87, and that the second mortgage had not
acquired priority over the mortgage purchased by *O.* [MOWAT,
V. C., *dubitante.*]

This was an appeal by a mortgagee, *Thomas Pittman,*
from the decree of the Court below, as reported *ante*
Volume XVII., page 631, confirming the report of the
Master finding that *Henry B. Ostrander* had priority
over the appellant in respect of a mortgage theretofore
assigned to *Ostrander.*

Statement

All the parties claiming any interest in the case
derived their title under one *John H. Conolly,* and the
deed through which he became entitled to the land in
question was registered in the year 1830.

He, by deed dated 10th February, 1852, quitted claim
or otherwise conveyed these lands to *John McSloy.*
This deed was not registered until the 16th October, 1857.

*John H. Connolly,* also by deed dated 1st May, 1854,
and registered 30th August, 1854, mortgaged these lands
in fee, to certain trustees, whom the plaintiffs represent.
As between them and *John McSloy* and those claiming
under him their title and priority as mortgagees were not
disputed.

---

* *Present.*—DRAPER, C.J., RICHARDS, C.J., MORRISON, J., WILSON, J.
MOWAT, V.C., GALT and GWYNNE, JJ.

On the 12th October, 1860, *John McSloy* mortgaged
these premises to *John H. Connolly* to secure payment
to him of $1520 and interest. This deed was registered
16th October, 1860.

On the 15th January, 1862, by deed registered on
29th of same month, *John McSloy* mortgaged the same
premises to *Thomas Pittman* to secure payment of
$329.

On the 5th April, 1862, *John H. Connolly* assigned
the mortgage of the 12th October, 1860, to *William
Eccles*. This assignment was registered on 7th April,
1862.

On the 28th May, 1862, *William Eccles*, by deed
registered on 30th of same month, assigned the same
mortgage to *George W. Pierce*.

On the 15th March, 1864, *John McSloy*, together
with several other parties, by deed registered 30th
October, 1865, bargained and sold all the estate, right,
title, &c., at law and in equity, as well in possession as
expectancy which they or either of them had in the same
premises to *Francis J. McSloy*.

On the 20th October, 1865, *George W. Pierce*, by
deed registered on 30th of same month, assigned the
premises conveyed to him by *William Eccles* to *Henry
B. Ostrander*, the respondent.

On the same 20th October *Francis J. McSloy* by
deed, registered on the same day as and next after the
deed last above stated, conveyed the same premises to
the respondent.

Ever since the registration of the mortgage of 1st
May, 1854, the legal estate in the premises remained

1871.  vested in the trustees under the marriage settlement

of *Shepherd Smith* and *Harriet* his wife; and whatever estate *John McSloy* took became vested in *John H. Connolly* by the mortgage deed of 12th October, 1860, subject to redemption. On the 20th October, 1865, in addition to the two instruments of that date already mentioned, there was a mortgage given by *Henry B. Ostrander* on the same lands to *George W. Pierce*, to secure to *Pierce* the payment of $1212, which was registered on the following day; being fully nine days before the registration of the deeds from *Pierce* and *Francis J. McSloy* to *Henry B. Ostrander* himself.

The Master, by his report, 8th June, 1870, found that the mortgage assigned by *Pierce* to *Ostrander* was, as against *Pittman*, a subsisting mortgage on the property and retained its priority over *Pittman's* mortgage. The Chancellor on appeal affirmed this report;—23rd

November following.

From this order of the Chancellor, *Pittman* appealed, on the grounds, that the evidence did not sustain the claim of *Henry B. Ostrander* for $2,472.55, principal and interest upon the mortgage made by *John McSloy* to one *John H. Connolly*, dated 12th October, 1860, which mortgage was on or about the 28th May, 1862, assigned to one *George W. Pierce*, who, on or about the 20th October, 1865, executed a deed of quit claim of the said mortgaged premises to the said *Henry B. Ostrander*; that the respondent never was the owner of the mortgage debt secured by the said mortgage, nor did he ever obtain an assignment of the said mortgage; that the respondent took the said deed of quit claim of the said mortgaged premises from the said *George W. Pierce*, for the purpose of getting in and perfecting his title as purchaser of the said premises, and not with any view of keeping the said mortgage alive, and the legal estate of the mortgagee, when conveyed to the said

*Ostrander*, merged in the fee of the said premises, which became vested in the said respondent, under and by virtue of the conveyance to him, made by one *Francis J. McSloy*, dated the 20th October, 1865; that the facts —that the said respondent executed a conveyance by way of mortgage, of 20th October, 1865, securing the sum of $1212, in part consideration for the quit claim deed to him above mentioned, and afterwards conveyed the said premises by deeds of bargain and sale, dated respectively 3rd December, 1866, to *James Ostrander* and *Russell H. Ostrander*, subject to said mortgage to *Pierce*, and not subject to the said mortgage to *Connolly*—shew clearly that the said respondent never contemplated nor had any intention of keeping the said mortgage to *Connolly* alive, but the said mortgage debt was satisfied by a cash payment made, and mortgage to *Pierce*, given by *Henry B. Ostrander* to the said *George W. Pierce* at the time of obtaining from him the quit claim deed as aforesaid; and the claim of *Henry B. Ostrander* is subsequent in priority to that of the appellant, and ought to have been so found by the Master.

Mr. *McDougall*, for the appeal.

It is contended on behalf of the appellant that the intention of the parties was, to pay off *Pierce's* mortgage, and to create a new mortgage for the unpaid balance of purchase money, which mortgage contains no reference or allusion to any existing incumbrance. He obtained also an assignment of the equity of redemption without any such reference. The effect of this was, therefore, that the first mortgage was not kept alive (a). *Ostrander's* evidence shews that he sold the property, and conveyed it as being free from all incumbrances other than the mortgage executed by himself in favor of *Pierce* on the occasion of his purchase from him.

1871.

Barker
v.
Eccles.

Statement.

---

(a) 1 Fisher on Mortgages, 397,

It is true *Pierce* states in his evidence that his intention was that the mortgage held by him should be kept
alive; the intention, however, of the owner of the estate
is what must prevail; that it is contended was clearly
shewn to be that the mortgage which he had obtained
the transfer of was not to be kept on foot.

He referred, amongst other authorities to *Astley* v.
*Mills* (a), *Tyler* v. *Lake* (b), *Hood* v. *Phillips* (c),
*Gower* v. *Gower* (d), *Tyrwhitt* v. *Tyrwhitt* (e), *Beattie*
v. *Grant* (f), *Henderson* v. *Mills* (g), *Mayhew* on Merger, 121.

Mr. *Ferguson*, contra.

DRAPER, C. J.—The presumable order of the three
conveyances of 20th October, 1869, seems to have been,
1st. The assignment by *Pierce* to *Ostrander* of the
mortgage securing $1520, for until that was executed

*Ostrander* had no interest in the property; 2nd. The
conveyance by *Francis J. McSloy* of the equity of
redemption; and last, the mortgage from *Ostrander* to
*Pierce* to secure to the latter $1212, which I assume
to have been the balance due to *Pierce* on the sale of the
mortgage.

The general rule is stated in *Hood* v. *Phillips* to
this effect, that where the same person becomes absolutely entitled to an estate and to a sum of money which
is charged upon it, the Court will deem the charge to
have become merged in the estate, or to have become
extinguished, unless it shall appear that the owner of the
estate and of the charge intended otherwise, and to shew
this intention direct and presumptive evidence may be
resorted to.

---

(a) 1 Sim 298.　　　　　　(b) 4 Sim. 851.
(c) 8 Beav. 513.　　　　　　(d) 1 Cox 53.
(e) 32 Beav. 249.　　　　　　(f) 18 Gr. 317.
(g) 11 Gr. 218.

In another case, *Tyrwhitt* v. *Tyrwhitt* (a), three tests are given to determine the intention of the owner of the charge ; 1. An actual expression of the intention ; 2. When the form and character of the acts done are consistent only with keeping the charge alive ; 3. Where it appears to be for the interest of the owner of the inheritance that it should be kept alive.

The case of *Grier* v. *Shaw* (b) may be referred to, to shew that under certain circumstances the Court will presume an intention on the part of the owner of a charge on his estate, that it should not merge where such merger would let in other charges in priority.

If the owner, on the other hand, mortgage the estate absolutely without noticing the charge, it will merge. And a charge secured by a term has been held to merge contrary to the admitted intention of the owner where he settled the estate, covenanting fully that it was free from incumbrances. (See *Fisher* on Mortgages, 2nd ed. 795, where *Tyler* v. *Lake* (c), and *Gower* v. *Gower* (d), are respectively cited in support of these positions.)

Were it necessary to decide this case upon the authority of decided cases, I must confess I have not yet made up my mind in support of the respondent's contention. See *Fisher* on Mortgages, 2nd edition, 786-7, referring to *Mocatta* v. *Murgatroyd*, *Greswold* v. *Marsham*, *Toulmin* v. *Sleeve*, *Watts* v. *Symes* (e). But it appears to me to fall within the proper construction of the Consolidated Statute of Upper Canada, chapter 87, section 1, which enacts that any mortgagee of freehold or leasehold property, or any assignee of such mortgagee may take and receive from the mortgagor or his assignee, a release of the equity of

---

(a) 32 Beav. 244 ; 9 Jur. N. S. 346.  (b) 10 Hare 76.
(c) 4 Sim. 351.  (d) 1 Cox, 53.
(e) 1 DeG. McN. & G. 240 ; S. C. 16 Jur. 114.

1871.

Barker
v.
Eccles.

redemption in such property, or may purchase the same under any power of sale in the mortgage, or any judgment or decree without thereby merging the mortgage debt as against any subsequent mortgagee.

*Ostrander*, being the assignee of the mortgage given by *John McSloy* to *John H. Connolly*, subsequently acquired the equity of redemption from *Francis J. McSloy*, the assignee of the mortgagor. The statute prevents a merger, and preserves the priority in favour of the respondent.

I think the appeal must be dismissed with costs.

MOWAT, V. C., intimated that he had not been able to see his way to the conclusion arrived at by the other Judges.

*Per Curiam.*—Appeal dismissed with costs. [MOWAT, V. C., *dubitante.*]

---

## MCGREGOR V. RAPELJE. [IN APPEAL.*]

*Marriage settlement—Collateral relations—Deed, sons to father.*

A widower, on his second marriage, executed a settlement which made provision for his children by his first marriage:
*Held*, [affirming the decree of the Court below] that the provision could not be defeated by a sale for value by the settlor.

A father having obtained a conveyance of the interest of his sons under a marriage settlement, for an alleged consideration, which did not exceed one-fifth of the value of such interest, and which was never paid, the transaction was set aside after the death of the settlor and one of the sons, in a suit by the devisees of the deceased son.

Statement. This was an appeal by the defendants from the decree made on the hearing, and reported *ante* Volume XVII., page 38.

---

* *Present.*—DRAPER, C.J., RICHARDS, C.J., MORRISON, J., WILSON, J., MOWAT, V.C., GWYNNE and GALT, JJ.

Mr. *Crooks*, Q.C., and Mr. *Hoskin*, for the appeal.

Mr. *Blake*, Q.C., and Mr. *S. Blake*, contra.

Mr. *Proudfoot*, for *Peter Wyckoff Rapelje*, in the same interest.

DRAPER, C. J.—*Duncan McGregor*, senior, being a widower with several sons, all infants, on the 8th of January, 1846, executed a deed, in contemplation of marriage with *Helen Rapelje*, in consideration of which marriage he conveyed to *A. A. Rapelje* (since deceased) and to defendant, *Peter W. Rapelje*, certain lands in fee to his own use, until the solemnization of the marriage; and thereafter in trust for *Helen Rapelje* for life, as a provision for herself, for the children of the settlor, and the children of the intended marriage, such life-estate to be in lieu of dower; and after the death of *Helen*, in trust for the children living at the date of the deed, or thereafter to be born, as tenants in common. The trustees had power to sell, and were to invest the proceeds for the benefit of the same parties.

The marriage took place. On the 2nd of November, 1861, the wife died, and on the 13th of December, 1861, the only child of the second marriage died unmarried and intestate, leaving her surviving her father and his two sons—*Duncan* the younger and the defendant *Abraham R. McGregor*. It is stated in the answer of the latter, that he had another brother, *John Alexander*, who died on the 25th of September, 1847, intestate and unmarried. The answer of *Peter W. Rapelje*, the surviving trustee, states that, at the date of the settlement, *Duncan* and *Abraham* were the only two living children of the settlor. *Duncan* was about two years older than his brother *Abraham*, who was born in 1834.

The settlor died (the date not proved), having made a will, dated the 8th of February, 1864, by which he devised to his son, the defendant *Abraham*, all his real and personal estate, subject to payment of his debts and legacies.

*Duncan*, the son, died before his father, having by will, dated the 21st of January, 1864, devised to the plaintiffs all his real estate upon trust.

In 1857 or 1858, *Duncan*, the father, acting under a power of attorney from the trustees of the settlement, sold to the Great Western Railway Company a part of the lands, and received $3,000, the purchase money. On the 16th of November, 1861, the defendant *Peter W. Rapelje*, as surviving trustee, filed a bill to compel him to pay over that money. Very soon after the death of his daughter *Helen*, *Duncan*, the father, obtained from his two sons a deed, dated the 16th of December, 1861, whereby they, for an alleged con-
sideration of $3,000, conveyed to him all their interest in the real estate and other funds in which they were interested under the settlement of January, 1846, which deed the father set up against the trustee, who thereupon abandoned the suit. The plaintiffs, however, ask no relief against him. *Duncan*, the son, was living with his father when this deed was executed. No consideration was paid at the time of the execution; but on the defence a bond was proved (by proof of handwriting, the sole subscribing witness being dead), dated the 16th of December, whereby *Duncan*, the father, bound himself to his two sons in a penalty of $3,000; conditioned to convey and assure to the obligees property sufficient in value to satisfy and discharge $3,000. It does not appear that either of the sons had any knowledge of the existence of this bond, nor is it shewn when it first came to light. It purports to have been witnessed by the same person who witnessed the execution of the deed of release from the sons. *Abraham R. McGregor*, in his deposition, swears that this deed was sent to him by his

father, with a request that he would sign and return it
by mail—that he signed it at Windsor—he cannot tell
at what date—he knew of no reason for signing it—did
not read it—did not consider that he was thereby
releasing his claims under the marriage settlement—
did not again hear of it until after his father's death—
though he subsequently acknowledged his signature to
it before *Henry Waters* (the sole subscribing witness to
it and the bond) at Chatham. He also swears he
received nothing for signing it, and that he did not
hear of the bond until after his father's death.

With regard to the execution by *Duncan*, the evidence is very meagre, and there is not a word which
shews any explanation given to him, or any more knowledge than his brother had of the contents, or object, or
effect of the release, nor that he received any consideration, or was aware of the existence of the bond.

On the part of the defence, the validity of so much
of the settlement as confers any benefit on the children
of the first marriage has been questioned as being a
voluntary settlement, and at an end by the sale to the
Great Western Railway Company of a certain part of
the land, as to which it appears to be assumed that the
sale was made by the settlor for a valuable consideration
paid to himself for his title to the property. It may be
gathered from the evidence that *Duncan*, the settlor,
acted in the arrangement with the Railway Company
under a power of attorney from the trustees, which may
have authorized him to execute a conveyance in their
name; and possibly such conveyance, so far from being
in derogation of the marriage settlement, may have been
an intended execution by the trustees or surviving
trustee of the power of sale vested in them by that
instrument. It is not likely the Railway Company
would have paid their money without a full investigation
of the title.

57—VOL. XVIII. GR.

But, however this may possibly be, no such point has been raised. The matter for our consideration as regards the settlement, being voluntary, and being annulled by the sale for value to the Railway Company, was argued on the assumption that the settlor had made this sale and conveyance.

The latest authority which I have seen on this question is referred to in the Court below—*Clarke* v. *Wright* (a). There it was held that a limitation in a marriage settlement made by a woman in favour of her illegitimate son was not fraudulent and void against a subsequent mortgagee. *Newstead* v. *Searles* (b) (the earliest case on the question, I believe) is referred to. This case is not approved of in the 14th edition of Sugden (c), where it is said that Lord *Mansfield*, in *Chapman* v. *Emery* (d), doubted Lord *Hardwicke's* saying, that where a woman about to marry a second husband, makes a settlement of her estate upon her children by her first husband, such settlement has been held good. With the greatest deference for that very learned writer, it appears to me Lord *Mansfield's* doubt applied to a passage just before cited from *Townshend* v. *Windham* (e), in these words : " If there is a voluntary conveyance of real estate or chattel interest by one not indebted at the time ; if that voluntary conveyance was for a child, and no particular evidence or badge of fraud to deceive or defraud subsequent creditors, that will be good, though the party afterwards becomes indebted." In *Chapman* v. *Emery*, the settlement was post nuptial, though prior to the mortgage, and *Newstead* v. *Searles* was not cited. But, in *Doe* v. *Routledge*, Lord *Mansfield* states the case of *Newstead* v. *Searles* without the slightest intimation of doubt or disapproval.

---

(a) 6 H. & N. 846 ; S.C. 7 Jur. N.S. 1032.
(b) 1 Atk. 266.                    (c) V. & P. 716.
(d) Cowp. 278, 280.                (e) 2 Ves. Senr. 10.

I feel bound to follow the decision in *Newstead*
v. *Searles*, which is fully sustained by *Clarke* v. *Wright*,
and of which *Blackburn, J.*, said, that he found no case
in which it had been questioned or disapproved.

The release is then the only point to be considered
as to the settlement, and this must, I think, be determined upon the principles on which courts of equity
usually act in cases of a gift or sale made by a son, of
his own estate, to his father.

Professedly this was a sale for a money consideration,
while in fact no such consideration ever passed, nor was
there any agreement between the parties that it should
pass. The father did not contemplate, as is plainly
apparent from his bond, which came to light after his
death, and of which the surviving son has sworn he was
till after that event ignorant, the payment of any
money consideration. Nor was the release founded
upon any previously made agreement or understanding
between these parties that it should pass. *Abraham*
never heard of it until he received the instrument by
mail in a letter from his father, requesting that he would
execute it; and he swears that he did execute it without
reading it, and without supposing that he thereby
released his claims under the settlement; and that he
never was paid any part of the expressed consideration.

Of the execution of the release by the other son,
*Duncan*, there is no direct proof; and what evidence
there is with regard to him generally, is calculated to
lead to the conclusion that he was a favorable subject
for the exercise of parental influence. The father's
own account of the transaction goes far to shew that he
did not explain the real effect of the deed to *Duncan*
any more than he did to *Abraham*. His assertion,
" the boys have perfect confidence in me, and they
know what the release is for," is contradicted by

1871.

McGregor
v.
Rapelje.

Judgment.

*Abraham*, and is unproved as regards *Duncan*, and is at variance with the language of the instrument itself, which represents a money consideration actually paid. Contrast these facts with the language of the Master of the Rolls, in *Cooke* v. *Lamotte* (a) : " In every transaction in which a person obtains by voluntary donation a benefit from another, it is necessary that he should be able to establish that the person giving him that benefit did so voluntarily and deliberately, knowing what he was doing ; and if this be not done, the transaction cannot stand.''

Under the circumstances, I fully adopt the opinion of the Court below with regard to this release. Even if the expressed consideration had been paid, it was wholly inadequate. I think the release has rightly been declared void as against both the sons ; and then the marriage settlement, even if voluntary, would be

unaffected so far as against the settlor and his heirs. Limitations in favour of collaterals are binding. See *Davenport* v. *Bishop* (b), on the argument of which case the appellant's counsel admitted as an exception to the rule in the case of *Johnson* v. *Legard* (c), the case where a father, by a settlement on his second marriage, made a provision for the children of the first. See also *Smith* v. *Cherrill* (d), as to the distinction between collateral relatives and children of the settlor by a former marriage.

As to laches—no ground for it.

Appeal dismissed, with this variation : that it be referred to the Master, to ascertain whether the settlor had three sons, or only two.

---

(a) 15 Beav. at p. 240.          (b) 1 Phil. 698.
(c) 3 Madd. 283.                  (d) L. R. 4 Eq. 390.

It was afterwards admitted that there had been four children entitled to share ; that two had died intestate, leaving their father their heir ; and that *Duncan's* (the son) share of the estate was one-fourth only.

The decree was varied accordingly ; and the defendants ordered to pay the costs of the appeal.

---

## Mossop v. Mason.—[In Appeal.*]

### *Sale of goodwill—Injunction.*

The defendant sold to the plaintiff the goodwill of the business of an innkeeper which he was carrying on in London, in this province, under the name of "Mason's Hotel," or "Western Hotel : "

*Held,* [affirming the decree of the Court below] that the sale of the goodwill implied an obligation, enforcible in equity, that the defendant would not thereafter resume or carry on the business of an innkeeper in London, under the name of "Mason's Hotel," or "Western Hotel ; " and would not resume or carry on the business of an innkeeper, under any name or in any manner, in the premises in question ; and would not hold out in any way that he was carrying on business in continuation of, or succession to the business formerly carried on by him under the said names, or either of them.

*Held,* also, [varying the decree of the Court below,] that a covenant in the agreement that the vendor should pay $4000 in the event of his carrying on business as an innkeeper within ten years, was void as an undue restraint of trade, but did not relieve the vendor from the implied obligation involved in the sale of the goodwill.

The appellant, *John Mason,* held the hotel in the town of London known as "Mason's Hotel" and the "Western Hotel," by an informal instrument in the nature of a lease, dated in January, 1865, at an annual rental of $800, for a term of five years ; and on the 1st January, 1868, he made an agreement under seal with the respondents, *Jonathan Mossop* and *Thomas Mossop* (the latter of whom subsequently left this pro-

Statement[1]

---

vince), to sell to them "all his goods, chattels, and effects, and good-will of the business carried on by him" in that hotel, for the sum of $2,003. He further agreed to pay $4,000 to the respondents if he directly or indirectly continued, commenced, or carried on, the business or calling of an innkeeper within the term of ten years.

This agreement was prepared by the respondents' solicitor, and on its production to be executed, the appellant's solicitor insisted that it should be confined in its restraint to London ; the appellant himself said it was not necessary, as he had no intention of resuming the business : the time was, however, limited to ten years, and then it was executed. No inquiry was made as to the appellant's title, but it was understood that he was a tenant, and that Mr. *Frank Smith* was his landlord. He told the respondents, in answer to an inquiry, that he held for five years, three of which had run out, and said he had no lease, but that *Smith* held a bond against him. It appeared that the appellant could not write ; he only put his mark to the instruments between him and the respondents, and between him and *Smith*.

As soon as the agreement with the respondents was executed, the appellant went out of possession, and the respondents entered, with the consent of the landlord, who, as respondents stated, accepted them as tenants from month to month. About nine months afterwards, the stables were burnt down by accident. The landlord did not rebuild, and, after some delay, the respondents gave up the premises to him. On the 1st October, 1868, they moved to the " City Hotel," situate in London, at some considerable distance from the " Western," and there carried on the same business of innkeepers.

Mr. *Smith* stated that one of the respondents spoke to him about the hotel before he took it from the appellant, and was told how long appellant's term had to run, but did not (according to Mr. *Smith's* recollection) ask about any writing. But he told this respondent, that as appellant had not spoken to him about the matter, he could say nothing about it. Soon after, both respondents came to him, but made no proposition. He made no agreement with them, and did not accept them as tenants. As soon as he heard of the fire he went to London, and told one of the respondents that he would at once have the stables rebuilt; that respondent seemed indifferent about it, and spoke of going to the "City Hotel," as they had not enough to do, and admitted that he had signed a lease the day before for the "City Hotel." *Smith* then went to the appellant and told him he did not release him from his agreement, and proposed to him to rebuild the stables larger, and to give him a new lease for seven years at $1,000 per annum. The appellant spoke of his obligation to respondents, and *Smith* said he would see him harmless.

The appellant thinking, as he stated, that the respondents were not able to indemnify him against the rent, if he had to pay under the agreement of 1865, took the premises again at an increased rent, and had thenceforward continued to carry on business there.

The respondents thereupon instituted this suit, for specific performance, and an injunction, and other relief.

An interlocutory motion was made for an injunction, as reported *ante* Volume XVI., page 302.

The cause was heard (see Volume XVII., page 360), when the following decree was pronounced :—

"1. This Court doth order and decree that a writ of injunction do issue out of this Court, perpetually restraining the defendant from resuming or carrying on

1871.

Mossop
v.
Mason.

Statement.

the business of an inn-keeper or hotel-keeper at or in
the neighbourhood of London, under the name of
" *Mason's* Hotel " or " Western Hotel," and from
resuming or carrying on the business of an inn-keeper
or hotel-keeper under any name, or in any manner, in
the premises at the corner of Mark Lane and Fullarton
Street, now or formerly occupied by him, and from in
any manner holding out that he is carrying on business
in continuation of, or succession to, the business carried
on by him under the said names, or either of them.

" 2. And the said defendant having submitted and
undertaken in and by the order made in this cause, and
bearing date the second day of December last, to stay,
or procure to be stayed, all proceedings at law for the
recovery of the unpaid purchase money upon the contract between the plaintiffs and the defendant in the
pleadings in this cause mentioned, until the hearing of
this cause, this Court doth order and decree that the
said stay of proceedings be continued.

" 3. And this Court doth order and decree that it be
referred to the Master of this Court at London to take
an account of the damage or loss sustained by the
plaintiffs by reason of the said defendant having resumed and carried on the business of an inn-keeper
or hotel-keeper in the premises at the corner of Mark
Lane and Fullarton Street, in the city of London, as
in the said pleadings mentioned, and to tax to the
plaintiffs their costs of this suit, and add them to the
amount of such damages.

" 4. And the said Master is also to take an account
of what is due to the defendant for principal money and
interest in respect of the unpaid purchase money upon
the said contract between the plaintiffs and defendant
and set the same off against the amount found due to
the plaintiffs for damages and costs as aforesaid.

"5. And this Court doth order that the party or 1871.
parties against whom the balance shall be found upon
taking such accounts do, within one month after the Mossop
said Master shall have made his report, pay to the party
or parties in whose favor the balance shall be found the
amount of such balance."

From this decree the defendant appealed on the
grounds that if the jurisdiction of the Court of Chancery,
in the absence of express contract, to restrain the vendor
of a good will from setting up anew the same business,
in the same place, depends on the power of the Court to
restrain the fraudulent use by the vendor of his vendee's
property, no case was made out for relief upon any such
ground ; and fraud, although alleged by the respondents,
was negatived by the evidence ; that the respondents
having taken an express covenant can have no right to
the relief granted on the ground of an implied covenant
or stipulation, or on any other ground than that to Statement.
which they are confined, namely, that of the express
covenant; that the express covenant is void as being in
restraint of trade ; that the appropriate remedy on the
express covenant is at law and not in equity ; that no
consideration was given for the sale of the goodwill
alleged to be evidenced by the writing ; that the respondents should have indemnified and saved harmless,
the appellant against the rent and other obligations
imposed on him in respect of the Western Hotel premises, but they refused so to do, and it was in consequence of such refusal and their conduct in the premises
that the appellant was obliged to do what he did in the
premises, and respondents should not under such circumstances be relieved in equity ; that the respondents
having left the premises the appellant was entitled to
commence the business of an innkeeper there ; that at
any rate, the respondents are not entitled to enjoin the
appellant from commencing anew and under a fresh
name the business of an innkeeper in the premises in

58—VOL. XVIII. GR.

question ; that the respondents were guilty of laches, and delay, and abandonment of their rights so as to disentitle them to equitable relief; that the respondents ought to be left to their remedy at law; and that the Court has no jurisdiction to restrain the action by the decree restrained.

In support of the decree the plaintiffs submitted, that having regard to the nature of the business, the relative positions of the parties, and the other circumstances established by the evidence, the said covenant is valid; that the said covenant is distributive, and so much of it as relates to a continuance of the business therein referred to is valid, and is in substance a covenant against carrying on such business within such a distance as to be in competition with the respondents; that the appellant is estopped by his conduct at the time of the execution of the said agreement from objecting to the respondents enforcing such covenant to the extent ordered by the decree; that the appellant represented, at the time of the purchase by the respondents of the said business, that he did not intend ever to enter into or engage in the said business again, and the appellant should now be compelled to make good such representation to the extent at least of not entering into competition with the respondents; that if the said covenant be, as the appellant contends, void, the plaintiffs are entitled to the relief afforded by the said decree, inasmuch as they are purchasers for value of the said goodwill; that the respondents did protect the appellant against the rent or obligations (if any) proved to have been imposed upon him in respect of the said " Western Hotel " premises, and never refused to indemnify and save harmless the appellant; that even if any lease to the appellant were proved, the appellant would be estopped from setting up any liability on his part in respect of the said "Western Hotel" premises, by his representations to the respondents that no lease thereof was in existence, and by his suppression of the fact of

its existence; that even if the appellant had been 1871.
allowed to remain, or were still under any such liability
to the owner of the said "Western Hotel" premises as
alleged, yet any contract of the respondents to indemnify
him against the same, did not arise from, and was not
referred to, in the said agreement, and was not a condition of the performance by the appellant of his said
covenant or agreement, but was enforcible by the
appellant as an independent agreement; that no justification was shewn by the appellant for the course he
pursued; and that the respondents leaving the premises
in which the appellant formerly carried on business did
not entitle the appellant to re-commence the said
business in the said premises.

Mossop
v.
Mason.

Mr. *S. Blake*, and Mr. *Meredith*, for the appellant,
in addition to the cases cited in the Court below, referred
to *Ward* v. *Byrne* (a), *Dickson* v. *Zizinia* (b), *The Great
Northern Railway Co.* v. *The Eastern Counties Railway Co.* (c), *Chissum* v. *Dewes* (d), *Smith* v. *Everitt* (e),
*Austin* v. *Boys* (f), *Addison* on Contracts, 632-3, and
889; *Broome's* Legal Maxims, 626, 631; *Drewry* on
Injunction, 234-5; *Kerr* on Injunction, 495.

Argument.

Mr. *Moss*, and Mr. *McGee*, contra, cited *The Leather
Cloth Co.* v. *Lorsont* (g), *Brigge* v. *Parkinson* (h),
*Mallon* v. *May* (i), *Green* v. *Price* (j), *Grace* v. *White-
head* (k), *England* v. *Downs* (l), *Hitchcock* v. *Coker* (m),
*Tallis* v. *Tallis* (n), *Jones* v. *Lees* (o), *Cooper* v. *Phibbs*
(p), *Garrard* v. *Frankel* (q), *Shackle* v. *Baker* (r).

(a) 5 M. & W. 548.　　　　(b) 10 C. B. 602.

(c) 9 Hare, 306.　　　　　(d) 5 Russ. 29.

(e) 27 Beav. 446.　　　　(f) 2 DeG. & J. 626.

(g) L. R. 9 Eq. pp. 354-5.　(h) 7 H. & N. 955.

(i) 11 M. & W. 653.　　　(j) 13 M. & W. 695; S. C. 16 M.

(k) 7 Gr. 591.　　　　　　& W. 346.

(l) 6 Beav. 269.　　　　　(m) 6 A. & E. 438.

(n) 1 E. & B. 391.　　　　(o) 1 H. & N. 189.

(p) L. R. 2 Eng. & Ir. App. 149. (q) 30 Beav. 445.

(r) 14 Ves. 468.

DRAPER, C. J.—This litigation, it appears to me, is
mainly attributable to the loose manner in which the
agreement of 1st January, 1868, has been drawn up.
Looking at that instrument in connection with the parol
evidence, the parties evidently contemplated not only
the sale of the goods and chattels in use at *Mason's*
hotel, " with the good will of the business theretofore
carried on by him " in the premises leased from *Smith,*
but an assignment also of whatever interest the appellant had in the house itself. The appellant might also
have required a covenant to indemnify him against rent
to fall due to the landlord. Other stipulations in relation to the premises, and the possibility of liability of
the appellant to the landlord, might reasonably have
been claimed. I think, also, that to have confined the
restriction on the appellant's carrying on business to
the limits of the city of London, or at most to a circle
extending a few miles round it, would have been acceded
to as expressing their true intention.

It is well settled that total restraints of trade are
absolutely bad, and that even partial restraints, if
nothing more appear, are presumably bad, though, if
the circumstances are set forth, the presumption may
be rebutted. And if there be simply a stipulation in
an instrument under seal that a trade shall not be
carried on in a particular place, there being no recital
in the deed, nor any averment shewing circumstances
which render the contract unreasonable, the contract is
good.

In the *Leather Cloth Co.* v. *Lorsont,* the principle
is thus stated : " Public policy requires that every man
shall be at liberty to work for himself, and shall not be
at liberty to deprive himself or the State of his labour,
skill, or talent, by any contract that he enters into.
On the other hand, public policy requires that when a
man has, by skill or by any other means, obtained

something which he wants to sell, he should be at
liberty to sell it in the most advantageous way in the
market, and in order to enable him to sell it advan-
tageously in the market, it is necessary that he should
be able to preclude himself from entering into competition with the purchaser ;" and the conclusion is
drawn that this public policy " enables him to enter
into any stipulation, however restrictive it is, provided
that restriction, 'in the judgment of the Court, is not
unreasonable, having regard to the subject matter of
the contract." In this case the restriction is of that
character which the Courts have decided to be contrary
to public policy. I refer also to the observations of
*Tindal*, C. J., in *Horner* v. *Graves* (b).

It has been suggested for the respondents that the
true construction of this agreement is only to restrain
the appellant from keeping an inn in London for ten
years ; and the whole surrounding circumstances, beginning with the fact that the respondents had been carrying
on business in Toronto before their purchase from the
appellant, down to the appellant's taking the new lease
of the " Western Hotel," are invoked in order to bring
about the construction contended for.

Conceding that the state of facts, and the situation
of the parties, at the time the contract was entered into,
may well be assumed to have been present to the minds
of the contracting parties, and should be regarded in
interpreting their language, this concession will not warrant the introduction of new stipulations, nor the alteration of those which were advisedly made part of the
contract, but which, in their legal consequences, defeat
what in all probability was intended.

The appellant's removal from London ; the landlord's
acceptance of rent from the respondents ; his absence

1871.

Mossop
v.
Mason.

Judgment.

---

(b) 7 Bing. 785.

from the province when the stables were burned; the
application, first to his agent, afterwards to himself,
to rebuild; the asserted refusal on his part, which,
however, he denies somewhat circumstantially; the
respondents' leaving the "Western" soon after, and
transferring their business to the "City Hotel," could
not have influenced the parties in regard to the agreement of the 1st January, 1868, though, as far as they
go, they may indicate how the parties understood it.
The facts immediately connected with the making of that
agreement appear to be, that the appellant was desirous
of giving up business as an hotel-keeper altogether,
and expressed that intention to the respondents and
others; that he arranged (and this is *Jonathan Mossop's*
evidence) with respondents to buy him out at a fair
valuation for his furniture and the goodwill of the
hotel; and that he was not to start business again.
One *Brunton*, an auctioneer, was agreed on by both

parties to make the valuation, and, I understand distinctly, he only valued the furniture and movables;
that nothing was said about a lease from *Smith*, though
the respondents saw him, and were told by him that the
appellant had the place for two years to come, which
the appellant also represented, and that he did not ask
for any indemnity as against *Smith*.

Then, do these circumstances and the agreement
enable the Court to construe this instrument as limited
in effect to restraining the appellant from keeping an
hotel for ten years within the city of London? My
answer must be in the negative. I think the covenant
is expressed according to the intent of both parties,
though no doubt in ignorance on both sides that by its
unlimited terms it was void, and I see nothing to lead
me to a construction limiting its generality except a
conviction that both parties meant to enter into a
valid agreement. But that might be said in most cases
where the agreement has been held void as against

public policy. There is no suspicion of fraud, but, in effect, the parties were *inopes consilii*, though each had a legal adviser.

As to goodwill; this term must vary in its definition according to the nature of the business with reference to which it is employed. It is inapplicable in some cases—for example, the business of a solicitor, which has no local existence, but is personal, depending upon the trust and confidence men may repose in his integrity and ability to conduct their affairs (a). Lord *Eldon*, in *Kennedy* v. *Lee* (b), points out distinct senses in which the term may be used. Mr. *Lindley* (c) says it is generally used to denote the benefit arising from connexion and reputation, and its value is what can be got for the chance of being able to keep that connexion and improve it. The present Lord Chancellor treats the name of a firm as a very important part of the goodwill, and says, "When a person parts with the goodwill of a business, he means to part with all that good disposition which customers entertain towards his particular shop or house of business, and which may induce them to continue their custom with it." (d) The name of the particular hotel would therefore be of value as connected with the goodwill of the business carried on therein, and that passed to the respondents to the extent of the appellant's right to possession as tenant, which was only for two years.

In the present case the goodwill was of an exceptional character: there was the public support and encouragement given to the hotel by habitual customers on account of its situation and convenience, and from the manner in which it was conducted, but to a greater or less degree dependent on the personal qualities of

---

(a) Austen v. Boys, 4 Jur. N.S. 719; 2 De G. & J. 626.
(b) 3 Mer. at 452.          (c) Part. p. 709.
(d) Churton v. Douglas, 5 Jur. N.S. at p. 890.

the appellant as a popular hotel keeper. One of the respondents says, " I don't think any one could do as well at the Western as *Mason*." Several witnesses concur in representing the appellant " to be very popular as a landlord." One adds, " It would take another man a long time to be as well known as *Mason*; the change of sign makes no difference as long as the man is there." The business which these popular qualities drew to the Great Western Hotel formed the goodwill, not so the personal qualifications of the appellant. He had the same right to use them as to use his personal industry and labour, as is said in *Churton* v. *Douglas*, next door " to the very place where the former business was carried on. And upon the authorities it is settled that it is the fault of those who wish for any protection against such a course that they do not take care to insert provisions to that effect in the deed, namely, that the business shall not be carried

Judgment. on *in the district* by the vendor."

If, therefore, the appellant had merely commenced a *new* business as an inn-keeper in the city of London, not in any way, by act or word, holding it out to be a resumption or continuance of his former business, the respondents could not, in my opinion, have maintained this suit. The only foundation of their case is, that having bought from him the goodwill of the business which he formerly carried on, he is now carrying on that identical business to their prejudice. I think they have proved this. I have endeavoured to explain what I consider to be the goodwill, distinguishing it from the advantages which the appellant derived from personal qualifications. He has resumed the business of an inn-keeper, not merely in London, but in the same house in which he carried it on when he sold the goodwill. A stranger might have rented these premises and have carried on the business of an innkeeper, and the respondents could have claimed nothing from him, for he had not contracted with them; he has sold them nothing, and received nothing from them. But the appellant could not, after an interval of a few months, avoid, even if desirous to do so, getting, to a greater or less degree, the public support and encouragement given to that hotel by its habitual customers—no doubt in numerous cases the very customers who had supported him before. It was scarcely possible under the circumstances but that he should resume a part of what he had sold, and he thus incurred the same responsibility as was incurred in *Churton* v. *Douglas*. Mr. *Frank Smith's* evidence shews that the appellant knew that he was about encroaching on his engagement with the respondents, but was induced to do so on the supposition that his agreement was void. I ground my judgment upon the conclusion that he has carried on the same business, on the same premises, and for two months in the same name. It seems to me a species of fraud on the purchasers of the goodwill. I shall only remark upon the evidence relating to the advertisements. The appellant says he knew nothing of the one in the *Advertiser*, though he heard it spoken of, and that he did order the one in the *Prototype* to be inserted. These advertisements shew what was the impression and belief among his friends, for it cannot be pretended they were not inserted in his interest. He did nothing to undeceive his friends, or to inform the public of the truth for more than two months after these publications, and after the bill was filed; and then he announces that his position is that of conducting a business neither connected with, nor in continuation of, any business formerly conducted on the premises.

I will briefly remark on another matter spoken to during the argument, namely, the alleged want of consideration for the sale of the goodwill. It is true no specific value was put upon the goodwill; the only pecuniary consideration was the price to be paid for the goods and chattels. But the appellant also obtained what he professed greatly to desire, namely, to part with the whole business; and not merely to sell his goods, but to be relieved altogether from the inn-keeping, with its charges and responsibilities, and as the respondents required time to pay the whole price, they agreed to keep the goods insured during that time. I think that a sufficient consideration might be inferred under the circumstances, and that the agreement having been executed so far on both sides, the appellant cannot now be heard to say he did not make a valid sale of the goodwill.

I am prepared, with one exception, to uphold the decree, though I should prefer omitting the words "*Mason's* Hotel" from the injunction, because I do not find that the appellant used that name for the hotel, though his own name was put as conducting it. This is, however, very unimportant. But I do not, as at present advised, concur in restraining the appellant from enforcing payment of the remaining part of the consideration money for the goods. When he gave a credit for eighteen months, the respondents agreed to keep the goods insured for the same term, which has expired more than a year. This debt is a legal debt,—the consideration for it was the goods. The respondent's claim is for damages, confessedly unliquidated; and *Smith* v. *Wootten* (a) is against staying the appellant's proceedings; and though the respondents' right to damages is clear in principle, there are many considerations arising upon the evidence which may materially reduce the claim.

The decree, so far as the 1st and 3rd clauses are concerned, should stand.

*Per Curiam.*—The decree to be varied by striking out the 2nd, 4th, and 5th clauses thereof; and adding to 3rd clause a direction for payment—with this variation, the decree is affirmed, and appeal dismissed with costs.

---

(a) 12 Gr. 200.

1871,

CHISHOLM V. EMERY.  [IN APPEAL.*]

*Will, construction of—Dying without issue—Personal trust.*

A testator devised certain real estate to his granddaughter; and, in
case of her dying without lawful issue, he directed the property to
be sold by his executors; and from the proceeds of such sales, and
from such other of his property as might be then remaining in their
hands, he directed certain legacies to be paid, and the remainder
to be applied at the discretion of his executors to missionary purposes:

*Held,* that the contemplated "dying without issue" was a dying
without issue living at the granddaughter's death.

This was an appeal from the order of the court
below, as reported *ante* Volume XVII., page 403.

*Ashman Pettit* died seized in fee of the lands in
question.

By his will, dated in May, 1842, he directed—            Statement.

(2.) For the maintenance of his wife, that she should
have possession, disposal, and profits of a defined
portion of his land until his granddaughter *Sarah
Eliza Emery* married, at which time his wife was to
give up her claim to the land to her granddaughter's
husband, and should receive instead thereof, during her
life, one-third of the profits of the whole of his farm.

(3.) That his wife should continue to have the possession of a part of his dwelling house and the use of
part of the other buildings on the lot.

(6.) That his granddaughter, upon her being married,
should have full possession of the aforesaid whole farm
and premises, with all the appurtenances and privileges

*Present.*—DRAPER, C.J., RICHARDS, C.J., HAGARTY, C.J., MORRISON,
J., WILSON, J., MOWAT, V. C., and GALT, J,

thereunto belonging (with the exception of the privileges granted to her grandmother as before expressed); and that she or her husband should pay unto her grandmother annually one-third of all the crops raised upon the farm, or a commutation equal to all the profits arising from the said land—to be in lieu of dower.

. (8.) Portions of his chattels (excepting what he gave his wife) were to be sold by his executors, and the proceeds applied for his granddaughter's education, and in other ways for her benefit, in the discretion of his executors, He then gave legacies to different persons. And in case his wife died before his granddaughter was married, the part of the farm which was to be appropriated to her maintenance was to be rented, and the rent added to the fund for the benefit of his granddaughter.

And he further directed that " in case of his granddaughter dying without lawful issue (or heir), the whole of the farm in his possession, after the death of his wife, should be sold ;" and he gave further legacies.

By indenture, dated the 2nd of April, 1862, made between *Sarah Eliza Van Norman* (the granddaughter), of the first part ; *Jonathan Mark Van Norman*, her husband, of the second part ; *Elizabeth Pettit*, widow of the testator, of the third part ; and *Daniel Black Chisholm* (the petitioner in this matter), of the fourth part ; after reciting the will, and that the parties of the first and second parts had agreed to sell the said lands to the party of the fourth part,—the party of the third part agreeing to release her interests,—the parties of the first and second parts, in consideration of £1,500 granted, &c., to the party of the fourth part, the same lands *habendum* in fee ; and the party of the third part, in consideration, &c., granted, released, and confirmed the same.

*Chisholm* petitioned the Court of Chancery that his title might be investigated and declared under the Act for Quieting Titles to Real Estate. Thereupon an order was pronounced (27th of June, 1870), whereby it was declared " that the said petitioner is not now entitled to a certificate declaring him the owner of the said lands in fee simple, subject only to the equity of redemption therein of the said *Joseph Birney* the younger and *John Land Birney;* and that *Sarah Eliza Emery* (now *Sarah Eliza Van Norman*) in the said will named, *did not under the said will take an estate tail in the said lands, but an estate in fee simple in the event of her dying without issue living at the time of her death, subject to be defeated by the executory devise over in the said will contained,* and doth order and decree the same accordingly. And it is further ordered that the said petitioner do forthwith, after taxation thereof, pay to the contestants one set of costs."

1871.<br>Chisholm<br>v.<br>Emery.

From this order the petitioner appealed.

Mr. *Blake*, Q.C., and Mr. *A. Hoskin*, for the appellant.

Mr. *James McLennan*, contra.

DRAPER, C. J.—I agree in the declaration which is appealed against, viz., that *Sarah Eliza Emery* (now *Van Norman*) did not, under the will of *Ashman Pettit*, take an estate tail in the lands devised, but took an estate in fee simple, subject, in the event of her dying without leaving issue at the time of her death, to be defeated by the executory devise in the will contained.

Sept. 8.<br><br>Judgment.

The devisor has, in the former part of the will, disposed of the fee simple of his farm ; but, in the latter part, he qualifies that disposition by the contingency of his granddaughter dying without lawful issue.

Chisholm
.v.
Emery.

The statute of Upper Canada (a) enacted that, in every devise of land, it shall be considered that the devisor intended to devise all such estate as he was seized of in the same land, whether fee simple or otherwise, unless it appear on the face of such will that he intended to devise only an estate for life, or other estate less than he was seized of at the time of making the will containing such devise.

The English statute (b) is substantially the same, except that after the words "in every devise of land," the words "without any words of limitation" are introduced.

This will does not in direct words give the estate to the granddaughter. It first gives to his wife, until the marriage of the granddaughter, a defined part of the testator's land, on the happening of which event his wife is to receive during her life time, in lieu of the land, one-third of the profits of the farm, with possession of part of the dwelling house and of other buildings. On the marriage of the granddaughter, she is to have full possession of the whole farm and premises, excepting the privileges granted to the testator's wife (I suppose as to part of the house and outbuildings), and the granddaughter or her husband are to pay annually to the testator's widow one-third of the crops raised, or a commutation for them, the will declaring that the privileges thus given are in lieu of dower.

Judgment.

Taking the different clauses of this will together, it must, in my opinion, be considered that the testator intended to devise all such estate as he was seized of, and therefore that the granddaughter took an estate in fee simple, subject to the charges in favor of her grandmother; and I think the words " dying without lawful issue or heir " afford in themselves very strong ground

---

(a) 4 Wm. 4, ch. 1, sec. 50; Con. St. U.C., ch. 82, sec. 12.

(b) 1 Vic., ch. 26, sec. 28.

for implying a gift in fee simple, there being in terms no previous limitation. There is no want of authority for such an implication.

I am also of opinion that the words " dying without lawful issue " mean without leaving lawful issue at her death.

The language of the Vice-Chancellor in the case of *Ex parte Davies* (a) appears to me to sustain this position. He says, " You are to look at the whole will, to see whether the testator, when he speaks of the devisee dying without leaving any lawful issue of his body, he is pointing to a failure of issue at the death of the devisee, or to an indefinite failure of issue. The words after an absolute devise in fee are 'in case my said son shall die without leaving any lawful issue of his body.' No doubt, before the Wills Act, these words would have made him tenant in tail, the words 'leaving,' &c., being held to mean a general failure of issue, and not that the time of the death of the devisee was fixed as the time of limitation."

This principle of construction by reference to the whole will was fully recognized in *Murray* v. *Addenbrook* (b), where Sir *J. Leach*, M.R. (and Lord *Lyndhurst*, afterwards, on appeal,) held that the words " failing male issue " were, upon the whole context of the will, to be construed " if there shall be no son then living."

In *Ex parte Hooper* (c), there was a devise to *A.* for life, remainder to all and every the children of her body, her heirs and assigns, as tenants in common ; but in case *A.* should die without leaving any issue of

---

(a) 2 Sim. N. S. at p. 120; 15 Jur. 1102. S. C.   See also 1 K. & J. 165.
(b) 4 Russ. 497.                    (c) 1 Drew. 264.

1871.  her body lawfully begotten, then over. *A.* had two
children, both of whom died before her; one died

leaving a child who survived *A.*; the other died without
issue: *Held,* that "leaving" meant "having," and that
the two children of *A.* took vested interests as tenants
in common in fee.

Again, in *McEnally* v. *Wetherall* (*a*), the words were,
"I leave to my brother *M. M.* my estate of *T.* and the
residue of all I possess, and in case he has no heir, my
estate and freehold to be given to the first heir-at-law,"
who was plaintiff in the action. The brother *M. M.*
had executed a disentailing deed, supposing that he was
tenant in tail; but it was held that the devise to the
first heir-at-law was an executory devise over after a
limitation in fee. I cannot help thinking the words
"dying without lawful issue or heir" are as strong as
"in case he has no heir.

In *Parker* v. *Birks* (*b*) there was a devise of real
estate to *W. S.*, his heirs and assigns, for ever; but in
case *W. S.* should die without child or children of his
body lawfully begotten, testator devised to the children
of *H. G.* on the decease of *W. S.* The present Lord
Chancellor observed, "In no case in which a clear
estate in fee simple has been limited by the first words,
has that estate been reduced to an estate tail in order
to construe the words of the gift over, on the death of
the devisee without issue, to be a remainder."

*Blinston* v. *Warburton* (*c*) has also a bearing upon
the present question, by reason of the charge in favour
of the grandmother.

The foregoing cases, with many others, are referred
to in *Coltsman* v. *Coltsman* (*d*), and the decision as to

---

(*a*) 15 Ir. C. L. Rep, 502.          (*b*) 1 K. & J. 156.
(*c*) 2 K. & J. 400.          (*d*) L. R. 3 E. & Ir. App. 121.

Flesk Castle sustains the opinion I have advanced. As
to Dick's Grove (the will came into operation before
the passing of the 1st Victoria), the first devise was
only for life, with a contingent remainder in the event
of the devisee for life dying without heirs of his body
living at his death.

The only remaining case I need notice is *Feakes* v.
*Standley* (a), which was referred to in the Judgment of
Vice Chancellor *Mowat*, but for a different purpose. It
may be that it is not to be reconciled with the authorities
above cited; but, if not, I do not think it can prevail
against them.

On the whole, I think it more fully consistent with
the whole tenor of the will, and having regard to the
fact that the legacies given by him out of the proceeds
of the sale directed to be made by the executors,—the
payment of which testator could not have meant should
await an indefinite failure of issue,—to hold that the
granddaughter took a fee simple subject to the provision
for the widow, and subject to the executory devise.

GWYNNE, J.—I am of opinion that the appeal should
be allowed. I do not find in the will any *direct* devise
of a fee simple nor indeed of any estate to the testator's
granddaughter; the only estate devised to her by the
will is that contained in the paragraph beginning "and
I further direct that in case of my granddaughter dying
without issue," &c.

The testator devises to his widow an estate for life, or
until his granddaughter, who as I understand was the
testator's sole heiress-at-law, should marry.

The 6th clause makes provision only in the event of

---

1871.

Chisholm
v.
Emery.

Judgment.

---

(a) 24 Beav. 485.

the granddaughter marrying, the effect of which provision I take to be that in the event of his granddaughter marrying, the estate of the widow shall be converted
into a charge upon the estate in fee simple, which, for
anything as yet stated in the will, would seem to be left
to *descend* upon the granddaughter. There is certainly
no *devise* to her of the fee simple.

The only estate as it appears to me which the granddaughter takes *under the will* is that devised by the
clause beginning "and I further direct that in case of
my granddaughter dying without lawful issue, the whole
of the farm now in my possession, after the death of my
beloved wife, shall be sold by my executors," &c.
Now, there being no estate of inheritance devised
by the will, unless it be by this clause, the estate so
devised must be an estate tail to enable the issue, if
there should be any of the granddaughter, to take
*under the will.*

This consideration, namely, that the issue of the
granddaughter would take nothing *under the will*,
unless there be an estate tail devised by this clause,
seems to me to be conclusive of the point. Moreover,
the general rule is, that the words " Dying without
lawful issue " constitute an estate tail unless they
be followed by a devise over, failing the issue, to some
persons or person upon whom it is clearly apparent
a personal, as distinguished from a transmissible, benefit
was intended to be conferred. Now I see nothing in
the devise over which can be said with certainty
to signify an intention of the testator to confer such a
personal benefit upon the devisees over. The devises
over are, " to my granddaughter's husband £250 ;
to *Aaron Durham Emery* £250 ; to *Sarah Amoret
Beach* £25 ; to my sister *Martha* £25." Now, unless
the granddaughter should be married she could have no
husband to take under this devise ; but supposing she

should have a husband or two husbands, and that both should die in her life-time, and that then she should die without issue, to whom would the devise over in such case go? I cannot say that I can see such a clear intention of conferring a personal benefit upon the devisees over as justifies us in departing from the general rule of construction of the words " dying without issue." But the first point, namely, that the issue of the granddaughter cannot *take under* the will otherwise than as heirs in tail, there being no estate of inheritance *devised* to the granddaughter unless these words constitute an estate tail in her, seems to me conclusive. I am of opinion, therefore, that the title of *Daniel Black Chisholm* is good, and that the appeal should be allowed.

*Per Curiam.*—Appeal dismissed with costs [GWYNNE, J., dissenting].

1871.

Chisholm
v.
Emery.

---

## DAVIDSON v. BOOMER.   [IN APPEAL.*]

*Will, construction of—Dower, annuity in lieu of.*

A testator, by his will, gave to his widow an annuity of $4,000 in lieu of dower. His will contained certain devises, and gave other legacies and annuities which the testator charged on the whole of his estate not before devised, and he empowered his executors to sell any of his property which they should think necessary; the widow elected to take the annuity.

*Held,* that having so elected, she was not entitled to dower out of any of the testator's lands, whether devised or not:

*Held,* also, that the legacies and annuities were payable primarily out of the personal estate.

This was an appeal from orders of the Court below in regard to the construction of the will of the late *Absalom Shade.* For reports on other points which

Statement.

---

*Present.*—DRAPER, C.J., RICHARDS, C.J., HAGARTY, C.J., MORRISON, J., WILSON, J., MOWAT, V.C., GWYNNE, J., and STRONG, V.C.

arose on this will, but which were not in question on the present appeal, see *ante* Volume XVI., pages 1 and 218.

The orders appealed from had reference to the following questions :—

(1.) Whether the widow of the testator *Absalom Shade* was, under his will, entitled to dower as well as to the annuity granted to her.

(2.) Whether the debts, legacies, and annuities of the testator were primarily chargeable or payable out of the personal estate of the testator, or out of a common fund composed of the personal estate and the real estate of the testator, or otherwise.

By his will the testator gave to his widow $4,000, to be paid to her in lieu " of dower annually during the term of her natural life." He also gave to her his household furniture, goods, and chattels, of what nature or kind soever, and wheresoever situate. He also gave to her in fee the house in which he resided, with the ground thereto attached, and all buildings thereon erected, and a flower garden.

After sundry other devises, legacies, and annuities— which legacies and annuities he made a charge upon the whole of his estate not before devised,—he empowered his executrix and executor " to sign all deeds and conveyances necessary to carry out this my will; also sign any and all discharges of mortgages and sell all property they may think necessary, except such as is hereinbefore devised."

The eighth clause of the will was as follows :— " I give, devise, and bequeath all the rest, residue and remainder, of my real and personal property to my executrix and executor hereinafter named, in trust to dispose thereof as to them may seem best, if not hereinafter provided for by a codicil in writing, to have and to hold to them, their heirs and assigns, for ever."

The testator added a codicil to his will, "to be taken as a part of my hereunto annexed last will and testament, and which will I in all respects, excepting wherein it is altered or changed by this codicil, do re-publish and confirm." By this codicil he gave certain sums of money, payable by certain fixed annual payments; to have and to hold to the donee of one of the gifts, " his heirs and assigns, for ever."

The widow elected to take the annuity of $4,000 in lieu of dower.

The following judgments were given on the points involved in this appeal by

SPRAGGE, C.—One of the points remaining undisposed of at the hearing was, whether under the will the realty and personalty constitute a mixed fund, to be applied *pro rata* in payment of legacies and annuities bequeathed by the will. It is not made a question whether realty as well as personalty is charged; it is clear that it is; but the question is, whether the two constitute a mixed fund.

The result of the authorities appears to be, that it is only where the will directs a conversion of the personal estate that the two are made to contribute *pro rata;* and as put by the learned annotator to Mr. *Jarman's* Treatise on Wills; a devise of real and personal estate to trustees, with a direction to pay, out of the issues, dividends, interest, and profits thereof, does not prevent the personal estate from being primarily liable.

This was settled by the decision of the House
of Lords, in *Boughton* v. *Boughton*, which was
followed in the case of *Tench* v. *Cheese* before Lord
*Cranworth*, Chancellor, and the Lords Justices, the
Lord Justice *Knight Bruce* saying that he entertained
some doubt upon it; but whether upon the doctrine or
upon its application to the case in question, does not
appear. The Lord Justice, however, in his judgment,
refers to *Boughton* v. *Boughton* as establishing this
distinction, " that where there is a mixed fund of real
and personal estate, the mere fact of the real and
personal estate being given together, does not constitute
them a mixed fund for the payment of debts, legacies,
or annuities, but that in order to effect that purpose
there must be a direction for the sale of the real estate,
so as to throw the two funds absolutely and inevitably
together, to answer the common purposes of the will."
*Boughton* v. *Boughton*, cited, as *Boughton* v. *James*,
was also followed by Lord *Romilly*, in *Ellis* v. *Bateman*.

I am referred by counsel for Mrs. *Boomer* to *Roberts*
v. *Walker*, before Sir *John Leach*, and to *Simmons*
v. *Rose*, before Lord *Cranworth;* but in neither of
those cases was a contrary doctrine held, for in both
of them there was a direction for sale. In the case
before me, there is no such direction; and I must hold,
in accordance with what I take to be the settled
law upon the point, that the personal estate is primarily
liable; and inasmuch as that is found to be, as I am
informed, sufficient to answer the debts, legacies, and
annuities charged by the will, there will be no resort
for that purpose to the real estate (a).

STRONG, V.C.—" I think it clear that the annuity
was given in lieu of dower in all the testator's lands,
and is not to be restricted to a satisfaction for dower in
those passing under the will. The cases on gifts in

---

(a) See further *ante* vol. xvii., p. 509.

lieu of thirds, such as *Pickering* v. *Stamford* (*a*), do not apply. The widow, as one of the persons to whom the Statute of Distributions gives the personal estate in the case of a failure of a gift of personalty, takes both the annuity and her statutory share, as the testator is only to be considered as purchasing the thirds for the benefit of his legatees. But in cases of realty, the testator is deemed to have purchased the dower for the benefit of whomsoever the estate may go to, whether it passes under the will or devolves upon the heir by operation of law. I refer to *Jarman* on Wills (*b*), and to *Lett* v. *Randall* (*c*).

Orders of the Court were taken out in pursuance of these judgments, the appellant, Mrs. *Boomer*, having elected to take the said annuity instead of dower, if she was not entitled to both; and the appellants being dissatisfied with such orders, brought this appeal.

Mr. *Crooks*, Q.C., and Mr. *S. Blake.*, for the appellants.

Mr. *McLennan*, Mr. *Moss*, Mr. *Drew*, Mr. *Cattanach*, and Mr. *Hoskin*, contra.

DRAPER, C. J.—I have felt some doubt, on a point of practice, as to whether the rules as to appeals have been sufficiently complied with. As an appeal from the Order 27th April, and the Decree of the 1st September, 1870, it seems proper; but there are no reasons of appeal given, and I do not understand for what reason they have been omitted. I do not desire to interpose any delay in giving judgment, but I do not wish to sanction any omission of the regular forms of proceeding whatever may have been the unexplained understanding between the parties.

Judgment.

---

(*a*) 3 Vesey, 332.  (*b*) 2nd ed., vol. i., p. 392.
(*c*) 3 S. & G. 83.

His Lordship then stated the questions raised and the provisions of the will as above set forth, and proceeded thus :—

The question whether the widow and her co-executor could claim the residue beneficially under the eighth clause of the will was not argued before us.*

If required to express my present opinion, I am compelled, not wholly without reluctance, to hold that the rest, residue, and remainder of the testator's real and personal property vested in the executrix and executor in trust, but that as the trust has never been declared, there is so far an intestacy.

My brother *Gwynne* has referred to a case of *Fenton* v. *Hankins* (a), where the testator bequeathed to *A. B.* and *C.*, as joint tenants, leaseholds upon certain trusts which did not exhaust the whole beneficial interest therein. He also bequeathed to the same parties certain bonds, mortgage deeds and stocks on trusts which did not exhaust the whole beneficial interest therein. He made *A. B.* and *C.* his executors, giving each £50. All the rest, residue, and remainder of his real and personal estate he gave to *A. B.* and *C.* as tenants in common, subject to any disposition he might thereafter by deed or writing duly executed, direct ; but he made no subsequent disposition. *Wood,* V. C., *inter alia,* observed that the gift to these persons as tenants in common, was an unusual form of gift to trustees. Then came the clause "subject," &c., which indicated an undecided state of mind, whether he would make a subsequent disposition. He did not say that he would make it, merely

*Judgment.*

---

* This had been previously decided against the widow and executor (*ante* vol. 16, p. 1,) and from that decision there had not been any appeal.

(a) 9 W. R. 300.

that he might make it, and the three persons would take
liable thereto. If the testator had expressed a clear
intention to make a further gift that might make a difference, but on this clause as it stood there was no trust
declared so as to oust the beneficial interest.

1871.

Davidson
v.
Boomer.

If, in that case, the clear expression of an intention
to make a further gift would have engrafted a trust
upon the otherwise apparent intention to benefit the
devisees; it appears to me *a fortiori* that a clear expression of an intention to devise *in trust* for any object the
testator might afterwards select and specify, must be
held to negative any intention to benefit the trustees.
Suppose a subsequent provision disposing of a part of
the remainder of testator's realty had been made by a
codicil referring to this eighth clause, is there any doubt
that a beneficiary under such codicil would have taken
as *cestui que* trust? and if so, could the eighth clause be
construed so as to make the executrix and executor
trustees as to one part and beneficiaries as to another.
The testator may not have contemplated, and probably
never imagined or intended, the result, which will follow
the language he has used as to this remainder; but I feel
compelled to hold that the legal effect of it is, to make
the executrix and executor trustees and not beneficiaries.

Judgment.

As in *Aston* v. *Wood* (a), the testator has given certain
property to persons *in trust*, but has omitted to mention
the trusts. The trustees named cannot take beneficially.
The gift then is certain, but there is no person to whom
the beneficial interest is given, and the remainder or
residue is not disposed of (b).

It is very probable that the testator did not contemplate dying intestate as to any part of his property, and

___

(a) L. R. 6 Eq. 421.
(b) Vide Corporation of Gloucester v. Wood. 3 Ha. 136.

61—VOL. XVIII. GR.

that he supposed that his executrix and executor would
take beneficially, if he made no other provision ; but the
words which he has used do not enable me to decide, that
such was his intention ; for he gives the residue to them
in trust.    In the words of the Lord Chancellor in *Briggs*
v. *Penny* (a), his " views and wishes may be left unexplained, such trust be left undeclared, but still in such a
case it is clear a trust was intended, and that is sufficient
to exclude the legatee from a beneficial interest.    Once
establish that a trust was intended and the legatee cannot
take beneficially.    If a testator gives upon trust, though
he never adds a syllable to denote the object of that
trust, or though he declares the trust in such a way as
not to exhaust the property, or though he declares it
imperfectly or though the trusts are illegal, still in all
these cases, as is well known, the legatee is excluded
and the next of kin take."

Judgment.
I conclude on the first question submitted to us that
the appellant Mrs. *Boomer* is not entitled to dower out
of the estate of her deceased husband, the testator, in
addition to the annuity given her by the will which she
elected to take.

On the second question I am of opinion that the debts
due and the legacies and annuities bequeathed by the
testator are primarily payable out of his personal estate.
They are constituted a charge on all his estate not specifically disposed of by the will, and there is a power
expressly given to the executrix and executor to sell real
estate and to sign all deeds and conveyances necessary
to carry out the will, but this is not sufficient to make
the real and personal estate a common or mixed fund

The leading cases are referred to in the Court below ;
and they so clearly establish the principles on which I

---

(a) 16 Jur. 94.

rest this conclusion, that I abstain from additional comment upon them

The judgment of the Court is confined to these two questions. On the other point I only express my own opinion.

In my opinion the appeal should be dismissed with costs.

RICHARDS, C. J., said he concurred in the judgment pronounced by his Lordship as to the result of this appeal. The effect of the eighth clause of the will, however, had not been discussed and therefore he did not express any opinion as to intestacy in respect of the residuary estate, not having made up his mind to either view on this part of the case; although it was possible that he might be driven by authorities to say that there was an intestacy.

HAGARTY, C. J.—I agree in dismissing the appeal on the points specially brought before ns. I wish to guard against being supposed to express any opinion on the effect of the residuary clause, as we are told the parties in litigation agree in their view of its operation.

GWYNNE, J.—The questions submitted upon this appeal have been argued upon the assumption that by the eighth paragraph of the testator's will, his residuary real and personal estate has been devised to the executrix and executor of his will as trustees only, and not as beneficiary devisees; and that no trust purpose, sufficient to exhaust the estate, being mentioned, the executrix and executor hold such residuary estate upon a resulting trust for the heirs-at-law and next of kin of the testator. If this assumption be well founded, I am of opinion that the judgments appealed from should be affirmed; but I am not prepared as at present advised to concur in such a construction of the paragraph referred to, nor, although the question as to the true construction of that paragraph has not been directly brought before us do I see how we can answer one of the questions submitted to us without opening the question as to the construction of the paragraph. The first question submitted to us is whether the widow of the testator is, under the terms of the will, entitled to dower as well as the annuity granted by the will? If she and the executor take the residue of the real estate undisposed of by the will *beneficially* and not as trustees, no question as to her having dower in those lands can arise; and yet it is as to her right to dower in lands devised to her and her co-executor by this eighth paragraph, that the question is raised. This question, therefore, as it seems to me, involves the necessity of our now putting a construction upon that paragraph.

In the absence of any argument upon this point I am not prepared to say that I am satisfied that the devise in the eighth paragraph of the will does not contain any expression importing an intention to confer a benefit upon the devisees therein named, viz., the executrix and executor of the will. There is no magic in the word *"trust"*—and if a beneficial purpose can be found in the sentence in which it is used, *that* purpose cannot by the use of the technical term be converted into a trust. Now, the testator, by this eighth paragraph of his will, gives, devises, and bequeaths all the rest, residue, and remainder of his real and personal estate to his executrix and executor thereinafter named, viz., his widow *Isabella J. Shade* and his friend *John Davidson, in trust*—and the paragraph proceeds to state the trust purpose to be, " to dispose thereof as to them may seem best, if not provided for by a codicil or writing, to have and to hold the same to them, their heirs and assigns for ever." Now, this inartistically constructed sentence appears to me to be fairly open to the construction that the testator's executrix and executor were to hold the residue of the real and personal estate upon trust, for such purpose as

the testator should thereafter declare by a codicil, and
if not so declared, or in so far as should not be so declared, then to have and to hold the same to his executor
and executrix, their heirs and assigns for ever, to dispose thereof as to them may seem best, which latter
words are sufficient to transfer the beneficial use. Accordingly it appears that by a codicil bearing date the
day after the date of the will, the testator bequeaths certain annuities and gifts of a considerable amount, which
are to proceed out of the residue devised by the eighth
paragraph of the will. If the case is to be decided
in the absence of any argument as to what is the true
construction of this paragraph, I am, as at present advised, of opinion that subject to the express purposes
specified in the codicil, there is a sufficient intention
apparent on the will that the executor and executrix
should take the residue beneficially, and that for this
reason no question as to the widow having or not having
dower in lands undevised can arise.

*1871.*

*Davidson v. Boomer.*

*Judgment.*

*Per Curiam.*—Appeal dismissed with costs.

---

## In re Wade,—Dee v. Wade.

### *Administration suit—Costs.*

Where one of the legatees was absent from the jurisdiction, and the
executors had been unable to discover him ; this was *held* a sufficient ground for the executors coming to the Court to obtain an
administration of the estate.

This was an administration suit, in which the usual
order had been obtained by the executors for the administration of the estate of *Robert Wade.* By the
Master's report, it was shewn that *Nathan Wade,* a
brother of the testator, was a specific legatee and was
also entitled to share in the residuary estate found to be
in the hands of the executors. The first report shewed
that *Nathan Wade* had not been heard from for several

years. When the case came on to be heard on further
directions, the Vice Chancellor refused the plaintiffs
(executors) their costs other than the costs of an application to pay the share of *Nathan Wade* into Court
under the Trustee Act.

Afterwards the executors made an application to the
Vice Chancellor to be allowed their costs, on which
application an order was made referring the matter back
to the Master to find what efforts had been made by the
executors to find *Nathan Wade*, and whether the executors
could have found him to serve him with their accounts.

The Master found that the executors had made efforts
to find *Nathan Wade*, but were unsuccessful. On the
matter coming on again,

Mr. *A. Hoskin*, for the plaintiffs, contended that the
executors were justified in applying for administration
because they were entitled to a release and discharge.
That the mere payment of his share into Court under
the Imperial Trustee Act (10 & 11 Vic. ch. 96) would
not release them. That they would be liable years
hence to be called on for an account by *Nathan Wade*,
and that, in any event, an account was necessary to
ascertain his share. He referred to *Barker* v. *Peile* (a).

Mr. *S. Blake*, for the defendants, contended that
payment into Court under the Imperial Trustee Act, and
advertising under the Canadian statute 29 Vic., cap 28,
for *Nathan Wade* would release the executors from
any liability to account to the latter.

Mr. *A. Hoskin*, in reply.—Sec. 27 of 29 Vic., cap. 28,
only provides for notice to creditors, and does not
provide that a distribution of assets after notice shall
bind legatees or parties entitled to the residuary estate.

---

(a) 2 Drew. & Sm. 341.

STRONG, V.C.—This is an administration suit instituted by the executors of *Robert Wade*. The usual administration order was made upon motion, and it did not appear upon the first report made by the Master to whom the case was referred that there was any sufficient ground for the institution of the suit, saving that *Nathan Wade*, one of the residuary legatees, and a brother of the testator, had not been heard of for many years, before the death of the testator or since, although efforts had been made to ascertain whether he was dead or alive. Upon the cause coming on to be heard on further directions on this report the plaintiffs were refused their costs; but subsequently an order was made, on their application, referring it to the Master to make further inquiries as to what efforts had been made to discover *Nathan Wade*. In pursuance of this order, the Master has made a report which shews that the executors did use proper efforts to discover *Nathan Wade*, and that the result of their inquiries was to leave it a matter of uncertainty whether he was living or not. Upon this last report I am of opinion that the executors are entitled to their costs out of the estate. It was argued on behalf of the defendants, that the executors could have protected themselves by paying the specific legacy left to *Nathan Wade* and his share of the residue into Court, under the provisions of the Trustee Act (*a*), which has been determined to be in force here. But I think the case of *Barker* v. *Peile* (*b*) is an answer to this objection. The executors are entitled to a final discharge upon dividing the assets remaining in their hands after payment of the debts of the estate; but, as Vice Chancellor *Kindersley* points out in this case of *Barker* v. *Peile*, the Trustee Act would not secure them full protection since they would still remain liable to a suit for an account by the person whose share was so disposed of in case he should be dissatisfied with the accounts.

1871.

In re Wade.

June 29.

Judgment.

---

(*a*) Imp. Stat.10 & 11 Victoria, cap. 96.    (*b*) 2 Drew and Smale, p. 341.

1871.     In the case of *White* v. *Cummins* (a), which has
always been regarded as a leading case as to the right
of an executor or administrator to have the estate
administered under the direction of the Court, Chancellor
*Blake* points out that the duties of a personal representative are two-fold; one to clear the estate by the payment of debts and liabilities; and the other to divide
the residue; and, whilst denying the right of the executor
or administrator to seek the protection of the Court in
the performance of these duties, unless he finds some
hindrance in completing the administration out of Court,
his Lordship, nevertheless, recognized the right of
the executor to come here if he met with any embarrass-
ment, either in applying or realizing the assets, or in
dividing the surplus. In the present case the impossibility of procuring a final discharge from *Nathan Wade*
seems to be a justification of this suit. I think, therefore, that I shall properly apply the rule laid down in
*White* v. *Cummins* by giving the executors their costs.

In re Wade.

Judgment.

---

## BROCKINGTON v. PALMER.

### *Injunction—Damages—Costs.*

Where a plaintiff filed a bill for an injunction and payment of damages;
and it appeared that the wrongful act complained of had, without
his knowledge, been discontinued before the suit was commenced:
*Held*, that the Court had not jurisdiction to make a decree for the
damages.

The defendant having neglected to inform the plaintiff of the discontinuance though applied to respecting it, before suit, the bill was
dismissed without costs.

Examination of witnesses and hearing at Brantford
spring sittings, 1871.

Mr. *Hardy*, for the plaintiff.

Mr. *McMahon*, for the defendant.

---

(a) 3 Grant 602.

STRONG, V.C.—This is a suit seeking an injunction to restrain a nuisance, and for damages. The plaintiff and defendant are inn-keepers, both occupying houses in the same street in the town of Brantford, the defendant's house being situated at a lower level than the plaintiff's. Before the defendant's occupation had commenced—some time in 1867—the plaintiff and other neighbouring proprietors in the street in question had, with the permission of the Town Council, laid down beneath the surface a box drain for the purpose of draining their cellars, for which purpose alone the drain was to be used. Sometime after the defendant's tenancy began he introduced a pipe leading from the laundry of his house into this drain. The consequence of this was, as was scarcely disputed, that, in December 1869, the drain became stopped and the plaintiff's cellar was thereby overflowed and he suffered damage. At this time the drain was opened, and it was ascertained beyond a doubt that the stoppage was caused by the accumulation of a mass of filth at the junction of the pipe, which the defendant had so introduced, with the main drain. Upon ascertaining this the defendant, who appears to have considered the drain to have been a public sewer, placed a fine wire seive over the mouth of the pipe leading from his laundry to the drain; and after this, no further obstruction was complained of for some time. Had nothing further occurred, it is quite clear, upon the plainest principles, that the plaintiff could not have maintained this bill, for an injunction filed in the month of May following. The injury having ceased, and there being no ground for apprehending a recurrence of it, the plaintiff's remedy for the damage caused to him by the overflow would have been an action at law. (a) In May 1870, however, the plaintiff's cellar was again overflowed by back-water from the drain, and the plaintiff's right to relief depends upon the manner in which this

1871.

Brockington
v.
Palmer.

June 20.

Judgment.

---

(a) Kerr on Injunctions, p. 338, and cases there cited.

62—VOL. XVIII. GR.

was caused. If it was caused by the pipe leading from the defendant's premises, as the former stoppage had been, the plaintiff would be entitled to an injunction ; if, on the other hand, it arose from the closing of the drain at its mouth by the direction of the town authorities, as the defendant contends, it would give the plaintiff no title to equitable relief. Upon the evidence I cannot find the fact to be that this second overflowing was caused by the defendant. It lies on the plaintiff to prove this, and I cannot presume it. The defendant says that in the spring he closed the mouth of the pipe altogether by nailing a board over it, and after this there was no communication between his house and the drain, except by means of the branch drain leading, as in all the houses in front of which the main 'drain ran, from the cellar, and with which no fault is found. The plaintiff asserts that this second injury must have been caused by the defendant from the nature of the sub-

stances which were floated into the cellar ; but I think, on the evidence of the witnesses, *Long*, *Kerter*, and *Brenner*, I must find, as I do, that the damage which the plaintiff suffered in May, 1870, was caused by the drain having been plugged at the mouth by the order of the corporation. Then the plaintiff, not being entitled to an injunction on the bill filed in May, 1870, the only remaining question is as to his right to damages in respect to the nuisance, admittedly caused by the defendant, from which he suffered in December, 1869.

The statute 28 Victoria, cap. 17, sec. 3, which is a re-enactment of one of the provisions of the English statute known as "Cairns' Act" has been the subject of several decisions in England, and it is now well settled that, unless the plaintiff shews himself to have been entitled to equitable relief at the date of the filing of his bill, he cannot have an assessment of damages here. In *Hindley* v. *Emery* (a), the present Lord Chancellor

(a) L. R. 1 Eq. Ca. at 54.

says: " It may be conceded that if all the mischief had
already been completed before the filing of the bill, this
Court would not have had jurisdiction to entertain the
suit for injunction, and, if that were so, could not grant
damages for the mischief done;" and in *Ferguson* v.
*Wilson* (a), Lord Justice *Turner* says, speaking of the
same enactment: "But that Act never was intended, as I
conceive, to transfer the jurisdiction of a Court of Law
to a Court of Equity. If, therefore, a plaintiff in a
suit in equity had no equitable right at the time of
filing the bill—for the case would be quite different if
there was an equitable right at the time of filing the
bill—so that the bill was altogether improperly filed in
equity, I am of opinion that the Act has no application."
From this it is clear the plaintiff cannot have a decree
for damages in respect of the wrong which was done to
him in December, 1869. The decree, however, for the
reasons stated by Lord Justice *Turner*, in *Robson* v.
*Whittingham* (b), may contain a declaration that the bill
is dismissed "*without prejudice to such right, if any,
as the plaintiff may have to bring an action at law.*"

I think it right to dismiss the bill without costs. The
defendant's conduct in taking no notice of the letters
which were written to him on behalf of the plaintiff
when the second obstruction occurred, instead of pointing out to the defendant, as he ought to have done, that
he had prevented the possibility of any injury arising
from his pipe by nailing on the board which he describes
in his evidence, and thus leading the plaintiff to the
knowledge of the true cause of the back-water, the
stoppage by the corporation, was calculated to mislead
the plaintiff, and to induce him to suppose that he was
suffering from a repetition of the former grievance.

*Per Curiam.*—Bill dismissed without costs.

*1871.*

*Brockington
v.
Palmer.*

Judgment.

---

(a) L. R. 2 Ch. App. at 88.      (b) L. R. 1 Ch. App. 442.

## SMITH v. KNIGHT.

*Will—Construction of.*

A will contained the following bequest: " To *Richard O. Knight* I
give my carpet, blankets, and whatever else I may have at his
house." *Held*, that mortgages and a bank deposit receipt, which
were in the house, did not pass.

Examination of witnesses and hearing at the spring
sittings at Chatham, 1871.

Mr. *James Bethune*, for plaintiff and next of kin.

Mr. *McLennan*, for defendant.

June 29.

Judgment.

STRONG, V.C.—The only question in this cause was
as to the construction of a legacy contained in the will
of the testatrix in favour of the defendant, *Richard O.
Knight*, who is one of the executors of the will.

This bequest is in these words : " To *Richard O.
Knight* I give my carpet, blankets, and whatever else I
may have at his house." The defendant *Knight* contends
that under this bequest certain mortgages belonging to
the testatrix, and also a bank deposit receipt for
moneys of the testatrix, which had been deposited by
the defendant *Knight*, in his own name, passed. The
defendant *Smith*, who is the testatrix's sole next of kin,
on the other hand, insists that these securities did not
pass, and that as the will contains no gift of residue,
the testatrix died intestate as regards them. Mr. *Bethune*,
for the next of kin, relied on the case of *Moore* v. *Moore*
(*a*), in which case it was held that a bequest " of all my
goods and chattels in Suffolk " did not include bonds in
the testator's house in that county, choses in action having no locality; and this case has never been questioned,

(*a*) 1 B. C. C. 127.

but was followed by the subsequent case of *Flemming* 1871.
v. *Brock* (a), which exactly resembles the present; where
Lord *Redesdale* held, that a gift of "all my property,
of whatever nature or kind the same may be, that may
be found in *A.'s* house except a bond of *B.* in my
writing box," did not pass a mortgage security, and
another bond and certain bankers' receipts, which were
in the house, on the same ground that choses in action
have no locality—and this although the exception of a
particular security might have warranted the implication
that it was intended to pass others.  These authorities
are decisive; and I need not refer to the other ground
on which it was contended that the mortgages and
receipt did not pass, namely, that the words "whatever
else" must be restricted to mean property "*ejusdem
generis*," with the articles specified; although I think
the weight of authority is with the next of kin in this
respect also.  The decree must therefore declare that
the mortgages and the bank receipt, and the money for
which it was given, did not pass under the will, and that
the testatrix died intestate as to the residuary and
personal estate not specifically bequeathed.

Smith
v.
Knight.

Judgment.

The defendant *Knight* must pay the costs up to the
hearing, the litigation having been caused by his
unfounded claim, in which I am of opinion he was so
clearly wrong, that I cannot order the costs to be paid
out of the estate. If the parties desire it, there must be
the usual decree for the administration of the estate, in
which case the subsequent costs must of course be
reserved.

---

(a) 1 Sch. and Lef., 318.

# DAVIDSON v. KIELY.

*Sheriff's deed—Insufficient description.*

A sheriff's deed described the property conveyed as "about fifteen
acres, more or less, being the whole of a block or piece of land
adjacent to the Grand Trunk Railway, being a part of lot number
twenty-seven in the first concession of South Easthope, now in the
town of Stratford."

*Held*, that this description was insufficient and the deed void.

Examination and hearing at Stratford spring sittings,
1871.

Mr. *Davidson*, for plaintiff.

Mr. *Iddington*, for defendants.

June 29.

Judgment.

STRONG, V. C.—The bill in this cause is filed to set
aside a sale for taxes made in February, 1863.
*Maurice Kiely* was the original purchaser, and the defendants are his sub-purchasers. Two of the defendants
only, *Clark* and *Hurley* have answered, and the bill
has been taken *pro confesso* against the others. The
answering defendants merely claim a lien for taxes paid
by *Kiely* and themselves since the purchase, and submit
to be redeemed.

As to the defendants against whom the cause was
heard *pro confesso*, it is clear that the bill, the allegations of which they admit, makes a sufficient case against
them, for it states not only that the land was illegally
assessed, but that the sheriff's deed described it as
"about fifteen acres more or less, being the whole of a
block or piece of land adjacent to the Grand Trunk
Railway, being a part of lot No. 27 in the 1st concession of South Easthope, now in the town of Stratford."
This is manifestly an insufficient conveyance under
Consolidated Statutes, Upper Canada, chapter 55, section

150.  The 4th section of Statute 27 Victoria, chapter 19, which was referred to at the hearing, cannot apply; for it was not passed until after the sale, though before the execution of the deed; but in any case it would afford no protection against a defect in the conveyance, and moreover it has not been pleaded.  The plaintiff is therefore entitled to a decree.  The only question raised at the hearing was as to the terms to be imposed upon the plaintiff.  All that the defendants claim is a lien for the taxes which have been paid since the purchase, and this they are clearly entitled to by force of the enactment contained in 33 Victoria, chapter 23, section 13.  An account must therefore be taken and apportionment made of the taxes paid by *Kiely* and the defendants, and these taxes and the purchase money with interest at 10 per cent. must be declared to form a lien upon the land.

As to the costs, the conduct of the defendants who have answered, in taking conveyances from *Kiely* who held under a deed bad upon its face, has tended to complicate the title of the plaintiff, and for that reason I cannot give them their costs, although they have very properly submitted to be redeemed.  The plaintiff's omission to make a tender, disentitles him to costs against any of the defendants.

*1871.*

*Davidson
v.
Kiely.*

Judgment.

---

## SKELLY v. SKELLY.

*Vendor's lien—Personal order for deficiency.*

In case of a decree for unpaid consideration money, the sale of the property should be provided for, and in case the same does not realize sufficient to pay the money with six years' arrears of interest there should be a personal decree for payment of the balance by the purchaser.

Where the amount in dispute is under $200 but the defendant is out of the jurisdiction, the plaintiff is entitled to costs on the higher scale.

Examination of witnesses, and hearing at the sittings of the Court at Barrie, in the spring of 1871.

Mr. *Crickmore.* for the plaintiff.

Mr. *D. McCarthy,* for defendant.

STRONG, V.C.—This case was reserved to consider some points raised as to the form of decree and the costs. The decree in this case is the usual decree to enforce the vendor's lien, the form of which should follow that approved of by the Court of Appeal in *Sanderson* v. *Burdett* (a), and should contain a personal order for the payment of any deficiency. The decree should direct the payment of interest from the date of the contract or at least six years' arrears should be allowed.

As to the costs, the plaintiff must have them upon the larger scale. I thought at the hearing, that, as this suit could clearly have been brought in the County Court, before the abolition of the equity jurisdiction, of that Court, although, by reason of the absence from the county of the defendant, it could not have been prosecuted there—the costs should be upon the lower scale; but my brother *Mowat,* to an unreported decision of whom I was referred, tells me he has decided that the necessity for serving the defendant out of the jurisdiction is sufficient to entitle the plaintiff to full costs, and I must follow that decision.

---

(a) *ante,* p. 417.

## BIEHN v. BIEHN.

*Partition—Charge for improvement.*

A father placed one of his sons in possession of certain wild land, and announced his intention of giving it to him by way of advancement. He died without carrying out this intention : meanwhile the son had taken possession, and by his improvements nearly doubled the value of the land.

*Held,* that the son was entitled to a charge for his improvements, and to have the land allotted to him in the division of his father's estate, provided the present value of the land in its unimproved state would not exceed his share of the estate.

In such a case, whether the son is not entitled to an absolute decree for the land. *Quære,*

Examination of witnesses, and hearing at the spring sittings, 1871, at Guelph.

Mr. *Miller,* for the plaintiff.

Mr. *Fitzgerald,* Mr. *Bowlby,* and Mr. *Kingstone,* for defendants.

STRONG, V. C.—This is a suit for the partition of the lands of *Moses Biehn,* who died intestate. The only point which arises for decision is one respecting the interest of *Moses D. Biehn,* one of the co-heirs, in certain lands in the township of Wallace, the legal title to which was in the intestate at the time of his death. It is not disputed by those of the co-heirs who are adult, and it has been satisfactorily proved against the infant defendants, that the intestate placed his son *Moses* in possession of this property which was then wild land, in 1864, and announced his intention of giving it to him by way of advancement, and that since that time the son has lived upon the land and made very valuable improvements upon it, worth nearly double the price of the land in its unimproved state. It is further proved that the father was ready to convey the land to the son, but died before his intention was carried out. Under this state of facts I thought that *Moses D. Biehn* was entitled

June 29.

Judgment.

63—VOL. XVIII. GR.

1871.   in equity, either to the land itself or at least to a lien
        for his expenditure in improving it, but I reserved judg-
Biehn    ment for the purpose of looking into the authorities
v.
Biehn.   —none having been cited on the argument.

Whilst I have had much doubt as to whether *Moses
D. Biehn* is not entitled to a decree declaring him
absolutely entitled to the land, I think it clear that he
is entitled to the lesser relief of a charge for his improvements upon the authority of the *Unity Joint Stock Bank
v. King* (a), the circumstances of that case being less
strong than those of the present, inasmuch as there was
there wanting any proof of an intention, on the part of the
father, to confer the ownership of the land upon his sons.

I think I am further justified in deciding that in
making partition the two half lots in Wallace being the
land of which *Moses D. Biehn* was put in possession by
Judgment.  his father, should be allotted to him, provided the present
value of this land in its unimproved state does not exceed
the value of the share of the lands to be divided to which
*Moses D. Biehn* is entitled. The decree will contain
declarations accordingly.

The same point came subsequently before the Court
in the suit of *Hovey* v. *Ferguson*, when the following
judgment was delivered by

August 23.   MOWAT, V.C.—As respects the lot claimed by *James
Hovey*, the decree will be the same as in *Biehn* v. *Biehn*,
lately decided by my brother *Strong*. I am not sure
that the authorities would not justify a decree in such
cases for the land itself, if a decree in the shape
which the Vice-Chancellor directed should not happen to
do full justice to the son. The point was not argued
there; at least, no authorities were cited. But if a son

_____

(a) 25 Beav. 72.

is entitled to the land itself, irrespective of the condition of the father's estate at the time of his death, I think that, in case of an intestacy, it would be most reasonable that the value of the land without the son's improvements should be deducted from his share of the estate; and I hope that it will be found that the Court has power to imply a condition of that kind in the verbal transaction between the father and the son, or that the Court may impose on the son that equity. For the present, I follow the view which my brother *Strong* acted upon, especially as I gather from *James Hovey's* answer that such a decree will be sufficient to secure to him his farm.

The plaintiffs, who are the widow and some of the heirs of intestate, claim that this lot should be partitioned with the other real estate of the intestate. *James*, in his answer, set up his claim to the lot; and counsel for one of the other defendants, who is in the same interest with the plaintiffs, contended that the question could not now be decided. The other defendants in the same interest as well as the plaintiffs, resisted the contention; and I am clear that it is competent for the Court to decide the question without a suit by *James Hovey*, or a reference to the Master. It is a matter for the discretion of the Court.

I think that the costs (as between party and party) of all parties up to decree should be paid out of the estate. In taxing these costs the Master will consider whether the costs of and incidental to the order made on motion were reasonably and properly incurred. No sale took place, and I have not before me the materials for judging whether the abortive proceedings were justifiable and reasonable.

I presume the parties are agreed as to the proper terms of the decree in other respects, as no other question was argued before me.

## MASON V. NORRIS.

### *Chattels—Injunction.*

The plaintiff and " *L* " were tenants in common of an oil well; they
filled an oil tank with oil equal in quantity to 2,400 barrels, of which
1,600 belonged to the plaintiff and 800 to defendant, and they agreed
that the oil was not to be sold under $5 a barrel; they were not
partners. *L*, without authority, contracted for the sale of all the
oil in the tank at $1.25 a barrel.

*Held*, on a bill against the purchaser that *L*. had no right to sell the
plaintiff's portion of the oil; that the defendant's removal of it
would be wrongful; but that as the oil was a staple commodity which
had not any peculiar value, and as there was no fiduciary relation
between the plaintiff and *L*, the plaintiff was not entitled to an
injunction; and that his only remedy was an action at law.

This was a motion for an injunction to restrain the
defendant from selling or removing certain quantities of
coal oil claimed by the plaintiff under the circumstances
appearing in the judgment of the Court.

Mr. *Bethune*, for the application.

Mr. *McLennan*, contra.

STRONG, V. C.—The plaintiff alleges, and I think he
also sufficiently, for the purposes of this motion, proves,
that he and a person named *Luce*, being tenants in
common of an oil well, agreed to construct, and did construct, a tank of sufficient capacity to contain 2,400
barrels of oil, and that they filled this tank with oil;
1,600 barrels of this oil being the plaintiff's, and the remaining 800 barrels belonging to *Luce*; upon the agreement that the oil was not to be sold until $5 per barrel
could be procured for it. That *Luce*, in fraud of the
plaintiff, sold to the defendants the plaintiff's oil together
with his own, at the price of $1.25 per barrel, and that
the defendants are now about to remove the oil from the
tank. Upon this state of facts the plaintiff asks for an
interlocutory injunction to restrain the defendants from
removing the oil.

I am of opinion that the agreement between the plaintiff and *Luce* did not constitute a partnership either *inter se* or as regards third persons. The evidence does not seem sufficient to make out that there was an ostensible partnership, and there was not in my judgment such a community of profit and loss as to create a partnership in the absence of express agreement. *Luce*, therefore, had no authority to bind the plaintiff; and the sale did not confer any legal title upon the defendants, who if they remove a greater quantity of the oil than the 800 barrels belonging to *Luce* will do so wrongfully. But I am unable to discover any ground on which to found the jurisdiction of this Court. The oil cannot be said to be of any peculiar value, being a staple commodity which can always be purchased, and therefore property in respect of any damage to which compensation can be had at law ; and I can discover no fiduciary relationship existing between the plaintiff and *Luce* which would warrant an interference on any such ground as the Court interfered in the case of *Pooley* v. *Budd* (a). *Luce* was not even entrusted with the possession of the oil as the plaintiff's agent, for according to the statement of *McIntyre* who made an affidavit read by the plaintiff on this motion, he, *McIntyre*, was left by the plaintiff in charge of the oil. If, therefore, the motion was to succeed I could suggest no case of threatened injury to chattels which the Court could not be called upon to restrain, and it is clear upon authority that in all but the two classes of cases I have indicated the Court ought not to interfere. I am aware of the *dictum* of Lord *Westbury* in the case of *Holroyd* v. *Marshall* (b), but I do not consider that would warrant me in granting an injunction. Moreover, I think the objection that *Luce* ought to have been a party is well founded. I refuse the motion.

---

(a) 14 Beav. 34.          (b) 10 H.L.C. 191.

# McLennan v. McDonald.

*Registry law—Priority—Notice.*

Where the registered owner of land had parted with his interest therein
·by an unregistered deed, a person who afterwards fraudulently took
and registered a conveyance from such registered owner, prior to
the Registry Act of 1865, knowing or believing that his grantor
had parted with his interest, was held not entitled to maintain his
priority over the true owner, though he did not know, or had no
correct information, who the true owner was.

Examination of witnesses and hearing at the autumn
sittings at Cornwall, 1871.

The suit related to the south half of lot number ten
in the ninth concession of Lancaster.

It appeared that, in 1820' or 1821 one *John
McDougall*, being the registered owner of the whole
lot, agreed verbally for the sale of it to *Alexander
McCrae* for £110. *McCrae* entered into possession,
and made some improvements. Afterwards, viz.,
in or about 1825, *McCrae* made a verbal agreement
with a cousin of his, one *Farquhar McLennan*,
that the latter should take the south half of the lot for
£60, and *McCrae* retain the north half for the balance
viz., £50. On this arrangement being communicated to
*McDougall*, he assented to it. *McLennan* entered into
possession of his half, cleared and cropped one or two
acres, and put up the walls of a house. He was an unmarried man, and used to live with *McCrae* on the north
half while attending to his own half; and whenever he
went away he left his portion of the lot in charge
of *McCrae*. Before *McCrae* paid his purchase
money, *McLennan* paid his, with the trifling exception
of 2s. 6d. for interest; and on the 15th of February,
1830, *McDougall*, having been so paid, executed to
*McLennan* a conveyance of the south half. A memorial
was also executed for registration but was never registered.

*McLennan* was in bad health at this time, and he died the same year, having first made his will, devising the land to his brother *Duncan* (then in Scotland), on condition that he should come to this country within twelve months after the testator's decease, and, if need be, maintain and support their sister *Margaret McLennan* in such a manner as should be satisfactory to his executors; and in case *Duncan* should fail to come to Canada within the period specified, he gave the lot to his sister *Margaret* herself, her heirs and assigns forever. This will was dated 23rd December, 1830. *Duncan* never came to this country. *Margaret* died about the year 1859, intestate and without issue. The suit was on behalf of her heirs. A relative paid *McDougall* the 2s. 6d.; and another relative paid the taxes from 1851 to 1860 or 1861. In 1866 he applied to pay those which had accrued after his last payment, and he then learned that the defendant *Archibald McDonald* had had the land assessed in his name, and that he claimed the land as his. These payments were made to preserve the property for *McLennan's* representatives when they should appear. The same relative had some notices put up in the adjoining village, warning persons against trespassing on the lot. The clearing was allowed to go into common, and became a resort for the cattle of the neighborhood. The wood, which was valuable, was preserved.

*John McDougall* died in or about 1851, and before *McCrae* had obtained a deed for his share of the lot. *McDougall's* eldest or only son *Donald* came of age about the time of his father's death. *Donald* had been told by his father to give *McCrae* a deed of the lot; and he accordingly executed to him a conveyance, which however covered *McCrae's* half only. About the year 1856 he came to live on part of lot 9, in the same concession as the lot in question, and resided there until his death (21st September, 1866). Some months before his death, viz., on the 23rd November, 1865, he executed a conveyance of the south half lot in question to the defendant *McDonald;* and the validity of this conveyance as against the representatives of *Farquhar McLennan,* was the question in this suit. The consideration was $100, $20 of which was paid to *McDougall* in his lifetime, and for the rest *McDonald* gave his promissory notes some time after receiving his conveyance. One of these notes, supposed to be the last of them, was produced, and bore date 17th September, 1866, and was payable in three years from date without interest The conveyance was registered on the 6th December, 1865, and *McDonald* claimed that he was a purchaser for value without notice, and that by virtue thereof and of the Registry law he was entitled to hold the property against the heirs of *Margaret McLennan.*

*McDonald* was examined, and made the following among other statements : " I am the owner of several lots. I have dealt a good deal in land. * * I was born in the township of Lancaster." After stating that he knew *Donald McDougall,* he proceeded to make the following statements bearing on the question of notice : " He and I met on the way, when I spoke of the purchase. I spoke first of making a bargain. I told him the place was to be sold for taxes. *I thought then it belonged to Alexander McCrae,* who owns the north half of the same lot. * * *Donald McDougall,* from whom I bought, was not in good circumstances at any time. I made no inquiries before I spoke to *Donald McDougall* as to the ownership of the lot. I do not recollect that I ever inquired of *Alexander McCrae.* I do not think I did. I never heard any other person spoken of as owner but *Alexander McCrae and John McDougall. Heard that McCrae had bought from John McDougall, but not that he had got a deed.* I heard that *McCrae* had bought, whether

the half or the whole lot I cannot say. I heard all this 1871.
before I spoke to *McDougall* about buying. It was McLennan
generally believed in the neighbourhood that *McCrae* v.
McDonald.
owned the whole lot." After his conversation with
*Donald* he searched the Registry, and found *John
McDougall* to be still the registered owner. Meeting
*Donald* after having ascertained that fact, he represents
the bargain to have come about in this way : " He
asked me if I had been at Alexandria, and if I was
satified. I said ' yes ' to both questions; I was satisfied as to his title ; *John McDougall* appeared to have
the title according to the Registry; *if he had given a
deed it was not recorded*. *Donald McDougall* asked
me if I was going to buy it. I offered him £20. I
was the first one that named a price. He said I must
add $20 to it. The bargain was concluded at that price
at once, and we appointed a day to meet in Alexandria
to complete the transaction. * * I never asked *Donald
McDougall* whether his father, *John McDougall*, had Statement.
given a deed to *Alexander McCrae*, because *Donald*
told me before that his father had told *him* to give
*McCrae* a deed. This was told me by *Donald* at our
first conversation. *Donald* did not give me any reason
for his father's telling him to give *McCrae* a deed. He
said he would give me as good a title as he had given to
*Alexander McCrae*. * * I never asked *Donald* whether
his father had given a deed to *McCrae* for the south
half, although *I thought the whole lot belonged to
McCrae*. * * *McCrae's* place is about a mile and a
half from mine. * * I do not know that *Donald
McDougall* ever looked after it. I do not think he
did. * * *Donald* was in poor circumstances ever since
I knew him."

The consideration named in the deed was £325.
This sum was put in at the instance of the defendant
*McDonald;* and the object was stated by him to have
been as follows :—" I put in the large sum as, in case I

64—VOL. XVIII. GR.

1871.   should sell, it would indicate the value.   *   *   I meant
~~~~   by putting the sum of £325 as the consideration in the
McLennan
   v.   deed, to shew that to any person offering to buy from
McDonald.
me, and to tell him I paid that for the land."

Mr. *D. B. McLennan* and Mr. *Harding*, for the
plaintiffs.

Mr. *James Bethune*, for the defendant.

Sept 27th.   MOWAT, V. C.—It appears that at the time of the
defendant's purchase his vendor had not the title deeds ;
that he was not in possession of any part of the property and never had been ; that, though living on the
adjoining lot, and in poor circumstances, he had never
pretended to exercise any act of ownership in respect of
this lot, and had never claimed the land in any way as
his ; and that the defendant had not paid the whole of
Judgment.   his purchase money when he received express notice of
the title of *Farquhar McLennan* and his representatives.   Indeed, the money does not appear to have been
legally paid yet ; for the greater part of it was paid
after *Donald* the grantor's death, and not, so far as is
shewn, to any one authorized as his personal representative to receive it.   But according to the decisions in
this country, these matters may not be sufficient against
the defence of a purchase for value, where the title is a
registered one (a).

Observations were made, during the argument, on the
smallness of the consideration.   On the one hand, the
consideration was said to be so small as to be merely
nominal, and as to shew that the parties did not suppose
that they were dealing in respect of a good title ; and
on the other hand, cases were cited to shew that the

---

(a) Ferres v. McDonald, 5 Gr. 313 ; Ferguson v. Kilty, 10 Gr. 102 ;
Moore v. Bank of British North America, 15 Gr. 319, and cases there
collected.

smallness of the consideration was not material to the
validity of the transaction. The cases so cited were cases
in which conveyances executed in good faith for a consideration considerably less than the value, were upheld
against creditors (*a*). The consideration here was certainly nominal as compared with the value of the land.
I think that the sum named in the deed should, after the
defendant's own explanation of his reason for naming it,
be taken, for the present purpose, as the value of the
property: the other evidence would not make the
value much less. The consideration to be paid was less
than one-tenth of this amount. The defendant afterwards paid $34 for arrears of taxes; but under the
covenants which he took from the grantor, an illiterate
man, who signed the deed with his mark, the latter was
bound to pay these arrears, and the defendant might
have deducted the amount from the $100 he was to pay.
For the purposes of a defence like that in question it is
not necessary to shew that the consideration paid was
adequate; but the smallness of the consideration may
be important evidence on the question of fraudulent
intent; purchases the consideration for which was so
small as to be only one-tenth of the value have
not been considered to be purchases within the meaning,
or entitled to the benefit, of the Statute 27 Elizabeth,
for the purpose of avoiding a prior voluntary conveyance executed in good faith (*b*). It may be a
question, too, whether, where actual notice is material
according to the Canadian cases, it must in a case
of this kind be express, or will be inferred where
the ignorance is wilful and is not merely the result of

1871.

McLennan
v.
McDonald.

Judgment.

(*a*) See Thompson v. Webster, 4 De G. & J. 600; Towend v. Toker,
L. R. 1 Ch. App. 446; Reaume v. Guichard, 6 U. C. C. P. 170.

(*b*) Upton v. Basset, Cr. Eliz. 445; Doe v. Rutledge, Cowp. 712;
Doe v. James, 16 East, 212; Metcalfe v. Pulvertoft, 1 V. & B. at 184;
Goff v. Lister, 14 Gr. at 460; Patulo v. Boyington, 5 U. C. C. P. at
137; see also How v. Weldon, 2 Ves, Senr. at 519, 520.

negligence (a). The conveyance in question was executed before the Registry Act of 1865 came into operation.

But the plaintiffs' case does not depend on the view which should be taken of these matters ; for it appears from the defendant's own testimony, that he bought believing that the land which he was buying belonged to *McCrae* at that very time. *McCrae* had been the original purchaser from *John McDougall ;* he had for 40 years been living on the adjoining half lot ; he had had the care of the south half for *Farquhar McLennan* while the latter was living and was away from the lot ; *McCrae* had from cousinly feeling continued in the care of it afterwards ; and both *Donald McDougall* and the defendant seem to have thought that *McCrae* was himself the true owner, and was entitled to a conveyance, if he had not already received a conveyance, of this south half. The defendant's reliance in buying appears clearly to have been, not that

*Donald* was the true owner, but that, no deed to the true owner having been registered, the defendant would be able, by getting a deed from *Donald* and registering it, to cut out the owner. In such a case, a purchaser's want of correct information as to who the true owner was, is wholly immaterial. It is no defence here any more than in criminal law, that a culprit supposed he was robbing *Peter* instead of *Paul* (b). The defence of a purchase for value is founded on the maxim that where there is equal equity the law must prevail ; and, so far from having an equal equity, a party has no equity at all against the true owners, if he bought knowing or correctly believing that his vendor had no title. To maintain this defence, before the Registry law, or under the Registry law applicable to this case, it was incumbent on the defendant to have shewn that he was a *bona fide* purchaser ; that his purchase was made honestly, in

---

(a) See Moore v. Bank of B. N. A., 15 Grant 319 ; May v. Chapman, 16 M. & W. at 361.

(b) See Taylor on Ev., ss. 68, 70.

the belief that his vendor was the true owner. A defence
of this kind (in the language of the Lord Chancellor in
*Jackson* v. *Rowe* (a) "must shew that, if the vendor had
not a good title, the party purchasing was imposed on at
the time of the purchase." That the defendant knew or
believed when he was buying, that he was committing a
fraud on somebody, is a conclusive answer to such a defence,
though he may have been mistaken as to who the
true owner was, or as to whom he was defrauding;
and may have fancied that he was defrauding his
neighbour *McCrae*, instead of the absent heirs of
*McCrae's* cousin and friend. The forms of plea
given for this defence in *Beames's* Pleas (b) and *Lewis's*
Equity Drafting (c) contain averments of the belief, as
to his vendor's title, which the purchaser had at the
time of his purchase; and in *Carter* v. *Pritchard*,
cited in Lord *St. Leonard's* book (d), it was expressly
held, that the plea "must aver the defendant's
belief that the person from whom he purchased was
seized in fee." On the other hand, I need hardly say
that no case was cited in which a defendant, though
confessing that at the time of buying he believed the
true or beneficial title to be in another and not in his
vendor, was allowed, notwithstanding, to retain his
ill-gotten advantage, merely because he had no notice
or information that the real owner was the plaintiff, or
who the real owner was (e).

Where a defendant's purchase was an honest one, the
true owner may still defeat it by shewing that such
purchaser had sufficient notice of his claim; though
he may, through negligence, or through not crediting
the information, or from any other cause, have been
led to disregard the notice. If he has received the
notice which the law applicable to the case requires,
he completes his purchase at the peril of the claimant

---

(a) 4 Russ. at 523.    (b) p. 342—343.    (c) p. 341.
(d) 14th ed. p. 788.    (e) See Goff v. Lister, 14 Gr. 456, *et seq.*

being able to make good his right; and the honesty and good faith of the purchase become as immaterial against the real title as they would be on a trial at law. Except in the case of an honest *bona fide* purchaser, the defence of a purchase for value is not valid either under the Registry law or otherwise; and the further question of notice of the particular claimant's title does not arise.

On the merits, therefore, I have a clear opinion against the defendant.

It appeared from the evidence that all of *Margaret McLennan's* heirs are not parties to the suit. She left a brother *Duncan* and a sister *Sarah*, both now dead. *Sarah's* children are parties to the suit; *Duncan's* children, except one, went many years since from Scotland to Australia; one was in this country some twenty years ago; and none of them has been heard of here for many years, so far as appears. The absence of these parties from the province would, under the old practice, be a sufficient reason for dispensing with them as parties (a); and, having reference to the 65th of the Consolidated Orders, I am clear that I ought not now to allow the objection which was taken at the hearing for want of parties.

Declare the impeached deed to be fraudulent and void in equity as against the heirs of *Margaret McLennan*; declare that as respects any legal estate which the defendant *Archibald McDonald* took under the same, he is a trustee of an undivided half of the land for the plaintiff and the other defendants, children and co-heirs of *Sarah McLennan*. Vesting order accordingly. Defendant *McDonald* will pay to all parties the costs of the suit.

*Judgment.*

---

(a) See the cases, Story Eq. Pl. sec. 78, *et seq.*

FERGUSON V. RUTLEDGE.

*Practice—General Order 554—Costs.*

The 554th General Order, as to filing a certificate of the applicability of the lower scale tariff, is directory; and the omission of it does not entitle a defendant, in case of the dismissal of the bill, to the higher scale costs, except for fees of Court actually paid.

Examination and hearing at autumn sittings at Guelph, 1871.

This was a suit which, before the abolition of the equity jurisdiction of the County Court, might have been brought in a County Court. On the hearing the bill was dismissed with costs; and the question was then suggested, whether such costs should not be on the higher scale, as the plaintiff had omitted to file a certificate as prescribed by the 554th General Order.

Mr. *Guthrie*, for the plaintiff.

Mr. *Hodgins*, for the defendant.

MOWAT, V. C.—Looking at the peremptory terms of the Statute (a), as well as to the language of the General Orders (10th September, 1869), I do not think that the omission is sufficient to subject the plaintiff to the payment of costs on the higher scale, except the fees of Court, as provided for by the 557th Order. I think that the 554th Order is to be treated as directory, and as intended for the objects referred to in the next three orders, and not as laying down a condition precedent which a plaintiff must observe in order to have the benefit of the Statute.

*Judgment.*

*Oct. 18th.*

---

(a) Law Reform Act, 1868, sec. 2.

## RICHARDSON V. ARMITAGE.

*Voluntary Conveyances' Act* (1868)—*Good faith.*

The Voluntary Conveyances' Act (1868) gives effect as against subsequent purchasers, to prior voluntary conveyances executed in good faith, and to them only; and a voluntary conveyance to a wife for the purpose of protecting property from creditors was held not to be good against a subsequent mortgage to a creditor.

Examination of witnesses and hearing at London, autumn sittings, 1871.

On the 7th November, 1868, the defendant *Francis Armitage* entered into a contract in writing with one *William Porte*, for the purchase from *Porte* of two village lots in Lucan at the price of $300, payable on the 1st January, 1870. On the 17th March, 1869, *Armitage* gave his promissory note to *Porte*, indorsed by a friend, for the amount of the purchase money, payable at the time so specified; and *Porte*, at the request of *Armitage*, conveyed the property to the wife of the latter in fee. The conveyance was registered 23rd March, 1870. *Armitage* executed, in favor of his wife, about the same time, an assignment of the contract of purchase.

Statement.

At the time of these transactions, *Armitage* was doing business as a grain dealer; and, feeling the business to be a precarious one, he had the conveyance made to his wife with a view (as was proved) to securing for himself and her a home which creditors could not reach in case he should be unsuccessful in his affairs. With the same view, he put up a house on the land, at a cost of $1100 or $1200, immediately after the making of the deed to his wife; and in this house they had ever since resided.

Meanwhile, the plaintiff had lent his name to *Armitage* as an indorser on accommodation paper to the extent of $6,000. Early in February, 1870, it was found that *Armitage* would be unable to pay; and the plaintiff had to give to the Montreal Bank, who held the accommodation paper, security for the amount on property of his own, and he had subsequently to pay the debt. About the time at which he had to give this security, he applied to *Armitage* for some counter-security, and he then for the first time learned that the title to the house and land was in Mrs. *Armitage*. The plaintiff thereupon applied to her for a mortgage on this property, and endeavoured to obtain in his favor the influence with her of some of her relatives. After some deliberation she consented to what he asked; and on the 11th February, 1870, she and her husband joined in a conveyance of the property to the plaintiff, taking back from him a bond conditioned for the re-conveyance of the property on the debt being paid by them in five years. On the 30th of March, 1870, an attachment in insolvency was issued against *Armitage*; and his wife's brother, *Thomas Hodgins*, was appointed assignee. Subsequently, Mrs. *Armitage* notified the plaintiff that she was a minor when she executed the deed; and on the 10th August, 1870, the present bill was filed.

Mr. *McLennan*, and Mr. *E. Parke*, for the plaintiff.

Mr. *Moss*, Mr. *McMahon*, and Mr. *Gibbons*, for the defendants.

Mowat, V. C.—The plaintiff, in his examination before the Master, stated that he had made use of no pressure to obtain the conveyance, and that it had been given to him voluntarily; and a conveyance obtained from an insolvent person by a creditor, under such circumstances, it was argued was void. But the terms "pressure" and "voluntary" were not used by the plaintiff in the sense which the argument requires; they were evidently employed by him to answer a charge or insinuation of

1871.

Ferguson
v.
Armitage.

October 18.

Judgment.

65—VOL. XVIII. GR.

1871.

Ferguson
v.
Armitage.

pressure by threats of criminal proceedings. But it is placed beyond controversy that the conveyance was not the spontaneous act of the grantors, but was made on the urgent application of the plaintiff, and not without reluctance on their part. Such a conveyance is not so voluntary an act as to be void under the insolvency law. Many cases, both in England and in Canada, shew that.

Previous to the conveyance to Mrs. *Armitage*, her husband was the equitable owner of the property; and *Porte* was trustee of it for him, subject to the payment of the purchase money. A voluntary conveyance of an equitable interest, as well as of a legal interest, is void against a subsequent purchaser or mortgagee; and a voluntary conveyance by the owner's trustee, at the request of his *cestui que trust*, is in the same position as a voluntary conveyance by the *cestui que trust* himself. On this point, *Barton* v. *VanHeythuysen* (a) is precisely in point.

Judgment.

The conveyance to the plaintiff is by the husband and wife jointly, and though in consequence of her infancy, the instrument is ineffectual as a conveyance by her, there is no reason why it should not be as effectual in the plaintiff's favor as if it had been a conveyance by the husband alone; and the conveyance to the wife having been voluntary, that single circumstance would have been sufficient but for the Voluntary Conveyances Act (1868), to give effect to the subsequent conveyance by the husband to the plaintiff as a mortgagee or purchaser *pro tanto*. The only point on which I reserved judgment was as to the applicability of that Act to the transaction in question.

Generally speaking, a deed to a man's wife gives him the benefit of the property as effectually as if the title was in himself; and if his creditors cannot touch it, the property is in a safer position for his own benefit than

---

(a) 11 Hare, 126.

property is which stands in his own name. It was no
doubt this view which led to the transaction which the
bill impeaches. The husband and wife with their family
occupy the property together; they have a common
interest in regard to the use which is made or which can
be made of it; the husband, if he should survive his
wife, has the property for his life ; and during their joint
lives she can only convey it with his concurrence. A
conveyance to a wife is in fact not a substantial parting
with the estate at all ; it is practically a mode of retaining it, and (according to the defendants' contention) of
more effectually retaining it, than if no conveyance of it
had been made by the husband. But the Voluntary
Conveyances Act (1868) does not as against subsequent
mortgages and conveyances, give effect to every voluntary conveyance, but only to such as are "executed in
good faith;" and I cannot think that such a conveyance
as that in question was "executed in good faith" in
the sense contemplated by the Legislature.

The expression may well be construed generally
as meaning "good faith" towards all the world, and
not merely towards future purchasers and the like. It
is not to be supposed, unnecessarily, that the Legislature
meant to interfere in favor of conveyances tainted with
bad faith towards creditors or others, any more than of
conveyances tainted with bad faith towards purchasers ;
while the language employed not only demands no such
construction, but, in order to be so construed, needs to
receive a restricted meaning not in accordance with the
grammatical signification of the words in which the
intention of the Legislature has been expressed. Before
the Act a man after executing a voluntary conveyance
in order to defeat creditors had a *locus pœnitentiœ*, and
of this I cannot presume that the Legislature meant to
deprive him.

Declare that the plaintiff has in equity the first charge
on the property as against the defendants, and that

Judgment.

subject thereto the defendant *Hodgins* is entitled as assignee in insolvency. Declare plaintiff entitled to the legal estate, subject to the right of redemption mentioned in the bond. Vesting order accordingly.

The decree must be without costs; or the plaintiff may, if he chooses, add the amount to his debt. I can make no personal decree for costs against the insolvent or his wife; and the case is not one for a personal decree for costs against the Assignee.

---

## GUMMERSON v. BANTING.

*Purchase under mistake—Payment for improvements.*

The rule, that a party in good faith making improvements on property which he has purchased, will not be disturbed in his possession, even if the title prove bad, without payment for his improvements, will be enforced actively in this Court, as well where the purchaser is plaintiff as when he is defendant; and that although no action has been brought to dispossess him.

The plaintiff had purchased from the widow and administratrix of the deceased *James Banting;* she having obtained administration with the will annexed on the executors named in the will renouncing probate.

On the heir-at-law obtaining majority an action of ejectment was brought against the plaintiff, under which he was turned out of possession; and he thereupon instituted the present suit, claiming to have a right, at all events, to the widow's estate in dower, and to have the amount which he had paid for the purchase of the property declared a lien and charge on the estate. After the bill was filed the widow died, so that the only question raised at the hearing was as to his right to a lien for the purchase money. The Court directed "that so far as the moneys paid by him to the personal repre-

sentative of the estate as purchase money of the land
assumed to be sold were properly applied in payment of
debts ; to that extent he may claim as a creditor of the
estate," but refused to " onerate the estate with the
value of the improvements made upon it by the plaintiff."

1871.
Gummerson
v.
Banting.

On settling the decree the plaintiff was dissatisfied
therewith, and had the cause set down to be spoken to
on the minutes.

Mr. *Wells,* for the plaintiff.

Mr. *Ferguson,* for the defendant.

SPRAGGE, C.—The question between the parties is,
whether a plaintiff, coming into this Court for relief; and
entitled to only such relief as is given to him in the
judgment in this case, can properly be allowed for
improvements of a permanent character made by him
upon the property which he purchased ; assuming that
he would be allowed for such improvements if he were a
defendant, as a term of the relief granted to the plaintiff : in other words, whether the position of the party
on the record makes any difference. The question
assumes that it is equitable as between the parties, that
the improvements should be allowed for, otherwise their
allowance to a defendant ought not to be made a term
of relief to a plaintiff.

Judgment.

Although upon this question the abstract equity is
assumed, I will refer shortly to some of the cases upon
the subject. The will in this case authorized the sale of
the testator's real estate for the payment of his debts
and for other objects. It named three executors.
None of the executors acted ; and administration with
the will annexed was granted to the widow of the testator ; and she, in the belief that she had the same power
under the will as was conferred upon the executors, sold

and conveyed the land to the plaintiff, who entered into possession : and he alleges that he has made large improvements of a permanent character upon the land, whereby its value has become greatly enhanced. It is the common case of a party purchasing under a mistake as to title ; and claiming to be allowed as against the true owner for improvements which he has made under such mistake.

Where the purchaser obtains the legal title, and the true equitable owner is put to come into this Court for relief, the Court has in several instances made it a term of relief that the purchaser should be allowed for improvements. That was the case in *Neesom* v. *Clarkson* (a). The Court, however, in that case put the title of the defendant to be allowed for improvements upon this, that it was his right to stand in the position of a mortgagee in possession. The person who took the con-

veyance there, believed that he had acquired the title ; he paid his purchase money and made improvements in that belief. I am not clear whether Sir *James Wigram* would have accorded him the position of mortgagee if he had not made such payment, though his language certainly is that he was of opinion that the person who acquired the legal title " would be entitled to be reimbursed his expenditure owing to the mistake." In *Bevis* v. *Boulton* (b), in this Court, an infant obtained relief only upon the like terms ; and several English cases are in that case referred to upon the point. As a general rule, and having due regard to the nature of the improvements, it is established that this Court regards it as equitable that a party making a purchase, under mistake as to title, should be allowed for improvements as against the true owner.

If it is equitable, it is a question which may fairly be asked whether there is any sound reason why the party

---

(a) 4 Hare 97.                    (b) 7 Grant 39.

having such equity may not come into a Court of Equity,
to enforce it, as well as have the benefit of it when he
happens to be a defendant. In one of the cases it is said
that a party making improvements under such circumstances has a lien upon the land for the improvements
he has made upon it. If that position is correct there
is no difficulty in the way of his filing his bill; he could
come into Court and enforce his lien. I confess I feel
some difficulty in getting at the lien. Lord *St. Leonards*
(*a*) explains how it is that a bargainee who has paid part
of his purchase money to his vendor who is unable to
make him a good title, has, as against his vendor, a lien
upon the land for the purchase money paid, thus: "The
right to a lien seems clear upon principle. In the case
of a vendor who has actually conveyed, the lien remains
although he has no longer the estate. The principle is
that the lien for the purchase money represented the
estate which in equity no longer was his: this right the
conveyance did not defeat. Now the purchaser upon the
execution of the contract, becomes in equity owner of
the estate and the money belongs to the vendor. If all
the money is paid he obtains the estate itself. The
money is in exchange for the estate. A deposit is
part payment. Therefore part payment *to that extent*
constitutes the purchaser actually owner of the estate:
consequently if the contract do not proceed, without the
fault of the purchaser, the seller, to recover the equitable
ownership, must repay the deposit, which representing
a portion of the interest in the property is a lien upon
it." By this reasoning, the lien of the purchaser for
purchase money paid is satisfactorily worked out: and,
as was observed by Sir *Richard Kindersley* in *Wythes*
v. *Lee* (*b*), in which the right to such lien was affirmed,
"If there is a right of lien, as that is a right in equity,
it follows that it must be capable of being enforced by
bill." I should have found difficulty in seeing how a

---

(*o*) V. & P. 14 ed. 671.  (*b*) 3 Dy. at 402.

lien can exist as against a party with whom the party claiming the lien has no contract, and whose title is paramount, especially if the equity being once placed upon the footing of lien, it might be held to draw after it all the legal consequences incident to lien, *inter alia* the right of enforcing it actively by sale of the land upon which the lien exists; and which might operate with great hardship upon the true owner: but I find in a late case of very high authority, *Cooper* v. *Phibbs* (a) before the House of Lords, that expenditure upon improvements made under mistake as to title are put very explicitly as constituting a lien against the true owner. Lord *Cranworth* in two passages applies to it the term lien; and Lord *Westbury* puts it very explicitly "now no doubt that expenditure constitutes a lien —a charge in the nature of a mortgage charge upon the property." The equity of the defendants to have the expenditure upon improvements allowed, was not

contended against in argument, nor was the nature of the equity, whether it constituted a lien or not, at all discussed: there is still the weight to be attached to the designation of the equity, by that term, by judges of very high authority.

In the old case of *Edlin* v. *Batalay* (b), the equity to be allowed for improvements was adjudged in favor of a plaintiff. The owner had brought ejectment, and it was "adjudged the purchaser (the plaintiff) should be relieved and hold the land till he be repaid his charges in building; discounting the profits received after the purchase;" and Mr. Justice *Story* in *Bright* v. *Boyd* (c), affirmed the doctrine broadly in favor of a plaintiff that he was entitled to such improvements, and that the amount by which the estate was enhanced in value is a lien and charge upon the estate.

---

(a) 2 E. & I. App. 166 et seq.　　　　(b) 2 Lev. 152.
(c) 2 Story, R. 605.

I do not myself think it is necessary to go so far in this case as to affirm that the expenditure upon improvements constitutes a lien upon the land, though, as I have said, lien would be a very plain ground upon which to put the equity to file a bill. But, independently of lien, it is established that it is equitable that the improver should have some allowance for his improvements. If so, it is inequitable for the owner to deprive him of the land without making him compensation. He has brought ejectment as was done in *Edlin* v. *Battlay*, and this bill is filed to prevent him from making such inequitable use of his legal title. I think the bill is sustainable on that ground. There is also much in favor of a bill being sustainable directly, and generally, to enforce compensation. I start again with this, that it has been adjudged to be equitable. If the party in whose favor the equity exists cannot enforce it, it must lie dormant until, what may never occur, the owner of the land has occasion to come to this Court, or to bring ejectment. If he has the legal title and possession, he would be in a position to ignore the equity. It would then be an equity still, but a useless abstract equitable right, an equity recognized indeed by the Court, but to which the Court declines to give effect, unless upon the happening of an accident, the owner having to come to the Court, or perhaps to go to a Court of law. This would be a great anomaly, an equity existing and recognized, but without a remedy.

The tendency of judicial decision is to do away with such anomalies. The enforcing of a wife's equity to a settlement at the suit of the wife herself or her trustees is an instance of this—*Story*, E. J., sec. 1414, and the authorities referred to—and there is the well known opinion of Sir *James Wigram*, expressed in several cases, that the position of a party upon the record makes no difference as to his equitable rights; and it is certainly in accordance with reason that it should be so.

1871.

Gummerson
v.
Banting.

Judgment.

66—VOL. XVIII. GR.

Mr. Justice *Story* in *Bright* v. *Boyd*, in affirming the right of a party to come into Court as plaintiff to be compensated for improvements says, "This is the clear result of the Roman Law," and he adds that in which I entirely agree, "and it has the most persuasive equity; and I may add common sense and common justice for its foundation."

I am referred to *Kilborn* v. *Workman* (a), a decision of my own in which I refused to allow to a purchaser coming into Court for a rescission of his contract, compensation for improvements made by him. I refused this upon the circumstances, and upon the authority of *McKinnon* v. *Burrows*, the point decided in which has since been decided otherwise in a case in England, *Bunny* v. *Hopkinson* (b): and I find in the same volume of Mr. *Grant's* Reports a decision by the late Chancellor, *Brunskill* v. *Clark* (c), in which compensation was adjudged to a purchaser plaintiff who had made improvements upon property purchased in ignorance of defects in title.

Upon the whole, the conclusion at which I arrive is that such relief may properly be given to a purchaser under mistake as to title coming into Court, as plaintiff, upon ejectment being brought by the owner, and I incline to think that it may properly be given where the owner is not bringing ejectment. The mode and extent of relief must always be a question depending upon the circumstances of each case. The Court will always be careful not to make a decree that will work injustice to the owner of the estate. The inquiry which I direct in this case will be the same as was directed by Mr. Justice *Story* in *Bright* v. *Boyd*, viz., that the Master ascertain the character and value of the improvements, by whom, and at what time made; also

---

(a) 9 Grant 255.      (b) 27 Beav. 565.      (c) 9 Grant 430.

the value of the rents and profits of the land on which 1871.
the improvements have been made, also the present
value of the improvements, and how far the value of the
land is increased by such improvements.

I do not give costs of this argument to either party;
not to the plaintiff, as he should have raised the question
at the hearing, and I gave him no costs at the hearing;
and not to *Charles Banting*, as I decide the point against
his contention. In other respects the costs will be as
already directed.

I find the three additional cases to which I have been
referred to be cases in which compensation for improvements has been sought by a purchaser *against his
vendor*.

That point I should think much more clear than the
one before me, where relief is sought without any contract, or encouragement, or standing by, against the
true owner.

Judgment.

---

## BARKER v. ECCLES. [IN APPEAL.]

[When this case was reported, *ante* page 440, an accidental
omission was made of the judgment of Mr. Justice
GWYNNE ; who, it will be perceived, dissented from
the decision pronounced by the majority of the Court.]

GWYNNE, J.—*Pittman's* mortgage having been registered upon the 29th January, 1862, every person who
after that acquired an interest in the mortgaged lands
did so with notice of that mortgage. Assuming, then,
that the transaction which took place upon the 20th
October, 1865, between *Pierce, McSloy,* and *Ostrander,*
was, that *Ostrander* first purchased from *Pierce* an

assignment of the *Conolly* mortgage, and having become
assignee of that mortgage, purchased the equity of
redemption from *McSloy* for the sum of $180, *Ostrander*
could not without the Consolidated Statute of Upper
Canada, (ch. 87,) have set up the *Conolly* mortgage
against *Pittman: Greswold* v. *Marsham* (a); *Mocatta*
v. *Murgatroyd* (b); and *Toulmin* v. *Steere* (c) are express upon this point. The payment by *Ostrander* to
*McSloy* of $180 for the purchase of the equity of
redemption (upon which *Pittman's* mortgage operated
as a charge), with the knowledge of the existence of
*Pittman's* mortgage, was in equity a fraud upon *Pittman*,
and equity therefore could not permit the *Conolly* mortgage to have been set up to the prejudice of *Pittman*,
upon whom this fraud had been committed.

Now the statute does not, in my judgment, authorize
that to be done which before the statute a Court of
equity would not have permitted to be done, because the
doing it would have operated as a fraud. All that the
statute authorizes is the *taking* a *release* of the equity
of redemption by a mortgagee or his assignee from the
mortgagor or his assignee, or the mortgagee or his
assignee *purchasing* the equity of redemption either
under a power of sale in the mortgage or at a sale
thereof under any judgment or decree, without *thereby*
—that is, by *taking the simple release* in the one case
or the *purchasing* the equity of redemption in the other,
—merging the *mortgage debt* as against any subsequent
mortgagee.

The *statute* does not authorize the owner of the equity
of redemption to acquire an earlier mortgage by assignment, and to set it up to defeat subsequent incumbrancers. To enable the statute to operate at all, it is
essential that the person acquiring the equity of redemp-

---

(a) 2 Ch. Cas. 170.        (b) 1 P. Wms. 393.        (c) 3 Mer. 210.

tion should be at the time a mortgagee or an assignee of
a mortgagee. It was therefore essentially necessary in
this case that it should be shewn that *Ostrander* had an
assignment of the *Conolly* mortgage—that is, of the
mortgage debt *before* he acquired the equity of redemption from *McSloy*. Now, granting the deed from *Pierce*
to *Ostrander* to have been executed before the deed
from *McSloy* to *Ostrander*, both having been executed
on the same day and as one transaction, the deed from
*Pierce* does not profess to assign the mortgage debt at
all ; it purports in consideration of $1,500 paid to
*Pierce*, the receipt whereof is thereby acknowledged,
" to grant, bargain, sell, transfer, and quit claim unto
*Ostrander* all *Pierce's* estate, right, title, interest, claim,
and demand both at law or in equity or otherwise however, and whether in possession or expectancy of, in, to,
or out of the south-half of lot No. 4, in the 7th concession
of the township of Dereham ; to have and to hold the
same unto and to the use of *Ostrander*, his heirs and
assigns for ever, subject to the reservations expressed in
the original grant thereof from the Crown." Now, this
transaction was effected through a lawyer, and the
marked difference between the language of the deed
from *Pierce* to *Ostrander* and that of the deeds from
*Conolly* to *Eccles* and from *Eccles* to *Pierce*, where the
indenture of mortgage and the mortgage debt are expressly in terms transferred and assigned, coupled with
the fact that the bargain and sale by *McSloy* to *Ostrander*
and the mortgage by *Ostrander* to *Pierce* were all
executed on the same day, at the same time, as one
transaction, satisfies my mind that there was no intention
to assign the mortgage debt by *Pierce* to *Ostrander*,
and that what was done, and was intended to be done,
was a sale of the land to *Ostrander*, effected by the
assignee of the first mortgage transferring the legal
estate, and the owner of the equity of redemption conveying by bargain and sale his estate—just as if the
owner of the equity of redemption had united with his

mortgagee in one deed to convey to a purchaser. This construction of the intention of the parties is, as it appears to me, the only one that is consistent with the fact of *Ostrander* executing a mortgage to *Pierce* to secure a balance of the purchase money, and with *Ostrander's* own statement in evidence of the transaction, and his admission that he " was to hold the mortgage" (by which I understand he was to have possession of it), "to shew how much he paid on the land, and that he supposes he overlooked the other" (that is *Pittman's*) mortgage, and that he " supposed that when *Pierce gave*" him, by which I understand *placed in his hands*, "the mortgage, *it shewed a part of the purchase money* [*he*] *gave for the land.*"

The statute, in my judgment, does not apply to a case of this nature. Its object, as it seems to me, is to protect a mortgagee who *takes a mere release* of the equity of redemption *in satisfaction of the mortgage debt*, or who *purchases* at a sale under a power in his mortgage, or at a sale under an execution issued upon a judgment or decree, in which cases the law will provide for a proper appropriation of the amount paid ; but that it is no more competent since the statute than it was before it was passed, for a mortgagee, with notice of a subsequent incumbrance, in fraud of the subsequent incumbrancer, to pay valuable consideration (which in justice should go to the subsequent incumbrancer) to the owner of the equity of redemption for the *sale* by him of such equity of redemption, and then to set up the prior incumbrance to the prejudice of the defrauded subsequent incumbrancer. I am of opinion, therefore, that the appeal should be allowed.

## LEE v. McKINLY.

*Will—Construction of—Election.*

A testator bequeathed a sum of money to his wife in lieu of all dower, &c., and revoked " all gifts or deeds or deed of gift of any real estate made by me at any time heretofore."

*Held,* that the widow was put to her election whether she would accept the bequest or retain an estate conveyed to her by a deed of gift during the lifetime of her husband.

Examination of witnesses and hearing at the autumn sittings, 1871, at Chatham.

Mr. *Maclennan,* for the plaintiff.

Mr. *S. Blake,* for the defendants.

STRONG, V. C.—This is a suit for payment of a legacy given by the testator *Edward Lee* to his wife. The bequest was in these terms :

Judgment.

" I do give and bequeath unto my wife $500 in lieu of all dower or thirds she may have in any of my property, lands, or tenements ; and I hereby revoke all gifts or deeds or deed of gift of any real estate made by me at any time heretofore to her, and charge my said executors with the payment of any legacy to her within six months after my decease ; provided she my said wife signify by writing her acceptance thereof within three months next ensuing my death."

The will contained a general devise of all the testator's lands. Two questions arose for decision ; the first, which I disposed of at the hearing, was as to the consequence of the plaintiff's omission to signify her acceptance of the legacy in writing within three months after the testator's death. I decided that this notification had only reference to the payment within six months, and

that its omission did not work a forfeiture of the legacy.
The remaining question was as to the effect of the
bequest on a deed of gift of certain lands made by the
testator to the plaintiff.

I think it clear that the plaintiff must elect. The
general devise by itself would of course not have been
sufficient to put the plaintiff to her election, for the very
plain reason that by a general devise the testator means
only to give what actually belongs to him. But here
there is first an intention expressed to avoid the deed of
gift, which if effected, would revest the lands in the
testator, and this being followed by a general devise of
all lands is equivalent to a devise by a specific description of the lands contained in the deed, which would
beyond all question have put the widow to her election.
The plaintiff must therefore elect in the usual manner.
Costs of all parties out of the estate.

---

## Re Mulholland.

*Quieting Titles Act.*

The Court will not grant a certificate to quiet the title of a party who
claims to be the legal owner in fee simple, but who is not in
possession of the land claimed, and is kept out of such possession
by a person who disputes the title of the claimant: in such a
case the claimant must first recover possession of the premises.

This was an application made by *Thomas Mulholland*,
under the Act for Quieting Titles to Real Estate, to quiet
the title to lot 19 in the 10th concession of the township of Brock. *Mulholland* claimed a title by possession
of twenty years and upwards by the parties through
whom he claimed. The contestant *Thomas Amey* was
at the time of filing the petition, and had ever since
continued, in possession of the north half of the lot, and
the contestant *Nicholas Dure* had had possession of the

south hàlf during the same time. The matter was before
the late Accountant as Referee, and he refused the
certificate to *Mulholland*, who appealed from his report.

On the appeal several questions were argued, but it is
unnecessary to refer to more than the one on which the
judgment turned. It was argued on behalf of the contestants that the Court could not entertain the application of
the claimant because he was out of possession; that
before he could apply to quiet his title he must first
obtain possession of the land; that the Act did not
contemplate quieting the title of a person out of pos-
sion and whose right to possession was disputed. ·

Mr. *Blake*, Q. C., and Mr. *Bain*, for the appeal.

Mr. *McMichael* and Mr. *Alfred Hoskin*, contra.

*Carson's* case (a) and *Re Bell* (b) were referred to.

STRONG, V. C.—This is a proceeding under the Act
for Quieting Titles, which came before me on an appeal
by the petitioner from the finding of the late Referee.
The question principally discussed was as to the effect
of the Statute of Limitations on the title. But on this
part of the case I need express no opinion, for it is very
clear upon the authorities that the appeal must be dismissed on another ground. It appears that the petitioner
is not in possession of the land in question, but that the
contestants are holding it adversely to him. This
objection, which was taken by the contestants' counsel
on the argument, and which is stated to have been also
urged in the office, must prevail.

The cases *Re Carson's* estates (c) and *Re Netter* (d),
decisions on the Imperial Act regulating the Landed

---

(a) 4 Ir. Eq. Rep. 555.    ·(b) 3 Chan. Chas. Rep. 239.
(c) 4 Ir. Rep. Eq. 555.    (d) 3 Ir. Rep. Eq. 504.

67—VOL. XVIII. GR.

1871.
Re
Mulholland.

Estátes Court in Ireland, an enactment in *pari materia* with the Act 29 V. cap. 25, clearly lay it down that a petitioner claiming title to an estate or possession cannot have the benefit of this mode of proceeding so long as another is in adverse possession of the land. These cases were followed by the Referee in *Re Bell* (a), as my brother *Mowat* tells me with his approval, and I must be guided by them also. I have not failed to consider Mr. *Blake's* argument that an action of eject-ment being now tried by a Judge without a jury, it can make no difference whether the claimant proceeds at law or under this Act as far as regards the mode of trial. To a certain extent this is true ; but the answer to the argument is, that a man cannot come here claiming an estate in possession whilst another person holds the possession adversely to him, as in that case he comes with a blot upon his title, and the effect of the certificate is not to establish him in the possession, *that* he must, in any event, recover at law ; and it is more convenient that the action should precede than that it should follow the granting of a certificate.

Judgment.

Appeal dismissed with costs.

---

### RE LANGTRY.

*Administration suit—Injunction—Costs.*

The fact that a creditor of an estate has proceeded at law after a decree for the administration of the estate of the testator has been obtained, is not sufficient to deprive him of his costs, either at law or of a motion in this Court to restrain his action.

This was an administration suit, the order for which had been obtained by the executor. After the order had been issued, a creditor of the estate had taken proceed-ings at law to enforce payment of his claim, whereupon

---

(a) Chy. Chambers, vol. iii., p. 239.)

the executor caused a notice of motion for an injunction
to restrain the action to be served, since which time the
creditor had not taken any further step in the action.

Mr. *Spencer*, for the executor, moved for an injunction accordingly.

Mr. *S. Blake,* contra, submitted to the order going, and asked for costs of the motion and at law.

STRONG, V. C.—The only question in this case was as
to the right of a creditor proceeding at law against an
executor, who had obtained an administration order, to
the costs of a motion to restrain his proceedings and
also to his costs at law. I think it clear that the creditor,
in the present case, who did not proceed at law after
notice of the decree, is entitled to these costs. The
case of *Bear* v. *Smith* (a), shews that a creditor is
entitled to his costs at law, even up to the date of the
service of a notice of motion to restrain him, Sir
*James Parker*, V. C., saying that a creditor, up to the
time an application to stop him is made, has "a right to
do what he can for himself."

It would seem to me also, on principle, to be the right
of a creditor to continue his proceedings at law until the
executor shews, by taking some proceeding to restrain
him, an intention to proceed under the decree. Moreover,
the creditor ought to have the right to appear on a
motion to restrain him, in order that proper terms may
be imposed on the executor, and that an order may be
drawn up shewing the grounds on which the proceedings
at law were stayed, as it may afterwards become of
importance to the creditor to be able to resume those
proceedings. It would appear therefore, that the creditor's proceeding at law, until notice of motion is served,
does nothing to disentitle him to his costs of the motion.

(a) 6 Jurist, 708.

1871.         If the creditor should offer resistance to the motion,
~~~~~      and should fail in his opposition; in such a case it would
Re
Langtry.   be proper to order him to pay the costs.   *Gardner* v.
*Garrett* (a) must, I think, have been a case of this kind;.
for otherwise, it is inconsistent with the cases of *White*
v. *Leatherdale* (b), and *Bear* v. *Smith*, before mentioned,
both decisions of very experienced Judges.

The respondent in this motion must therefore have
his costs at law up to the date of service of notice of
motion, and also his costs of the motion.

----

## TRUESDELL V. COOK.

*Statute of Limitations—Adverse possession—Bill to deliver up deeds.*

The owner of land put his father in possession in 1847, under a parol
agreement that the father should clear up and cultivate the land,
taking to his benefit the profits thereof.   The father remained in
undisturbed possession until his death, which occurred in 1870:
*Held*, that the father had obtained a title by length of possession;
and a bill filed to obtain the delivery up of certain deeds executed
between the father and another son, was dismissed with costs.

Examination of witnesses and hearing at the autumn
sittings at Kingston, 1871.

Mr. *Blake*, Q. C,, Mr. *James Maclennan*, and Mr.
*Peter Cameron*, for plaintiff.

Mr. *Moss* and Mr. *Deacon*, for defendants.

Judgment.     STRONG, V. C.—The bill in this case seeks to have
certain deeds delivered up as clouds upon the plaintiff's
title.   The material facts are as follows :  The plaintiff
purchased the land in question and obtained a conveyance of it in 1842, and lived on it, being absent at

----

(a) 20 Beav. 469.                    (b) 1 W. R. 405.

intervals from 1842 until 1845 or 1846. The plaintiff's
father, *William Truesdell*, also went to live on the
land in 1842, and continued there up to the time of
his death within the last year. The bill alleges—
and there is evidence to establish it—that the plaintiff's
purchase deed was destroyed by his father some time
anterior to the date of the plaintiff leaving the place
in 1845 or 1846. There is also proof of the plaintiff's
father having been left by the plaintiff in exclusive
possession of the land, when the plaintiff removed
in 1845 or 1846, upon the agreement that he (the
father) should take care of the land and clear and
fence some portion of it, in return for which he was
to have the profits. Some admissions, within twenty
years, by the father of the plaintiff's title are proved;
but these are mere parol admissions made not to the
plaintiff or to any person acting on his behalf but to
third persons. It is also attempted to be shewn that
some fifteen or sixteen years ago there was an interruption of the father's possession by the entry of the
plaintiff's brother, *William Truesdell*, under the plaintiff's authority. After the father, *William Truesdell's*
possession had lasted more than twenty years, he made
a conveyance to the defendant *John Cook*, who immediately afterwards conveyed to *William Truesdell*, the
father, and the defendant *Margaret*, his wife, for their
lives and the life of the survivor, with remainder to the
infant defendant, *William Henry Cook*. The plaintiff
subsequently to these conveyances, brought an action of
ejectment against his father, which was tried at Brock-
ville, at the Spring Assizes of 1870, and resulted in the
plaintiff being nonsuited. Since this the plaintiff has
brought another action of ejectment, which is now pending. The bill prays that the conveyances made to and
by the defendant, *John Cook*, may be delivered up to be
cancelled, and removed from the registry.

On behalf of the defendants, Mr. *Moss* objected first,

that this was a mere ejectment bill, which the Court has
no jurisdiction to entertain; and secondly, that the
Statute of Limitations was a bar to the plaintiff; *William
Truesdell*, the father, having acquired a prescriptive
title to the land; or at all events that the plaintiff's
right was barred by reason of his having been out of
possession for more than twenty years. I am of opinion
that the bill must be dismissed on both grounds. I am
of opinion that in a proper case where the plaintiff,
having a legal title has done all he possibly can to assert
his title at law, a bill may be maintained in this Court to
compel the delivering up of a deed which appears to be
void at law, provided it is a registered instrument. I find
no authority for saying that the existence of an unregistered deed, passing no interest, and not appearing
to be a link in the title, can give ground for the jurisdiction; but the registration has such a tendency to
embarrass the title of the true owner that there would

be a great want of remedy if this Court could not decree
cancellation in such a case. But I think it very clear
that in a case like the present, where the plaintiff is out
of possession and the defendants, or some of them, are in
possession, claiming adversely to the plaintiff, a bill like
the present cannot succeed. Such was the opinion of
my brother *Mowat* in the case of *Shaw* v. *Ledyard* (a).
In Lord *Redesdale's* Treatise on Pleading, at p. 54, the
law of the Court as to the jurisdiction to order the delivery
of title deeds is laid down as follows: "If the title to the
possession of the deeds and writings which the plaintiff
prays possession depends on the validity of his title to the
property to which they relate, and he is not in possession
of that property, and the evidence of his title to it is in
his own person, or does not depend on the production of
the deeds and writings of which he prays the delivery,
he must establish his title to the property at law before
he can come into a Court of equity for delivery of

_____

(a) 12 Grant 382.

the deeds or writings." This rule is recognized by my
brother *Mowat* in *Shaw* v. *Ledyard*, as being applicable to a case like the present, where the cancellation
of a deed, prejudicially affecting the title, is sought by a
plaintiff asserting a legal title to the fee simple in
possession, whilst other persons are in actual adverse
possession—although my learned brother in that case
thought the doctrine did not apply, inasmuch as the
land there being uncultivated and not in the actual possession of any person, the plaintiff had it not in his power
to bring an action at law. If the bill here had prayed
for re-execution of the destroyed deed, the case might
have been different; but the only relief asked for is the
delivery up of the deeds executed to and by the defendant *John Cook.*

The defence of the Statute of Limitations is also fatal
to the plaintiff's case. It was argued that the plaintiff's
father was in possession as a mere caretaker or servant
of the plaintiff, in which case time does not run against
the true owner; but I am of opinion that this is not the
correct result of the evidence. I concede that where it
is shewn that a contract of hiring exists between the
parties, and the possession has been incidental to that
contract, the statute does not operate. But where, as
in the present case, no such relationship existed between
the parties and the party in possession has been let in
upon the terms of performing certain services upon the
land, taking in recompense the profits of the land, a
tenancy at will is created. Therefore in the present
case the statute began to run at the expiration of a year
after the sole possession of *William Truesdell*, the
father, commenced, which was not later than the end
of the year 1847. The recognition of the plaintiff's
title, spoken of by the witnesses, *Snider* and Mrs. *Cross*,
were manifestly insufficient acknowledgments to prevent
the operation of the statute; for first, they were not in
writing, and secondly, they were not made to the
plaintiff or to any agent acting for him.

1871.

Truesdell
v.
Cook.

Judgment.

The alleged occupation of *William Truesdell*, the son, I also adjudge to be ineffectual as an interruption of the father's possession, It appears that *William Truesdell*, the son, was upon the land merely to assist his father, whose servant he must have been, since the crops grown whilst he lived upon the land, during all which time his father's possession remained as before, were taken by the father to his own use. The statute therefore applies, and the plaintiff's title is barred, which is the same result as that which was arrived at by the learned Judge who tried the action of ejectment. The bill must be dismissed with costs.

---

## WILLIAMS V. JENKINS.

*Purchase by agent—Principal and agent—Parol evidence—Resulting trust.*

The plaintiff agreed with *J.* to purchase a mining lease for their joint benefit, the consideration for which was to be the testing of the ore at the crushing-mill of the plaintiff, and at his expense. In pursuance of this arrangement, *J.* did arrange for the lease, but took the agreement therefor in his own name. The ore was, as agreed upon, tested at the crushing-mill of the plaintiff, and at his expense, but *J.* attempted to exclude the plaintiff from any participation in the lease, asserting that he had obtained the same for his own benefit solely :

*Held*, that the true agreement could be shewn by parol ; and that the plaintiff was entitled to the benefit of the agreement.

Statement.    Examination of witnesses and hearing at the sittings of the Court at Belleville, in the autumn of 1871.

This was a suit to enforce a trust in respect of a license or lease of a mining right in some lands in the township of Marmora. The lease in question was made by the defendant *Palmer* to the defendant *Jenkins*, on the 23rd December, 1870, *Palmer* himself being a lessee of the lode, part of which was the subject of the lease in question in the cause. The plaintiff asserted that the

lease was procured in pursuance of an agreement between himself and *Jenkins* that *Jenkins* should obtain
the lease in their joint names, and for their joint behoof;
and that the consideration given *Palmer* was the testing
of the ore, which was gold-bearing quartz, at the
crushing-mill of the plaintiff. The plaintiff further
asserted that a release made by *Jenkins* to *Palmer*
just before the filing of the bill, and after both *Palmer*
and *Jenkins* had become aware of the plaintiff's intention to press his claim, was in fraud of the plaintiff, and
ought not to be regarded as any bar to the plaintiff's
right to relief.

1871.<br><br>Williams<br>v.<br>Jenkins.

Mr. *Moss* and Mr. *Dickson*, for the plaintiff.

Mr. *English*, for the defendants.

STRONG, V. C.—At the conclusion of the hearing I
stated that I found the facts in the plaintiff's favor, as
I could not have failed to do after hearing the evidence
and observing the demeanour of the witnesses, particularly the unsatisfactory examination of both the
defendants. I am satisfied that there was a deliberate
intention on the part of both *Jenkins* and *Palmer* to
cheat the plaintiff. I reserved my judgment, however, to
look into the law, as I thought the Statute of Frauds
might be a bar to the plaintiff's right to a decree. I
have come to the conclusion, however, after considering
the authorities, that it constitutes no defence. The
evidence of the agency of *Jenkins* was clearly parol,
and the case of *Bartlett* v. *Pickersgill* (a) certainly
establishes that where an agent for purchase makes
a contract and takes a conveyance in his own name,
no part of the consideration being paid by the principal,
and there being no part performance, the fact of the
agency being proved by parol only, the Statute of

Judgment.

_____

(a) 1 Cox, 15, and 4 East, 577, *n*.

68—VOL. XVIII. GR.

Frauds applies, and the agency cannot be established; and this case is quoted with approval by late text-writers of authority (a).

This case of *Bartlett* v. *Pickersgill* has, however, lately undergone some criticism by the Lords Justices in the case of *Heard* v. *Pilley* (b), which last case, in its facts, much resembles the present. Lord Justice *Selwyn* there says; "Assuming the case of *Bartlett* v. *Pickersgill* to be good law, it cannot, I think, be considered as laying down any such general proposition as is contended for by the defendants. At all events, it would be subject to qualifications, especially to those which are mentioned by Lord *St. Leonards* (c). I cannot accede to the argument urged in reply, that under these circumstances, when the agent goes to the principal and says, 'I will go and buy an estate for you,' it is not a fraudulent act on his part afterwards to buy the estate for himself, and deny the agency. I think that would be an attempt to make the Statute of Frauds an instrument of fraud;" and Lord Justice *Giffard* says: "I cannot help adding, as regards the case of *Bartlett* v. *Pickersgill*, that it seems to be inconsistent with all the authorities of this Court, which proceed on the footing that it will not allow the Statute of Frauds to be an instrument of fraud." Without, however, assuming that *Heard* v. *Pilley* has overruled *Bartlett* v. *Pickersgill*, I think I may distinguish this case from it as the Lords Justices distinguished *Heard* v. *Pilley*. In *Bartlett* v. *Pickersgill* there had been a completion of the purchase by a conveyance: here, as in *Heard* v. *Pilley*, there has been no formal grant. This alone would, in my judgment, be sufficient to warrant a decree for the plaintiff. But there are other grounds. In the first place, I think it cannot be said that the principle

---

(a) Lewin on Trusts, 5th ed. p. 133; Dart on Vendors, 4th ed. p. 882.

(b) L. R. 4 Ch. App. 548.  (c) V. & P. 14th ed. p. 145.

on which Lord *Rosslyn* decided *Foster* v. *Hale* (a), and
Sir *James Wigram* decided *Dale* v. *Hamilton* (b),
however it may have been found fault with by text-
writers, has ever been judicially overruled; and if not,
it applies in the present case, since the evidence shews
that the agreement between the plaintiff and *Jenkins*,
of which I must hold *Palmer* to have had ample notice,
was, that *Jenkins* should obtain the lease for the joint
benefit of himself and the plaintiff, and that the lode
should be worked by them in partnership.

But perhaps the safest answer to the Statute of
Frauds is to be found in the fact that the consideration
for the agreement was wholly paid by the plaintiff. It is
proved that the only consideration given to *Palmer*
for this lease, or agreement for lease, was the testing
of the ore at the crushing-mill of the plaintiff. This
test was had at the sole expense of the plaintiff. It is
well established that where the purchase money, or any
part of it, is paid by the principal, parol evidence of
agency is let in on the ground of resulting trust; and
although I doubted at the time of the argument, I am
now convinced that, the agreement having been made
by *Palmer* in consideration of this test to be made at
the plaintiff's mill, and at the plaintiff's expense, as
was afterwards done, the case is not distinguishable
from one in which the price is actually paid by the
principal in money; so that there is here, in my opinion,
a resulting trust expressly excepted by the 8th section
of the Statute of Frauds.

There will, therefore, be a decree for plaintiff, with
costs.

1871.
Williams
v.
Jenkins.

Judgment.

---

(a) 5 Ves. 308.    (b) 5 Hare 369.

THE ONTARIO SALT COMPANY V. THE MERCHANTS
SALT COMPANY.

*Contract in restraint of trade—Demurrer—Ultra vires.*

Several incorporated companies and individuals, engaged in the
manufacture and sale of salt entered into an agreement, whereby
it was stipulated that the several parties agreed to combine and
amalgamate under the name of " The Canadian Salt Association," for
the purpose of successfully working the business of salt manufacturing and to further develope and extend the same, and which
provided that all the parties to it should sell all salt manufactured
by them through the trustees of the association, and should sell
none except through the trustees:

*Held,* on demurrer, that this agreement was not void as contrary to
public policy or as tending to a monopoly or being in undue
restraint of trade; that it was not *ultra vires* of such of the contracting parties as were incorporated companies, but was such in
its nature as the Court would enforce.

Demurrer for want of equity.

Mr. *Crooks,* Q. C., and Mr. *James Maclennan,* for the
demurrer.

Mr. *Blake,* Q. C., and Mr. *Garrow,* contra.

The grounds of demurrer and points relied on by
counsel are stated in the judgment of

Judgment.    STRONG, V. C.—The bill in this case is filed by the
Ontario Salt Company and five other companies, all
incorporated under the provisions of the general Acts
of the Legislature relating to joint stock companies, and
several individuals as plaintiffs, against the Merchants
Salt Company, a corporation also constituted under the
general Acts referred to; and it seeks to have the
defendants restrained from doing certain acts in contravention of covenants contained in an indenture made
between the plaintiffs and defendants. This indenture
the bill alleges to have been entered into " with the view

of successfully working the business of salt manufacturing, and to further develope and extend the same, and
for the purpose of procuring and assuring combined
action and mutual protection in their said business."
By the indenture the plaintiffs and defendants agreed
" to combine and amalgamate and unite under the name
of the Canadian Salt Association for the purposes stated
in the recital of the said agreement of mutual protection
in the general management of salt operations, for the
purpose of selling on such terms as to secure as far as
possible a fair share for their capital invested in such
operations, and generally for the purposes of combined
action and mutual protection in all matters relating to
the manufacture and sale of salt in Canada and elsewhere." The bill further states as follows : " The said
agreement provided for the appointment of trustees
from among and by whom a president and vice-president
were to be appointed ; and the said trustees were also to
appoint and provide for the payment of such other
officers or agents as they might deem necessary for fully
and effectually carrying out the agreement," and that in
pursuance of the agreement trustees and officers were
appointed. It is also alleged by the bill that " the
agreement provides that all the parties to it should sell
all salt manufactured by them through the trustees of
the association, and should sell none except through
the said trustees ;" and that no party should be permitted to withdraw from the agreement until six months
after its date, and then not until after three months'
notice.

This bill was demurred to for want of equity. Upon
the argument of the demurrer, the learned counsel for
the defendants insisted upon the following points : *First*,
that the agreement set forth in the bill was contrary to
public policy as tending to a monopoly. *Secondly*, that
it was void as being in undue restraint of trade. *Thirdly*,
that it was a contract *ultra vires* of the defendants and

Judgment.

such of the plaintiffs as are incorporated companies.
*Fourthly*, that it was an agreement of such a peculiar
nature that, even though binding at law, this Court would
not enforce it; and lastly, that the Court ought to decline
to interfere on the ground of hardship.

I am of opinion that on none of these grounds ought
this demurrer to be allowed.

It is out of the question to say that the agreement
which is the subject of this bill had for its object the
creation of a monopoly, inasmuch as it appears from the
bill that the plaintiffs and defendants are not the only
persons engaged in the production of salt in this province,
and therefore the trade in salt produced here by other
persons, and in salt imported from abroad, will remain
unaffected by the agreement, except in so far as prices
may possibly be influenced by it.   The objection on this
head is rather that the agreement has for its object the
raising the price of salt, and for that reason is illegal, as
constituting the old common law offence of "engrossing,"
or at least is void as being against public policy.

Engrossing is defined to be "the getting into one's
possession or buying up large quantities of corn or other
dead victuals with intent to sell them again." (a)   In
the case of the *King* v. *Waddington* (b), the defendant
was convicted of the offence of trying to raise the price
of hops in the market, by telling sellers that hops were
too cheap, and planters that they had not a fair price for
their crops, and for contracting for one-fifth of the produce of two counties, when he had a stock on hand
and did not want to buy, but merely to speculate how
he could enhance the price.   And *Waddington* was
imprisoned for four months and fined £500.   Mr. Justice
*Grose*, in pronouncing sentence, saying, that "It would

---

(a) Benjamin on Sales, p. 386.          (b) 1 East. 143.

be a precedent of *most awful moment* for this Court to declare that hops, which are an article of merchandise, and which we are compelled to use for the preservation of the common beverage of the people of this country, are not an article the price of which it is a crime by undue means to advance." The common law which was so severely applied in this case has since been abolished in England by the statute 7 and 8 Vic. cap. 24; and although I have been unable to discover that any similar legislation has taken place in this country, I cannot suppose that a law which would strike at a vast number of transactions which, with manifest benefit and profit to the community, are daily being entered into without the least suspicion on the part of those engaged in them that they are doing wrong, would now be applied as part of our common law. As regards the United States, Mr. *W. Story*, in his Treatise on Sales, at p. 647, says: " These three prohibited acts" (referring to engrossing and the kindred offences of forestalling and regrating) " are not only practised every day, but they are the very life of trade, and without them all wholesale trade and jobbing would be at an end. It is quite safe, therefore, to consider that they would not now be held to be against public policy." I must therefore conclude that long usage has brought about such a change in the common law since the decision in the *King* v. *Waddington*, that even if it could be said that the object of the parties to the agreement in question here was to enhance the price of salt, the contract would be neither illegal nor against public policy.

Were I to hold this agreement void on any such ground, I should be laying down a rule, which if applied, would cause great inconvenience in trade, and one, the necessity for which would at this day be discountenanced by all public and scientific opinion.

I am far, however, from saying that if this doctrine

1871.

Ontario Salt Co. v. Merchants Salt Co.

Judgment.

of the *King* v. *Waddington* is still to be considered as
law, it would reach such an agreement as this. I think
a distinction would be found in the consideration that
here the article, the price of which was to be regulated,
was not to be purchased in the market, but was actually
to be produced by the parties themselves, and this pro-
duct they could not be compelled to part with except on
their own terms. Then the object of the agreement was
not unduly to enhance the price, but as it is expressly
alleged in the bill, to enable the parties by concerted
action to combat an attempt on the part of foreign
producers and manufacturers unduly to depreciate it. I
know of no rule of law *ever* having existed which prohibited a certain number (not all) of the producers of a
staple commodity agreeing not to sell below a certain
price—and nothing more than this has been agreed to
by the parties here.

Further, it is expressly alleged in the bill that the
effect of the deed was to constitute a partnership; and
if this is so, there can be nothing objectionable in the
stipulation that all the salt produced—which is to form
the partnership stock—should be sold through the agency
of the trustees. The first objection therefore fails.

I cannot either agree that this contract is void on
grounds of public policy, as being in undue restraint of
trade. The law on this subject is now well settled, though
there is sometimes much difficulty in applying it. *Primâ
facie* every contract in restraint of trade is void; but if
an agreement appears to be for a partial restraint only,
for valuable consideration and reasonable, the law
sanctions it.

Here there is certainly some restraint imposed by the
parties upon themselves, for they agree not to sell except
through the intervention of the common agents, such
salt as they may produce. But this is a partial restraint

only; they put no restriction on their right to continue the manufacture, neither do they stipulate not to sell at all, but merely not to sell except through the medium of particular persons. Then the mutual obligations imposed by the contract constitute a sufficient consideration.

The remaining question, as to how far the restraint is reasonable, introduces the only difficulty to be found in the case. In *Horner* v. *Graves* (a), *Tindal*, C. J., explains the sense in which the expression *reasonable* is to be used in this connection, as follows:—"We do not see how a better test can be applied to the question, whether reasonable or not, than by considering whether the restraint is such only as to afford a fair protection to the interest of the party in favor of whom it is given, and not so large as to interfere with the interests of the public."

The question then here is, whether or not this agreement does do hurt to the public interest? The authority principally relied on by Mr. *Crooks* was the case of *Hilton* v. *Eckersley* (b). There a bond entered into by the millowners of a certain district in Lancashire, conditioned to carry on their works in regard to wages, and the engaging of labourers and time of work, according to the resolutions of a majority for a period of twelve months, was held void as being in undue restraint of trade, and so contrary to public policy. It is to be observed that in *Hilton* v. *Eckersley* each millowner completely surrendered his right of carrying on trade without restraint to the majority of the associates, who could at any moment they thought fit close the mills altogether. Before, however, pointing out how far short of the restraint imposed in *Hilton* v. *Eckersley* the present agreement falls, I will refer to some general

1871.

Ontario Salt Co v. Merchants Oil Co.

Judgment.

(a) 7 Bing. at 743.          (b) 6 E. & B. 47.

observations of Judges of high authority, which shew how carefully courts of justice ought to proceed in determining what is and what is not against public policy. In this same case of *Hilton* v. *Eckersley*, we find Lord Campbell using this language: "I enter upon such considerations with much reluctance and with great apprehension when I think how different generations of Judges and different Judges of the same generation have differed in opinion upon questions of political economy and other topics connected with the adjudication of such cases; and I cannot help thinking that where there is no illegality in bonds and other instruments at common law, it would have been better that our Courts of justice had been required to give effect to them, unless where they are avoided by Act of Parliament."

When one finds that Lord Campbell, notwithstanding these striking observations, decided that the obligors were not bound by their bond, it is impossible not to

feel the force of the somewhat quaint illustration of *Burrough*, J., in *Richardson* v. *Mellish* (a), where he says: "Public policy is an unruly horse, and when once you get astride it, you never know where it will carry you."

Again, commenting on *Hilton* v. *Eckersley*, the editors of *Smith's* Leading Cases, Mr. Justice *Willes* and Mr. Justice *Keating* say (b): "The law upon this subject is, it must be confessed, in an unsatisfactory state, and there seems but too much ground to fear that, unless checked by a firm determination to uphold men's acts when not in violation of some known rule of law, and to treat decided cases having a contrary tendency as exceptional, it may degenerate into the mere private discretion of the majority of the Court as to a subject of all others most open to difference of opinion and most

---

(a) 2 Bing. at 252        (b) 4 edit. vol. 1, p. 286.

liable to be affected by changing circumstances." And
in *Richardson* v. *Mellish*, already cited, *Best*, C. J.,
says : " I am not much disposed to yield to arguments of
public policy. I think the Courts of Westminster Hall
have gone much further than they were warranted in
doing on questions of policy. They have taken on
themselves sometimes to decide doubtful questions of
policy, and they are always in. danger in so doing,
because Courts of law look only at the particular case,
and have not the means of bringing before them all those
considerations which enter into the judgments of those
who decide on questions of policy. I admit that if it
can be clearly put upon the contravention of public
policy, the plaintiff cannot succeed ; but it must be
unquestionable—there must be no doubt."

After reading the extracts which I have just quoted, it
requires no argument to demonstrate that decided cases,
unless the facts exactly resemble those of the case for
determination, are of but little assistance in questions of
this kind. I think, therefore, that *Hilton* v. *Eckersley*
may be disposed of by saying that the only proposition
of law which it affirms is the familiar one that contracts
in restraint of trade, though partial, are nevertheless
void if unreasonable—that is against public policy.
That the particular contract there in question was void
on that ground, in no way assists to prove that the totally
dissimilar contract in question here is also to be held
bad. The rule of law is plain—the difficulty is in
applying it.

I must therefore inquire whether in the present case
there is "without doubt" an "unquestionable" interference with the public interests by reason of the
execution of this deed.

In the first place, it must be remembered, that there
is here no submission to the will of a majority, but that

1871.

Ontario Salt
Co.
v.
Merchants
Salt Co.

Judgment.

all are placed on an equal footing. Then there is no restriction on the sale of the salt, but it is all to be placed in the hands of the trustees, whose duty it is to sell to the best advantage, the interest of all being alike. What is this more than two persons carrying on the same trade binding themselves not to undersell each other? And can it be said that such an agreement would be in restraint of trade? The only distinction between such a case and this is, that in the case put the parties would be subject to the inconvenience of having constantly to adjust the prices with the risk of frequent disagreements, whilst in the present case that is obviated by leaving it to the judgment of a common agent. Suppose two producers of any article agree to consign all their produce to the same agent and to leave that agent to sell for the same price. How would public policy be infringed by such an arrangement? The argument on the part of the defendants might be pushed so far as to make a partnership between two persons carrying on the same trade illegal as tending to lessen competition. That a contract to charge the same prices is not an improper restraint of trade, was determined by high authority in the case of *Hearne* v. *Griffin* (a). That was the case of an agreement between two coach masters not to oppose each other and to charge the same prices, and it was contended that it was an undue restraint. But Lord *Ellenborough* held the contract to be valid, saying: "How can you contend that it is in restraint of trade; they are left to charge what they like, though not more than each other. This is merely a convenient mode of arranging two concerns which might otherwise ruin each other." I see no difference in principle between that case and the present. Here, it is true, as I have already remarked, that the regulation of price is left to third parties, the trustees, whose obligations are alike to all the constituents. If authority is

---

(a) 2 Chitty's Repts. 407.

to be referred to, the case of *Wickens* v. *Evans* (a), cited by Mr. *Blake*, is strongly in favor of the plaintiffs resembling this case as it does in many of the essential facts.

I do not follow Mr. *Crooks* in his argument that the number of persons associated in this arrangement made a difference. It appears on the face of the bill that they are not all the salt producers in the Province, and it also appears that salt, other than the produce of the wells of the plaintiffs and defendants, can be, and is supplied to the public. This being so, I think it makes no difference that this agreement was entered into by twenty persons engaged in the trade instead of only two.

Did I even think otherwise than I do, that this arrangement was injurious to the public interests, I should hesitate much before I acted on such an opinion, for I should feel that I was called on to relieve parties from a solemn contract, not by the mere application of some well established rule of law, but upon my own notions of what the public good required—in effect to arbitrarily make the law for the occasion. I can conceive no more objectionable instance of what is called Judge-made law, than a decision by a single Judge in a new and doubtful case that a contract is not to bind on the ground of public policy.

Mr. *Crooks* further argued that the deed was not binding as being *ultra vires* of the several parties who are companies incorporated under the Provincial Acts relating to joint stock companies. Upon the allegations of the bill, I must assume that so far as the individual members of these companies are concerned, they assented to the arrangement and to the execution of the deed. Then I take the rule to be that these companies, like all corporations, are regulated as to their powers by the instrument of their creation; and that if not expressed

---

(a) 3 Y. & J. 318.

in the statute, it is to be implied that they are to engage in no undertaking foreign to the object for which they are created. So far I go with the learned counsel for the defendants. But I cannot agree that this arrangement is foreign to the purpose of companies incorporated for the purpose of producing, manufacturing, and selling salt. I regard the agreement as one providing for a particular mode of selling salt, and therefore as being quite consistent with the objects of the company, and in fact tending to the better accomplishment of those objects. I do not think the companies have surrendered their rights in any respect. Their internal affairs will still be managed as usual, and their business will not, under the agreement, be interfered with, save in the single matter of selling. The cases determining the validity of traffic agreements, as they are called, between competing railway companies, providing that the gross earnings shall go into a common purse and be divided in certain agreed proportions, are in point

to shew that this deed is not *ultra vires*.

It was argued by Mr. *Maclennan* that, even assuming the agreement to be legal and binding, the case was not a proper one for the interference of a Court of equity. I must decide against this objection also. The breach of the agreement complained of by the bill is, the sale of salt in contravention of the covenant not to sell except through the trustees. The right to an injunction to restrain a breach of a negative covenant stands on a different footing from a right to specific performance, and ever since 1852, when Lord *St. Leonards* decided, *Lumley* v. *Wagner* (a), I believe there has been no doubt but that the breach of such a covenant as this would be enjoined.

It was lastly urged that the hardship of the agreement on the defendants constituted a defence. I cannot see the

---

(a) 1 Deg. M. & G. 604.

slightest foundation for such an objection. All parties under this deed have equal rights and equal liabilities. The demurrer must be overruled with costs.

## THE ONTARIO SALT COMPANY v. THE MERCHANTS SALT COMPANY.

*Injunction—Corporate seals—Partnership.*

Several proprietors of salt wells entered into an undertaking to sell their products through trustees, and in no other way; and a written agreement to this effect was executed by all the parties, except one, who was resident in England, and carried on his business here through an agent; the business was carried on under the agreement, notwithstanding his non-execution of the deed, and one of the other parties having subsequently attempted to act in contravention of the agreement, it was *held* that the delay of the absent party to sign the contract could not be set up as an answer to a motion for an injunction restraining the contravention.

Some of the parties executing a deed were corporate bodies, and the witnessing clause was expressed, "In witness whereof, the said parties hereto have hereunto set their hands aed seals," &c, and the seals were all simple wafer seals.

*Held*, that in the absence of evidence shewing these not to be the proper corporate seals of the companies, this was a sufficient sealing on the part of the incorporated companies.*

After the decision of the demurrer, which has just been reported, a motion was made for an injunction in the terms of the prayer of the bill by

Mr. *Spencer* and Mr. *Garrow*, for the plaintiffs.

Mr. *Crooks*, Q. C., Mr. *Hayes*, and Mr. *Holmested*, contra.

SPRAGGE, C.—I have read the judgment of my brother *Strong* upon the argument of the demurrer, and

* See also as to the point of what is a sufficient sealing of an instrument: Hamilton v. Dennis, *ante* volume xii. p. 325.

1871.

Ontario
Salt Co.
v.
Merchants
Salt Co.

of course consider the points which he has decided
conclusively determined, so far as this application is
concerned, unless presented by evidence in a shape
substantially different from that in which they are
presented by the Bill; and upon reading the affidavits
on both sides upon this application, I do not find that the
points which were, before my learned brother upon the
demurrer are substantially varied by the affidavit evidence.

There are, however, some points which did not arise
and were not determined upon the demurrer. The non-
execution by *Ranesford* of the instrument by which this
association was constituted is one of these. It appears
sufficiently, I think, that it was considered an important point by those who formed the association that
*Ranesford* should join it; so important indeed, that it
is at least doubtful whether the defendants would have
entered into it, but for the expectation that *Ranesford*

Judgment. would have been a party to it. It is even put more
strongly in the affidavit of Mr. *Hayes*, that it was upon
the assurance of a leading promoter of the undertaking
that *Ranesford* would join it, and upon the condition
that he would join it, that the defendants became parties
to the association; and it is stated that it was not before
the 10th of October that the defendants became aware
that he had not joined it. He is named as a party in
the instrument of association.

This association was, in its legal effect, a partnership;
and there can be no doubt that if one or several parties
enter into articles of copartnership in which another or
other parties are named as partners, and the party or
parties so named do not join and execute the articles,
it is only a contemplated not a perfected partnership.
Here *Ranesford* was not only named, but there was a
distinct understanding, if not a condition, that he should
be a party to the association. He was the largest

manufacturer in, what has been called the salt region, and his co-operation in the objects of the association was deemed material if not essential to its success.

On the other hand are these facts. *Ranesford*, at the time of the entering into this association (1st July last), was a resident of London, England, and always was so and still is so, conducting his business of boring for, and manufacturing salt by an agent in Canada; and it was well understood that the operations of the association were not to await his becoming a party to the association, but were to be proceeded with at once; and as a matter of fact the association did go into operation; and *Ranesford's* agent in Canada acted under the articles of association as if *Ranesford* himself had actually and formally become a party to it.

The necessary result of what was agreed to be done, and of what was done was, that the necessary time for *Ranesford* to become a party to the instrument of Association was to be allowed; the business of the association not to be in abeyance in the meantime but to be proceeded with. If the defendants had within such necessary time done the acts which are complained of in this suit, I am of opinion that they ought to have been enjoined. I think the question upon this point is, whether a reasonable time has elapsed.

It is urged that it was as much the duty of the defendants as of the plaintiffs to procure *Ranesford's* execution of the instrument. It appears from the affidavits that the defendants were not the promoters of the association, and that they became parties to it, their officers making it a point that *Ranesford* should also become a party. This, I think, threw upon the promoters the duty of seeing that he became a party: or, supposing it was not the peculiar duty of any party to see to this, it could hardly be a consequence that all

70—VOL. XVIII. GR.

other parties should remain bound for an indefinite
period as partners in an enterprise, while a person whose
partnership was at the least considered important, was
not a party. All this time the relations of *Ranesford*
with the association have been of an anomalous character; he has had the advantages of membership of this
association without its liabilities, and with the power, so
far as appears from anything that is disclosed in the
case, of acting independently of it at any time that he
might think fit.

On the other hand is this: that the defendants, who
were represented by a very active agent (Mr. *Hayes*),
at the board of the association never made any
objection to the absence of Mr. *Ranesford*. He says
indeed that he had assumed that *Ranesford* had executed the instrument, until informed to the contrary
on the 10th of October; but so little importance was
attached to its non-execution that, in a letter written
seven days afterwards by the defendants' manager, in
which he announces the determination of the defendants' board of directors not to remain in amalga-
mation any longer, unless the defendants were allowed
themselves to sell a certain quality of salt, he
makes no allusion to the non-execution of the instrument by *Ranesford*, but concludes with a hope "that
this matter will be arranged at once so as to meet our
views:" and, in a letter written the day following by
Mr. *Hayes* himself, the non-execution by *Ranesford* is
not in terms alluded to. His letter sets forth several
grounds of complaint by the defendants against the
association. The two first would have suggested the
objection, if thought an essential one: "1st. That all
the manufacturers have not come in, and this was a
fundamental part of the understanding. 2d. All the
wells have not signed the agreement." Other objections
follow, which are matters of internal management. Those
which I have quoted do not point to the objection now

raised. They point to the fact of some manufacturers
of salt continuing to manufacture outside of the association. The second as well as the first points to this
only. It is the first objection put in another shape,
that *all* manufacturers have not joined the association;
that was the gravamen of the objection. There is
nothing in either of these two letters pointing to the
non-execution of the instrument by *Ranesford*. Immediately after this the defendants withdrew from the
association and committed the acts in contravention of
the instrument of association which are now sought to
be enjoined.

These two letters appear to me to be strong evidence
that the defendants had all along acquiesced in the
position of *Ranesford* with the association; and I must
take them to have had knowledge of what that position
was. They withdrew for reasons which certainly did not
warrant their withdrawal; and the sufficiency of which
is not now contended for, and then set up this non-
execution by *Ranesford*, which is evidently an afterthought. I must hold them to have acquiesced with
knowledge; and that they are not now entitled to set up
this non-execution by *Ranesford*, as entitling them to
act in contravention of their agreement.

It is objected further, that the instrument is not duly
executed under the corporate seal of the defendants, or
of the other parties to it who are corporate bodies. The
parties to it are some of them individuals and some of
them corporate bodies, and the witnessing part runs
thus: "In witness whereof, the said parties hereto have
hereunto set their hands and seals." A number of seals
are affixed, with nothing upon the face of them to denote
what they are. Opposite one of them—or rather of
more than one of them—are the words, the Merchants
Salt Company of Seaforth, limited, *M. P. Hayes*,
Secretary and Treasurer," Opposite others are the

Judgment.

names of officers of salt companies, describing them by abbreviations to be such. The objection is, that these seals are not shewn to be corporate seals; but what does appear is, I think, *primâ facie*, sufficient. These seals, as well as the seals set opposite the names of individuals, parties to the instrument, are described as the seals of the parties. "the said parties hereto have hereunto set their hands and seals"—some of those parties being individuals and some corporate bodies. There is no evidence that these seals are not the seals of these corporate bodies. The point arose in an American case: *Mill Dam Foundry* v. *Hovey* (a), and this was the language of the Court: "Now seals are in fact affixed to the instrument produced, and the legal presumption is that they were placed there as the seals of the parties. That presumption must prevail until it be rebutted by competent evidence. It has been said that the seal does not appear to be one of a corporation. But a corporation as well as an individual person may use and adopt any seal. They need not say that it is their common seal. This law is as old as the books."

I think the plaintiffs are entitled to an injunction, and that this is not a case in which the balance of convenience is in favor of leaving the defendants to conduct a separate, independent business, in contravention of the articles of association to which they became parties.

---

(a) 21 Pick. Rep. 417, 428.

# WILKIE V. THE CORPORATION OF THE VILLAGE OF CLINTON.

*Municipal council—Rates—Injunction—Separate accounts.*

The limit of two cents in the dollar demanded by the Municipal Act of 1866 as the maximum of assessment, includes the special sinking fund rate to be levied in respect of past debts.

Where for the purpose of erecting a market house, a municipal council would require to levy a rate which would exceed the amount of two cents in the dollar allowed to be imposed by section 225 of the Act, it was *held* that a ratepayer was entitled to an injunction restraining the erection of the building by the council.

It is culpable neglect of duty on the part of municipal officers not to see that separate accounts for special rate, sinking fund, and assessments for general purposes are kept as directed by the statute.

Motion for injunction to restrain the defendants the Corporation from paying, and the other defendants (the contractors) from receiving any moneys on account of the contract for the erection of the market house and town hall in the said village; and also restraining the Corporation from proceeding to collect or receive the rates imposed for the payment of such building.

Mr. *S. Blake* and Mr. *D. McDonald*, for the motion.

Mr. C. *Moss*, contra.

SPRAGGE, C.—In my view of this case it may be conceded to the defendants that a by-law for the expenditure of moneys for the putting up of a market place, the money expended to be paid within the year, was within the competence of the Town Council.

Nov. 15.

Judgment.

The case seems to turn upon this: whether the limit of two cents in the dollar imposed by the Municipal Act of 1866, section 225, as the maximum of assessment, comprises under the terms " debts of the Corporation,

whether of principal or interest, falling due within the
year," the special sinking fund rate required by the
statute to be imposed when money is borrowed upon the
credit of the Municipality under section 226.

The statute of 1849 contained clauses similar to sections 225 and 226 in the Act of 1866, except that no
limit was placed to the assessment and levy by the
Council upon the ratable property of the Municipality.
In the former as in the latter statute, it was made the
duty of the Municipal Council to assess and levy each
year a sufficient sum to pay all valid debts of the Corporation, whether of principal or interest, falling due
within the year : then follows the restriction, "but no
such council shall assess and levy in any one year more
than an aggregate rate of two cents in the dollar on the
actual value, exclusive of school rates ; and if in any
municipality the aggregate amount of the rates necessary for the payment of the current annual expenses of
the municipality, and the interest and principal of the
debts contracted by such municipality, at the time of the
passing of this Act shall exceed the said aggregate rate
of two cents in the dollar on the actual value of such
ratable property, the council of such municipality shall
levy such further rates as may be necessary to discharge
obligations already incurred, but shall contract no
further debts until the annual rates required to be
levied within such municipality are reduced within the
aggregate rate aforesaid." If the sinking fund rate
falls within this restriction, the two cents in the dollar
will be exceeded by the expenditure which is sought to
be restrained.

The words of the Act are " valid debts of the corporation, whether of principal or interest;" and it is
contended that the sum, which the municipality is
required by law to raise and set apart yearly as a
sinking fund for the gradual repayment of moneys

borrowed, is not a *debt* within the meaning of the Act. I do not agree in this. I think the word must be taken as used in its most comprehensive sense, as something due from one to another. I find it defined in the Imperial Dictionary as " that which is due from one to another, whether money, goods, or service, which one person is bound to pay or perform to another." I take the word to be used in the same sense as the word "obligations," in the latter part of the clause.

It is an incident of the money borrowed, part of the contract of lending; it is due to the creditor, that so much shall be set apart yearly towards his eventual payment. Its being done, adds to his security; its omission impairs it. I cannot doubt that he has such an interest in its being done as would entitle him to compel its being done. It is something incident, as I have said, to the debt, which the municipality is bound to provide for. Its nature is to create a trust fund; and the municipality is a debtor to the fund year by year as moneys become payable to that fund. It is, in my opinion, a debt of the municipality in the most proper sense of the term, and without giving to the word used any strained construction.

That it is used in this sense in the Act is further apparent from this, that it is the only clause in the Act by which it is made the duty of municipal councils, or by which they are empowered to assess and levy upon the ratable property of the municipality. It is the mode pointed out by the statute for providing means for carrying on the affairs of the municipality. If funds are not raised in this way they cannot, so far as the Act goes, be raised at all.

It appears to me the proper solution of the question is this: the sinking fund is comprehended in that, to meet which the council is to assess and levy upon the ratable

1871.

property. The limit of that assessment is two cents in
the dollar, and the expenditure in question overruns that
amount, and ratepayers therefore are entitled to an
injunction. I do not think, looking at all that has
occurred, that there has been any such lying by or delay
as should disentitle the plaintiffs to what they ask.

The matter may not be of any great practical importance, as the by-law which is to be submitted to the
ratepayers during the present month may solve the
difficulty.

I think I ought not to dispose of this case without
observing upon the utter disregard of the provisions of
the statute, disclosed in the evidence, on the part of
those officers of the municipality whose duty it is to see
to the keeping of its accounts. The separate accounts,
so pointedly required by section 230 of the Act, seem
not to have been kept; but special rates, sinking fund
account, and rates and assessments for general purposes,
appear to have been mixed up together. The directions
of the statute are so explicit, that it was nothing less
than most culpable neglect of duty not to follow them.

---

## WALLACE v. MOORE.

*Dower—Mode of estimating damages.*

The mere fact that at the death of, or alienation by, the husband, his
lands were of no rentable value, is not alone sufficient to disentitle
the widow to claim damages, if the land has been subsequently
made rentable by reason of improvements or otherwise either by the
heir or vendee; as in such a case a portion of the rent is attributable to the land.

Appeal by the defendant from the report of the
Master, at Brantford. The grounds of appeal appear
in the judgment.

Mr. *McGregor*, for the appeal.

Mr. *E. B. Wood*, contra.

SPRAGGE, C.—In my opinion the Master has taken
the value of the dower of Mrs. *Moore* upon an erroneous
principle, so far as the arrears of dower are concerned.
It is evident from the terms of his report, that he has
taken the value of the land as the basis of his calculation,
and fixed the value of the dower by a rate, as to one
portion six per cent.; as to another five per cent. upon the
value of the land. It is manifest that the result arrived
at may be very different from the annual value.

The mode adopted by the Master is not reasonable, nor
is it in accordance with the statute. The 21st section of
the Act 32 Victoria chapter 7, speaks of the mode of
arriving at the allowance for arrears of dower, or fixing
a yearly sum in lieu of an assignment of dower by
metes and bounds, as "estimating damages for the
detention of dower or the yearly value of the lands."
The damages for the detention of dower must be the loss
sustained by the widow by reason of her proportion of
rents, or of the value of occupation, not having been paid
to her. The words "yearly value" speak for themselves; and the third sub-section of section 31 makes the
meaning of the Act, if possible, still more clear. It provides, that in cases where from circumstances an assignment by metes and bounds cannot be made, there shall
be assessed "a yearly sum of money, being as near as
may be one-third of the clear yearly rents of the
premises, after deducting any rates or assessments payable thereon." Nothing can indicate more clearly the
intention of the Legislature that the compensation to the
widow should be one-third of the yearly value or yearly
rents received—not a percentage upon the gross value.
I need hardly say that the principle of compensation
prescribed by sub-section 3 of section 31 is to be

observed wherever an assessment is to be made, whether
of arrears of dower or in lieu of an assignment by metes
and bounds.

A portion of the property of which the widow in this
case is dowable consists of village lots in Norwichville, a
considerable and increasing village. Of these lots only
one had buildings upon it at the death of the husband ;
the rest were vacant and of no annual value, producing
no rents or profits ; but the Master has taken the gross
value of the whole of them and upon that value has
fixed a percentage. In regard to the arrears of dower
this is, so far as the vacant lots are concerned, compensating the widow, where she has sustained no loss. So
far therefore as the arrears of dower are concerned, I
think the Master has proceeded upon an erroneous
principle. The 21st section does not in terms deal with
such a case as is presented by the decree in this suit.

It provides for arrears of dower ; and for fixing the value
of future dower in lieu of assignment by metes and
bounds ; but does not provide for fixing a gross sum in
lieu of an annual payment for future dower. Here the
decree directs the Master to find the value of the dower
as well as the arrears. This value of the dower must
mean its value for the future. This admits of different
considerations, and I do not see what principle can be
adopted in the case of the village lots other than that
which the Master has taken, and no other has been
suggested. Her right, independently of the decree,
would be to have her dower assigned by metes and
bounds or by parcels, upon the principle prescribed in
sub-section 2 of section 31. The value directed by the
decree to be ascertained is in lieu of that right ; and it
would be ignoring that right and palpably unjust to say,
because certain property has yielded no annual profit
hitherto, her dower in it is of no value. Obviously it is
of some value. Suppose buildings put upon these lots,
the rentable value would be compounded in part of the

value of the buildings; and in part of the value of the land, and so much of the rentable value of the whole as is properly attributable to the land is the rentable value of the land. It may be the building that gives the rentable value to the land, but still it is the rentable value of the house and land, and not of the house only; for the house elsewhere than on the land might be of much less annual value than the house and land together, and would be certainly of some less annual value.

Then as to the farm property. Section 21 of the Act deals with arrears of dower, and also prescribes the mode of fixing the yearly value of dower for the time to come; but, as I have said, it makes no provision for ascertaining the gross value in one sum. That I apprehend must still be done by taking the value of the life of the dowress. The yearly value of the land must be taken in the mode pointed out by the 21st section. It may be that in this case, at the date of the death of the husband, the farm property was in so bad a condition that its annual value was very small; one witness puts it, as worth nothing at that date. I do not think that this clause of the Act calls for an estimate of value based upon the actual condition and productiveness of the property at the date of the husband's death. Such a construction would lead to consequences certainly not contemplated by the Act. For instance, farm property might, from bad husbandry, from neglect of land, buildings, and fences, have fallen into such a condition that its productiveness would not at the time repay the cost of cultivation; and yet, with repair and good husbandry, the annual value might be very considerable. And so with house property, it might at the death of the husband be in such a state of dilapidation as to be literally untenantable; and its rentable value while in that condition scarcely anything; while, if put in repair or let upon an improving lease, it might bring a large rental.

It would be at once unjust, and not according to the spirit of the Act, in any such cases to compute the allowance to the widow upon the actual annual value at the date of the death of the husband. The mischief to be remedied was, the widow, under the law as it then stood, being dowable of permanent improvements; usually, buildings put upon the land by the heir or devisee, or alienee of the husband. This was felt to be unjust as well as against public policy in deterring the proprietor of the land from improving his property; and so the clause enacts in the first place that the value of permanent improvements made after death or alienation shall not be taken into account. It is upon the concluding part of the clause that any doubt can exist. It enacts that the estimate shall be made upon the " state of the property" at the time of alienation or death, allowing for rise in value. The " state of the property" here spoken of means, as I read the clause, its state without permanent improvements as distinguished from its state with permanent improvements. Reading the whole together, and looking at the mischief it was intended to remedy, I think it would be pushing this clause beyond its object and meaning if it were interpreted to mean anything more than that permanent improvements made after the death of, or alienation by the husband should be excluded from consideration—in the words of the first part of the clause, should "not be taken into account." Any other interpretation would operate unjustly against the dowress; for instance, in the case of farm or house property in a dilapidated condition at the time of death or alienation. The clause applies to arrears of dower as well as to fixing a money value in lieu of an assignment by metes and bounds, and this case might occur: land might descend or be devised, being at the time of death in a dilapidated condition, and the heirs or devisee might lease, allowing the first year's rent to the tenant for restoration and repair, and reserving a good money rental for the

residue of the term. It would be most unjust if the
dowress, coming after some years for her arrears of
dower, should be confined to what the land would
actually produce in the way of ground rental or profit
at the death of her husband. Instead of getting one-
third she might not get one-tenth of what had come to
the hands of the heirs or devisees since the death
of her husband, if the Act were to receive a more strict
interpretation against the dowress than that which I put
upon it. Regard, too, should be had to the character of
the improvements made. The language of the Act is
"permanent" improvements, and it is the value of the
land apart from improvements of that character that is
to be estimated.

I do not think it well to attempt to define more particularly how the estimate of value should be made.
What I mean to decide is, that the actual productiveness
of property at the date of alienation or death is not, in
my judgment, necessarily its yearly value within the
meaning of the Act. •

It must be referred back to the Master to review his
report. It is not a case in which I think it is proper to
give costs of this appeal to either party.

CANADA PERMANENT BUILDING AND SAVINGS' SOCIETY
v. YOUNG.

*Specific performance—Misdescription in advertisement—Compensation for
deficiency.*

The advertisement of sale of a farm described the property as being
"96 acres cleared and cultivated, a good log house, and frame
barn 60 by 32 on the premises; also, driving-shed." Upon a survey
of the property being made, it appeared that the quantity of
cleared land was 74¾ acres under cultivation and legal fence, and
12¼ acres of pasture land, with some girdled trees standing, and a
few logs lying upon it, which had never been cultivated and could
not be until the logs should be removed: the dimensions of the
barn were 50 feet by 30, and there was no driving-shed upon the
property. On a bill filed by the vendors for specific performance of
the contract:

*Held*, independently of a stipulation in the conditions of sale providing
for errors in the advertisement, that these differences were such as
entitled the purchaser to be compensated therefor: and the
vendors, having disputed the purchaser's right to such compensation, were ordered to pay the costs of the suit.

Examination of witnesses and hearing at St. Catha-
rines, Autumn Sittings, 1871.

Mr. *Proudfoot*, for the plaintiffs.

Mr. *Moss*, for the defendant.

Nov. 15.      SPRAGGE, C.—I have examined the cases to which I
was referred at the hearing, and am confirmed in the
Judgment. opinion that I then expressed, that the defendant is
entitled to compensation.

The bill is for specific performance by vendors of real
estate, sold by auction, against the purchaser.

The land sold is a farm in the township of Binbrook,
one of the conditions provided that " If any mistake be
made in the description of the premises, or any other
error whatsoever shall appear in the above particulars,

such mistake or error shall not annul the sale, but a
compensation or equivalent shall be given or taken, as
the case may require ; such compensation or equivalent
to be settled '' by arbitrators in a mode set out in the
condition.

In the advertisement of sale, the farm is described as
having " 90 acres, cleared and cultivated, a good log
house, and frame barn 60 by 32, on the premises, also
driving shed.'' The part of the description which I
have set out, is that which is objected to as erroneous.

It turns out that there were 74¾ acres under good cultivation and legal fence, and 12¼ acres of pasture land,
with some girdled trees upon it, and a few logs lying
upon it. This piece of land has never been cultivated,
and will not be fit for cultivation until the logs are
removed. The dimensions of the barn are 50 feet by
30 ; there was no driving shed on the place ; there was
what a witness described as " a kind of broken down
shed not used.'' A new shed has been put up since the
sale.

The defendant does not resist specific performance ;
but insists that it should be " with compensation in
respect of the particulars in which the premises fall short
in fact from what they were by the advertisement represented to be.''

The difference in the dimensions of the barn is certainly a substantial difference ; the quantity of cleared
land, too, is less in fact than it was described to be, and
part of it not in the condition described ; and there was
no driving shed.

The answer to the defendant's claim for compensation
is, that he was not deceived. I do not think this is
made out in fact. The only evidence upon it is that of

Mr. *Tomlinson*, the plaintiffs' agent at the sale, who
says that he had a conversation with the defendant
before the sale on the same morning; that he said
something about the description in the advertisement
not being correct; that the quantity of land was not so
much as described, and something about the barn and
shed, which the witness did not remember particularly.
He says that it was hard to understand him.

This is very faint evidence, or rather no evidence at
all of the defendant being himself acquainted with the
premises, so as to have knowledge of what they really
were—such knowledge as to correct the erroneous
description given in the advertisement. It is in evidence
that it was spoken of in the audience, that the description was inaccurate, and it was probably from this
that the defendant spoke to *Tomlinson*. This was before
the sale, and during its progress the agent drew the
defendant's attention to the compensation clause.

It is suggested that *Bell*, a son-in-law of the defendant,
and who was at the time living on the place, was the
defendant's agent at the sale, and that he knew the
actual state of the farm. I think *Bell* was not his
agent at the sale; and if he were, knowledge is not
brought home to the agent, except as to the driving shed.
*Bell* swears he did not know the dimensions of the
barn, nor the quantity of land cleared. As to the
latter indeed, the clearing was so irregular (as appeared
by a map put in at the hearing), that it would require
actual measurement and calculation to get at the quantity.
Upon neither point was it a matter patent to the senses,
as it was in one respect in *Dyer* v. *Hargrave.* (a) There
the land was described as being in a ring fence, when
it was in fact intersected by other lands; but this was
well known to the purchaser. Sir *William Grant* said,

---

(a) 10 Ves. 506.

"he saw the farm before he purchased. He was willing to purchase it by private contract. He had lived in the neighborhood all his life. This variance is the object of sense." The defendant in that case resisted specific performance on account of this variance, and of two other variances between the particulars and the actual condition of the premises. As to these other variances, the observations of Sir *William Grant* are so apposite to this case that I cannot do better than quote them: (a) "The two other objections admit a different consideration; for they are such as a man may have an indistinct knowledge of; and he may have some apprehension, that in those respects the premises do not completely correspond with the description; and yet the description may not be so completely destroyed as to produce any great difference in his offer." Just what Sir *William Grant* describes may have probably passed through the mind of the defendant in this case; and he would feel all the more safe when referred to the clause providing for compensation.

There is another case which was before Lord *Langdale*, *King* v. *Wilson*, (b) which applies particularly to the variance in the dimensions of the barn. The purchaser was at the time of the sale the tenant and occupier of a freehold house in Islington, which was described in the particulars as 46 feet in depth, when in fact the depth was only 33 feet. It was urged that the difference was so great that it must have attracted the attention of the purchaser; that there could have been no deception as the purchaser was in possession, and must have seen the mistake and known the real dimensions; but Lord *Langdale* held him entitled to be compensated for the difference, observing: "Now, I don't know that persons in the occupation of premises are in the habit of measuring them. I think you would

Judgment.

(a) Page 509.  (b) 6 Bea. 124.

72—VOL. XVIII. GR.

find very few persons who know the exact depth and frontage of their premises."

*Lethbridge* v. *Kirkman* (a) was an action to recover back a deposit. One of several objections to the sale was, that in the particulars of sale the premises were described as upwards of 217 feet in depth; one of the conditions of sale however was, that the quantities "were to be taken more or less;" and the Court did not think that the small discrepancy as to the measurement (which was actually 204 feet) was material. The question of compensation did not arise at all. I do not think the case material upon the question before me. Lord *Brooke* v. *Rounthwaite* (b) was a much stronger case for refusing compensation than this case can be pretended to be. Sir *James Wigram* said that he had found great difficulty in bringing his mind to believe that it was not a mere afterthought of the defendant. But he says: "If, however, there has been a misrepresentation, I cannot refuse the defendant the benefit of that ground of defence either in the way of compensation or of a decree dismissing the bill, merely upon such a speculation."

I think I should come to the conclusion that the purchaser in this case would be entitled to compensation, even if there were no provision for it in the conditions of sale. Where a party takes upon himself to make a representation in order to effect a sale and enhance his price, it is to be assumed, *prima facie,* that the purchaser buys upon the faith of that representation being true, and the onus is upon the seller to shew very clearly, when he desires to save himself from the consequences of his representation, that the purchaser's own knowledge of the thing sold was so clear and accurate, that he must have known the real condition of the thing

(a) 25 L. J. Q. B, 89.          (b) 5 Hare 298.

sold, and could not have been misled by the representation. The evidence in this case fails altogether to
shew any such knowledge in the purchaser.

Then as to the clause of compensation. It is framed,
in part at least, in the interest of the vendors, in order
to prevent the rescission of the contract of sale by reason
of mistake in the description of premises sold or other
error; but that the purchaser shall have compensation
in lieu thereof. This surely entitles the purchaser to
compensation where there is mistake in description or
other error as much as it enables the vendor to require
him to take compensation instead of a rescission of the
contract. It is distinctly a part of the contract; and
is no doubt made a part of the conditions of sale, for
the sake of its effect upon intending purchasers. Its
effect is almost necessarily to induce them to offer a
higher price; and it appears from the evidence of *Hoey*,
a bidder at the sale, that it had that effect upon him.
One of the great "dampers" to a sale by auction, is
*uncertainty* in regard to the thing sold. It will always
bring a higher price, if the purchaser can depend upon
what he bids for, and will not be held to his purchase,
unless he does get what he bids for, or compensation for
that wherein it may fall short of what it is represented
to be. The plaintiffs must pay the costs.

## GOODFELLOW V. ROBERTSON.

*Investment by agent of money in land—Lunacy.*

*A.* received $1,200 belonging to his son-in-law *R.*, and invested it with other money of *A.'s* own in the purchase of a farm, which cost $3,200. *R.*, with his family, went into possession of the farm, and *A.*, the father-in-law, by his will devised the farm to *R.'s* wife and son jointly for the life of the wife, with remainder to the son in fee, subject to the payment of $200 to a daughter of *R.*, and of $600 to another person. It was assumed in the cause that *R.* was at the time of the purchase and thenceforward of unsound mind and unable to give a valid assent to the transaction ; and the Court held that on that assumption he was entitled to the $1,200 as against *A.'s* estate, and that the devise to his wife and son were no satisfaction of the claim ; and also that he was probably entitled to a charge on the land for the debt.

But the Court directed inquiries whether *R.* was at the date of the transaction of mental capacity to assent to the purchase ; and if so, whether he did assent thereto : also, inquiry as to the occupation of the land by *R.* and his family before the death of *A.*, and the value of such occupation.

Hearing on further directions.

Statement. .This was a suit brought for the administration of the estate of *Adam Goodfellow*. In the Master's office it was claimed on behalf of the defendant *James Robertson*, that he was entitled to a charge for $1200 on a lot of land in the township of Essa (devised by *Adam Goodfellow*) under the following circumstances :—In and before December, 1855, *James Robertson* was the owner of one hundred acres of wild land in the township of Maryborough. *Robertson* was then married to a daughter of *Adam Goodfellow*. At this time there was some question amongst the family as to the mental condition of *Robertson*, and *Adam Goodfellow* being anxious that his daughter should settle near him, the Maryborough land was sold to *John Goodfellow* (a son of *Adam*) for $1200. *Adam Goodfellow* in December, 1855, purchased the land in Essa, and this sum of

$1200 was applied in part payment of the purchase money, which was in all $3200. The balance of the purchase money was paid by *Adam Goodfellow*, and the conveyance of the Essa land was taken by him in his own name. Immediately on this purchase *Robertson* and his family went into occupation of the Essa land and had continued in possession ever since. *Adam Goodfellow* died in 1865, and by his will, amongst other devises, devised the Essa land to his daughter *Mary Robertson,* (wife of *James Robertson*), and *Adam Robertson*, his son, jointly, during the natural life of *Mary Robertson,* and after her death he gave the land to *Adam Robertson,* subject to the payment of $600 to another daughter of *Adam Goodfellow*, and $200 to a daughter of *James Robertson*. It did not appear in the Master's office what was the mental condition of *James Robertson* in December, 1855; nor whether he was in a condition to give, or had given his consent to such application of the $1200. There was evidence that the $1200 had been applied in the purchase of the Essa land, and that *Robertson* and his family had been living on it. The Master merely reported the fact of the claim made by the guardian of *James Robertson*. When the matter came on for further directions, it was claimed on behalf of *James Robertson* that there was a resulting trust in his favour, and that he was entitled to a charge on the Essa land, and this was the only question argued.

Mr. *A. Hoskin,* for plaintiff, the executor of *Adam Goodfellow.*

Mr. *J. Bain* appeared for *James Robertson,* a defendant.

Mr. *Badgerow,* for other defendants.

SPRAGGE, C.—This case, upon the point argued, is a very peculiar one. Some sixteen years ago, *James*

*Robertson*, a party defendant to this suit, exhibited, it is said, symptoms of unsoundness of mind. *Adam Goodfellow*, the testator, was his father-in-law, and being anxious for the welfare of his daughter and her family, made an arrangement out of which this question has arisen. *Robertson* was the owner of a lot in Maryborough. His father-in-law was desirous that he and his family should be near him, partly—perhaps principally—from the state of his mind, and purchased with a view to their benefit a lot in Essa, the purchase money being $3,200. The Maryborough lot was sold for $1,200 to a son of *Adam Goodfellow*, which sum was paid on account of purchase money to the vendor of the Essa lot. The difference between that and the whole purchase money was to be provided by *Adam Goodfellow*, and for the purposes of this question it may be taken that it was so provided. The conveyance of the Essa farm was made to *Adam Goodfellow*, and he by his will devised it to his daughter, *Robertson's* wife, and her son *Adam*, for life, with remainder to the son in fee, subject to the payment of two sums of money, one to a daughter of the testator of $600, and another of $200 to a granddaughter named *Robertson*.

It is contended, that to the extent of $1,200, there was a resulting trust in favor of *Robertson*, whose money it was, it being the purchase money of the Maryborough lot. The only doubt as to this could be from the circumstance of its being part only and not the whole of the purchase money, and from the mental condition of the person to whom the money belonged. These circumstances alone differ it from the ordinary case. The money being only a portion of the purchase money would not, it appears, prevent the application of the rule, *(a)* nor as I incline to think would the mental condition of the owner of the money.

---

*(a)* Wray v. Steele, 2 V. & B. 388.

It could scarcely lie in the mouth of a person so appropriating his money to deny it in a case where the application of the rule would be for the benefit of the owner of the money; it is a trust resulting by operation of law, and it does not seem to be necessary to prove that the money was advanced by its owner in order to its application in the purchase of the land. If such proof were, necessary, an assenting mind on his part would necessarily have to be shewn; and in the case of the money of a lunatic, the rule could not apply. In nearly all the cases certainly the money was advanced to the nominal purchaser for the purpose of making the purchase; but there are some cases in which this was not the case; *Ryall* v. *Ryall* (a) was one of these. It was a case in which an executor applied certain moneys of the estate in the purchase of lands. The question made was, whether it was a charge upon the lands purchased. Lord *Hardwicke* directed an inquiry, and appeared to rely upon its being a trust by operation of law. There is also a case of *Bennet* v. *Mayhew*, which is cited first in 1 *Brown's* Chan. Cases 232, and again in 2 B. C. C. 287, and where it is stated that a steward had laid out moneys remitted to him, in the purchase of land, and as is stated in the second volume without any direction to lay out the money in land, yet the Court presumed that he purchased for his principal, and directed an inquiry whether any of the money had been laid out in land. And Lord *St. Leonards* says: "If the trust money is traced, the *cestui que trust* may claim either the property purchased or the money." (b) The difficulty appears to have been in tracing the money into the land, because, as Lord *Hardwicke* said, in *Ryall* v. *Ryall*, it has no ear-mark, though, as he adds, the Court had done so in some cases. It must, however, I apprehend, be necessary to trace the very money itself into the purchase, and that it is admitted was the case here.

1871.

Goodfellow
v.
Robertson.

Judgment.

---

(a) 1 Atk. 59.  (b) V. & P. 14 ed. 708.

I do not know, however, that it is material in this case on behaif of the lunatic to shew a resulting trust in his favor. It is not desired on his behalf to get at the land itself—that is devised to a portion of his family. The claim I understand is for so much of the money of the lunatic as came to the hands of the testator, $1,200, whatever use he made of it. If *Robertson* was at that time lunatic, he could not have assented to the advance and application of the money; and so the testator had in his hands $1,200 of the moneys of the lunatic, and used it in a way which did not relieve him from liability to account for it, and that money is still due from his estate. Is it any answer to this to say that he applied it towards the purchase of an estate, which he has devised to the lunatic's wife and one of the lunatic's children. In the will he treats this land as his own, and devises it as a matter of bounty to his daughter and grand-child, and

this is the more apparent from his charging it with bequests in favor of others. If this be a correct view, *Robertson* is a creditor of the testator's estate for the amount in question, being for so much money received to his use; and the doctrine of resulting trusts has not necessarily any application.

I do not know whether it is material in the interest of *Robertson* to establish the sum of money in question as a charge upon this land. *Ryall* v. *Ryall*, to which I have referred on another point, is in favor of its being a charge; and there is a dictum of Sir *William Grant*, in *Lench* v. *Lench* (a), also in its favor. "Then as to the other ground that the purchase was made with the trust money, all depends upon the proof of the fact: for whatever doubts may have been formerly entertained upon this subject, it is now settled that money may in this manner be followed into the land

---

(a) 10 Ves. 517.

in which it is invested." I had occasion to consider this point in a case before me of *Merchants' Express Co.* v. *Morton (a)*, which was not a case of trust moneys. The case is certainly more likely to arise in the case of trust moneys, and has so arisen in several cases. *Lench* v. *Lench,* is a case of trust moneys, so also was *Sowden* v. *Sowden (b)*, and so was *Lechmere* v. *Lechmere (c)*, which is well summarized in note 3 to *Sowden* v. *Sowden*. But in *Bennett* v. *Mayhew* the money was not trust money, except in the sense of its being money received by an agent for his principal; and in *Ryull* v. *Ryall* it was money of an estate come to the hands of an executor. The reasons upon which the money was held traceable into the land in *Lechmere* v. *Lechmere* and *Sowden* v. *Sowden* do not apply to *Bennett* v. *Mayhew* or to *Ryall* v. *Ryall*, and if made a charge in those cases I confess I see no good reason why the rule should not apply in an ordinary case of money in the hands of one person belonging to another being used in the purchase of land. There will, of course, always be the difficulty of tracing the money into the land ; and it is only where it can be so traced that there can be a charge, *Pitt* v. *Pitt (d)*, *Neesom* v. *Clarkson (e)*, and *Maddison* v. *Chapman (f)* are examples of the Court establishing charges upon lands, on the advance of moneys in respect of the lands under circumstances, which made it equitable that such charges should be established; and these charges were established upon no particular equitable principle, but upon the general one that it was equitable, under the circumstances, that the charges should be established.

There is also the case of *Barrack* v. *McCullock (g)*, establishing that whatever may be seized in execution

1871.

Goodfellow
v.
Robertson.

Judgment.

(a) 17 Gr. 274.               (b) 1 Br. C. C. 582.

(c) Cas. Tem. Talb. 80.       (d) T. & R. 180.

(e) 4 Hare, 97.               (f) 1 J. & H. 470.

(g) 3 K. & J. 110.

by creditors may be traced into stock or land and may be got at by creditors under 13 Elizabeth (a).

I confess, however, that I am not so clear either upon this point, or upon the point of there being a resulting trust, as upon the point of there being a debt which may be claimed on behalf of the lunatic against the estate of the testator; and unless it is necessary (as to which I am not informed) in the interest of the lunatic to rest his case upon one of these other grounds, I should prefer to rest my judgment in his favor, simply upon the ground of a debt due by the testator's estate.

There is another aspect which the case may present, but which has not been noticed in argument. If *James Robertson* had been sane, and the $1,200 had been advanced with his assent towards the purchase of the Essa farm, he could not, I apprehend, now claim that [sum as a debt against the estate of *Goodfellow.* He would be entitled to such an interest in the land purchased as so much of the purchase money would represent, and this would satisfy the justice of the case; while claiming the $1,200 as a debt of the estate would be a hardship upon those entitled to it. This would be so, because *Goodfellow*, in devising the land as he did beneficially for members of the lunatic's family, might well have considered that he was doing much more than repaying so much of the purchase money as had come to his hands from *Robertson*, for the legacies charged upon the land by his will were less than half the purchase money advanced by him. So far as the interest of *Robertson* is concerned, apart from that of members of his family, devisees under *Goodfellow's* will, this would be as advantageous to him as for the amount to be established as a debt against the estate of *Goodfellow*; but the question is, is *Robertson* com-

(a) Sug. V. & P. 14 Ed. 706.

pellable to do this? If I could see my way to compel this
course, I would do so; but I confess I cannot. There is
still another aspect of the case which has not been
presented to me. Suppose it should appear to be more
for the interest of *Robertson* that a resulting trust
should be established, will not the Court establish such
resulting trust? If *Goodfellow* had devised to a
stranger, such an inquiry would be proper. The
devise being as it is, may, or may not make a difference,
very possibly it may.

It may turn out upon inquiry that *Robertson* was, at
the date of this transaction, of mental capacity to
assent to the application of this money towards the
purchase of the Essa farm, and that in fact he did so
assent. If these inquiries are answered in the affirmative, the case will be clear of the difficulties to which
I have alluded. As yet, there is no proof one way or
the other upon these points. It has been rather taken
for granted that he was of unsound mind at that date.
There will be an inquiry upon the two points that I
have indicated. There will also be an inquiry as to
the circumstances of the occupation of the Essa farm
by the lunatic and his family before the death of
*Goodfellow*, and the value of such occupation. Without
information upon this point, I am not in a position to
say whether or not any charge can properly be made
on behalf of the estate for such use and occupation.
The costs, in respect of this claim against the estate,
and further directions will be reserved.

*1871.*

Goodfellow
v.
Robertson.

Judgment.

## RIDLEY v. SEXTON.

*Principal and agent—Compensation—Interest.*

R., who was engaged in the lumber business, employed S. as his agent, and by letter agreed to pay him $10 per $1,000 cubic feet on all timber which S. manufactured for him, which rate (the letter said) "includes purchasing, superintending the making, and attending to the shipping of the same," R. paying all travelling expenses. S. bought a quantity of timber for R., which was not manufactured under the superintendence of S.

*Held,* that he was entitled to a reasonable compensation for this service; and there having been considerable delay in enforcing payment, caused by R. having obtained an injunction restraining S. from proceeding at law, it was *held* that he was entitled to interest on the amount of his claim.

Appeal from the Master's report by the plaintiffs.

Mr. *Maclennan,* for the appeal.

Mr. *S. Blake* and Mr. *Barker,* contra.

Nov. 29.  SPRAGGE, C.—The position of the parties appears to
Judgment. have been this: Mr. *Rae* was a gentleman of business habits, residing in Hamilton, and putting his wife's means, or a portion of them, with the assent of her trustees, to profitable use in the getting out and shipping of timber. *Sexton* the defendant, as is evident from the nature of his employment, and from his being continued in it for a series of years by Mr. *Rae,* was selected as a person skilled in what is termed the "getting out" of timber and shipping it for market; including therein the purchase of the timber standing in the woods, the cutting and manufacturing the same into timber, and marking, measuring, and shipping the same. The cutting, manufacturing, marking, measuring, and shipping was, as appears by the letters which constitute the agreement and by the evidence, to be done under the supervision of *Sexton;* and the purchasing of stand-

ing timber was a matter for the exercise of his personal skill and judgment.

The measure of his remuneration for these services was agreed to be by a commission on the quantity of timber, purchased, manufactured, and shipped, at the rate of $10 per 1,000 cubic feet; and if all the timber purchased by *Sexton* had been manufactured and shipped by him, there would probably have been no question between the parties. The question arises out of this, that three large parcels of standing timber were purchased by *Sexton* for *Rae*, and at his instance, which were not manufactured by *Sexton* into timber, the manufacturing and other processes, including shipping, being performed by other persons employed by *Rae*, and not through any default, so far as the evidence shews, on the part of *Sexton*. I may here observe, that the actings of *Rae* in all these dealings with *Sexton* are adopted by the trustees, and the case is argued as if he had been acting all through in his own right.

The two letters by which the contract is evidenced were written by *Rae ;* one in the shape of a proposal by *Rae* to employ *Sexton*, and the other in the shape of an acceptance by *Sexton* of *Rae's* proposal. The latter is evidently meant as a simple acceptance of the terms proposed by *Rae*. *Rae's* letter says: " In reference to our transactions of last year, I am willing to pay you in the same way this year, $10 per 1,000 cubic feet on all timber you manufacture for me this season;" and then, as if to avoid misconception, it proceeds, " which rate includes purchasing, superintending the making, and attending to the shipping of the same, I paying all your travelling expenses," &c. This contract was for one season only ; but the dealings of the parties appear to have continued upon the same terms from year to year until October, 1866, when a new contract was entered into, which however throws no light upon the question between the parties.

Mr. *Maclennan's* contention is, that *Sexton* was the general agent of *Rae* in the getting out of timber in the western part of Canada, and that the $10 per 1,000 feet on all timber manufactured and shipped by him was intended to cover all services rendered by him as such agent; that it was a mode of compensation for all services as such agent; that the parties could not have contemplated any further compensation; and he puts the case of a merchant agreeing to compensate a clerk by a commission on a particular branch of business to cover all services rendered by him. Such an agreement of course might be made; but I see nothing in this agreement or in the dealings of the parties to indicate that the *pro rata* compensation agreed upon was to cover any services besides those specified.

But in one view no services other than those specified were rendered by *Sexton,* and so the question, in the shape put by Mr. *Maclennan,* does not arise. The main thing to be done was the manufacture of timber, and that was to comprise the hewing timber trees into timber, and the other processes specified in the letters of December, and was to comprise also the purchase of any standing timber that might be so manufactured; but not the purchase of any other standing timber. Suppose a written direction sent by *Rae* to *Sexton* to purchase a quantity of standing timber, and suppose it to be expressed to be for some purpose other than its manufacture into timber, it would surely be open to *Sexton* to refuse to execute the commission; or, if he accepted it, to stipulate for a compensation for the service. There is nothing in the agreement requiring *Sexton* to make such a purchase gratis, or indeed to make it all.

I have said that the services rendered by *Sexton* in the purchase of these parcels of timber were services specified in the agreement. I think they were so, because I take it from the evidence that they were purchased for the purpose of being manufactured by *Sexton* into timber under the agreement which was then continued to be acted upon by the parties; and if so, there is this, that the completion of the purpose for which they were purchased was intercepted by *Rae*. *Sexton* had rendered a service in making the purchase; the mode of compensation contemplated by the agreement was defeated by the act of *Rae*. This could not in reason defeat the right of *Sexton* to be compensated for the value of the services he had rendered.

But suppose these purchases of timber are not to be regarded as made in order to their being manufactured by *Sexton*—their purchase was a service outside of the agreement altogether—for it is clear from its terms that the purchase of timber was only in order to its manufacture. The words " purchasing, superintending the making, and attending to the shipping of *the same*," proves this, the words " the same," being clearly referrible to the timber to be manufactured by *Sexton*. If the purchases were outside of the agreement, *Sexton's* right to be compensated for his services in the matter was clear. There was nothing to give *Rae* a right to the whole of his time and services; and the case put of a merchant's clerk, does not seem to me to apply.

The principle laid down by Lord *Cranworth*, then Baron *Rolfe*, in his charge to the jury in the case of *Marshall* v. *Parsons* (a), and which is quoted by Mr. *Addison*, in his book on Contracts (b), has some application to this case. The marginal note shews sufficiently the facts and the question submitted to the jury.

Mr. *Maclennan* argued this point strenuously as well ingeniously for the plaintiff, or I should have given less consideration to it than I have done. I confess it

1871.

Ridley
v.
Sexton.

Judgment.

---

(a) 9 C. & P. 656.          (b) p. 589.

appears clear to me that *Sexton* was entitled to some compensation for his services rendered in the purchase of the timber in question.

Then it is contended for the plaintiffs that, assuming *Sexton* to be entitled to some compensation for his services in the purchase of timber, the Master, in allowing him a commission on such purchases, has proceeded upon an erroneous principle.

The evidence shews it to have been a principle of compensation by no means unusual in the timber business. To this there is the evidence of *De Coe*, *McRae*, and *Langstaff*. The evidence of *Cook* is not against it; for, while speaking of his own practice to pay by time, he gives an estimate of what would be reasonable upon a payment by quantity. Some of the witnesses speak of the rate of compensation being in proportion to the goodness of the bargain made; and it is a practical reason for that mode of compensation, that it would be a powerful incentive to the agent to make the best possible bargain for his principal. It is to be observed, too, that a *pro rata* compensation was the mode agreed upon between the parties for compensating for the services provided for in the agreement. There are other witnesses indeed who speak of their practice being different—*Neelon*, *Calvin*, *Campbell*, and *McAlister*—but the witnesses were themselves practically conversant with the business, and the men employed by them, though engaged sometimes in the purchase of timber, were in every sense in a subordinate position, rather foremen than agents for their employers; while in the case of *Sexton*, his employer relied solely upon his knowledge, skill, carefulness, accuracy, and good management; and he was obliged to rely upon these qualities, for he was entirely incompetent himself to transact such business.

This is abundantly clear from the evidence. *Rae*
himself spoke of his own incompetence. In answer to a
suggestion from *De Coe*, in reference to one *Hunt*, he
said that *Hunt* was not his agent to buy timber—that
he knew no more about it than he (*Rae*) did; and he
went on to say that *Sexton* was his managing man, and
whatever he said that the timber they were speaking of
was worth, that was the price they would give. To
another witness also *Rae* spoke of *Sexton* and of his
purchase of timber; that he was a good judge of standing timber and a good lumberman, and of his having
purchased large quantities for him, and of obtaining a
large section very cheap. This was to the witness
*McRae*. The same witness says : " I consider the most
important part of an agent's services is the exercise of
judgment in buying of standing timber." There is also
the evidence of *Langstaff*, who says " Mr. *Rae* was a
commercial man and good financier, but did not pretend
to know anything of the timber business." There is a
good deal more scattered through the evidence which
shews that *Sexton* was really the managing agent in
making the purchase of timber, and that his skill and
judgment were wholly relied upon by *Rae* in making
the purchases. All this is material upon the question
of *amount ;* but it is also material as shewing the
footing upon which he was in this matter with *Rae*,
and that it was essentially different from that of the
persons spoken of by *Neelon*, *Calvin*, and others, as
employed by them, and for the present I use it for
this latter purpose. Looking at the evidence to which
I have been directed upon this point, there appears
to me to have been furnished to the Master more
material upon which to form a judgment as to what
would be a proper *pro rata* allowance, than as to what
would be a proper allowance for time, care, and labor ;
and there is quite enough to warrant the Master in
adopting the principle of compensation which he has
adopted.

As to the *amount* allowed, I ought to be well satisfied
that it is excessive before I overrule the judgment of the
Master in regard to it. I confess that the amounts
when first named to me by counsel did appear large;
and I am not sure that I should myself, if in the Master's
place, have allowed so much. Yet, I cannot say that
the Master was wrong, and he has evidently acted with
care and discrimination in making the allowance. To
take the case of the *Cameron* purchase : the Master has
allowed $600, being $4 per 1,000 feet upon the quantity
*actually used* by *Lynch*, a manufacturer for *Rae*, viz.,
150,000 feet. The estimated quantity purchased was
700,000 feet; the sum allowed upon that quantity would
have been at the rate of about 75c. per 1,000 feet.
Still, $600 seems a large sum; but the examination of
the land occupied a considerable time being in parts of
two or three years. He was assisted by *Rae's* men;
but the whole was done under his immediate supervision.

The land was in six or seven different townships, and
almost every lot had to be examined. The time and
labor which *Sexton* gave to the work was very considerable. The amount to be paid was large, and the
responsibility resting upon him, as his judgment and
accuracy had to be alone relied upon, was great; and
the bargain that he made was a very good one for *Rae*,
and *Rae* had the benefit of the purchase to the extent
of the whole quantity purchased, not only to the extent
of that used. I have referred already to *Sexton's*
qualifications for the work, and *Rae's* own entire ignorance of the business. I have to add that it appears
from the evidence that he was not only a competent but
a very diligent and painstaking agent. He is described
as allowing no idleness on the part of the men;—as a
strict overseer.

On the purchase of timber from Mr. *Gzowski*, the
Master has allowed $2 per 1,000 feet; on that purchased
from *Langstaff*, $2.50. Part of the evidence upon the

subject of all these allowances was taken before the Master himself. He has allowed less than the average of what upon the evidence appears to have been paid upon other purchases; and I cannot say upon the whole that he has allowed too much.

No special argument was addressed to me in relation to the allowance for the purchase of staves, Mr. *Maclennan* agreeing that they should abide the result of the allowance for the purchase of standing timber.

A further objection is, that the Master has allowed interest upon the amount which he finds due to *Sexton.* Interest was claimed by *Sexton* in the Master's office upon the yearly balances due from time to time; but interest has been allowed by the Master only from the time of the filing of the declaration in the action at law, in which declaration there was a count for interest. The proceedings in the action at law were stayed by the injunction in this suit; but for the injunction, the cause would have come on for trial at the Spring Assizes for 1869. I think the material point is, whether interest would have been recoverable at law. It was a legal demand on the part of *Sexton*, and I apprehend a debt within the meaning of the statute. *Blogg* v. *Johnson* (a) was not a case of a legal demand. *Turner* v. *Burkenshaw* (b) was the converse of this case in some respects; there the agent was the party indebted, and interest was claimed against him. It was refused on the ground that there had been no demand of payment. In the matter of *Powell's* Trusts (c), and the Earl of *Mansfield* v. *Ogle* (d) were cases of arrears of annuities, which stand upon a peculiar footing, annuities being, as was said by Lord Justice *Turner* in the latter case, partly principal and partly interest, and so far as they consist of interest

(a) L. R. 2 Ch. App · 225,　　　(b) Ib. 488.
(c) 10 Hare 134.　　　(d) 4 De. G. & J. at 42.

the Lord Justice saw no difference between arrears of annuity and the arrears of interest on a mortgage debt. To allow interest in such a case would, he conceived, be a dangerous precedent. In the former case he spoke of the discretion which Courts of Equity had exercised in allowing interest upon such arrears, and saw no reason why the statute allowing juries to exercise discretion in certain cases should be taken to have altered the rule by which the discretion of a Court of Equity was guided. I do not think that that language applies to this case.

It is urged for the plaintiff that *Sexton* was 'an accounting party. True, he was so as to moneys which he received from *Rae*, in order to apply them in the business in which he was *Rae's* agent; and if he had been in arrear in respect of those moneys and *Rae* had made a demand, I incline to think there is nothing in the cases to prevent interest being allowed to him. *Turner* v. *Burtenshaw* is rather in favor of the allowance of interest in such a case than against it; and in the old case of *Boddam* v. *Riley*, (*a*) which was a case between partners, and was of course before the statute, Lord *Thurlow's* language was: "I take it, nothing but what arises from a contract, agreement, or demand of a debt, can give rise to a demand of interest, and this court in these cases follows a Court of law." In regard to the debt, however, which was the subject of the action at law, and upon which the Master has allowed interest, *Sexton* was not an accounting party. His suit was for a debt for services rendered, and it was certainly competent to the jury to allow interest upon it from the filing or service of the declaration—I suppose they were contemporaneous. In other words interest was properly allowable from that date; and and if one may speculate upon what a jury would

---

(*a*) 1 Bro. C. C. 239.

have done, I should say a jury would probably, almost certainly, have allowed interest.

I think, too, that there is a great deal in this, that the injunction obtained by the plaintiff intercepted *Sexton's* recovery at law, and I think the Master was right in placing him as far as he could in the same position as he would have occupied at law if he had been left to pursue his remedy there; and as was said in *Boddam* v. *Riley*, "this Court in these cases follows a Court of law." Even if a *jury* had not allowed interest, it would have been, as put by Mr. *Blake*, only a postponement of the allowance for a short time, inasmuch as a judgment at law carries interest; and it is to be assumed that judgment would have been recovered according to the ordinary course of the Court; and that it would have been for the amount which is in this Court adjudged to be due.

It is very unfortunate that no light is thrown upon any of the questions involved in this appeal by the books and papers of the parties. I cannot say this is the fault of one party more than of the other, but so it is.

I do not find that the Master is wrong upon any of the points upon which his report is objected to. The appeal must be dismissed with costs.

## SAUNDERS V. STULL.

*Answering demurrable bill charging fraud—Sale by fraudulent grantee—
Decree against married woman.*

A bill charging a defendant with fraud, and not praying relief
against him as to costs or otherwise, is demurrable.

Charges of fraud do not justify answering a demurrable bill; and
where the defendant to such a bill answered, and the cause went to
a hearing, the bill was dismissed without costs.

A conveyance void against creditors was made through a third party
to the owner's wife; the husband afterwards became insolvent and
joined his wife in a sale of the property to a purchaser without
notice; a conveyance to the purchaser was executed and registered,
and the purchsaer gave to the wife a mortgage for part of the
purchase money, and paid her the residue in cash. On a bill by the
assignee in insolvency he was declared entitled to the mortgage,
and to any of the money which still remained in the wife's hands,
and to any property, real or personal, which she had purchased
with the residue and still owned; but the Court refused to direct
an inquiry as to whether she had separate estate, in order to charge
the same with any of the residue which had been spent by her, or
with the costs of the suit.

Statement. The plaintiff was assignee in insolvency of *James
Frederick Stull* and *George W. Stull*. *James F. Stull*
and one *Oliver* had been partners in trade as country
shop-keepers. In November, 1868, *Oliver* died, and
*George W. Stull* bought out their stock-in-trade, &c., for
$1800, on credit; and immediately afterwards, viz:
29th December, 1868, he executed a conveyance of his
farm (being almost his only means) to his mother-in-law,
*Catherine Oliver*, for the nominal consideration of $50,
and she immediately conveyed the farm, by way of
gift to *George's* wife, *Annie Cullen Stull*. *George*
carried on the business in his own name until the
11th of May, 1869, when he took *James Frederick
Stull* into partnership with him. On the 17th of
November, 1869, an attachment in insolvency was
issued against both partners. On the 22nd of June,
1870, *George W. Stull* and his wife, both of whom were

defendants, sold the farm to *George Lyons*, another
defendant, for $3400, subject to some prior charges,
which *Lyons* was to pay. For $900 of the purchase
money he gave Mrs. *Stull* a mortgage on the property,
and the balance he paid to her. All the deeds were duly
registered.

The bill was to have the various conveyances set
aside as fraudulent and void against creditors; or that
Mrs. *Stull* should be declared a trustee of the proceeds
for the plaintiff.

The cause came on for the examination of witnesses
and hearing at the sittings of the Court at Guelph in
the autumn of 1871.

Mr. *Moss* and Mr. *Guthrie* for the plaintiff.

Mr. *Hodgins* and Mr. *Peterson* for the defendants
*Lyons*, Mrs. *Stull*, and Mrs. *Oliver*.

Mr. *Saunders*, for the defendant *George W. Stull.*

MOWAT, V. C.—At the close of the argument on the
hearing, I expressed my opinion that the defendant
*Lyons* was a purchaser for value, without notice, and that
the bill must, as against him, be dismissed with costs.

It was admitted that the bill must be dismissed
against Mrs. *Oliver ;* and the only question as to her
was as to her costs. The bill charged her with having
been a party to the impeached transactions for the
fraudulent purpose of defeating creditors, but the bill
did not pray any relief against her as to costs or otherwise. The bill was therefore demurrable (*a*); and it was

---

(*a*) LeTexier v. Margravine of Anspach, 15 Ves. at 164; 1 Danls.
Pr. 4th ed. 283, 499; Morgan & Davey on Costs, 278.

1871.　held by the Master of the Rolls in *Nesbitt* v. *Berridge* (a),

Saunders
v.
Stull.

that a defendant is not justified in neglecting to demur because the bill contains charges of fraud. That case was reheard by the Lord Chancellor (b); and though the Jurist report of his judgment as to costs is a little obscure, I am satisfied (c) that it was only as to the supplemental bill that His Lordship, varied the decree as to costs, and that he did not dissent from what' the Master of the Rolls had said and done in dismissing the original bill as to certain defendants without costs on the ground that though charged with fraud they should have demurred. The case is cited in the text books (d) as an authority for that rule, and I have found no report of a contrary case. I shall, therefore, dismiss the bill against Mrs. *Oliver* without costs.

Judgment.

As respects Mrs. *Stull*, I stated at the close of the argument that, though she may have been guilty of no moral fraud, yet, as against the plaintiff, she could not maintain her right to the property; and that the creditors are entitled to the mortgage of $900, The plaintiff's counsel claimed that she should also be charged with the money which she had received, and with the costs of the suit. He asked leave to amend his bill, if necessary, charging that she had separate estate ; and he claimed a reference to the Master to inquire what separate estate she had. I think that he is entitled to a decree for any part of the purchase money which may be still in her possession or power, and for any property, real or personal, into which she has mediately or immediately converted the same, and which she now, owns. There may be a reference to the Master to ascertain these particulars ; in which case he will state any special circumstances, and further directions and costs of the

---

　:(a) 32 Beav. 282.　　　　　(b) 10 Jur. N. S. 53,

　(c) S. C. 12 W. R. 283.

　(d 1 Danl. 4th ed. 499; Morgan & Davey, 21.

reference may be reserved. But I find no reported case which would warrant my directing an inquiry whether Mrs. *Stull* has separate estate, in order to charge it with what she has spent of the purchase money, or with the costs of the suit (*a*).

This defendant's counsel argued that some of the creditors had, by their conduct, precluded themselves from sharing in this property. It is not necessary to consider the effect of the evidence in that respect, as the conduct of these creditors can be no bar to the plaintiff's suit, and as the creditors referred to must be parties to any proceeding for trying the question as to them.

It was said that the impeached transaction was valid as between Mrs. *Stull* and her husband ; that she would be entitled to any surplus which might remain after paying creditors ; and that the Court should take the administration of the funds into its own hands, and direct the Master to ascertain what creditors are entitled to participate in it. But that is not the practice (*b*) ; and if that course is sometimes taken, it is under circumstances which, I think, have no application to the present case (*c*). I do not see much chance of there being a surplus ; but if there should be a surplus, and if Mrs. *Stull* is entitled to it ; or if she can shew that any of the creditors have disentitled themselves to participate in the produce of the property in question, I leave her to enforce her rights in these respects by such proceedings as she may be advised ; sufficient not appearing to make it necessary or expedient, in my judgment, to depart from the usual practice. The decree, however, may be expressed to be without pre-

---

(*a*) Hogan v. Morgan, 1 Hog. 250.

(*b*) See Townsend v. Westacott, 4 Beav. 58 ; Columbine v. Penhall, 1 Sm. & G. at 257 ; Barling v. Bishopp, 29 B. at 421 ; &c.

(*c*) See Bott v. Smith, 21 B. at 517 ; Tucker v. Hernaman, 1 Sm. & G. 394 ; S. C. 4 D. M. & G. 395.

75—VOL. XVIII. GR.

1871.

Saunders
v.
Stull.

judice to any question as to Mrs. *Stull's* right to the
surplus (*a*), or as to her right to set up the disqualifica-
tion of any of the creditors to participate in the fund.
There will be no costs against *Stull* or his wife up to
decree.

---

### THE MERCHANTS BANK OF CANADA v. CLARKE.

*Fraud on creditors—Reality of sale—Corroborative evidence.*

In the case of a sale by an insolvent person to a relative, attended by
suspicious circumstances, the reality and *bona fides* of the transaction should not be rested on the uncorroborated testimony of the
parties to the impeached transaction.

To maintain a sale impeached by creditors, it is not sufficient
in this Court to prove that the transaction was really intended
to pass the property; for, as laid down by the Court of Error
and Appeal in *Gotwalls* v. *Mulholland,* "although the sale may
have been *bona fide,* with intent to pass the property, yet if
made with intent by vendor and purchaser to defeat and delay
creditors, it would be void."

Statement.

This was a suit by execution creditors of one *Moses
C. Clarke* to set aside, as fraudulent against creditors,
a conveyance made by him to his son, the defendant
*George F. Clarke,* on the 29th July, 1870, of all his
real estate, consisting of twenty acres of land in the
township of West Oxford, on which the debtor resided;
and a lot of land in Ingersoll, which was in possession
of a tenant at a rent. The defendant *George F. Clarke*
insisted that the conveyance was made to him in pursuance of a *bonâ fide* sale of the property for $3,000 cash,
which he paid; and he denied that the purpose of the
transaction was to defraud or delay creditors.

It was admitted that the liabilities of the father at
this time greatly exceeded the value of his property.

---

(*d*) See French v. French, 6 DeG. M. & G. at 103.

He had been indorsing for one *Samuel J. Read*, a country shopkeeper, and was on *Read's* paper to the amount of $8,000 or upwards. At the time of the transaction in question, *Read* was in insolvent circumstances, and he had been sued by some of his creditors and was pressed by others. He went into insolvency on the 6th October afterwards, and his estate paid eight cents on the dollar. On the 28th July, *Moses C. Clarke* had been served with the plaintiffs' writ in respect of a note of $945, dated 21st June, 1870, made by *Read*, payable a month after date, and indorsed by *Moses C. Clarke*. This was the debt for which the plaintiffs afterwards recovered their judgment. *Moses C. Clarke*, it appeared, had been served shortly before with another writ in respect of a note of $400; and his position in consequence was alarming and exciting him. On the 28th July, the day on which he was served with the writ on the $945 note, he went to Aylmer, where his son was residing, and which was about twenty-five miles from his own residence; and the deed in question was executed on the following day at St. Thomas.

1871.

Merchants Bank v. Clarke.

The case came on for the examination of witnesses and hearing at the Autumn Sittings (1871), at Woodstock.

Mr. *S. Blake* and Mr. *T. Wells*, for the plaintiffs.

Mr. *Crooks*, Q. C., and Mr. *John McLean*, for the defendants.

MOWAT, V. C.—[After stating the facts of the case as above] There is no evidence whatever except that of the parties themselves that this transaction was really a sale, or that the alleged purchase money was paid; and it has frequently been observed, that transactions of this kind ought not to be held sufficiently established by the uncorroborated testimony of the parties to it (a). I

December 6.

Judgment.

---

(a) See Douglass v. Ward, 11 Gr. 39 : Ball v. Ballantyne, *Ib.* at 202; Stevenson v. Franklin, 16 Gr. at 142,

cannot say that either the deposition of the father
(which was taken in Michigan under a commission), or
the evidence of the son (which was given before myself
at the hearing), was entirely satisfactory; or that I
could with propriety attach to this testimony any exceptional weight.

There is, on the other hand, in the transaction much
which, viewed from a judicial standpoint, is not free from
reasonable suspicion. The position of the father at the
time with reference to his liabilities, I have mentioned.
Besides his real estate, he had a mortgage for $300,
which he sold to his son, and was paid for, on the same
occasion that his real estate was conveyed to his son.
His only remaining means appear to have been a little
farm stock, viz., a cow, a calf, and two pigs; and
his household furniture. His private debts, exclusive
of his liabilities as indorser, amounted to about $1,000.
That was his position when he made his appearance at

his son's house in Aylmer. There, according to the
account of both, the father proposed to sell the property
to the son for $3,000. The sale was to be free from
dower. They say that the father had been talking some
months before of selling; but no other witness is produced
who heard any such talk; and both defendants say that
the father had never before proposed to the son to sell to
him; and the son states that before this time he " had
no thought of purchasing." They both say, that the son
did not ask his father what he wanted the cash down for,
and that the father did not say. The son accepted the
proposal without first offering less than the father had
proposed. The son states, that he did not know the value
of the properties; that he made no inquiry about them
except of his father; and that he had no examination
made of the title. The father was fifty-five or sixty
years old, was a farmer at this time, and had never followed any other business but farming or teaming; and he
is not pretended to have been at the time contemplating,

or to have been supposed by the son to be contemplating, any new business. He had bought the twenty acre parcel a few years previously; it was but a few months since he had finished building the house on it; and he resided there with his wife and three daughters, one of the daughters being grown up. Both father and son admit, that at the time of the transaction between them, it was not intended that the father or his family should remove from the place; that it was, on the contrary, agreed that they should remain; that nothing was said about paying any rent; and that the crops then on the place were to be the father's. The defendant was (he says) to have a release of his mother's dower; but the conveyance drawn contains no provision for that purpose; and the allegation is, that the whole consideration was paid without getting this release or applying for it; nor did the son afterwards apply for it. A receipt for the purchase money, or the supposed purchase money, which is on the deed, was signed by the father; it acknowledges payment on the day of the date of the deed; but it is admitted that no money was paid on that day. The defendant says that he paid $1,900 of the amount to his father at Aylmer on the following day in the presence of *A. C. Brown*; but neither *Brown* nor any one else except the father is called to corroborate this statement. The father does not recollect the amount of the first payment. The deed was registered on the 1st August. The son says that he paid the remaining sum of $1,100 a few days afterwards, at his own house in Aylmer, when no one else was present. The father says, that he did not count the money which was paid on either occasion; that others counted it for him; but he does not name these others, nor is any one called to corroborate the story. The son says, that he had $2,500 at this time in his cash box (at first he said in his safe) at his house, and that the amount had been accumulating for some months; but no one is produced who

saw this money, or who knew of his having it, or
who states any facts which by inference might
afford to the Court some corroboration of the statement of his having it. The son admits that he has
no book containing any entry respecting this money,
or any portion of it; respecting his having it; or
respecting his paying it to his father. The son is a
physician, and practises in partnership with another
professional gentleman; and he also had for a year been
carrying on, through a clerk, a small general store in
Aylmer; but the $2,500, or any part of it, does not
appear in either set of books. The son says, that
he kept the money derived from his professional
business and his shop business distinct from his private
money transactions, and that of these last he has never
kept any record. But while he had this large sum in
his hands (as he says), and before the transaction in
question, he had been negotiating for a loan of $2,000
from a gentleman at St. Thomas; and when he received

this money shortly after his purchase was completed and
paid for, he put the borrowed money into his shop
business, as appears from the cash book of that business.
The loan was at ten per cent. Further, no one is produced who saw the $1,900 or the $1,100, or any money,
with the father. The father says that he paid $1,000
of the money to his creditors; but he cannot recollect
the name of but one of these creditors: to him, he says
that he paid $300 or $400; the rest he says that he
gave to his wife, but no other evidence of this is given;
no one is produced who saw the money, or any money,
with her.

The deed purported to be an immediate transfer of
the property and would (according to its purport) entitle
the defendant to the crops then in the ground. The
private arrangement, that the father should notwithstanding retain possession, and that he should have the crops
for his own use, fixes on the transaction one of those

" badges of fraud" which in such cases are deemed of great weight. Indeed, the son says, that his object was to keep the West Oxford place in the family for the benefit of his mother, and that he did not change this intention until his father and mother had left the country. It was some time after they had left before he endeavored to obtain any rent from the Ingersoll property.

The whole account of the defendants is so unlike what takes place in the case of real purchases made in good faith, that I think it impossible, on the uncorroborated evidence of the parties, to hold that the transaction in question is proved to have been a real sale, intended *bona fide* to pass the property.

Whether the sale was real or only colorable, that the father's purpose was to prevent his property from being seized for his liabilities as indorser, seems to me an irresistible conclusion from the facts in evidence. His liabilities at the time were more than double what he was worth; and, if the transaction was as real as it purports to have been, his abrupt journey on the very day of being served with a writ, to propose the sale to his son, without any previous negotiation or correspondence on the subject; his demand of cash for the whole price; the hurry with which the transactions of the sales of the property and of the mortgage were completed; and the entire absence of any suggestion even now to account for all this on any other supposition than his desire to save his property from his creditors, place the motive of his conduct beyond reasonable question. I think that on the whole evidence I ought further to hold the son to have been a party to his father's purpose.

If all which is suspicious and defective in the case as it stands could have been cleared up by other evidence, it it to be regretted that the evidence was not given. My decision must be based wholly on the materials which are before me.

It was argued, that, though the transaction were real, yet, if entered into by both parties for the purpose of defrauding or delaying creditors, it is void. On that point there has been great diversity of judicial opinion. The last decision which I know of, is by the Chancellor of this Court, who held in *Wood* v. *Irwin* (a), that the sale would be void, and affirmed that the Court of Appeal had not in *Smith* v. *Moffatt* (b) decided anything to the contrary. Before the latter case, such sales had always been held by this Court to be invalid. The point was first considered and so held, I believe, in *McMaster* v. *Clare*, when the Court was composed of Chancellor *Blake*, Vice Chancellor *Esten*, and the present Chancellor (then Vice Chancellor *Spragge*) (c). The English decisions in equity, with the single exception of *Hale* v. *The Omnibus Company*, are to the same effect. There are, on the other hand, at common law, both in England and here, decisions to the contrary. But the Court of Appeal in *Crawford* v. *Meldrum* (d) set aside a conveyance, though the transaction was clearly real as between the parties, and was intended to pass the property; but the consideration was inadequate; and the grantor was insolvent, as the grantee knew.

In *Gottwalls* v. *Mulholland* (e) there was no inadequacy; and the following was there stated by *Draper*, C.J., speaking for the whole Court, to be the rule in such cases : " As the law stands, the charge would more clearly have expressed our views if it had been to the effect, that, although the sale may have been *bona fide* with the intention to pass the property, yet if made with intent by vendor and purchaser to defeat and delay creditors, it would be void against the defendants ; but if made, as the facts in this case shew, to dispose of the property ratably amongst all his creditors, it is valid."

---

(a) 16 Gr. 398.     (b) 28 U. C. Q. B. 486.
(c) 7 Gr. at 558.     (d) 3 E. & A. 101.
(e) Ib. 200.

That must be treated to be the law until the Court of Appeal unequivocally reverses its own conclusion, should it ever do so. *Smith* v. *Moffatt* (a) was cited as having that effect, but that case does not warrant such a construction. It does not profess to be the result of any change of opinion since the previous case had been decided.

There was a difference of opinion in the Court there as to what the effect of the Judge's charge had been. But the Chief Justice of the Court stated his opinion of the law as follows: "It appears to me that all the defendants had a right to ask was contained in the learned Judge's direction; for it involved necessarily the inquiry whether the consideration was substantial in reference to the value of *Dolsen's* interest in the property at the time he conveyed to *Smith;* whether that consideration was paid in order to acquire the title, and not to give color to a scheme to defeat and delay creditors; and whether the object of *Smith* and of *Dolsen* was to defeat and delay creditors; *in other words, whether the transfer of the property would have taken place if the intention to defeat and delay creditors had not existed in the minds of both these parties at the time of the transfer, and these acts were in furtherance of that intention.*"

Judgment.

Chancellor *VanKoughnet*, in his judgment, referred to the language of *Willes*, J., in *Pennell* v. *Reynolds* (b), as stating the Chancellor's view of the correct rule. There *Willes*, J., had said that "before we hold that a deed conveying property in consideration of a present advance which bears a substantial proportion to the value of the property is invalid, we must be satisfied that there exists an intention to defeat and delay, and consequently to defraud the creditors. And that

(a) 28 U. C. Q. B. 486.     (b) 11 C. B. N. S. at 722.

76—VOL. XVIII. GR.

that object must be the object not only of the bankrupt but also of the person who is dealing with him. "A person dealing *bona fide* with the bankrupt would be safe, unless he knows, or from the very nature of the transaction must be taken necessarily to have known, that the object was to defeat and delay the creditors, the deed cannot be impeached." His Lordship Chancellor *VanKoughnet* stated that he concurred in that statement of the law: so that his view was, that the reality of the transaction was not sufficient to sustain it if its purpose was fraudulent.

The present Chancellor (then Vice Chancellor) *Spragge* delivered an elaborate and able judgment to the same effect; and, construing the Judge's charge differently from the rest of the Court, his opinion was in favor of the appellant.

The Chief Justice of the Common Pleas stated that he concurred in much that had been said by Vice Chancellor *Spragge*, and he added: "I assume, and the case on both sides was argued on the assumption, that the charge was in truth substantially what in his (Vice Chancellor *Spragge's*) judgment it should have been."

Mr. Justice *Wilson* and Mr. Justice *Morrison* concurred with Chief Justice *Draper;* and that Mr. Justice *Wilson*, in so concurring, did not understand that he was taking a different view, is manifest from his judgment in the Court below in *Gottwalls* v. *Mulholland* (a). There, speaking for the majority of the Court (Chief Justice *Richards* and himself), he had said (among other things to the same effect): "We do not think that the case of *Wood* v. *Dixie* determined that the intent and object with which a sale was made were not inquirable into so long as the parties really intended to pass the

---

(a) 15 U. C. C. P. at 70.

property by the sale and for a sufficient consideration. 1871.
\* \* If a sale were made with the express purpose of
removing goods, which could be conveniently seized from
the reach of creditors, and giving an equivalent for
them in money in order that it might not be seized, or
might not be as conveniently seized as goods, or with
the intent that the money might be thrown by the debtor
into the fire, or that the debtor might forthwith abscond
with it, or for property situated in a foreign country, or
not falling into possession for several lives, it can
scarcely be said that this would be a *bona fide* sale," &c.

Mr. Justice *Gwynne's* opinion was the only one, in
*Smith* v. *Moffatt*, which is distinctly and unequivocally
opposed to what had been laid down in *Gottwalls* v.
*Mulholland*. I believe that I myself was present at the
argument in *Smith* v. *Moffatt*, but from the pressure of
my other judicial work, I happened to be unable to
give the case attention afterwards, and I was not
present when judgment was given. The Chief Justice
(*Richards*) also was absent.

It is plain, therefore, that if a majority of the Judges
in Appeal now take a different view of the law from that
laid down in *Gottwalls* v. *Mulholland*, the judgments in
*Smith* v. *Moffatt* do not say so.

Two late English cases were cited for the defendant.
*Alton* v. *Harrison* (a) was one of these : but that case
was merely that a *bona fide* mortgage to certain
creditors was good against an expected sequestration ;
and that under the 13th Elizabeth a debtor may prefer
one creditor to another. The debtor there had a legal
right to postpone the sequestrating creditor to other creditors, if he thought fit : but the case is no authority for
sustaining a sale, which is designed to defeat creditors,

---

(a) L. R. 4 Ch. App. 622.

1871.

Merchants
Bank
v.
Clarke.

for the benefit of the vendor personally. *Bayspoole* v. *Collins* (a) was, I believe, the other case referred to. That was a case under 27th Elizabeth, and merely established that, though a prior voluntary conveyance is void against a subsequent sale or mortgage, yet a small consideration is sufficient to maintain the priority of the former.

In view of all the authorities, I feel bound to hold that the rule laid down by the Court of Appeal, in *Gottwalls* v. *Mulholland*, which also is in accordance with the whole course of decision in this Court up to that time, and with the late decision of the Chancellor, in *Wood* v. *Irwin*, is the rule by which this Court continues to be governed.

Judgment.

Whether, therefore, the transaction was real or colorable, I must hold it void against the plaintiffs. There will be the usual decree. The plaintiffs will add their costs to their debt.

---

## McCARTY v. McMURRAY.

*Fraud on creditors—Unpaid purchase money—Estoppel.*

An insolvent person sold his land to his brother; a creditor filed a bill impeaching the sale as fraudulent; part of the consideration was said by the defendants to be a pair of horses and waggon of the value of $200; but the parties had fraudulently given out after the sale that these horses were still the horses of the brother who had bought the land, and in this way had misled the plaintiff and other creditors:

*Held,* that this brother was estoppel from afterwards setting up against the creditor that the $200 had been paid in that way; and, the plaintiff's debt being less than that amount, he was *held* entitled to a decree for payment, or in default, a sale of the land

Examination of witnesses and hearing at the sittings at Woodstock, in the Autumn of 1871.

---

(a) L. R. 6 Ch. App. 228.

On the first November, 1869, the plaintiff, for the accommodation of *Robert McMurray*, joined him in a promissory note for $75 to one *McLeod*. The note fell due on the 4th February, 1870, and on the 10th the payee' commenced a suit thereon against both makers. On the 10th March, 1870, he obtained judgment for $94.25. On the 24th, the plaintiff paid the amount, and took an assignment of the judgment; and at the time of filing the bill he had in the hands of the sheriff of Oxford executions against the lands and goods of the principal debtor *Robert McMurray*. The latter had no goods, and the bill was filed to obtain payment out of certain land which the debtor had conveyed on the 30th March, 1870, to his brother *James Farley McMurray*. This land was *Robert's* only property. The bill impeached the conveyance as fraudulent against creditors. The two brothers were defendants. They both swore at the hearing, that the conveyance was in pursuance of a sale to *James*, and was not colorable, or executed with intent to defraud creditors. Their evidence as to the reality of the alleged sale was to some extent confirmed by the evidence of the gentleman who drew the conveyance. It was proved that *Robert* was at the time insolvent.

1871.

McCarty
v.
McMurray.

Mr. *Spencer* and Mr. *T. Wells*, for the plaintiff.

Mr. *S. Blake* and Mr. *Ball*, for the defendants.

MOWAT, V. C.—I incline to think that there was a real sale.

Dec. 6.

Judgment.

The defendants say that the whole of the purchase money was paid; $200 of it in a pair of horses and waggon. There is no evidence but their own of the payment of this $200, or of the sale to *Robert* of the horses and waggon in satisfaction of that amount; and it is clear from the evidence, that if this was part of the bargain, it was concealed from the public for the express purpose of preventing Robert's creditors from seizing these chattels. From the time of the transaction the horses continued to be spoken of by both brothers as being still the property of James; they were kept afterwards in James's stable, and were fed there on his hay, even during periods that Robert had them in use; sometimes James used them himself; and when Robert used them, James gave out that he had lent them to Robert. I am satisfied that by means of this scheme, they managed to mislead the plaintiff and other creditors, and to prevent the horses from being seized as Robert's. Whatever, therefore, the fact may be as to the ownership of these chattels, I ought to hold James to be estopped from now saying (when it suits his purpose) that he had sold the horses to Robert as part of the bargain respecting the land. It is impossible to permit him to blow hot and cold. As Judgment. between the plaintiff and James, $200 of the alleged purchase money must be treated as not having been paid, and as being now a lien on the land, to the benefit of which the plaintiff is entitled.

The bill proceeds on the ground that the transfer of the land was colorable; but, as I have no doubt that all the facts are sufficiently before me, there seems no reason why I should not make a decree according to the rights of the parties as I gather them from the evidence. The decree, however, will not be drawn up for three weeks, to give the defendant an opportunity to make such application to me as he may be advised.

This sum of $200 being more than sufficient to satisfy the plaintiff's debt, it is unnecessary to consider whether it sufficiently appears that the sale would have taken place in the absence of a fraudulent intent; or to observe upon the general question as to the validity of a sale which might have taken place at all events, but which, by the fraudulent contrivance of the parties, is carried out in such a way as in part to deceive creditors.

. Unless within three weeks the defendant satisfies me that he should have an opportunity of giving further evidence, the plaintiff will take a decree for his debt and costs (lower scale) ; and, in default, for a sale of the land.

---

## CONNOR v. McPHERSON.

*Tax sales—Five Years' arrears—Lapse of time.*

On a bill impeaching a tax sale on the ground that no portion of the taxes had been due for five years before the issuing of the treasurer's warrant, it appeared, that the first year's taxes had been imposed by a by-law passed in July, 1852 ; that the collector's roll was not delivered until after August, 1852 ; and that the treasurer's warrant was dated 10th July, 1857 :
*Held,* that the sale was invalid.

Where a plaintiff files a bill praying relief on the ground of a legal title in himself, no shorter lapse of time than would be a bar at law is an obstacle to relief in equity.

By the Assessment Act of 1866, owners had four years to impeach a tax deed : By an Act passed in 1869, all actions for that purpose were stayed until after the following session of the Legislature ; and by another Act of the same session all previous Assessment Acts were repealed, amended, and consolidated, with a reservation of rights had or acquired under the repealed Acts; by one of the clauses of the amended Act the limit appointed for bringing actions was two years :
*Held,* that an owner, who had less than two years of his four remaining when the Acts of 1869 were passed, had like others two years thereafter to bring his suit.

This cause came on for the examination of witnesses and hearing at the sittings of the Court at Sarnia, in the Autumn of 1871. Statement.

The plaintiff claimed to be the owner of the west half of number thirteen in the eighth concession of Enniskillen;

and this suit was to set aside as clouds on her title, (1st) a deed by the Sheriff to one *David McColl* in pursuance of an alleged sale of the land for taxes; and (2nd) a subsequent deed of the land from *McColl's* devisee to the defendant *McPherson*, dated 22nd March. 1865. The land was wild at the time of the tax sale, and had continued so up to the time of the hearing; neither *McColl* nor *McPherson* had ever been in actual possession. The plaintiff's title was admitted subject to the question of the validity of this tax sale.

The sale was for the taxes from 1852 to 1856. The alleged by-laws imposing the taxes for 1852 were dated respectively, the 9th and 27th July, 1852. The collector's roll was not delivered to the collector until after August of that year. The warrant for the sale was dated 10th July, 1857; and the plaintiff insisted, among other things, that no portion of the taxes had at that date been due for five years, and that the sale was therefore void.

Mr. *Kennedy*, for the plaintiff.

Mr. *J. Bethune*, for the defendants.

Dec. 6.

Judgment.

MOWAT, V. C.—It was contended by the defendants, that the taxes were due at the beginning of the year 1859, though the by-laws imposing them for that year had not then been passed; or that if such taxes were not due, within the meaning of the Statute, before the passing of the by-laws, they became due the moment the by-laws were passed. But *Ford* v. *Proudfoot* (a) and *Bell*. v. *McLean* (b) are against this contention, and are sufficient to make out the sale in question to be in point of law invalid. The provision at the end of section 1 of 27th Victoria, ch. 19, is not retrospective.

(a) 9 Gr. 478.     (b) 18 U. C. C. P. 416.

It is unnecessary to consider other objections which the plaintiff's counsel urged against the sale.

The delay of the plaintiff in commencing a suit was relied on as a bar to the plaintiff's right to relief. After the sheriff's sale *McColl* paid the taxes for two years; and thence no taxes were paid by anybody for several years. In 1864 the land was again sold for taxes, when the plaintiff, through her agent, became the purchaser. In the following year the defendant paid the redemption money; and since that time all the taxes have been paid by the plaintiff. In 1870 the defendant *McPherson* sold wood off the lot, and this is the first time that anything was done on the land by any of the claimants. On the 3rd November, 1870, the present suit was commenced. Whether under these circumstances the defendant, if his legal title was good, could have resisted a suit brought on purely equitable grounds, it is unnecessary to consider; for it is on her strict legal title that the plaintiff founds her claim to a decree; and in such a case a lapse of time which is no bar to the legal title, is no obstacle to the relief which the holder of the legal title can claim in equity. It was contended for the defendants, that by the Assessment Act of 1866 (a) the plaintiff was bound to bring her suit either at law or in equity within four years after the passing of that Act. The Assessment Act of 1869 (b) repealed that Act. The 155th section of this Act of 1869 provided, that a tax deed should be valid unless questioned before some court of competent jurisdiction within two years after the passing of this Act. The four years which the plaintiff had by the Act of 1866, expired (according to the defendant's contention) in August, 1870. Chapter 35 of the Acts of 1869 stayed until the end of the then next ensuing session all suits impeaching tax sales. The repeal of the Act of 1866 by chapter 36 passed in 1869 was

---

(a) 29–30 Vic., ch. 53, sec. 156.      (b) 32 Vic. ch. 36.

1871.     subject to a reservation of " all rights, proceedings or
~~~~~     things legally, had, acquired, or done under" it; and it
Connor    provided that " all things begun but not completed there-
v.
McPherson. under may be continued to completion" as if the repeal-
ing Act had not been passed. It is clear that by the
Assessment Act of 1869 the Legislature took from the
operation of the 155th clause of the Act of 1866 something
of the rights of those owners who had more than two
years of their four still unexpired; and the exceptional
Act, chapter 35, made an important inroad on the rights
of all to whom the 155th section applied. I think it impossible. to hold under these circumstances, that the
saving clause (a) in chapter 36 was intended to except
section 155 of the previous Act from the operation of the
repeal, so far as relates to owners who like the plaintiff had then less than two years to bring their suits. I
think that the two years should be construed as intended to apply equally to all.

Judgment.

The defendant *McPherson* stated in his evidence that he
had sold timber off the lot in 1870; and plaintiff's counsel
asked for a reference as to the amount so sold; and that if
necessary the bill should be amended for that purpose.
The defendant's counsel cited *Cook* v. *Jones* (b) to shew
that no amendment would be permitted in cases like the
present; but I do not think that that case applies. The
defendant stated that he had sold the wood off from
twenty-two to twenty-four acres at the rate of $6 an
acre. The plaintiff may take a decree for (say) $138,
or may take a reference at her own risk as to costs. No
actual amendment of the bill need be made. The defendant is to have credit for the particulars mentioned in the
13th section of 33 Victoria, chapter 23.

The bill charges that the sheriff's sale was fraudulent.
It does not appear that the costs of either side have

_____

(a) Sec. 204.          (b) 17 Gr. 488.

been increased by this charge; but if they have, the 1871.
plaintiff should pay such increase. The rest of her costs
she may have (a).

## FORREST V. LAYCOCK.

*Mortgage by husband and wife—Dower after mortgage—Compromise
valid against creditors—Practice—Lower scale of costs.*

The release of a wife's dower to a purchaser is a good consideration
for the grant of a reasonable compensation to the wife; and such a
grant made *bonâ fide* is valid against the husband's creditors.

Where a wife joins in a mortgage of her husband's estate as a security
to the mortgagee, and for no other purpose, she parts with her
dower so far only as may be necessary for that purpose, and she is a
necessary party to a subsequent sale by the husband free from dower.

A wife joined in a mortgage of her husband's estate to secure a loan
of one-fourth or one-fifth of the value of the property, and he
subsequently sold the property; his wife claimed to be entitled
to dower, and refused to join in the conveyance without a
reasonable compensation being made to her; her right to dower
being supposed by all parties to exist, her husband had a piece of
land conveyed to her, which she accepted, and thereupon she signed
the conveyance of the mortgaged estate. The transaction appearing to have been for the interest of creditors, it was held to be
valid, independently of the question whether her claim to dower
was in such a case well founded in point of law or not.

The costs of a suit by a judgment creditor, to whom less than $200 is
due, to obtain payment of his own debt alone out of property
alleged to have been conveyed away to defeat the plaintiff's claim,
are taxable according to the lower scale, no matter what the value
of the property may be.

Examination and hearing at the sittings at Woodstock,
in the Autumn of 1871.

It appeared that on the 6th September, 1870, the Statement.
plaintiff recovered in a Division Court a judgment
against *Joseph Laycock* for $95.68 debt, and $6.38
costs. Having taken the necessary steps for the pur-

(a) See Blest v. Brow, 8 Jur. N. S. 602 ; Jones v. Ricketts, Ib. 1198;
Staniland v. Willott, 3 McN. & G, 664 ; Pledge v. Buss, Johns 663

pose, he had in the hands of the sheriff of Oxford a *fi. fa.* against *Laycock's* lands ; and the object of the bill was, to obtain payment out of a piece of property in the village of Embro, claimed by the debtor's wife, *Mary Laycock*, as hers. The husband and wife were the defendants to the suit.

It appeared that Mr. *Laycock* had been for many years a miller at Embro. He owned and carried on there a flouring mill, an oatmeal mill, and a saw-mill. He had also a farm of 50 or 55 acres adjoining the mills. Some years ago he mortgaged this property, or part of it, to one Dr. *Austin*. In or about 1866, this mortgage was discharged, and another was made to Dr. *Fuller* for $3,000, part of the money having been required to pay off Dr. *Austin's* mortgage. In March, 1869, being desirous of paying off Dr. *Fuller's* mortgage, and of raising more money, *Laycock* sold the fifty acres to
Statement. one *Campbell* for $2,000, and mortgaged the residue, the mill property, to one *McLeod* for $1,500. Two months after this, a freshet carried away the dam ; money was borrowed from one *Young* for the rebuilding of the dam ; and a second mortgage on the mill property was given to him to secure the loan. *Laycock* proceeded to rebuild, and when he had the dam nearly finished another freshet carried off all his work. Once more he set about renewing it. This time he got the dam finished ; and the mills were again at work, when a third freshet came, and once more carried all away.

Mrs. *Laycock* had joined in all the mortgages of the property, and in the deed to *Campbell*. The mortgages to *McLeod* and *Young* were under the Act respecting Short Forms of Mortgages. In both these mortgages the conveyance by the husband and the release by the wife were expressed to be subject to the proviso for redemption. The other mortgages were not produced at the hearing. At the time of executing, and before

executing, these several instruments, Mrs. *Laycock*
spoke to her husband about her dower, and on each
occasion she received from him some assurance
which quieted her for the time. She was twenty
years younger than her husband; they had a large
family; from 1867 or 1868 he had been in poor
health; and he did not appear to have managed his
affairs very successfully. On account of his failing
circumstances, Mrs. *Laycock's* anxiety to secure some
provision for herself seems to have come to a head at the
time of the sale to *Campbell;* and she refused to join
in that sale until her husband had promised her that on
the sale of the mill property, which he was then contemplating and probably endeavoring to effect, he would
make to her compensation for her dower in respect of
both properties.

1871.

Forrest
v.
Laycock.

Before the last accident occurred to the dam, he had
bargained for the sale of the mill property to one
*Knott* for $8,500; but, the dam having been carried
away the day before the matter was to be closed, *Knott*
threw up the bargain. *Laycock* then contracted to sell
to *Midgeley* for $6,500, out of which *Midgeley* was to
pay the mortgages; for $1,000 he was to convey the
property now in question; and the balance he was to
pay on or before the first April then next. Mrs.
*Laycock* refused to sign off her dower unless she was
paid for it. She claimed to be entitled to compensation for her dower in the fifty acres also which had
previously been sold to *Campbell.* $1,000 was con-
sidered to be the value of her dower; and, that being
the value of the property now in question, she agreed to
accept this property in satisfaction of her claims. This
being assented to, she executed the deed to *Midgeley,*
and the conveyance of the property in question was
made by *Midgeley* to her. Soon afterwards she entered
with her family (numbering twelve in all) into possession
of this property; and she had continued with them in
possession ever since.

Statement.]

1871.

Forrest
v.
Laycock.

A considerable part of *Midgeley's* purchase money was applied in payment of *Laycock's* debts, and there was no evidence affecting Mrs. *Laycock* to shew that there were any other debts besides those paid and the amount due to the plaintiff. Mr. *Laycock* was called as a witness against himself by the plaintiff, and he gave his evidence with the utmost apparent honesty, but in considerable seeming weakness of mind and body. He said that there remained some debts unpaid—the amount of them (if such there were) was not suggested, nor to whom any of them were due. Of the money received from *Midgeley*, what was not employed in paying debts was expended in the support of the family during the first few months after the sale; and by the time the plaintiff sued and obtained his judgment, all had been expended.

Statement. The plaintiff's debt was not paid, because he claimed $300 (or $500), and would take no less, though the amount really due to him was, as appeared from the judgment, less than $100. He was at the time in possession of the oatmeal mill, under some verbal agreement for applying the profits to pay the debt. The mill was not going, but he refused to give up possession without payment of the amount on which he was insisting; and *Laycock* was in consequence obliged to allow to *Midgeley*, by way of compensation for the delay, $100 out of the purchase money, the sum so allowed being of itself more than the amount of the plaintiff's true debt as established by the judgment.

The bill claimed payment of the judgment out of the property conveyed to Mrs. *Laycock*; the grounds on which this relief was sought being, "that no part of the consideration given to *Midgeley* for the conveyance to Mrs. *Laycock* was her property, but (the whole consideration) was the property of the defendant *Joseph*

*Laycock.*" The bill charged that the conveyance to
Mrs. *Laycock* was made to her for her husband's benefit,
and to defraud his creditors.

Mr. *S. Blake* and Mr. *Ball*, for the plaintiff.

Mr. *Barrett* and Mr. *Richardson*, for defendant
*Mary Laycock.*

MOWAT, V. C.—[After stating the facts as above] I
have no doubt that the conveyance to Mrs. *Laycock* was
meant to be for her benefit, and for her separate use. I
have no doubt that the transaction was an honest one ;
that it ha'd no fraudulent purpose; that there was no idea
of, by that means or any other, avoiding payment of the
plaintiff's debt; that in the sale to *Midgeley*, as in all
the previous transactions relating to the husband's property, all parties thought that Mrs. *Laycock* was
entitled to dower, and thought that her joining in the
conveyance was essential to making a good title free
from dower; that she would not have joined in the
conveyance to *Midgeley* without receiving this compensation; that *Midgeley* (unless compelled) would not
have accepted a conveyance without her signature ;
that the piece of property which she got was considered
by all parties at the time to be a reasonable compensation for her dower ; and that *Midgeley* would not
have given even $5,500 for the property subject to
her dower. I have no doubt that the intention of both
Mr. and Mrs. *Laycock* at this time was that all the
husband's debts should be paid out of the balance of the
purchase money, and that they expected it would be
sufficient to pay them. I am satisfied that the non-
payment of the plaintiff's debt, at the same time as the
other debts were paid, arose from the exorbitant sum
which he claimed.

I am clear that the release of a wife's dower to a

1871.    purchaser is a good consideration for the grant of a
——————   reasonable compensation to her, and that such a grant
Forrest
  v.     made *bona fide* is valid against the husband's creditors.
Laycock.
         I refer to *Lavender* v. *Jackson* (a) and *Arundel* v.
         *Phipps* (b), and to the observations to be found in
         *Sugden* on Vendors (c) and *Park* on Dower (d).

But it was said in argument that, Mrs. *Laycock*
having previous to the sales to *Campbell* and *Midgeley*
joined in mortgaging the property, she had thereby,
according to the English decisions, parted with her
dower absolutely ; and that the conveyance to her was
therefore wholly without consideration. These mortgages are not mentioned in the bill as having had this
effect; but the bill charges that no consideration moved
from her ; and the plaintiff's counsel claimed to be
entitled to urge the argument.

Judgment.      It is to be observed that, by the terms of the only two
mortgages which I have seen, Mrs. *Laycock's* release of
dower was not absolute, but was subject, like her husband's
grant, to the proviso for redemption ; and that neither
instrument contains any express provision as to the
reconveyance of the property on payment, or as to the
uses on which the land was to be held by the mortgagee
subject to redemption ; and that the arguments against
the wife which in the English books are founded on the
forms in use there may not apply with the same force
to these mortgages.

With reference to the doctrine of the English law,
Lord *Wensleydale,* in his book on Dower, states (e),
" that a fine is not necessarily an absolute bar to a title
of dower ; but that a woman may still continue dowable
(notwithstanding her having joined on levying a fine)

---

(a) 2 Lev. 137.                    (b) 10 Ves. 139.
(c) 11 ed. pp. 935, 936.           (d) p. 211.
                    (e) 207.

either, first, where that fine in its own nature only
created a charge or chattel interest; or, secondly, where,
although the fine itself imported a grant of the fee, the
use of that fine either resulted to or was declared in
favor of the husband, subject only to the charge, &c.
This the writer apprehends to be the correct mode of
stating the doctrine of Courts of law; but it seems to
be the understanding of the profession that Courts of
equity carry the point still further in favor of the
dowress; and that cases may occur where a fine,
although an absolute bar at law, would in equity, upon
the ground of its having been levied for a particular
purpose only, be restrained from operating to exclude
the widow from her dower, except to the extent of the
particular purpose originally contemplated."

1871.

Forrest
v.
Laycock.

In illustration of the doctrine of equity the learned
author refers to, and states, several cases which I have
examined. The first of them is an anonymous case
reported in 2 Eq. Ca. Ab. 385, where the general
principle was recognized that, where a wife joined with
the husband in a fine in order to make a mortgage, the
fine, though a bar at law, was not necessarily a bar in
equity. The next case referred to is *Naylor* v. *Baldwin*
(a) (15 Chas. 1.,) where the Court declared that if [the
wife] levied the fine only to secure the lease [the mortgage,] no debt could bar her except the debt on the
lease." *Dolin* v. *Coltman* (b) is the next case in point
of time (1684); and there the right of the wife, notwithstanding the fine, was again recognized. The last case
(in point of time) of the cases mentioned in the book on
Dower is *Jackson* v. *Parker* (c), before Sir *Thomas Sewell*,
Master of the Rolls. There, as in the other cases, the
husband had made a mortgage by lease and release, and
fine, in which the wife had joined, and the proviso was,
that, if the husband and wife should pay, the mortgagee

Judgment:

---

(a) 1 Ch. Rep. 130.      (b) 1 Vern. 294.      (c) Ambl. 687.

1871.
Forrest
v.
Laycock.

would reconvey to them, their heirs and assigns. A subsequent clause declared the uses of the fine (subject to the mortgage debt) to be to the husband, his heirs and assigns. After the husband's death the question arose, what interest the wife took in the equity of redemption ; and, though the wife's name was mentioned in the proviso, it was held that the equity of redemption was not thereby given to her and her husband jointly; and though her name was not mentioned in the subsequent clause, but her husband's only, she was held entitled to her dower. In stating this case afterwards in the House of Lords, Lord *Redesdale* gave an explanation of it, which was in part as follows: (*a*) "Upon a contest for redemption the Court would regard the ownership of the estate previous to the mortgage ; and in that view the husband would be considered as the person entitled to redeem, the wife being entitled to redeem only in respect of her

Judgment. interest, which would have been only a right to dower if she had survived her husband. In such case she would have been entitled to have had the estate redeemed for the purpose of letting in her dower, but there her right ended."

After stating at some length the cases (not including the case in the House of Lords) the learned writer of the book on Dower observes as follows (*b*) : "Whether at the present day Courts of Equity would admit of extrinsic evidence that it was the agreement or intention of the parties, that the fine should only conclude the wife as against the incumbrancer; or whether they would render such evidence unnecessary by presuming an agreement to that effect in every case where a fine is levied as part of a mortgage transaction, is perhaps doubtful. * * On this point the student should consider the cases where a fine by husband and wife of the

---

(*a*) 1 Bligh. at 124.          (*b*) p. 212.

wife's jointure lands, has been restrained in equity to the particular purpose."

In *Jackson* v. *Innes*, in the House of Lords (a), Lord *Redesdale* expressly declared that, where a fine is levied to a mortgagee, cases of jointure and dower, and other cases which he mentions, depend on the same principle ; and the law as to all he stated in these words : " It must now be admitted as an established principle, to be applied in deciding upon the effect of mortgages of this description, whether it be the estate of the wife or the estate of the husband, if the wife joins in the conveyance, either because the estate belongs to her, or because she has a charge by way of jointure or dower out of the estate, and there is a mere reservation in the proviso for the redemption of the mortgage, which would carry the estate from the person who was owner at the time of executing the mortgage ; or where the words admit of any ambiguity ; that there is a resulting trust for the benefit of the wife, or for the benefit of the husband, according to the circumstances of the case."

I was referred after the argument to a passage in the notes to *Powell* on Mortgages, p. 286 (b), as favoring the plaintiff's case. The learned editor, however, refers there to a fuller discussion of the subject in a subsequent part of the book, and, on referring to this part, I find that the view of the learned editor corresponds with that given in the extracts which I have taken from the book on Dower. He states that it is the general understanding of the profession, " that a fine, unless an absolute bar at law, may, in equity, on the ground of its having been levied for a particular purpose, be restrained from operating to exclude the widow from her dower except to the extent of the particular purpose contemplated ;" and the learned writer considered this "general

---

(a) 1 Bligh. at 126.    (b) 6th Ed. by Coventry.

opinion " to be " confirmed and enforced " by the cases which he cites (a). He thinks it established that in equity " the fine may operate as a total or a partial bar to dower, according to the intention of the parties." He adds : " Whether a corresponding statement can be made as to the operation of a fine in a Court of law the cases do not warrant us in deciding ; but no sound reason occurs why a Court of law should not adopt this equitable principle, and restrict the effect of the fine to the purpose intended in the same manner that it restrains the operation of any other species of conveyance" (b). I refer for like statements of the law to *Roper's* Husband and Wife, 2nd Ed., by *Jacob*, p. 536 *et seq.*, and *Bright's* Husband and Wife, p. 525, &c.

There are thus in favor of the wife the decisions in the old cases ; and the opinions of Sir *Thomas Sewell*, Master of the Rolls, in *Jackson* v. *Parker*, and afterwards of Lord *Redesdale* in the House of Lords ; and there is, I believe, no decision or judicial opinion to the contrary.

All the text writers state the doctrine in the same way with, so far as I can discover, the single exception of Mr. *Jarman*, who expressed a strong opinion to the contrary in his article on Fines in *Bythewood's* Conveyancing (c). He also gives there the opinions of three conveyancing counsel to whom the point had been referred in 1816. One of these is in favor of the wife ; the name of the counsel is not given, but he is called " a gentleman of great experience;" and it is said of him that " there is no gentleman whose opinion deserves greater attention than his." The other two opinions were by Mr. *Hayes* and Mr. *Bell* (both eminent lawyers, certainly), and were the other way. Mr. *Jarman* admits, that there had been a " difference of opinion "

---

(a) p. 675.　　(b) p. 676a; see also pp. 678, 680a, 732, 739.
(c) Vol. 4, 2nd ed. p. 173.

on the subject; that "some of the opinions in the early cases may seem to support the doctrine against which (his) observations are directed;" that extra-judicial opinions of Sir *Thomas Sewell* and Lord *Redesdale* were expressed to the same effect; and that "their statement of the doctrine had been accepted without hesitation by the most approved writers on the subject," referring to Jac. Rop. H. & W. 537; Coote on Mortgages, 548; Patch 175; 2 Cov. Pow. Mort. 675.

Every thing in the shape of judicial authority or opinion being thus in favor of the wife; the most approved writers on the subject having (with one exception) adopted the same view; and the same having been the general opinion of the profession up to the time at which Mr. *Coventry* published his very learned and valuable notes to Mr. *Powell's* work; and the books containing no evidence that the opposite opinion ever became general; I do not see how it would be possible for me, as a Canadian Judge, to hold, in a contested case, and after looking into the authorities, that this opposite opinion is, notwithstanding, the law of the Court. To my mind, too, the reasoning on which the opinion in favor of the wife is rested, is more satisfactory than the reasoning by which the opposite opinion is supported.

It was not contended that the mortgages in the present case contain any indication that Mrs. *Laycock* intended thereby to part with her dower for any other purpose than the security of the mortgagee; and it is perfectly clear that, in fact, she had no such intention.

I do not say that it is necessary for the wife's defence that the Court should decide this point in her favor. A *bona fide* compromise is sustainable as against creditors as well as others. A reasonable settlement of a claim made and acceded to in good faith may be valid, though it should be decided afterwards that the law was differ-

Judgment.

1871.    ent from what the parties had assumed it to be.    For

Forrest.
v.        all that appears in the present case, it was for the interest
Laycock.  of *Laycock's* creditors that his wife should receive from
him $1000 in satisfaction of her claim, even though, in
case of a contest, there had been a prospect of making
out the claim to be unsustainable (*a*).

Having reference to the ages, and the state of health,
of the husband and wife respectively, in connection
with all the other circumstances to which I have referred,
I cannot say, upon any evidence before me, that, in any
view of the extent to which Mrs. *Laycock* may be
considered to have been entitled to claim dower, the
compensation agreed to was excessive, or was so unreasonable as to invalidate the transaction.    I think
that the plaintiff's bill should be dismissed with costs.

THE VICE CHANCELLOR was afterwards applied to
Judgment. with respect to the scale on which the costs should be
taxed.    He said that it must be the lower scale ; that
the County Court Act gave jurisdiction to that Court in
case of equitable relief being sought " for or by reason
of any matter whatever, when the subject matter involved
does not exceed the sum of $200 ;" that the subject
matter in a case of this kind must be taken to be the
amount due on the judgment in respect of which equitable
relief is sought ; and the amount here was considerably
less than $200; that the bill was for the payment of the
plaintiff's debt only, and did not allege nor was it proved
against Mrs. *Laycock* that there were any other debts ;
that the case was analogous to that of a mortgagee or
registered judgment creditor, provided for by the previous
sub-section (No. 4), who might have sought in the County
Court a foreclosure or sale of the debtor's property
whatever the value of it, so long as the sum claimed to
be due to the plaintiff did not exceed $200.

(*a*) See Heap v. Tonge, 9 H. 90 ; Stapelton v. Stapelton, and notes,
2 Wh. & T. 755.

### SMART v. McEWAN.

*Mortgage, purchase of without notice—Priority.*

An assignee of a mortgage cannot as against a prior equity set up the plea of purchase without notice.

The registered owner of land mortgaged the same, and afterwards conveyed the property absolutely to a purchaser, who registered before such mortgage, giving back a mortgage to secure purchase money; and subsequently the vendor assigned his mortgage to a purchaser who had no notice of the prior mortgage:

*Held,* that the purchaser's mortgage in the hands of the assignee was subject to the lien or charge of the vendor's mortgagee.

Examination of witnesses and hearing at Lindsay, Autumn Sittings, 1871.

Mr. *Moss* for the plaintiff.

Mr. *C. S. Patterson* and Mr. *Dennistoun*, for the defendant.

STRONG, V. C.—The plaintiff, sues as executor of a Mr. *Gage. Charles B. Orde* being in debt to *Gage*, who had incurred liabilities as a surety for him, made to *Gage* a mortgage of the land in question. Then, the mortgage being a perfected security, so far as the parties to it were concerned, though not registered, *Orde* conveyed to *Cuthbert*, who had no notice, and who registered, thus cutting out the mortgage to *Gage;* and *Cuthbert* then gave *Orde* a mortgage to secure the purchase money. This mortgage *Orde* registered, and afterwards, through the agency of his attorney *Ernest Orde*, assumed to assign it for value to the defendant, who had no notice of any equity in favor of *Gage.* The plaintiff, representing *Gage*, claims to have a charge on this mortgage. I disposed at the hearing of all the questions of fact and law arising, excepting that as to the plaintiff's right to this charge or lien. I have been unable to find any authority, and I have been referred to none by the learned counsel who appeared in the cause.

Judgment.

I have therefore to decide the case on principle, and I adhere now to what I said at the hearing, namely, that the mortgage to *Gage* being void as against *Cuthbert* only, and a valid and subsisting instrument between the parties to it, it binds any interest in the lands which *Orde* has.

I am aware that in cases, under the statute 27th Elizabeth, chapter 4, where a voluntary deed was avoided by a subsequent conveyance for valuable consideration, the purchase money in the hands of the settlor was not bound by the trusts of the first settlement: *Townend* v. *Toker* (a), establishes this, although the doctrine does not seem altogether to have received the approval of Lord Justice *Turner*. But this case differs in two respects: first, there is here still in the mortgagor's hands an interest in the land itself, which, I think, must be considered bound in the same way as the interest of a person who, having no title, makes a

mortgage, and afterwards himself acquires a charge on the same land, would be bound. The subsequently accruing interest feeds the title under the first deed. This circumstance, that here there is this actual interest in the land in the original mortgagor, is sufficient of itself to take this case out of the authority of cases proceeding on the statute of 27th Elizabeth. But, secondly, the plaintiff is a purchaser for value, and not a mere volunteer, so that the principle on which those cases seem to have proceeded cannot apply.

The plaintiff's equity being established, it binds the defendant, although he took the transfer of the mortgage from *Orde* without notice and for value; for I adhere to my decision in the case of *Ryckman* v. *The Canada Life Assurance Company* (b), founded on the authorities there quoted, that an assignee of a mortgage cannot set up a defence of purchase for value without notice; and, moreover, here the legal

_____

(a) L. R. 1 Ch. App. 446          (b) 17 Gr. 550.

estate did not pass, as *Ernest Orde* had no authority to convey it, his power of attorney not being sufficiently extensive to authorize such an act.

There must be the usual decree, as in the case of a derivative mortgage treating the mortgage given by *Orde* to *Gage*, as constituting a charge on that from *Cuthbert* to *Orde*. The costs of the suit will be added to the debt as in an ordinary case.

---

## WRIGHT V. RANKIN.

*Implied agency—Secret profit—Conflict of testimony.*

W. was the owner (subject to a mortgage) of property which *M.* wished to buy; *R.* becoming aware of this, entered into friendly negotiations with both, and bargained with *W.* to take $3,500, and with *M.* to give $5,600 for the property; *R.* concealed this difference from the parties. *W.* conveyed to *M.*; on her signing the deed, *R.'s* attorney paid to her the $3,500 (less the mortgage debt), and on the deed being delivered to *M.* she (*M.*) paid to *R.'s* attorney the $5,600. The facts afterwards coming to the knowledge of W. she filed a bill against *R.* claiming the balance of the $5,600; and it appearing that in the negotiations he had given *W.* to understand that he was acting in her interest, and had no personal interest of his own, the plaintiff was *held* entitled to a decree against *R.* for such balance with interest and costs.

There may be agency, and its duties and liabilities, without express words of appointment or acceptance; and where a party in negociating between two persons, the one desiring to sell, the other to buy certain land, gave the former to understand that he was acting in her interest, it was *held*, that she was entitled to the full price which he obtained for the land, though it exceeded the amount which he had obtained her consent to accept.

In such a case, there being a conflict as to what had passed in the conversations, and no other witness of them being produced, it was *held* that, other things being equal, the version of the deceived party should be accepted in preference to that of the other party.

Examination of witnesses and hearing, at the sittings of the Court at Sandwich, in the Autumn of 1871.

1871.

Wright
v.
Rankin.

On the 18th of November, 1870, the plaintiff, Mrs. *Wright*, and her husband executed, at or near Windsor, a conveyance of some land in the township of Sandwich to Mrs. *McKinstry*, wife of Commodore *McKinstry*, a resident of Detroit. The consideration expressed in the conveyance was $5,600; and that amount was, on a subsequent part of the same day, paid at Detroit by Mrs. *McKinstry* to the defendant *Frank Evans Marcon* for Mrs. *Wright* (as Mrs. *McKinstry* supposed). *Marcon*, however, paid $2,100 of the amount to the defendant *Arthur Rankin*, or to his use; and the suit was to recover the amount from *Rankin* and *Marcon*.

The defendants claimed that Mr. *Rankin* was entitled to this money; that he had bought the property from Mrs. *Wright*, for his own benefit, at $3,500, which was paid or accounted for to her when she signed the deed, and was afterwards made good out of the $5,600; that he resold to Mrs. *McKinstry* for the $5,600 for his own benefit; and that the conveyance was made by Mrs. *Wright* to Mrs. *McKinstry* direct for the mere purpose of avoiding the unnecessary expense of two conveyances. The plaintiff met these statements by alleging, that *Rankin* professed to be acting as her agent in negociating the sale to Mrs. *McKinstry;* that he pretended to her (or to her husband, who was acting for her,) that $3,500 was all that Mrs. *McKinstry* was willing to give or had agreed to give; and the plaintiff alleged, that she was not aware of the truth until after the receipt of the money by *Rankin*.

Mr. *S. Blake* and Mr. *O'Connor*, for the plaintiff.

Mr. *Hodgins* and Mr. *Dougall*, for the defendants.

December 6.   MOWAT, V. C.—[After stating the facts as above].
As the deed purports to be a sale from Mrs. *Wright*
Judgment. to Mrs. *McKinstry* direct, and as the sum of $5,600 is

therein expressed to be the consideration for which
the conveyance is made; and as that clearly appears
from the evidence to have been Mrs. *McKinstry's*
understanding of the transaction at the time, the onus
of proving the contrary is upon the defendant who
asserts it.

The negotiations for the sale by Mrs. *Wright*, and
for the purchase by Mrs. *McKinstry*, were conducted
by Mr. *Rankin* with each, or with the husband of each;
and the *Wrights* and *McKinstrys* had no communication
with one another. But it is clear that the *McKinstrys*
thought that they were buying from Mrs. *Wright*; and
it is also clear that the *Wrights* had no idea that they
were selling to Mr. *Rankin* for his own benefit, if at all.
It is clear also that not only was Mr. *Rankin* aware of
the impression of the *Wrights* in that respect, but he
believed that but for that impression they would not sell.
Part of his evidence, given on his own behalf, was as
follows: "On the first occasion of speaking to Mr.
*Wright* about the property, I asked him if he was disposed
to sell the property by private sale," (it was then under
advertisement for sale by auction on the 19th of
November, Mr. *Wright* having met with losses which
appear to have made an early sale an object to him,)
"for, if he was, I thought that I could find him a purchaser. * * The reason why I said I would find him
a purchaser was, that if he had known I was the purchaser he would have been suspicious, and would have
asked more. He knew that I bought and sold property,
and that I did not want this property for my own use.
He would, therefore, have believed that I saw something
could have been made of it, and perhaps he would not
have sold it to me at all."

A receipt was proved, dated 16th November, 1870,
which Mr. *Rankin* wrote out when he afterwards closed
the bargain with Mr. *Wright*, and which receipt

Mr. *Wright* signed after Mr. *Rankin* had read it to
him.   This document begins as follows : " Received
from *Arthur Rankin* the sum of $100 on account of
his purchase from me of 19 acres," &c.   The property
is then described, and the terms of the bargain are
stated, except that no price is named.

It was argued for the defendants that this mention of
the purchase as "his," namely, *Rankin's,* shews that Mr.
*Wright* then understood that *Rankin* was the purchaser,
and that he was purchasing for himself.  To this argument it was answered, amongst other things, that Mrs.
*Wright* deposed that she had heard *Rankin* reading
the paper before her husband signed it, and that she
understood that it named Commodore or Mrs. *McKinstry*
as the purchaser.   It was further pressed upon my
attention, that the Commodore in his evidence had
sworn that that was as he also understood the paper
when it was read to him.   Mr. *Rankin,* however, distinctly swore that he read the paper truly on both
occasions.   The explanation of the contradiction probably is, that, as neither Mrs. *Wright* nor the Commodore
suspected that Mr. *Rankin* was claiming to be the
purchaser from Mrs. *Wright,* both overlooked the word-
ing of the paper in the particular now under consideration.   At all events, purchases by an agent in his own
name are common transactions.

I think that the form of the receipt is insufficient to
outweigh the effect of the statements which I have quoted
from Mr. *Rankin's* evidence, corresponding, as those
statements do, with the tone of all the other evidence
in the cause ; and, on the whole, I am clear that I
must hold that the evidence negatives- the position
taken by Mr. *Rankin* in his answer, denying (in the
words of the answer,) "that I in any way led him
(*Wright*) to believe that I was not purchasing on my
own account"  But that conclusion does not dispose of

the case ; I have to consider Mr. *Rankin's* relation to the plaintiff in the transaction.

Mrs. *Wright*, in her deposition, related two conversations as having occurred between her husband and Mr. *Rankin* at Mr. *Wright's* house. Mr. *Rankin* denied the first of these conversations *in toto*, and stated that he was but once in the house, viz. when the receipt was written and signed. Mrs. *Wright* also stated several particulars as having occurred on the latter occasion ; which Mr. *Rankin* distinctly denied. I know nothing whatever of Mrs. *Wright* except what appeared before me in this case. She seemed to be an educated and intelligent lady, and she gave her evidence with every appearance of truthfulness and candor ; and, in view of all the circumstances, I do not see how I can refuse to give to her the benefit of the principle laid down by the Master of the Rolls in *Lane* v. *Jackson* (a) and other cases. His Lordship observed : " I have frequently stated that where the positive fact of a particular conversation is said to have taken place between two persons of equal credibility, and one states positively that it took place, and the other as positively denies it, I believe that the words were said, and that the person who denies their having been said, has forgotten the circumstance. By this means I give full credit to both parties."

*Judgment.*

I have further to bear in mind that in Mr. *Rankin's* negotiations with the *Wrights*, he had in view an undisclosed scheme for his own profit, while he allowed and led her and her husband to suppose that he had no personal interest in the matter. He had on that account a great advantage over them in the negociations. By acute management, he prevented them from suspecting that he had any personal interest in the sale which they were

---

(a) 20 B. at 539.

negotiating; or that there was any occasion for vigilance
on their part against him; or any occasion for applying
personally to the purchasers, or for negotiating with
them directly, or for preserving evidence of the character
in which Mr. *Rankin* was acting. These considerations
afford special reason why, in the absence of any evidence
corroborating Mr. *Rankin's* version of what passed
between him and the plaintiff's husband in her hearing,
I ought to hold Mrs. *Wright's* version to be that on
which the decree of the Court must proceed.

Mrs. *Wright* deposed that in the first conversation
which she mentioned, "her husband said that he had
perhaps better leave the matter in his (Mr. *Rankin's*)
hands, as he (Mr. *Rankin*) could make a better bargain
than he (Mr. *Wright*) could do himself, and as he (Mr.
*Wright*) knew the parties. Mr. *Rankin* replied that he
thought he could. . . . Mr. *Rankin* said that he dared
say he could make a better bargain with the Commodore
than Mr. *Wright* could." She further stated that no
sum was named on that occasion; that at the second
interview at the house, "Mr. *Rankin* assured Mr.
*Wright* that he could not get any more than
$3,500; that the Commodore was not willing to give
more. He said that the Commodore or Mrs. *McKinstry*
had authorized him to pay $100, if Mr. *Wright* had
accepted the $3,500. . . . The offer of $3,500 was
accepted on Mr. *Rankin's* assurance that that was all
they (the Commodore and Mrs. *McKinstry*) were willing to give." Mr. *Rankin*, in his deposition, contradicted these statements of Mrs. *Wright*. Mr. *Wright*
offered himself as a witness, but his evidence was
objected to by the defendants, and I held it inadmissible.

Now, while there are several details in regard to
which there is a conflict of testimony between Mrs.
*Wright* and Mr. *Rankin*, yet the only point material to
the plaintiff which can be said to be disputed or disputa-

ble on the evidence is, whether, during the negotiations, or before the transaction was completed, Mr. *Rankin* gave the *Wrights* to understand that he was acting for them in the sale to Mrs. *McKinstry*, that he was endeavoring to get for them the best price which the *McKinstrys* could be prevailed on to give. If he gave the *Wrights* so to understand, or if he knowingly allowed them so to understand, it is clear that he thereby made himself so far their agent that he must, in a case like this, give up to them any profit which he was secretly making in the transaction, though they may have used no express words appointing him their agent, and though he may have carefully avoided any express acceptance of agency (a). In regard to the fact, I think that the proper conclusion from the whole evidence is, that Mr. *Rankin* did give the plaintiff (through her husband) so to understand, and that the sale of the property at $3,500 was procured by that means.

' Judgment.

The result is, that the plaintiff is entitled as against *Rankin* to the decree which she seeks.

I suggested at the hearing whether *Rankin's* agency for Mrs. *McKinstry* did not raise a question if she was not the person entitled to the $2,100; but, on reflection, I am clear that Mr. *Rankin's* liability to the plaintiff has nothing to do with his possible liability to Mrs. *McKinstry*. Possibly he may be liable to Mrs. *McKinstry* for $2,100, on the ground that he might have got the property for her at $3,500; or at all events that he did get it at that price, though by means which were irregular. If the better to accomplish the object in view, Mr. *Rankin*, unfortunately, chose to be considered by each party, or allowed himself to be considered by each party, as acting in the interest of that party, he

(a) See cases collected in Cameron v. Barnhart, 14 Gr. 661.

may perhaps have rendered himself liable to each as if he had been agent for that party only. But as to Mrs. *McKinstry* I determine nothing ; she is no party to this suit ; and counsel for the defendants was probably right in contending that she could not properly be made a party to it, either by way of amendment or otherwise. Mr. *Rankin,* in giving his evidence, claimed that the transaction, as respects both the plaintiff and Mrs. *McKinstry,* was, on his part, legitimate, and of a kind which is common enough. All that I have to decide is, that as between him and Mrs. *Wright,* upon the evidence given, the transaction, so far as he derived a profit from it, is not (in my opinion) sustainable in this Court.

As to the defendant *Marcon,* I incline to think that the plaintiff has not made out a sufficient case for a decree against him. He was not solicitor for her. He was solicitor for the *McKinstrys.* He probably knew that the *McKinstrys* considered that they were buying from the plaintiff, and not from Mr. *Rankin ;* and that they supposed that the whole of the $5,600 was going to the plaintiff ; and he did not undeceive them, considering that his duty to Mr. *Rankin,* whose solicitor also he was, required this reticence. Whether this reticence has made him liable to the *McKinstrys* or not, it is quite another question whether he is liable to the plaintiff. There is no evidence that she or her husband supposed that Mr. *Marcon* was acting to any extent for her. Mr. *Marcon* knew that the *Wrights* were not aware that Mrs. *McKinstry* was to pay $5,600, and he was aware that Mr. *Rankin* desired that they should not know ; but a resale by a purchaser at an advanced price before he obtains his conveyance, or the concealment of the advanced price from his vendor when a conveyance is obtained from him direct to the sub-purchaser, is not necessarily an illegal transaction ; and it does not appear that Mr. *Marcon* was aware of those other circumstances in the

negotiation between Mr. *Rankin* and the *Wrights* which
disabled *Rankin* from making a profit out of the
transaction; or was aware of any circumstances which,
as between Mr. *Rankin* and the *Wrights*, would make
the transaction, in point of law, a fraud on the *Wrights*.
I do not see, therefore, on what legal principle I could
hold Mr. *Marcon* to be liable to the plaintiff.

The decree will dismiss the bill as against *Marcon*
without costs; and will direct the payment by *Rankin*
to the plaintiff of $2,100, with interest from 18th of
November, 1870, and of the plaintiff's costs of the suit
as respects all the defendants..

*1871.*

Wright
v.
Rankin.

Judgment.

---

## DEWAR v. SPARLING.

*Covenant not to sue—Release obtained from plaintiff by defendant's
attorney.*

A stipulation not to sue one of two judgment debtors is no discharge
of the other, though there should be no express reservation of rights
as against such other.

The plaintiff recovered a judgment against two defendants, each of
whom made a conveyance of his property. The plaintiff filed bills
impeaching the conveyances respectively as fraudulent; in the one
suit the plaintiff obtained a decree; and the other suit he settled,
consenting to the bill therein being dismissed without costs:
*Held*, that these circumstances did not necessarily imply a settlement
or discharge of the debt.

The only further evidence of the terms of the settlement was contained
in a letter from the plaintiff to his solicitors, stating as to the
second suit, that he had settled with the defendants, taking $45
costs, and agreeing not to prosecute the suit, or look to the
defeudants therein for any portion of the judgment; and the letter
inquired, "What about *lis pendens*? Will not bill have to be
dismissed to have it removed?"
*Held*, that the judgment against the other debtor was not discharged.

An old man whose mental faculties had been somewhat impaired by
age, being in difficulties with his son, applied for advice to the
attorney of persons against whom he had recovered a judgment for
one debt and a verdict for another debt; the attorney obtained

from him a release of the two debtors without any consideration, and without his having any other advice in regard to the transaction ; and the only evidence of what had passed between the two was the evidence of the attorney himself, the client being dead : *Held*, that the release could not be maintained in equity.

This was an appeal by the defendants *Sparling* against the Master's report, finding $630.24 to be due to the plaintiff, and $705.84 to be due to *Thomas Robinson*, who was made a party in the Master's office. The contention of the appellants was, that the Master should have found that there was no sum due to either the plaintiff or *Robinson*.

Mr. *Wells* and Mr. *S. Blake*, for the appellants.

Mr. *C. S. Patterson*, for the plaintiff.

Mr. *Ferguson*, for *Robinson*.

The authorities cited are, with others, given in the judgment.

December 6.

Judgment.

MOWAT, V. C.—The plaintiff's claim was on a judgment recovered by him against the appellant *William Sparling*, who is a defendant, and one *Joseph Orr*, who is not a party to this suit. The bill was against *William Sparling* and his sons, to set aside as fraudulent a conveyance made to his sons. The plaintiff filed another bill against *Orr* and another party to set aside as fraudulent another conveyance, which *Joseph Orr* had executed in favor of his co-defendant. The plaintiff obtained a decree in the suit against the *Sparlings;* and he afterwards came to an arrangement with *Orr*, which the appellants' counsel contended had the effect of discharging the judgment against the appellant *William Sparling* as well as against *Orr*.

This contention may be treated as rested on two grounds. The facts as to one are these : The plaintiff's solicitor, in the Chancery suit against *Orr*, sent to the defendants' solicitors a memorandum stating that "the suit had been settled between the parties," and consenting to a dismissal of the bill without costs. An order to that effect was accordingly obtained on the 3rd June, 1871. This order is expressed to be made "on the application of the defendants, and on reading the consent of the plaintiff's solicitor herein." I am clear that these circumstances alone would not be a discharge of the debt, even as respects *Orr*. They would merely operate, at most, as an agreement to abandon the plaintiff's claim against the property mentioned in the bill.

But it is said that the agreement between the parties went beyond that. The only other evidence which was given of the agreement is contained in a letter from the plaintiff to his solicitors, dated 15th April, 1871. This letter is as follows: "*Dewar* v. *Orr*. The defendants called to-day, and I settled with them; taking $45 costs, and agreeing not to prosecute suit or look to them for any portion of judgment. . . . What about *lis pendens ?* Will not bill have to be dismissed to have it removed?" What, then, the plaintiff agreed to was, that he would not prosecute the Chancery suit of *Dewar* v. *Orr ;* that he would consent to its dismissal if necessary; and that he would not look to the defendants therein for any part of his judgment. Such an agreement is not distinguishable for the present purpose from the ordinary covenant not to sue; and it is a clearly settled rule, that a covenant not to sue one of two joint debtors does not release the other, even though there may be no express reservation of the covenantor's rights against the other (*a*). It is only in case of a release or

Judgment.

---

(*a*) Fitzgerald v. Trout, 11 Mod. 234 ; Lacy v. Kynoston, Holt 178 ; 1 Lord Ray. 699 ; 12 Mod. 551 ; Dean v. Newhall, 8 T. R. 168 ; Hutton v. Eyre, 6 Taunt. 289 ; Thomas v. Courtney, 1 B. & Ald. 1 ; Walmsley v. Cooper, 11 A. & E. 216.

discharge, as distinguished from a mere stipulation not to sue, that such a reservation is material.

Counsel for the appellants cited *Cheetham* v. *Ward*(a), *Nicholson* v. *Revell* (b), and *Webb* v. *Hewitt* (c). These were cases in which the one debtor had been absolutely released or discharged, and are not cases of a covenant not to sue. So far as any of the cited cases contain any thing which seems to support the appellants' contention, they are not consistent with other reported cases, including the latest (d). According to the weight of authority, including the latest cases both in law and equity, the leaning should not be in favor of construing a stipulation to be a release rather than a covenant not to sue, but should be the reverse; and stipulations which were in form releases have been construed, in view of the whole agreement, as mere covenants or stipulations not to sue, so as to prevent their operating as discharges of

other persons whom there was no intention of discharging; so that, as Sir *G. M. Giffard* said, in *Greene* v. *Wynn* (e), even where parties put into a "deed words which standing alone amount to a release, the Court will not give that effect to them, but will take the whole of the deed together and effectuate that which was the real intention of the parties." ( f )

The appellants' counsel cited *Cocks* v. *Nash* (g) also. That case decided merely, that parol evidence was inadmissible (at law) to shew that a release under seal was given to the releasee on an undertaking by the defendant (not under seal) that the release should not operate to discharge him (h); and the Lord Chief Justice

---

(a) 1 B. &. P. 633.      (b) 4 A. & E. 683.      (c) 3 K. & J. 442.

(d) See Solly v. Forbes, 2 Bro. & B. 338; Exp. Gifford, 6 Ves. 805; Thompson v. Lack, 3 C. B. N. S. at 551; Kearsley v. Cole. 12 M. & W. 128; North v. Wakefield, 13 Q B. 536; Price v. Barker. 4 E. & B. 760; Defries v. Smith, 10 W. R. 189; Green v. Wynn L. R. 7 Eq. 28.

(e) 7 Eq. at 82.      (f) See 3 C. B. N. S, at 552, &c.

(g) 9 Bing. 341.      (h) S. P. Exp. Glendinning, Buck. 517.

expressly said (a), that if there had been a covenant not
to sue instead of a release, there would have been no
difficulty in the plaintiff's case.

ᵥ The appellants' counsel referred to the right of
*William Sparling*, under the Mercantile Law Amendment Act, to an assignment of the judgment in casé of
his paying the amount. The debtors *Orr* and *Sparling*
did not occupy to the plaintiff the relation, one of
principal and the other of surety. They were joint
debtors. In such a case, it appears from *Hall* v.
*Hutchons* (b), *Wyke* v. *Rogers* (c), *Jenkins* v. *Robertson*
(d), and *Reade* v. *Lowndes* (e), that the right of each of the
debtors to an assignment of the joint judgment when
he pays it does not relieve one debtor from his liability
to the creditor on such a dealing with the other debtor
as took place here.

There is no doubt that it was not the intention of the
parties to the agreement that the plaintiff's remedy
against the appellant should be interfered with; and I
agree with the Master that their agreement has not that
effect.

The appeal as to the claim of *Thomas Robinson*
remains to be considered. ᵢ His claim is in respect of
certain judgments, one recovered by his father *William
Robinson* in his lifetime, and the other obtained after
his death on a verdict which had been recovered in his
lifetime. The appellants' objection to the allowance of
the claim is, that *William Robinson*, on the 15th June,
1870, executed a release of all claims which he had
against *William Sparling*. The respondent answers,
that before that date the respondent had become

---

(a) 9 Bing., at p. 346.
(b) 3 M. & K. 426.          (c) 1 DeG. McN. & G. 408.
(d) 2 Drew 341.  See *Duff* v. *Barret*, 15 Grant 632.
(e) 23 Beav. 361.

equitable assignee of the debts; ·that the release to *William Sparling* was without consideration ; and that it was invalid even against the releasor.   The respondent *Thomas Robinson* is the administrator of his father's estate.

The appellants' counsel contended that there was no assignment to *Thomas Robinson.*  The Master found against that contention.; and it was unnecessary for him to decide as to the validity of the release as against the releasor.   I shall remark upon the latter question only.

Assuming, then, that there was no prior assignment to the respondent, have the appellants established a valid release to *William Sparling ?*   In examining this question I must exclude from consideration the evidence of the parties on their own behalf, the same being inadmissible in consequence of the death of *William Robinson.*

At the time of the release, *William Robinson,* the releasor, was an old man of seventy or upwards, and was infirm of body.    His mental faculties, also; had been impaired by old age—to what extent the evidence is conflicting, and it is unnecessary to decide. Three years before this time he had been induced to transfer to his son all his property, except (as the appellants' counsel contended, and as for the present purpose I assume) the judgment which he had theretofore recovered against *William Sparling* and *Orr,* and the other debt for which judgment was recovered against the same parties subsequently.   Of the former judgment he had made an assignment to the present plaintiff, under alleged circumstances of which I shall say nothing, as, since the death of the assignor, the plaintiff very properly reassigned the judgment to the administrator.    The consideration for the transfer to the son was his agreement to maintain his father and mother for the rest of their lives ; but the arrangement did not work well; the

old man became greatly dissatisfied with his son's conduct, and, I am afraid, not wholly without reason; and
the father's real or fancied grievances were the frequent
topic of his conversation.

This was the relation of the father and son, when the
last action was brought against *Sparling* and *Orr.* The
action was in the father's name, but was carried on by
the son. The father was in attendance as a witness for
the plaintiff, having been, as it seems, subpœnaed for
that purpose. After the verdict had been given, the
old man and the defendant's attorney got into communication out of Court. (The attorney is not a solicitor in the present suit). The old man told the
attorney his grievances, and asked his advice. The
attorney sympathised, or professed to sympathise,
with him; undertook to act for him against his son;
and advised him to release *Sparling* and *Orr* from
the two debts — the one for which judgment had
previously been recovered, and the other for which a
verdict had that day been rendered. To all this the
old man consented, without any other professional
advice, or, in fact, any other advice whatever. The
attorney, on the same day, prepared a general release
of *Sparling* and *Orr,* and got the old man to execute it.
A few days afterwards the attorney prepared a separate
release of each of the parties, *Sparling* and *Orr*, and
got the old man to execute these releases also.

In all this the conduct of the attorney was most
irregular. If the old man had desired to execute such a
release, he should have been required to get some other
attorney to act for him in that matter. It is too plain for
argument that it was in the interest of *Sparling* and *Orr*
(whose attorney he had been for several years) that the
attorney advised the releases, and induced the old man to
execute them. It is pretended that in his conversation
with the attorney he said that the suits were unjust, and

that he wished to put a stop to them; but he had been press-ing these claims for years ; they were, according to the appellants' contention, the only means which the old man had, except his son's agreement for maintenance; and the sudden discovery, after seeing the attorney, that the claims were unjust, and the sudden wish not to enforce them, are extremely suspicious. It is said that the old man expressed a wish to get rid of law altogether; yet, while for this purpose he was voluntarily releasing strangers from a judgment and a verdict which he had actually obtained, he was giving instructions for com-mencing actions against his own son. No one was present at the interview between him and the attorney when the agreement for the release was come to between them ; and no one but the attorney can now tell what the latter said with reference to it. *Sparling, Orr*, and one of their witnesses were present when the release was ready to be executed; and the despairing helplessness

of the old man at this time, and the power over him which the attorney had managed already to acquire, appear from an incident to which this witness deposes. The old man, he says, " put up his hands in an imploring way and said he threw himself on [the attorney's] pro-tection." But if anything said to have previously passed between him and the attorney could, in equity, have given validity to the release, what had so passed would need to be proved by independent testimony of the clearest and most satisfactory kind. It would be contrary to all propriety to maintain such a transaction after the death of the party, on the sole evidence of the attorney by whom, under circumstances like the present, the release had been procured (a). After getting the releases exe-cuted, the attorney commenced two actions for the father against his son—one on the agreement for maintenance, and the other for an alleged assault. Neither action

---

(a) See Walker v. Smith, 29 Beav. at 396 ; Bank of Montreal v. Wilson, 2 Chan. Cham. 117 ; &c.

was tried; and in November, 1870, five months after giving the releases, the old man died at the house of one of the appellants, where he had been residing for the principal part of this interval; and the Master has allowed the appellants for the old man's board.

The case, then, is that of a helpless old man who had parted with his property, applying to the appellants' attorney for advice, and of this attorney taking advantage of the opportunity to advise, and obtain for his clients, releases of the debts in question without consideration. The release of these debts was a gift of them; and I am clear that the well known principles which regulate voluntary donations apply to such a case. The often quoted statement of these principles by the Master of the Rolls in *Hoghton* v. *Hoghton* (a) was as follows: "Wherever one claims by voluntary donation a large pecuniary benefit from another, the burthen of proving that the transaction is righteous ... falls on the person taking the benefit. But this proof is given, if it be shewn that the donor knew and understood what it was that he was doing. If, however, besides the obtaining of this voluntary gift from the donor, the donor and donee were so situated towards each other that undue influence might have been exercised by the donee over the donor, then a new consideration is added; and the question is not, to use the words of Lord *Eldon* in *Huguenin* v. *Baseley*, 'whether the donor knew what he was doing, but how the intention was produced;' and though the donor was well aware of what he did, yet if his disposition to do it was produced by undue influence, the transaction would be set aside."

In the present case, plainly, the donor (or releasor) and the donee's attorney "were so situated towards each other that undue influence might have been exer-

---

(a) 15 B. at 299.

cised by the" donee's attorney "over the donor;" and it
is perfectly manifest that the old man's "disposition" to
execute the release "was produced by undue influence,"
within the meaning of the decisions on that subject.
Undue influence by the donee's attorney is the same
thing as undue influence by the donee himself. I
have had occasion to observe elsewhere, that "it has
been held in many cases," several of which I cited,
"that deeds of gift in favor of third persons, however
innocent, cannot be maintained if procured through
influence on the part of another, which under the circumstances would have rendered a deed of gift to the latter
void." It is clear beyond all question that a voluntary
transfer of these debts to the attorney himself would not
have been maintainable against the releasor; and a
voluntary release obtained from him through the attorney's means in favor of the appellant *William Sparling*,
is in the same position. I have no hesitation in holding
that it is impossible to maintain a release of actions
obtained by the releasee's attorney under the circumstances in evidence here.

Judgment.

I am therefore of opinion that the appeal, as to the
claims of both the plaintiff and *Robinson*, must be dismissed with costs.

## Northwood v. Keating.

*Evidence of party—Alterations in deed—Onus of proof.*

In a suit against a widow by the assignee of a mortgage purporting to be executed by her late husband, and herself, the plaintiff proved their signatures and that of the subscribing witness, who also was dead; the Judge by whom the defendant had been examined verified his certificate, though he did not recollect the circumstances ; the document was a patched instrument, and the parts were not referred to in the attesting clause or otherwise authenticated :

*Held*, on rehearing, [reversing the decree of Vice Chancellor *Mowat*,] that the unsupported evidence of the defendant, though believed by the Vice Chancellor, was not sufficient to disprove the execution of the instrument by her, nor to throw on the plaintiff the onus of proving that the patching of the instrument had been before execution.  [Mowat, V. C. dissenting.]

This was a suit of foreclosure brought by the assignee of a mortgage, or alleged mortgage, dated 14th April, 1858, expressed to be made between *Thomas Keating*, Statement. since deceased, and his wife, the defendant *Mary M. Keating*, of the first part, and *Robert S. Woods* and *William Northwood*, of the second part.   The mortgage purported to secure the mortgagees in respect of a promissory note of £140, theretofore indorsed by them for *Thomas Keating*.   The mortgaged property belonged to Mrs. *Keating ;* and on the mortgage was indorsed a certificate by the County Court Judge as to the due execution by the defendant, &c.   The promissory note mentioned was held at the time by the Bank of Upper Canada, and had been overdue for more than a year.

The defendant by her answer disputed the mortgage ; and alleged, that she had never to her knowledge signed it ; that if her signature was attached thereto it had been obtained by fraud and deception, namely, by procuring her to sign under the impression that she was executing an instrument for some other purpose; that she never had been asked to sign such a document, and had not

been informed that she was doing so ; that she had never
received any benefit of the promissory note, or of the
moneys which had been obtained thereby, or for which
the same had been given ; that she had not been aware of
the existence of the mortgage until after her late husband's death, or about 30th September, 1864, when one
*John B. Williams*, informed her that there was such a
document in existence ; that upon the day on which the
mortgage purports to bear date, her husband had
requested her to sign a mortgage to secure certain
money due to *Robert S. Woods*, and *John B. Williams*,
the executors of her father's estate ; that she had signed
no other document on that day to her knowledge ; and
that, if her signature had been obtained to the mortgage
in question, it must have been so obtained by fraudulently
representing the same as being a part of the mortgage
to the executors.

Statement.     The cause having been put at issue came on for the
examination of witnesses and hearing at the sittings of
the Court at Chatham, in the Spring of 1870.

Judge *Wells*, before whom Mrs. *Keating* had executed
the mortgage, was examined as a witness and swore :—
" My certificate is indorsed on the produced mortgage A.
I recollect one evening about eight o'clock, Mr. *Keating*
came to me to take his wife's examination at his house. I
went and examined her as the certificate mentions, and
she gave her consent. I have no doubt that the certificate
truly states what is mentioned in it. I have no recollection
that this is the mortgage, though I have no doubt of the
fact. She was examined apart from her husband. That
is always so in such cases. I don't remember this particular mortgage ; I dont remember the time of the year
nor who were present ; I think there was a lady or two in
the room ; I don't remember any one else. If this is the
mortgage executed at the time, I recollect it was executed
at Mr, *Keating*'s house ; I can't, by looking at it, identify
it. From my certificate, I presume that Mrs. *Keating*

consented. I knew nothing whatever of the transaction
between the parties ; I don't recollect of her acknowledging
any other instrument before me but on the occasion mentioned ; I don't recollect seeing the instrument executed.
Part of the certificate is in my own handwriting. I
can't say whether the instrument is in the same condition
now as it was when I took the acknowledgment." To the
Court.—" My custom in such cases is to look at the
instrument to see what it is ; to state the nature of it
to the party, and then ask as to the consent; I have no
doubt that I did so in this case as in other cases."

Mrs. *Keating* was also examined in the cause ; and in
her evidence she swore :—" I recollect signing a mortgage in, I think, 1858. My husband asked me if I
would sign a mortgage to *Woods* and *Williams*, as
executors to my father's estate, for some money that
my husband had got from the executors; it was from
my father's estate ; I think that the amount was
$500. I replied, " You know that it was never my
intention to mortgage my house." He said, ' I know
that ; but he had got into trouble by indorsing for a
person named *Berryman*, and if I would sign this mortgage,
it would be the means of protecting the property against
the bank,' for he had indorsed at the bank. He said that
I must not be uneasy ; that it was not with the intention
of selling the property but of protecting it; that they had
no intention of selling it. I then said that I would sign
this mortgage, but for one reason only (as I told him)
namely, because the money had been got from my father's
estate ; and I did not wish the children to whom the
money was left to be able to say that I had one dollar
more than was my due. He then said, he would go for
somebody to witness my signature. I said, " Not to-
night." He said, " Oh ! yes, it may as well be done at
once." He went out and returned in about half-an-hour
with Judge *Wells* and Mr. *Miller*. A few minutes after
they came, the Judge asked me into the next room. He
then asked me two or three questions respecting, I suppose,
the paper I was about to sign. The first question was,
' Was I aware of what I was about to do or sign ?' I

answered that 'l was.' I gave that answer, thinking
that I was signing a mortgage to *Woods* and *Williams*.
His next question was, ' Had I been influenced by any
one, or was I doing it of my own free will?' I answered,
that ' I had not been influenced, and that I was doing it
of my free will.' In the other room I signed a paper.
My husband, Judge *Wells*, and Mr. *Miller* were all present
when I signed; I understood that I was signing a mortgage to *Woods* and *Williams*, as executors of my father's
estate. That is all I understood I was signing. I think
my name to paper B. is in my handwriting; I cannot say
whether it is mine or not. I do not recognize paper A. as
one I had seen before; I know nothing of that paper; I
may have signed it; I would not have known whether I
had to sign once or more than once for one mortgage; I
did not know. No one then or before spoke to me of
giving such a mortgage or security as the mortgage now
in question (A.) I signed B. at my own house, between
nine and ten o'clock in the evening. The business may
have taken ten minutes altogether—not more. All three

gentlemen then went away. I did not read over the
papers which I signed, nor did any one read them to me
—not a word. The Judge did not take the papers into
the private room into which we went together: they were
in the room which we left. When we returned they were
there. After being signed, I think that my husband
folded them and put them in his pocket. I never executed
any mortgage on any other occasion. The first time that
my husband spoke to me about the bank, was the same
evening that I signed. All that he said was, that he had
indorsed for *Berryman*, and that the effect was to protect
the property against the bank; he mentioned no one else
but *Berryman* for whom he had indorsed; he did not name
the amount he had so indorsed. I was satisfied to execute
a mortgage for the purpose which my husband mentioned. There was no conversation between my husband
and myself except what I have mentioned. Nothing was
said of the value of the property; I think there were two
papers there, but whether I signed two I do not recollect.
The signatures to A. and B. both look like mine; I can't
say that either is more like than the other. No other

question was asked me by Judge *Wells* except those I have
mentioned. My memory is pretty good when anything
interests me particularly as this did. It was on the 30th
September, 1864, that I first heard of the mortgage now in
question (A.) I recollect Mr. *Campbell* serving me with
papers before that. I looked at the names, date, and
amount mentioned in the papers, but did not further read
the papers. Two papers were served upon me; the dates
were the same and the amounts, except a difference of
$30. *Woods* and *Williams*'s names were on one paper, and
*Woods* and *Northwood*'s were on the other paper. I concluded from the resemblance that they related to the same
mortgage; but, seeing *Northwood*'s name on the one paper
impressed me, as I had not heard of his name in the
matter before, and I did not know what it meant. When
my husband came in, I gave him the papers, saying that
I had got them from Mr. *Campbell*. I asked him why
Mr. *Northwood*'s name was there? He said that when he
got the money from *Woods* and *Williams*, *Northwood* was
indorser, and that the papers had to be drawn out in that
way. I did not ask him for any explanation as to the
amounts. I thought the difference might be costs or
interest; I asked him no further questions. When I
handed him the papers, he said he knew about them, and
I think he threw them down as if indifferent about them.
I took no step in respect of the mortgage in question from
1864, when I first heard of it My recollection is quite
distinct as to Judge *Wells* not taking the papers with him
when he went with me into the other room. When I
executed the mortgage, I did not know to what extent I
was charging the property; I knew nothing more than
what my husband told me, as I have already mentioned.
My husband had told me sometime before of his getting
the money from my father's trustees. The amount, as he
told me, was $500; I never disputed the mortgage to the
executors. Mr. *Williams* told me on the 30th September,
1864, of the mortgage in question (A.). He was at my
house, and I was asking him if there was no way of
settling the mortgage to the executors, so as to stop the
interest? and in the course of the conversation, he said,
'what would be the use of my settling the executor's

*1871.*

*Northwood
v.
Keating.*

*Statement*

1871.  mortgage, for there was still *Northwood's* mortgage against
the property? I only said that I had never signed such a
mortgage; that was the first I had ever heard of it; this
was about two days after my husband's death." In answer
to a question by the Court, she said; "I am quite sure
that the Judge did not tell me to whom the mortgage was:
he did not mention a name. I have lived on the property
from 1858 to the present time."

Northwood
v.
Keating.

The memorial of the mortgage A., it was admitted by
both parties was executed by Mr. *Keating* alone.

Vice Chancellor *Mowat* before whom the case was
heard dismissed the bill with costs (a), and the plaintiffs
thereupon set the cause down for rehearing before the
full Court.

Mr. *Blake*, Q. C., for the plaintiff.

Mr. *Maclennan*, for the defendant Mrs. *Keating*.

Judgment.     SPRAGGE, C.—I think it proved beyond any reasonable
doubt that the signature to the plaintiff's mortgage is
that of Mrs. *Keating*. Her case must be that she signed
the paper upon the representation, and in the belief, that
it was part of the same instrument which she had agreed
to execute, viz., the mortgage to *Jacobs's* executors. I
agree with the conclusion at which my brother *Strong*
has arrived, and, substantially, in the reasoning by which
he arrives at it. My learned brother having gone very
fully into the case, I propose to be very brief. My
brother *Mowat* gives implicit credit to the evidence of
Mrs. *Keating*, and he has, of course, had better means
of judging of her evidence than the other members of
the Court have had. I am bound to assume that her
intelligence, her demeanour, and all the circumstances
attending the giving of her evidence, were such as pro-

---

(a) See *ante* volume xvii., page 347.

perly to impress upon the mind of my learned brother an undoubting belief in her veracity. But assuming all this; and even assuming further that she really intended honestly to speak the whole truth; it does not follow that she was strictly accurate in what she said. Her recollection certainly was not perfect. Take this short passage of her evidence " I think that there were two papers there; but whether I signed two, I do not recollect." Now it is certain that there were two papers, and certain also that she signed them both. Her evidence is all matter of memory; and memory, not of things that occurred merely, but, and that chiefly, that certain things did not occur. Her memory was at fault as to the facts to which I have referred. Can we feel so entirely assured that it is not at fault as to other facts, as to be safe in pronouncing that the County Court Judge is wrong? We have the alternative of either supposing that Mrs. *Keating's* memory is at fault, or that the Judge departed in this instance from what was obviously his duty as well as his practice; and of which he speaks so confidently as to say, and to reiterate, that he has no doubt that it was done in the instance in question. I should go more into this part of the case but that my brother *Strong* has treated so fully as well as ably the point in question, and I agree with my learned brother's observations as to the extreme danger of setting aside an instrument upon the unsupported testimony of a person affected by it if it stands, and who would be benefited by its being set aside.

So strongly, indeed, did my brother *Mowat* feel this, that he found it necessary in his first judgment to resort to what he conceived to be the corroborative evidence furnished by an inspection of the mortgage itself, without which, as my learned brother himself admits, he should not be prepared to set it aside.

It is certainly a very slovenly document; and if such a document had been prepared by a London stationer, as

was the case in *Kennedy* v. *Green* (a), it would be open
to more grave suspicion than it is. But unfortunately,
a great deal of the conveyancing in, the country parts
especially, of Upper Canada, is slovenly in appearance;
and this was more the case at the time this paper was
drawn than it is now.

I confess I do not see in this paper such grounds of
suspicion as strike my brother *Mowat*. The defendant's
theory I understand to be, that *Keating* presented to his
wife two instruments, having represented that he was
going to ask her to execute one; and that he led her to
believe that these two papers constituted one document:
that they were in fact one instrument executed in duplicate. If this were his design, one would certainly expect,
that he would as far as possible make the two papers
resemble one another, and this he might easily have
done, for the matter of the recital, for the introduction of
which the first leaf of the printed form was cut in two,

might just as well have been introduced in the proviso
for redemption. In the shape in which it is, it would absolutely court inquiry. Both these mortgages are before us.
Suppose them presented to any one, lawyer or layman, as
duplicates or counterparts, it would be seen at a glance
that they were not so. They are not, as in *Kennedy* v.
*Green*, in a shape to hide anything, or to aid in deception;
but in a shape that renders it patent to any casual observer
that they were not what it is now suggested that *Keating*
represented them to be. If he intended any such representation he took unnecessary pains to convict himself
of misrepresentation, to suggest inquiry, and put his wife
upon her guard. There could be no possible motive for
preparing this slovenly document, when, if he intended a
fraud upon his wife, a mortgage similar to the one which
is not disputed would have answered his purpose much
better. Or, again, if the theory be, that it was altered
between its execution by the wife and its delivery to Mr.

---

(a) 3 M. & K. 699.

*Woods, Keating,* besides committing a second fraud, took unnecessary pains to prepare and deliver a document in such a shape as ought in the judgment of my learned brother, to have put Mr. *Woods* upon inquiry.

To my mind the mortgage being in the shape in which it is, is not corroborative of Mrs. *Keating's* testimony ; but, if any thing, the reverse.

With regard to the delay in bringing this suit, and the consequent loss of the evidence of Mr. *Keating* and Mr. *Miller,* it is certainly very unfortunate ; but I think it is not chargeable, wholly at least, upon the plaintiff. The forbearance to press it against *Keating* may probably have been due to his importunities; and after his death there would be a natural repugnance to press the matter against the widow; and on the other hand, is not the delay and the loss of *Miller's* evidence at any rate due in part to herself? In September, 1864, she was distinctly informed that the plaintiff held this mortgage against her. She had no reason to suppose that he was guilty of any wrong in regard to it, or that he was aware that she denied its genuineness. In common fairness she should have informed him that she denied her execution of the instrument. If she had done this, we should have had several years less of delay, or of forbearance, whichever it may properly be called ; and we should have had the evidence of the subscribing witness·

I think the decree should have been for the plaintiff.

MOWAT, V. C.—The question of fact in this case was, whether the mortgage on which the bill was filed is the defendant's deed? It is not necessary to discuss the evidence on which I arrived at the conclusion that the deed was not hers, or was not proved to be hers, except so far as the process may have involved some question of law; for beyond that, we do not on a rehearing interfere with judgments on matters of fact. Is there any rule which forbade my making a decree in the defendant's favor on her own testimony without some further corroboration than the other facts of the case afford?

My judgment proceeded on the ground, that, as against the credited evidence of the party to be charged, a paper in the pieced, patched, and unauthenticated condition of the alleged mortgage, purporting to secure an antecedent debt, and not (so far as appears) attempted to be enforced for upwards of eleven years after its supposed execution, is not on the same footing as an instrument would be which shewed on its face nothing that was irregular or that the law or practice regards as suspicious, and which had, with the knowledge of the parties, been acted upon according to its purport from the time of its execution. I did not question that, as the law now stands, in the case of deeds, there is, ordinarily, a presumption that alterations, though not authenticated in the attestation clause or otherwise, were made before execution; but I thought that, if that presumption applied at all to an instrument in the state of the instrument in question, and after the delay which had taken place, it was a presumption which the evidence of the party, that she had not executed, or had not knowingly executed, such a deed, if credited by the Judge or jury trying the issue, was sufficient *prima facie* to rebut and neutralize, and that such evidence, if believed, was sufficient to throw on the plaintiff the onus of giving extrinsic evidence that the instrument was in the same state when executed as it is now.

The plaintiff's counsel, at the hearing at Chatham, admitted (as I stated in my judgment) that Mrs. *Keating* meant to speak the truth; and counsel argued against the accuracy of her recollection only. But there was no probability that she could believe what she swore to unless what she swore to was true; and having seen her in the witness-box and heard her examination and cross-examination, I believed her story; and, no extrinsic evidence having been offered by the plaintiff, I thought that the defendant was entitled to my judgment. The question was a legal one ; and if it had been tried at law, and a jury had found as I did, and if the Judge had been satisfied as I was, I apprehend that the verdict would not have been disturbed.

After reconsidering the case with the light of the further argument which was presented at the rehearing, I see no reason for thinking that I was wrong in my view of either the law or the fact.

I am not aware that it has ever been laid down in the Common Law Courts that the testimony of a party must be corroborated by other evidence. The necessity for corroboration in any Court, and the extent of the corroboration to be exacted, must depend on the nature of the case. If a party is sought to be charged by virtue of a transaction which was accomplished and dealt with afterwards in a way to deprive the party of the means of corroboration, it would be contrary to the spirit of the Act admitting parties to be witnesses, and would be required by no sound principle, to hold, that the evidence of the party deserved no more consideration than that of a party who was claiming to have sold goods, or paid money, or obtained a gift, or created a trust, which it was his own fault if he was without the means of establishing except by his own unsupported oath. A person may innocently, and without any suspicion on his part, be entrapped into a deed under circumstances which make corroboration of his own evidence difficult or even impossible ; and to hold, that, however truthful he may be known to be, and however a Judge or jury may feel his evidence to be honest and accurate, it cannot, as a matter of law, prevail, would be affording unnecessary and, I respectfully think, unjustifiable facilities to imposition, for the benefit of the dishonest, or the protection of the imprudent.

1871.

Northwood
v.
Keating.

Judgment.

Mrs. *Keating* swore, that the paper or papers which she signed was or were produced as constituting the one mortgage which she admits having consented to execute, and which she has never disputed; and she signed in the undoubting belief that that was the case. If what she swore is true, the obtaining her signature to the produced paper was a fraud, and does not bind her. That is not questioned. "The position that, if a grantor or covenantor be deceived or misled as to the actual contents of the deed, the deed does not bind him, is supported by many authorities," as was pointed out by Mr. Justice *Byles* in delivering the judgment of the Court in *Foster* v. *McKinnon* (a); and whether one of the papers signed by Mrs. *Keating* was altered after she had signed it, or was at the time misrepresented to her, is immaterial. In either case the deed was not in law hers.

The rule in ancient times was that the onus of offering extrinsic evidence, in regard to apparent alterations in an instrument, was in all cases on the party relying on the instrument, whether it was a deed, will, or any other kind of instrument; and this rule still prevails in the case of wills, bills, or notes; but now, as Lord *Cranworth* said, in *Simmons* v. *Rudall* (b), "in the case of deeds, the authorities *seem* to shew, that, when there are interlineations, the presumption is, that they were made before execution." In *Williams* v. *Ashton* (c), the present Lord Chancellor said, that that view had only recently been adopted. In *Doe* v. *Catomore* (d), Lord *Campbell* gave this statement of what appeared on the subject in the books: "In Co. Litt. 225 b, it is said, that 'of ancient time if the deed appeared to be rased or interlined in places material, the Judges adjudged upon their view the deed to be

---

(a) L. R. 4 C. P. at 711.          (b) 1 Sim. N. S. at 136.
(c) 1 J. & H. at 118.              (d) 16 Q. B. 745.

void. But of latter time the Judges have left that to the jurors to try whether the rasing or interlining were before the delivery.' In a note (1) [136], upon this passage in *Hargrave* and *Butler's* edition of *Coke* upon *Littleton*, it is laid down : 'It is to be presumed that an interlining, if the contrary is not proved, was made at the time of making the deed.' " The principle of this is said to be, that "a deed cannot be altered after it is executed, without fraud or wrong ; and the presumption is against fraud or wrong." But an unauthorized alteration of a bill, note, or will, by a person who is to profit by the alteration, would equally be a fraud and wrong.

When it is thus said, that, in the case of a deed, the alteration is now, in the absence of any evidence either way, presumed to have been made before execution, this does not mean an absolute, imperative, or violent presumption ; and, under circumstances, it may on the contrary be a presumption of a very mild type. In the case from which I have just quoted, the interlineations were not material interlineations ; but Baron *Parke*, in the absence of any extrinsic evidence, left it to the jury to inspect the deeds, and he directed the jury to judge from the deeds themselves whether they had been altered before or after execution. The defendant's counsel objected to this charge and moved against the verdict for misdirection, arguing that the deeds were inadmissible without extrinsic evidence as to the time at which the alterations had been made ; but the Court in *Banc* held otherwise.

That there is danger of alterations being wrongfully made is the reasonable ground of the ancient rule as respects all instruments, and of the rule which still prevails with respect to wills, bills, and notes. No doubt the danger exists, to some extent at all events, in the case of deeds also, and is enhanced, and (according to the

*1871.*

*Northwood v. Keating.*

*Judgment.*

1871.     passage which in my judgment I cited from *Shepherd's*
          Touchstone).is "most dangerous and the deed thereby
Northwood  most suspicious     *     *    when it is a deed-poll, and
   v.
Keating.   there is but one part of the deed, and where the rasure
          or other alteration is in any material part of the deed."
          The instrument in question was of the class thus
          designated as "most dangerous and most suspicious;"
          and it is beyond all question that the various parts of
          the patched instrument (if its execution were honestly
          obtained) should, as a matter of propriety and reasonable
          caution, have been authenticated by the usual means.
          Without that authentication, the document was most
          unbusinesslike, and was most disgraceful to a convey-
          ancer. A far less irregular document was held, in
          *Kennedy* v. *Green* (a), to make inquiry a duty on the
          part of the persons dealing with property. I take the
          rule to be, that, wherever there is anything irregular in
          deeds, it is the duty of parties, taking an interest under
Judgment. or through such deeds, to make inquiries. The chief
          irregularities in *Kennedy* v. *Green* were not in the body
          of the deed, but on the back of the deed; yet the follow-
          ing are the terms in which the judgment of the Lord
          Chancellor dealt with them: "The back of the deed
          was checkered all over with suspicious appearances.
          The title of the deed, not in the engrossing hand, but
          written in a somewhat slovenly way, and with the words
          of the title of different sizes, beget a suspicion of hurry
          and imperfection in the preparation of the instrument.
          When does a stationer ever send such a blank indenture
          out of his office, unless when pressed for singular
          despatch? Then the receipt written across one fold into
          a second square sideways, and the signature in like
          manner running into the second square. But, above all,
          the receipt removed far from the top, and leaving such
          a space as might by the holder of the deed, supposing
          that space to have been left in blank, have been filled

          ─────────────────────────────

                    (a) 3 M. & K. at 721.

up in any manner he chose. This was at once a circumstance to excite the greatest, the most jealous suspicion.
Had a cheque been originally written with an inch of
blank to the left hand of the sum, would not all who saw
it start at the risk run by the maker, and would not the
maker, on his attention being drawn to it, nay, even the
holder, take the precaution of drawing a line or two
over the blank? But suppose a banker had discounted
a cheque with a sum as 'one hundred' interlined, would
any Judge direct any jury to let that banker recover
against the maker, though full value had by him (the
banker) been paid for it? All the cases have decided the
contrary, and held that *every unusual circumstance is a
ground of suspicion, and prescribes inquiry;* and I hold
the receipt written here in a way to enable any person
to commit a gross fraud—a way for that reason never
adopted—was abundant ground for suspicion, and
demanded inquiry and explanation."

Let us call to mind now the state of the deed
here when handed to the mortgagees. There is not
a tittle of evidence as to the state in which it was when
signed; but when afterwards handed by the husband to
the mortgagees, it wanted on its face the ordinary and
recognized safeguards against fraud and imposition.
It consisted of two leaves of unequal length, and united
by a wafer only; the first leaf was in three distinct
pieces, united with gum or paste, and contained most
material parts of the instrument; yet was not identified;
and no part of it was authenticated by the signatures
or initials of the parties or witnesses, or in any other
way. In the case of such a paper, I perceived no reason
why the evidence of the party, if believed, should not
be sufficient to throw the onus of further extrinsic
evidence on the grantee; and I so held.

If the security had been for a contemporary advance
instead of an antecedent debt, or even if its acceptance

83—VOL. XVIII. GR.

1871.

Northwood
v.
Keating.

Judgment.

had been a consideration for time to pay a good debt, I more than doubt if the mortgagees would· have been content to accept an instrument in this state without further inquiry. I do not believe that any lender of money, whether in the legal profession or out of it, possessing habits of ordinary caution, would have advanced his money on such security without first obtaining some authentication of the first leaf and its various parts, or without some communication with Mrs. *Keating* on the subject; for there had been no communication whatever with her beforehand. But as the receiving of the instrument took away nothing from the grantees, and involved the advance of no money, and the foregoing of no remedy, they had no interest in ascertaining that all was right; they had no incitement to vigilance and caution in accepting the paper as it was; they would gain nothing by finding that all was wrong. This consideration, not unnaturally, enabled

suspicion to sleep, and prevented the inquiry which ordinary caution would otherwise have suggested, and which, if made or proposed, might have saved this lady her property without the expense and anxiety of this suit. An unwillingness to disappoint parties who have advanced money on the faith of a deed regular on its face, has nothing to do with parties who accept, for an antecedent debt, and without any fresh consideration, a deed in the state in which this one was when given to the supposed mortgagees.

Against Mrs. *Keating* two circumstances were relied upon. The first was the service upon her of the notices in December, 1863, five years and a-half after the date of the transaction. If her evidence is true, she had not had the slightest cause for any suspicion of the fraud which she now declares had been practised upon her. It is said that this notice must have made her aware of the fraud, if fraud there was; and that her silence on the subject is evidence that she knew that she

had executed the mortgage in question. I think that
her silence shews no such thing, even if the notice had
made her aware of a fraud having been practised upon
her. It would not be a natural and necessary thing
that a wife should proclaim such heartless wickedness
on the part of her husband, even if she had discovered
it; and her silence would not have the effect of setting
up against her an instrument which she had not really
executed (a).

But she says that she did not infer from the
notices that there were two independent mortgages;
and I think her evidence as given in my reported judgment is natural and entirely credible. We read the
notice now as lawyers, and also with the knowledge that
there were in existence two separate and distinct instruments for two separate and distinct debts. But would
an unsuspecting woman, who was unacquainted with law
or with business, and who knew that she had executed
but one mortgage, and that to her father's executors,
necessarily infer from these formal and technical notices
that a fraud or a forgery had been committed upon her,
and that her husband's explanation of the two notices
was false? I think that such an assumption on my
part would be unreasonable and unwarranted.

Judgment.

Nine months afterwards her husband died; and then
for the first time she was told and understood that there
was this second mortgage. She at once denied that she
had ever executed such a mortgage; and she has so
insisted ever since. But the mortgagees left her in
undisturbed personal possession of the mortgaged
premises for five years more, bringing no suit and making no demand upon her. If before the husband's death
they had actually proceeded to sell, the purchaser, if
well advised, would have required some further document

---

(a) See Lewin on Trusts, 5 ed., pp. 371, 661, 662, &c.

from Mrs. *Keating,* or some authentication of this one, or might as a matter of precaution have personally or by his solicitor have put himself in communication with her. An inquiry then would have been carried on with the advantage of her husband being alive, and of the subscribing witness being alive, and of the memories of all being less blunted than the memories of the survivors may be supposed to have become five or six years later.

Plaintiff's counsel endeavored to charge the delay on the defendant. That is the second circumstance to which I referred as having been relied upon in opposition to her evidence. It was contended that by reason of the delay every presumption should be made in the plaintiff's favor. But the reverse is the true position. Mrs. *Keating* was all this time in possession of the property; and the alleged mortgage, though certainly a cloud on her title, was no more than a cloud. The

mortgagees, on the other hand, were out of possession, and do not appear to have ever had any benefit from their supposed mortgage; it had, up to this time, been to them a piece of paper and no more; and the duty of vindicating their right in respect of the property was beyond all question on them; Mrs. *Keating's* only duty was to defend herself in case of being attacked. The omission of a woman and widow to voluntarily engage in a Chancery suit for the removal of a cloud on her title to property of which she was in undisturbed enjoyment, is something very different from the delay for eleven years by two business men, one of them a lawyer, to act in any substantial way on a mortgage which they held.

I think that if Mrs. *Keating's* evidence required corroboration, it was not uncorroborated, within the meaning of any recognized or sound rule on the subject of corroboration. I think that her evidence was corroborated by the state of the alleged mortgage, and by the absence of the customary and proper identification of the patched portions by a memorandum in the attestation clause and otherwise; and I think that her evidence may be regarded as receiving further corroboration from the long delay of the mortgagees. I think that this corroboration is all that should be demanded in a case of this kind, if the Court or jury believe the witness.

At law a single witness is sufficient, if believed, to convict of most crimes, or to sustain any civil suit; and the Statute has placed a party on the same footing with respect to competency as any other witness. It is in only a few exceptional cases that corroboration is technically necessary. One even interested witness, whom we know or believe to be honest and careful, may produce a stronger and more reliable conviction than several other witnesses would do. The number of the witnesses, or their disinterestedness, are only elements to be taken into account. They afford no certain test of truth.

The question at issue might have been tried at law; but reference was made to the late cases in Equity respecting corroboration. Lord *Romilly* in one case (*a*) laid it down, with respect to gifts by a client to his solicitor, that "in all these cases you must not take into account the evidence of the recipient himself; the gift must be established by separate and independent evidence." But that ruling rests on grounds applicable to that class of cases only. Again, in *Bentley* v. *McKay* (*b*), the same learned Judge said, that "it would be a very dangerous thing to set aside or reform a deed fourteen years and more after its execution, and which has been acted upon during that period, upon no other testimony than that of the persons who executed and are bound by the deed. and who will benefit by the deed being altered. I certainly do not know that this Court

(*a*) Walker v. Smith, 29 B. at 396.          (*b*) 31 B. at 158.

has ever so acted in any case." There the deed had been continuously acted upon during the whole of the fourteen years; and in such a case the argument was as strong for requiring additional evidence, as the inaction of the mortgagees for eleven years under the instrument in question here, affords reason for an opposite course. The testimony of parties on their own behalf in administration suits has also been held to require support; for "if it were otherwise," as the Master of the Rolls observed, in *Grant* v. *Grant* (a), "any stranger might come and swear that any testator owed him a sum of money." There a wife claimed certain chattels as gifts from her deceased husband ; with respect to most of these she proved the gifts by independent testimony, as well as by her own oath; and the Court, for that reason, accepted her own unsupported oath with respect to the remaining articles. In *Down* v. *Ellis* (b), the rule that the Court does "not act on

the unsupported testimony of a party in his own favor," was again referred to by the same learned Judge. The plaintiff there claimed money which was standing in the funds in the name of her deceased daughter. The plaintiff alleged, that the stock was bought, partly with her savings, partly with her daughter's savings ; and that the agreement between them was, that the dividends of the whole fund should be paid to the plaintiff during the joint lives of the plaintiff and her daughter, and that the survivor should take the whole capital. But the only direct evidence of these allegations was the plaintiff's oath; and the chief support which her testimony received from independent testimony was, proof that the plaintiff had received the dividends for a considerable period, under a revocable power of attorney from the daughter and her husband. The Master of the Rolls, however, held the plaintiff's case to be sufficiently established.

---

(a) 34 B. 627.                    (b) 35 Beav. 578.

1 think that these cases help to shew that I violated
no principle of law or equity in the decree which I
pronounced; and I continue of opinion that that decree
was right.

STRONG, V. C.—The mortgage, the foreclosure of
which is sought by the bill in this cause, purports to
have been given as an indemnity to the mortgagees, the
plaintiff and the defendants *R. S. Woods* and *William
Northwood*, against their liability as sureties for *Thomas
Keating*, the late husband of the defendant *Mary M.
Keating*. This instrument is dated the 14th April,
1858, and is expressed to be made between *Thomas
Keating* and his wife, the defendant *Mary M. Keating*,
of the first part, and the mortgagees already named of
the second part, and the property affected by it is the
estate of the defendant *Mary M. Keating*. This mortgage has indorsed upon it a certificate by the Judge of
the County Court of Kent of his examination of the
defendant Mrs. *Keating*, which certificate is dated the
19th of April, 1858. The instrument was registered on
the 21st of April, 1858. The defendant Mrs. *Keating*,
by her answer, states her defence as follows: she says
that she never to her knowledge signed the mortgage,
and that if her signature is attached thereto, the same
was obtained by fraud and deception practised upon her
by the parties interested, by procuring her to sign the
same under the impression that she was executing an
instrument for some other purpose. That she was not
aware that the plaintiff and the defendants *Woods* and
*William Northwood* held a mortgage against her
property until after her late husband's death, or about
the 30th of September, 1864, when one *John B.
Williams* informed her that there was such a document
in existence. That upon the day the mortgage purports
to bear date her husband requested her to sign a
mortgage to secure certain moneys due to *Woods* and
*Williams*, as executors of *George Jacobs;* but that she

signed 'no other document on that day to her knowledge;
and if her signature was obtained to the mortgage now
in question, it must have been obtained by fraudulently
representing the same as being a part of the mortgage
to the executors of *Jacobs.*

The cause was heard at the sittings at Chatham, in
the spring of 1870, before my brother *Mowat,* who
made a decree dismissing the bill, and that decree has
heen reheard before this Court.

The execution of the mortgage is, I think, sufficiently
proved.  The subscribing witness to the mortgage deed,
*Miles Miller,* died suddenly after the institution of the
suit, and shortly before the hearing, after he had been
served at the instance of the plaintiff with a subpœna to
give evidence in this cause; but his signature is proved.
The defendant *Woods,* who is called for the plaintiff,
says that Mrs. *Keating* admitted her execution of the

mortgage to the executors (Exhibit B), and comparing
the signature to this last mortgage with that to the
instrument in question, he says he believes them to be
signed by the same person.   But Mrs. *Keating* herself
does not venture to deny her signature.  She says:
"My name to it looks like my signature."  And again,
" I may have signed it.'"  Further, the County Court
Judge, Mr. *Wells,* after refreshing his memory by looking
at the certificate, says, that although he has no independent recollection of the particular instrument in question,
yet from seeing his name set to the certificate, he has
no doubt that Mrs. *Keating* was examined by him, as
stated in the certificate on the day named, and that in
accordance wlth his custom in such cases, he looked at
the instrument, saw what it was, and stated the nature
of it to Mrs. *Keating.*  This evidence is quite sufficient
to establish that the instrument was duly explained to
Mrs. *Keating* before its execution. (*a*)   Then observa-

---

(*a*) Taylor on Evidence, Ed. 3, p. 1139.

tions have been made, both in the judgment of my learned hrother and at the bar, upon the appearance of the instrument, which, as I understand the argument, is said to be in such a state as to raise a presumption that it has been altered since execution. It consists of a printed form filled up in the handwriting of *Keating*, the defendant's husband, who is stated to have been a lawyer's clerk, and to have been used to prepare deeds and legal documents. The form, which originally consisted of one whole sheet, is cut into half sheets, and the first of these half sheets is cut in two, and a piece of paper is let in between the divided parts and attached to them with some adhesive matter, and the two leaves are united with a wafer. The instrument certainly presents a slovenly and unusual appearance; but I have seen many documents affecting property, of much greater value than I take this property to be, even more carelessly prepared. The insertion of the piece of paper in the first sheet, a device which is frequently adopted, was obviously with the object of gaining space, for the recitals, which the printed form did not afford. The union of the leaves with a wafer cannot be more objectionable than if they had been tied together with riband; and I have never understood that a deed written on several sheets or half sheets of paper, and tied together with tape or riband, not fastened with a seal, is on that account to be presumed to have been altered since execution, or to be deemed to be in such a condition as to make it incumbent on the party propounding it to shew in addition to the ordinary evidence of execution, that it was in the same state at the time of sealing. I see no reason why the same presumption should not be applied to this instrument, which is applied when a deed appears to have been altered or interlined; and in such a case it is well settled that the alteration or interlineation will be presumed to have been made before execution (a). I am of opinion, therefore, that the plaintiff makes out

---

(a) Doe Tatum v. Catomore, 16 Q. B.

his case as regards the execution, and that his evidence is *prima facie* sufficient to prove the mortgage to be the deed of the defendant Mrs. *Keating*.

The question then arises, does the defendant prove the execution to have been procured by the fraudulent misrepresentation alleged in the answer? As I have already pointed out, the case made by Mrs. *Keating* is, that the execution of the mortgage was procured by the fraudulent misrepresentation that it was part of the mortgage which she had agreed to give to the executors of her father. There is therefore here no room to contend that this case is one of a class of which *Cook* v. *Lamotte* (a) may be taken as an example, in which a party seeking relief under a deed, the legal execution of which he has established, is called on to do something more, namely, to rebut a presumption against the validity of the instrument in equity arising from the relationship of the parties, the absence or insufficiency of consideration or the want of independent advice; for this doctrine does not apply to transactions between husband and wife (b). And here, moreover, the mortgage, though procured through the intervention of the husband, is a security to innocent purchasers for value. *Cobbett* v. *Brock* (c) is very explicit on this last point. The defence, therefore, is one of direct actual fraud, committed not by the mortgagees or any of them, but by the husband of the mortgagor, the principal debtor, for whom the mortgagor became a surety; for there is not the slightest pretence for saying that there was any complicity on the part of the mortgagees in any representation which the husband may have made, and Mrs. *Keating* herself states that she never spoke to any of them on the subject of the mortgage. The case is therefore narrowed to one of fraud by the husband in

---

(a) 15 Beav. 234.    (b) Nedby v. Nedby, 5 De G. & S. 377.
    (c) 20 Beav. 524.

procuring the execution of this mortgage by a trick.
The only witness called for the defence was Mrs.
*Keating* herself; and if the fraud is made out, it must
necessarily be by her own evidence either standing alone
or with such confirmation as may be derived from the
circumstances. Now, placing the most implicit faith in
Mrs. *Keating's* testimony, giving her credit for having
spoken the truth in every particular, I must say that it
falls far short of that indubitable proof which all courts
of justice require before avoiding a solemn instrument
like a deed appearing to be well executed and *prima
facie* proved, on the ground of fraud in its execution,
proof of which is especially required to be strong and
clear where the alleged fraud is of the species complained
of in the present case—misrepresentation by word of
mouth alleged to have been made upwards of twelve
years anterior to the examination of the single witness
who is called to establish it. What Mrs. *Keating* says
in her evidence is, that nothing was ever said to her
about this mortgage of the plaintiffs—that all that was
spoken of was the mortgage to the executors. What
she undertook by her answer to prove, and what she
must prove, in order to invalidate the plaintiff's mortgage is, that she did in fact execute two instruments, it
being stated to her that both were parts of the same
transaction, namely, the mortgage to the executors; but,
so far from proving this, these are Mrs. *Keating's* own
words: "I think that there were two papers there, but
whether I signed two, I do not recollect."

Is it compatible with the strictness of proof which is
required in cases of this description to hold that Mrs.
*Keating*, who has no recollection of having signed this
mortgage, and remembers nothing having been said
as to any document other than the mortgage to the
executors, should be taken to have proved the positive
misrepresentation alleged?

Northwood
v.
Keating.

The fallacy of determining that Mrs. *Keating* proves
the fraud is, I think, apparent. She does not prove
any positive act or statement with reference to this
impeached deed. All she says in effect is: "I don't
remember signing this deed, nor having been spoken to
about it; therefore, if I did sign it, I feel sure that it
must have been on the representation that it was part of
the mortgage to the executors." She does not swear
that any such representation was really and in truth
made, but she *infers* that if she did sign the mortgage,
she must have been induced to do so by misrepresentation. This is not proof, but argument. I think the
fair conclusion from Mrs. *Keating's* evidence is, that as
she had forgotten the fact of having signed a second
document, she has also forgotten the circumstances
which led to her signing it. I am of opinion that this
testimony, giving the witness credit for having spoken
the truth, is insufficient to support the allegation of actual
fraudulent misstatement on which the defence is based.

Judgment.

But even if Mrs. *Keating's* evidence did clearly sub-
stantiate the defence, would it be of itself sufficient to
found a decree upon, having regard to the fact that the
subscribing witness to the deed, and *Keating*, who procured its excution, were both dead at the time of the hearing? If the attesting witness *Miller* had been alive, and
had been examined, and after hearing his evidence, as
well as that of Mrs. *Keating*, my brother *Mowat* had
thought fit to give credit to the defendant's testimony in
preference to that of the other witnesses, I should have
thought it right—considering the principles which ought
to regulate all appellate jurisdictions in reviewing the
decisions of questions of fact, depending on the credibility
of witnesses who have been examined in presence of the
primary court—to have held his finding conclusive. (a)

---

(a) Santacana v. Ardevol, 1 Knapp 269; Reid v. Aberdeen New-
castle and Hull Steamship Co., L. R. 2 P. C. 245; Gray v. Turnbull,
L. R. 2 S. Ap. 53; The "Julia," 14 M. P. C. 210; Sanderson v.
Burdett, 18 Grant 417.

But here the plaintiff has, by death, lost the evidence
of the attesting witness, and also that of *Keating*, the
husband. This, I apprehend, justifies the application of
the principle of the cases which are cited in the
judgment of my learned brother. (*a*) I consider that
these authorities only apply where, as in the present
case, a claim is attempted to be maintained or resisted
on the unsupported evidence of one party after the loss
of evidence by the other party, for I do not understand
that there is anything in these decisions to prevent the
Court in a case where there has been no loss of evidence
from making a decree founded on the testimony of a
party only. The English Acts regulating the law of
evidence do not, as does the Statute of this Province,
disqualify a party from giving evidence in his own
behalf, where the other party to the transaction is dead;
and I understand the cases just quoted not as laying
down any rule of law as to the competency of witnesses,
but as shewing that on grounds of policy weight will not
be given to the unsupported evidence of parties in their
own interest, where the other side is incapacitated from
meeting it by the death of witnesses. Most of the cases
cited were administration suits, in which creditors sought
to establish debts by their own evidence; and it was
held that they could not do so after the death of the
debtors, the parties with whom they had contracted.
This applies here as regards both *Miller* and Mr.
*Keating*. The Vice Chancellor, however, admits this
doctrine, and says if he had had to depend on Mrs.
*Keating's* evidence alone, he would not have made this
decree, and my learned brother relies on the state of
the mortgage deed as a sufficient confirmation of the
direct testimony. But if the due execution of the
instrument in the state in which it now exists is to be
taken as proved *prima facie*, as I have already expressed

---

(*a*) Walker v. Smith, 29 Beav. 396; Bentley v. McKay, 31 Beav.
15; Grant v. Grant, 34 Beav. 623; Down v. Ellis, 35 Beav. 578;
Hartford v. Power, I. L. R. 3 Eq. 602.

the opinion that it must be, I am unable to see how the
appearance of the deed can be any confirmation of Mrs.
*Keating's* evidence given for the purpose of shewing that
it never was duly executed.  In my opinion, so to argue,
is to give no weight to the presumption which the law
makes in favor of the due execution of a sealed instrument, and to make it incumbent on the plaintiff to
account for the appearance of the document, and this
the decided cases already referred to and the maxim,
"*omnia præsumuntur rite esse acta,*" shew that he is not
required to do.

Further, but even if the defendant had made
out a *prima facie* case by her own evidence, I should
have thought that the evidence of Judge *Wells* would
have outweighed it.  It is true that this witness has no
independent recollection of this particular deed, but considering his official position, that his connection with this
transaction was in the performance of a judicial act, that
he recorded the result of his examination in a certificate
signed at the time, and that he states it was his
invariable practice in taking these examinations to look
at the deed, and explain its contents to the examinant, I
think his evidence more than counterbalances that of
Mrs. *Keating*, given in support of her own case.  Therefore, in my judgment, the defence entirely fails.

The sufficiency of the certificate of examination
indorsed on the mortgage was objected to on four
distinct grounds.  First, because the certificate had
been altered by the Judge, since he signed it, by inserting the place of his residence.  This cannot vitiate the
certificate if it was originally sufficient, though no doubt
it was a very irregular and improper thing to have done.
Then it is said the certificate contains no sufficient
description of the Judge.  The answer to this is, that it
might be shewn, as it has been, *aliunde*, that he had
jurisdiction; and this being so, section 4 of Statute 22

Victoria, chapter 35, applies, and renders the omission harmless. The want of any statement in the certificate, as it was originally signed, of the place at which the examination was had is also cured by the same section : *Robinson* v. *Byers.* (a)

1871.

Northwood
v.
Keating.

And section 2 of the same Act is an answer to the last objection to the certificate, namely, that it appears to have been signed on a day subsequent to that of the execution of the deed : *Monk* v. *Farlinger.* (b)

The conclusion is, that the decree must be reversed, and a decree of foreclosure pronounced in its stead. The plaintiff is entitled to a direction for the immediate payment of his costs up to the hearing, and also to the costs of this re-hearing.

Judgment.

---

## JONES v. BECK.

*Mortgage—Subsequent conveyance of portions—Exoneration.*

A registered owner of Whiteacre and Blackacre and other lands mortgaged all to the plaintiff: the owner then sold Whiteacre to *B.*, and afterwards Blackacre to *K.*, covenanting in each case against all incumbrances. The various instruments were respectively registered immediately after their execution

*Held*, that *B.'s* right, as between him and *K.*, was to throw the whole mortgage, and not merely a ratable part, on Blackacre.

Rehearing before the full Court.

The material facts appeared to be as follows : On the first of February, 1848, the Hon. *George S. Boulton*, being the registered owner of B, C, and other lots of land, mortgaged them to the plaintiff, and the mortgage was duly registered. On the 31st December, 1851, Mr. *Boulton* sold and conveyed B to one of the

---

(a) 13 Grant. 388.                    (b) 16 U. C. C. P.

defendants, the Rev. *J. W. Beck*, with covenants against incumbrances. This conveyance was also duly registered. Afterwards, namely, on the 10th July, 1863, the mortgagor, for valuable consideration, conveyed C to the other defendants *James* and *Michael Kenary*, with like covenants against incumbrances. Both purchases were made and completed without actual notice of the prior mortgage. At the hearing of the cause, *Strong*, V. C., made a decree, which in effect, as between the defendants, threw the plaintiff's mortgage on lot C, the property secondly sold, in exoneration of B, the lot sold first. The *Kenarys* objected to this, and reheard the cause. On the rehearing, it was contended on their behalf that, as between the purchasers of B and C, the lots should have been charged ratably with the mortgage debt.

Mr. *S. Blake*, for the plaintiff.

Mr. *Moss*, for the defendants *Kenary*.

Judgment.

SPRAGGE, C.—In the cases of *Davis* v. *White* (a) and *Barker* v. *Eccles* (b), I expressed my views on the points argued on this rehearing; and I have seen no reason for changing the opinion I then formed. I think the decree of my brother *Strong* was right, and should be affirmed.

MOWAT. V. C.—It is not disputed that, as between Mr. *Beck* and the mortgagor and his heirs, Mr. *Beck* was entitled in equity to throw the whole mortgage on C in exoneration of B, which he had sold free from all incumbrances.

The registration of the mortgage and of Mr. *Beck's* conveyance was notice of this equity in respect of C to

---

(a) 16 Gr. 312.                    (b) 17 Gr. 277.

all subsequent purchasers of C, according to the doctrine held by the late Vice Chancellor *Esten* in *Boucher* v. *Smith* (a).

That case is in favor of the *Kenarys* on the question as to whether the mortgagor by selling the remaining property could affect and diminish the equity of *Beck* in respect of that lot; for the learned Vice Chancellor appears to have intimated that in such a case the two purchasers should bear the charge ratably. But in the subsequent case of *Bank of Montreal* v. *Hopkins* (b), his Honor came to the opposite conclusion, and stated the rule to be, "that when a mortgagor alienates the equity of redemption in part of the lands, the rights and obligations of the mortgagor and purchaser in regard to the discharge of the mortgage debt as between themselves depend entirely on the terms of the agreement between them. When the mortgagor undertakes to discharge the mortgage wholly as between themselves, the mortgage debt is thrown upon the remainder of the estate retained by him, and any one purchasing part of such remainder must accept it subject to this burden."

Judgment.

The present Chancellor took the same view in the subsequent cases of *Davis* v. *White* (c) and *Barker* v. *Eccles* (d); and it was adopted by my brother *Strong* on the hearing of the present case. That also I think was the decree in the latest English case which was cited to us, though Mr. *Moss* contended the contrary. I refer to *Beavor* v. *Luck* (e).

The previous English authorities are not uniform; but having considered them all, and also the remarks upon them by the text writers, I am of opinion that the better doctrine is that which has ever since the late Vice

(a) 9 Gr. at 354, 355.  (b) *Ib.* p. 495.
(c) 16 Gr. at 314.  (d) 17 Gr. at 280.
(e) L. R. 4 Eq. 548, 549.

Chancellor's decision in *Montreal Bank* v. *Hopkins* been maintained in this country, namely, that a subsequent purchaser from the mortgagor, with notice, ought not to be, and is not, in a better position than the mortgagor himself as respects the equity in question.

The result is, that the decree should be affirmed with costs.

*Per Curiam.*—Decree affirmed with costs.

---

### CRABB v. PARSONS.

*Equitable pleadings at law.*

Where in a suit at law either party files an equitable pleading at any stage of the suit, and the judgment of the Court is given thereon, neither party will be allowed afterwards to file a bill in respect of the same matter on the ground that the same had been insufficiently pleaded in the action at law.

Accordingly, where the equitable pleading in question was by way of rebutter :

*Held*, that the judgment at law was conclusive.

Motion for injunction to restrain proceedings at law.

Statement.　The facts appearing on the motion were as follows : On the 9th of October, 1868, *Parsons* commenced an action in the Court of Queen's Bench against *Crabb*, upon a contract for the purchase by *Crabb* from *Parsons*, of a steam engine, boiler, and shaftings, for $450.

*Crabb*, amongst other answers to the action, pleaded a set-off upon two promissory notes made by *Parsons* to a firm in Montreal, and by it indorsed to *Crabb*, amounting together to about $850.

To this plea *Parsons* replied, that the alleged set-off did not accrue within six years.

*Crabb*, amongst other rejoinders to the replication, pleaded as to the defence of the Statute of Limitations to the set-off, a rejoinder on equitable grounds to the effect that on the 6th of December, 1862, before the notes were barred by the Statute of Limitations, *Parsons* commenced an action in the Court of Queen's Bench upon the contract then sued on; that *Crabb* pleaded to the said action the same plea of set-off as pleaded by him in the second suit in respect of the same two promissory notes, which were then not barred by the Statute of Limitations, and thereupon gave *Parsons* notice to reply to said plea within eight days; that *Parsons* did not reply thereto within the time limited, and took no steps whatever in that suit from the filing of the plea until the month of October, 1868, when the notes became barred by the Statute, and then *Parsons* discontinued that action and commenced the action now sought to be restrained; that the plea in the original action was not replied to, and proceedings therein were wholly suspended and stayed by *Parsons*, and judgment of *non pros* was not signed against him therein, as might have been done, at *Parsons*' special instance and request, and for his sole benefit; that it was agreed between *Parsons* and *Crabb* that, in consideration of judgment not being signed on that plea, the two notes should and would be so set-off against *Parsons's* claim, and the same were thereupon mutually set-off and allowed against such claim; that at such special instance and request on *Parsons's* part, and for no other reason, the proceedings in the former suit were and continued to be wholly stayed and suspended; that *Crabb*, relying on such request and agreement, and on the fact that *Parsons* had admitted the correctness of the set-off, and the right of *Crabb* to a set-off against his claim, and had therefore abandoned his said claim, and did not intend to proceed further with the action, took no further steps or proceedings therein or for the recovery of the set-off; that it was wholly unjust and inequitable that *Parsons* should be allowed to maintain his present action at law and defeat *Crabb's* set-off by pleading the Statute of Limitations to the set-off founded on these promissory notes.

To this rejoinder, *Parsons* for a surrejoinder on equitable grounds, pleaded that *Crabb* waived and forfeited his rights under the alleged agreement set out in the rejoinder by giving *Parsons*, before the discontinuance of the first and the commencement of the second action, namely, on the 30th of September, 1868, a term's notice of his intention to proceed in such first action by entering judgment of *non pros* against *Parsons* therein for want of a replication, and by accepting the costs of defence taxed to him on *Parsons's* rule to discontinue.

*Parsons* also demurred to the rejoinder on the grounds, amongst others, that the facts set forth were not sufficient to constitute an equitable set-off, and were not sufficient in law to prevent the operation of the Statute of Limitations, and were no answer to the replication.

*Crabb* took issue in law upon the demurrer, and for a rebutter on equitable grounds to the above surrejoinder, pleaded that he did not waive and forfeit his rights under the agreement as alleged, because *Parsons* agreed with him immediately after the pleading of the plea of set-off in the first action that he (*Parsons*) would, within a reasonable time thereafter, pay *Crabb* the costs thereof; that *Parsons* did not within a reasonable time pay said costs; and that thereupon, in order to recover those costs, and for no other purpose, and without waiving or forfeiting his rights under said agreement, *Crabb* gave the notice set out in the surre-joinder.

*Crabb* also demurred to the surrejoinder on various grounds.

The demurrers were (with other demurrers arising out of other parts of the pleadings in the suit not material to be stated here) argued before the Court of Queen's Bench, during Michaelmas Term, 1870, and during Easter Term, 1871, judgment was given for *Crabb* upon *Parsons's* demurrer to the rejoinder, and for *Parsons* upon *Crabb's* demurrer to the surrejoinder.

On the 1st September, 1871, the plaintiff (*Crabb*) filed his bill in this cause, setting out substantially the same facts as are above set forth, but alleging further that *Parsons*, besides agreeing to pay the costs of the former suit, as set out in the rebutter, agreed to pay *Crabb* $20, which he failed to do, and praying that the defendant (*Parsons*) should be enjoined from further proceeding with his action at law, or from pleading therein the replication of the Statute of Limitations to the plaintiff's set-off.

The action was entered for trial at the County of York Assizes, commencing on the 17th of October, 1871, and *Crabb* thereupon moved for an injunction.

Mr. *Spencer*, for plaintiff.

Mr. *C. Moss*, for defendant.

In addition to the cases mentioned in the judgment, counsel referred on the point of the right of plaintiff to maintain a suit in equity, after having set up the same defence at law, to *Farebrother* v. *Welchman* (a), *Leuty* v.

_____

(a) 3 Drew 122.

Crabb
v.
Parsons.

*Hillas (a), Waterlow* v. *Bacon (b), Boulton* v. *Cameron
(c),* and as to delay in moving to, *Thorp* v. *Hughes (d),
North Eastern Railway Company* v. *Martin (e),
Maclure* v. *Ripley (f), Scotson* v. *Gaury (g), Salisbury*
v. *Metropolitan Railway Co. (h).*

SPRAGGE, C.—It appeared to me, upon the argument on this application, that the point, so far as the
plaintiff's case was concerned, was narrowed to this:
whether the waiver set up by the defendant in this suit,
to the agreement pleaded by the plaintiff, both of these
pleadings being upon equitable grounds, and the judgment of the Court of Law upon this pleading of waiver,
was a bar to the same waiver being set up in this Court;
and the learned Counsel for the plaintiff conceded that
his case was narrowed to this point: but he contended
that the defendant in that suit, and the plaintiff in this,
omitted to state, by way of rebutter, that part of the
Judgment. agreement alleged to be waived was that *Parsons,*
plaintiff in that suit, was to pay $20 as well as the
costs.    The plaintiff, setting up the waiver, stated that
*Parsons* was to pay the costs: *Crabb,* plaintiff in this
suit, demurred to that pleading insisting that the proceedings set up as a waiver of the agreement were not
a waiver, but were taken only in order to the recovery
of his costs; and the Court held the proceedings to be
a waiver; and looking at the grounds of the decision, I
have no doubt it would have been the same if it had
been stated in the pleading of either party that the
proceedings set up as waiver, had been taken in order to
recover the $20, as well as the costs.

Mr. *Spencer's* contention amounted to this, as I put it
to him, that he had failed at common law through bad

(a) 4 Jur. N. S. 1166.        (b) 2 L. R. Eq. 514.
(c) 9 Gr. 297, in moving.     (d) 3 M. & C. 742.
(e) 2 Ph. 758.                (f) 13 Jur. 353 ; 2 Mac. & G. 276 n.
(g) 1 Ha. 99.                 (h) 39 L. J. Chy. 429.

eqyitable pleading, and that that being the cause of his failure at law, it gave him a right to bring the same equitable matter before this .Court ; and he referred me to two cases : *Craig* v. *The Gore District Mutual Insurance Company* (a), and *Evans* v. *Bremridge* (b), in support˘of his contention. I have looked at these cases, and do not think that they warrant this Court in adjudicating upon the question of waiver upon any grounds presented by this bill. The Court of Law was with *Crabb* upon the agreement set up by him, being a good answer in equity to the pleading to which it was set up, the Statute of Limitations; but against him upon the pleading setting up a waiver of that agreement.

Since the argument my attention has been directed to the˘Common Law Procedure Amendment Act of 1866. The third section, after reciting that doubts existed as to the effect of equitable defences pleaded in suits at law, enacts, that "if the defendant in any suit at law shall plead any equitable defence, and judgment shall be given against such defendant upon such equitable plea, such judgment shall be pleadable as a good bar and estoppel against any bill filed by such defendant, in equity, against the plaintiff, or representative of such plaintiff, at law in respect to the same subject matter which has been brought into judgment by such equitable defence at law." I read the words "equitable plea," in this enactment, as meaning equitable *pleading*, so that if a legal bar were pleaded, and the plaintiff, by replication, set up something to which the defendant pleaded matter in equity as an equitable answer to the replication by way of rejoinder, such rejoinder would be an equitable plea within the statute. I put this by way of illustration : if the defendant's equitable pleading shall come at a later stage of the pleadings between the parties, it would still, I apprehend, be within the

(a) 10 Grant 137.          (b) 27 L. T. 8.

statute, for the same reason would apply. Here the defendant pleaded a rebutter, setting up matter why, on equitable grounds, the matter alleged as a waiver of the agreement should not be a good answer to it, and he also demurred to the pleading setting up the waiver.

Assuming for a moment that the language of the Act does not in its terms exactly apply to the pleadings of the defendant at law, it settles a principle which is, in my judgment, fully applicable to this case. It is that a defendant at law, choosing to set up what he conceives to be equitable matter in the suit at law, and putting himself upon the judgment of the Court of Law, in regard to such equitable matter, has elected to stand by it, and must abide by it.

I think a Court of Equity should apply the principle of that enactment to any case in which a defendant at law has submitted to the judgment of a Court of Law matters which, in his judgment, constitute an equitable answer to what is alleged against him at law, and, upon which the Court of Law adjudicates, at whatever stage of the proceedings at law he may take this course. The principle of the enactment appears to be this, that he shall not try his fortune in one Court and, failing there, commence a suit in respect of the same matter in another. The words of the section exclude any such distinction as is contended for by the plaintiff's Counsel here. The judgment at law is made a good bar and estoppel in respect to the same "subject matter" which has been brought into judgment by the equitable defence at law. Here the subject matter was the agreement and its waiver.

Apart from the statute, I think the cases would properly lead to the same conclusion.

The injunction to restrain proceedings at law must be refused.

## DAY v. BROWN.

*Conflicting evidence, Master's finding on—*

Where the evidence given before a Master is conflicting, his judgment on it is, in general, accepted by the Court as correct: and not to be reversed on appeal.

Masters should be careful not to attach too much weight to oral testimony in opposition to evidence of facts and circumstances.

Rehearing of order pronounced by Vice Chancellor *Strong* dismissing an appeal from the report of the Master at Brantford, at the instance of the plaintiff.

Mr. *V. McKenzie*, for the appeal.

Mr. *Bowlby* and Mr. *Fitch*, contra.

The judgment of the Court was delivered by

SPRAGGE, C.—This rehearing is of an order made Judgment. by my brother *Strong*, overruling objections taken by the plaintiff, to the report of the Master at Brantford.

The Master allowed a sum of $800 as paid in one sum by one of the defendants to the plaintiff, and which sum the plaintiff swears was not paid. The fact of payment was sworn to by three several witnesses, who were examined *viva voce* in the presence of the Master, and who swore that they were present and saw the payment made, giving time, place, and circumstances in relation to the payment.

Mr. *McKenzie* points out, with great force and ingenuity, several circumstances tending to throw suspicion upon the fact of this alleged payment having been made; but all these circumstances were, no doubt, presented to the Master, and pressed upon his attention, as outweighing the direct evidence of payment; and

86—VOL. XVIII. GR.

we must assume that he considered them maturely, and
gave such weight to them as in his judgment they were
entitled to. If these circumstances were of such a
nature as necessarily to outweigh any direct evidence of
payment, so that it was evident that, consistently with
proved circumstances, the alleged payment could not
have been made, we should be forced to the conclusion
that the witnesses must have been untruthful (they could
not have been mistaken), and that the Master erred in
giving credit to them.

But the circumstances here were not of such cogency;
they were only suspicious, and the Master having
himself seen the witnesses, having observed their demeanour, and not only their answers, but their mode of
answering; their appearance, manner, and the many
minor circumstances attending the examination of witnesses which give to, or detract from the value of oral testimony, had materials for forming a more correct judgment
as to the weight to be attached to it, than any one from
merely reading the evidence can possibly have. If upon
an appeal involving the question of the weight to be
attached to oral testimony, the Judge hearing the appeal
should overrule the Master, he would run a great risk of
being in the wrong; and setting aside the judgment
of the Master in a case where, from his superior means
of forming a correct judgment, he would be the more
likely to be right. We think that the learned Vice
Chancellor, in overruling this appeal, proceeded upon a
correct principle, and that his order must be affirmed,
and with costs.

I take occasion, however, to make this observation
(in which, I believe, my learned brothers concur), that
there is perhaps a proneness, with some, at any rate, of
the Masters of the Court, to give overmuch weight to
oral testimony, and too little weight to conduct and to
circumstances. The tendency of almost all minds is

to place faith in witnesses whose appearance and bearing indicate truthfulness; but circumstances may shew that witnesses apparently truthful are really false, and no one who has been conversant with the examination of witnesses can fail to have observed how his faith in an apparently truthful witness has been shaken upon his being subjected to the test of a searching cross-examination, or confronted with the evidence of other witnesses, or with proved circumstances; when, if his evidence had been left unassailed, it would have been considered perfectly reliable. Conduct and circumstances are crucial tests of the truthfulness of testimony, and should be very carefully considered, and due weight should be given to them by those who, in a judicial position, have to draw their conclusions upon matters of fact from all the evidence, of whatever nature, that is before them.

It is perhaps scarcely necessary to add, that the great weight necessarily attached by the Court to the finding of the Masters upon facts in which they have had the advantage of being themselves present and hearing the evidence of witnesses, should make them anxiously careful to come to a right conclusion. The Court *must* place great faith in their carefulness and judgment; and if they fail in these, the consequence must be, in many cases, a miscarriage of justice.

1871.

Day
v.
Brown.

Judgment.

## McKINNON V. ANDERSON.

*Mortgage—Suit to redeem—General Order 466.*

Where a second mortgagee files a bill of redemption, and makes default
in paying at the time appointed, the mortgagor (as well as the first
mortgagee) has, under the General Order 466, the option of having
a day thereupon appointed for redemption of the first mortgage by
the mortgagor.

The judgment on the original hearing before Vice
Chancellor *Mowat* is reported *ante* Volume XVII.,
page 636.    The defendant *Anderson*, reheard the
cause.

Mr. *Hodgins*, for *Anderson*.

Mr. *English*, for the plaintiff.

SPRAGGE, C.—The decree in *Graham* v. *Anderson*
Judgment. directs accounts of the amount due on the mortgage of
*Graham* to *Anderson*, and the amount due on the
mortgage of *McKinnon* to *Anderson*, reserving further
directions and costs.

The decree on further directions directs the amount
found due on the mortgage of *Graham* to *Anderson*,
together with *Anderson's* costs, in all $600.26, to be paid
by *Graham*, plaintiff, and *Hime* : upon payment,
*Anderson* to convey to *Graham* and *Hime* : in case of
default, bill to be dismissed: in case of payment, the Court,
having caused an account to be taken of the amount due
on the *McKinnon* mortgage, and for costs, being $546.89,
orders that that amount be paid by *McKinnon*: upon
payment, *Graham* and *Hime* to convey to *McKinnon* :
in default of payment, *McKinnon* to be foreclosed.

The decree might have directed that, upon default by
*Graham* and *Hime*, *McKinnon* should have a day to
redeem *Anderson*, which would have been upon payment

of the *Graham* mortgage and interest, and upon payment also of *Anderson's* costs, as is directed by the decree in *Graham* v. *Anderson.*

The decree in this suit gives him those costs ; but the learned Vice Chancellor thought he should have no costs in this suit, in *pœnam* for not taking his remedy in the other suit : that, at least, is one of the grounds upon which costs have been refused to him.

Where there are two courses of procedure, one more expensive than the other, and the one that is the less expensive will serve the proper purposes of a party as well as that which is more expensive ; and he yet chooses to take that course which is the more expensive, he is properly limited to the costs of that which is the less expensive. But does that rule apply to such a case as this ? In the first place, I do not see that it was not quite as open to *McKinnon* as to *Anderson* to have the decree put in the shape in which it is now suggested on behalf of *McKinnon* that it should have been put. It was a decree on further directions. Being after decree, all parties to the suit were in the position of actors. I assume that all parties had notice of the settling of the minutes. If it was settled without notice by the plaintiff *Graham*, *Anderson* is no more answerable for the shape of it than *McKinnon* ; and if it was settled with notice, *McKinnon* is as much answerable for its shape as *Anderson* is.

There is nothing in the General Order to prevent any party availing himself of its provisions. But either party, or both, may have advisedly abstained from doing so. *McKinnon* may have preferred not to be put to redeem so soon ; and we find, in fact, that the bill in *Graham* v. *Anderson* was dismissed in November, 1868, and that it was not until June, 1870, that *McKinnon* filed his bill to redeem ; and he may have been glad, in the event of *Graham* and *Hime* not redeeming, to take the chance of further time, rather than have to redeem at once. On the other hand, *Anderson* may have been well content with the investment of his money, and not have desired to call it in; and such, indeed, appears to have been the case, for he has not called it in at all. Both these suits are for redemption.

In order to apply the rule which has been invoked to deprive *Anderson* of his costs, a party must be shewn to have taken a course which he ought not to have taken; that he was wrong, as a matter of conduct, in taking that course. In fact, *Anderson* took no course actively; he only abstained from something which would have had the effect of lessening the amount of costs against *McKinnon*, but which something it was equally competent for *McKinnon* to do, and which probably he would have done if, upon the whole, he had

thought it more for his interest to do it. I think *Anderson* had a perfect right to leave the decree to stand as it was, and that he may have done so for reasons of which this Court cannot disapprove, cannot fasten upon, as wanton, or in any respect wrong; and I think further, that *McKinnon* may fairly be looked upon as an assenting party to, (certainly not dissenting from), that which was done; and that it does not lie in his mouth to complain of it.

My brother *Mowat* suggests that it was not the right of *McKinnon* to take the decree in the shape that he now suggests that *Anderson* should have taken it, inasmuch as *Anderson* would not, in that case, be entitled, as against *Graham*, to his costs, as he would be upon the dismissal of *Graham's* bill. That would be so certainly; but then why should *Anderson* be visited *in pænam* for not taking a course which would have the same effect, viz., depriving him of his remedy for his costs against *Graham?* The objection to

*McKinnon* taking that course would be removed by
his paying those costs to *Anderson*. And they are
costs which he ought to pay if he took that course,
being costs which he would have to pay in case he redeemed; and by taking that course he would in effect
be declaring his intention to redeem.

It is fair to add as an evidence that *McKinnon*
advisedly abstained from having inserted in the decree
the provision that he now says ought to have been
inserted because he wished for further time to pay his
mortgage debt; that it was through his default that
*Graham* and *Hime* were foreclosed, for his mortgage
was past due; and he had only to furnish to them what
he owed upon his mortgage, and they would have been
enabled to pay *Anderson*. There was only the one
debt, and it was in fact his debt, and is indeed so put
in the first judgment of the learned Vice Chancellor.
The decree, he thought, should be " the same (except as
to costs) as if *McKinnon* were the original owner, and
had executed both mortgages; that is, had executed
first a mortgage to *Anderson* to secure the sum named
in the mortgage by the *Grahams* to *Anderson*, and
afterwards, a mortgage to the *Grahams* for the balance
of what is payable by *McKinnon* on his mortgage to
them." It would have been quite consistent with the
judgment to have given only one day to redeem to
*Graham* and *Hime* and to *McKinnon*. There are,
then, two reasons why, as I think, *Anderson* was not
bound to take the course that has been suggested : one,
that he was not bound to call in his mortgage money,
and his abstaining from doing it was not a wrong for
which he can be visited in *pœnam ;* the other, that he
was not bound to forego his remedy for costs against
*Graham*. I may add a third, for *McKinnon* might have
taken that course himself upon payment of *Anderson's*
costs. So far as to the costs.

The point as to the two per cent. additional interest
does not appear to have been open when the decree now
appealed from was before my brother *Mowat*. It had
been raised before the Master, and also upon the hearing
on further directions in *Graham* v. *Anderson*, and raised
by *Anderson*, and adjudged against him; *McKinnon*, as
well as *Graham*, being parties to that suit, and interested in the question. It is therefore *res judicata*.

If my brother *Mowat* had refused *Anderson*
his costs of this suit solely on the ground of his not
taking the decree in *Graham* v. *Anderson* in the shape
suggested, I should have been in favour of varying the
decree by giving him his costs. But my learned brother
says in his judgment, "The defendant has also set up
various claims by answer, which have not been substan-
tiated;" and he says that there were circumstances of
conduct on the part of *Anderson*, to which he has not
particularly adverted in his judgment, which ought, in
his opinion, to deprive him of his costs. That brings
the case to this, that my learned brother would, as a
matter of discretion, have deprived *Anderson* of his
costs, apart from the course that he conceived he ought
to have taken in the suit of *Graham* v. *Anderson*; and
with the exercise of that discretion we cannot, on rehearing interfere.

The result is, that the decree must be affirmed; but,
as it was not unreasonable for *Anderson's* counsel to
suppose that he was deprived of his costs, principally,
at least, because he did not, in *Graham* v. *Anderson*,
take the course suggested, and could not know that if
that point were out of the case he would not have had
his costs, I think the decree should be affirmed, without
costs.

STRONG, V.C.—I think this decree should be affirmed
in all respects. I do not, however, agree with the Vice

Chancellor that *Anderson*, the first mortgagee, was bound, instead of taking an order simply dismissing the bill in the suit of *Graham* v. *Anderson*, to have gone on and foreclosed his mortgage in that suit under the provisions of the General Order 466. I think he had the right to elect as he did to have the bill simply dismissed ; therefore, this did not constitute a ground for depriving him of his costs in this suit. But the course the defendant adopted in the suit of *Graham* v. *Anderson* was not the sole ground for refusing the costs. It appears that the defendant, by his answer, set up several unfounded claims, and my brother *Mowat* was of opinion that by so doing the defendant had disentitled himself to costs. In this I agree, more especially as the conduct of the defendant seems to have been harsh and oppressive.

I think it very clear that the question raised as to the two per cent. extra interest must also be adjudged against the defendant. That question having been determined between the same parties in the suit of *Graham* v. *Anderson* is *res judicata*. Moreover, I am of opinion, that in no case could *Anderson* enforce the payment of this extra interest, since the agreement to pay it is not binding, there being no undertaking to forbear or other valuable consideration for the plaintiff's promise to pay it. The decree must be affirmed with costs.

# INDEX

# PRINCIPAL MATTERS.

---

## ACCEPTANCE OF TITLE.
See "Vendor and Purchaser." 2.

---

## ACQUIESCENCE.
See "Nuisance."

---

## ADMINISTRATION.

Where a testator dies in a foreign country leaving assets in this Province, the Court, at the instance of a legatee, will restrain the withdrawal of the assets from the jurisdiction, notwithstanding that there may be creditors of the testator resident where the testator was domiciled at the time of his death; and that there are no creditors resident in this Province.

### Shaver v. Gray, 419.

---

## ADMINISTRATION SUIT.

1. The plaintiff and another bought from a testator's executors and trustees certain real and personal estate; the real estate was subject to a mortgage which the vendors agreed to pay; the purchasers paid their purchase money, but the vendors applied the same to pay other debts of the testator, and left the mortgage in part unpaid; the plaintiff having bought out his co-purchaser filed a bill against the executors; a decree by consent was made, giving the plaintiff a lien on the testator's assets, ordering the defendants to pay personally what the plaintiff should fail to realize from the assets, and directing the accounts and inquiries usual in an administration suit; the estate was insufficient to pay all creditors: before the making of the decree a creditor of the estate had obtained judgment

against the executors, and the sheriff seized and sold goods of the testator in their hands :

*Held*, that the plaintiff had no right to prevent the creditor from receiving the money.

**Henry v. Sharp, 16.**

3. Under the ordinary administration decree in respect of a testator's real and personal estate, the Master may take an account of timber cut with which the defendants are chargeable.

**Stewart v. Fletcher, 21.**

3. In an administration suit, the executors were charged with so much of the expenses of the reference as was incurred in the Master's office in establishing charges which they disputed.                                       *Ib.*

4. Where one of the legatees was absent from the jurisdiction, and the executors had been unable to discover him ; this was *held* a sufficient ground for the executors coming to the Court to obtain an administration of the estate.

**Dee v. Wade, 485.**

5. The fact that a creditor of an estate has proceeded at law after a decree for the administration of the estate of the testator has been obtained, is not sufficient to deprive him of his costs either at law or of a motion in this Court to restrain his action.

**Re Langtry, 530.**

See also "Practice." 1.

## ADVANCES TO AND BY AGENTS.
See " Agent and Trustee."

## ADVERTISEMENTS OF SALE.
See " Insolvency." 1.

[MISDESCRIPTION IN.]
See " Specific Performance," 3.

## ADVERSE POSSESSION.
See "Statute of Limitations," 5.

## AGENT, ADVANCES TO AND BY.
See " Agent and Trustee."
" Investment of Money by Agent."

## AGENT AND TRUSTEE.

*M.* was administrator of the estate of *S.* and was managing the real estate for the heirs; he was also one of the executors and trustees of *E.*; there was a sum of $808.55 due for taxes on some property of the *S.* estate, and *M.* paid the same with money of the *E.* estate, directing the agent of that estate to charge the amount to the *S.* estate; *M.* did not enter the amount in his accounts with the *S.* estate as a loan, and, on the contrary, in the accounts which he rendered he took credit for the amount as a payment by himself: the heirs knew nothing of the loan until some time afterwards; they had not authorized *M.* to borrow money; and he was at the time indebted to them as agent in a sum exceeding the amount of the taxes; *M.* afterwards died insolvent, and indebted to both estates:

*Held*, in appeal, that the *E.* estate could not hold the heirs of the *S.* estate liable for the $808.55, and was not entitled to a lien therefor on the property in respect of which the taxes were payable.

Ewart v. Steven, 35.

## AGENCY.

### [EVIDENCE OF.]
See "Joint Purchase," 2.

### [IMPLIED.]

1. There may be agency, and its duties and liabilities, without express words of appointment or acceptance; and where a party in negotiating between two persons, the one desiring to sell, the other to buy certain land, gave the former to understand that he was acting in her interest, it was *held*, that she was entitled to the full price which he obtained for the land, though it exceeded the amount which he had obtained her consent to accept.

Wright v. Rankin, 625.

2. In such a case, there being a conflict as to what had passed in the conversations, and no other witnesses of them being produced, it was *held* that, other things being equal, the version of the deceived party should be accepted in preference to that of the other party. *Ib.*

See also "Secret Profit."

## AGREEMENT.

### [CONSTRUCTION OF.]
See "Vendor and Purchaser," 4·

## ALTERATIONS IN DEED.

In a suit against a widow by the assignee of a mortgage purporting to be executed by her late husband, and herself, the plaintiff proved their signatures and that of the subscribing witness, who also was dead ; the Judge by whom the defendant had been examined verified his certificate, though he did not recollect the circumstances ; the document was a patched instrument, and the parts were not referred to in the attesting clause, or otherwise authenticated :

*Held*, on rehearing [reversing the decree of Vice-Chancellor *Mowat*,] that the unsupported evidence of the defendant, though believed by the Vice-Chancellor, was not sufficient to disprove the execution of the instrument by her, nor to throw on the plaintiff the onus of proving that the patching of the instrument had been before execution. [MOWAT, V.C., dissenting.]

Northwood v. Keating, 643.

---

## AMENDMENT.

1. In a suit for specific performance, the evidence having clearly established the bargain as alleged by the plaintiff though his bill omitted to state the terms and mode of payment as agreed upon ; the Court offered him the alternative of taking a decree for specific performance, with payment of purchase money in hand ; or to amend his bill, setting up the exact terms of the bargain.

Gillatley v. White, 1.

2. The defence of the Statute of Limitations being allowed at the hearing to be put in by supplemental answer :

*Held*, on rehearing, that the plaintiff should have an opportunity of controverting this defence.

McIntyre v. The Canada Co. 367.

See also " Usury," 1, 2.

---

## ANNUITY IN LIEU OF DOWER.

See " Will," 6.

---

## ANSWERING DEMURRABLE BILL.

A bill charging a defendant with fraud, and not praying relief against him as to costs or otherwise, is demurrable.

Saunders v. Stull, 590.

Charges of fraud do not justify answering a demurrable bill; and where the defendant to such a bill answered, and the cause went to a hearing, the bill was dismissed without costs.

Saunders v. Stull, 590.

---

## APPEAL BY MARRIED WOMAN.
See "Practice," 2.

---

## ASSETS, DEFICIENCY OF.
See "Administration Suit," 1.

---

## ASSIGNEE FOR VALUE.
[WITHOUT NOTICE.]
See "Mortgage," &c., 4, 6, 7.

---

## ASSIGNEE IN INSOLVENCY.
See "Reversionary Interest."

---

## BRACKET BOARDS.
The use of bracket boards on a mill-dam is such an easement as the Statute of Limitations will protect.

Campbell v. Young, 97.

---

## BUILDING SOCIETIES.
Building Societies are virtually exempted from the operation of the usury laws.

The Freehold Permanent Building and Savings Society v. Choate, 412.

In mortgages taken by a building society for advances to borrowing members, it is not necessary to express in the instruments how much of the interest reserved is a bonus in respect of the sum advanced, and how much for interest. *Ib.*

---

## CANAL INTERSECTING ROAD.
See "Injunction." 1.

---

## CHANCERY, JURISDICTION OF.
The Court of Chancery has no jurisdiction to give relief to sureties on a recognizance in a criminal proceeding.

Rastall v. The Attorney General (In Appeal), 138.

## CHARGE FOR IMPROVEMENTS.

See "Partition," 1.

———◆———

## CHARITABLE USES.

A testator bequeathed £100 to the Society of St. Vincent de Paul, and directed the residue of his estate to be converted into cash, and paid to the House of Providence. These were voluntary unincorporated associations.

*Held*, that so far as they could be paid out of personalty these legacies were good ; and should be paid over to the persons having the management of the pecuniary affairs of the institutions named.

### Elmsley v. Madden, 386.

———◆———

## CHATTEL MORTGAGE.

1. An immaterial variation between a chattel mortgage and the copy subsequently filed does not invalidate the re-filing.

### Walker v. Niles, 210.

2. A mistake in the number of the lot where the chattels were, was held to be immaterial under the circumstances. *Ib.*

3. The statement annexed to the affidavit filed with the copy of the mortgage, did not give distinctly all the information required by the Act, but the affidavit and statement together contained all that was necessary : *Held*, sufficient. *Ib.*

4. The statement contained an item of $2.25 as paid for re-filing, which the mortgagee had no right to charge : *Held*, not to vitiate the instrument. *Ib.*

5. A chattel mortgage was given for $1070 ; it afterwards appeared that the amount was made up in part of a promissory note made and given by the mortgagee to the mortgagor at the time of the execution of the mortgage and not paid for some months afterwards :

*Held*, that in the absence of fraud the mortgage was valid. *Ib.*

———◆———

## CHATTELS.

See " Injunction," 2.

———◆———

## COLLATERAL RELATIONS.

See " Marriage Settlement," 1.

## COMPENSATION.

[FOR DEFICIENCY.]
See " Specific Performance," 3.
[FOR SERVICES.]
See " Principal and Agent."

---

## COMPROMISE.

[VALID AGAINST CREDITORS.]
See " Dower," 8.
"Mortgage," &c., 5.

---

## CONFLICT OF TESTIMONY.

See " Agency, Implied," 2.
"Master's Finding on."

---

## CONSTRUCTIVE NOTICE.

See " Registry Law, 1."

---

## CONTEMPORANEOUS COVENANT.

See " Parol Agreement," 3.

---

## CONTRACT.

" Specific Performance," 1.

---

## CONTRACT IN RESTRAINT OF TRADE.

Several incorporated companies and individuals, engaged in the manufacture and sale of salt entered into an agreement, whereby it was stipulated that the several parties agreed to combine and amalgamate under the name of " The Canadian Salt Association," for the purpose of successfully working the business of salt manufacturing and to further develope and extend the same, and which provided that all parties to it should sell all salt manufactured by them through the trustees of the association, and should sell none except through the trustees :

*Held*, on demurrer, that this agreement was not void as contrary to public policy or as tending to a monopoly or being an undue restraint of trade ; that it was not *ultra vires* of such of the contracting parties as were incorporated companies, but was such in its nature as the Court would enforce.

The Ontario Salt Co. v. The Merchants' Salt Co. 540.

## CORPORATE SEALS.

Some of the parties executing a deed were corporate bodies, and the witnessing clause was expressed, " In witness whereof, the said parties hereto have hereunto set their hands and seals," &c., and the seals were all simple wafer seals.

*Held*, shat in the absence of evidence shewing these not to be the proper corporate seals of the companies, this was a sufficient sealing on the part of the incorporated companies. The Ontario Salt Co. v. The Merchants' Salt Co. 540.

---

## CORROBORATIVE EVIDENCE.

See " Reality of Sale."

---

## COSTS.

The costs payable out of an estate to persons not trustees thereof, were directed to be taxed between party and party only.

### Gray v. Hatch, 72.

See also " Administration Suit," 3, 5.
" Amendment."
" Damages."
" Dower."
" General Orders."
" Information Suit."
" Insolvency."
" Jurisdiction."
" Lower Scale of Costs."
" Practice."

---

## COVENANT, CONSTRUCTION OF.

[IN EQUITY.]
See " Riparian Proprietors," 2, 3, 4.

---

## COVENANT NOT TO SUE.

A stipulation not to sue one of two judgment debtors is no discharge of the other, though there should be no express reservation of rights as against such other.

### Dewar v. Sparling, 633.

See also " Discharge of one of several joint Debtors."

---

## CRIMINIAL CASES, RECOGNIZANCE IN.

See " Recognizance," &c.

## DAMAGES.

1. Where a plaintiff filed a bill for an injunction and payment of damages ; and it appeared that the wrongful act complained of had, without his knowledge, been discontinued before the suit was commenced :

*Held,* that the Court had not jurisdiction to make a decree for the damages.

**Brockington v. Palmer, 488.**

2. The defendant having neglected to inform the plaintiff of the discontinuance though applied to respecting it, before suit, the bill was dismissed without costs. .                    *Ib.*

See also " Dower," 7.
" Trust," 1, 2.

## DECREE AGAINST MARRIED WOMAN.

See " Married Woman."

## DEEDS.

### [SONS TO FATHER.]

A father having obtained a conveyance of the interest of his sons under a marriage settlement, for an alleged consideration, which did not exceed one-fifth of the value of such interest, and which was never paid, the transaction was set aside after the death of the settlor and one of the sons, in a suit by the devisees of the deceased son.

**McGregor v. Rapelje (In Appeal), 446.**

### [ALTERING.]

See "Alterations in Deeds."

### [BILL TO DELIVER UP.]

See "Statute of Limitations," 5.

## DEFICIENCY OF ASSETS.

See " Administration Suit," 1.

## DEFICIENCY, COMPENSATION FOR.

See " Specific Performance," 3.

## DEFICIENCY, PERSONAL ORDER FOR.

See " Vendor's Lien,"

## DEMURRER.

See ".Contract in Restraint of Trade."

—•—

## DISCHARGE OF ONE OF SEVERAL JOINT DEBTORS.

1. The plaintiff recovered a judgment against two defendants, each of whom made a conveyance of his property. The plaintiff filed bills impeaching the conveyances respectively as fraudulent; in the one suit the plaintiff obtained a decree; and the other suit he settled, consenting to the bill therein being dismissed without costs :

*Held*, that these circumstances did not necessarily imply a settlement or discharge of the debt.

**Dewar v. Sparling, 633.**

2. The only further evidence of the terms of settlement was contained in a letter from the plaintiff to his solicitors, stating as to the second suit, that he had settled with the defendants, taking $45 costs, and agreeing not to prosecute the suit, or look to the defendants therein for any portion of the judgment; and the letter inquired, "What about *lis pendens?* Will not bill have to be dismissed to have it removed?"

*Held*, that the judgment against the other debtor was not discharged.      *Ib.*

See also " Covenant not to sue."

—•—

## DIVISION COURT.

On an interpleader in the Division Court the jurisdiction of the Judge is not confined to the question of legal property : he may determine the claimant's right to an equitable interest.

**McIntosh v. McIntosh, 58.**

—•—

## DIVISION OF LOSSES.

See "Partnership," 2.

—•—

## DOUBLE MAINTENANCE.

See "Will," 3.

—•—

## DOWER.

1. A widow entitled to dower commenced an action therefor against a tenant, to whom, without express authority, the property had been leased by a Receiver in this Court.

*Held*, that she was not at liberty to proceed in such action without the leave of the Court.

**Coleman v. Glanville, 42.**

2. A testator devised his farm to his widow for life, determinable upon her marrying again, and gave to her a certain portion of the dwelling house situate thereon; and subject to this estate of the widow in the portion of the house, the will shewed an intention that the rest of the house and the farm should be kept in entirety, and be personally occupied and enjoyed by his sons until the youngest should attain the age of twenty-one.

*Held*, that the widow must elect between the provision made for her by the will and dower.

*Held*, also, that a second marriage, after having elected to take under the will, would not resuscitate the right to dower.

Coleman v. Glanville, 42.

3. In such a case the widow remained on the farm, and received some small sums of money for her own use, but had never had set apart for her exclusive enjoyment the portion of the house devised to her:

*Held*, that these acts did not amount to that deliberate and well-considered choice made with a knowledge of rights and in full view of consequences, which is necessary to constitute an election. *Ib.*

4. Where the annual value of a widow's dower was not large, and she made no demand for it, but resided on the property with her son, the heir, during his life, she having no intention of claiming dower, a claim for arrears against his estate after his death was refused.

Phillips v. Zimmerman, 224.

5. In case of land of which a widow is dowable, but in which her dower has not been set out, if the timber is cut down she is entitled to the income arising from one-third of the amount produced.

Farley v. Starling, 378.

6. In such a case the widow had reason to apprehend that the owner intended to fell the whole of the wood; it was shewn that in fact he had no such intention; but he had an opportunity of undeceiving her, and did not avail himself of it:

*Held*, that proof that he had not the intention imputed to him, did not exempt him from liability to the costs. *Ib.*

7. The mere fact that at the death of, or alienation by, the husband, his lands were of no rentable value, is not alone sufficient to disentitle the widow to claim damages, if the land has been subsequently made rentable by reason of improvements or otherwise either by the heir or vendee; as in such a case a portion of the rent is attributable to the land.

Wallace v. Moore, 560.

8. The release of a wife's dower to a purchaser is a good consideration for the grant of a reasonable compensation to the wife ; and such a grant made *bonâ fide* is valid against the husband's creditors.

Forrest v. Laycock, 611.

9. Where a wife joins in a mortgage of her husband's estate as a security to the mortgagee, and for no other purpose, she parts with her dower so far only as may be necessary for that purpose, and she is a necessary party to a subsequent sale by the husband free from dower.                           *Ib.*

[ANNUITY IN LIEU OF.]
See " Will," 6.

———•———

## DYING WITHOUT ISSUE.
See " Will," 5.

———•———

## ELECTION.
See " Dower," 2, 3.
" Will," 8.

———•———

## EQUITABLE CLAIM.
See " Division Court."

———•———

## EQUITABLE PLEADINGS AT LAW.

1. Where in a suit at law either party files an equitable pleading at any stage of the suit, and the judgment of the Court is given thereon, neither party will be allowed afterwards to file a bill in respect of the same matter on the ground that the same had been insufficiently pleaded in the action at law.

Crabb v. Parsons, 674.

2. Accordingly, where the equitable pleading in question was by way of rebutter :
*Held*, that the judgment at law was conclusive.          *Ib.*

———•———

## EQUITY OF REDEMPTION.
[RELEASE OF.]
See " Mortgage," &c., 3.

———•———

## ESTATE TAIL.
See " Will, Construction of." 1.

## ESTOPPEL.
See " Fraud on Creditors," 2.

---

## EVIDENCE.

In a suit by the assignee of a mortgage, brought against the mortgagors (who had covenanted with the assignee that the whole mortgage money was due), one of the mortgagors is not a competent witness to prove a payment to the mortgagee in his life time.

### Hancock v. McIlroy, 209.

---

## EVIDENCE OF PARTY.
See "'Alterations in Deed."

---

## EXECUTION CREDITOR.
See " Administration Suit,"' 1·

---

## EXECUTORS.

[COSTS OF.]
See " Administration Suit," 3.

[LIABILITY OF, IN RESPECT OF REAL ESTATE.]
See " Will," 2.

---

## EXONERATION.
See " Mortgage," &c., 8.

---

## FIXTURES.

**1.** On the sale of a woollen factory and machinery, it was stipulated that until the purchase money should be fully paid, the vendees were not to remove the machinery. The vendors afterwards executed a conveyance to the purchasers, and the latter to secure the unpaid purchase money, executed a mortgage which purported to be of the factory only, and did not mention the machinery :

*Held,* that the covenant against removing the machinery remained in force :

*Held, also,* that the mortgage covered not only the machinery which were fastened with nails or screws, but also machines which were kept in their place by cleats, as well as the plates and paper used with the press.

### Crawford v. Findlay, 51.

2. The purchasers resold, their vendee having notice of the covenant, and the vendee subsequently became insolvent.

*Held*, that his assignee in insolvency was not at liberty to remove the machinery by reason of non-registrasion under the Chattel Mortgage Act or otherwise.

See also " Landlord and Tenant."

## FOREIGN TESTATOR.

See "Administration."

## FRAUD ON CREDITORS.

1. To maintain a sale impeached by creditors, it is not sufficient in this Court to prove that the transaction was really intended to pass the property : for, as laid down by the Court of Error and Appeal in *Gotwalls* v. *Mulholland,* " although the sale may have been *bona fide*, with intent to pass the property, yet if made with intent by vendor and purchaser to defeat and delay creditors, it would be void."

2. An insolvent person sold his land to his brother ; a creditor filed a bill impeaching the sale as fraudulent ; part of the consideration was said by the defendants to be a pair of horses and waggon of the value of $200 ; but the parties had fraudulently given out after the sale that these horses were still the horses of the brother who had bought the land, and in this way had misled the plaintiff and other creditors :

*Held*, that this brother was estoppel from afterwards setting up against the creditor that the $200 had been paid in that way, and the plaintiff's debt being less than that amount, he was *held* entitled to a decree for payment, or in default, a sale of the land.

See also " Mortgages," &c. 4.

## FURTHER DIRECTIONS, DISMISSAL OF BILL ON.

On further directions, a bill was dismissed with costs, as respected some of the original plaintiffs ; they having no right to sustain such a bill.

## GENERAL ORDERS.

1. The 554th general order, as to filing a certificate of the applicability of the lower scale tariff, is directory ; and the

omission of it does not entitle a defendant, in case of a dismissal of the bill to the higher scale costs, except for fees of Court actually paid.

**Ferguson v. Rutledge, 511.**

2. Where a second mortgagee files a bill of redemption, and makes default in paying at the time appointed, the mortgagor (as well as the first mortgagee) has, under the General Order 466, the option of having a day thereupon appointed for redemption of the first mortgage by the mortgagor.

**McKinnon v. Anderson, 684.**

---

### GOOD FAITH.

See " Voluntary Conveyances Act, (1868.)"

---

### GOODWILL, SALE OF.

The defendant sold to the plaintiff the goodwill of the business of an innkeeper which he was carrying on in London, in this province, under the name of "Mason's Hotel," or " Western Hotel :"

*Held*, [affirming the decree of the Court below] that the sale of the goodwill implied an obligation, enforcible in equity, that the defendant would not thereafter resume or carry on the business of an innkeeper in London, under the name of " Mason's Hotel," or " Western Hotel ;" and would not resume or carry on the business of an innkeeper, under any name or in any manner, in the premises in question ; and would not hold out in any way that he was carrying on business in continuation of, or succession to the business formerly carried on by him under the said names, or either of them.

*Held*, also, [varying the decree of the Court below,] that a covenant in the agreement that the vendor should pay $4000 in the event of his carrying on business as an innkeeper within ten years, was void as an undue restraint of trade, but did not relieve the vendor from the implied obligation involved in the sale of the goodwill.

**Mossop v. Mason, 453.**

---

### GREENHOUSE & MACHINERY.

See " Landlord and Tenant."

---

### HUSBAND AND WIFE.

See " Dower," 9.
" Mortgage," &c., 5

## IMPROVEMENTS.

[CHARGE FOR.]
See " Partition," 1.

[PAYMENT FOR.]
See " Purchase under Mistake."

---

## INCUMBRANCES, COVENANT AGAINST.

See " Vendor and Purchaser," 1.

---

## INFORMATION SUIT.

In a suit by the Attorney General, on the relation of certain parties (reported *ante*, Volume XV., page 304,) the defendant was ordered on argument to pay the costs of the relators.

### The Attorney General v. Price, 7.

---

## INDIAN LANDS.

The Act respecting Indian Lands authorized the Governor in Council to declare applicable thereto the Act respecting timber on public lands; an order in Council was issued accordingly; eight years afterwards another Act was passed which contained a clause authorizing the Governor in Council to declare the Timber Act applicable to Indian lands, and to repeal any such order in Council and substitute others, and another clause authorizing the Governor in Council to make regulations and impose penalties for the sale and protection of timber on Indian Lands:

*Held*, that the Timber Act continued in force until revoked or altered by a new order in Council.

### The Attorney General v. Fowlds, 433.

---

## INJUNCTION.

1. An Act of Parliament having provided that it should be lawful for a Canal Company to cut a channel across a certain highway, and to erect, keep, and maintain a safe and commodious bridge across the canal; and the bridge, after being erected, having become unsafe through the default of the Canal Company, an incorporated Road Company acquired the road, made several endeavours to get the bridge repaired, but all of them having failed, through the insolvency of the Canal Company, the Road Company at length commenced the erection of a fixed bridge, which would have the effect of impeding the navigation of the canal:

*Held*, [reversing the decision of the Court below,] that they had not any right to do so, and a permanent injunction was granted restraining them [SPRAGGE, C., and MOWAT, V. C., dissenting.]

### The Town of Dundas v. The Hamilton and Milton Road Co., 311.

2. The plaintiff and *L.* were tenants in common of an oil well; they filled an oil tank with oil equal in quantity to 2,400 barrels, of which 1,600 belonged to the plaintiff and 800 to defendant, and they agreed that the oil was not to be sold under $5 a barrel; they were not partners. *L.*, without authority, contracted for the sale of all the oil in the tank at $1.25 a barrel.

*Held*, on a bill against the purchaser, that *L.* had no right to sell the plaintiff's portion of the oil; that the defendant's removal of it would be wrongful; but that as the oil was a staple commodity which had not any peculiar value, and as there was no fiduciary relation between the plaintiff and *L*, the plaintiff was not entitled to an injunction; and that his only remedy was an action at law.

### Mason v. Norris, 500.

See also " Administration Suit," 5.
" Dower," 6.
" Goodwill," 1.
" Partnership," 3.
" Municipal Council."

---

### INSOLVENCY.

1. Advertisements by assignees in insolvency for the sale of property of the insolvent should describe the property and state the title with the distinctness required in equity in the case of advertisements by trustees and other officials.

### O'Reilly v. Rose, 33.

2. In case of a sale by an assignee in insolvency being open to objection on the part of the creditors, the remedy of objecting creditors is by application to the County Court Judge; not by suit in Chancery in the first instance. *Ib.*

3. An insolvent compounded with his creditors, and had his goods restored to him; he thereupon resumed his business with the knowledge of his assignee and creditors, and contracted new debts. It was subsequently discovered that he had been guilty of a fraud which avoided his discharge, whereupon he absconded, and an attachment was sued out against him by his subsequent creditors;

*Held,* that they were. entitled to be paid out of his assets in priority to the former creditors.

### Buchanan v. Smith, 41.

4. In such a case the assignee, as representing the former creditors, was ordered to pay the costs of a suit brought by the subsequent creditors to enforce their rights. *Ib.*

---

## INSUFFICIENT DESCRIPTION.

See " Sheriff's Deed."

---

## INTEREST.

See " Principal and Agent."
" Sale of Notes."

---

## INTERPLEADER.

See " Division Court."

---

## INVENTION, PATENT FOR.

See " Patent for Invention."

---

## INVESTMENT OF MONEY BY AGENT.

*A.* received $1,200 belonging to his son-in-law *R.*, and invested it with other money of *A.*'s own in the purchase of a farm, which cost $3,200. *R.*, with his family, went into possession of the farm, and *A.*, the father-in-law, by his will devised the farm to *R.*'s wife and son jointly for the life of the wife, with remainder to the son in fee, subject to the payment of $200 to a daughter of *R.*, and of $600 to another person. It was assumed in the cause that *R.* was at the time of the purchase and thenceforward of unsound mind and unable to give a valid assent to the transaction; and the Court held on that assumption he was entitled to the $1,200 as against *A.'s* estate, and that the devise to his wife and son were no satisfaction of the claim; and also that he was probably entitled to a charge on the land for the debt.

But the Court directed inquiries whether *R.* was at the date of the transaction of mental capacity to assent to the purchase; and if so, whether he did assent thereto; also, inquiry as to the occupation of the land by R. and his family before the death of A., and the value of such occupation.

### Goodfellow v, Robertson, 572,

## JOINT PURCHASE.

1. Where a purchase was made by a person in his own name but in reality for the benefit of another, a personal decree against both, for the payment of the purchase money, was held to be correct.

Sanderson v. Burdett, 417.

2. Parol evidence of the agency was held admissible, and the purchaser, who entered into the contract in his own name, and who was a defendant, was held a good witness on behalf of the plaintiff against his co-purchaser, the other defendant. *Ib.*

## JURISDICTION.

Where the amount in dispute is under $200 but the defendant is out of the jurisdiction, the plaintiff is entitled to costs on the higher scale.

Skelly v. Skelly, 495.

See also " Insolvency," 2.

## JURISDICTION OF CHANCERY.

The Court of Chancery has no jurisdiction to give relief to sureties on a recognizance in a criminal proceeding.

Rastall v. The Attorney General, 138.

## LANDLORD AND TENANT.

A greenhouse, conservatory, and hothouse, affixed to the freehold, were held not to be removable by a tenant. Also, the glass roofs.

But machinery for heating these houses, which rested by its own weight on bricks, and was not fastened to the freehold, was held to be removable. Also, the pipes passing from the boilers through a brick wall into adjoining buildings.

Gardiner v. Parker, 26.

## LAPSE OF TIME.

Where a plaintiff files a bill praying relief on the ground of a legal title in himself, no shorter lapse of time than would be a bar at law is an obstacle to relief in equity.

Connor v. McPherson, 607.

## LIEN FOR UNPAID PURCHASE MONEY.

The principle that a vendor, by taking from a purchaser an indorsed note as security for unpaid purchase money does not thereby lose his vendor's lien, is equally applicable where the security given is a bond, in which a third person joins as surety.

Shennan v. Parsill, 8.

## LIMITATIONS, STATUTE OF.

See " Lapse of Time."
" Statute of Limitations."

## LOSSES, DIVISION OF.

See " Partnership."

## LOWER SCALE OF COSTS.

The costs of a suit by a judgment creditor, to whom less than $200 is due, to obtain payment of his own debt alone out of property alleged to have been conveyed away to defeat the plaintiff's claim, are taxable according to the lower scale, no matter what the value of the property may be.

Forrest v. Laycock, 611.

## LUNACY.

See " Investment of Money by Agent."

## MAINTENANCE, DOUBLE.

See " Will," 3.

## MARRIAGE SETTLEMENT.

A widower, on his second marriage, executed a settlement which made provision for his children by his first marriage :
*Held,* [affirming the decree of the Court below,] that the provisions could not be defeated by a sale for value by the settlor.

McGregor v. Rapelje, 446.

## MARRIED WOMAN.

[APPEAL BY.]
See " Practice," 2, 3.

[DECREE AGAINST.]

A conveyance void against creditors was made through a third party to the owner's wife ; the husband afterwards became

insolvent and joined his wife in a sale of the property to a
purchaser without notice ; a conveyance to the purchaser was
executed and registered, and the purchaser gave to the wife a
mortgage for part of the purchase money, and paid her the residue in cash. On a bill by the assignee in insolvency he was
declared entitled to the mortgage, and to any of the money
which still remained in the wife's hands, and to any property,
real or personal, which she had purchased with the residue and
still owned ; but the Court refused to direct an inquiry as to
whether she had separate estate, in order to charge the same
with any of the residue which had been spent by her, or with
the costs of the suit.

Saunders v. Stull, 590.

## MASTER'S FINDING ON CONFLICTING TESTIMONY.

1. Where the evidence given before a Master is conflicting,
his judgment on it is, in general, accepted by the Court as correct : and not to be reviewed on appeal.

Day v. Brown, 681.

2. Masters should be careful not to attach too much weight
to oral testimony in opposition to evidence of facts and circumstances. *Ib.*

## MASTER'S REPORTS.

To avoid expense, questions which arise in the Master's
office on the construction of a will should, where practicable,
be left for decision by the Court on further directions, instead
of being brought before the Court by way of appeal from the
Master's report.

Scott v. Scott, 66.

See also, " Practice," 4.

## MERGER.

See " Priorities," 2.

## MILL DAMS.

See " Parol Agreement," 2.
" Riparian Proprietors," 2, 3, 4.

## MISDESCRIPTION IN ADVERTISEMENT.

See " Specific Performance," 3.

## MISTAKE.

See " Chattel Mortgage," 2.

---

## MORTGAGE, MORTGAGOR, MORTGAGEE.

1. Where a sale takes place under a power contained in a mortgage, and the sale is not properly conducted through the fault of the solicitor, the mortgagor, or any other party interested as well as the mortgagee, has a right to institute proceedings complaining thereof.

### Howard v. Harding, 181.

2. First mortgagees with a power of sale released portions of the mortgaged property to the mortgagor:
*Held*, that this did not give priority to a subsequent incumbrancer, with respect to the remainder of the property; but might render the first mortgagees responsible to the second for the fair value of the parcels released.

### The Trust and Loan Company of Canada v. Boulton, 234.

3. A., who was greatly addicted to drinking, gave to B. a mortgage to secure a small debt; the property was worth at least seven times the debt; and the rent of half the property, for three years, would have paid off the claim: but five years before the debt was payable, A., without any additional consideration, released his equity of redemption to B.; and B. was allowed to remain in possession for seven or eight years after the mortgage debt was paid off by rents. A majority of the Judges of the Court of Appeal were of opinion; and *held*, [affirming the decree of the Court below,] that the facts and evidence shewed that the release was given on a parol trust, for the benefit of the mortgagor and his family, and that to set up the release as an absolute purchase, was a fraud on the part of B. against which the Court should relieve, notwithstanding the lapse of time and the death of some of the witnesses.

### Crippen v. Ogilvie, 253.

4. An insolvent person executed to his son a mortgage for $1000, of which $400 was a pretended debt to the son, and $600 a pretended debt to his mother. The son subsequently, under an arrangement with the father, transferred the mortgage to C., who was the holder of notes of the morgagor to the amount of $600, which he gave up to the mortgagee, and he paid in cash $400 to the mortgagee. C. had notice of the character of the mortgage, but the transaction with him was *bona fide*:

*Held*, that he was entitled to claim for the full amount of the security, in priority to subsequent execution creditors of the mortgagor. [MOWAT, V. C., dissenting.]

Totten v. Douglas, 341.

5. A wife joined in a mortgage of her husband's estate to secure a loan of one-fourth or one-fifth of the value of the property, and he subsequently sold the property ; his wife claimed to be entitled to dower, and refused to join in the conveyance without a reasonable compensation being made to her ; her right to dower being supposed by all parties to exist, her husband had a piece of land conveyed to her, which she accepted, and thereupon she signed the conveyance of the mortgaged estate. The transaction appearing to have been for the interest of creditors, it was held to be valid, independently of the question whether her claim to dower was in such a case well founded in point of law or not.

Forrest v. Laycock, 611.

6. An assignee of a mortgage cannot as against a prior equity set up the plea of purchase without notice.

Smart v. McEwan, 623.

7. The registered owner of land mortgaged the same, and afterwards conveyed the property absolutely to a purchaser, who registered before such mortgage, giving back a mortgage to secure purchase money ; and subsequently the vendor assigned his mortgage to a purchaser who had no notice of the prior mortgage :
*Held*, that the purchaser's mortgage in the hands of the assignee was subject to the lien or charge of the vendor's mortgagee.–*Ib.*

8. A registered owner of Whiteacre and Blackacre and other lands mortgaged all to the plaintiff: the holder then sold Whiteacre to *B.*, and afterwards Blackacre to *K.*, covenanting in each case against all incumbrances. The various instruments were respectively registered immediately after their execution.
*Held*, that *B.*'s right, as between him and *K.*, was to throw the whole mortgage, and not merely a ratable part, on Blackacre.

Jones v. Beck, 671.

See also "Fixtures," 1, 2.
"General Orders," 2.

———

## MUNICIPAL COUNCIL.

Where for the purpose of erecting a market house, a municipal council would require to levy a rate which would exceed

the amount of two cents in the dollar allowed to be imposed
by section 225 of the Municipal Act, it was *held* that a
ratepayer was entitled to an njunction restraining the
erection of the building by the co ncil.

### Wilkie v. The Corporation of Clinton, 557.

## MUNICIPAL OFFICERS.

It is culpable neglect of duty on the part of municipal
officers not to see that separate accounts for special rate,
sinking fund, and assessment for general purposes are kept as
directed by the statute.

### Wilkie v. The Corporation of Clinton, 557.

## NOTES.

See " Sale of Notes."

## NOTICE.

See " Registry Law," 1, 2.

## NOVELTY.

See " Patent for Invention."

## NUISANCE.

In 1861, while the defendant was engaged in erecting
buildings for a tannery on land adjoining the plaintiff's
premises, the plaintiff encouraged the defendant to proceed
with his project; the buildings were proceeded with, and
business in them was commenced the same year; in 1863
additions were made to the buildings with the plaintiff's
knowledge and acquiesence ; and the plaintiff made no complaint about the business until 1868, though all this time it had
been carried on, and the plaintiff had been residing on the
premises adjoining :
*Held*, [affirming the decree of the Court below,] that by his
conduct he had debarred himself from obtaining relief in
equity on the ground of a tannery being a nuisance.

### Heenan v. Dewar, 438.

## ONUS OF PROOF.

See " Alteration in Deed."

## PAROL AGREEMENT.

1. A parol agreement in reference to land partly performed, by execution of deeds, was enforced.

### Shennan v. Parsill, 8.

2. *C* contemplated the erection of a saw mill on land which he owned, but he required the privilege of backing water on the lands of four other persons having lands farther up [the stream ; from three of these persons he obtained, through the agency of the fourth of them (*E*), the right, by deed, of backing the water to whatever extent would be occasioned by a dam nine feet high. The fourth (*E*) verbally gave the same right, but executed no writing. *C* thereupon erected a dam seven feet six inches high, but finding this insufficient he some years afterwards desired to raise it further.

*Held*, by the Court on appeal [SPRAGGE, C., and MOWAT, V. C., dissenting], that *E.'s* agreement was not binding to any greater extent than *C.* had taken advantage of in erecting his original dam.

### Hendry v. English, 119.

3. An alleged parol agreement said to have been entered into contemporaneously with a covenant under seal, was not permitted to control the covenant, the parol agreement having been proved by one witness only, whose intention to speak the truth was admitted on all hands, but the accuracy of whose recollection was not confirmed by other evidence.

### Lewis v. Robson, 395.

- ◆ -

## PAROL EVIDENCE.

See " Purchase by Agent."

———◆———

## PAROL TRUST.

See "Mortgage," &c., 3.

———◆———

## PARTIES.

A vendor devised his estate to trustees, and on a division of the estate among the *cestuis que* trust the trustees conveyed to one of them the sold property : these facts appeared on a bill by the purchaser against the grantee for specific performance : the defendants set up by answer that the executors and trustees were necessary parties : the Chancellor at the hearing overruled the objection and the Court of Appeal sustained the decree. [DRAPER, C. J., and GWYNNE and GALT, JJ., dissenting.]

### Butler v. Church, 190.

## PARTITION.

1. A father placed one of his sons in possession of certain wild land, and announced his intention of giving it to him by way of advancement. He died without carrying out this intention : meanwhile the son had taken possession, and by his improvements nearly double l the value of the land.

*Held*, that the son was entitled to a charge for his improvements, and to have the land allotted to him in the division of his father's estate, provided the present value of the land in its unimproved state would not exceed his share of the estate.

2. In such a case, whether the son is not entitled to an absolute decree for the land. *Quære.* *Ib.*

See the same point.

----

## PARTNERSHIP.

1. In partnership suits the defence of the Statute of Limitations is not available unless six years have elapsed before the filing of the bill since the dealings of the partners wholly ceased.

2. A partnership was formed between two civil engineers and architects, the profits of which were to be divided in shares of three-fifths and two-fifths. During the continuance of the partnership they invested moneys of the partnership in the purchase of real estate, which resulted in a loss :

*Held*, that the loss was to be borne by the partners in the same proportions as they were to share the profits and loss of their other business. *Ib.*

3. Several proprietors of salt wells entered into an undertaking to sell their products through trustees, and in no other way ; and a written agreement to this effect was executed by all the parties, except one, who was resident in England, and carried on his business here through an agent ; the business was carried on under the agreement, notwithstanding his non-execution of the deed, and one of the other parties having subsequently attempted to act in contravention of the agreement, it was *held* that the delay of the absent party to sign the contract could not be set up as an answer to a motion for an injunction restraining the contravention.

## PART PERFORMANCE.
See " Parol Agreement."
" Specific Performance," 2.

## PATENT FOR INVENTION.
The plaintiff had obtained a patent for an improved gearing for driving the cylinder of threshing machines ; and the gearing was a considerable improvement ; but, it appearing that the same gearing had been previously used for other machines, though no one had before applied it to threshing machines— it was *held* [affirming the decree of the Court below,] that the novelty was not sufficient under the Statute to sustain the patent.

Abell v. McPherson, 437.

## PLEADING.
*Quære*, whether, in order to exclude parol evidence of a contract it is necessary for a defendant who denies the contract to claim the benefit of the Statute of Frauds.

Butler v. Church, 190.

See also " Parties," 1.
" Usury," 2.

## PERSONAL DECREE.
See " Joint Purchase," 1.

## PERSONAL ESTATE.
See " Will, " 6.

## PERSONAL ORDER FOR DEFICIENCY.
" See Vendor's Lien."

## PERSONAL TRUST.
See " Will," 5.

## PERSONALTY.
See " Charitable Uses."

## POWER.
See " Will," 1.

## PRACTICE.

1. In case a creditor brings an administration suit after being informed that there are no assets applicable to the payment of his claim, if the information appear by the result to have been substantially correct, he may have to pay the costs of the suit.

### The City Bank v. Scatcherd, 185.

2. Where a married woman defended a suit in Chancery without a next friend, it was held that the husband and wife could appeal to the Court of Error and Appeal without any next friend.

### Butler v. Church, 190.

3. On an appeal against the report of the Master by a married woman and her husband, defendants in the suit, it is not necessary that the married woman should have a next friend ; such case differing from an application by a married woman alone.

### Hancock v. McIlroy, 209.

4. An objection of the Statute of Limitations cannot be made by an appellant against the Master's report without having been taken before the Master.

### Brigham v. Smith, 224.

See also " Amendment."
       " Answering Demurrable Bill."
       " Evidence."
       " Further Directions."
       " General Orders."
       " Master's Reports."

## PRINCIPAL AND AGENT.

R., who was engaged in the lumber business, employed S. as his agent, and by letter agreed to pay him $10 per 1,000 cubic feet on all timber that S. manufactured for him, which rate (the letter said) " includes purchasing, superintending the making, and attending to the shipping of the same," R. paying all travelling expenses. S. bought a quantity of timber for R. which was not manufactured under the superintence of S.

*Held*, that he was entitled to a reasonable compensation for this service ; and there having been considerable delay in enforcing payment, caused by R. having obtained an injunction restraining S. from proceeding at law, it was *held* that he was entitled to interest on the amount of his claim.

### Ridley v. Sexton, 580.

See also " Joint Purchase," 2.
       " Purchase by Agent."

## PRIORITIES.

1. Two mortgages were successively taken and registered which, by mistake, omitted a certain parcel of ground which both were meant to contain. The second mortgage was subsequently assigned for value, without actual notice of the first mortgage ; and the assignee afterwards under a decree of this Court in a suit to which the joint mortgagees were not partners acquired the legal estate from the original vendor's grantee, who was entitled to hold it for unpaid purchase money :

*Held*, that the assignee of the second mortgage was entitled as against the first mortgagee to hold the legal estate until the second mortgage should be paid.

### The Merchants' Bank v. Morrison, 382.

[Reversed on appeal. See *post* vol. xix., p. 1.]

2. There were two mortgages on certain land. *O.*, having notice of the second mortgage, bought the first mortgage, and, at or about the same time, the equity of redemption, and gave to the party who was selling to him the first mortgage a new mortgage for the sum *O.* was to pay therefor. *O.* conveyed portions of the land to his sons in terms subject to the mortgage which he had so given ; and he afterwards paid that mortgage off :

*Held*, [affirming the decree of the Court below,] that these facts were not sufficient evidence of an intention to merge under the statute 22 Victoria, chapter 87, and that the second mortgage had not acquired priority over the mortgage purchased by *O.*

### Barker v. Eccles, 440.

See also " Registry Law," 2.

——◆——

## PURCHASE BY AGENT.

The plaintiff agreed with *J.* to purchase a mining lease for their joint benefit, the consideration for which was to be the testing of the ore at the crushing mill of the plaintiff, and at his expense. In pursuance of this arrangement *J.* did arrange for the lease, but took the agreement therefor in his own name. The ore was, as agreed upon, tested at the crushing-mill of the plaintiff, and at his expense, but *J.* attempted to exclude the plaintiff from any participation in the lease, asserting that he had obtained the same for his own benefit solely.

*Held*, that the true agreement could be shewn by parol ; and that the plaintiff was entitled to the benefit of the agreement.

### Williams v. Jenkins, 536.

## PURCHASE UNDER MISTAKE.

The rule that a party in good faith making improvements on property which he has purchased, will not be disturbed in his possession, even if the title prove bad, without payment for his improvements, will be enforced actively in this Court, as well where the purchaser is plaintiff as where he is defendant; and that although no action has been brought to dispossess him.

### Gummerson v. Banting, 516.

## QUIETING TITLES' ACT.

The Court will not grant a certificate to quiet the title of a party who claims to be the legal owner in fee simple, but who is not in possession of the land claimed, and is kept out of such possession by a person who disputes the title of the claimant: in such a case the claimant must first recover possession of the premises.

### Re Mulholland, 528.

## RATES.

The limit of two cents in the dollar demanded by the Municipal Act of 1866 as the maximum of assessment, includes the special sinking fund rate to be levied in respect of past debts.

### Wilkie v. The Corporation of Clinton, 557.

See also "Municipal Council."

## REALITY OF SALE.

In the case of sale by an insolvent person to a relative, attended by suspicious circumstances, the reality and *bona fides* of the transaction should not be rested on the uncorroborated testimony of the parties to the impeached transaction.

### The Merchants' Bank v. Clarke, 594.

## RECEIVER.

See "Dower," 1.

## RECOGNIZANCE IN CRIMINAL CASES.

A recognizance which was expressed to be the joint and several recognizance of the prisoner and his sureties was acknowledged by the sureties only; and the prisoner was discharged without his acknowledgment first having been obtained:

*Held*, that the sureties were liable. [SPRAGGE, C., MOWAT and STRONG, V. CC., dissenting.]

Rastall v. The Attorney General, 138.

See also "Jurisdiction of Chancery."

---

## REDEMPTION, SUIT FOR.

See "General Orders," 2.

---

## REGISTRY LAW.

1. The registration of a deed is not constructive notice of the grantor's interest in land not comprised in it; and has not the same effect in that respect as actual notice of the registered deed might have.

The Merchant's Bank v. Morrison, 382.

2. Where the registered owner of land had parted with his interest therein by an unregistered deed, a person who afterwards fraudulently took and registered a conveyance from such registered owner, prior to the Registry Act of 1865, knowing or believing that his grantor had parted with his interest, was held not entitled to maintain his priority over the true owner, though he did not know, or had no correct information, who the true owner was.

McLennan v. McDonald, 502.

---

## RELEASE OF PORTIONS OF MORTGAGE PREMISES.

See "Mortgage," &c., 2.

---

## RELEASE OF EQUITY OF REDEMPTION.

See "Mortgage," &c., 3.

---

## RELEASE OF SUIT.

### [WITHOUT ADVICE.]

1. Differences having arisen between parties, trustee and *cestui qui trust*, the latter (*A.*) obtained against *B.* (the trustee) a decree for an account, and large sums were in dispute between them: while the reference was pending, *B.* got a release of the suit prepared for *A.*'s signature: a friend brought *A.* to *B.*'s office, and *B.* there induced *A.* to sign the release in consideration of $150 which he promised to pay; on a subsequent day *A.* went for the money, and then at *B.*'s request executed

a quit claim deed of all his interest in the land. There was no evidence of the true state of the accounts at the time of these transactions: *A.* was sober when he entered into them, and he understood their nature; and *B.* had no fraudulent purpose therein: *B.* was a person of large business experience; *A.* had little, if any, business experience, and his habits were intemperate and thriftless; and he executed the two instruments without the knowledge of his solicitor, and without advice:

*Held.* that the instruments were void in equity.

**The Edinburgh Life Assurance Co. v. Allen, 425.**

2. An old man whose mental faculties had been somewhat impaired by age, being in difficulties with his son, applied for advice to the attorney of persons against whom he had recovered a judgment for one debt and a verdict for another debt; the attorney obtained from him a release of the two debtors without any consideration, and without his having any other advice in regard to the transaction; and the only evidence of what had passed between the two was the evidence of the attorney himself, the client being dead:

*Held,* that the release could not be maintained in equity.

**Dewar v. Sparling, 633.**

---

## REMOVAL OF TRUSTEE.
See "Trust," &c., 3.

---

## RETAINER, RIGHT OF.
See "Vendor and Purchaser," 1.

---

## REVERSIONARY INTEREST.

An insolvent's reversionary interest in an estate passes to his assignee, and entitles the assignee to maintain a suit in a proper case for the appointment of new trustees, and for an account of the estate: But the Court refused to make an order for the sale of such reversionary interest.

**Gray v. Hatch, 72.**

---

## RIPARIAN PROPRIETORS.

1. The use of bracket boards on a mill dam is such an easement as the Statute of Limitations will protect.

**Campbell v. Young, 97.**

2. On a sale of a mill site the vendor covenanted to secure to the vendee sufficient water for certain manufacturing purposes; the deed did not state how the water was to be supplied; but a dam was then standing which afforded the necessary supply, and it did not appear that the covenantor had any other way of securing it:

*Held*, that he or any one claiming under him was not entitled to a decree for the removal of this dam without supplying sufficient water in some other way.

*Held*, also, that the grantee, his heirs and assigns, were entitled to use the water for other purposes, provided no more was used than the specified manufactures had required and used.

Rosamund v. Forgie, 370.

3. After the conveyance, other persons, unconnected with either party, erected mills above the dam, and used part of the water: *Held*, that this did not relieve the grantor, or those claiming under him by subsequent deeds, from the obligation to supply his first grantee with water, so far as the maintenance of the dam was a discharge of this obligation. *Ib.*

4. Certain riparian owners filed a bill against another riparian owner to restrain him from maintaining a dam; other persons were interested in maintaining the dam, whom the plaintiffs did not prove any title to interfere with; and one of the plaintiffs had sold a mill site to the defendant on verbal representations which implied that he was to have the benefit of the dam: The Court *held*, that if the plaintiffs had any claim against the defendant, the proper course was to leave them to their legal remedy against him; and the bill was dismissed with costs. *Ib.*

## SALE.

See " Mortgage," &c., 1.
" Solicitor."

## SALE OF NOTES.

A loan of money was made for two months at two per cent. a month, at the expiration of which time it was contemplated a new arrangement would be made. After the expiry of the two months, no other arrangement having been effected, the Court held the lender entitled to claim interest at the rate originally agreed upon, and to sell the notes held by him as security, to repay himself the amount of his claim; subject only to the question whether he had sold the notes for the best price that could be obtained for them; and as to which the Court directed an inquiry before the Master.

——◆——

## SALES OF PORTIONS OF MORTGAGED LANDS.

See " Mortgage," &c., 8.

——◆——

## SALE OF WHEAT, PART OF A LARGER QUANTITY.

See "Warehouseman's receipt."

——◆——

## SALE, TRUSTEE FOR.

*A.* executad to *B.* a deed of his property in trust, (amongst other things) to convert the same into money. *B.* under the assumed authority of this deed mortgaged the property:

*Held*, that the mortgage was not authorized by the trust for sale, and was only valid to the extent of *B.'s* beneficial interest (if any) in the premises.

——◆——

## SECRET PROFIT.

*W.* was the owner (snbject to a moregage) of property which *M.* wished to buy; *R.* becoming aware of this, entered into friendly negotiations with both, and bargained with *W.* to take $3,500, and with *M.* to give $5,600 for the property; *R.* concealed this difference from the parties. *W.* conveyed to *M.*; on her signing the deed, *R.'s* attorney paid to her the $3,500 (less the mortgage debt), and on the deed being delivered to *M.* she (*M.*) paid to *R.'s* attorney the $5.600. The facts afterwards coming to the knowledge of *W.* she filed a bill against *R.* claiming the balance of the $5,600; and it appearing that in the negotiations he had given *W.* to understand that he was acting in her interest, and had no interest of his own, the plaintiff was *held* entitled to a decree against *R.* for such balance with interest and costs.

——◆——

## SEPARATE ACCOUNTS.

See " Municipal Officers."

## SET-OFF.

See " Vendor and Purchaser, I."

———◆———

## SHERIFF'S DEED.

A sheriff's deed described the property conveyed as " about fifteen acres, more or less, being the whole of a block or piece of land adjacent to the Grand Trunk Railway, being a part of lot number twenty-seven in the first concession of South East-hope, now in the town of Stratford."

*Held*, that this description was insufficient and the deed void.

Davidson v. Kiely, 494.

———◆———

## SOLICITOR.

In case of a sale under a power in a mortgage the solicitor of the mortgagee cannot become the purchaser, though the proceedings for the sale were not taken in his name, and it was not shewn that any loss had occurred by reason of his being the purchaser.

Howard v. Harding, 181.

———◆———

## SPECIFIC PERFORMANCE.

1. In pursuance of a verbal agreement for the sale of lands, the purchase money being payable by instalments, to be secured by mortgage on the premises bargained for and other lands owned by the purchaser; a deed and mortgage were drawn up, which were signed and sealed by the vendor and mortgagor respectively—neither instrument referring to the other, and the deed expressing that the purchase money had been paid. The vendor and mortgagor took away the respective instruments signed by them for the purpose, as alleged, of procuring the execution thereof by their respective wives. The vendor subsequently refused to perfect the transaction, and on a bill filed by the purchaser for specific performance :

*Held*, that the conveyance so executed by the vendor was a sufficient contract of sale within the Statute of Frauds ; that the presumption on the face of such instrument was that the purchase money had been paid ; which being admitted by the plaintiff to be incorrect, the purchaser was entitled to a decree for specific performance, paying the price in hand.

Gillatley v. White, 1.

2. Continued possession by a tenant coupled with acts inconsistent with his previous tenancy, is sufficient part performance to let in parol evidence of a contract of sale.

### Butler v. Church, 190.

3. The advertisement of sale of a farm described the property as being " 96 acres cleared and cultivated, a good log house, and frame barn 69 by 32 on the premises ; also, driving-shed." Upon a survey of the property being made, it appeared that the quantity of cleared land was 74¾ acres under cultivation and legal fence, and 12¼ acres of pasture land, with some girdled trees standing, and a few logs lying upon it, which had never been cultivated and could not be until the logs should be removed : the dimensions of the barn were 50 feet by 30, and there was no driving-shed upon the property. On a bill filed by the vendors for specific performance of the contract :

*Held,* independently of a stipulation in the conditions of sale providing for errors in the advertisement, that these differences were such as entitled the purchaser to be compensated therefor : and the vendors, having disputed the purchaser's right to such compensation, were ordered to pay the costs of the suit.

### The Canada Permanent Building Society v. Young, 566.

See also " Parol Agreement, 1."

—————

### STATEMENT.

See " Chattel Mortgage," 4.

—————

### STATUTE OF FRAUDS.

See " Pleading."
" Specific Performance," 1.
" Timber Limits."

—————

### STATUTE OF LIMITATIONS.

1. The use of bracket boards on a mill dam is such an easement as the Statute of Limitations will protect.

### Campbell v. Young, 97.

2. A person who had been in possession of lands for upwards of 20 years, wrote to the heir of the true owner, acknowledging his title as such heir:

*Held*, that such acknowledgment having been made after the title by possession was complete, did not take away the statutory right which possession gave.

### McIntyre v. The Canada Co., 367.

3. An acknowledgment to a party's trustee is sufficient to take a case out of the Statute of Limitations. *Ib.*

4. *P.* being in possession of land of which he was not the owner, made a verbal gift of the land to *C.*, but afterwards ejected him. *C.* then obtained a conveyance from the owner. More than 20 years had elapsed from the time that the Statute of Limitations began to run in favor of *P.* against the true owner:

*Held*, that *C.'s* possession did not interrupt in *C.'s* favor the running of the Statute; that the owner being barred, *C.*, his grantee, was barred also. *Ib.*

5. The owner of land put his father in possession in 1847, under a parol agreement that the father should clear up and cultivate the land, taking to his benefit the profits thereof. The father remained in undisturbed possession until his death, which occurred in 1870:

*Held*, that the father had obtained a title by length of possession; and a bill filed to obtain the delivery up of certain deeds executed between the father and another son, was dismissed with costs.

### Truesdell v. Cook, 532.

—◆—

## STATUTE, REPEAL OF.

### [BY IMPLICATION.]
See " Indian Lands."

—◆—

## SUBSEQUENT CREDITORS.
See " Insolvency," 3.

—◆—

## SUIT TO REDEEM.
See " General Orders," 2.

## SUIT, RELEASE OF.

See " Release of Suit."

——◆——

## SUPERSTITIOUS USES.

A bequest by a member of the Roman Catholic Church of a sum of money for the purpose of paying for masses for his soul. is not void in this Province.

### Elmsley v. Madden, 386.

——◆——

## TAXES.

1. The devisee of a life estate in all a testator's property, is bound to keep down the annual taxes on the land, and they form a first charge on the devisee's interest.

### Gray v. Hatch, 72.

2. By the Assessment Act of 1866, owners had four years to impeach a tax deed : by an Act passed in 1869, all actions for that pnrpose were stayed until after the following session of the Legislature ; and by another Act of the same session all previcus Assessment Acts were repealed, amended, and consolidated, with a reservation of rights had or acquired under the repealed Acts ; by one of the clauses of the amended Act the limit for bringing actions was two years :

*Held*, that an owner, who had less than two years of his four remaining when the Acts of 1869 were passed, had like others two years thereafter to bring his suit.

### Connor v. McPherson, 607.

——◆——

## TAX SALES.

On a bill impeaching a tax sale on the ground that no portion of the taxes had been due for five years before the issuing of the treasurer's warrant, it appeared that the first year's taxes had been imposed by a by-law passed in July, 1852 ; that the collector's roll was not delivered until after August, 1852 ; and that the treasurer's warrant was dated 10th July, 1857 :

*Held*, that the sale was invalid.

### Connor v. McPherson, 607.

See also " Taxes."

## TAX TITLES.

1. *Held*, per *Richards*, C.J , *Wilson*, J., *Mowat*, V.C . *Gall*, J .
and *Strong*, V.C., that the Statute 27 Victoria, chapter 19,
section 4, cures all errors as regards the purchaser at a tax
sale, if any taxes in respect of the land sold had been in arrear
for five years; this rule apples where an occupied lot has been
assessed as unoccupied.

### The Bank of Toronto v. Fanning (In Appeal), 39 .

2, In a suit to impeach a sale of land for taxes, it appeared
that about 20 or 30 acres of the lot were cleared and fenced,
and a barn was erected thereon, into which hay made on these
twenty acres was stored in winter, by the person occupying
the adjoining lot under the authority of the proprietor ; no one
resided on the 20 acres ; the owner was resident out of the
country and had not given notice to the assessor of the township to have his name inserted on the roll of the township :

*Semble*, that the lot should have been assessed as occupied.

[*Draper*, C.J., *Hagarty*, C.J., and *Gwynne*, J., dissenting,
who were of opinion that the lot was properly assessed as
non-resident.]                                        *Ib.*

---

## TIMBER,

### [ACCOUNTS OF]

See Administration suit,' '2, 3.

### [DOWER IN RESPECT OF.]

See "Dower," 5.

---

## TIMBER LIMITS.

The plaintiff, being entitled, according to the usage of the
Crown, to a license for certain timber limits, on the 3rd December, 1863, took out a license in the name *J. N. & Co.*, and
delivered the same to them upon a verbal agreement for obtaining advances on the security thereof ; *J. N. & Co.* procured
these advances from a bank, and deposited the license by way
of security. In December, 1864, the plaintiff took out a new
license in the name of *J. N. & Co.*, and they assigned the
same to the bank as a further security. The plaintiff having
made default, the bank sold the limits with the knowledge of,
and without any objection by, the plaintiff :

*Held*, in appeal, that though there was no writing shewing
the agreement between the plaintiff and any of the other

parties, the sale was binding on him ; and a bill impeaching it was dismissed with costs. [*Draper*, C. J., and *Spragge*, C., dissenting.]

## TITLE.

[QUESTION OF.]
See " Vendor and Purchaser," 3.

[SHEWING GOOD.]
See " Vendor and Purchaser," 4, 5.

## TRUE COPY.
See " Chattel Mortgage," 3.

## TRUSTEE TO SELL.
See " Sale, Trustee for."

## TRUST, TRUSTEE, AND CESTUI QUE TRUST.

1. Where a trustee is authorized to invest in either of two specified modes, and by mistake invests in neither, the measure of his liability is the loss arising from his not having invested in the less beneficial of the authorized modes.

2. Two years before the passing of the Act relaxing the usury laws (22 Vic. ch. 85), a trustee who was authorized to invest on mortgage or in government securities, made an investment in Upper Canada Bank stock, under the impression that such an investment was within his authority ; the stock ultimately turned out worthless; and the trustee submitted to account for the principal with compound interest, at six per cent. :
*Held*, that this was the extent of his liability, though eight per cent. might have peen obtained on mortgages.    *Ib.*

3. The insolvency of a trustee, or his leaving the country in debt to reside in a foreign country, is a sufficient ground to remove him from the trust.

4. By virtue of a will *A.* had a life interest in certain lands, with remainder to the plaintiff in fee. The land was afterwards sold at sheriff's sale under circumstances which made

the sale void in Equity, and the purchaser a trustee for the devisees. *A.* (the life-tenant) for valuable consideration conveyed his life-interest to the purchaser:

*Held*, that the plaintiff could not claim the benefit of that transaction.

Gilpin v. West, 228.

5. It is the duty of a trustee for sale to use all diligence to obtain the best price; and where a trustee sold property at private sale, without previous advertisement, at a price lower than other persons were willing to give, and did not first communicate with these persons, though informed of offers of the higher price made by them to one of the *cestuis que* trust; the trustee was held responsible for the loss.

Graham v. Yeomans, 238.

6. In such a case, the absence of any fraudulent motive in the trustee is no defence; nor is evidence of witnesses that the property was worth no more than the trustee obtained for it.

*Ib.*

7. The trustee deposed that he had disbelieved the statement of the *cestuis que* trust:

*Held*, no excuse for not testing the truth of the statement by reference to the parties. *Ib.*

See also, " Sale, Trustee for."

---

## ULTRA VIRES.

See " Contract in restraint of Trade."

---

## UNAUTHORIZED INVESTMENT.

See " Trust," &c., 1, 2.

---

## UNOCCUPIED LANDS.

See " Tax Titles."

---

## UNPAID PURCHASE MONEY.

See " Fraud on Creditors," 2.
"Lien for Unpaid Purchase Money."

## USURY.

1. An assignment to the Trust and Loan Company of a valid existing mortgage bearing more than eight per cent. interest, is not necessarily void.

### The Trust and Loan Company of Canada v. Boulton, 234.

2. The Court will not at the hearing of a cause allow an amendment or supplemental answer to let in evidence necessary for a defence of usury. *Ib.*

See also " Building Societies."

---

## VENDOR'S LIEN.

In case of a decree for unpaid consideration money, the sale of the property should be provided for, and in case the same does not realize sufficient to pay the money with six years' arrears of interest there should be a personal decree for payment of the balance by the purchaser.

### Skelly v. Skelly, 495.

---

## VENDOR AND PURCHASER.

1. On the sale of land, which was subject to a prior mortgage which the vendor had given, and which was not then due, the vendor executed a covenant to the purchaser *B.* covenanting that he had not incumbered the property, and the purchaser *B.* executed a mortgage for his unpaid purchase money. The intention was, that the vendor should pay the prior mortgage, but he failed to do so ; after it became due, he sold and assigned *B.'s* mortgage to the plaintiff, who had notice of all the facts: the plaintiff afterwards obtained an assignment of the prior mortgage, and *B.* paid off the same :

*Held,* that *B.* was entitled to apply on his mortgage the money so paid by him to the plaintiff. [*Strong,* V. C., dissenting.]

### Henderson v. Brown, 79.

2. An abstract of title and the title deeds having been sent to a purchaser in November, 1869, at his own request, for the purposes of examination and advice, he retained the same for a considerable time, intimated no objection to the title, and in correspondence with the vendor's solicitors implied that he was content with the title : but in June, 1870, he claimed the right of investigating it afresh :

*Held,* that by the lapse of time and the letters which he had written he had impliedly accepted the title.

### Rae v. Geddes, 217.

3. On a sale by a person whose title is derived under a Chancery purchase, a question as to whether the legal estate was effectually conveyed to him under such purchase is, on a subsequent sale of the property, a question of conveyance, not of title.

Rae v. Geddes, 217.

4. *A.* agreed to sell to *B.* "all his right, title, and interest," in certain specified property " owned by" *A.*, and to " give a a good and sufficient deed of the said land free of all incumbrances :"

*Held*, that the vendor was bound to shew a good title.

Gordon v. Harnden, 231.

5. Before an abstract was asked for, the purchaser had sold small portions of the land, and he and his vendees had cut down some of the wood thereon ; but the vendor, notwithstanding, promised afterwards to give an abstract as demanded, and delivered an abstract accordingly :

*Held*, that the plaintiff was entitled to have this abstract verified. *Ib.*

## VOLUNTARY CONVEYANCES' ACT (1868.)

The Voluntary Conveyances' Act (1868) gives effect as against subsequent purchasers, to prior voluntary conveyances executed in good faith, and to them only ; and a voluntary conveyance to a wife for the purpose of protecting property from creditors was held not to be good against a subsequent mortgage to a creditor.

Richardson v. Armitage, 512.

## WAREHOUSEMANS' RECEIPT.

A warehouseman sold 3,500 bushels of wheat, part of a larger quantity which he had in store, and gave the purchaser a warehouseman's receipt under the statute, acknowledging that he had received from him that quantity of wheat, to be delivered pursuant to his order to be indorsed on the receipt. The 3,500 bushels were never separated from the other wheat of the seller :

*Held*, by the Court of Appeal [*Spragge*, C., *Morrison*, and *Gwynne*, JJ., dissenting] that the purchaser had an insurable interest.

Box v. The Provincial Insurance Co., 280.

## WHEAT, SALE OF, PART OF A LARGER QUANTITY.

See " Warehouseman's Receipt."

## WILL, CONSTRUCTION OF.

1. A testator devised certain property to his son *A*., and to the heirs of his body lawfully to be begotten, with power to appoint any one or more of such heirs to take the same :

*Held*, that *A*. took an estate tail ; that there was no trust in favor of his children ; and that mortgages therefore executed by him took precedence of the claims of the children under an appointment which he afterwards executed in their favor.

The Trust and Loan Company of Canada v.
Fraser, 19.

2. A testator devised his farm to minor childern, and directed that his executors should rent the same ; that no timber should be cut except for the use of the premises ; and that the executors should have full power to carry the will into effect :

*Held*, that it was the duty of the executors to prevent the executrix from cutting the timber for other purposes.

Stewart v. Fletcher, 21.

3. A testator (amongst other things) devised certain lands to each of his two younger children, and directed that the rents should be and remain to his widow or executors for the education and up-bringing of the devisees respectively until they were twenty-one, &c. ; and he also left all his dividends and profits of his bank stock, &c., to his widow and executors for the same purpose. The residue of his estate was to be divided equally amongst all his chilhren. The rents of the lands devised to one of the younger children were alone more than sufficient for his education and maintenance :

*Held*, notwithstanding, that he was entitled to a share of the dividends bequeathed ; that the whole income derived from the stocks being given, the gift could not, in favor of the residuary legatees, be construed as conditional on being needed for the purpose specified.

Denison v. Denison, 41.

4. The testator, after devising a parcel of land to each of his three sons, directed his executors to collect the debts due to him, and out of the money so collected to pay his debts, funeral and testamentary expenses and legacies ; and he charged the deficiency on two of the parcels which he had devised ; by a subsequent part of his will, he gave his household furniture, and other personal chattels, to his wife for her own use, except the piano, which he gave to one of his daughters ; there was no other residuary clause in the will.

*Held*, that the whole of the testator's residuary estate, except the debts due to him and the piano, went to the wife, exonerated from the debts which the testator owed.

Scott v. Scott, 66.

5. A testator devised certain real estate to his granddaughter; and, in case of her dying without lawful issue, he directed the property to be sold by his executors; and from the proceeds of such sales, and from such other of his property as might be then remaining in their hands, he directed certain legacies to be paid, and the remainder to be applied at the discretion of his executors to missionary purposes:

*Held*, that the contemplated " dying without issue " was a dying without issue living at the granddaughter's death.

Chisholm v. Emery (In Appeal), 467.

6. A testator, by his will, gave to his widow an annuity of $4,000 in lieu of dower. His will contained certain devises, and gave other legacies and annuities which the testator charged on the whole of his estate not before devised, and he empowered. his executors to sell any of his property which they should think necessary; the widow elected to take the annuity.

*Held*, that having so elected, she was not entitled to dower out of any of the testator's lands, whether devised or not:

*Held*, also, that the legacies and annuities were payable primarily out of the personal estate.

Davidson v. Boomer (In Appeal), 475.

7. A will contained the following bequest: " To *Richard O. Knight* I give my carpet, blankets, and whatever else I may have at his house." *Held*, that mortgages and a bank deposit receipt, which were in the house, did not pass.

Smith v. Knight, 492.

(See same point.—Collins v. Collins, 24 L.T.N.S., 780.)

8. A testator bequeathed a sum of money to his wife in lieu of all dower, &c., and revoked " all gifts or deeds or deed of gift of any real estate made by me at any time heretofore."

*Held*, that the widow was put to her election whether she would accept the bequest or retain an estate conveyed to her by a deed of gift during the lifetime of her husband.

Lee v. McKinly, 527.

# COURT OF ERROR AND APPEAL.

## General Rules and Orders.

I. Upon, from, and after this date, all Rules heretofore made, and now in force, regulating the practice and proceedings in civil cases in this Court are annulled ; and the following Rules made under the authority of the Consolidated Statute of Upper Canada, chapter thirteen, section sixty-four, are substituted for the same.

II. That, unless otherwise specially ordered, the security to be given in all cases of Error and Appeal, shall be personal, and by bond, and may be in the form given in the Rule numbered seven ; and shall be filed in the office of the Clerk of the Court appealed from, in Toronto.

III. That the security required by the Consolidated Statute of Upper Canada, chapter thirteen, section fifteen, shall be by bond to the respondent or respondents in the sum of four hundred dollars ; such bond to be executed by

the appellant or appellants, or one or more of
them, and by two sufficient sureties (except in
special cases, such as absence from the province,
lunacy of the appellant, or other cases of similar
difficulty, to be established by affidavit to the
satisfaction of the court appealed from, or a
Judge thereof; when an additional surety, in place
of the appellant, may be received, by Rule, or
Order of such Court or Judge) ; and the condition
of the bond shall be to the effect, that the appellant
or appellants shall and will effectually prosecute
his or their appeal, and pay such costs and
damages as shall be awarded in case the judgment or decree appealed from shall be affirmed
or in part affirmed.

IV. That when the judgment to be appealed
from directs the payment of money, and the
appellant desires to stay the execution thereof,
then the bond shall be in double the amount of
such judgment ; unless the same shall be in debt
on bond for a penal sum, or upon a warrant of
attorney, or *cognovit actionem*, or otherwise,
exceeding the sum really due, in which case the
bond shall be only in double the true debt, and
costs ; and the amount so recovered and of such
true debt and costs shall be stated in the condition,
or recital to the condition, of the bond, immediately after the statement of the nature of the action ;
and the condition shall be to the effect that the
appellant shall effectually prosecute such appeal,
and if the judgment appealed from, or any part
thereof, shall be affirmed, shall pay the amount

directed to be paid by such judgment, or the part of such amount as to which such judgment shall be affirmed, if it be affirmed only in part, and all damages which shall be awarded against the appellant in the appeal ; provided always that, in cases where the security to be given shall be in a sum above two thousand dollars, it shall be in the discretion of the Court appealed from, or of a Judge thereof, to allow security to be given by a larger number of sureties, apportioning the amount among them as shall appear reasonable ; and provided further, that, where the amount by the judgment directed to be paid exceeds $10,000, it shall be in the discretion of such Court or Judge to allow security to be given for such amount less than double as shall appear reasonable.

V. That when the judgment appealed from shall be in an action of ejectment, the security required by the last preceding Rule shall be taken in double the yearly value of the property in question ; and in cases where the matter in question ; shall relate to the taking of any annual or other rent customary, or other duty or fee, or any other such like demand of a general and public nature affecting future rights, the amount in which such security shall be taken, in addition to the security required for costs, shall be fixed by order of the Court appealed from, or a Judge thereof.

VI. That in all other cases falling within any or either of the exceptions contained in the sixteenth section of the said statute, chapter thirteen, the security shall be personal and by bond, and the condition shall be made suitable to the circumstances, and shall, as well as the bond and the recitals and condition required under the Rules numbered four and five, contain such further and other conditions as shall be directed by any special order in that behalf made by the Court appealed from, or by a Judge thereof.

VII. The bond may be in the following form, to be varied as occasion may require under any of the foregoing rules :—

Know all men by these presents. that we, (naming all the obligors, with their places of residences and additions,) are jointly and severally held and firmly bound unto (naming the obligees, with their places of residence and additions,) in the penal sum of          dollars, for which payment. well and truly to be made, we bind ourselves, and each of us by himself, our, and each of our heirs, executors and administrators, respectively, firmly by these presents.

Witness our respective hands and seals, the         day of          in the year of our Lord, 18

Whereas the (appellant) complains, that in the giving of judgment in a certain suit in her Majesty's Court of Queen's Bench, (or of *Common Pleas*, as the case may be,) in the Province of Ontario, between (naming the parties to the cause) in a plea of        , manifest error hath intervened ; wherefore the (appellant) desires to appeal from the said judgment to the Court of Error and Appeal.

Now the condition of this obligation is such, that if the (appellant) do and shall effectually prosecute such appeal, and pay such costs and damages as shall be awarded, in case the judgment aforesaid to be appealed from shall be affirmed, then this obligation shall be void, otherwise to remain in full force.

VIII. That the parties to every such bond as sureties shall, by affidavit respectively, make oath that they are resident householders or freeholders in Ontario, and severally worth the sum mentioned in such bond, over and above what will pay and satisfy all their debts ; which affidavit may be in the following form :

*In the (style of Court.)*

A. B., plaintiff,    I, E. F., of          , make oath and
         vs.          say, that I am a resident inhabitant
C. D., defendant.     of Ontario, and am a householder
in, (or a freeholder in          ,) and that I am worth the
sum of          , (the sum mentioned as the penalty, or such
sum as the deponent is bound in,) over and above what will
pay all my debts ; and I J. H., of          , make oath and
say, that I am a householder in          , (or a freeholder
in          ,) and that I am worth the sum (as in the former
case) of          , over and above what will pay my debts.

The above-named deponents, E. F. and G. H., were sworn at, &c., the          day of          18   , before me.
                                        , Commissioner, &c.

IX. That in case of appeals from the Courts of law, fourteen days' notice shall be given of the time and place at which application will be made to the court from whose judgment it is intended to appeal, or, in vacation, to a Judge, for the allowance of such security, which notice shall contain the names and additions of the obligors.

X. That the allowance of such security may be opposed by affidavit, but that in the absence of any such opposition the affidavit above-mentioned shall be sufficient, in the discretion of the judge, to warrant the allowance thereof.

XI. That if allowed. the officer of the Court shall endorse on such bond the word "allowed," prefixing the date and signing his name thereto ; upon which such security shall be deemed perfected.

XII. That in every appeal from either of the Courts of Common Law upon a special case, the appellant shall prepare and file with the Clerk of the proper Court, at his office in Toronto, a true copy of such case, and of the judgment or decision of the court appealed from, and shall give immediate notice in writing of such filing to the opposite party.

XIII. That in every appeal from the decision of either of the Courts of Common Law, upon a rule to enter a verdict or nonsuit on a point reserved at the trial, or upon a motion for a new trial upon the ground of misdirection, or upon a rule whereby a by-law or any part of a by-law has been quashed, the, appellant shall prepare and file with the Clerk of the proper Court, as aforesaid, a statement of the case, the pleadings, evidence, and affidavits, or so much thereof as shall be necessary, and of the rule, order, judgment, or decision of the Court, together with the reasons of appeal, and shall give immediate notice in writing of such filing to the opposite party.

XIV. That the respondent may, within eight days after being served with such notice, apply

to any Judge of the Court appealed from, for
a summons to alter and amend the special case,
or the statement so filed, which Judge, on the
return of such summons, may approve or modify
the same as to him shall seem proper.

XV. That if no such application be made
within eight days next after the day of service
of the notice, the copy of the special case, or the
statement so filed, shall be deemed correct for
the purpose of the appeal.

XVI. That before the expiration of eight
days from the service of notice, or if a Judge's
summons has been obtained under the foregoing
Rule number fourteen, then within four days after
such summons shall have been disposed of, or
within such longer time as may be fixed by the
Judge, the respondent shall file with the Clerk
of the Court whose decision is appealed against,
his reasons against such appeal.

XVII. Unless the appellant shall, with the
memorandum required by the thirty-third section
of the aforesaid statute, chapter thirteen, file, a
copy of his grounds of appeal, the respondent
may, by notice in writing, demand the same ;
and if the grounds of appeal are not filed within
eight days after service of such demand on the
appellant, his attorney or agent, the appeal,
upon proof by affidavit of the service of the
demand, and that the grounds of appeal were
not filed as above required, shall be dismissed

with costs ; but the appellant may, within the
eight days, apply to the Judge for further time to
file his reasons, and the Judge may, in his discretion, allow the same.

XVIII. That unless the respondent shall,
within eight days after the filing of the appellant's grounds of appeal and notice in writing
thereof given to him, his attorney or agent, file
his joinder thereto, and reasons for sustaining the
judgment, the appellant, may, in writing, demand
the same ; and unless the respondent file such
joinder and reasons within eight days after the
service of such demand, the respondent shall be
precluded from filing the same without the leave
of the court, or a judge thereof, first had and
obtained upon a rule *nisi* or summons ; and
the Court of Error and Appeal will proceed
*ex parte* to hear the cause on the part of the
appellant, and to give judgment thereon without
the intervention of the respondent.

XIX. That the case, so stated and settled,
together with the reasons of appeal and affidavit
of service, shall forthwith be delivered by the
Clerk of the Court, whose decision is appealed
against, to the Clerk of the Court of Error and
Appeal.

XX. That when error on the record is
suggested and alleged, copies of the transcript of
the judgment, with the suggestion and denial of
error, and when any case has been stated and

settled under the foregoing Rules numbered twelve and thirteen, copies of such case, with the reasons for and against the appeal, and the opinions delivered by the Judges, shall be printed ; and such copies shall be deemed to be the printed cases of the appellant and respondent respectively.

XXI. That as soon as the transcript of judgment or case settled shall have been delivered to the Clerk of the Court of Error and Appeal, and not less than four days before the day appointed by the Court for the actual hearing of causes, (or before the first day appointed for the then next sittings of the Court,) the case may be set down for hearing on the application of either party, and notice of such setting down shall be forthwith given to the opposite party.

XXII. That in appeals from the Court of Chancery all securities, under the fifteenth section of the aforesaid statute, section thirteen, shall be personal, by bond with sureties; which bond shall, as near as may be, be in the form of the bond given in the foregoing Rule number seven, and shall (together with an affidavit of justification in the form *mutatis mutandis* given in the foregoing Rule number eight) be filed with the Registrar of the said Court; and notice thereof shall be served on the respondent, his solicitor or agent ; and such security shall stand allowed unless the respondent shall, within fourteen days, move the said Court to disallow the same.

A special application shall be necessary to stay the proceeding under any of the exceptions in the sixteenth section of the said act, chapter thirteen.

XXIII. That in every case appealed from Chancery, a copy of the pleadings and evidence, or so much thereof respectively as is material for the purposes of the appeal, shall be printed, together with the opinions delivered by the Judges on the case, and the reasons of appeal, and the reasons for supporting the decree or order; which printed copies shall, for all purposes, be considered the printed cases of the appellant and respondent respectively. The parties may join together in procuring the printing of such copies, one whereof shall be handed to the Registrar of the said Court, whose duty it shall be to examine the same and, if necessary, to correct it and the copy so examined by the Registrar, shall be marked by him with the words, "examined and approved;" to which he shall sign his name, and he shall forthwith deliver that copy to the Clerk of the Court of Error and Appeal.

XXIV. That where one ground of the appeal is the rejection of evidence or the reception of improper evidence, such evidence shall, where practicable, be printed in a separate part of the book, and with an extra wide margin, and be distinguished by an appropriate heading and marginal note.

XXV. That in appeals from the Court of Chancery, if the parties do not agree as to what the printed case should contain, either party may apply to a Judge of the said court in Chambers, upon notice to all parties interested, which notice is to be served according to the practice of the said court; and thereupon the Judge will give directions as to what is to be printed.

XXVI. That the said Court or a Judge thereof shall also have the like power of making Orders for the expediting or conducting of proceedings in appeals from the Court of Chancery, as either Court of Law or a Judge thereof has in the case of appeals from such Court of Law ; and in case of non-compliance with any such Order, the Court of Chancery or a Judge thereof may order the case to stand dismissed, or to be proceeded with *ex parte*, as the case may require, and as would be the course in the like case on an appeal from either Court of Law.

XXVII. That in all appeals from any of the said courts, the appellant shall, within one month after the allowance of the appeal bonds, deliver to the Clerk of this Court the printed cases for the use of the Judges ; and shall, at the time of such delivery, enter the case with the said Clerk for hearing at the then next ensuing sittings of this Court ; and that, in case of neglect or omission by the appellant to comply with this rule, the respondent may, upon filing with the said Clerk a sworn copy of the order of allowance of the appeal bond, or a certificate from the Clerk of the Court appealed from of the day on which such allowance was made, or on which the bond stood allowed (as the case may be), obtain from the Clerk of this Court a certificate of such neglect or omission ; and thereupon the appeal shall stand dismissed with costs without further order.

XXVIII. Upon the application of the appellant, supported by affidavit, and after hearing the respondent, if he does not consent to such application, the Court appealed from or a Judge thereof, may give further reasonable time for delivering the printed cases, and entering the Appeal for hearing as required by the foregoing Rule.

XXIX. The Clerk of the Court of Error and Appeal shall receive no appeal books unless they are printed on good paper, on one side of the paper only, and in demy-quarto form, with small pica type leaded.

XXX. That the Court appealed from or a Judge thereof shall allow any bond, notice, appeal, or other proceeding, taken or observed under these rules and orders, to be amended whenever such amendment shall to such Court or Judge seem reasonable.

XXXI. That this Court may, in its discretion, postpone the hearing until any future day during the same sittings, or at any following sittings.

XXXII. That if either party neglect to appear
at the proper day to support or resist the appeal, the Court may hear the other party, and may
give judgment without the intervention of the
party so neglecting to appear, or may postpone
the hearing upon payment of such costs as the
court shall direct.

XXXIII. That all Rules and all Orders of
this Court, in cases appealed, shall bear date on
the day of the judgment or decision being pronounced, and shall be signed by the Clerk of
the Court.

XXXIV. That the same fees and allowances
shall be taxed in Appeal by the Clerk of the Court
of Error and Appeal, for attorneys and solicitors,
or any officer of the said Court, as are allowed
for similar services in the Court from which
the appeal is brought; and that counsel fees
shall be taxed as follows: In appeals of a simple
nature, or where judgment is given at the close
of the argument, the Officer is to tax a fee not
exceeding forty dollars to the senior counsel,
and not exceeding twenty dollars to the junior,
for the hearing of the appeal; in more important or difficult cases, the fee to the senior
counsel shall not exceed eighty dollars, and to
the junior fifty dollars; within these limits, the
fee shall be in the discretion of the taxing officer;
and in all cases the amount of the counsel fees
taxed by him shall be subject to be reduced on
application to a Judge of the Court appealed

from.  Not more than fees to two counsel are to
be taxed to any party entitled to be heard on an
appeal.

XXXV. That the security to be given in cases
of appeal to her Majesty in Privy Council, shall
be personal, and by bond to the respondent or
respondents, such bond to be executed by the
appellant or appellants, or one or more of them.
and by two sufficient sureties, (except in special
cases, as mentioned in the foregoing Rule, number
three,) in the penal sum of two thousand dollars,
the condition of which bond shall be to the effect
that the appellant or appellants shall and will
effectually prosecute his and their appeal, and
pay such costs and damages as shall be awarded
in case the judgment or decree appealed from
shall be affirmed, or in part affirmed ; and in
cases from Chancery, application to the Court of
Appeal to stay proceedings shall be by motion
and notice, which motion, if granted, shall be
upon terms as to security, under the sixteenth
section of the aforesaid statute, chapter thirteen,
or otherwise, as the circumstances or nature of
the case may require.

XXXVI. That the bond referred to in the
foregoing Rule, number twenty-nine, shall be in
the following form :—

Know all men by these presents, that we, (naming all the
obligors, with their places of residence and additions,) are
jointly and severally held and firmly bound unto, (naming
the obligees, with their places of residence and additions,) in

the penal sum of          dollars, for which payment, well
and truly to be made, we bind ourselves, and each of us by
himself, our, and each of our heirs, executors and administrators, respectively, firmly, by these presents.

Witness our hands and seals respectively, the          day of
in the year of our Lord, 18  .

Whereas (the appellant) alleges, that in the giving of
judgment in a certain suit in her Majesty's Court of Error
and Appeal, in Ontario, between (the respondent) and
(the appellant), manifest error hath intervened, wherefore
(the appellant) desires to appeal from the said judgment to
her Majesty, in her Majesty's Privy Council.

Now the condition of this obligation is such, that if (the
appellant) do and shall effectually prosecute such appeal, or
pay such costs and damages as shall be awarded, in case the
judgment aforesaid to be appealed against shall be affirmed, or
in part affirmed, then this obligation shall be void, otherwise
shall remain in full force.

XXXVII. That in every case of appeal to her
Majesty in Council, the obligors, parties to any
bond as sureties, shall justify their sufficiency by
affidavit in the manner and to the same effect as
is required by the foregoing Rule number eight.

WM. H. DRAPER, C. J., APPEAL.
WM. B. RICHARDS, C. J.
JOHN H. HAGARTY, C. J. C. P.
JOSEPH C. MORRISON, J.
ADAM WILSON, J.
O. MOWAT, V. C.
JOHN W. GWYNNE, J.
THOMAS GALT, J.
S. H. STRONG, V. C.

Lightning Source UK Ltd.
Milton Keynes UK
UKHW041035070119
334942UK00011B/1874/P